WELCOME TO THE BALLROOM no.9 | TOMO TAKEUCH

Contents

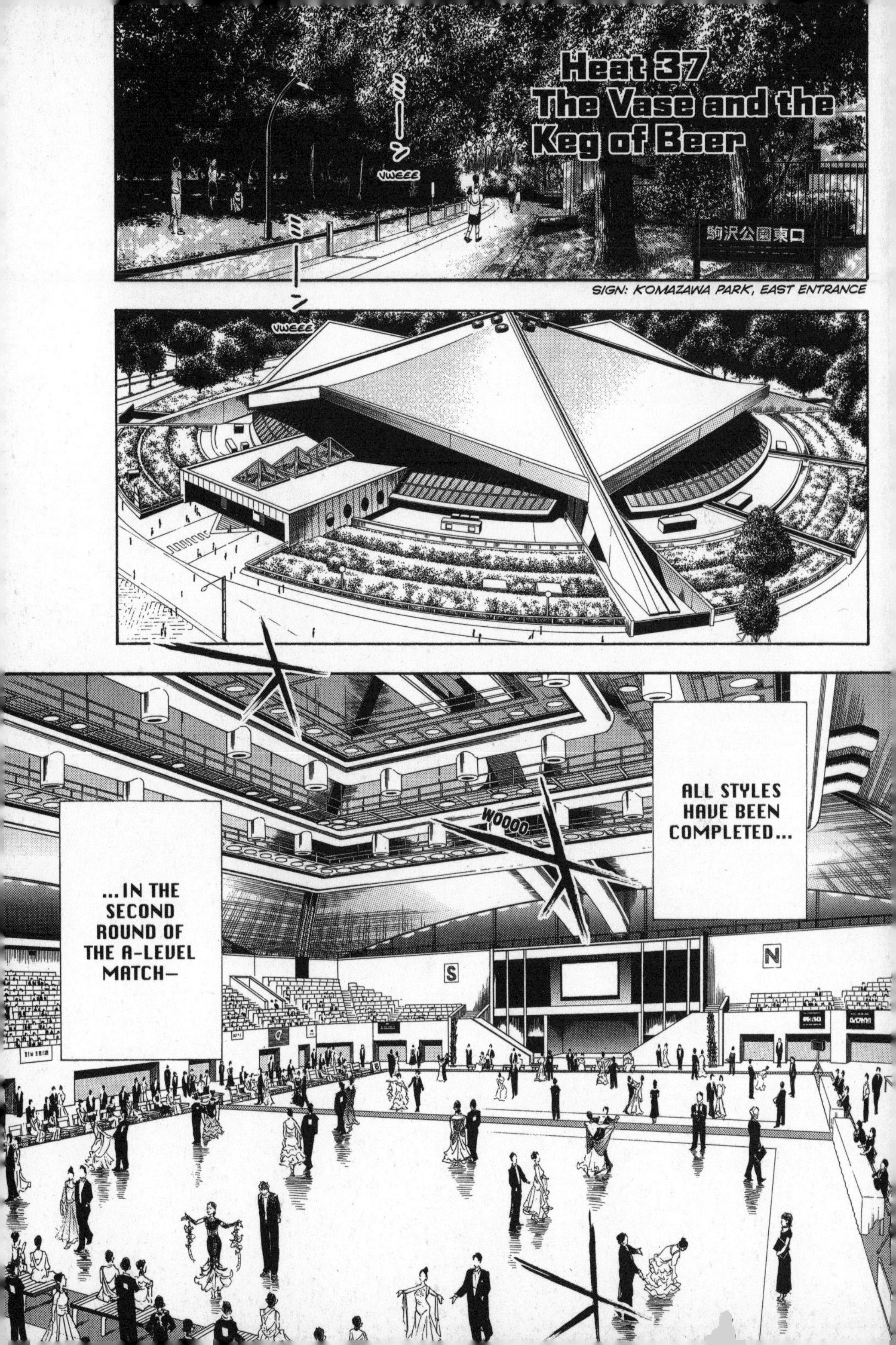
Heat 37
The Vase and the Keg of Beer
ミーン
VWEEE
駒沢公園東口
SIGN: KOMAZAWA PARK, EAST ENTRANCE
ミーン
VWEEE
ALL STYLES HAVE BEEN COMPLETED...
...IN THE SECOND ROUND OF THE A-LEVEL MATCH—
WOOOO
S
N

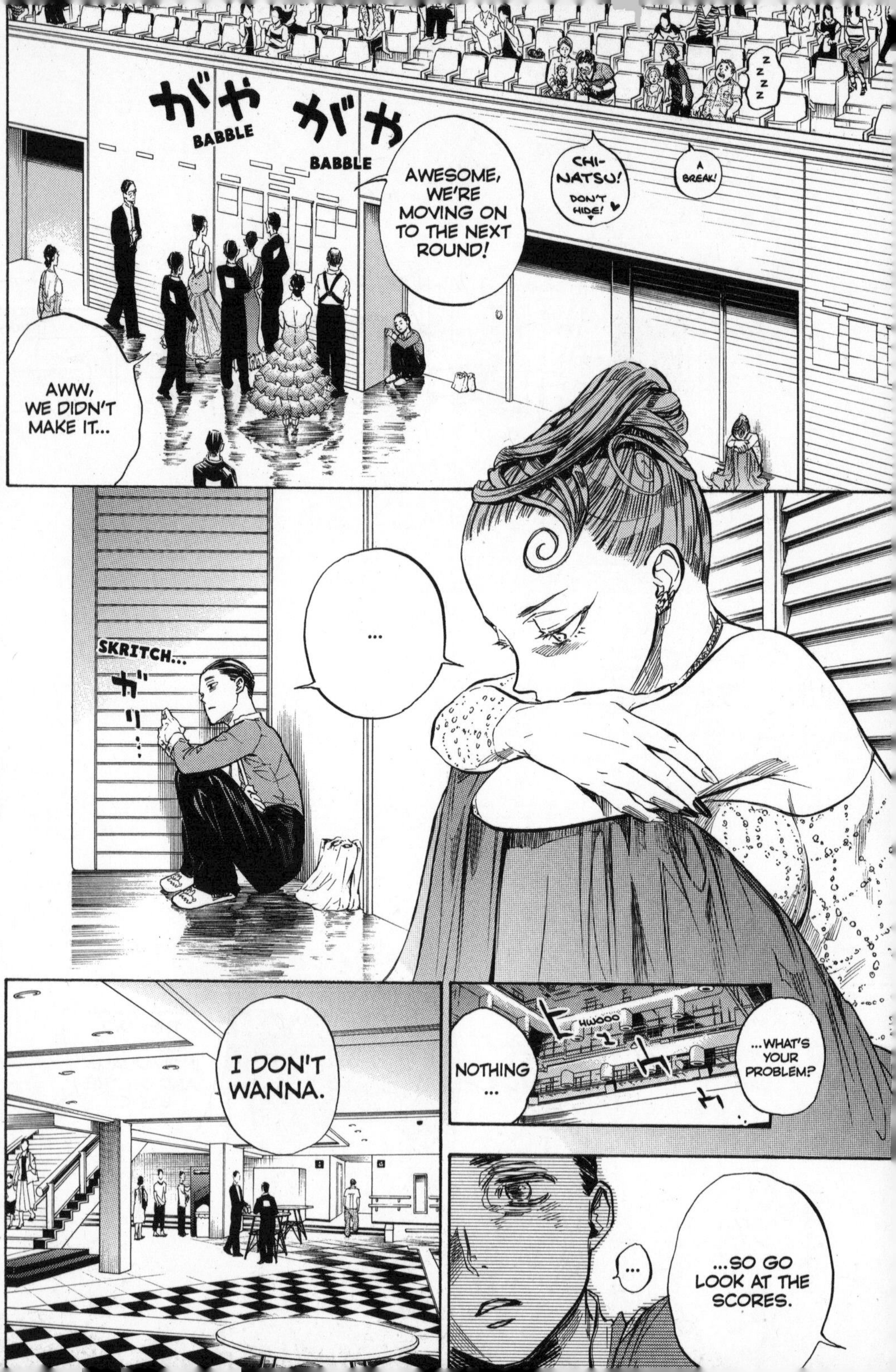
Z Z Z
A BREAK!
CHI-NATSU! DON'T HIDE! ♥
AWESOME, WE'RE MOVING ON TO THE NEXT ROUND!
ガヤ
BABBLE
ガヤ
BABBLE
AWW, WE DIDN'T MAKE IT...
...
SKRITCH...
ガリ…
...WHAT'S YOUR PROBLEM?
HWOOO
NOTHING ...
...SO GO LOOK AT THE SCORES.
...
I DON'T WANNA.

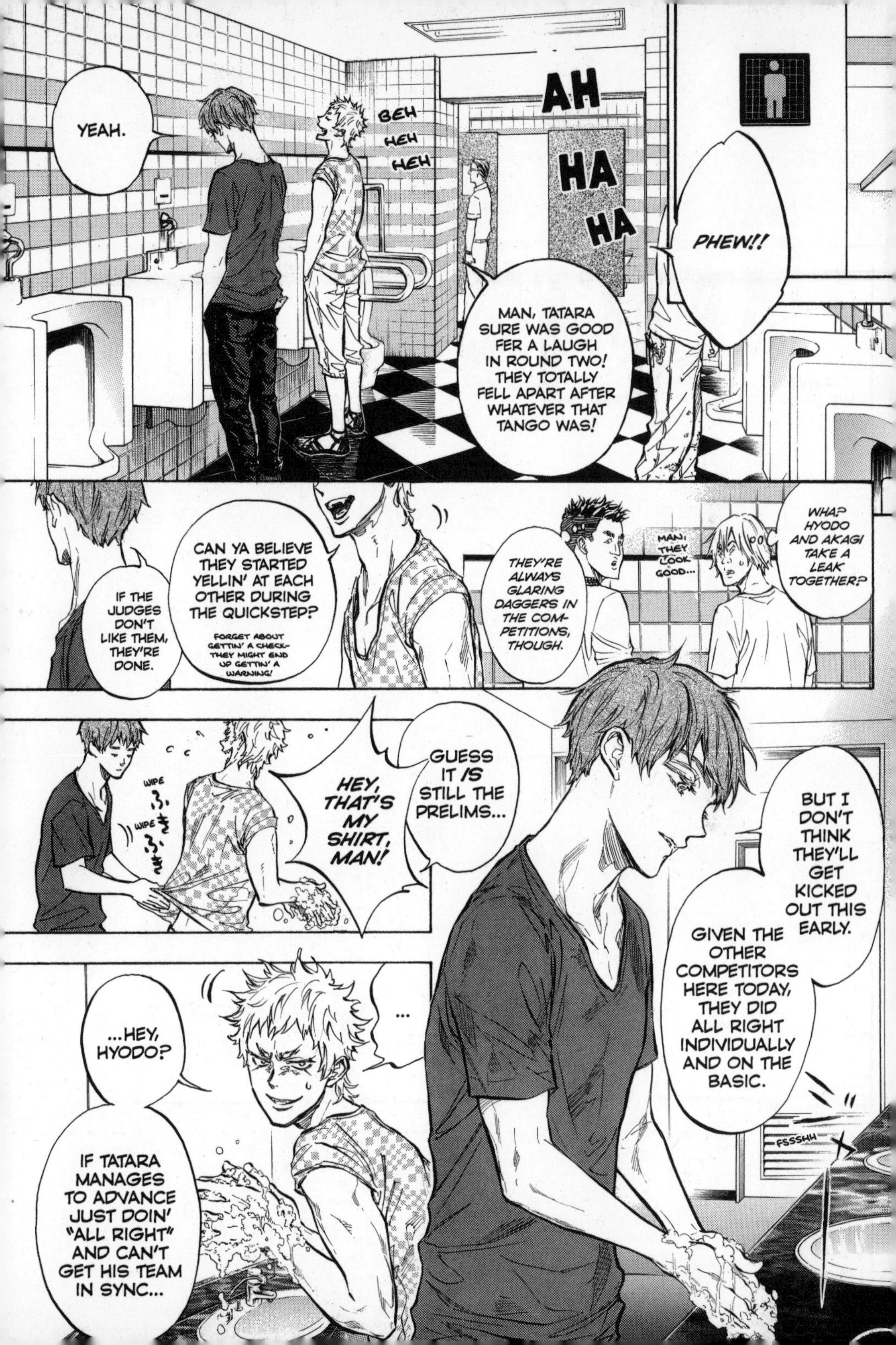

PHEW!!
AH HA HA
MAN, TATARA SURE WAS GOOD FER A LAUGH IN ROUND TWO! THEY TOTALLY FELL APART AFTER WHATEVER THAT TANGO WAS!
BEH HEH HEH
YEAH.
WHA? HYODO AND AKAGI TAKE A LEAK TOGETHER?
MAN! THEY LOOK GOOD...
THEY'RE ALWAYS GLARING DAGGERS IN THE COMPETITIONS, THOUGH.
CAN YA BELIEVE THEY STARTED YELLIN' AT EACH OTHER DURING THE QUICKSTEP?
FORGET ABOUT GETTIN' A CHECK-THEY MIGHT END UP GETTIN' A WARNING!
IF THE JUDGES DON'T LIKE THEM, THEY'RE DONE.
BUT I DON'T THINK THEY'LL GET KICKED OUT THIS EARLY.
GIVEN THE OTHER COMPETITORS HERE TODAY, THEY DID ALL RIGHT INDIVIDUALLY AND ON THE BASIC.
FSSSHH
GUESS IT IS STILL THE PRELIMS...
HEY, THAT'S MY SHIRT, MAN!
WIPE ふき
WIPE ふき
...
...HEY, HYODO?
IF TATARA MANAGES TO ADVANCE JUST DOIN' "ALL RIGHT" AND CAN'T GET HIS TEAM IN SYNC...

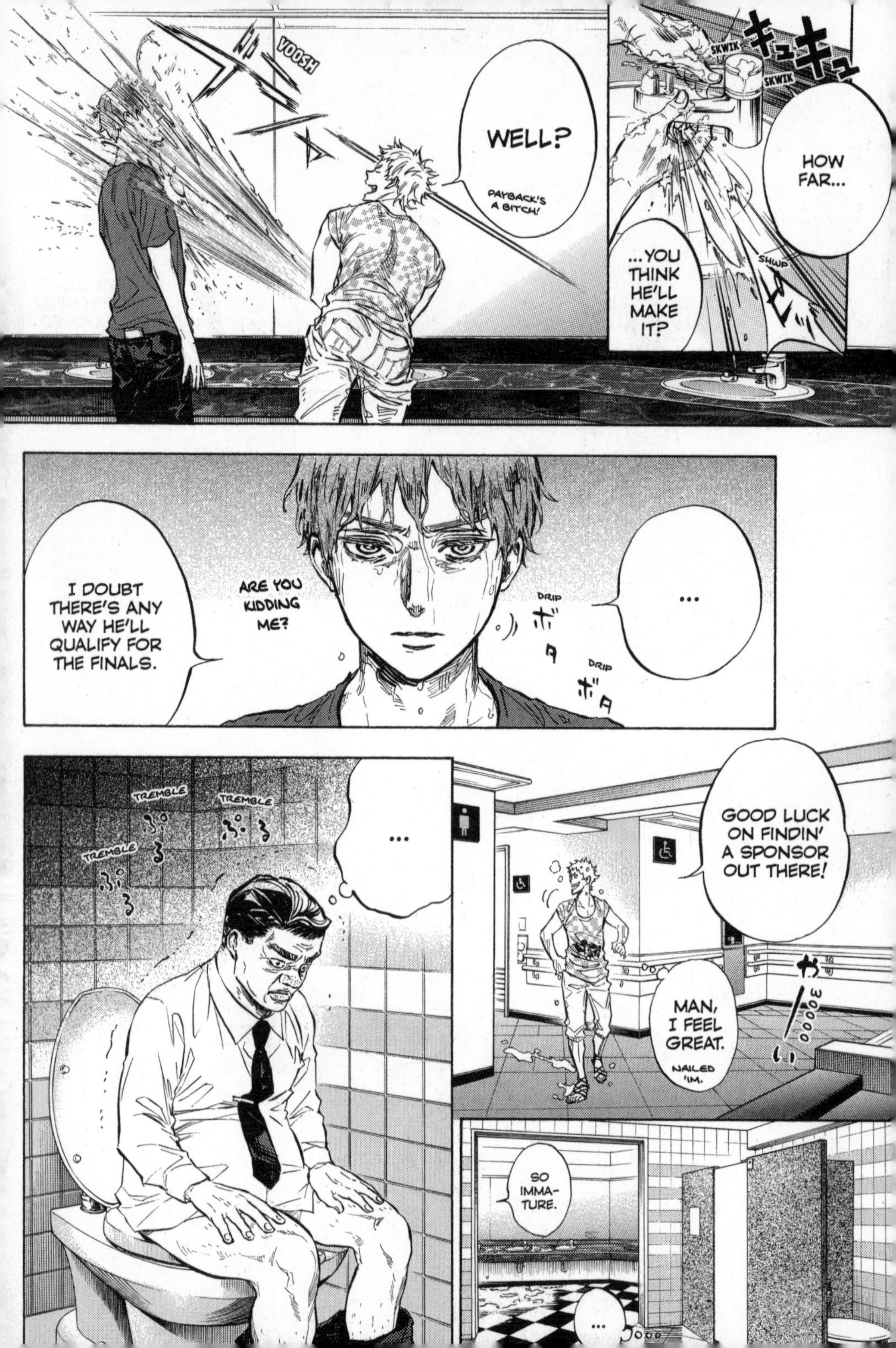
SKWIK
キュキュ
SKWIK
HOW FAR...
...YOU THINK HE'LL MAKE IT?
SHWP
VOOSH
WELL?
PAYBACK'S A BITCH!
...
DRIP
ボタ
DRIP
ボタ
ARE YOU KIDDING ME?
I DOUBT THERE'S ANY WAY HE'LL QUALIFY FOR THE FINALS.
GOOD LUCK ON FINDIN' A SPONSOR OUT THERE!
WOOOO
MAN, I FEEL GREAT.
NAILED 'IM.
SO IMMA-TURE.
...
...
TREMBLE
TREMBLE
TREMBLE

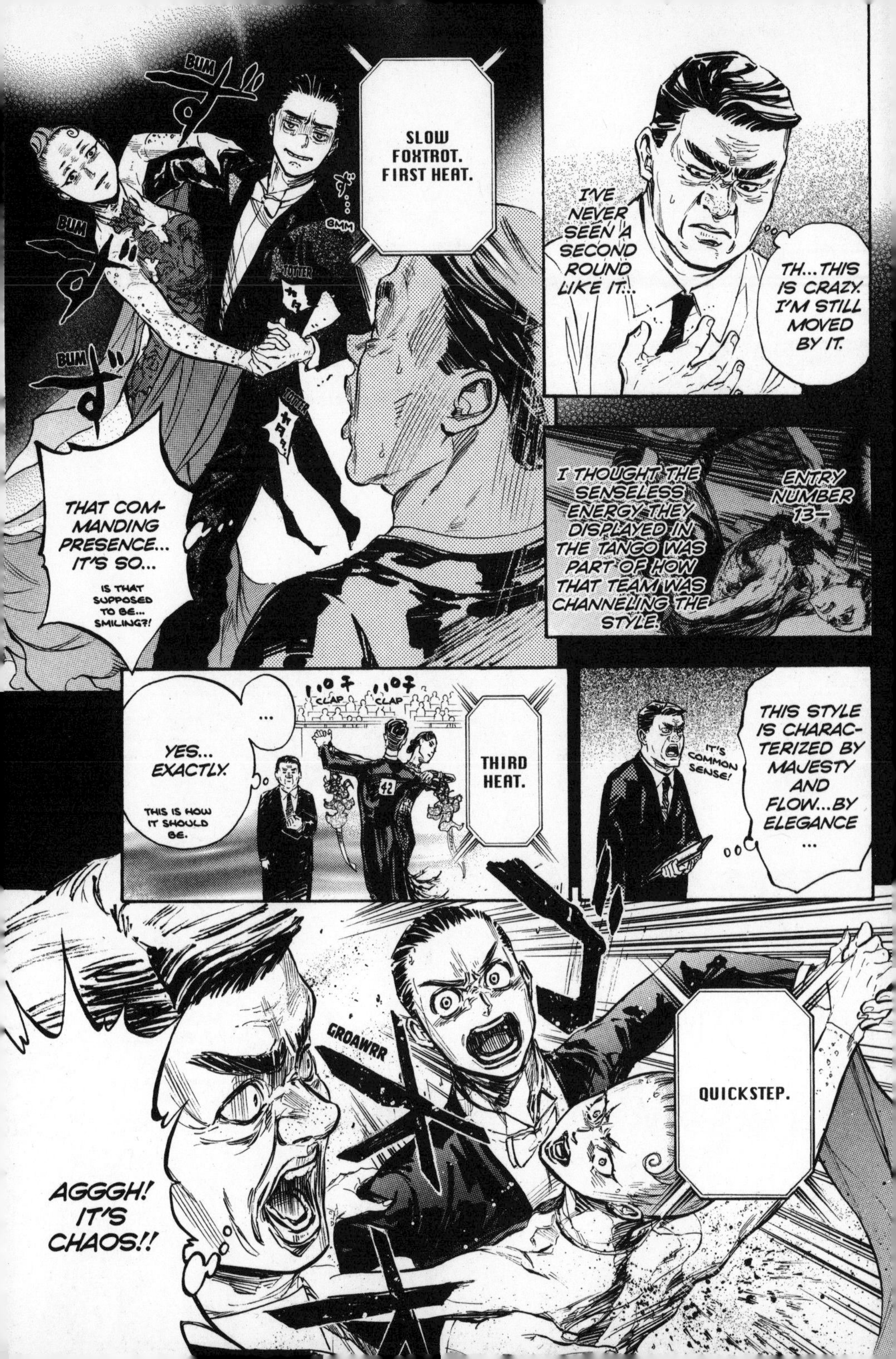
TH...THIS IS CRAZY. I'M STILL MOVED BY IT.
I'VE NEVER SEEN A SECOND ROUND LIKE IT...
ENTRY NUMBER 13—
I THOUGHT THE SENSELESS ENERGY THEY DISPLAYED IN THE TANGO WAS PART OF HOW THAT TEAM WAS CHANNELING THE STYLE.
SLOW FOXTROT. FIRST HEAT.
BMM
BUM
TOTTER
BUM
TOTTER
BUM
THAT COM-MANDING PRESENCE... IT'S SO...
IS THAT SUPPOSED TO BE... SMILING?!
THIS STYLE IS CHARAC-TERIZED BY MAJESTY AND FLOW...BY ELEGANCE ...
IT'S COMMON SENSE!
THIRD HEAT.
CLAP
CLAP
...
YES... EXACTLY.
THIS IS HOW IT SHOULD BE.
QUICKSTEP.
GROAWRR
AGGGH! IT'S CHAOS!!

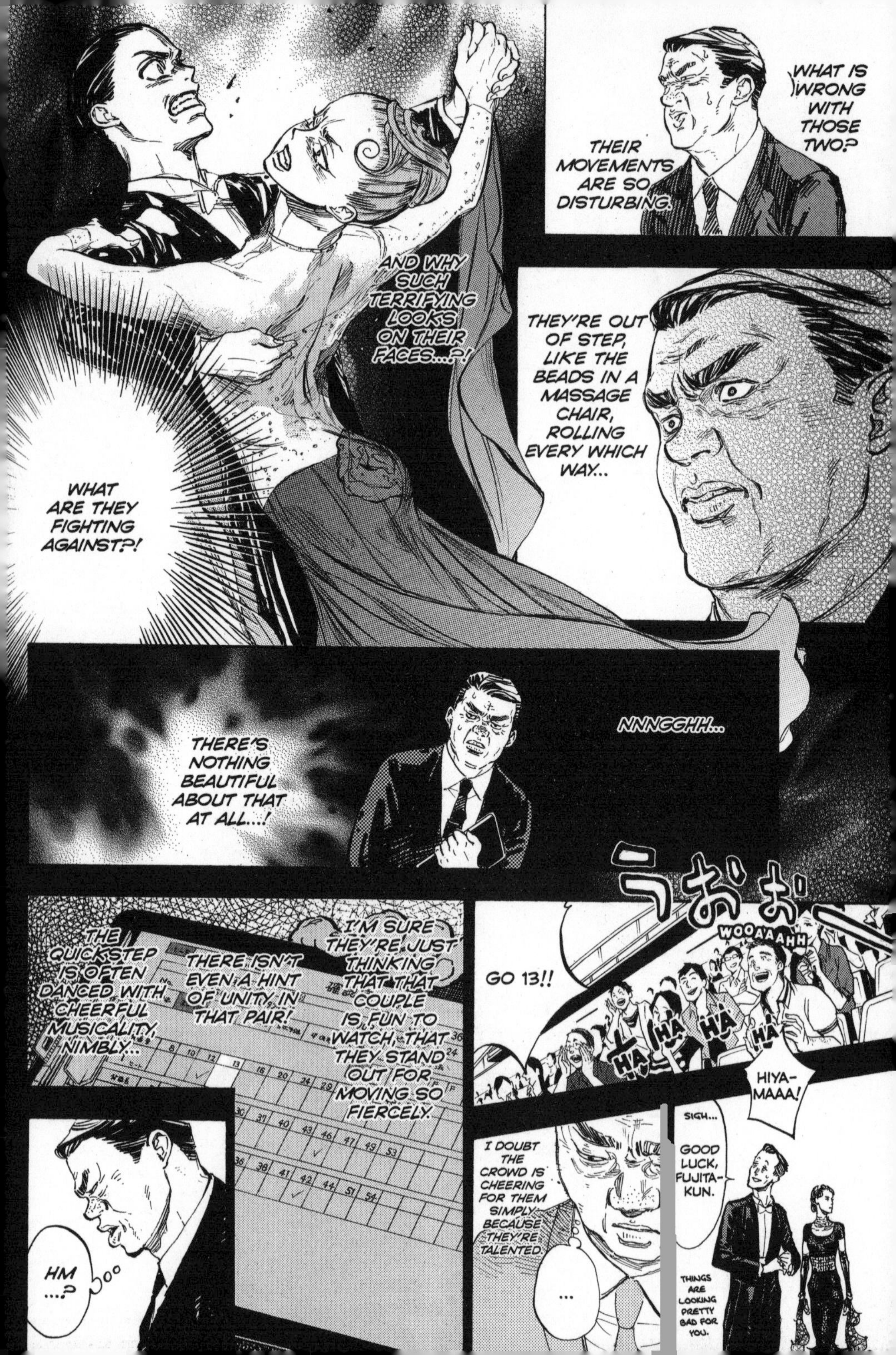
WHAT IS WRONG WITH THOSE TWO?
THEIR MOVEMENTS ARE SO DISTURBING.
THEY'RE OUT OF STEP, LIKE THE BEADS IN A MASSAGE CHAIR, ROLLING EVERY WHICH WAY...
AND WHY SUCH TERRIFYING LOOKS ON THEIR FACES...?!
WHAT ARE THEY FIGHTING AGAINST?!
NNNGGHH...
THERE'S NOTHING BEAUTIFUL ABOUT THAT AT ALL...!
うおぉ
WOOAAAHH
GO 13!!
HA HA HA HA
HIYA-MAAA!
I'M SURE THEY'RE JUST THINKING THAT THAT COUPLE IS FUN TO WATCH, THAT THEY STAND OUT FOR MOVING SO FIERCELY.
THERE ISN'T EVEN A HINT OF UNITY IN THAT PAIR!
THE QUICKSTEP IS OFTEN DANCED WITH CHEERFUL MUSICALITY, NIMBLY...
SIGH...
GOOD LUCK, FUJITA-KUN.
THINGS ARE LOOKING PRETTY BAD FOR YOU.
I DOUBT THE CROWD IS CHEERING FOR THEM SIMPLY BECAUSE THEY'RE TALENTED.
...
HM ...?

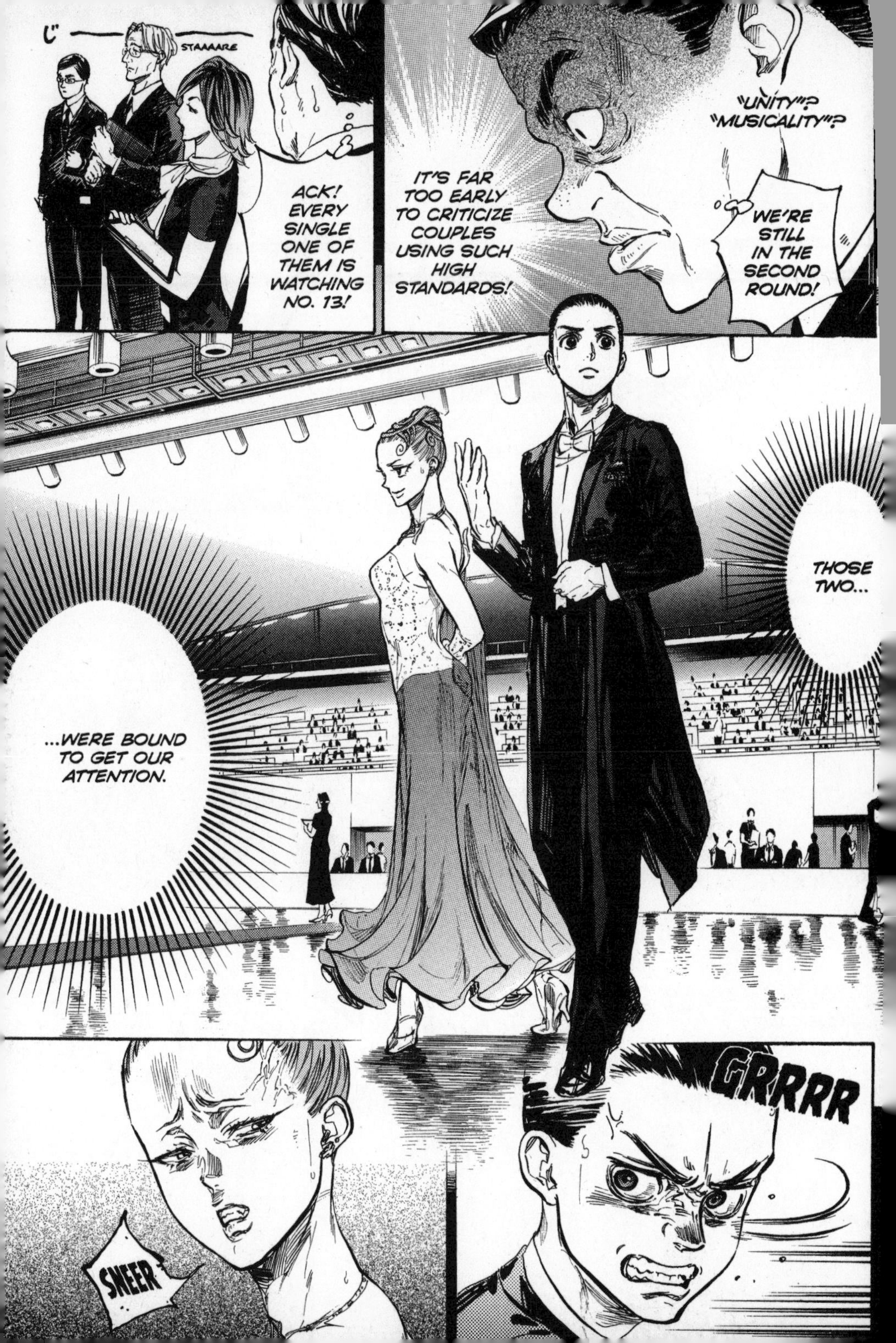
"UNITY"? "MUSICALITY"?
IT'S FAR TOO EARLY TO CRITICIZE COUPLES USING SUCH HIGH STANDARDS!
WE'RE STILL IN THE SECOND ROUND!
じ
STAAAARE
ACK! EVERY SINGLE ONE OF THEM IS WATCHING NO. 13!
THOSE TWO...
...WERE BOUND TO GET OUR ATTENTION.
GRRRRR
SNEER

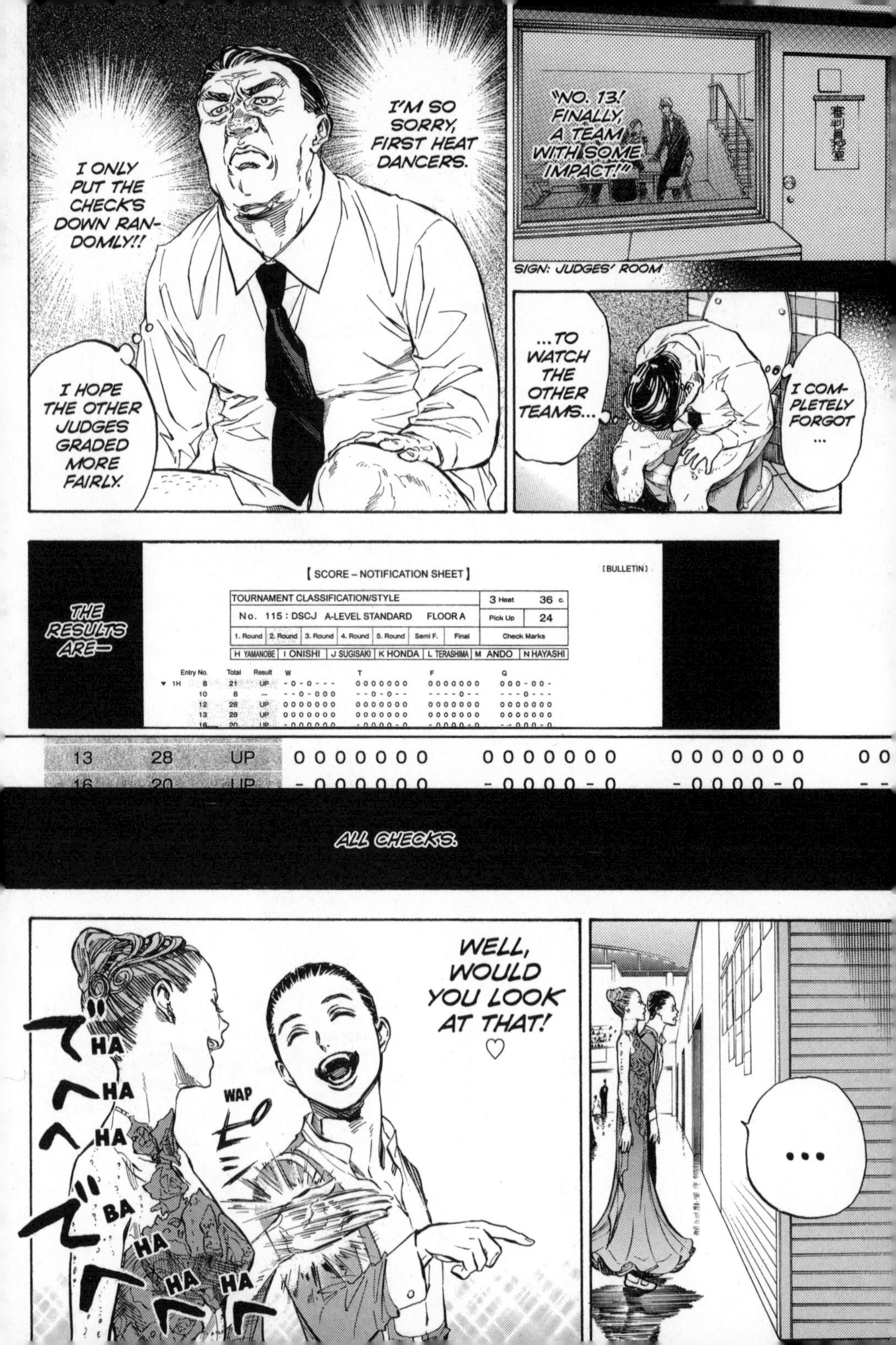
"NO. 13! FINALLY, A TEAM WITH SOME IMPACT!"
SIGN: JUDGES' ROOM
I'M SO SORRY, FIRST HEAT DANCERS.
I ONLY PUT THE CHECKS DOWN RANDOMLY!!
I HOPE THE OTHER JUDGES GRADED MORE FAIRLY.
I COMPLETELY FORGOT...
...TO WATCH THE OTHER TEAMS...
THE RESULTS ARE—
[BULLETIN]
【SCORE – NOTIFICATION SHEET】
TOURNAMENT CLASSIFICATION/STYLE
No. 115 : DSCJ A-LEVEL STANDARD FLOOR A
3 Heat 36 c.
Pick Up 24
1. Round 2. Round 3. Round 4. Round 5. Round Semi F. Final Check Marks
H YAMANOBE I ONISHI J SUGISAKI K HONDA L TERASHIMA M ANDO N HAYASHI
Entry No. Total Result W T F Q
▼ 1H 8 21 UP - 0 - 0 - - - 0 0 0 0 0 0 0 0 0 0 0 0 0 0 0 0 0 - 0 0 -
10 8 — - - 0 - 0 0 0 - - 0 - 0 - - - - - - 0 - - - - - 0 - - -
12 28 UP 0 0 0 0 0 0 0 0 0 0 0 0 0 0 0 0 0 0 0 0 0 0 0 0 0 0 0 0
13 28 UP 0 0 0 0 0 0 0 0 0 0 0 0 0 0 0 0 0 0 0 0 0 0 0 0 0 0 0 0
13 28 UP 0 0 0 0 0 0 0 0 0 0 0 0 0 0 0 0 0 0 0 0 0 0 0
ALL CHECKS.
WELL, WOULD YOU LOOK AT THAT! ♡
HA HA HA BA HA HA HA
WAP
...

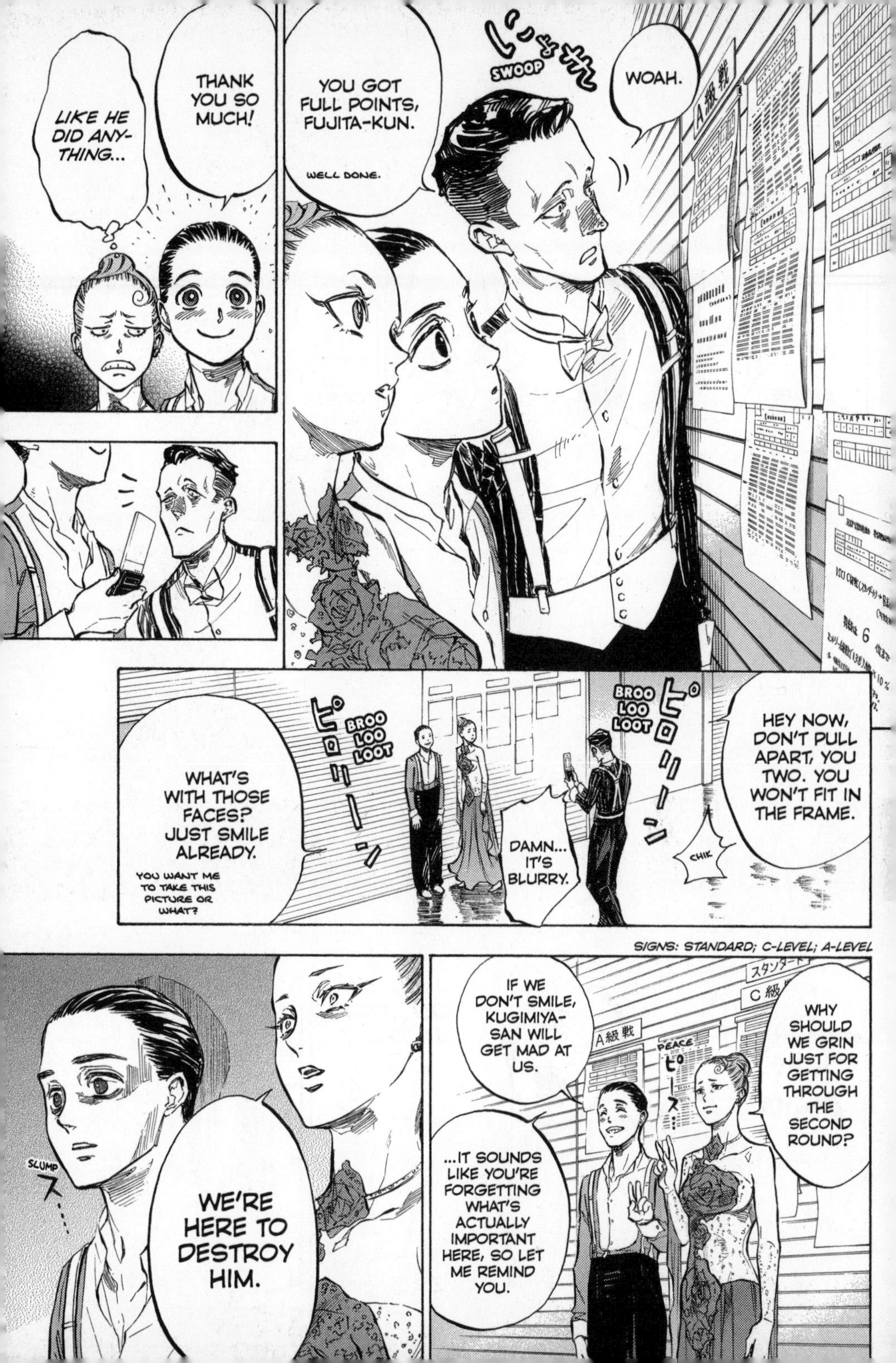
WOAH.
SWOOP
YOU GOT FULL POINTS, FUJITA-KUN.
WELL DONE.
THANK YOU SO MUCH!
LIKE HE DID ANY-THING...
HEY NOW, DON'T PULL APART, YOU TWO. YOU WON'T FIT IN THE FRAME.
CHIK
BROO LOO LOOT
DAMN... IT'S BLURRY.
BROO LOO LOOT
WHAT'S WITH THOSE FACES? JUST SMILE ALREADY.
YOU WANT ME TO TAKE THIS PICTURE OR WHAT?
SIGNS: STANDARD; C-LEVEL; A-LEVEL
WHY SHOULD WE GRIN JUST FOR GETTING THROUGH THE SECOND ROUND?
IF WE DON'T SMILE, KUGIMIYA-SAN WILL GET MAD AT US.
PEACE
...IT SOUNDS LIKE YOU'RE FORGETTING WHAT'S ACTUALLY IMPORTANT HERE, SO LET ME REMIND YOU.
WE'RE HERE TO DESTROY HIM.
SLUMP

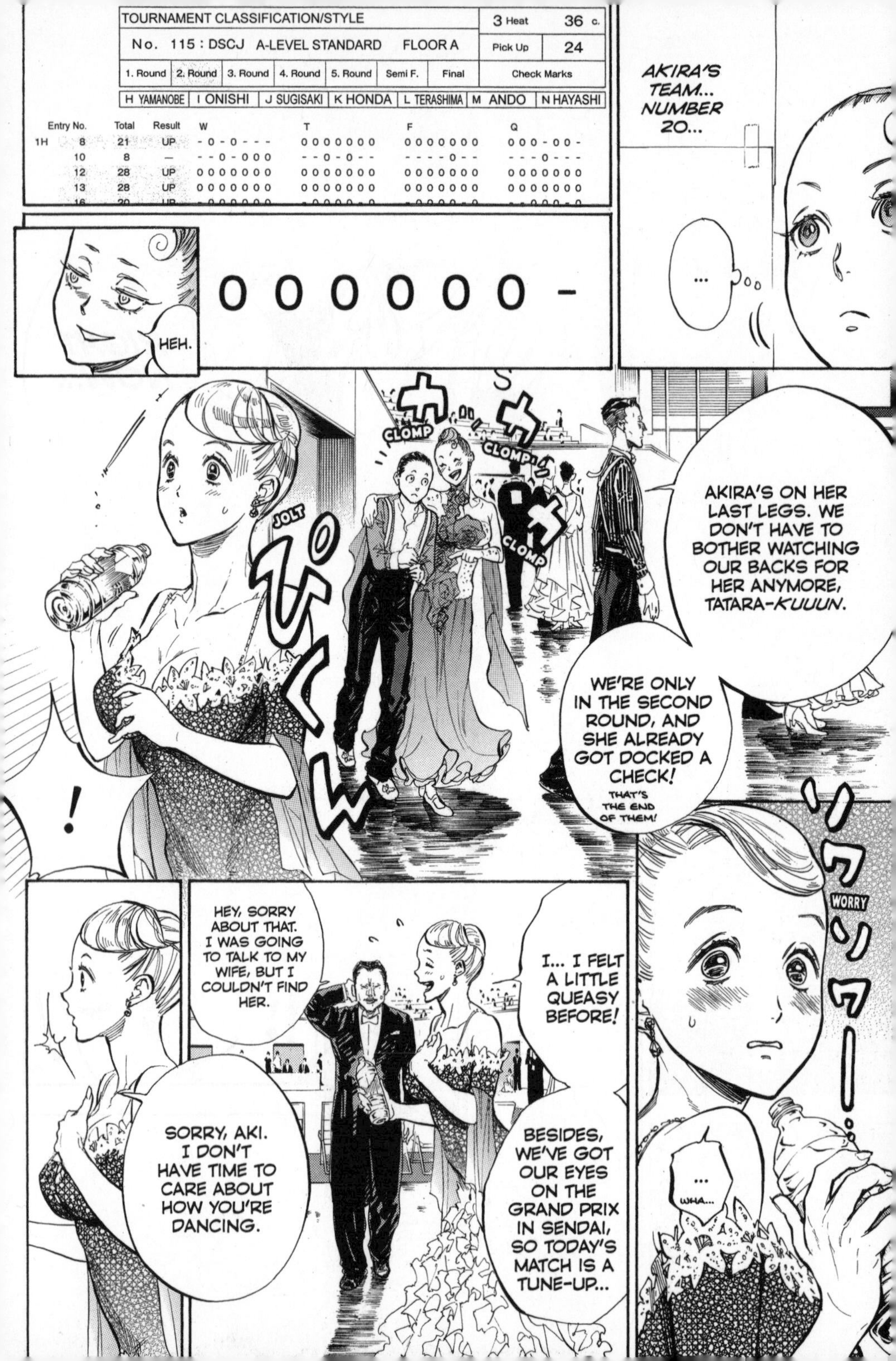
AKIRA'S TEAM... NUMBER 20...
...
TOURNAMENT CLASSIFICATION/STYLE
3 Heat 36 c.
No. 115 : DSCJ A-LEVEL STANDARD FLOOR A
Pick Up 24
1. Round 2. Round 3. Round 4. Round 5. Round Semi F. Final
Check Marks
H YAMANOBE I ONISHI J SUGISAKI K HONDA L TERASHIMA M ANDO N HAYASHI
Entry No. Total Result W T F Q
1H 8 21 UP - 0 - 0 - - - 0 0 0 0 0 0 0 0 0 0 0 0 0 0 0 0 0 - 0 0 -
10 8 — - - 0 - 0 0 0 - - 0 - 0 - - - - - - 0 - - - - - 0 - - -
12 28 UP 0 0 0 0 0 0 0 0 0 0 0 0 0 0 0 0 0 0 0 0 0 0 0 0 0 0 0 0
13 28 UP 0 0 0 0 0 0 0 0 0 0 0 0 0 0 0 0 0 0 0 0 0 0 0 0 0 0 0 0
0 0 0 0 0 0 -
HEH.
AKIRA'S ON HER LAST LEGS. WE DON'T HAVE TO BOTHER WATCHING OUR BACKS FOR HER ANYMORE, TATARA-*KUUUN*.
WE'RE ONLY IN THE SECOND ROUND, AND SHE ALREADY GOT DOCKED A CHECK!
THAT'S THE END OF THEM!
CLOMP
CLOMP
CLOMP
JOLT
!
WORRY
...
WHA...
I... I FELT A LITTLE QUEASY BEFORE!
HEY, SORRY ABOUT THAT. I WAS GOING TO TALK TO MY WIFE, BUT I COULDN'T FIND HER.
BESIDES, WE'VE GOT OUR EYES ON THE GRAND PRIX IN SENDAI, SO TODAY'S MATCH IS A TUNE-UP...
SORRY, AKI. I DON'T HAVE TIME TO CARE ABOUT HOW YOU'RE DANCING.

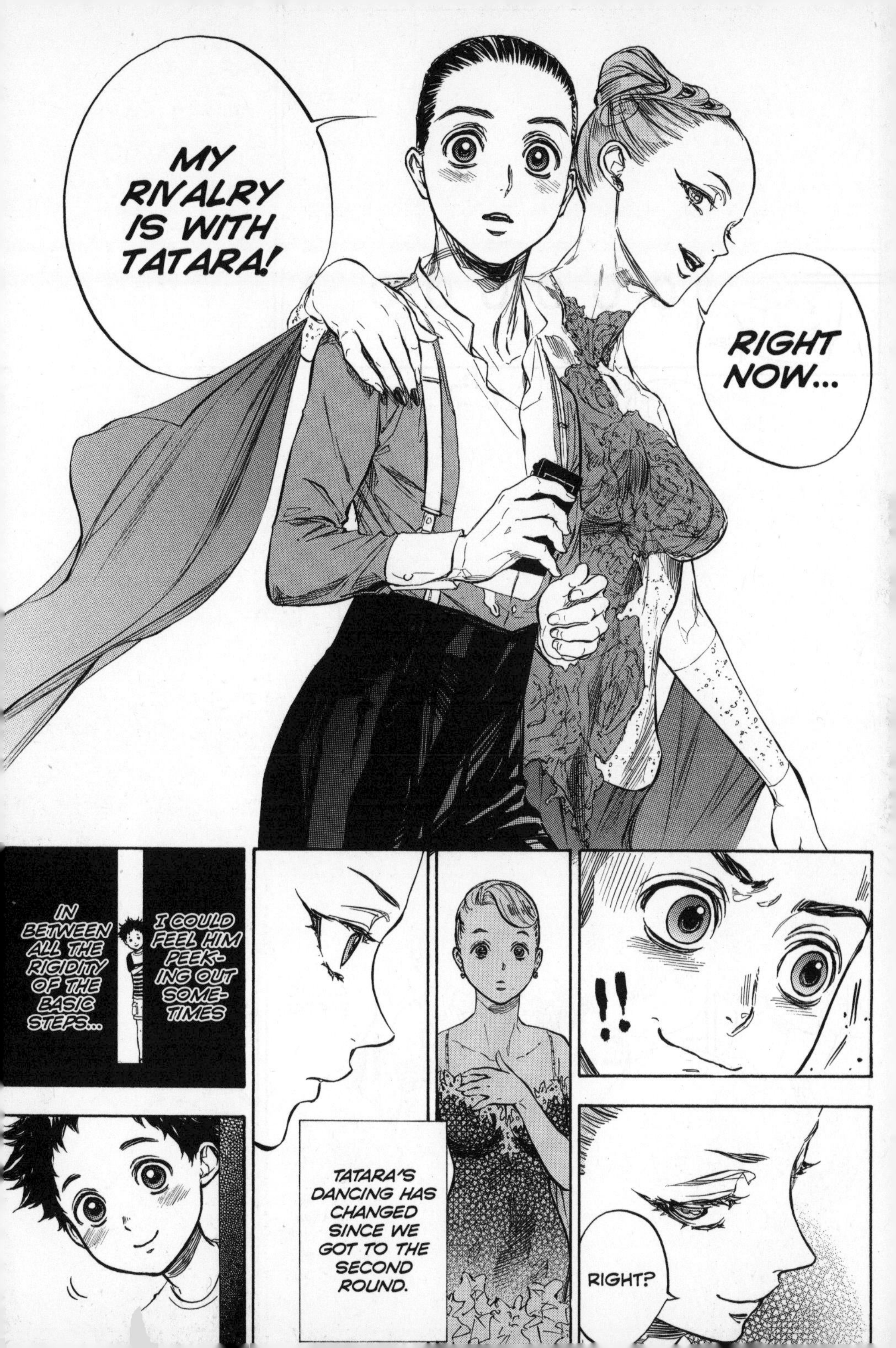
RIGHT NOW...
MY RIVALRY IS WITH TATARA!
!!
RIGHT?
TATARA'S DANCING HAS CHANGED SINCE WE GOT TO THE SECOND ROUND.
I COULD FEEL HIM PEEK-ING OUT SOME-TIMES
IN BETWEEN ALL THE RIGIDITY OF THE BASIC STEPS...

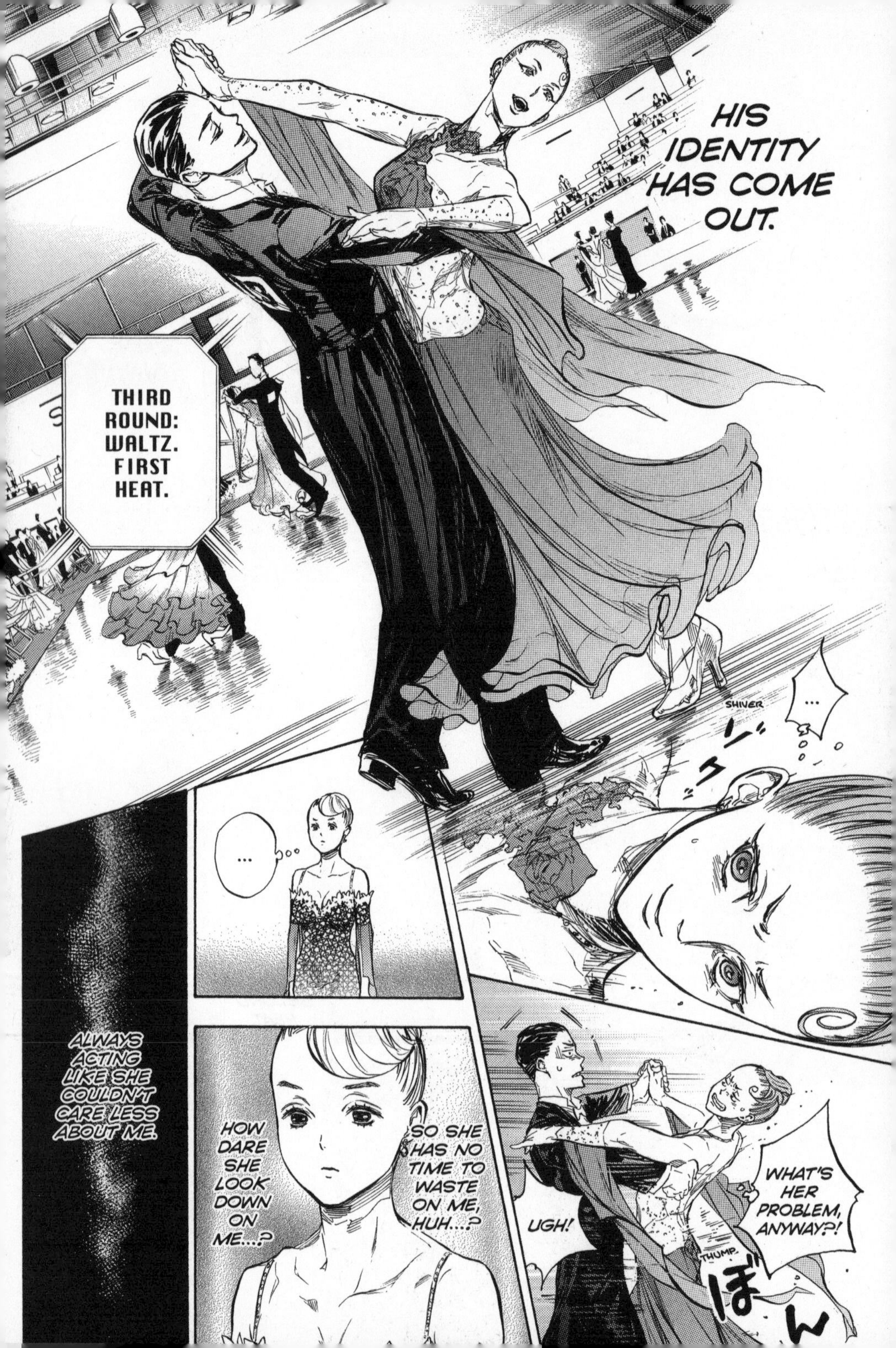
HIS IDENTITY HAS COME OUT.
THIRD ROUND: WALTZ. FIRST HEAT.
SHIVER
...
...
WHAT'S HER PROBLEM, ANYWAY?!
UGH!
THUMP
SO SHE HAS NO TIME TO WASTE ON ME, HUH...?
HOW DARE SHE LOOK DOWN ON ME...?
ALWAYS ACTING LIKE SHE COULDN'T CARE LESS ABOUT ME.

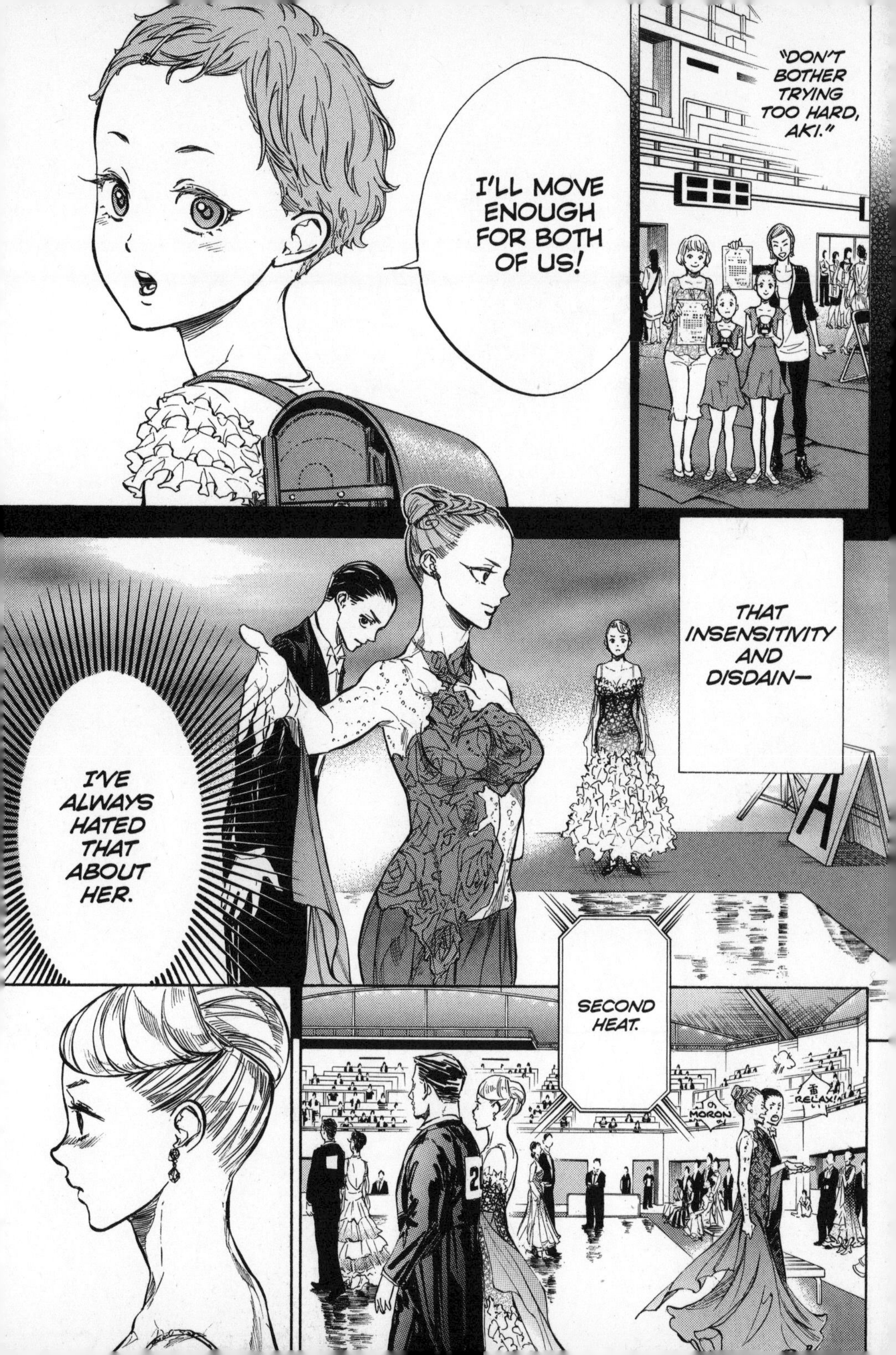
"DON'T BOTHER TRYING TOO HARD, AKI."
I'LL MOVE ENOUGH FOR BOTH OF US!
THAT INSENSITIVITY AND DISDAIN—
I'VE ALWAYS HATED THAT ABOUT HER.
SECOND HEAT.
RELAX!
MORON.

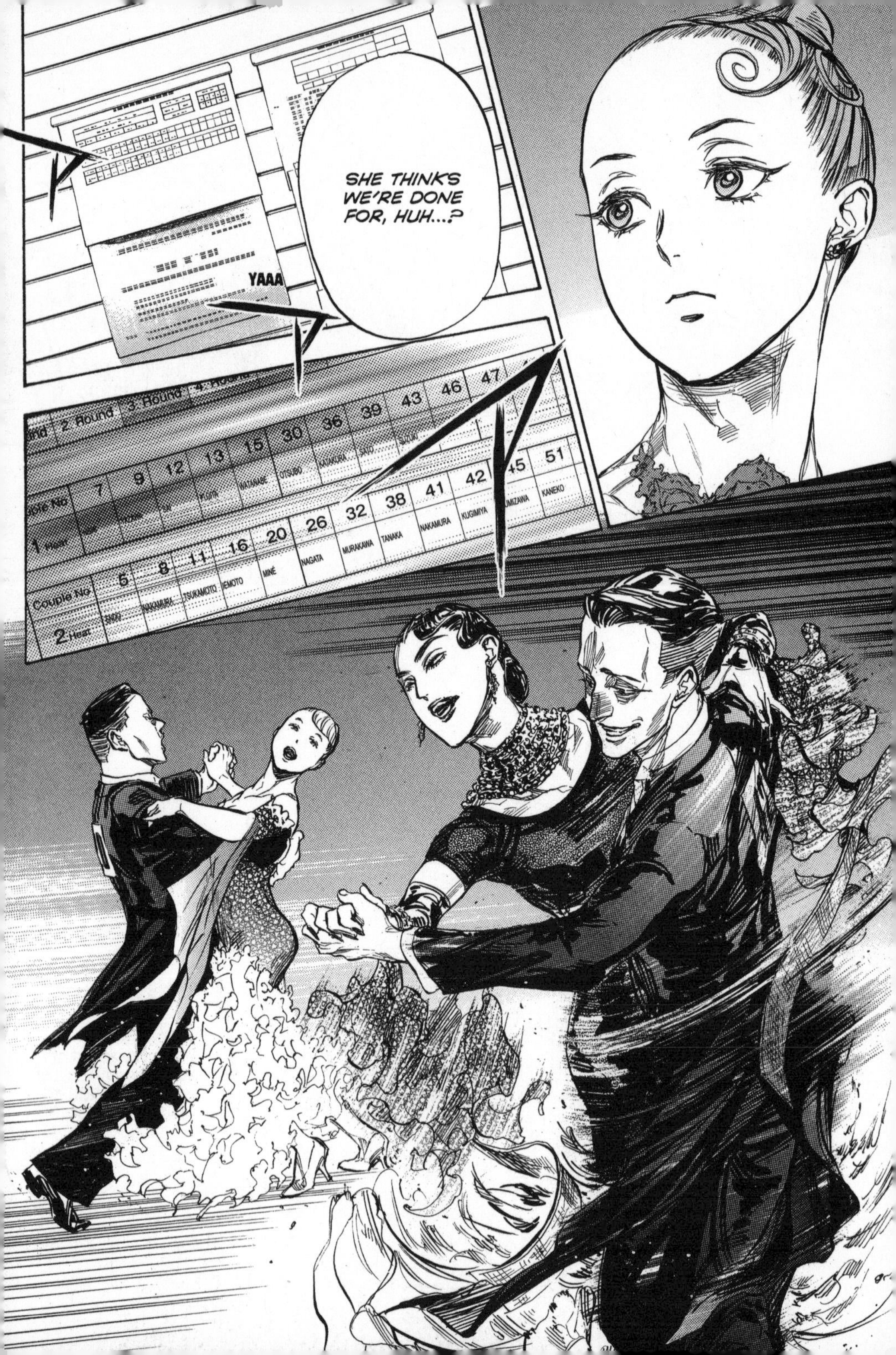
SHE THINKS WE'RE DONE FOR, HUH...?
YAAA

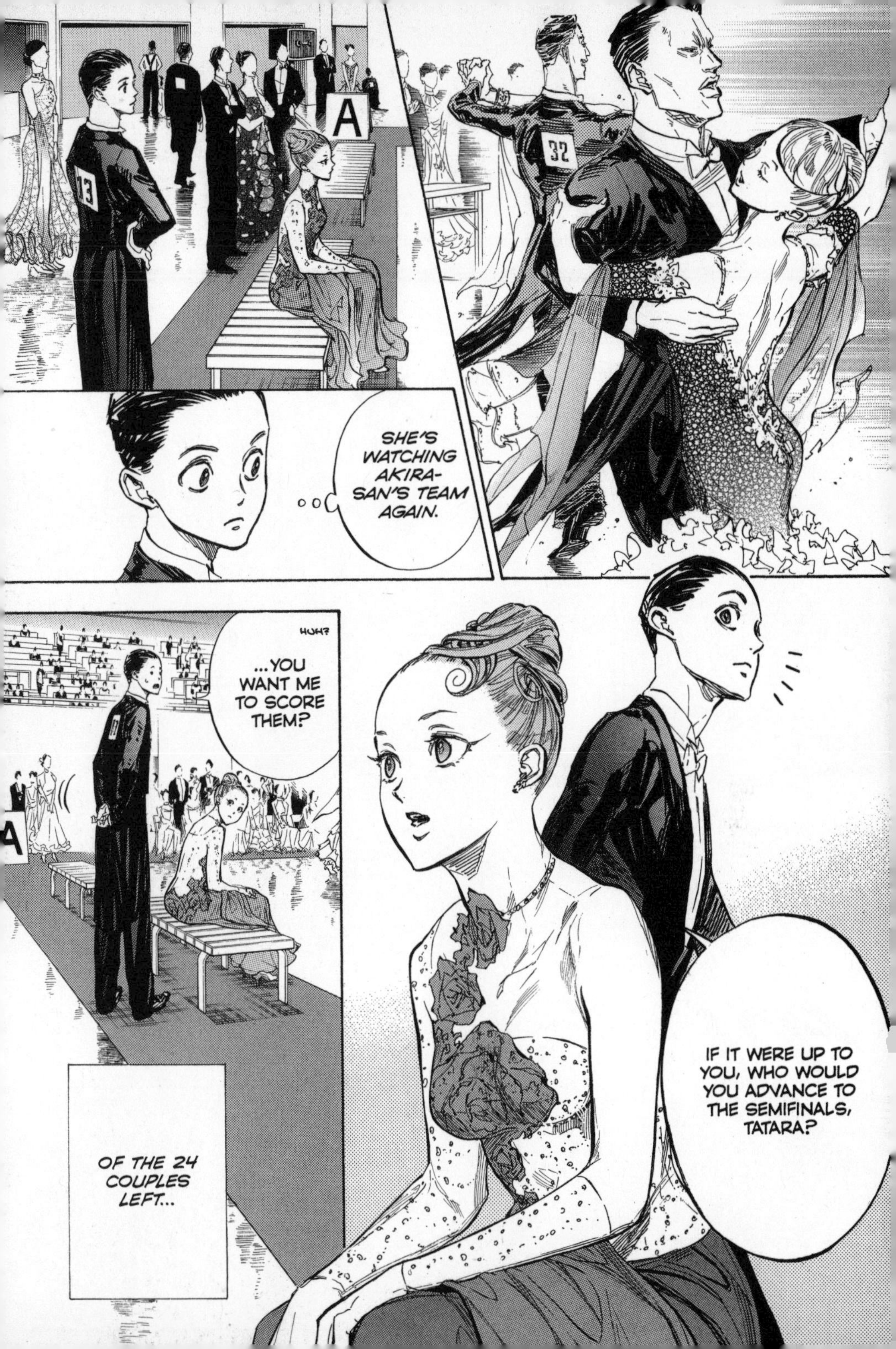

SHE'S WATCHING AKIRA-SAN'S TEAM AGAIN.
IF IT WERE UP TO YOU, WHO WOULD YOU ADVANCE TO THE SEMIFINALS, TATARA?
HUH?
...YOU WANT ME TO SCORE THEM?
OF THE 24 COUPLES LEFT...

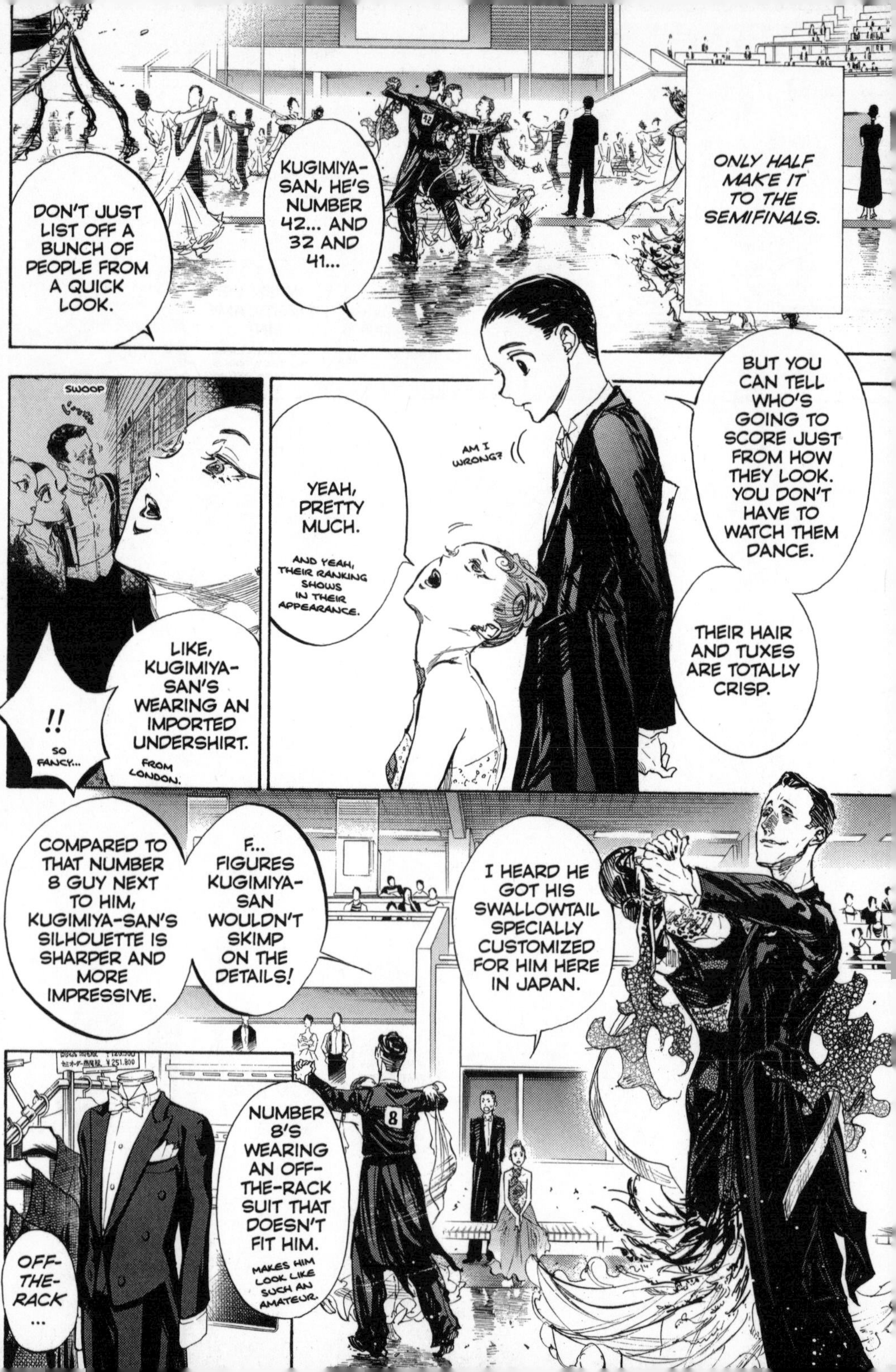
ONLY HALF MAKE IT TO THE SEMIFINALS.
KUGIMIYA-SAN, HE'S NUMBER 42... AND 32 AND 41...
DON'T JUST LIST OFF A BUNCH OF PEOPLE FROM A QUICK LOOK.
BUT YOU CAN TELL WHO'S GOING TO SCORE JUST FROM HOW THEY LOOK. YOU DON'T HAVE TO WATCH THEM DANCE.
THEIR HAIR AND TUXES ARE TOTALLY CRISP.
AM I WRONG?
YEAH, PRETTY MUCH.
AND YEAH, THEIR RANKING SHOWS IN THEIR APPEARANCE.
SWOOP
LIKE, KUGIMIYA-SAN'S WEARING AN IMPORTED UNDERSHIRT.
FROM LONDON.
!!
SO FANCY...
I HEARD HE GOT HIS SWALLOWTAIL SPECIALLY CUSTOMIZED FOR HIM HERE IN JAPAN.
F... FIGURES KUGIMIYA-SAN WOULDN'T SKIMP ON THE DETAILS!
COMPARED TO THAT NUMBER 8 GUY NEXT TO HIM, KUGIMIYA-SAN'S SILHOUETTE IS SHARPER AND MORE IMPRESSIVE.
NUMBER 8'S WEARING AN OFF-THE-RACK SUIT THAT DOESN'T FIT HIM.
MAKES HIM LOOK LIKE SUCH AN AMATEUR.
OFF-THE-RACK...

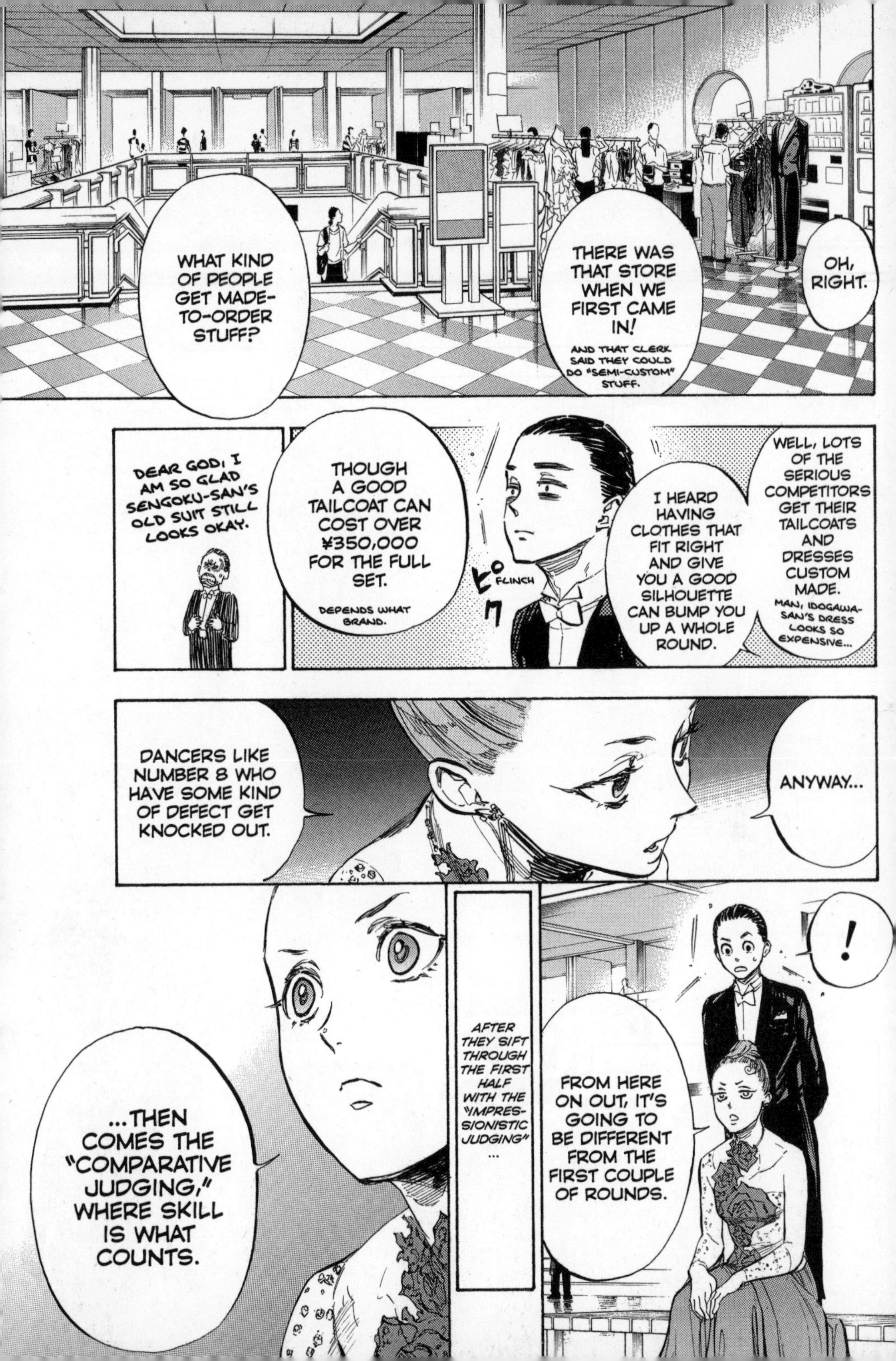
OH, RIGHT.
THERE WAS THAT STORE WHEN WE FIRST CAME IN!
AND THAT CLERK SAID THEY COULD DO "SEMI-CUSTOM" STUFF.
WHAT KIND OF PEOPLE GET MADE-TO-ORDER STUFF?
WELL, LOTS OF THE SERIOUS COMPETITORS GET THEIR TAILCOATS AND DRESSES CUSTOM MADE.
MAN, IDOGAWA-SAN'S DRESS LOOKS SO EXPENSIVE...
I HEARD HAVING CLOTHES THAT FIT RIGHT AND GIVE YOU A GOOD SILHOUETTE CAN BUMP YOU UP A WHOLE ROUND.
FLINCH
THOUGH A GOOD TAILCOAT CAN COST OVER ¥350,000 FOR THE FULL SET.
DEPENDS WHAT BRAND.
DEAR GOD, I AM SO GLAD SENGOKU-SAN'S OLD SUIT STILL LOOKS OKAY.
ANYWAY...
DANCERS LIKE NUMBER 8 WHO HAVE SOME KIND OF DEFECT GET KNOCKED OUT.
!
FROM HERE ON OUT, IT'S GOING TO BE DIFFERENT FROM THE FIRST COUPLE OF ROUNDS.
AFTER THEY SIFT THROUGH THE FIRST HALF WITH THE "IMPRESSIONISTIC JUDGING"...
...THEN COMES THE "COMPARATIVE JUDGING," WHERE SKILL IS WHAT COUNTS.

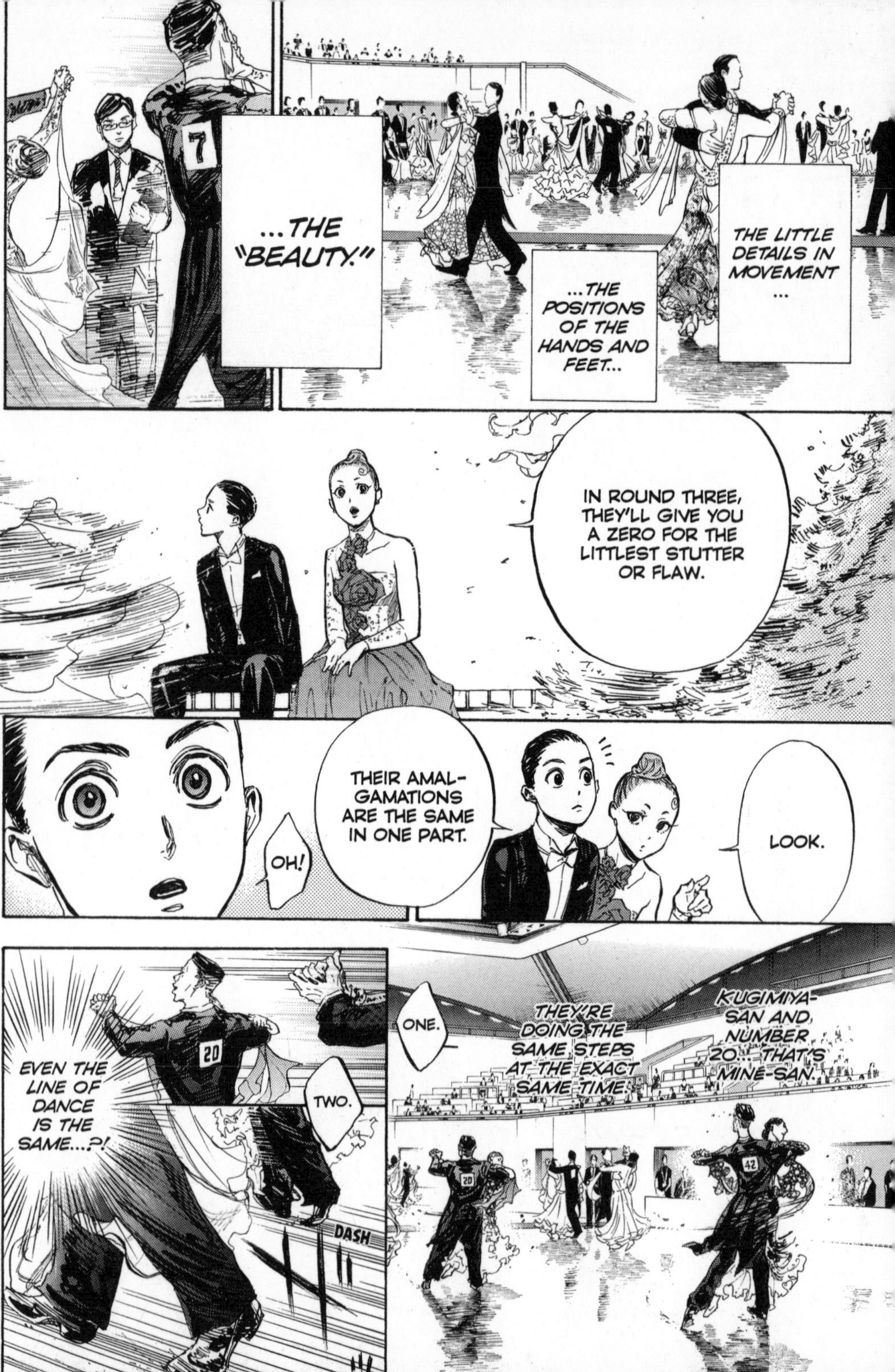
THE LITTLE DETAILS IN MOVEMENT...
...THE POSITIONS OF THE HANDS AND FEET...
...THE "BEAUTY."
IN ROUND THREE, THEY'LL GIVE YOU A ZERO FOR THE LITTLEST STUTTER OR FLAW.
LOOK.
THEIR AMAL-GAMATIONS ARE THE SAME IN ONE PART.
OH!
KUGIMIYA-SAN AND NUMBER 20... THAT'S MINE-SAN.
THEY'RE DOING THE SAME STEPS AT THE EXACT SAME TIME.
ONE.
EVEN THE LINE OF DANCE IS THE SAME...?!
TWO.
DASH

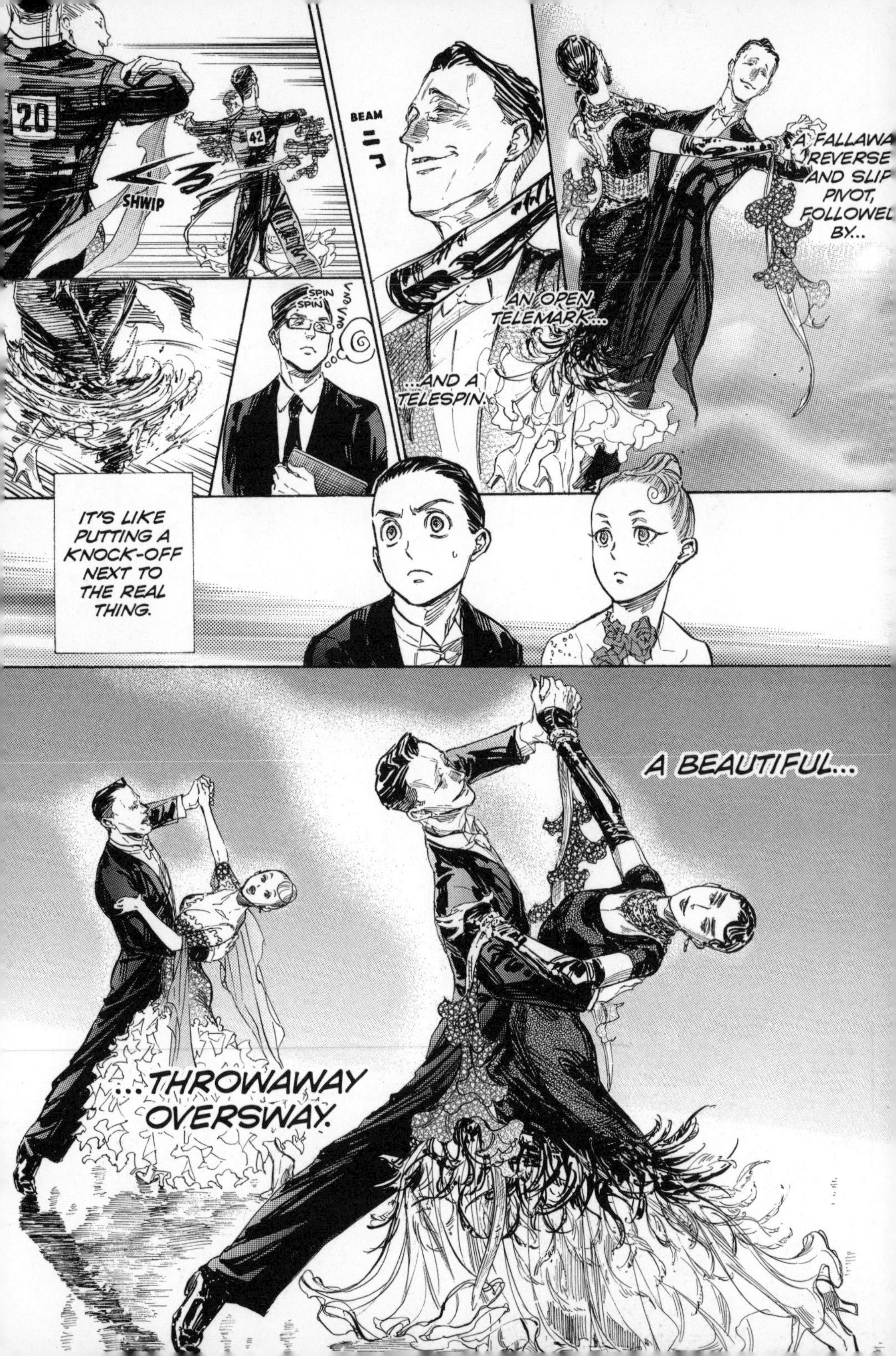
A FALLAWA REVERSE AND SLIP PIVOT, FOLLOWEL BY...
BEAM
ニコ
SHWIP
AN OPEN TELEMARK...
...AND A TELESPIN.
SPIN
SPIN
IT'S LIKE PUTTING A KNOCK-OFF NEXT TO THE REAL THING.
A BEAUTIFUL...
...THROWAWAY OVERSWAY.

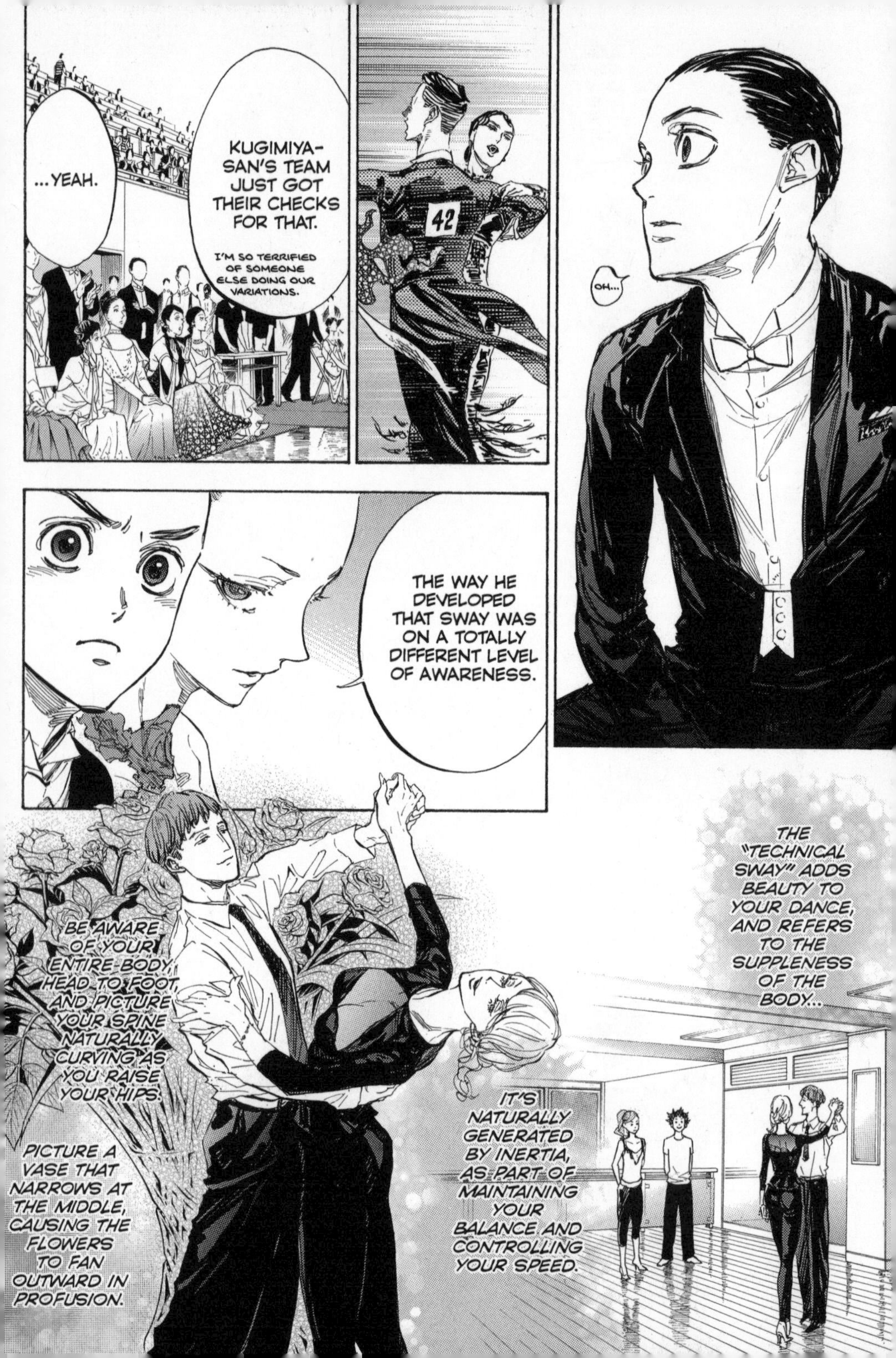
OH...
KUGIMIYA-SAN'S TEAM JUST GOT THEIR CHECKS FOR THAT.
I'M SO TERRIFIED OF SOMEONE ELSE DOING OUR VARIATIONS.
...YEAH.
42
THE WAY HE DEVELOPED THAT SWAY WAS ON A TOTALLY DIFFERENT LEVEL OF AWARENESS.
THE "TECHNICAL SWAY" ADDS BEAUTY TO YOUR DANCE, AND REFERS TO THE SUPPLENESS OF THE BODY...
IT'S NATURALLY GENERATED BY INERTIA, AS PART OF MAINTAINING YOUR BALANCE AND CONTROLLING YOUR SPEED.
BE AWARE OF YOUR ENTIRE BODY, HEAD TO FOOT, AND PICTURE YOUR SPINE NATURALLY CURVING AS YOU RAISE YOUR HIPS.
PICTURE A VASE THAT NARROWS AT THE MIDDLE, CAUSING THE FLOWERS TO FAN OUTWARD IN PROFUSION.

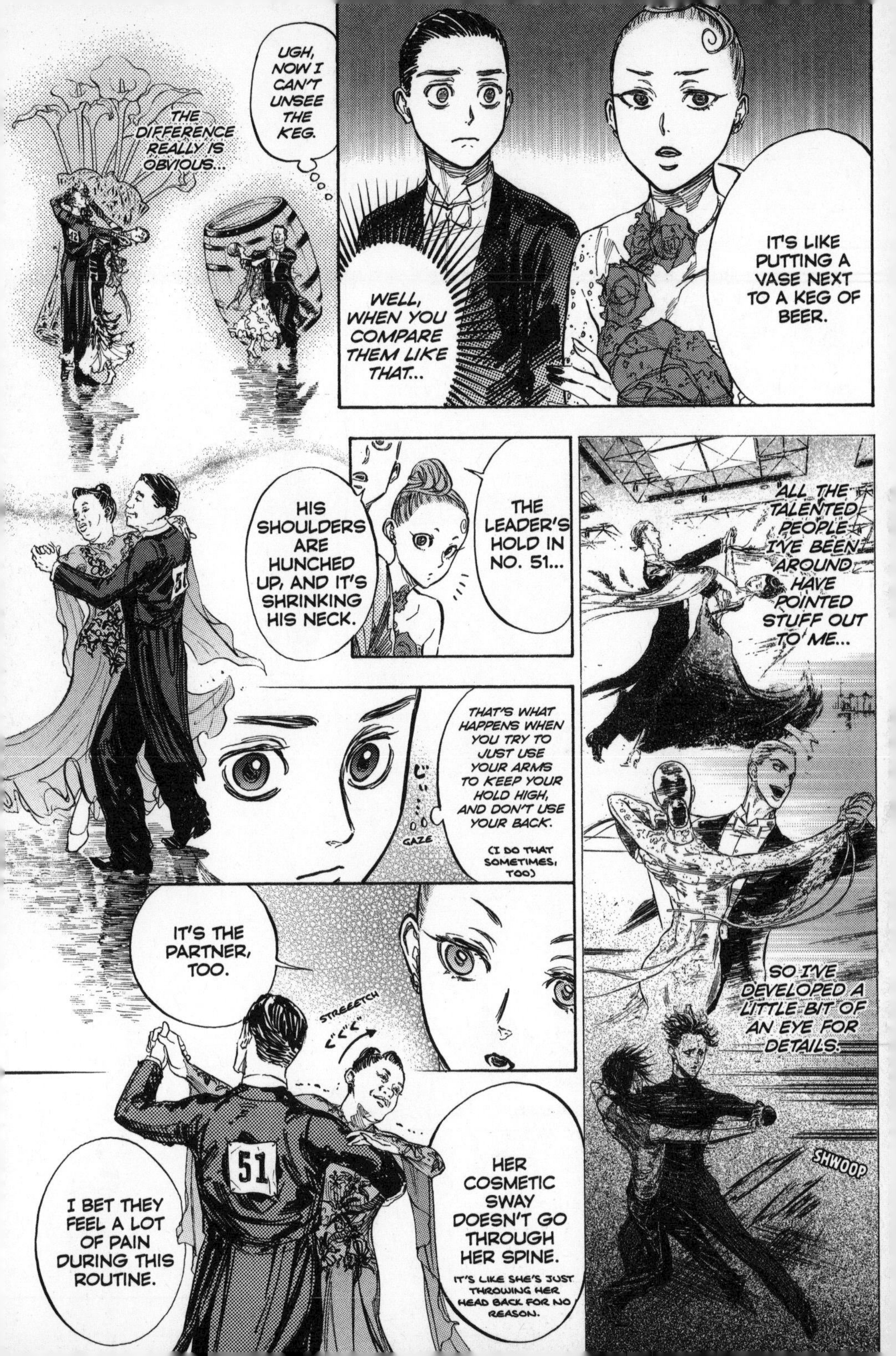

IT'S LIKE PUTTING A VASE NEXT TO A KEG OF BEER.
WELL, WHEN YOU COMPARE THEM LIKE THAT...
UGH, NOW I CAN'T UNSEE THE KEG.
THE DIFFERENCE REALLY IS OBVIOUS...
ALL THE TALENTED PEOPLE I'VE BEEN AROUND HAVE POINTED STUFF OUT TO ME...
SO I'VE DEVELOPED A LITTLE BIT OF AN EYE FOR DETAILS.
SHWOOP
THE LEADER'S HOLD IN NO. 51...
HIS SHOULDERS ARE HUNCHED UP, AND IT'S SHRINKING HIS NECK.
THAT'S WHAT HAPPENS WHEN YOU TRY TO JUST USE YOUR ARMS TO KEEP YOUR HOLD HIGH, AND DON'T USE YOUR BACK.
(I DO THAT SOMETIMES, TOO)
GAZE
IT'S THE PARTNER, TOO.
STREEETCH
HER COSMETIC SWAY DOESN'T GO THROUGH HER SPINE.
IT'S LIKE SHE'S JUST THROWING HER HEAD BACK FOR NO REASON.
I BET THEY FEEL A LOT OF PAIN DURING THIS ROUTINE.

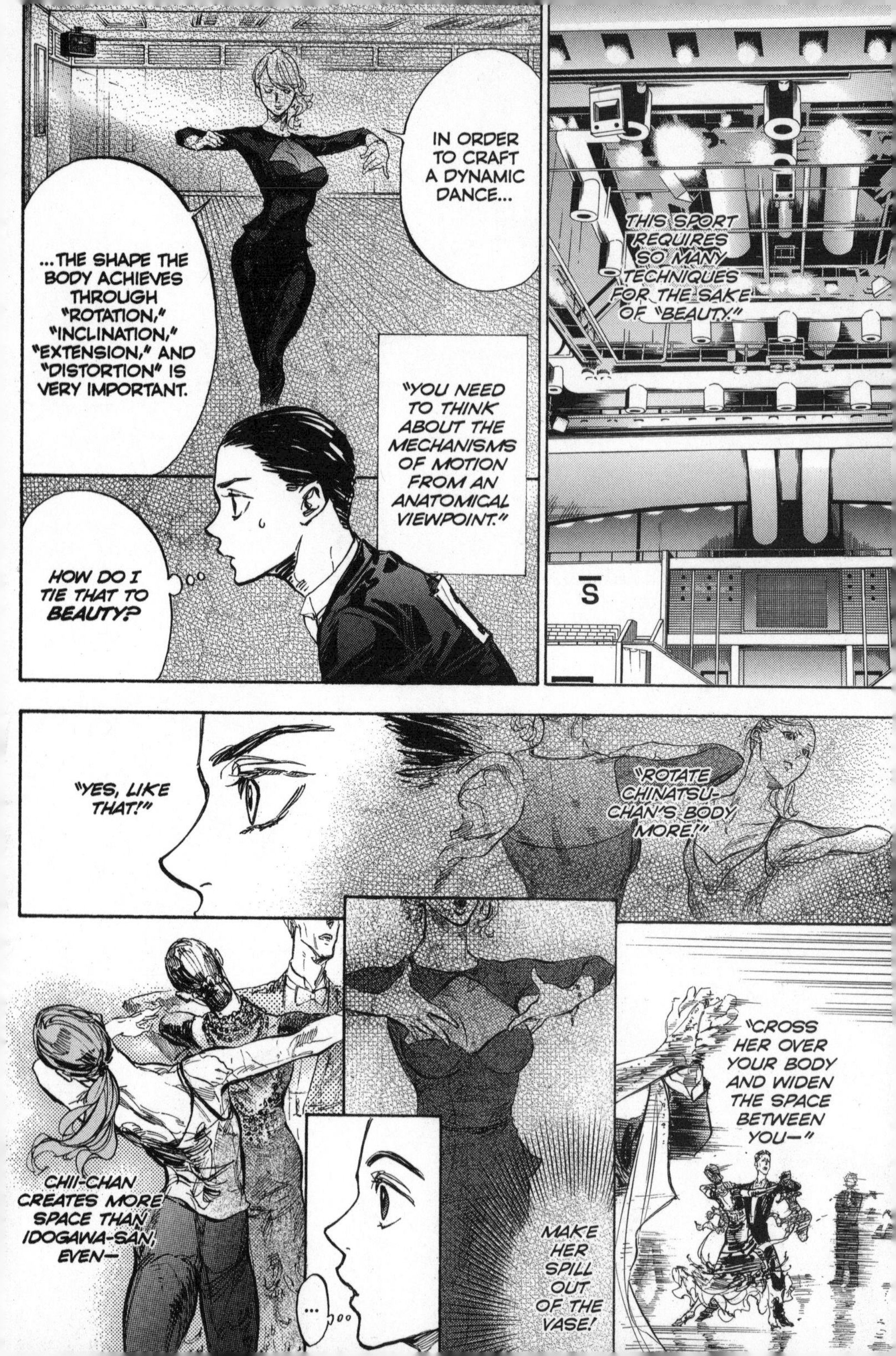

THIS SPORT REQUIRES SO MANY TECHNIQUES FOR THE SAKE OF "BEAUTY."
S
IN ORDER TO CRAFT A DYNAMIC DANCE...
...THE SHAPE THE BODY ACHIEVES THROUGH "ROTATION," "INCLINATION," "EXTENSION," AND "DISTORTION" IS VERY IMPORTANT.
"YOU NEED TO THINK ABOUT THE MECHANISMS OF MOTION FROM AN ANATOMICAL VIEWPOINT."
HOW DO I TIE THAT TO BEAUTY?
"ROTATE CHINATSU-CHAN'S BODY MORE!"
"YES, LIKE THAT!"
"CROSS HER OVER YOUR BODY AND WIDEN THE SPACE BETWEEN YOU—"
MAKE HER SPILL OUT OF THE VASE!
...
CHII-CHAN CREATES MORE SPACE THAN IDOGAWA-SAN, EVEN—

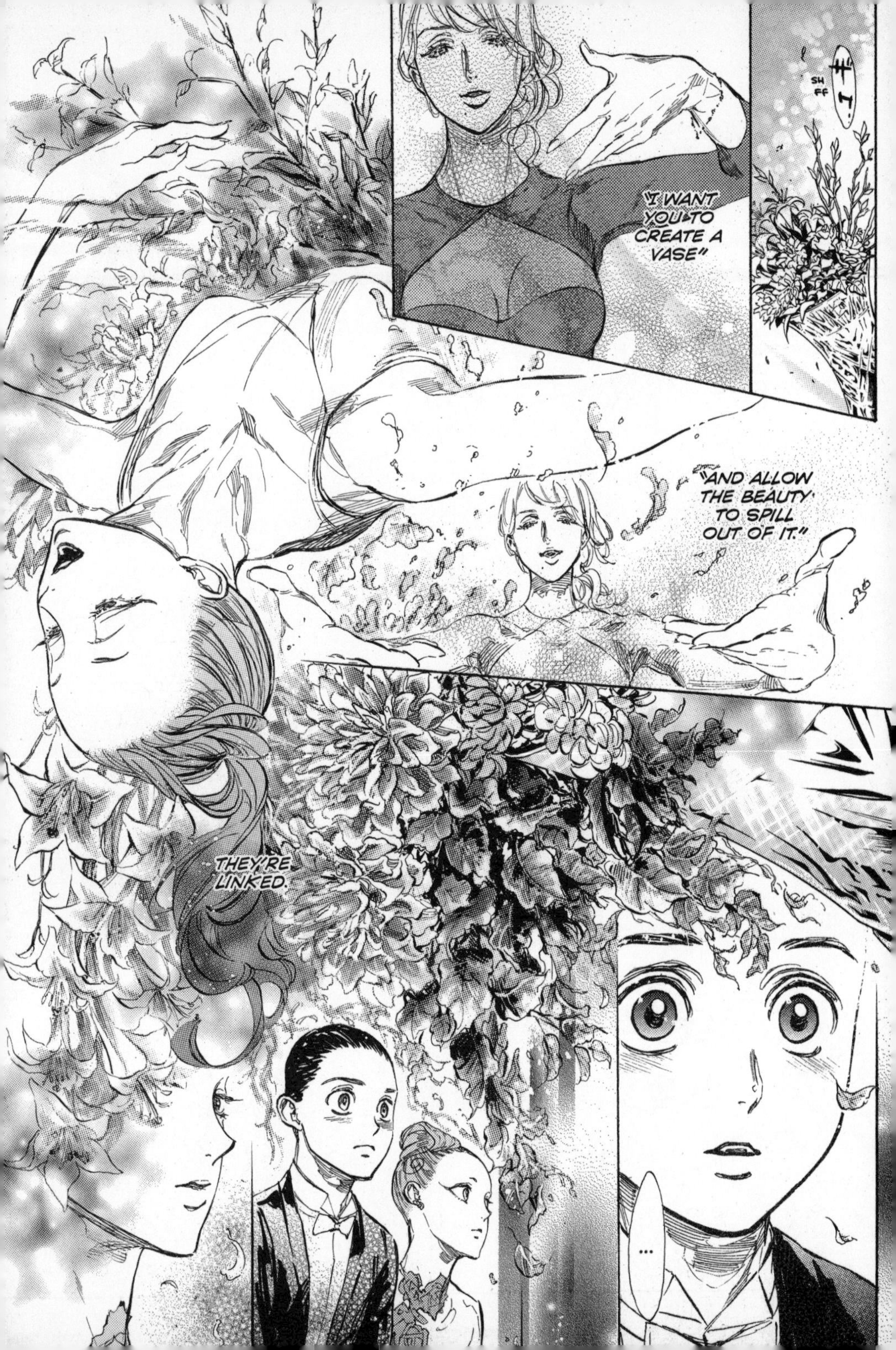
SHFF
"I WANT YOU TO CREATE A VASE"
"AND ALLOW THE BEAUTY TO SPILL OUT OF IT."
THEY'RE LINKED.
...

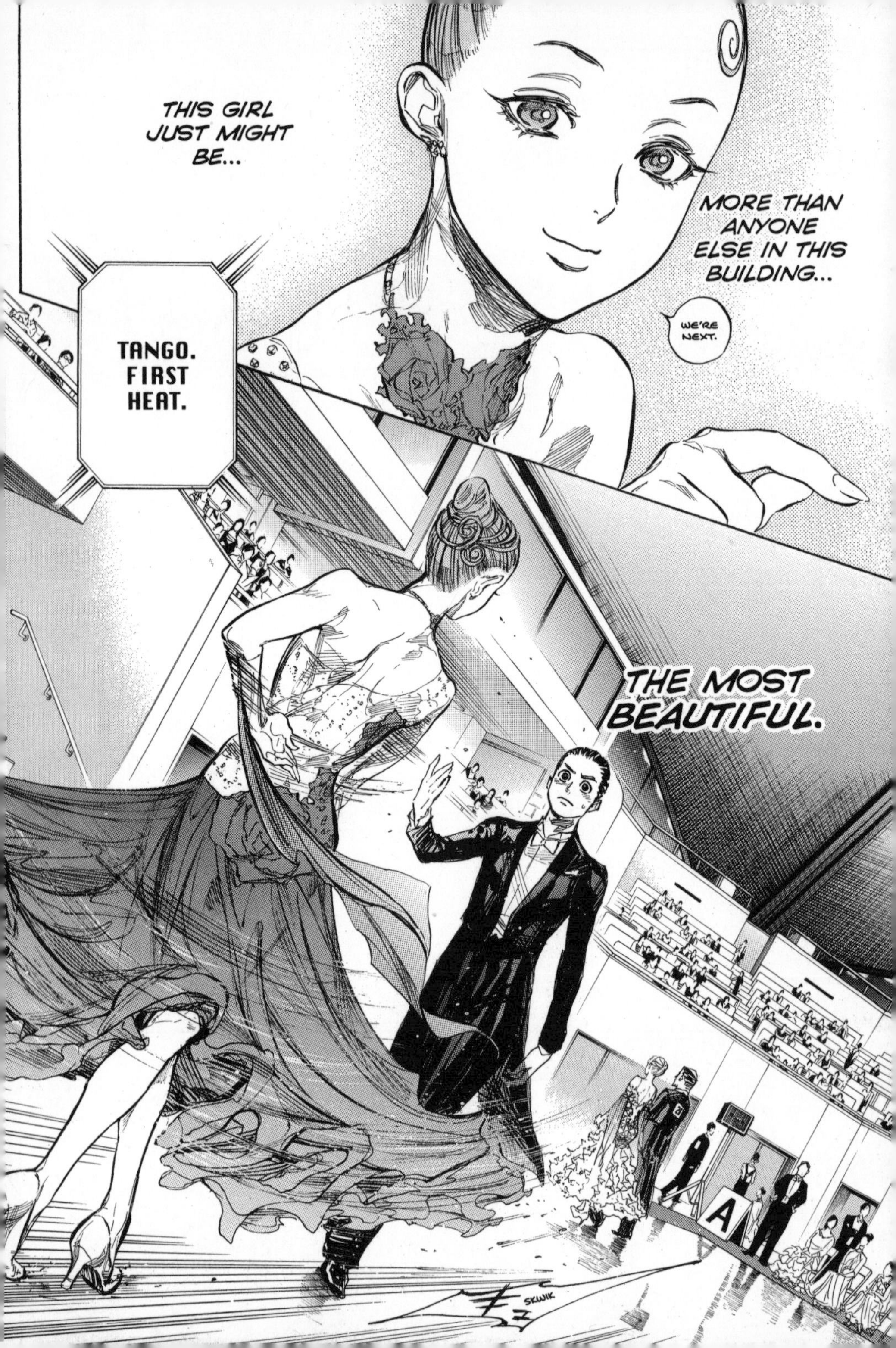
THIS GIRL JUST MIGHT BE...
MORE THAN ANYONE ELSE IN THIS BUILDING...
WE'RE NEXT.
THE MOST BEAUTIFUL.
TANGO. FIRST HEAT.
SKWIK

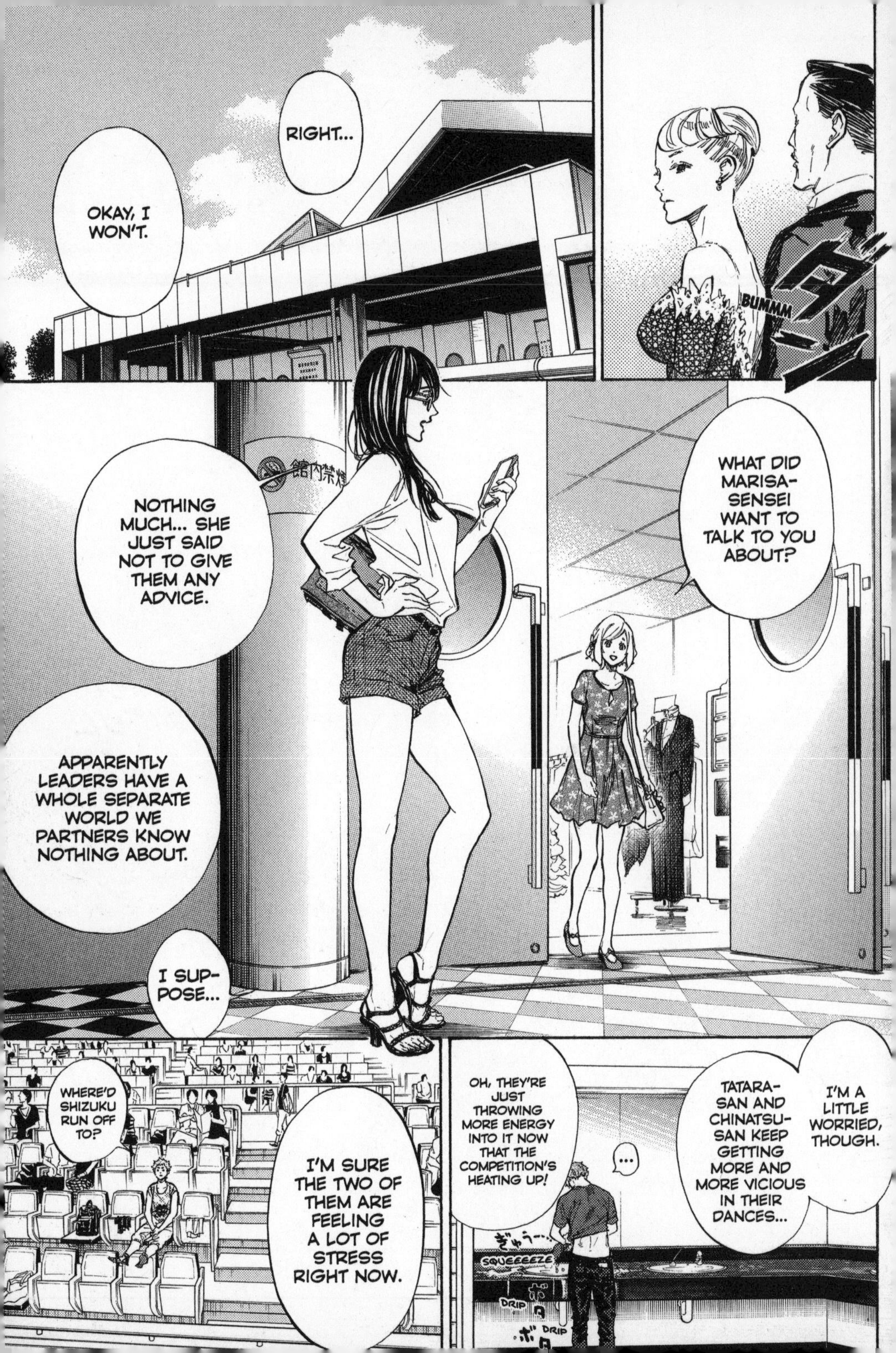
BUMMM
RIGHT...
OKAY, I WON'T.
WHAT DID MARISA-SENSEI WANT TO TALK TO YOU ABOUT?
NOTHING MUCH... SHE JUST SAID NOT TO GIVE THEM ANY ADVICE.
APPARENTLY LEADERS HAVE A WHOLE SEPARATE WORLD WE PARTNERS KNOW NOTHING ABOUT.
I SUP-POSE...
I'M A LITTLE WORRIED, THOUGH.
TATARA-SAN AND CHINATSU-SAN KEEP GETTING MORE AND MORE VICIOUS IN THEIR DANCES...
OH, THEY'RE JUST THROWING MORE ENERGY INTO IT NOW THAT THE COMPETITION'S HEATING UP!
...
SQUEEEEZE
DRIP
DRIP
WHERE'D SHIZUKU RUN OFF TO?
I'M SURE THE TWO OF THEM ARE FEELING A LOT OF STRESS RIGHT NOW.

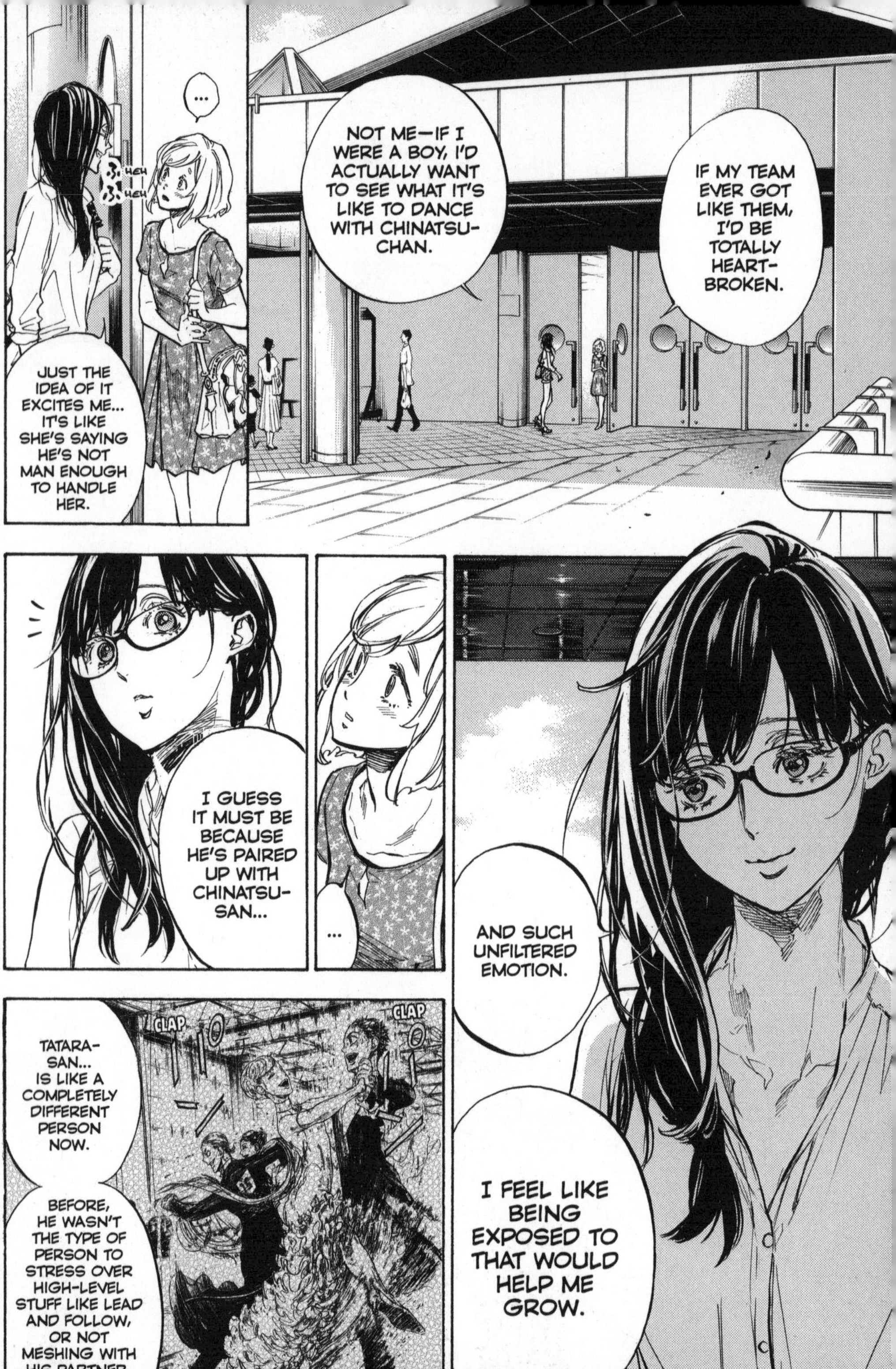
IF MY TEAM EVER GOT LIKE THEM, I'D BE TOTALLY HEART-BROKEN.
NOT ME—IF I WERE A BOY, I'D ACTUALLY WANT TO SEE WHAT IT'S LIKE TO DANCE WITH CHINATSU-CHAN.
...
ふ HEH
ふ HEH
JUST THE IDEA OF IT EXCITES ME... IT'S LIKE SHE'S SAYING HE'S NOT MAN ENOUGH TO HANDLE HER.
...
I GUESS IT MUST BE BECAUSE HE'S PAIRED UP WITH CHINATSU-SAN...
CLAP
CLAP
TATARA-SAN... IS LIKE A COMPLETELY DIFFERENT PERSON NOW.
BEFORE, HE WASN'T THE TYPE OF PERSON TO STRESS OVER HIGH-LEVEL STUFF LIKE LEAD AND FOLLOW, OR NOT MESHING WITH HIS PARTNER.
AND SUCH UNFILTERED EMOTION.
I FEEL LIKE BEING EXPOSED TO THAT WOULD HELP ME GROW.

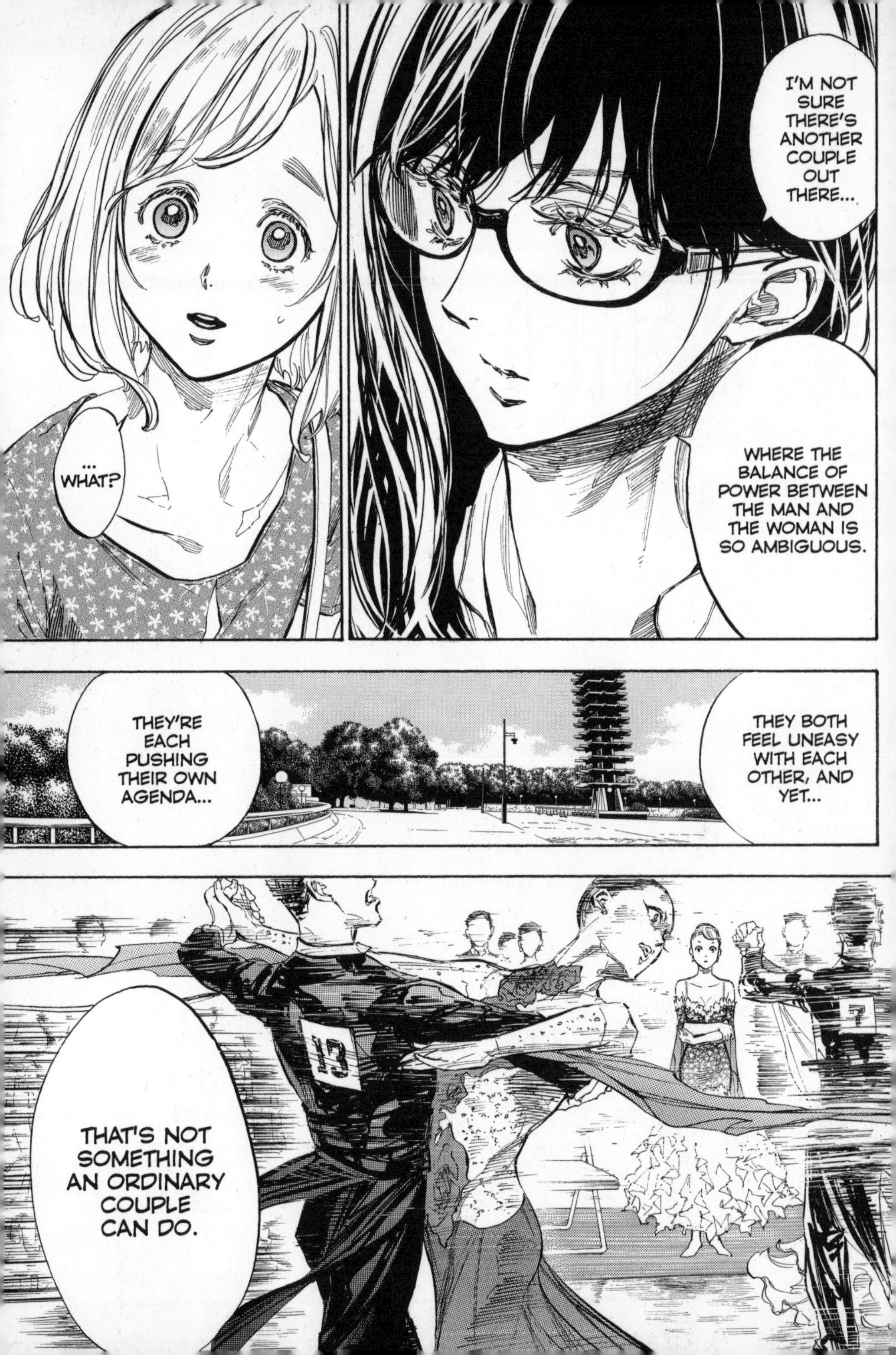
I'M NOT SURE THERE'S ANOTHER COUPLE OUT THERE...
WHERE THE BALANCE OF POWER BETWEEN THE MAN AND THE WOMAN IS SO AMBIGUOUS.
... WHAT?
THEY BOTH FEEL UNEASY WITH EACH OTHER, AND YET...
THEY'RE EACH PUSHING THEIR OWN AGENDA...
THAT'S NOT SOMETHING AN ORDINARY COUPLE CAN DO.

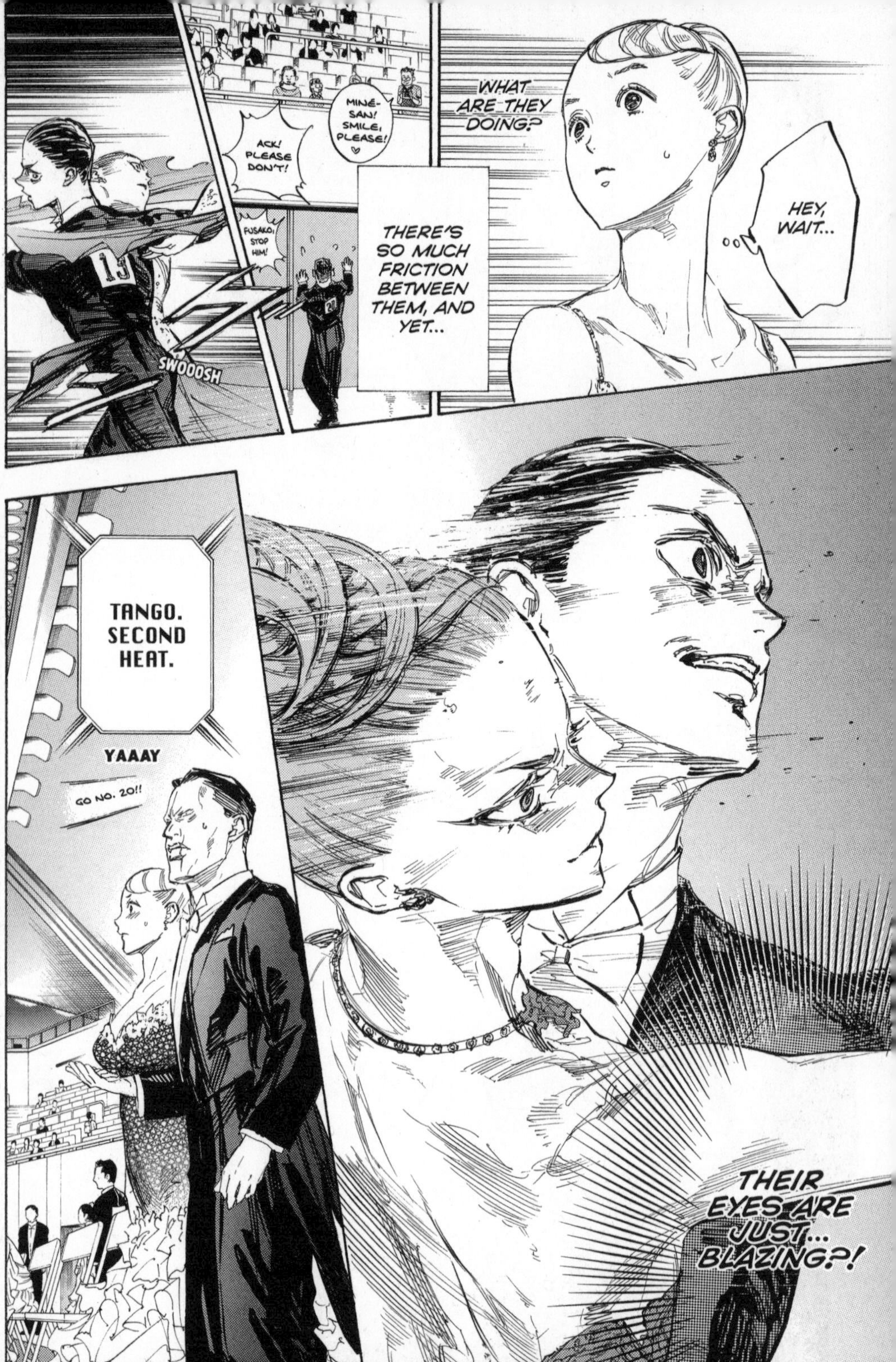
WHAT ARE THEY DOING?
HEY, WAIT...
MINÉ-SAN! SMILE, PLEASE! ♥
FUSAKO! STOP HIM!
THERE'S SO MUCH FRICTION BETWEEN THEM, AND YET...
ACK! PLEASE DON'T!
SWOOOSH
THEIR EYES ARE JUST... BLAZING?!
TANGO. SECOND HEAT.
YAAAY
GO NO. 20!!

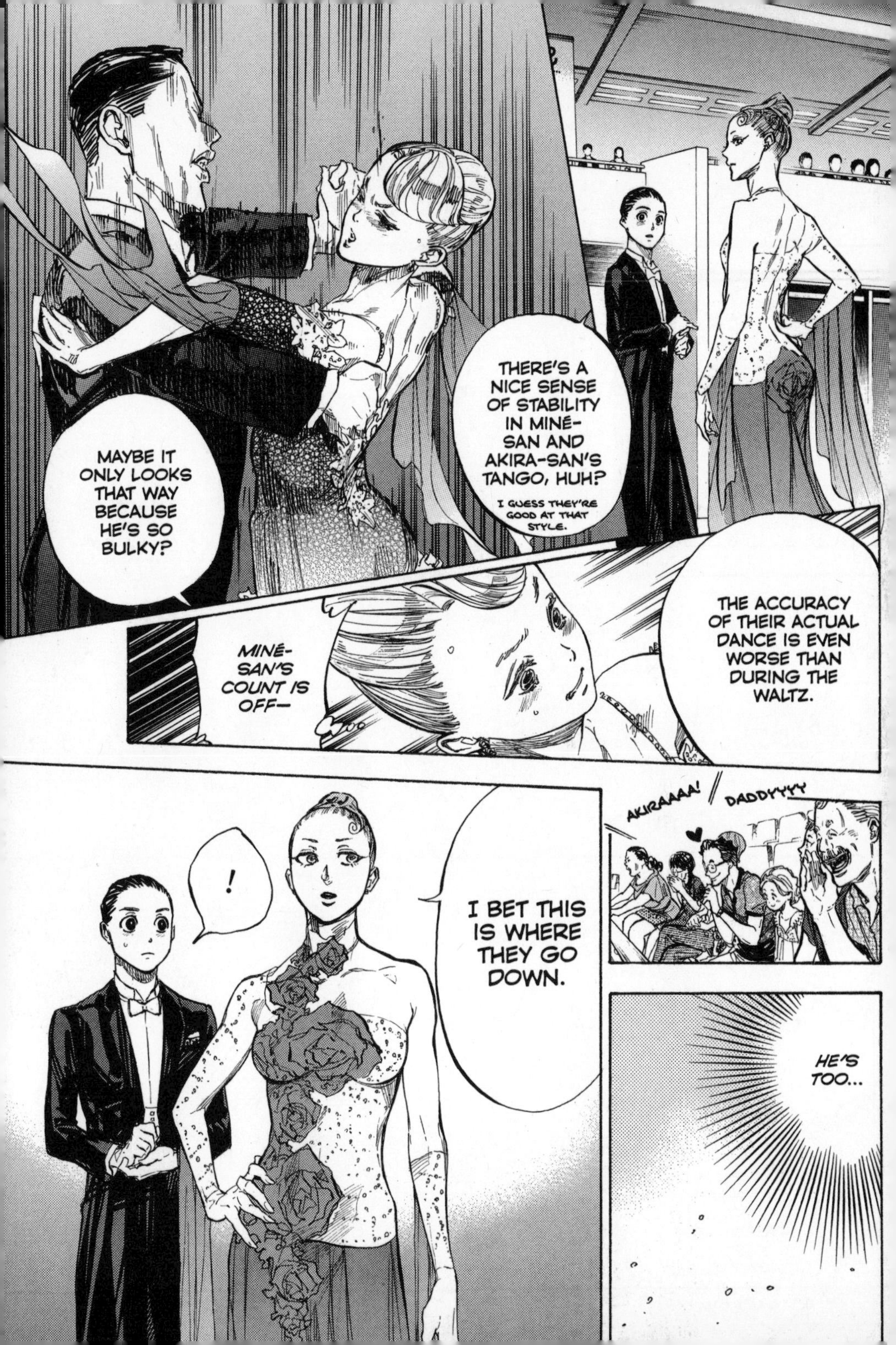
THERE'S A NICE SENSE OF STABILITY IN MINÉ-SAN AND AKIRA-SAN'S TANGO, HUH?
I GUESS THEY'RE GOOD AT THAT STYLE.
MAYBE IT ONLY LOOKS THAT WAY BECAUSE HE'S SO BULKY?
THE ACCURACY OF THEIR ACTUAL DANCE IS EVEN WORSE THAN DURING THE WALTZ.
MINÉ-SAN'S COUNT IS OFF—
DADDYYYY
AKIRAAAA!
HE'S TOO...
I BET THIS IS WHERE THEY GO DOWN.
!

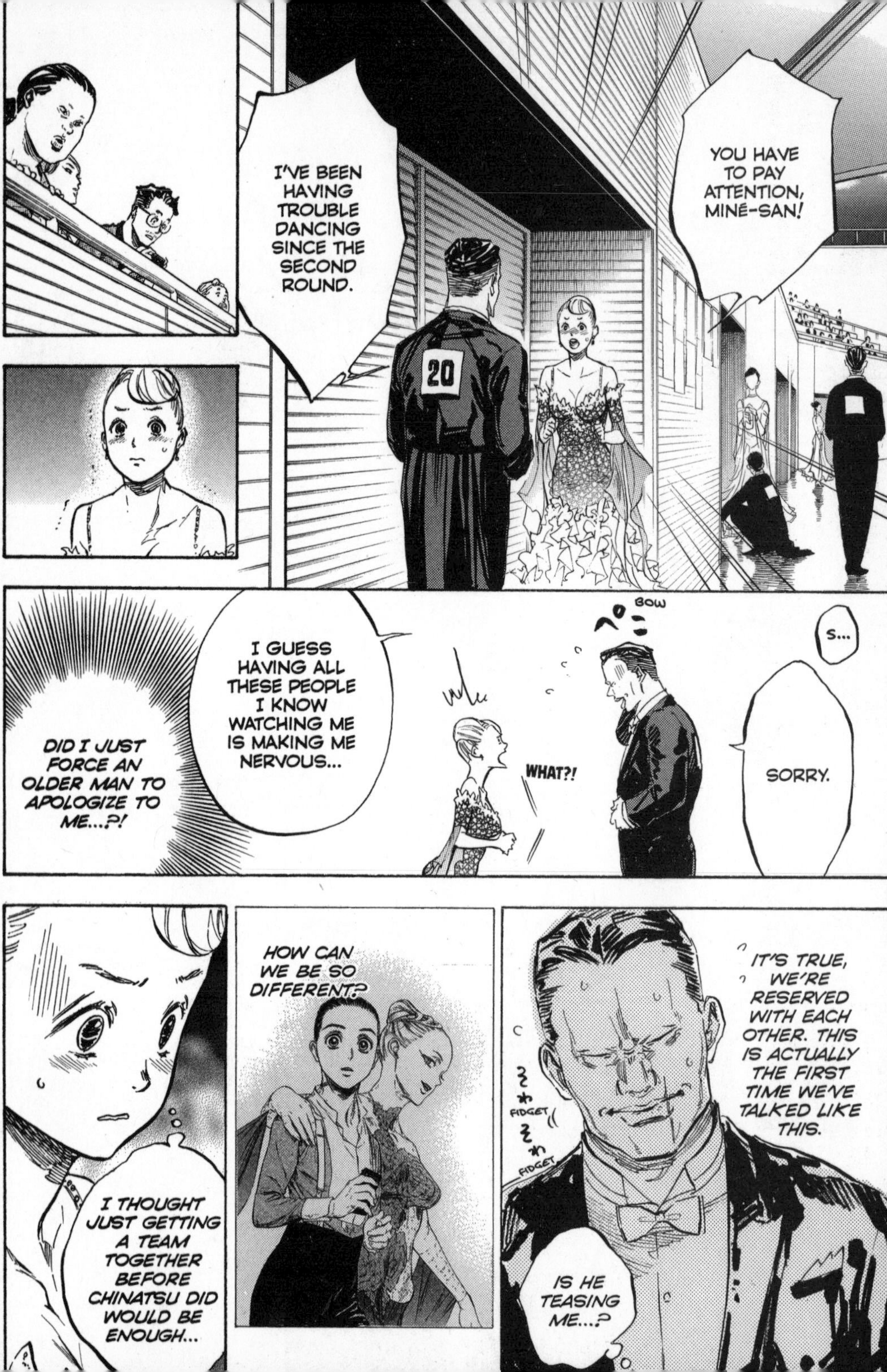
YOU HAVE TO PAY ATTENTION, MINÉ-SAN!
I'VE BEEN HAVING TROUBLE DANCING SINCE THE SECOND ROUND.
20
S...
BOW
SORRY.
WHAT?!
I GUESS HAVING ALL THESE PEOPLE I KNOW WATCHING ME IS MAKING ME NERVOUS...
DID I JUST FORCE AN OLDER MAN TO APOLOGIZE TO ME...?!
IT'S TRUE, WE'RE RESERVED WITH EACH OTHER. THIS IS ACTUALLY THE FIRST TIME WE'VE TALKED LIKE THIS.
FIDGET
FIDGET
IS HE TEASING ME...?
HOW CAN WE BE SO DIFFERENT?
I THOUGHT JUST GETTING A TEAM TOGETHER BEFORE CHINATSU DID WOULD BE ENOUGH...

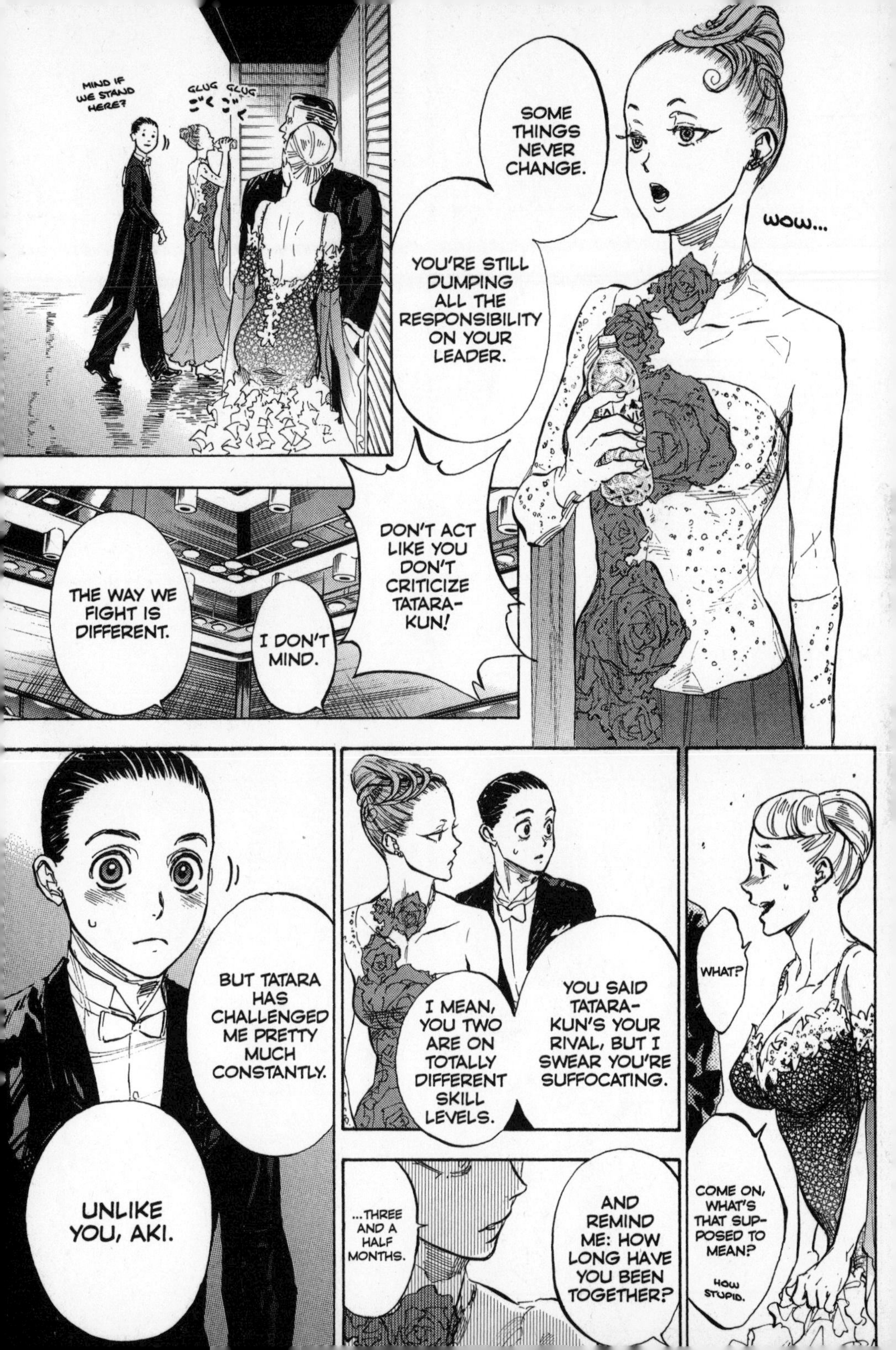
SOME THINGS NEVER CHANGE.
YOU'RE STILL DUMPING ALL THE RESPONSIBILITY ON YOUR LEADER.
WOW...
GLUG GLUG
ごくごく
MIND IF WE STAND HERE?
DON'T ACT LIKE YOU DON'T CRITICIZE TATARA-KUN!
I DON'T MIND.
THE WAY WE FIGHT IS DIFFERENT.
WHAT?
COME ON, WHAT'S THAT SUP-POSED TO MEAN?
HOW STUPID.
YOU SAID TATARA-KUN'S YOUR RIVAL, BUT I SWEAR YOU'RE SUFFOCATING.
I MEAN, YOU TWO ARE ON TOTALLY DIFFERENT SKILL LEVELS.
AND REMIND ME: HOW LONG HAVE YOU BEEN TOGETHER?
...THREE AND A HALF MONTHS.
BUT TATARA HAS CHALLENGED ME PRETTY MUCH CONSTANTLY.
UNLIKE YOU, AKI.

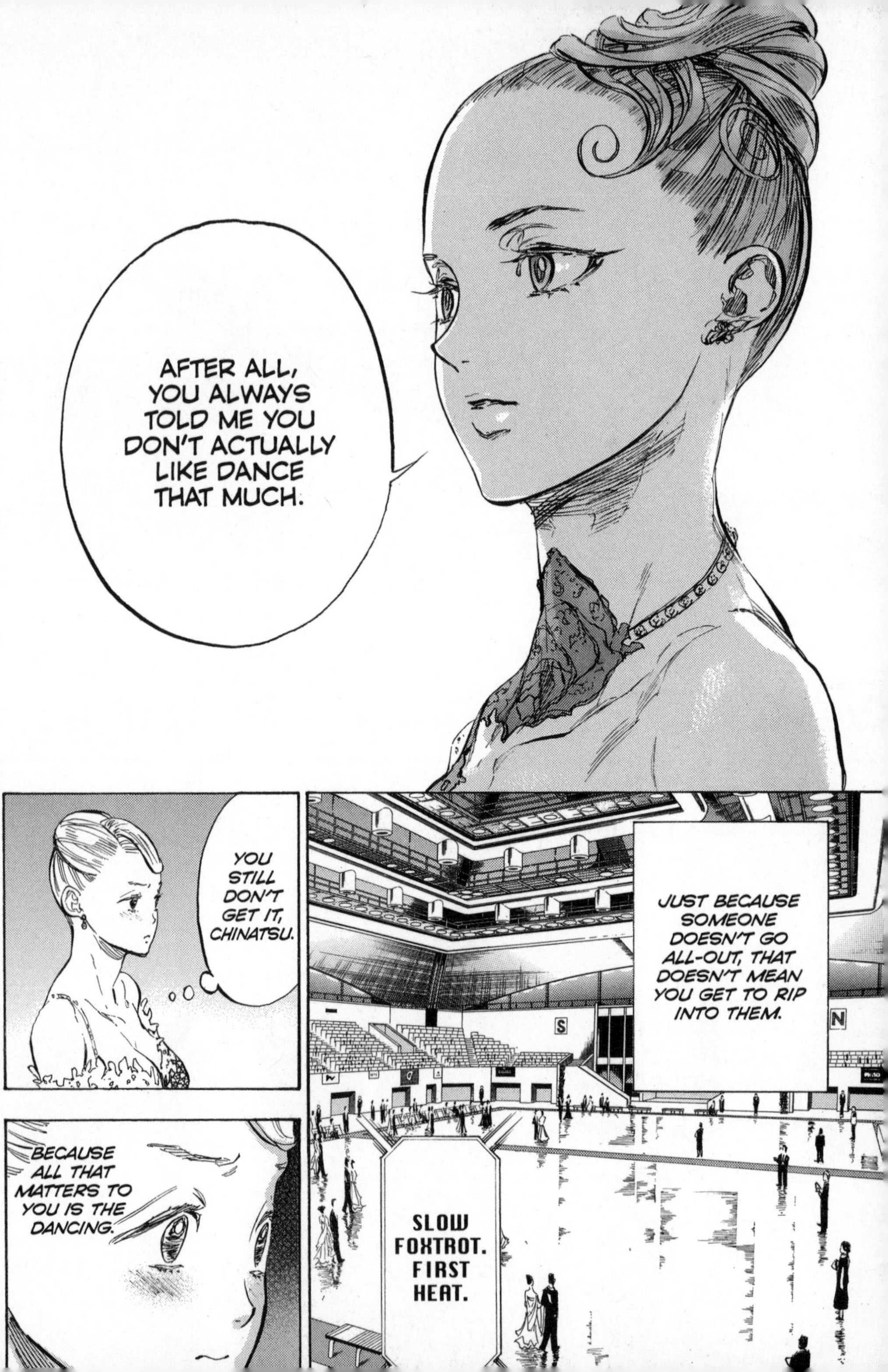

AFTER ALL, YOU ALWAYS TOLD ME YOU DON'T ACTUALLY LIKE DANCE THAT MUCH.
JUST BECAUSE SOMEONE DOESN'T GO ALL-OUT, THAT DOESN'T MEAN YOU GET TO RIP INTO THEM.
SLOW FOXTROT. FIRST HEAT.
YOU STILL DON'T GET IT, CHINATSU.
BECAUSE ALL THAT MATTERS TO YOU IS THE DANCING.

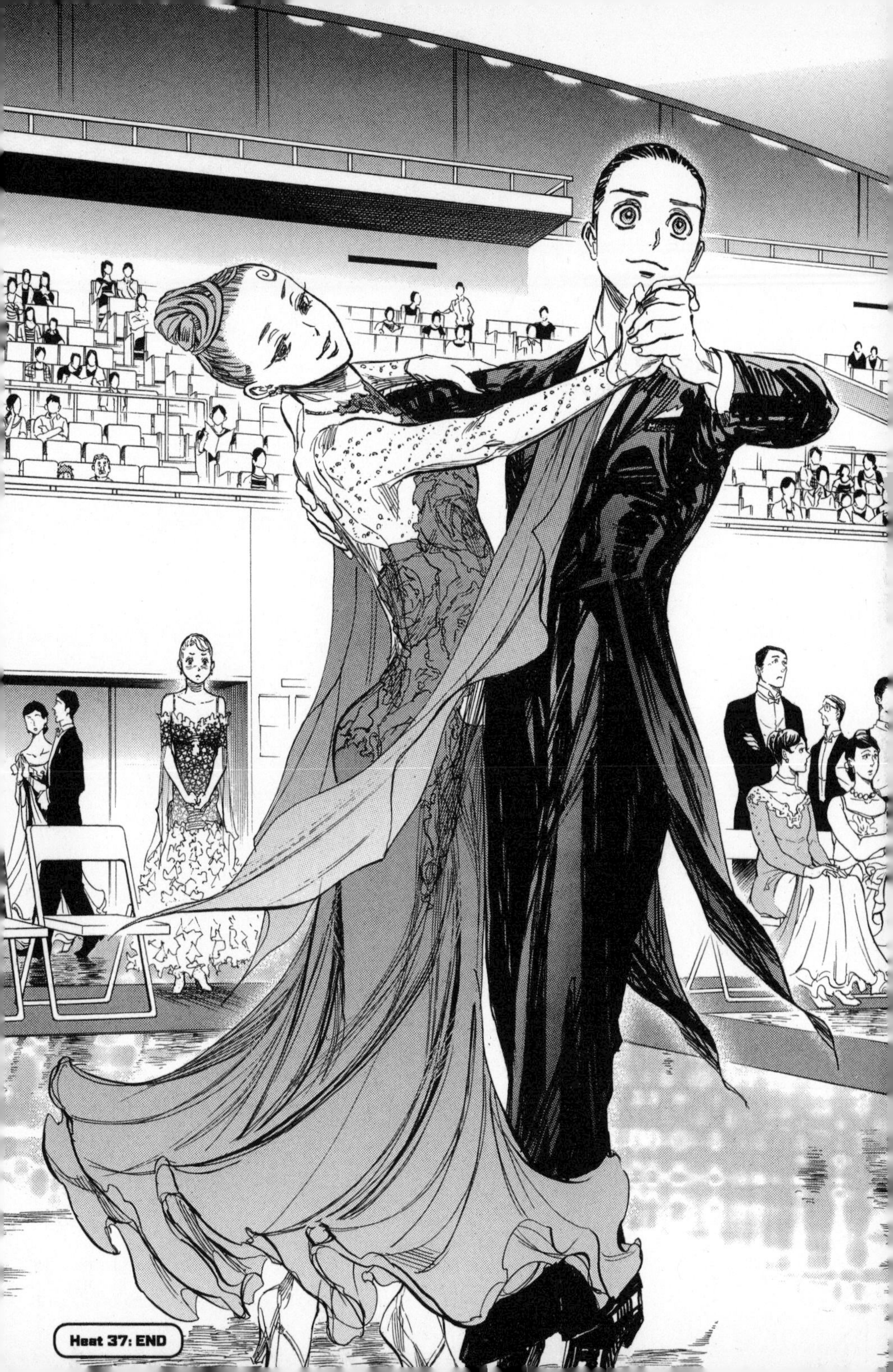
Heat 37: END

WELCOME TO THE BALLROOM

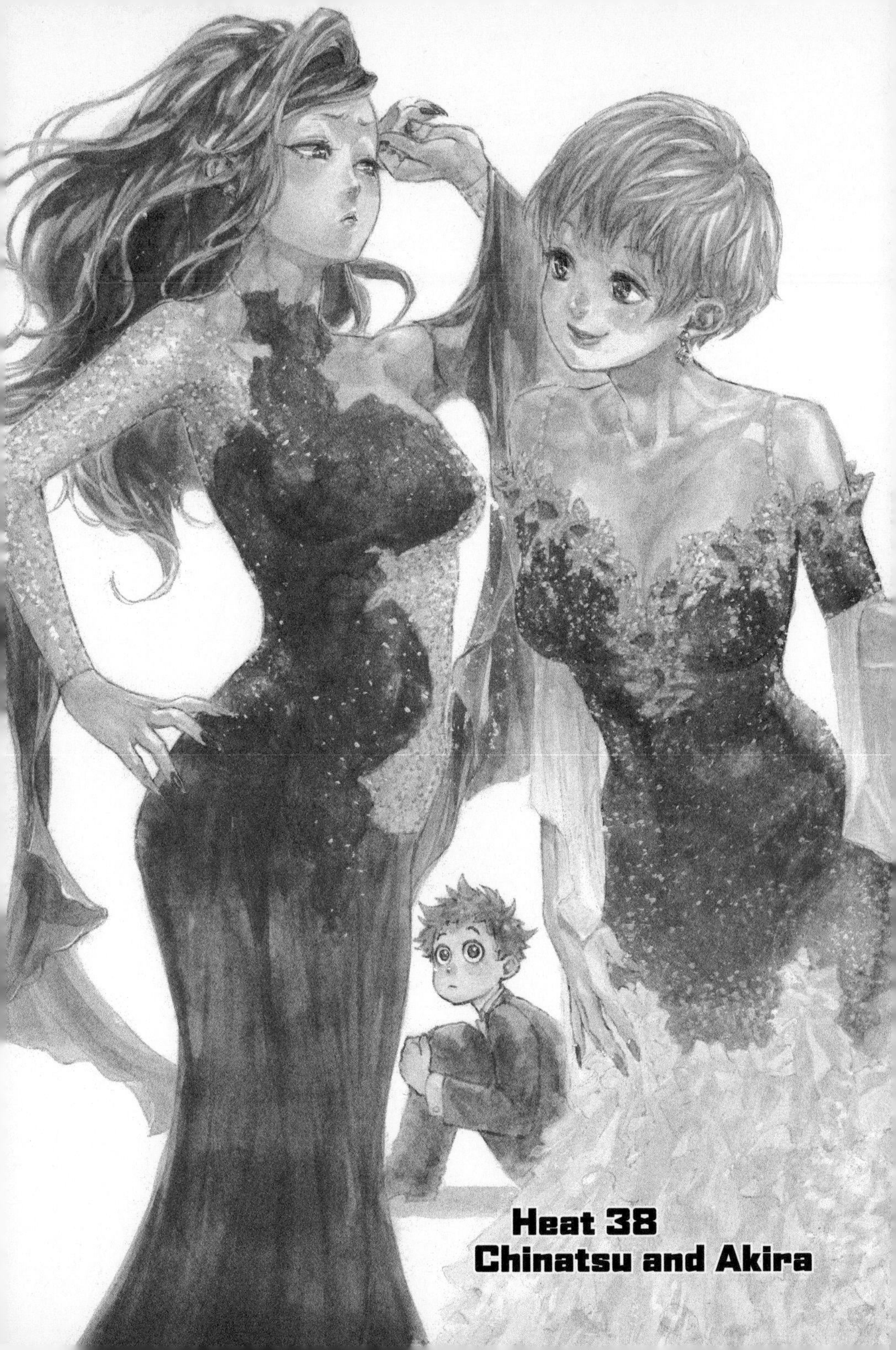

Heat 38
Chinatsu and Akira

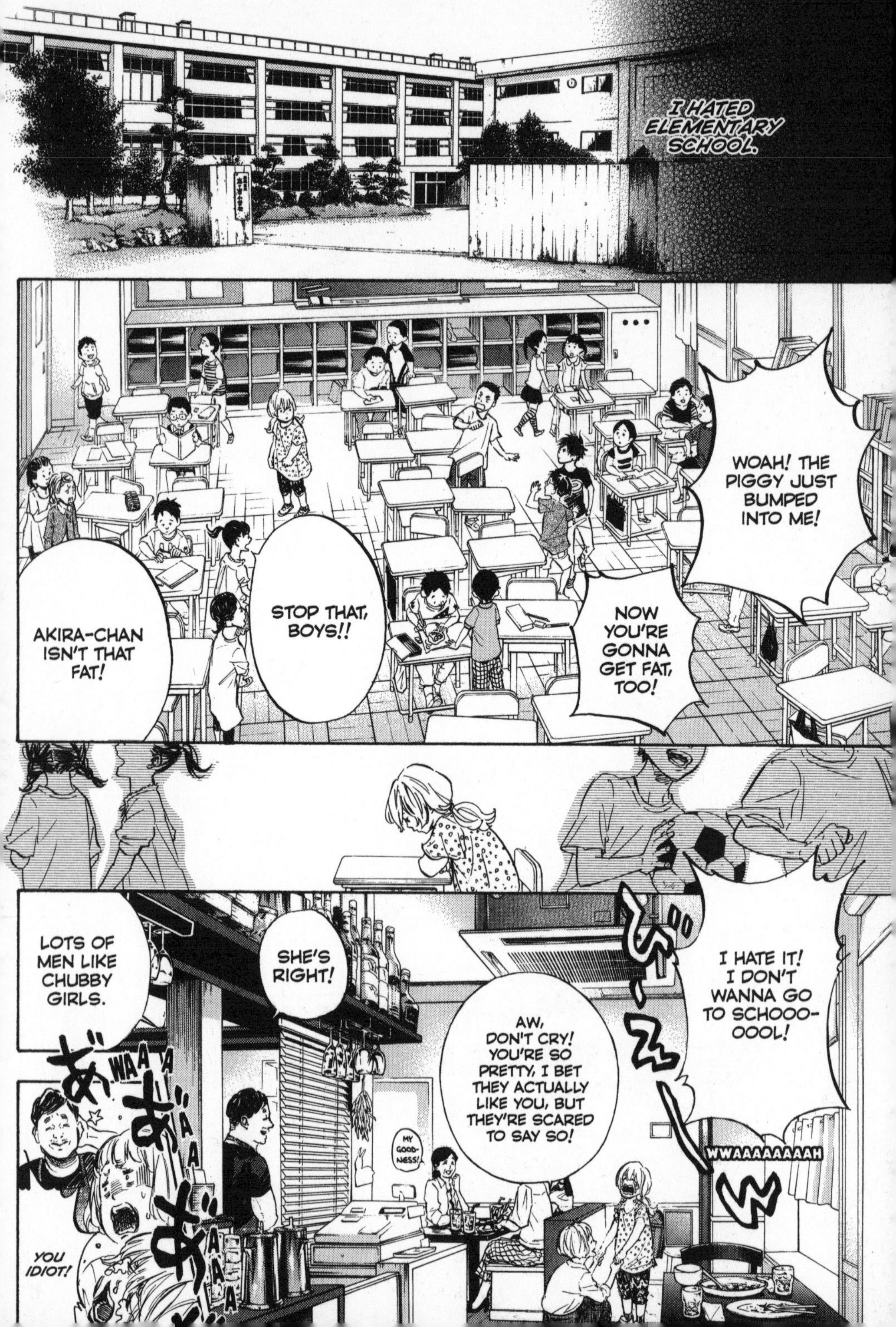
I HATED ELEMENTARY SCHOOL.
WOAH! THE PIGGY JUST BUMPED INTO ME!
NOW YOU'RE GONNA GET FAT, TOO!
STOP THAT, BOYS!!
AKIRA-CHAN ISN'T THAT FAT!
I HATE IT! I DON'T WANNA GO TO SCHOOO-OOOL!
WWAAAAAAAAH
AW, DON'T CRY! YOU'RE SO PRETTY, I BET THEY ACTUALLY LIKE YOU, BUT THEY'RE SCARED TO SAY SO!
MY GOOD-NESS!
SHE'S RIGHT!
LOTS OF MEN LIKE CHUBBY GIRLS.
WAAAA
YOU IDIOT!

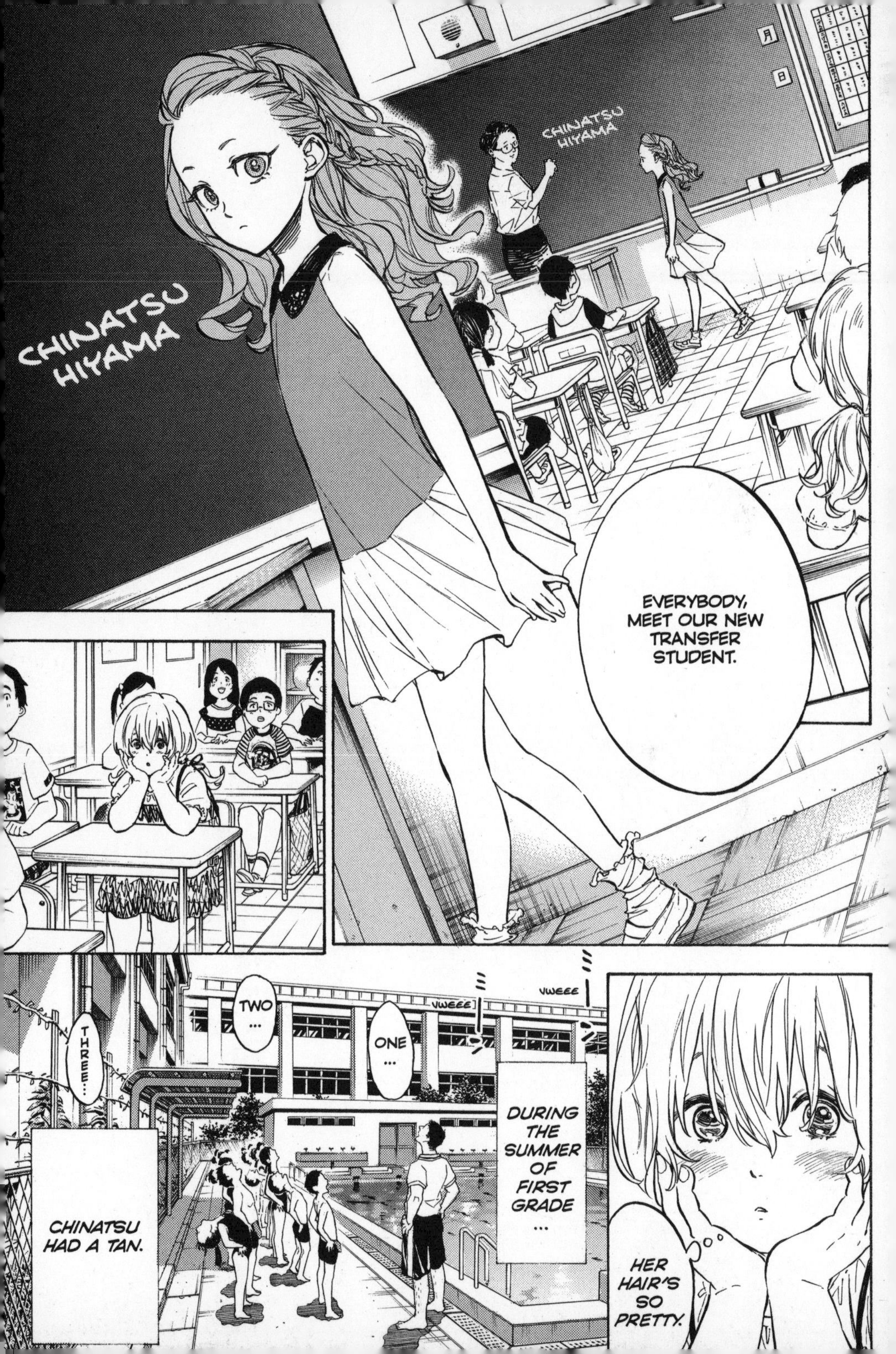
CHINATSU HIYAMA
CHINATSU HIYAMA
EVERYBODY, MEET OUR NEW TRANSFER STUDENT.
HER HAIR'S SO PRETTY.
VWEEE
VWEEE
ONE ...
TWO ...
THREE...
DURING THE SUMMER OF FIRST GRADE ...
CHINATSU HAD A TAN.

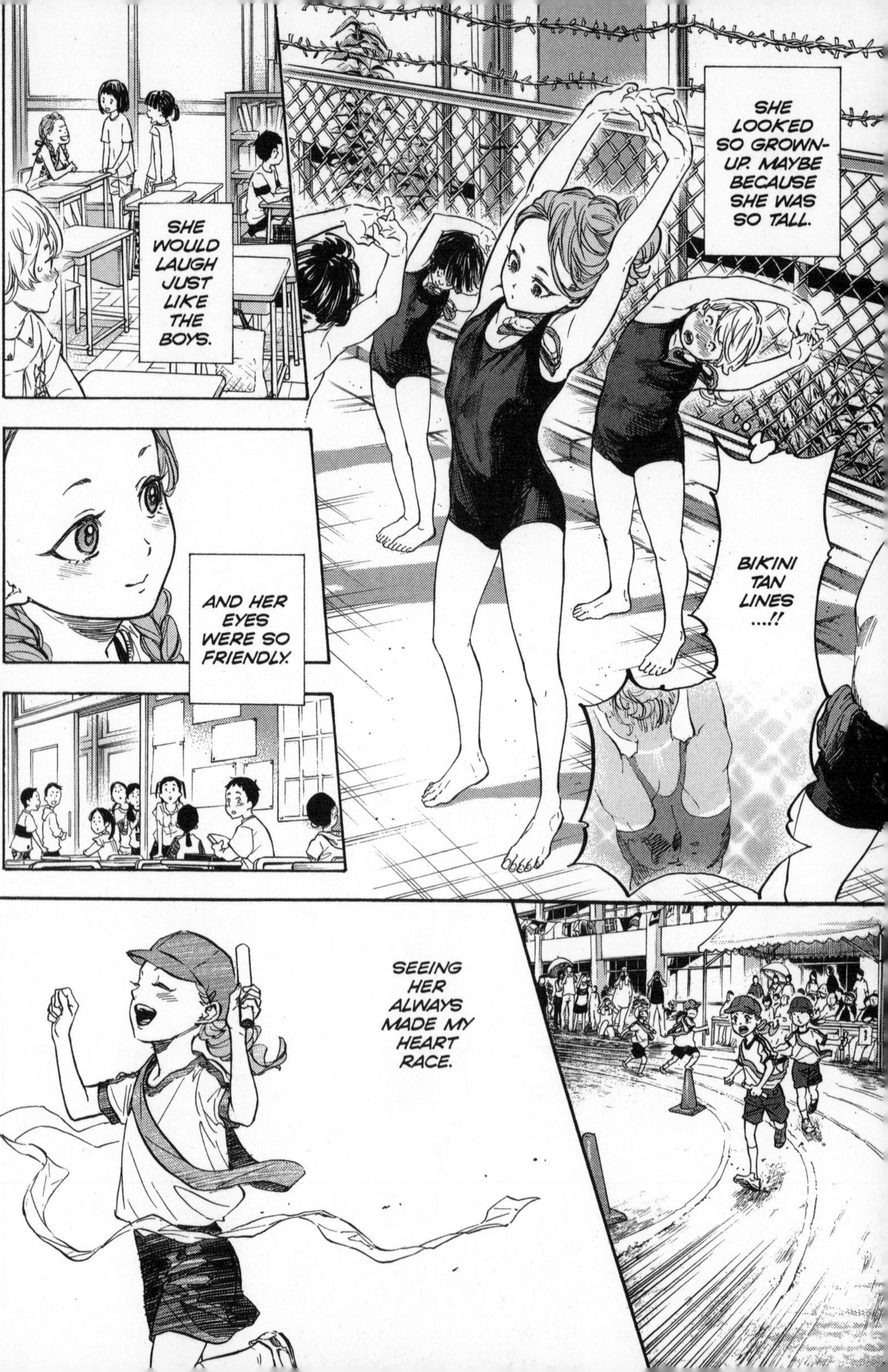
SHE LOOKED SO GROWN-UP. MAYBE BECAUSE SHE WAS SO TALL.
BIKINI TAN LINES ...!!
SHE WOULD LAUGH JUST LIKE THE BOYS.
AND HER EYES WERE SO FRIENDLY.
SEEING HER ALWAYS MADE MY HEART RACE.

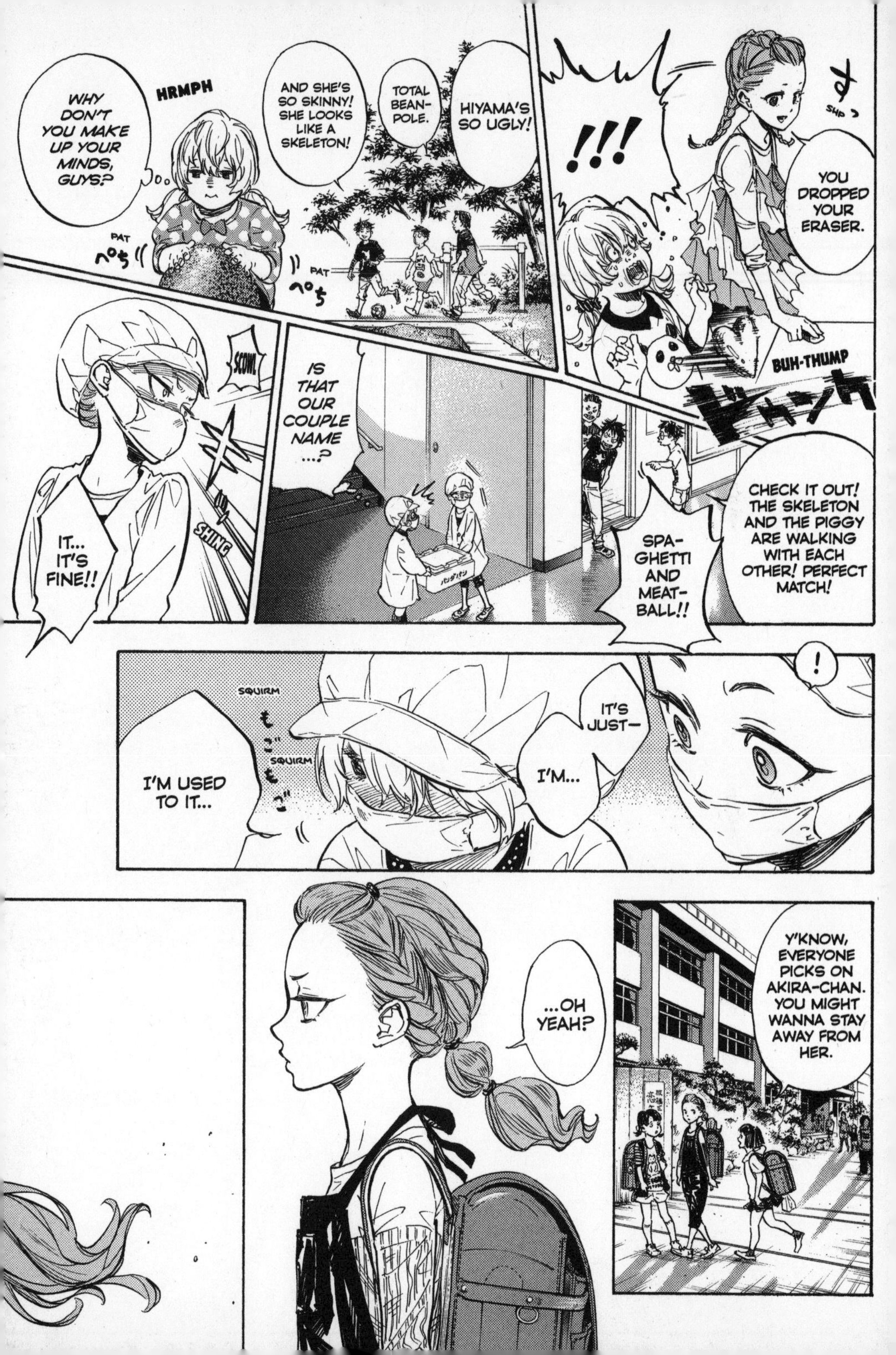

!!!
SHP
YOU DROPPED YOUR ERASER.
BUH-THUMP
HIYAMA'S SO UGLY!
TOTAL BEANPOLE.
AND SHE'S SO SKINNY! SHE LOOKS LIKE A SKELETON!
HRMPH
WHY DON'T YOU MAKE UP YOUR MINDS, GUYS?
PAT
PAT
CHECK IT OUT! THE SKELETON AND THE PIGGY ARE WALKING WITH EACH OTHER! PERFECT MATCH!
SPA-GHETTI AND MEAT-BALL!!
IS THAT OUR COUPLE NAME ...?
SCOWL
SHING
IT... IT'S FINE!!
!
IT'S JUST—
I'M...
SQUIRM
SQUIRM
I'M USED TO IT...
Y'KNOW, EVERYONE PICKS ON AKIRA-CHAN. YOU MIGHT WANNA STAY AWAY FROM HER.
...OH YEAH?

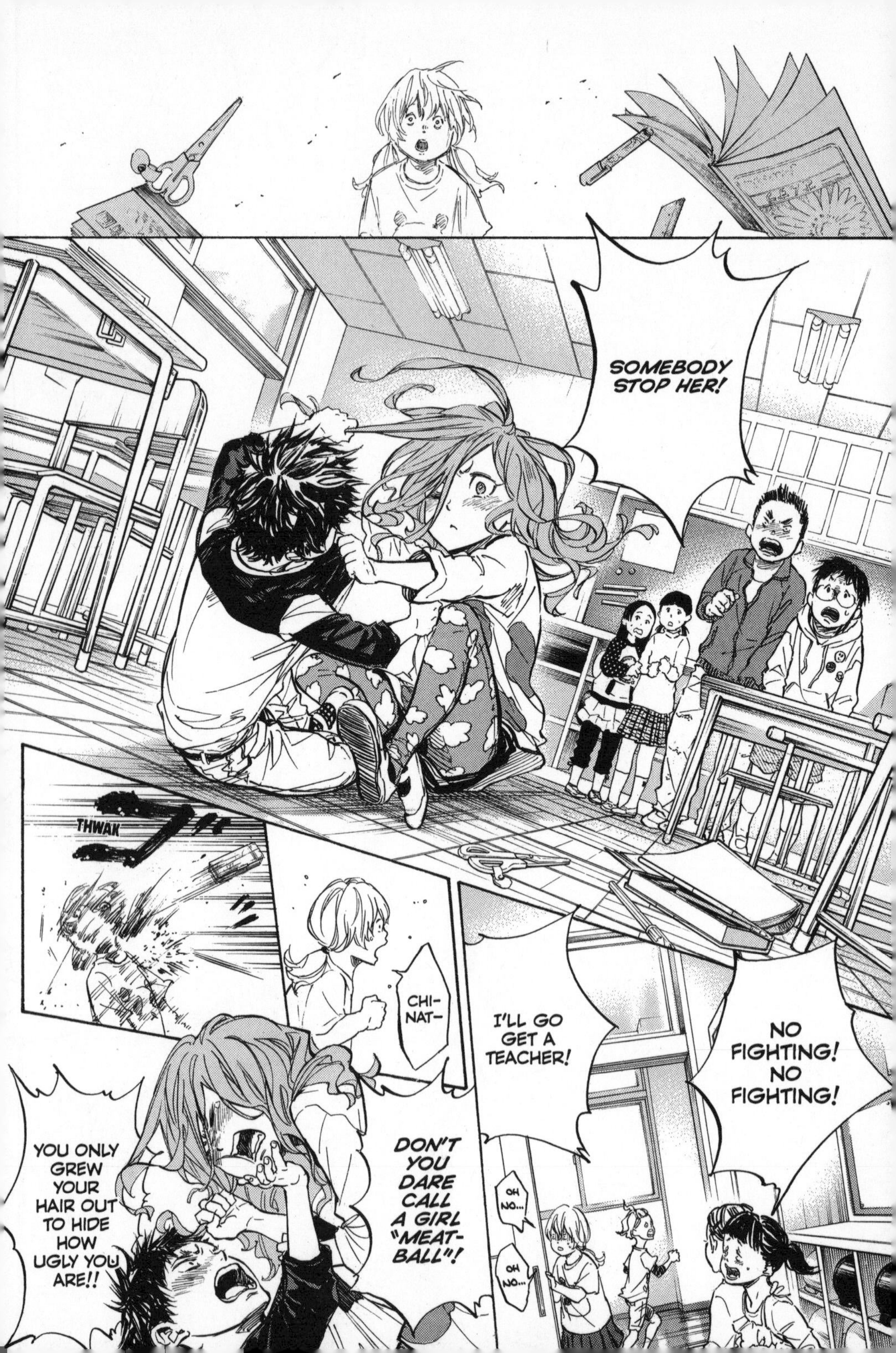
SOMEBODY STOP HER!
NO FIGHTING! NO FIGHTING!
I'LL GO GET A TEACHER!
OH NO...
OH NO...
CHI-NAT-
THWAK
DON'T YOU DARE CALL A GIRL "MEAT-BALL"!
YOU ONLY GREW YOUR HAIR OUT TO HIDE HOW UGLY YOU ARE!!

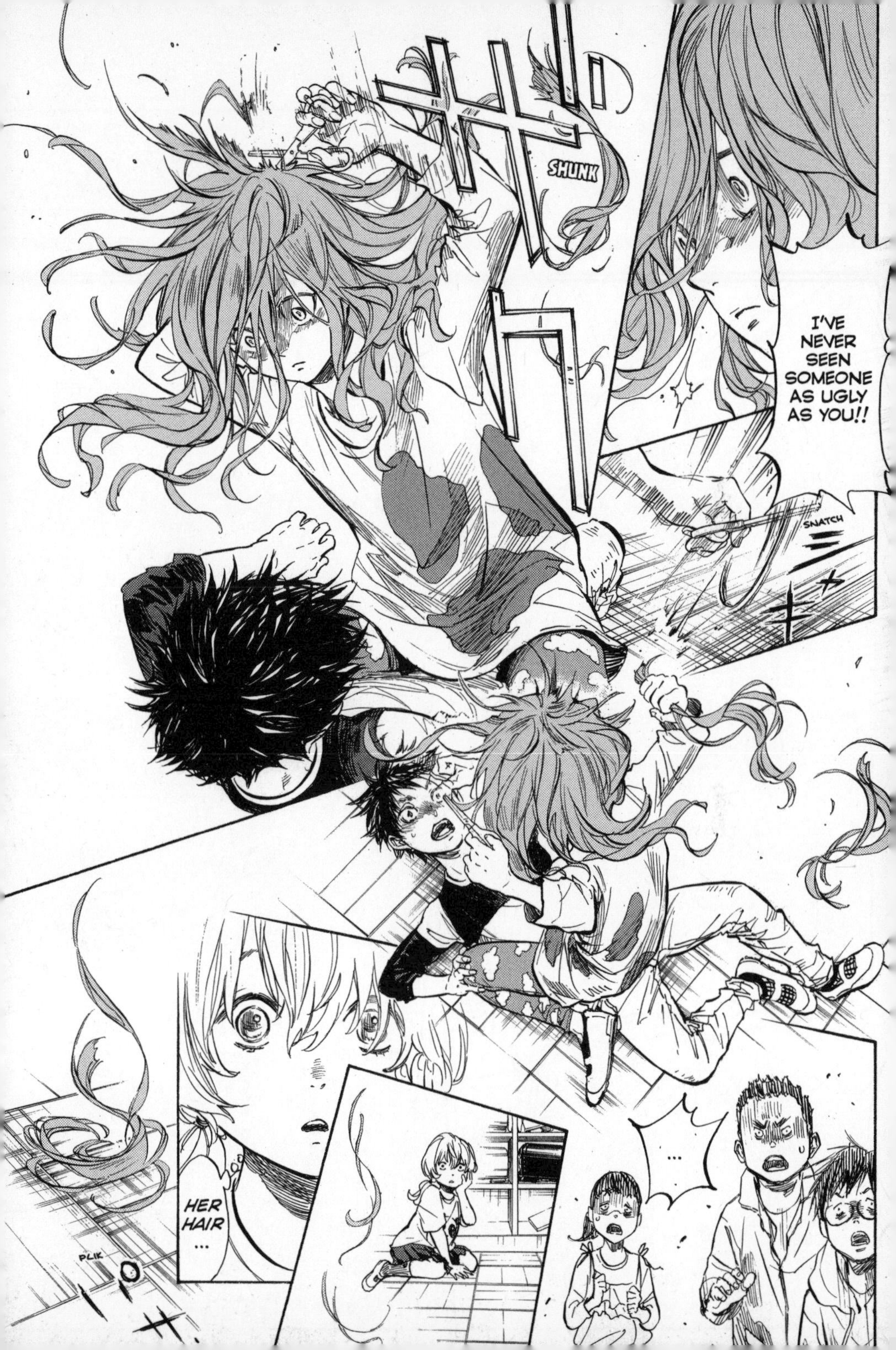
I'VE NEVER SEEN SOMEONE AS UGLY AS YOU!!
SNATCH
SHUNK
...
HER HAIR ...
PLIK

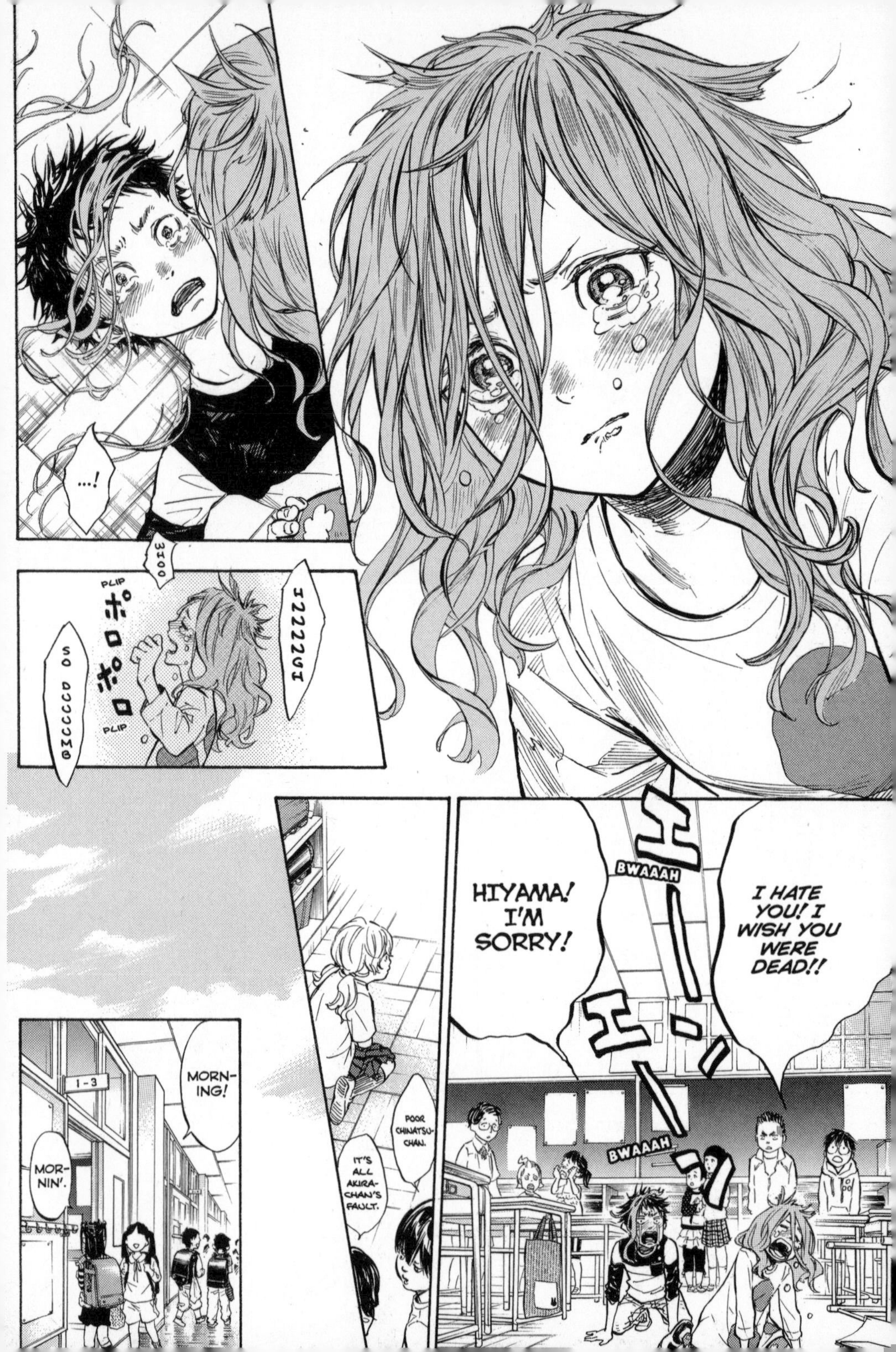
...!
PLIP
PLIP
SO DUUUUUMB
I HATE YOU! I WISH YOU WERE DEAD!!
BWAAAH
HIYAMA! I'M SORRY!
BWAAAH
POOR CHINATSU-CHAN.
IT'S ALL AKIRA-CHAN'S FAULT.
MORN-ING!
1-3
MOR-NIN'.

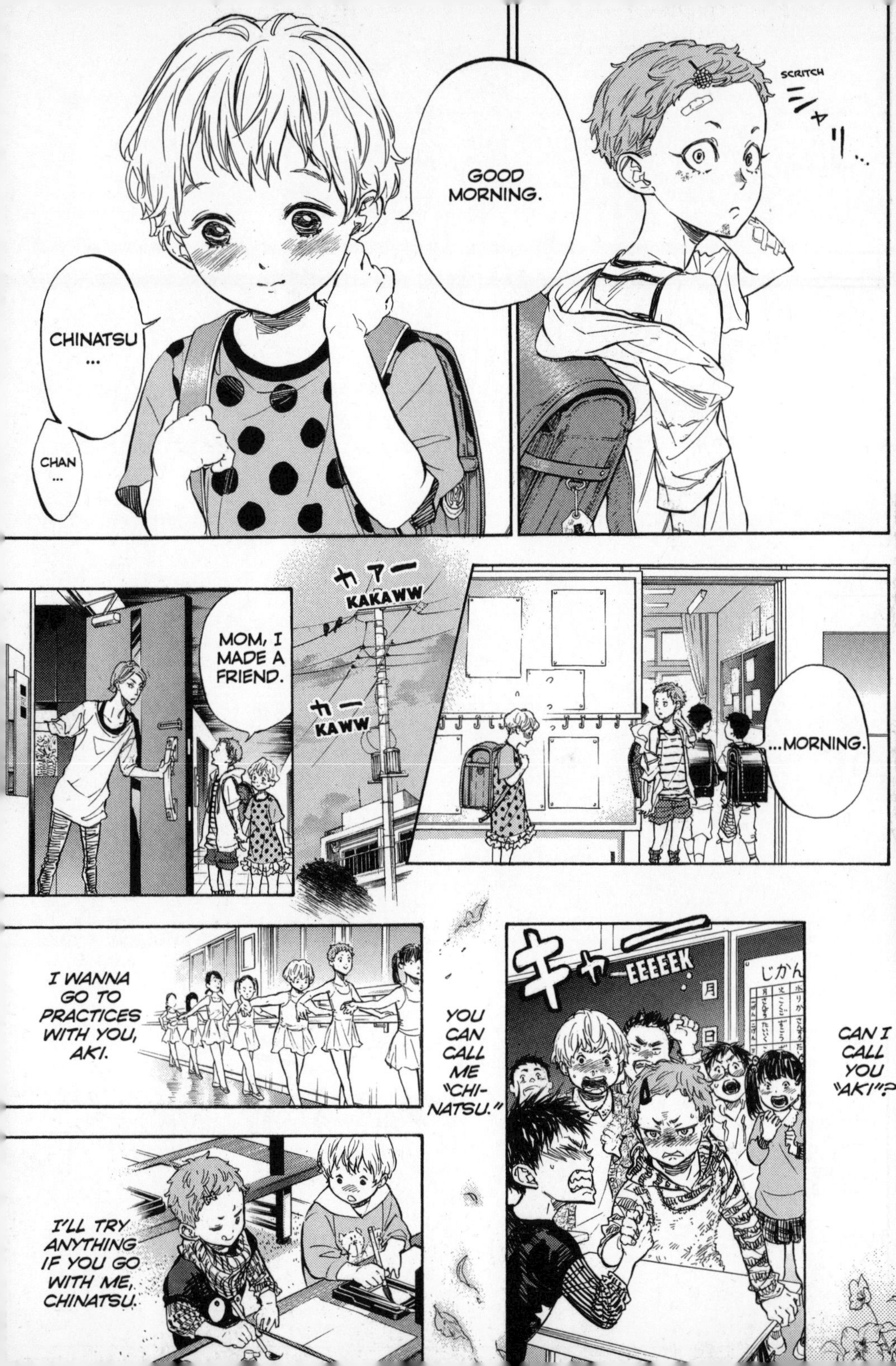
SCRITCH
シャリ…
GOOD MORNING.
CHINATSU …
CHAN …
…MORNING.
カァー
KAKAWW
カー
KAWW
MOM, I MADE A FRIEND.
キャー
EEEEEK
CAN I CALL YOU "AKI"?
YOU CAN CALL ME "CHI-NATSU."
I WANNA GO TO PRACTICES WITH YOU, AKI.
I'LL TRY ANYTHING IF YOU GO WITH ME, CHINATSU.

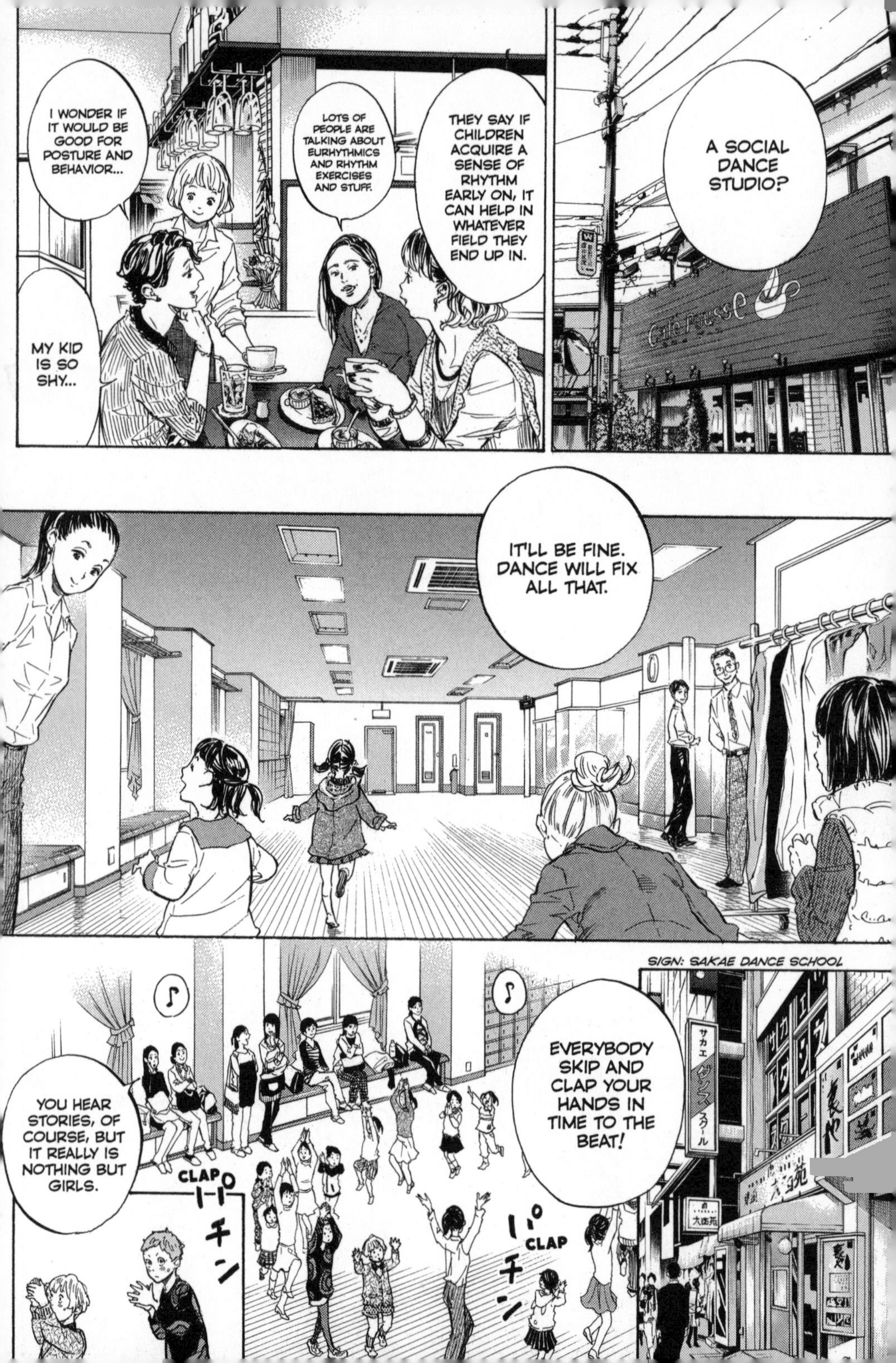
A SOCIAL DANCE STUDIO?
THEY SAY IF CHILDREN ACQUIRE A SENSE OF RHYTHM EARLY ON, IT CAN HELP IN WHATEVER FIELD THEY END UP IN.
LOTS OF PEOPLE ARE TALKING ABOUT EURHYTHMICS AND RHYTHM EXERCISES AND STUFF.
I WONDER IF IT WOULD BE GOOD FOR POSTURE AND BEHAVIOR...
MY KID IS SO SHY...
IT'LL BE FINE. DANCE WILL FIX ALL THAT.
SIGN: SAKAE DANCE SCHOOL
サカエ ダンス スクール
EVERYBODY SKIP AND CLAP YOUR HANDS IN TIME TO THE BEAT!
♪
♪
パチン
CLAP
YOU HEAR STORIES, OF COURSE, BUT IT REALLY IS NOTHING BUT GIRLS.
CLAP
パチン

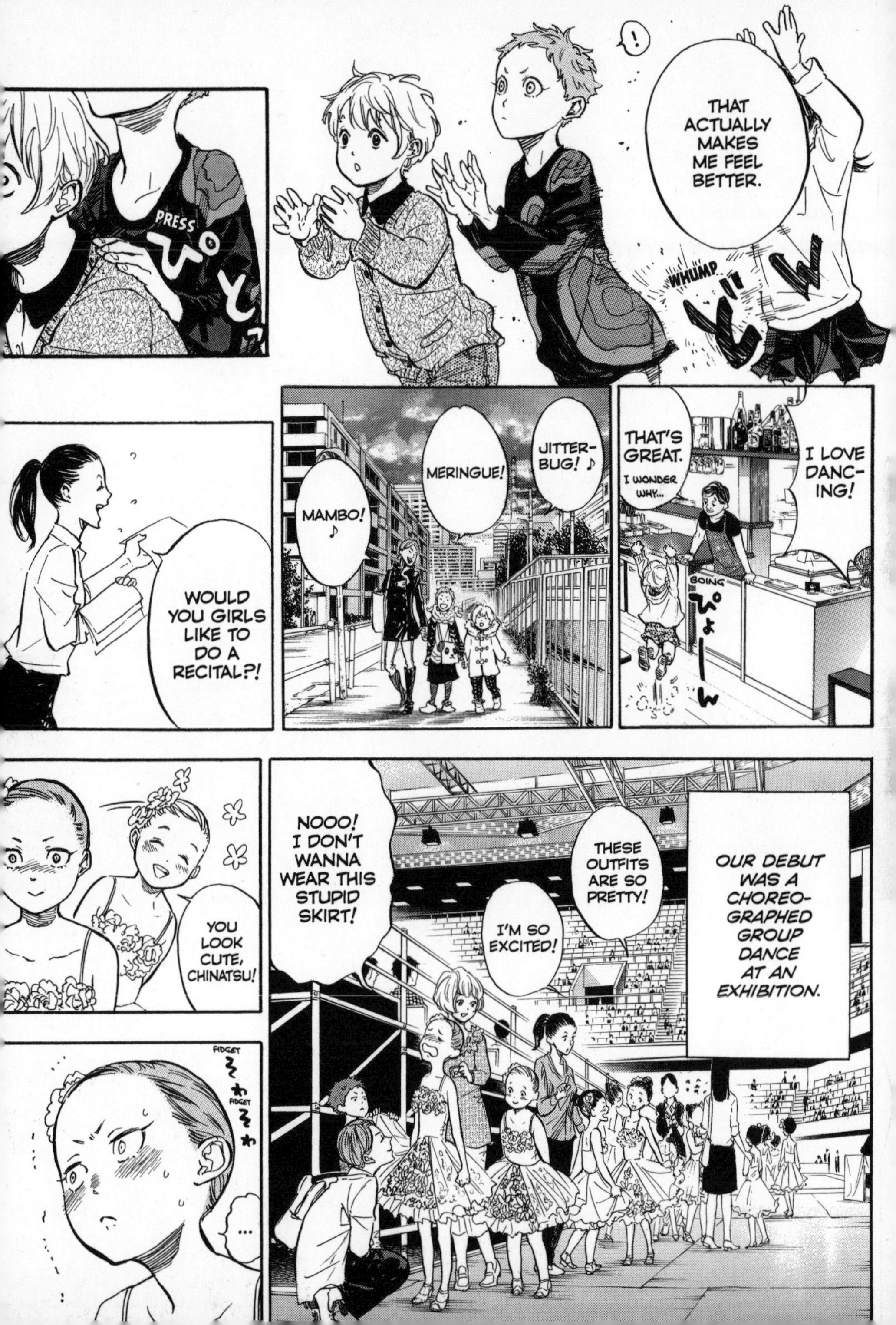
!
THAT ACTUALLY MAKES ME FEEL BETTER.
WHUMP
PRESS
I LOVE DANCING!
THAT'S GREAT.
I WONDER WHY...
BOING
JITTER-BUG! ♪
MERINGUE!
MAMBO! ♪
WOULD YOU GIRLS LIKE TO DO A RECITAL?!
OUR DEBUT WAS A CHOREOGRAPHED GROUP DANCE AT AN EXHIBITION.
THESE OUTFITS ARE SO PRETTY!
I'M SO EXCITED!
NOOO! I DON'T WANNA WEAR THIS STUPID SKIRT!
YOU LOOK CUTE, CHINATSU!
FIDGET
FIDGET
...

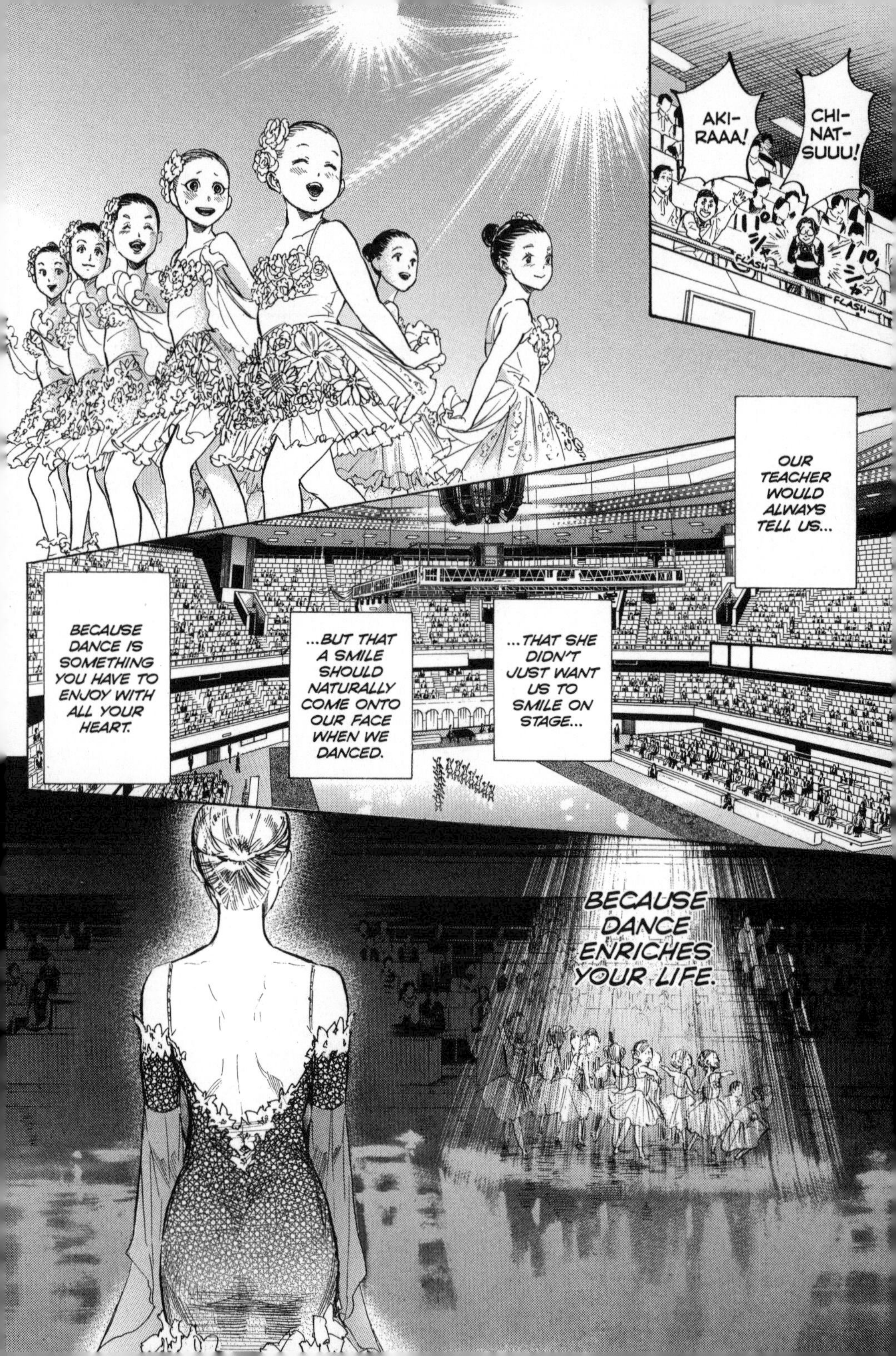
CHI-NAT-SUUU!
AKI-RAAA!
FLASH
FLASH
OUR TEACHER WOULD ALWAYS TELL US...
...THAT SHE DIDN'T JUST WANT US TO SMILE ON STAGE...
...BUT THAT A SMILE SHOULD NATURALLY COME ONTO OUR FACE WHEN WE DANCED.
BECAUSE DANCE IS SOMETHING YOU HAVE TO ENJOY WITH ALL YOUR HEART.
BECAUSE DANCE ENRICHES YOUR LIFE.

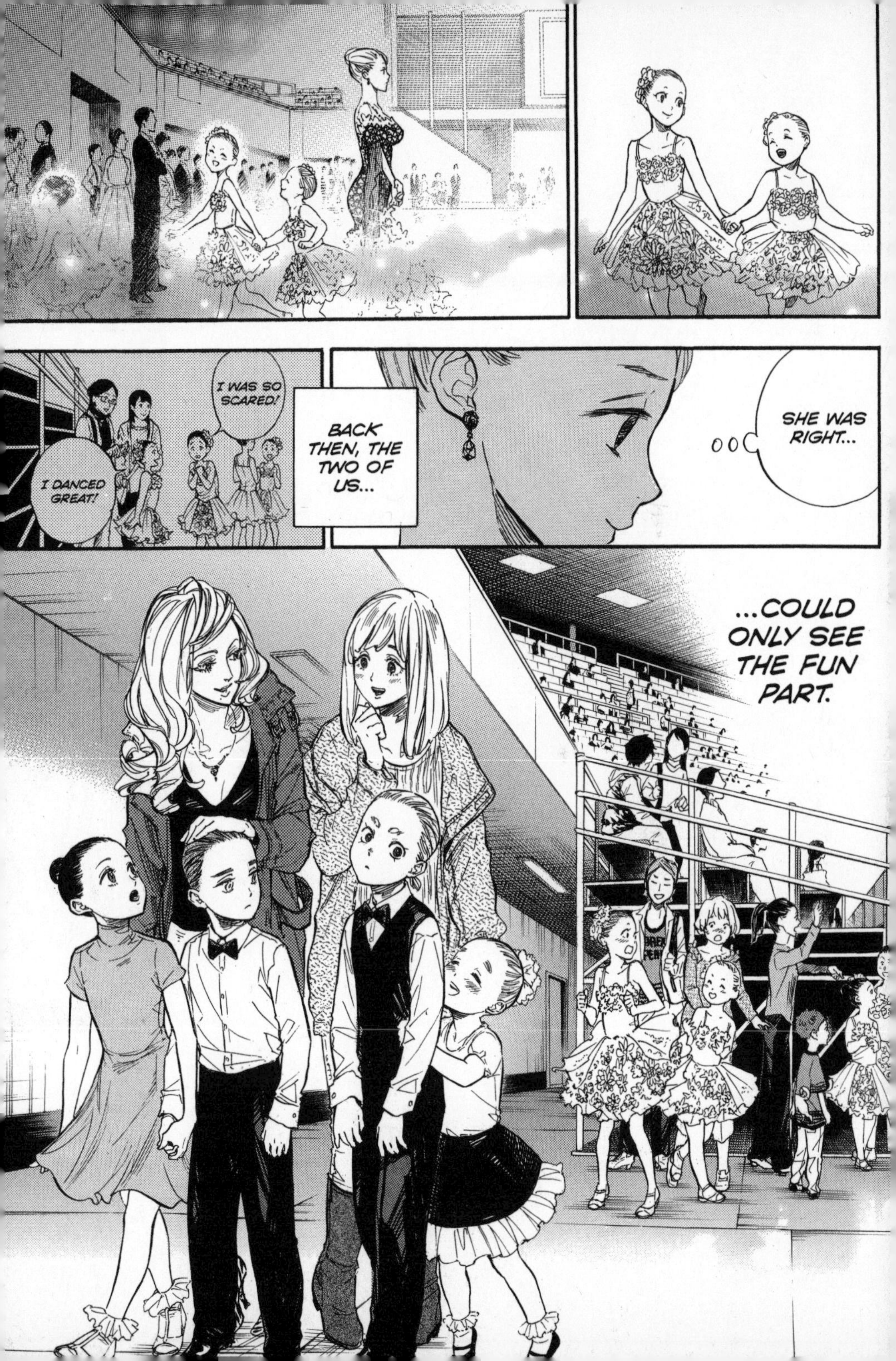
SHE WAS RIGHT...
BACK THEN, THE TWO OF US...
I WAS SO SCARED!
I DANCED GREAT!
...COULD ONLY SEE THE FUN PART.

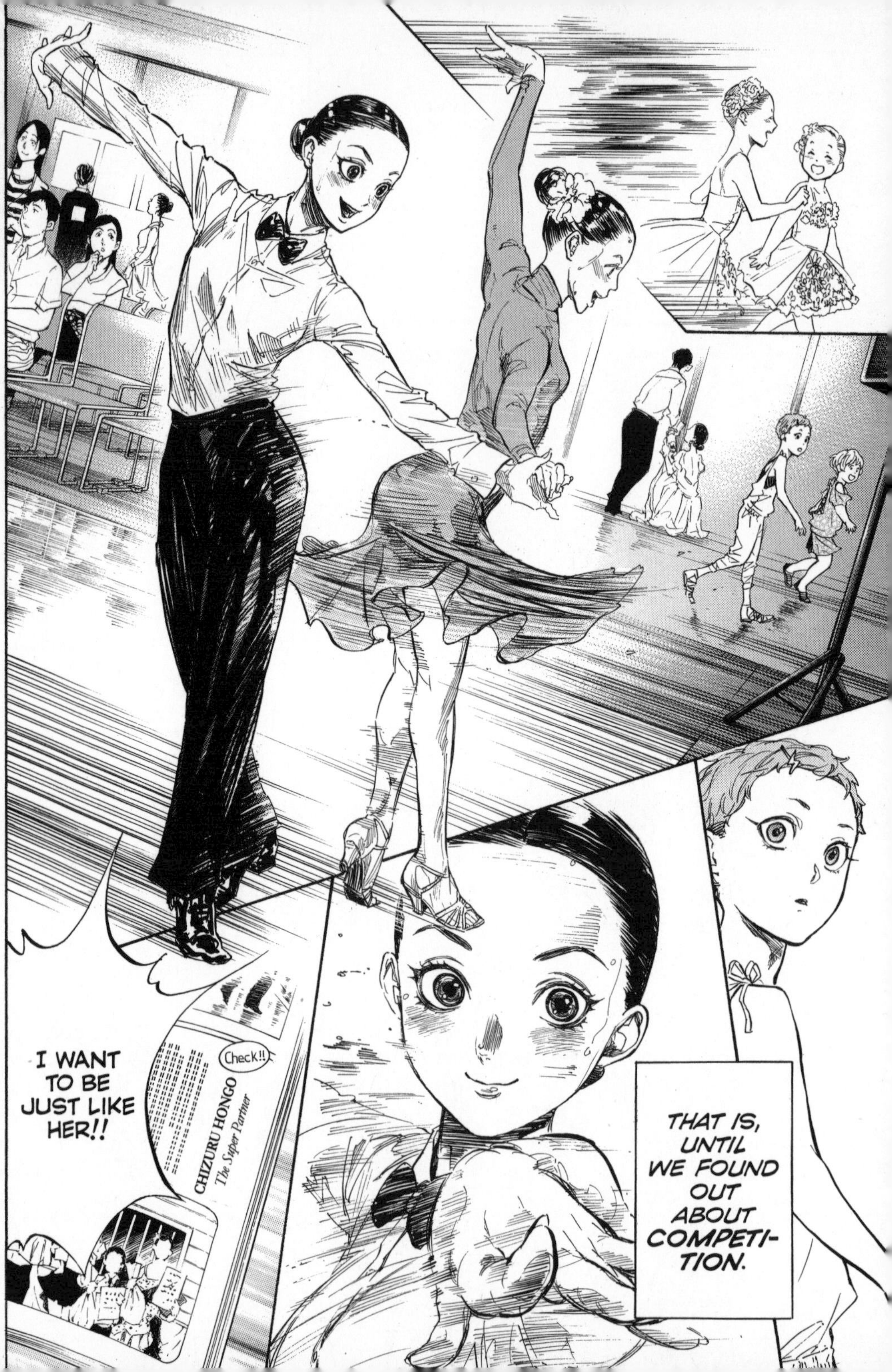
THAT IS, UNTIL WE FOUND OUT ABOUT COMPETITION.
Check!!
CHIZURU HONGO
The Super Partner
I WANT TO BE JUST LIKE HER!!

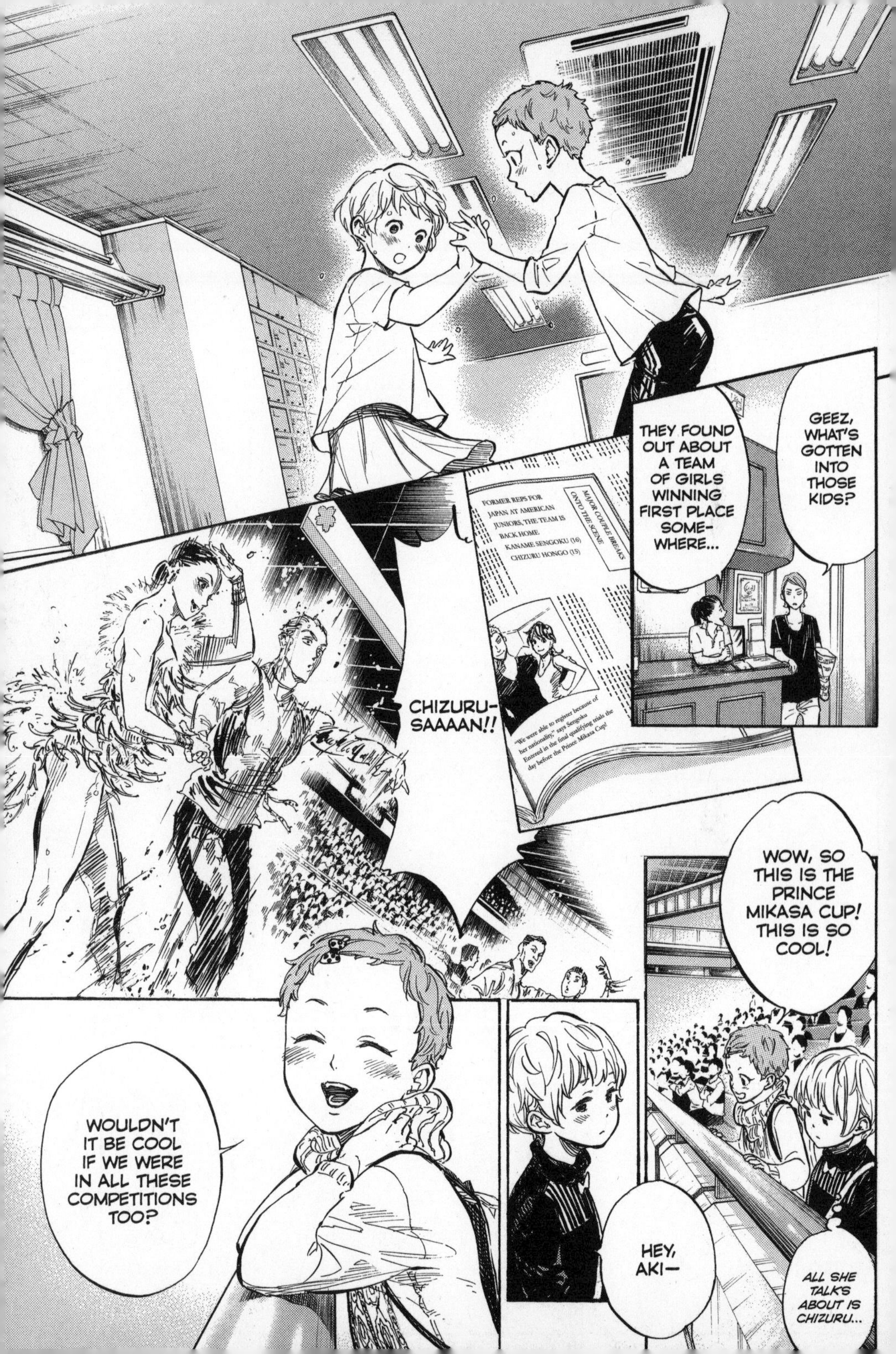
GEEZ, WHAT'S GOTTEN INTO THOSE KIDS?
THEY FOUND OUT ABOUT A TEAM OF GIRLS WINNING FIRST PLACE SOME-WHERE...
MAJOR COUPLE BREAKS ONTO THE SCENE
FORMER REPS FOR JAPAN AT AMERICAN JUNIORS, THE TEAM IS BACK HOME
KANAME SENGOKU (16)
CHIZURU HONGO (15)
"We were able to register because of her nationality," says Sengoku
Entered in the final qualifying trials the day before the Prince Mikasa Cup!
CHIZURU-SAAAAN!!
WOW, SO THIS IS THE PRINCE MIKASA CUP! THIS IS SO COOL!
ALL SHE TALKS ABOUT IS CHIZURU...
HEY, AKI—
WOULDN'T IT BE COOL IF WE WERE IN ALL THESE COMPETITIONS TOO?

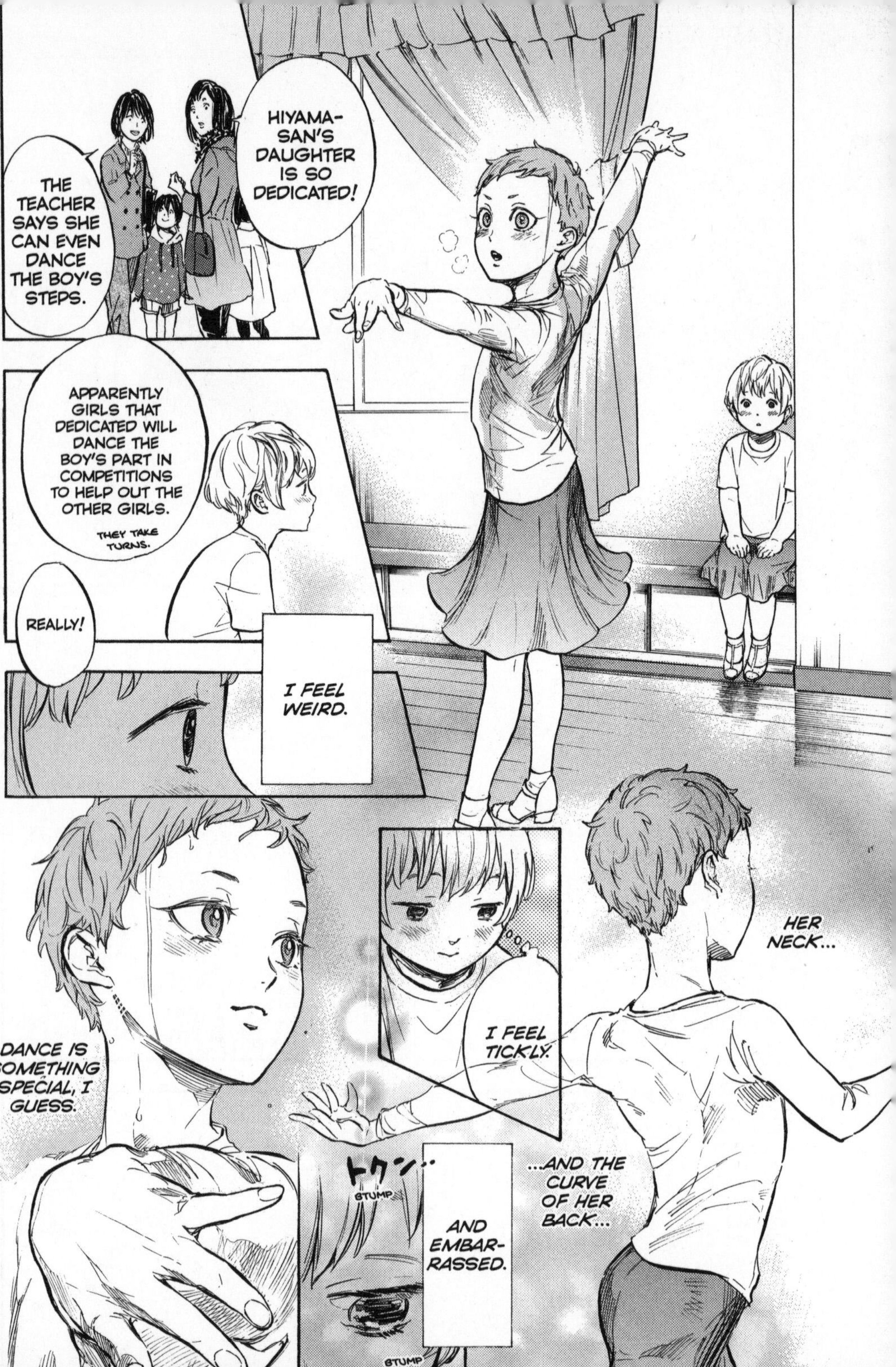
HIYAMA-SAN'S DAUGHTER IS SO DEDICATED!
THE TEACHER SAYS SHE CAN EVEN DANCE THE BOY'S STEPS.
APPARENTLY GIRLS THAT DEDICATED WILL DANCE THE BOY'S PART IN COMPETITIONS TO HELP OUT THE OTHER GIRLS.
THEY TAKE TURNS.
REALLY!
I FEEL WEIRD.
HER NECK...
...AND THE CURVE OF HER BACK...
I FEEL TICKLY.
トクン…
STUMP
AND EMBARRASSED.
STUMP
DANCE IS SOMETHING SPECIAL, I GUESS.

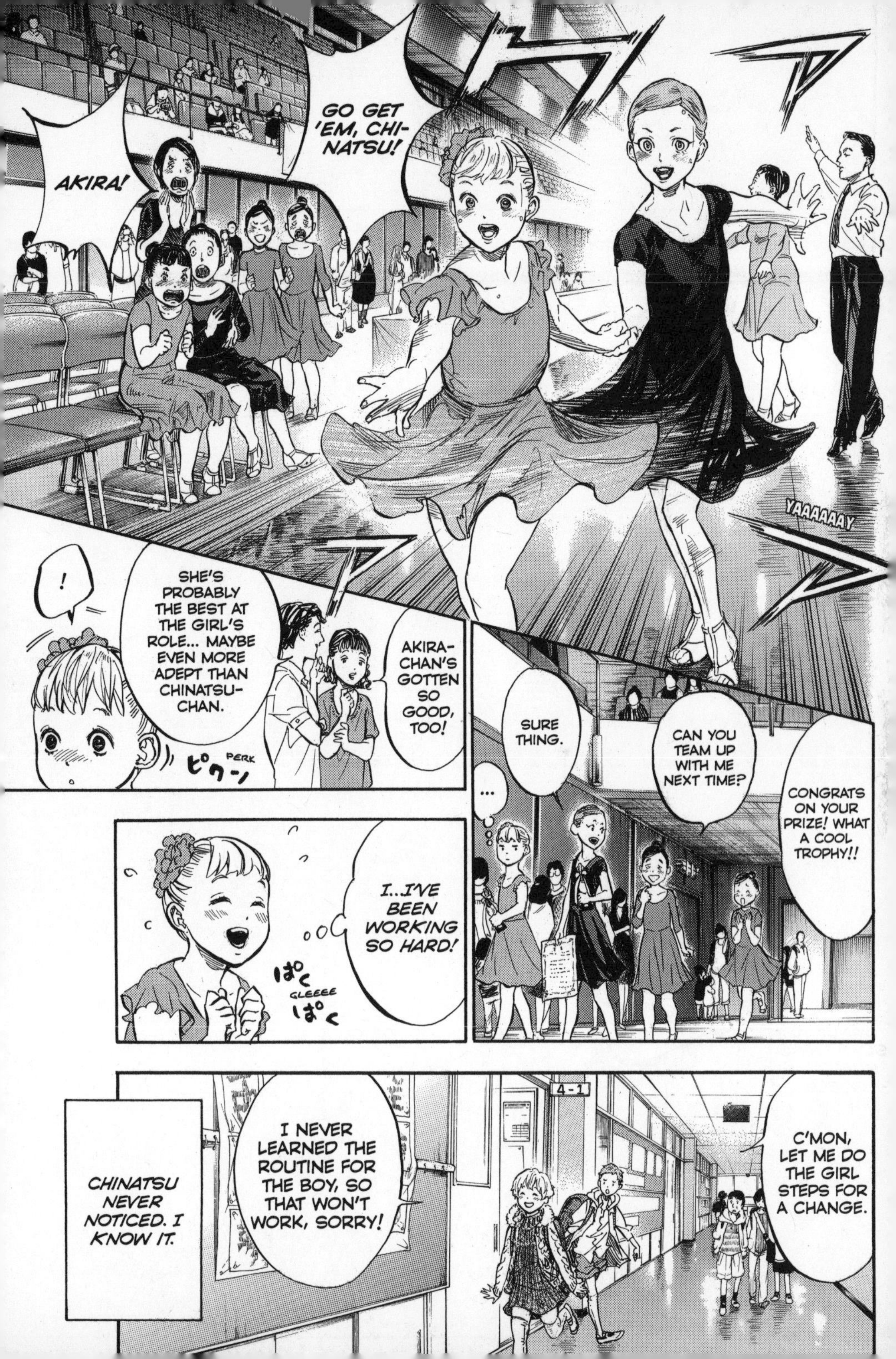
GO GET 'EM, CHI-NATSU!
AKIRA!
YAAAAAAY
CONGRATS ON YOUR PRIZE! WHAT A COOL TROPHY!!
CAN YOU TEAM UP WITH ME NEXT TIME?
SURE THING.
...
AKIRA-CHAN'S GOTTEN SO GOOD, TOO!
SHE'S PROBABLY THE BEST AT THE GIRL'S ROLE... MAYBE EVEN MORE ADEPT THAN CHINATSU-CHAN.
!
ピクーン
PERK
I..I'VE BEEN WORKING SO HARD!
ぱくぱく
GLEEEE
C'MON, LET ME DO THE GIRL STEPS FOR A CHANGE.
I NEVER LEARNED THE ROUTINE FOR THE BOY, SO THAT WON'T WORK, SORRY!
CHINATSU NEVER NOTICED. I KNOW IT.
4-1

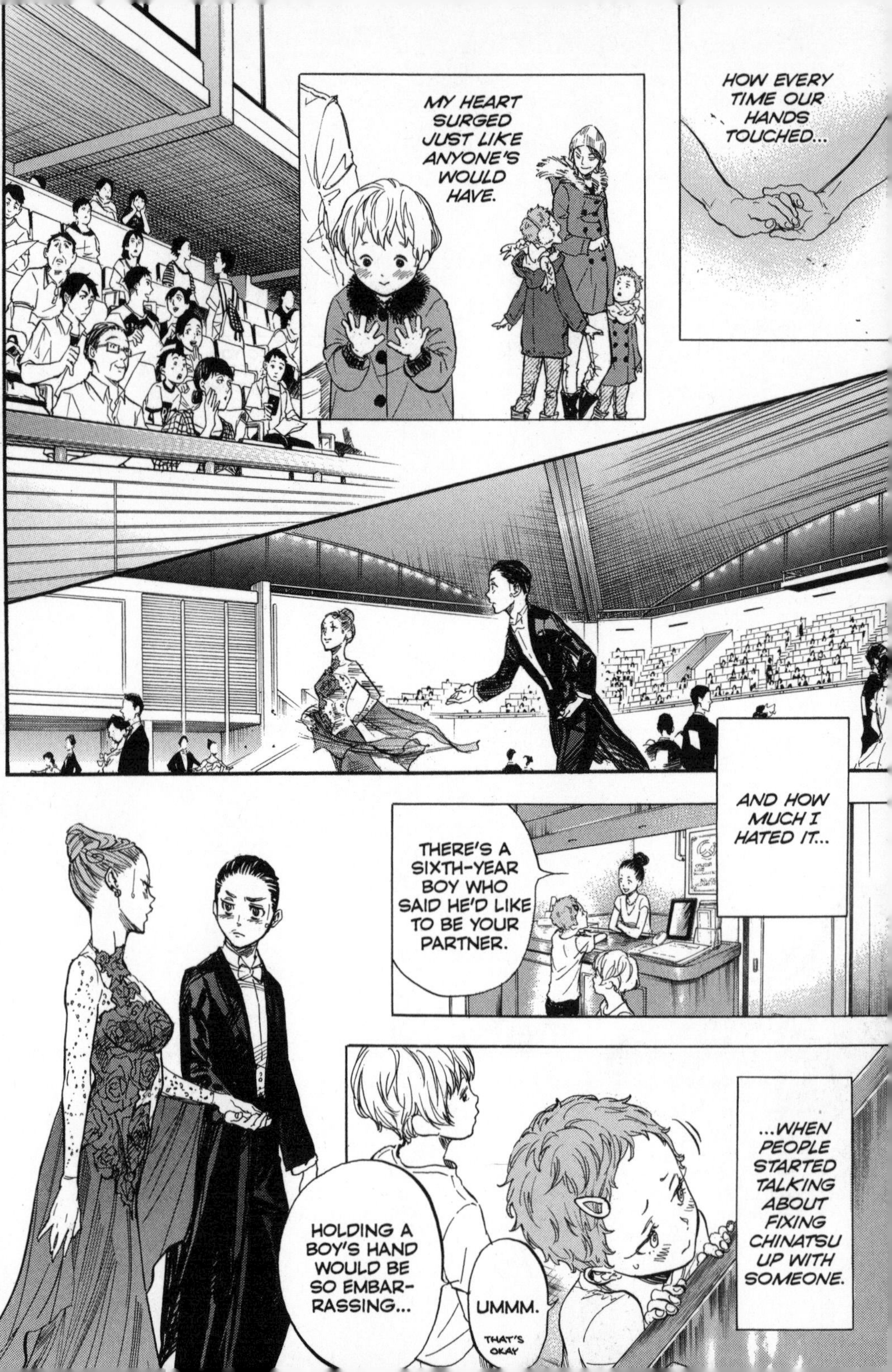
HOW EVERY TIME OUR HANDS TOUCHED...
MY HEART SURGED JUST LIKE ANYONE'S WOULD HAVE.
AND HOW MUCH I HATED IT...
THERE'S A SIXTH-YEAR BOY WHO SAID HE'D LIKE TO BE YOUR PARTNER.
...WHEN PEOPLE STARTED TALKING ABOUT FIXING CHINATSU UP WITH SOMEONE.
HOLDING A BOY'S HAND WOULD BE SO EMBAR-RASSING...
UMMM.
THAT'S OKAY

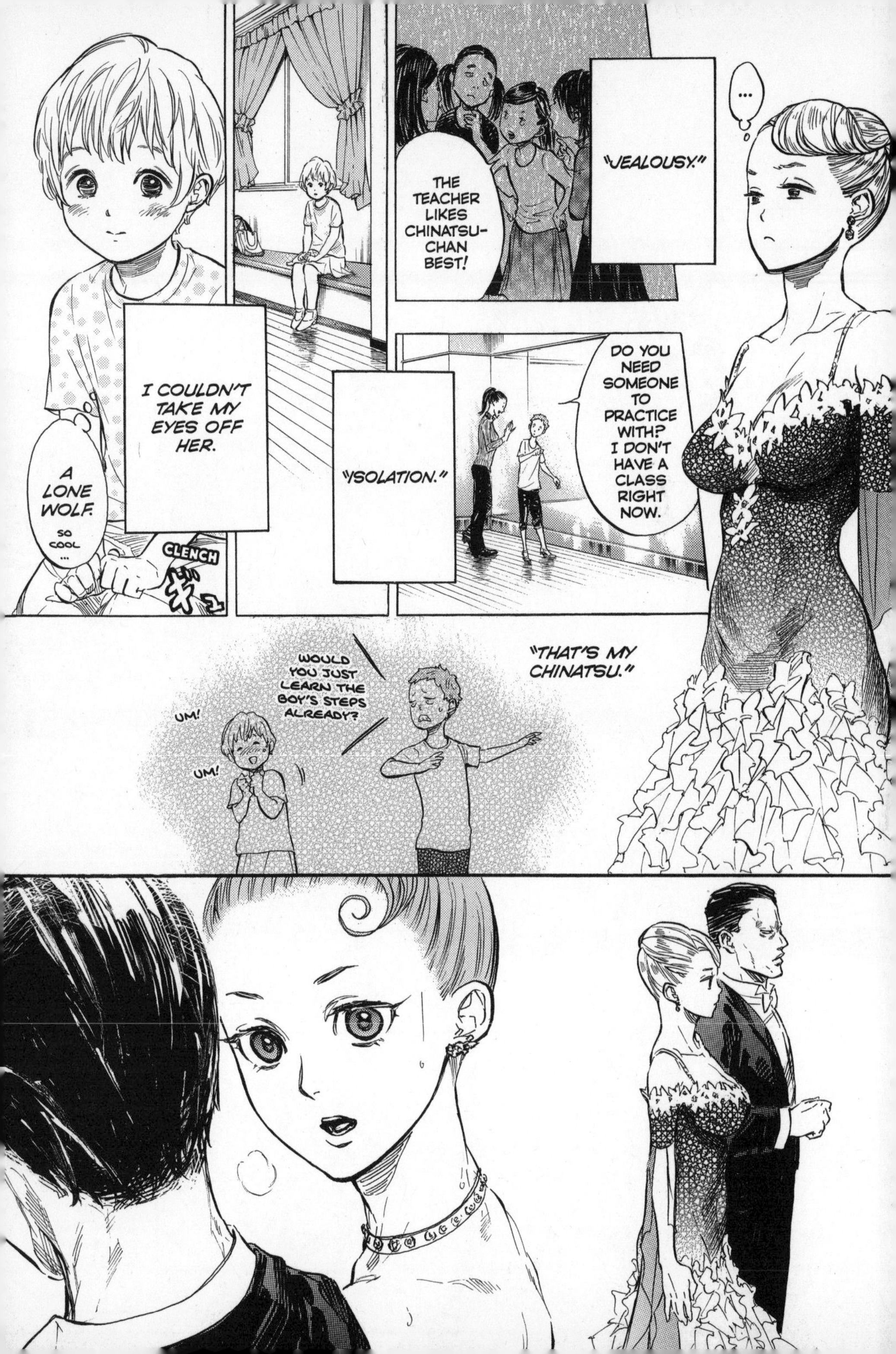
...
"JEALOUSY."
THE TEACHER LIKES CHINATSU-CHAN BEST!
DO YOU NEED SOMEONE TO PRACTICE WITH? I DON'T HAVE A CLASS RIGHT NOW.
"ISOLATION."
I COULDN'T TAKE MY EYES OFF HER.
A LONE WOLF.
SO COOL...
CLENCH
"THAT'S MY CHINATSU."
WOULD YOU JUST LEARN THE BOY'S STEPS ALREADY?
UM!
UM!

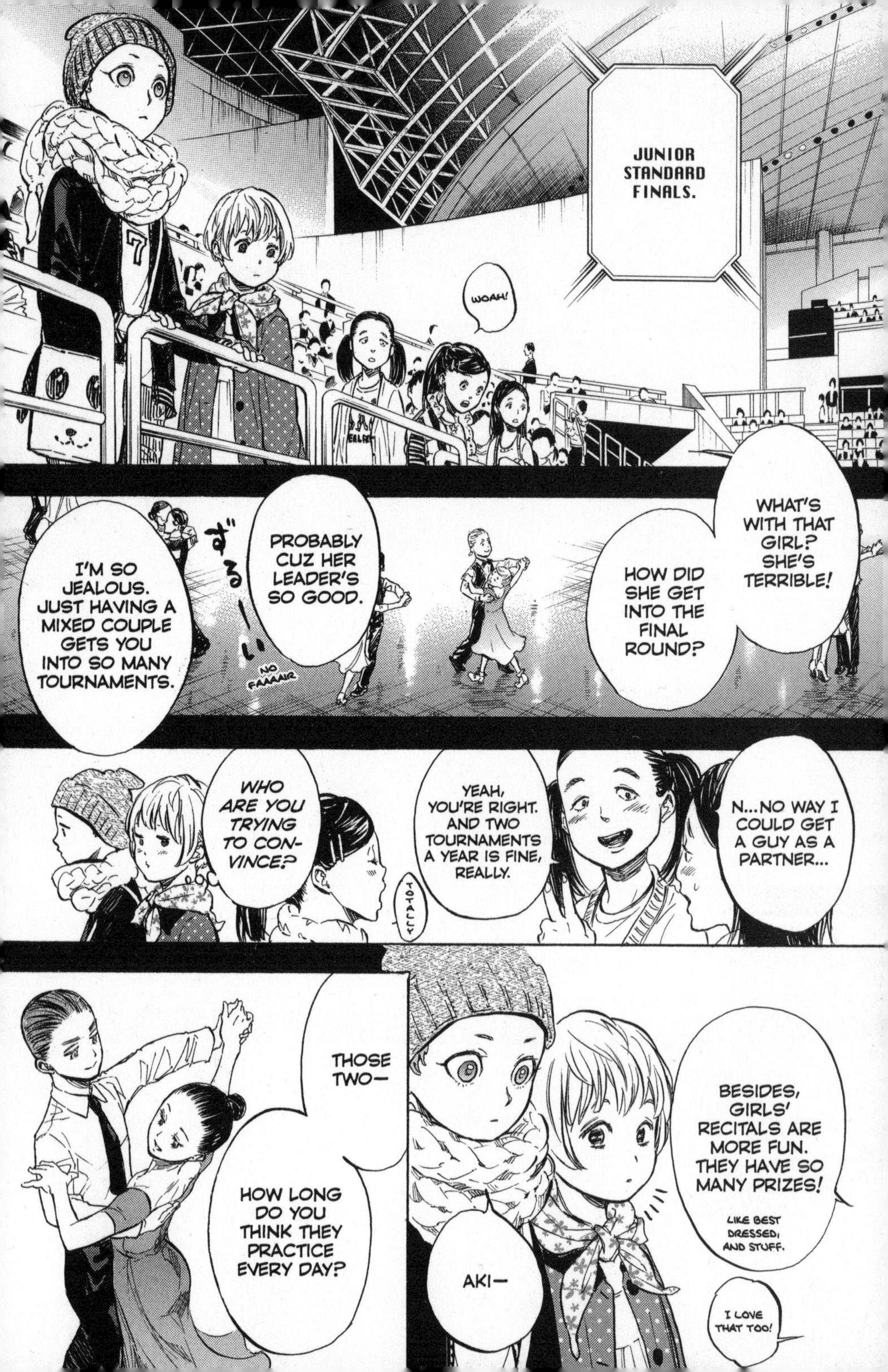
JUNIOR STANDARD FINALS.
WOAH!
WHAT'S WITH THAT GIRL? SHE'S TERRIBLE!
HOW DID SHE GET INTO THE FINAL ROUND?
PROBABLY CUZ HER LEADER'S SO GOOD.
ずるい
NO FAAAAIR
I'M SO JEALOUS. JUST HAVING A MIXED COUPLE GETS YOU INTO SO MANY TOURNAMENTS.
N...NO WAY I COULD GET A GUY AS A PARTNER...
YEAH, YOU'RE RIGHT. AND TWO TOURNAMENTS A YEAR IS FINE, REALLY.
TOTALLY
WHO ARE YOU TRYING TO CONVINCE?
BESIDES, GIRLS' RECITALS ARE MORE FUN. THEY HAVE SO MANY PRIZES!
LIKE BEST DRESSED, AND STUFF.
I LOVE THAT TOO!
AKI—
THOSE TWO—
HOW LONG DO YOU THINK THEY PRACTICE EVERY DAY?

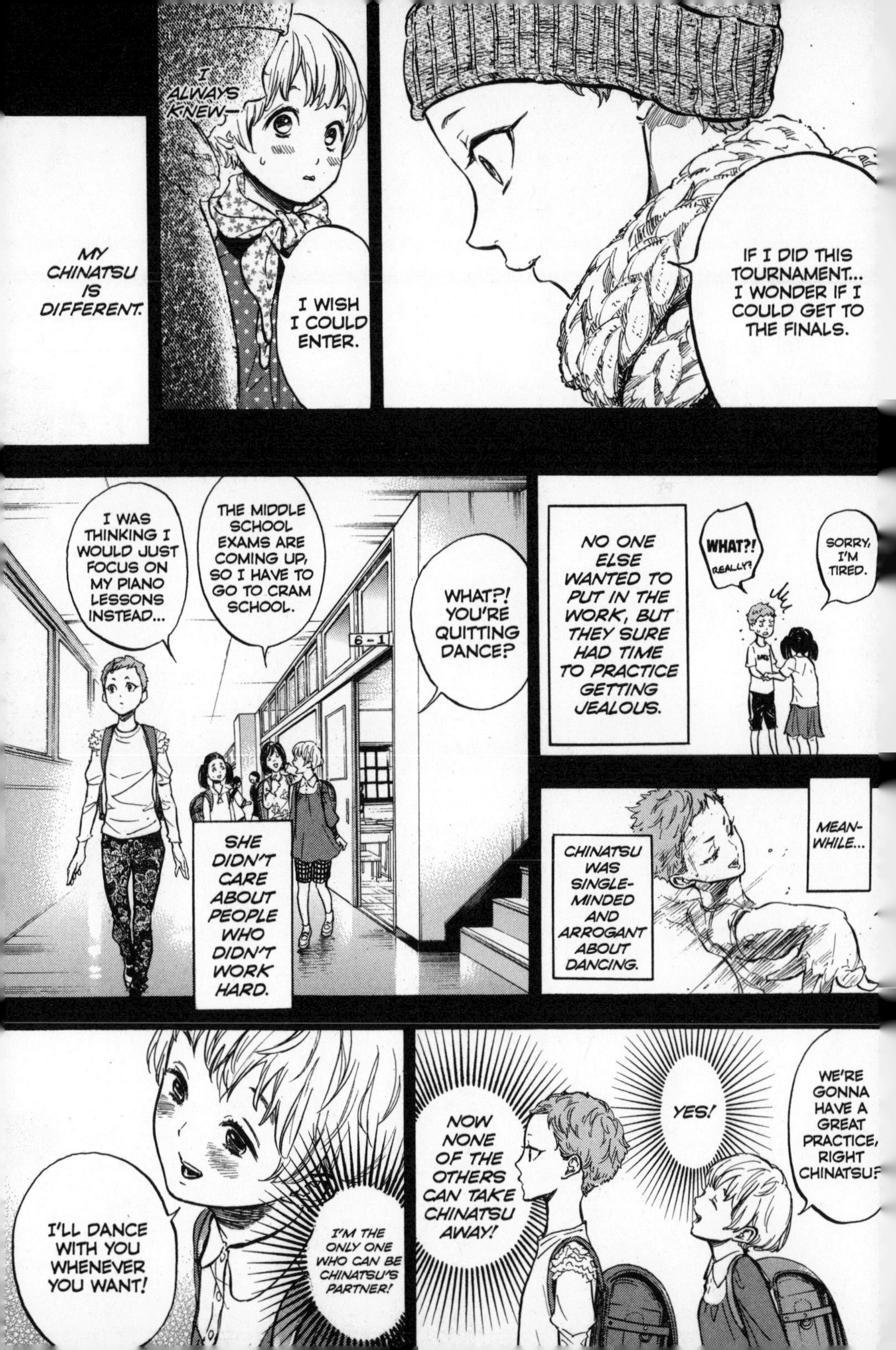
IF I DID THIS TOURNAMENT... I WONDER IF I COULD GET TO THE FINALS.
I ALWAYS KNEW—
I WISH I COULD ENTER.
MY CHINATSU IS DIFFERENT.
SORRY, I'M TIRED.
WHAT?! REALLY?
NO ONE ELSE WANTED TO PUT IN THE WORK, BUT THEY SURE HAD TIME TO PRACTICE GETTING JEALOUS.
MEAN-WHILE...
CHINATSU WAS SINGLE-MINDED AND ARROGANT ABOUT DANCING.
WHAT?! YOU'RE QUITTING DANCE?
THE MIDDLE SCHOOL EXAMS ARE COMING UP, SO I HAVE TO GO TO CRAM SCHOOL.
I WAS THINKING I WOULD JUST FOCUS ON MY PIANO LESSONS INSTEAD...
6-1
SHE DIDN'T CARE ABOUT PEOPLE WHO DIDN'T WORK HARD.
WE'RE GONNA HAVE A GREAT PRACTICE, RIGHT CHINATSU?
YES!
NOW NONE OF THE OTHERS CAN TAKE CHINATSU AWAY!
I'M THE ONLY ONE WHO CAN BE CHINATSU'S PARTNER!
I'LL DANCE WITH YOU WHENEVER YOU WANT!

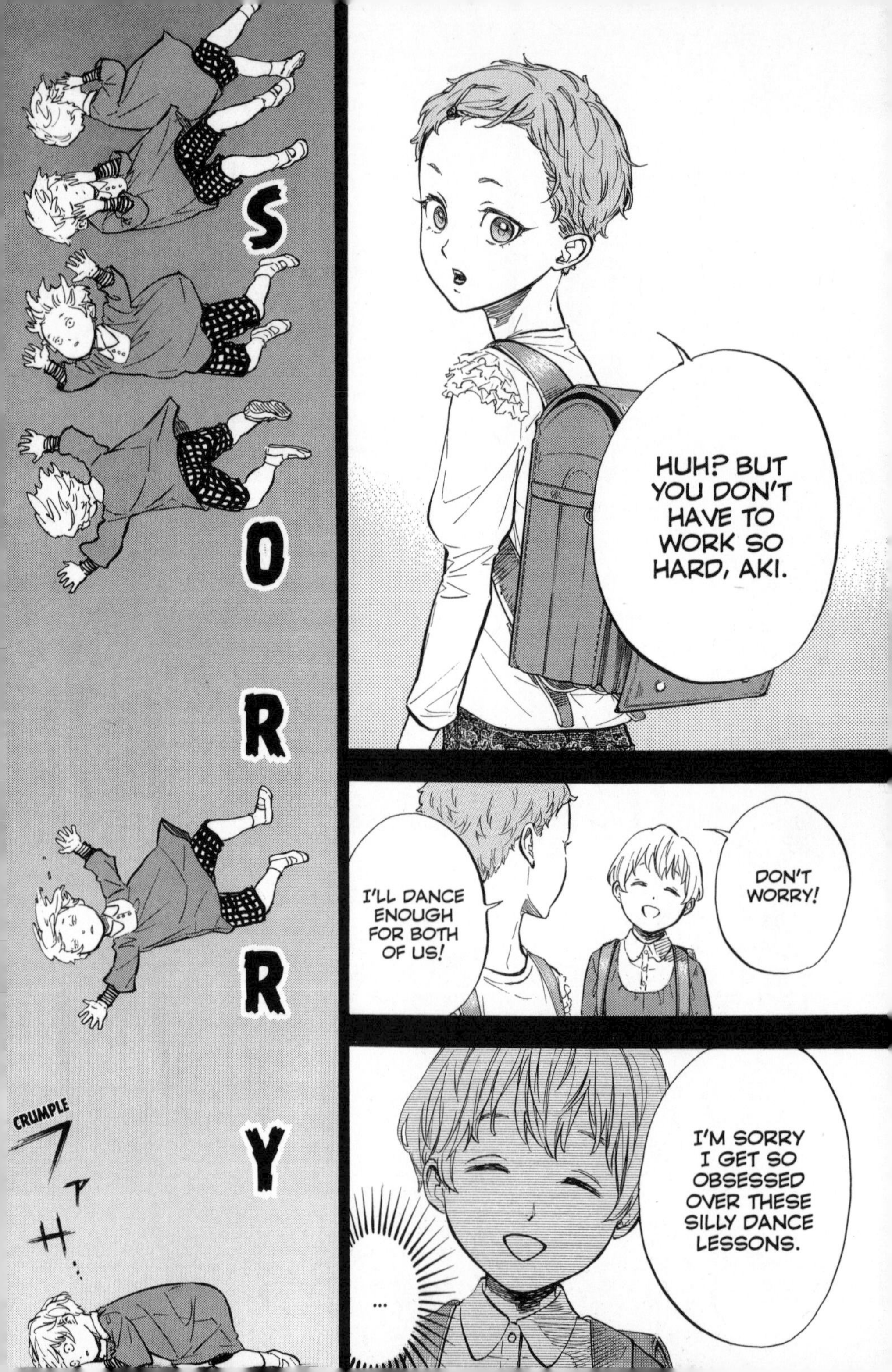
HUH? BUT YOU DON'T HAVE TO WORK SO HARD, AKI.
DON'T WORRY!
I'LL DANCE ENOUGH FOR BOTH OF US!
I'M SORRY I GET SO OBSESSED OVER THESE SILLY DANCE LESSONS.
...
SORRY
CRUMPLE
...

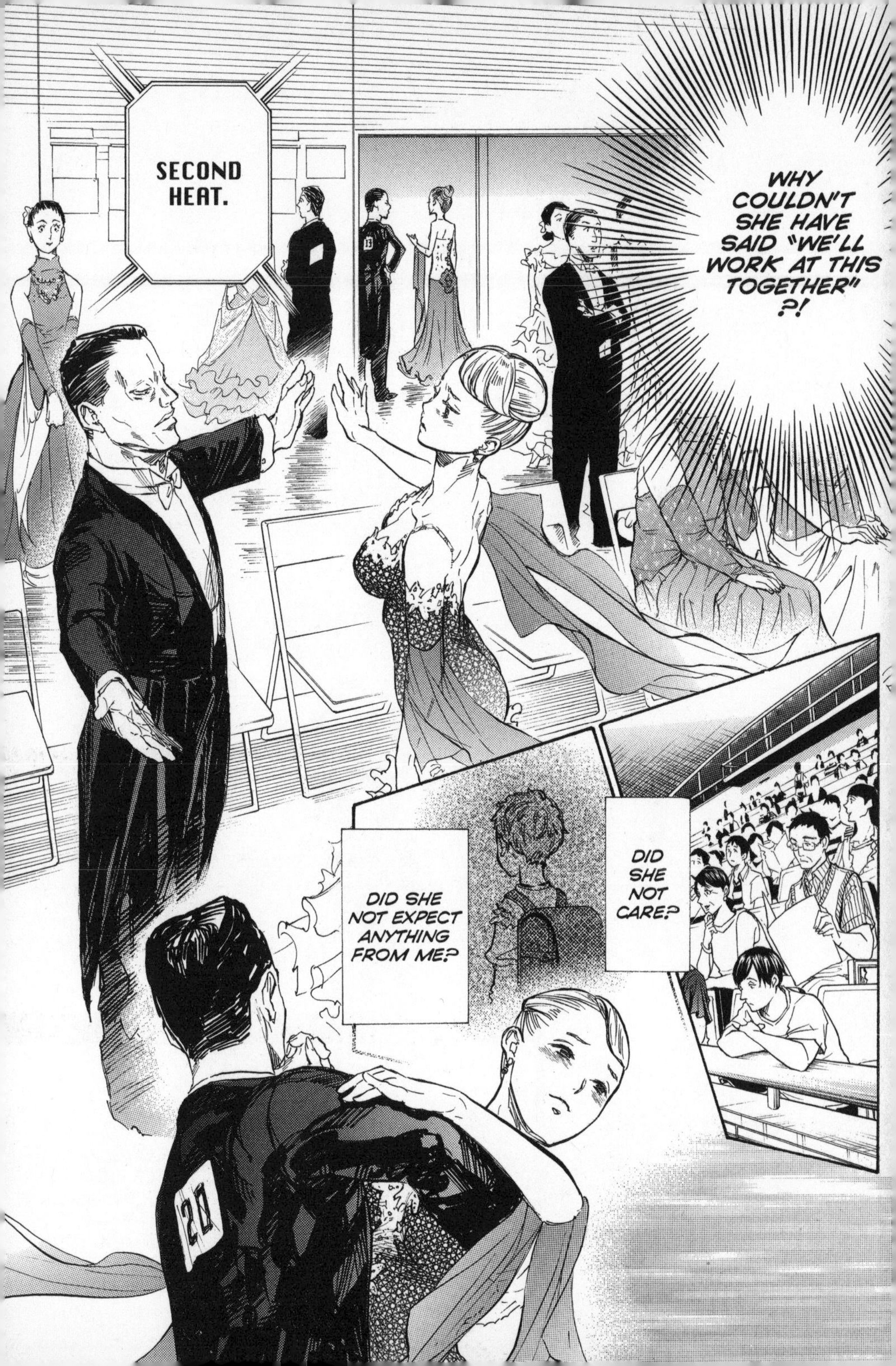
WHY COULDN'T SHE HAVE SAID "WE'LL WORK AT THIS TOGETHER"?!
SECOND HEAT.
DID SHE NOT CARE?
DID SHE NOT EXPECT ANYTHING FROM ME?
20

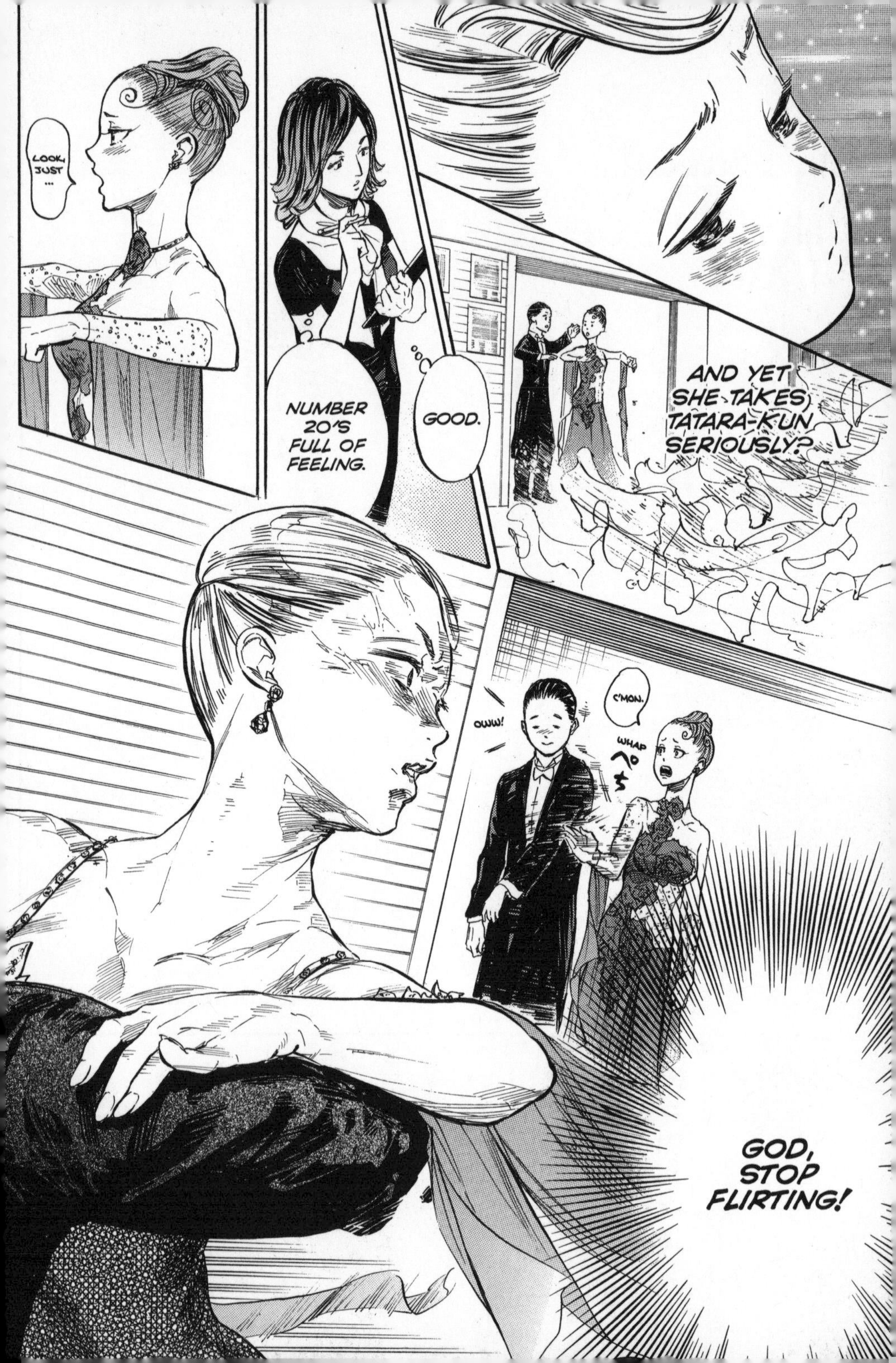
AND YET SHE TAKES TATARA-KUN SERIOUSLY?
GOOD.
NUMBER 20'S FULL OF FEELING.
LOOK, JUST ...
C'MON.
OWW!
WHAP
GOD, STOP FLIRTING!

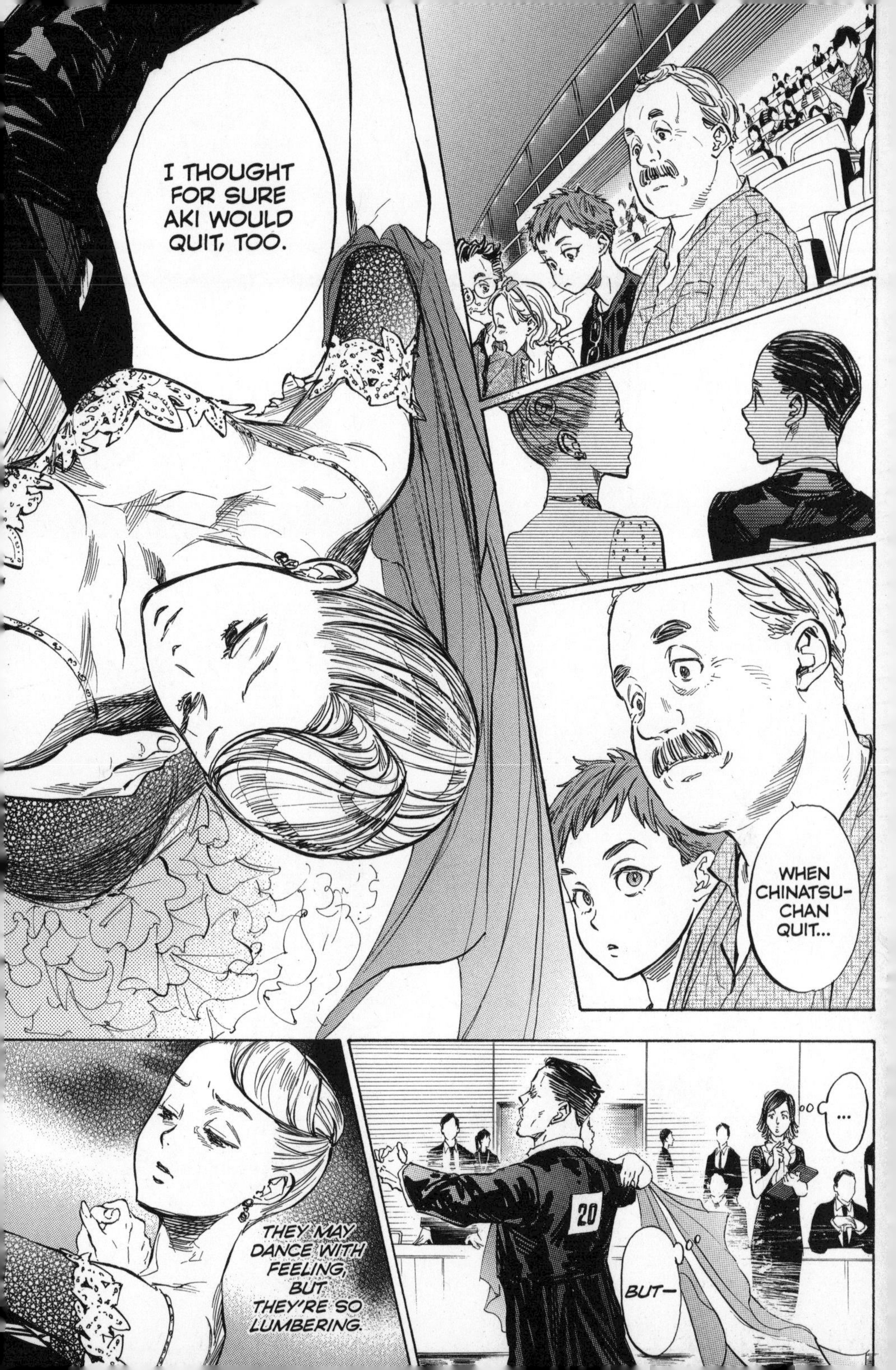
I THOUGHT FOR SURE AKI WOULD QUIT, TOO.
WHEN CHINATSU-CHAN QUIT...
...
BUT—
THEY MAY DANCE WITH FEELING, BUT THEY'RE SO LUMBERING.
20

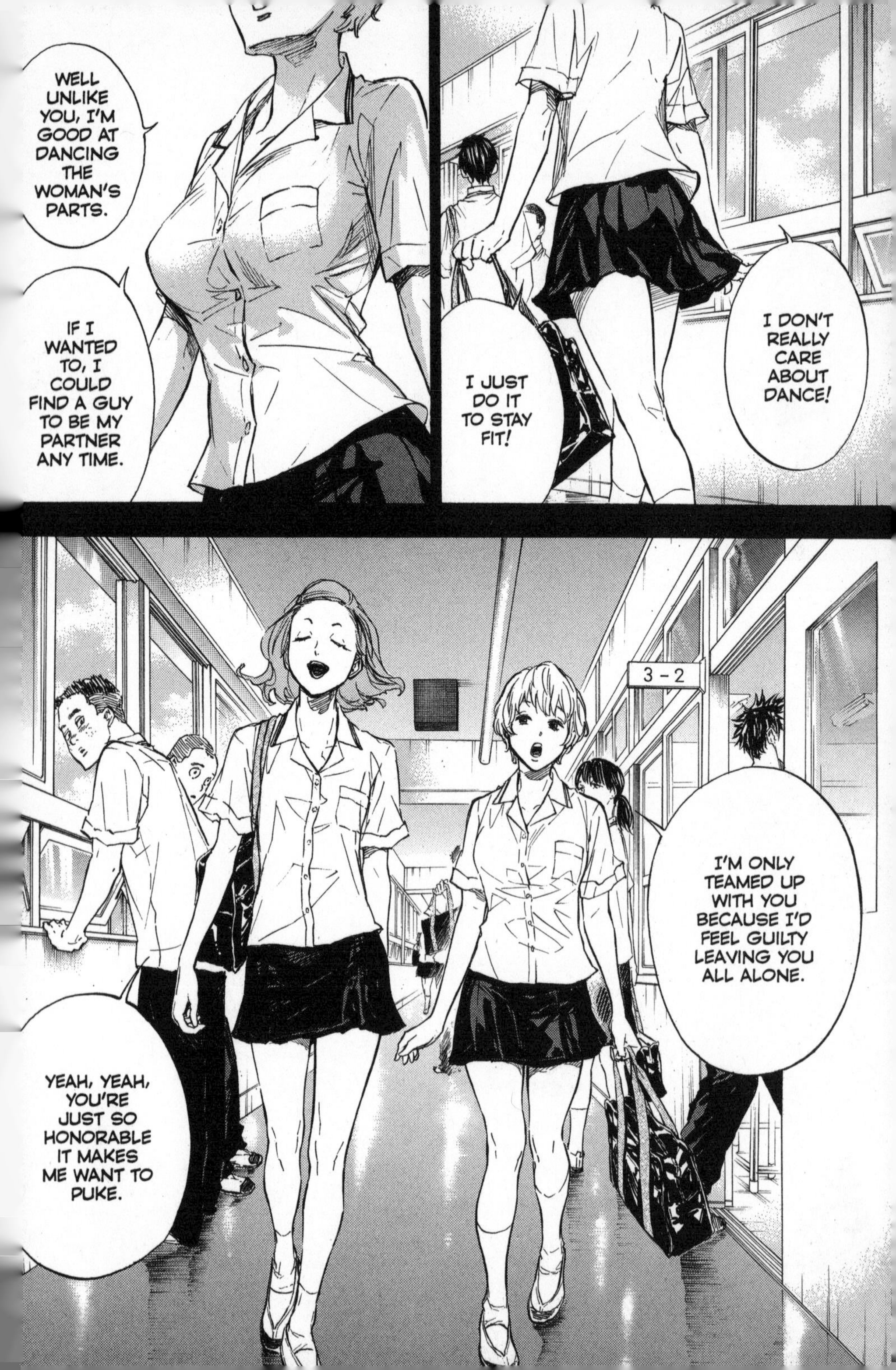
I DON'T REALLY CARE ABOUT DANCE!
I JUST DO IT TO STAY FIT!
WELL UNLIKE YOU, I'M GOOD AT DANCING THE WOMAN'S PARTS.
IF I WANTED TO, I COULD FIND A GUY TO BE MY PARTNER ANY TIME.
3-2
I'M ONLY TEAMED UP WITH YOU BECAUSE I'D FEEL GUILTY LEAVING YOU ALL ALONE.
YEAH, YEAH, YOU'RE JUST SO HONORABLE IT MAKES ME WANT TO PUKE.

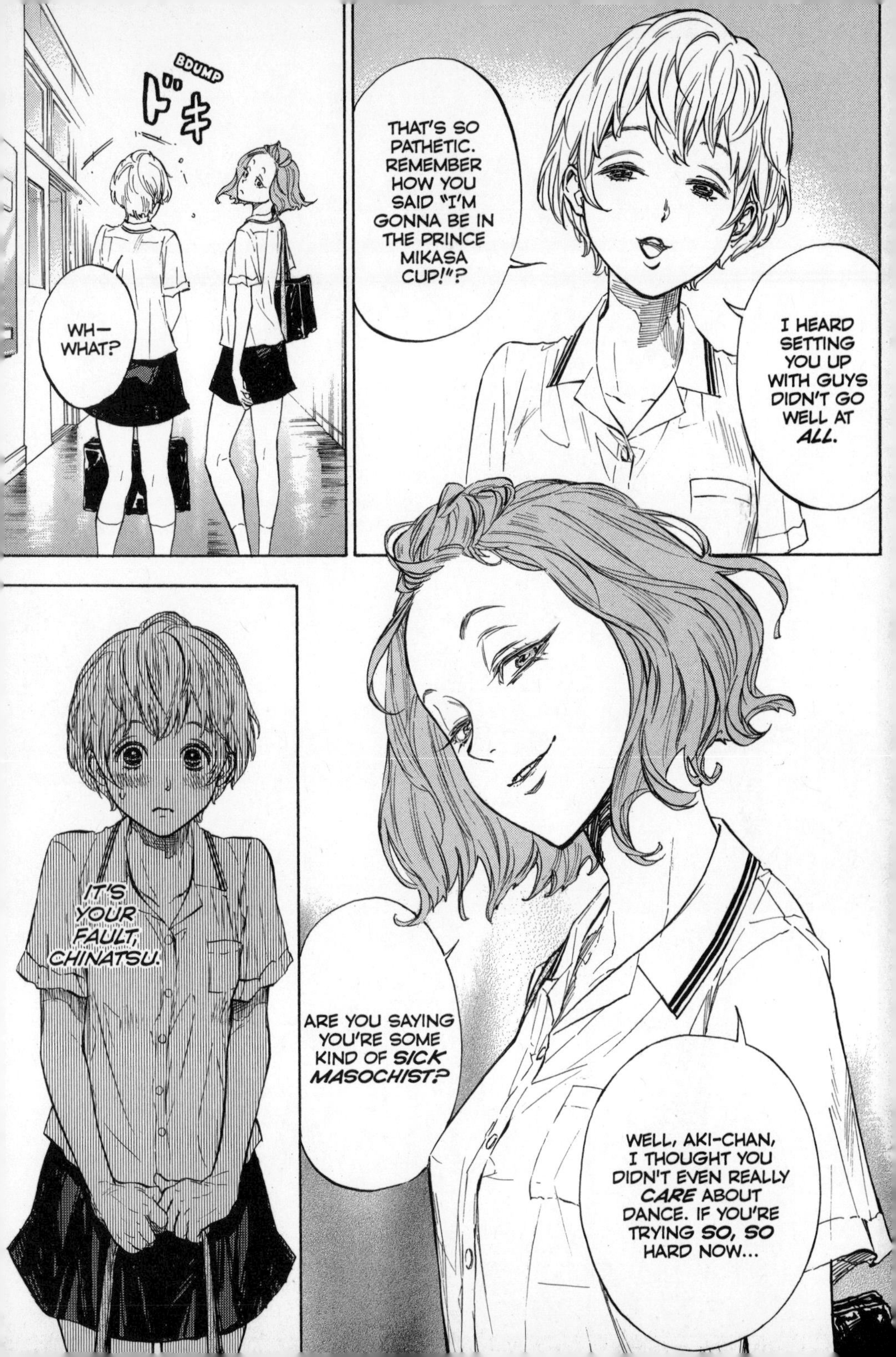
I HEARD SETTING YOU UP WITH GUYS DIDN'T GO WELL AT *ALL*.
THAT'S SO PATHETIC. REMEMBER HOW YOU SAID "I'M GONNA BE IN THE PRINCE MIKASA CUP!"?
BDUMP
ドキ
WH—WHAT?
WELL, AKI-CHAN, I THOUGHT YOU DIDN'T EVEN REALLY *CARE* ABOUT DANCE. IF YOU'RE TRYING *SO, SO* HARD NOW...
ARE YOU SAYING YOU'RE SOME KIND OF *SICK MASOCHIST?*
IT'S YOUR FAULT, CHINATSU.

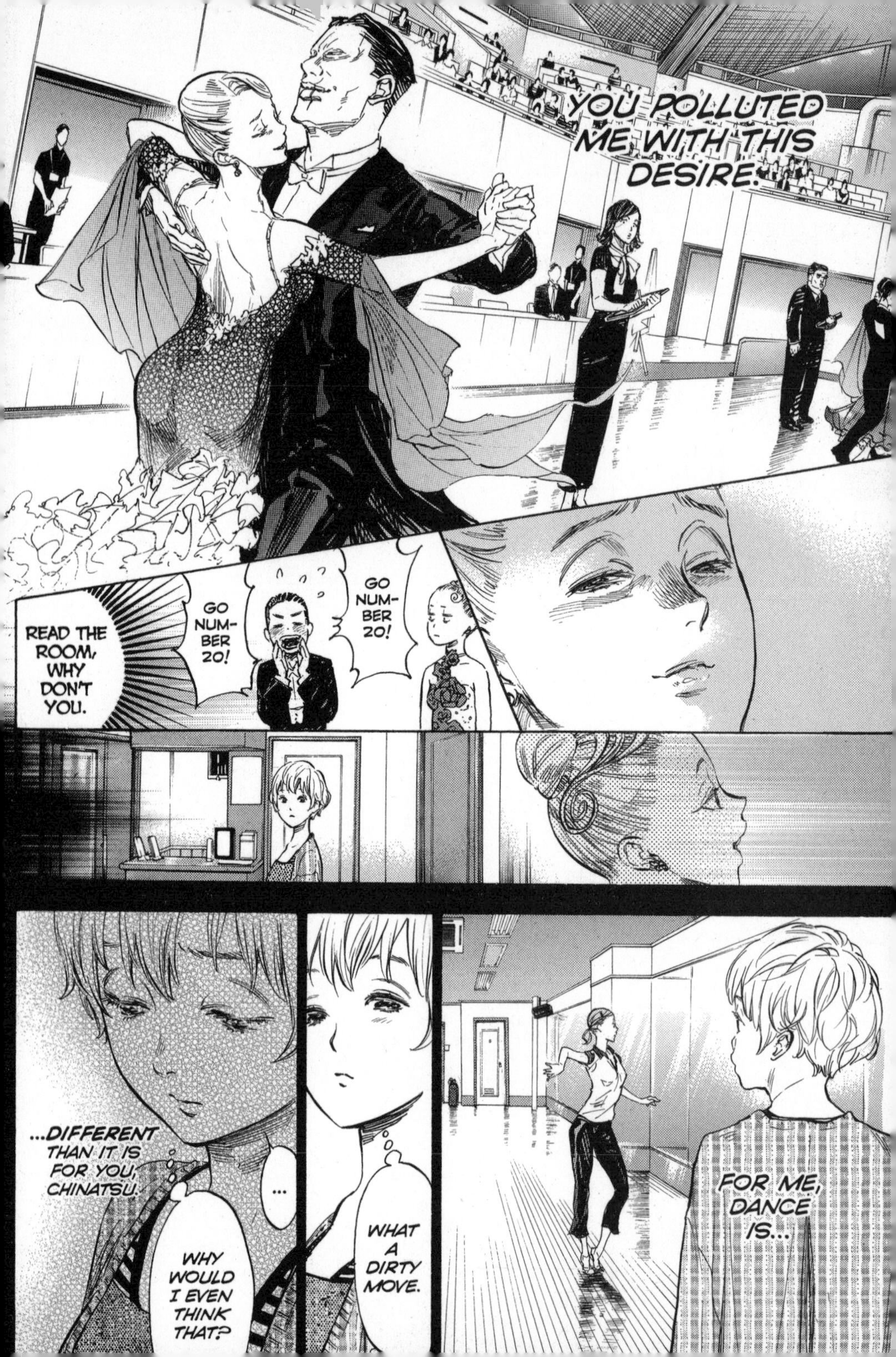
YOU POLLUTED ME WITH THIS DESIRE.
GO NUM-BER 20!
GO NUM-BER 20!
READ THE ROOM, WHY DON'T YOU.
FOR ME, DANCE IS...
WHAT A DIRTY MOVE.
...DIFFERENT THAN IT IS FOR YOU, CHINATSU.
...
WHY WOULD I EVEN THINK THAT?

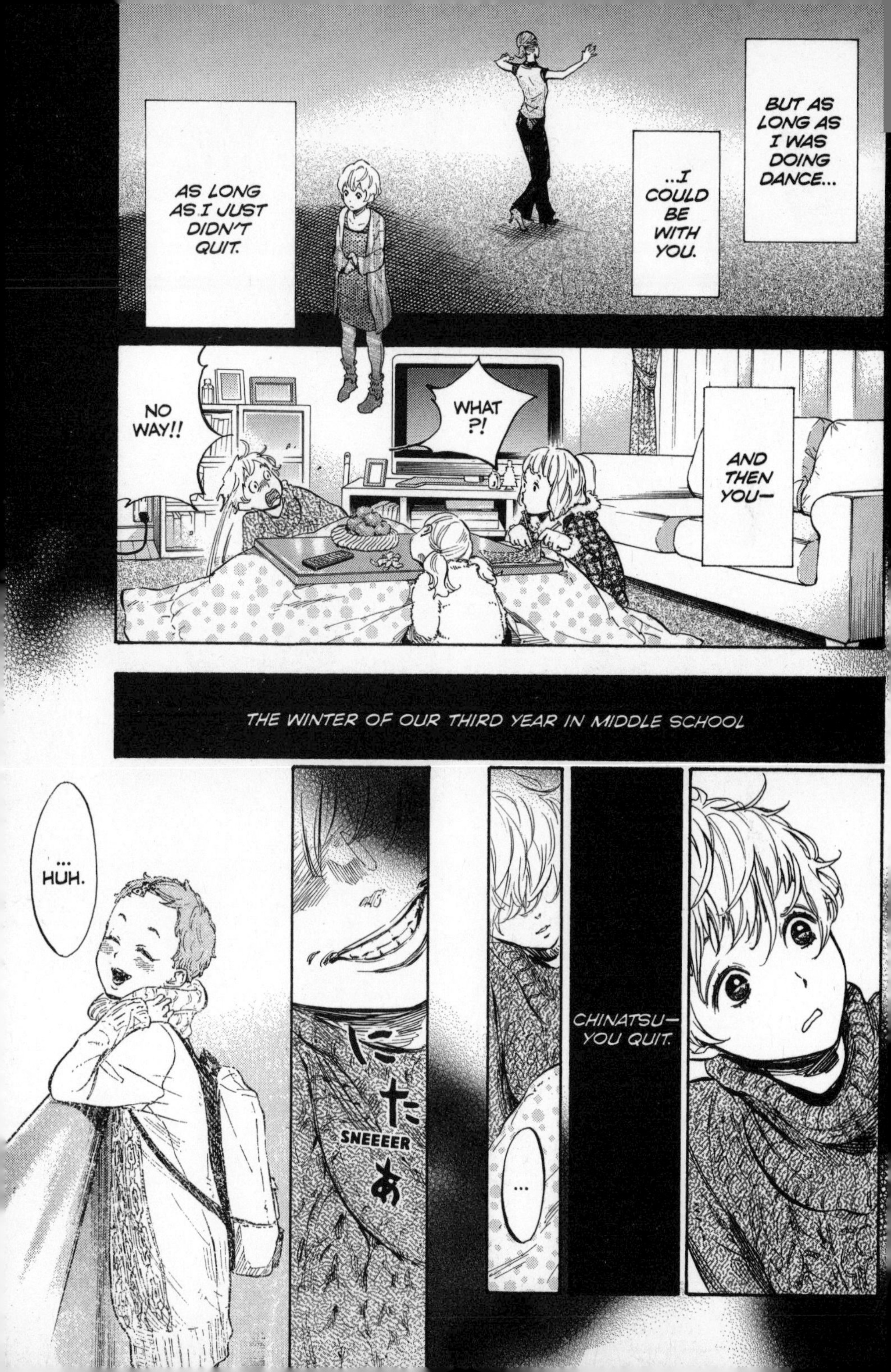
BUT AS LONG AS I WAS DOING DANCE...
...I COULD BE WITH YOU.
AS LONG AS I JUST DIDN'T QUIT.
AND THEN YOU—
WHAT ?!
NO WAY!!
THE WINTER OF OUR THIRD YEAR IN MIDDLE SCHOOL
CHINATSU— YOU QUIT.
...
にた
SNEEEER
あ
...HUH.

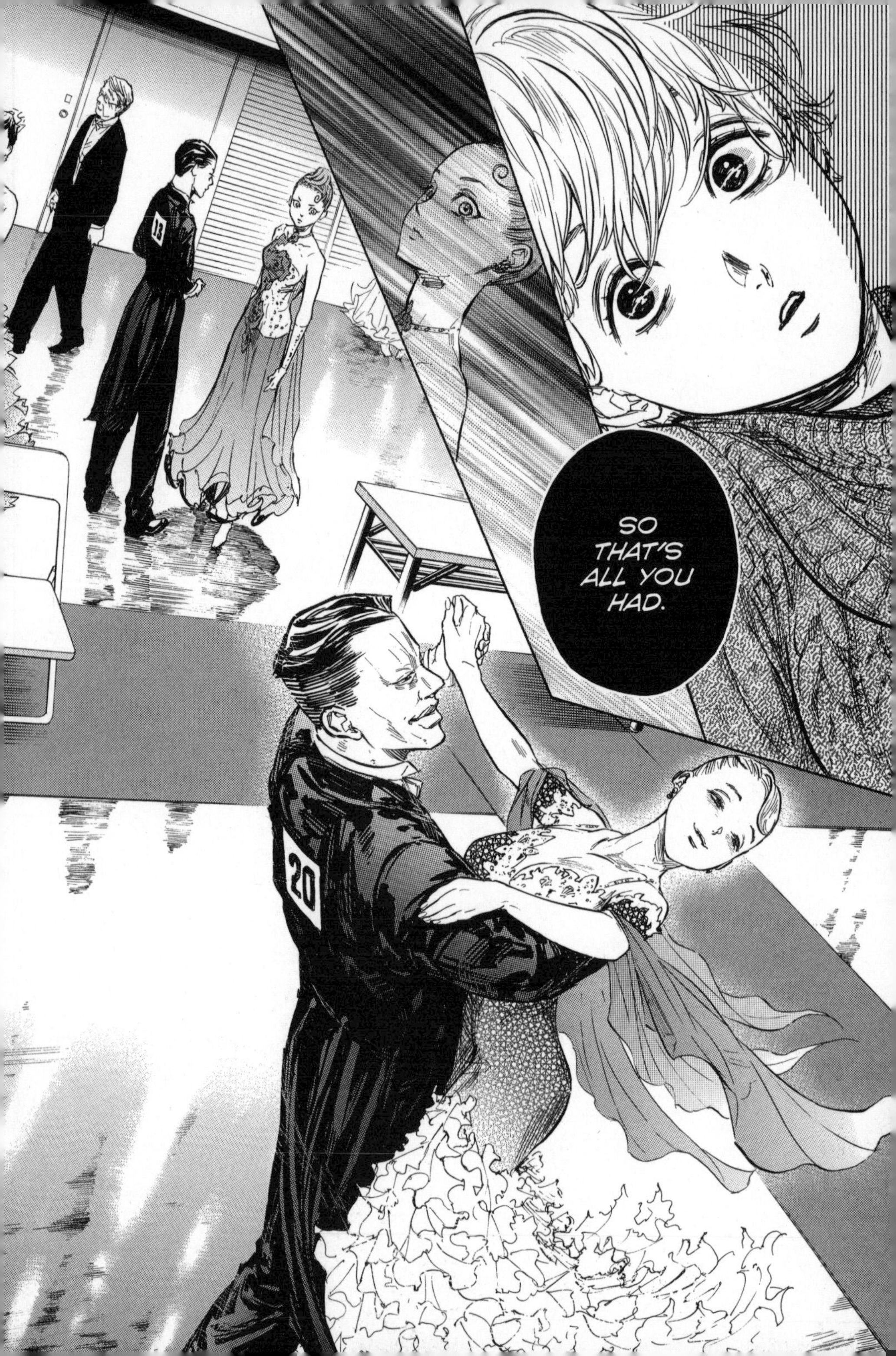
SO THAT'S ALL YOU HAD.

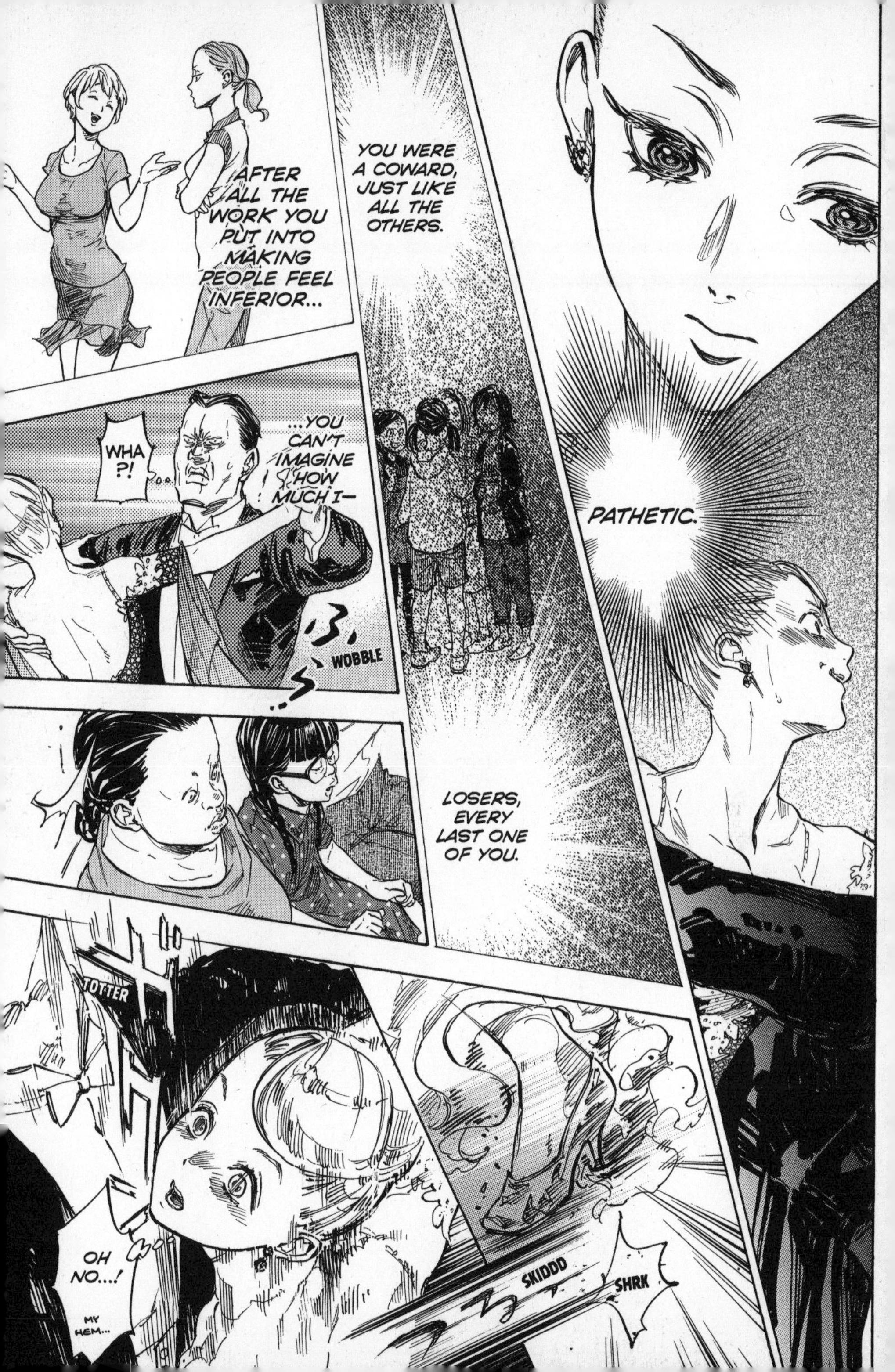
PATHETIC.
LOSERS, EVERY LAST ONE OF YOU.
YOU WERE A COWARD, JUST LIKE ALL THE OTHERS.
AFTER ALL THE WORK YOU PUT INTO MAKING PEOPLE FEEL INFERIOR...
...YOU CAN'T IMAGINE HOW MUCH I—
WHA ?!
WOBBLE
SHRK
SKIDDD
TOTTER
OH NO...!
MY HEM...

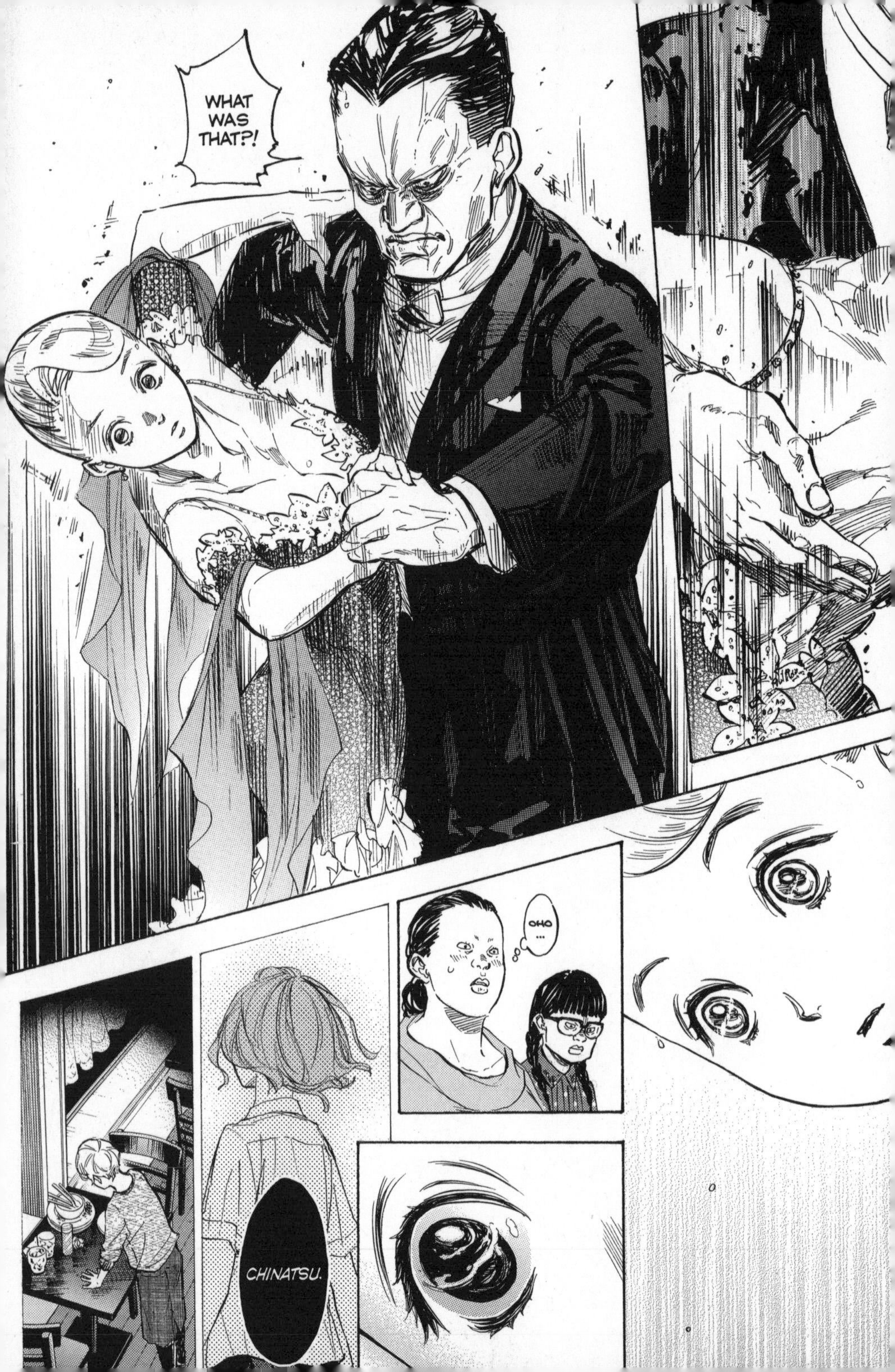
WHAT WAS THAT?!
OHO ...
CHINATSU.

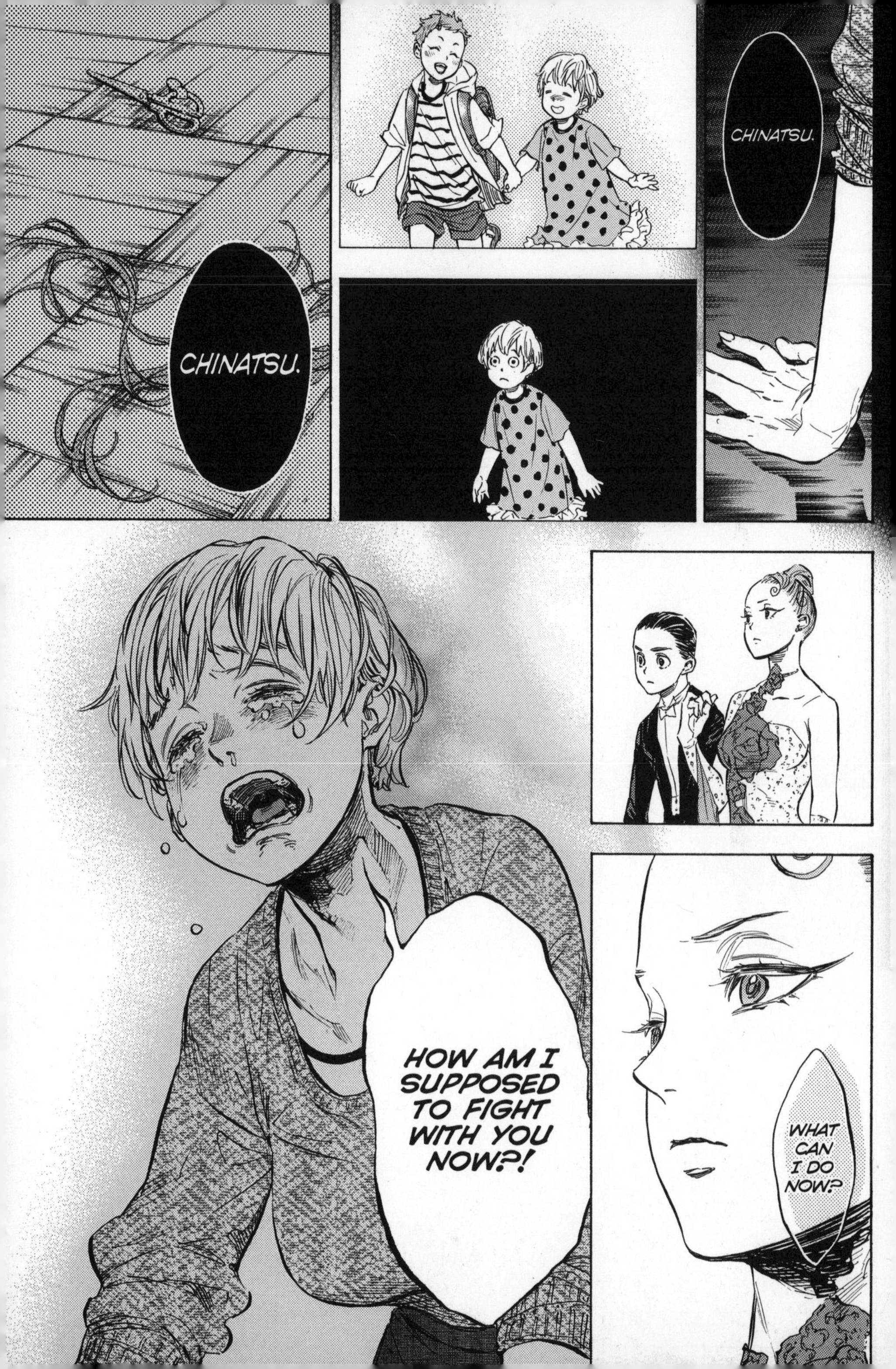
CHINATSU.
CHINATSU.
WHAT CAN I DO NOW?
HOW AM I SUPPOSED TO FIGHT WITH YOU NOW?!

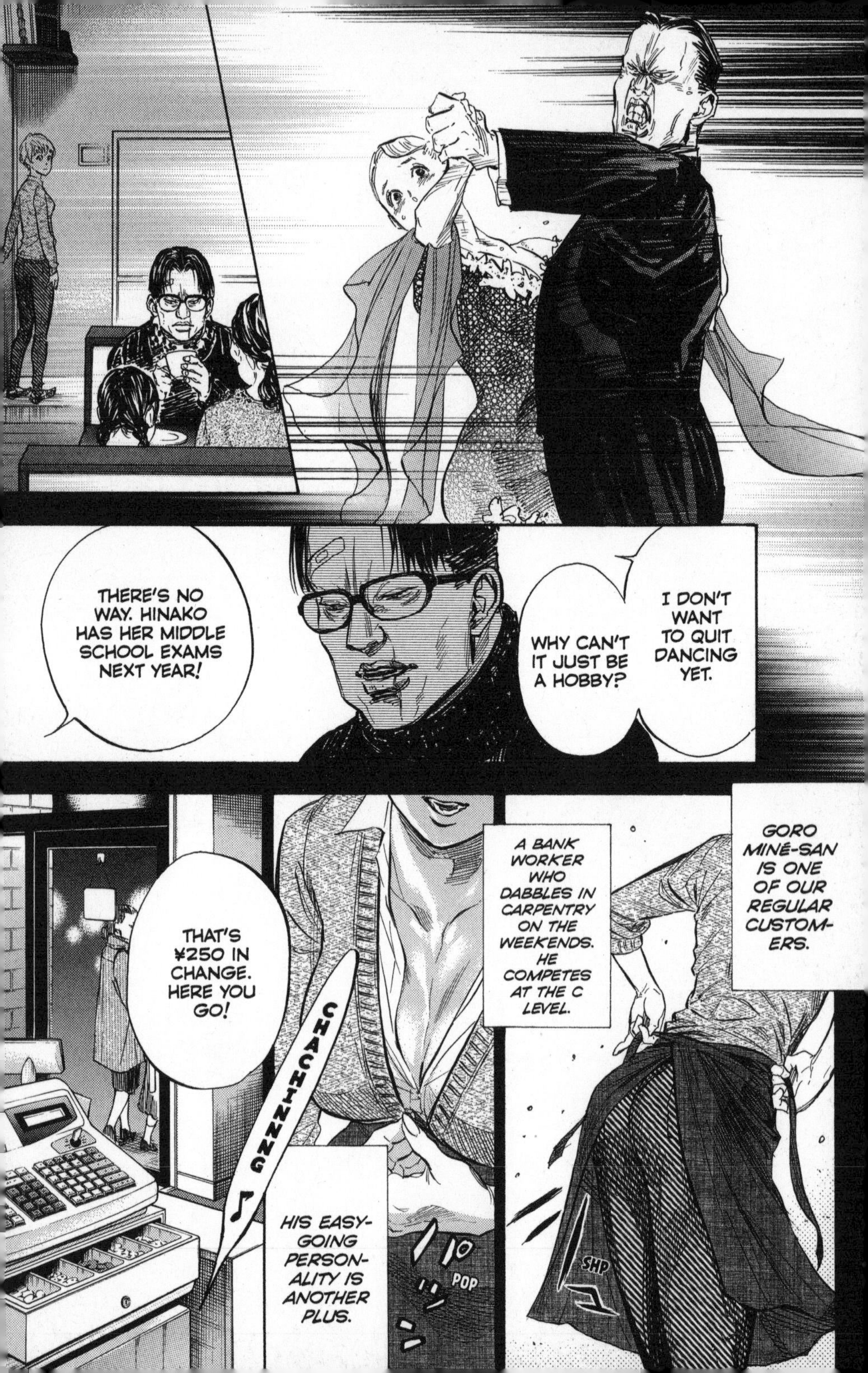

I DON'T WANT TO QUIT DANCING YET.
WHY CAN'T IT JUST BE A HOBBY?
THERE'S NO WAY. HINAKO HAS HER MIDDLE SCHOOL EXAMS NEXT YEAR!
GORO MINÉ-SAN IS ONE OF OUR REGULAR CUSTOMERS.
A BANK WORKER WHO DABBLES IN CARPENTRY ON THE WEEKENDS. HE COMPETES AT THE C LEVEL.
SHP
HIS EASY-GOING PERSONALITY IS ANOTHER PLUS.
POP
CHACHINNNG ♪
THAT'S ¥250 IN CHANGE. HERE YOU GO!

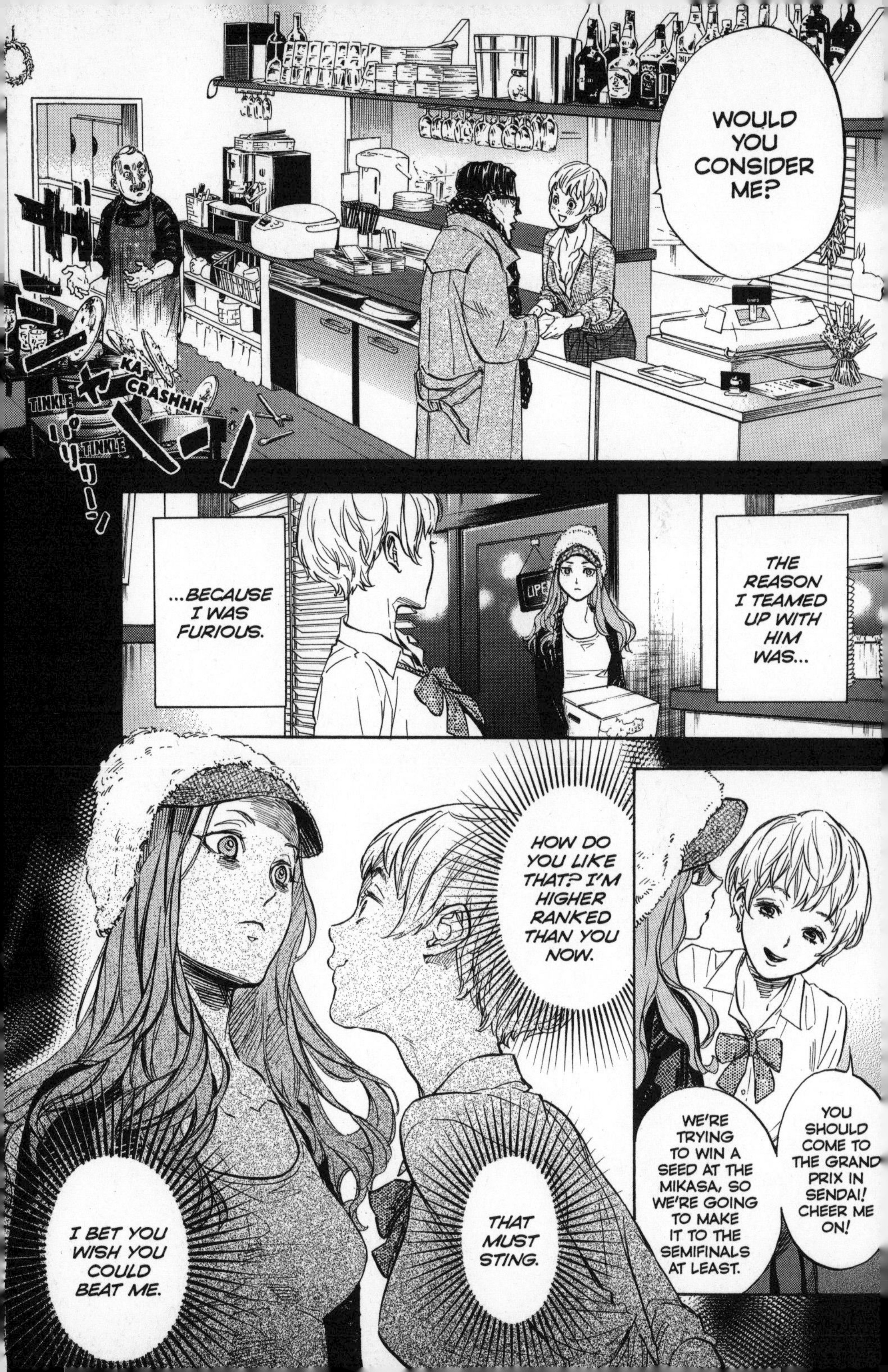
WOULD YOU CONSIDER ME?
KA CRASHHH
TINKLE
TINKLE
THE REASON I TEAMED UP WITH HIM WAS...
...BECAUSE I WAS FURIOUS.
YOU SHOULD COME TO THE GRAND PRIX IN SENDAI! CHEER ME ON!
WE'RE TRYING TO WIN A SEED AT THE MIKASA, SO WE'RE GOING TO MAKE IT TO THE SEMIFINALS AT LEAST.
HOW DO YOU LIKE THAT? I'M HIGHER RANKED THAN YOU NOW.
THAT MUST STING.
I BET YOU WISH YOU COULD BEAT ME.

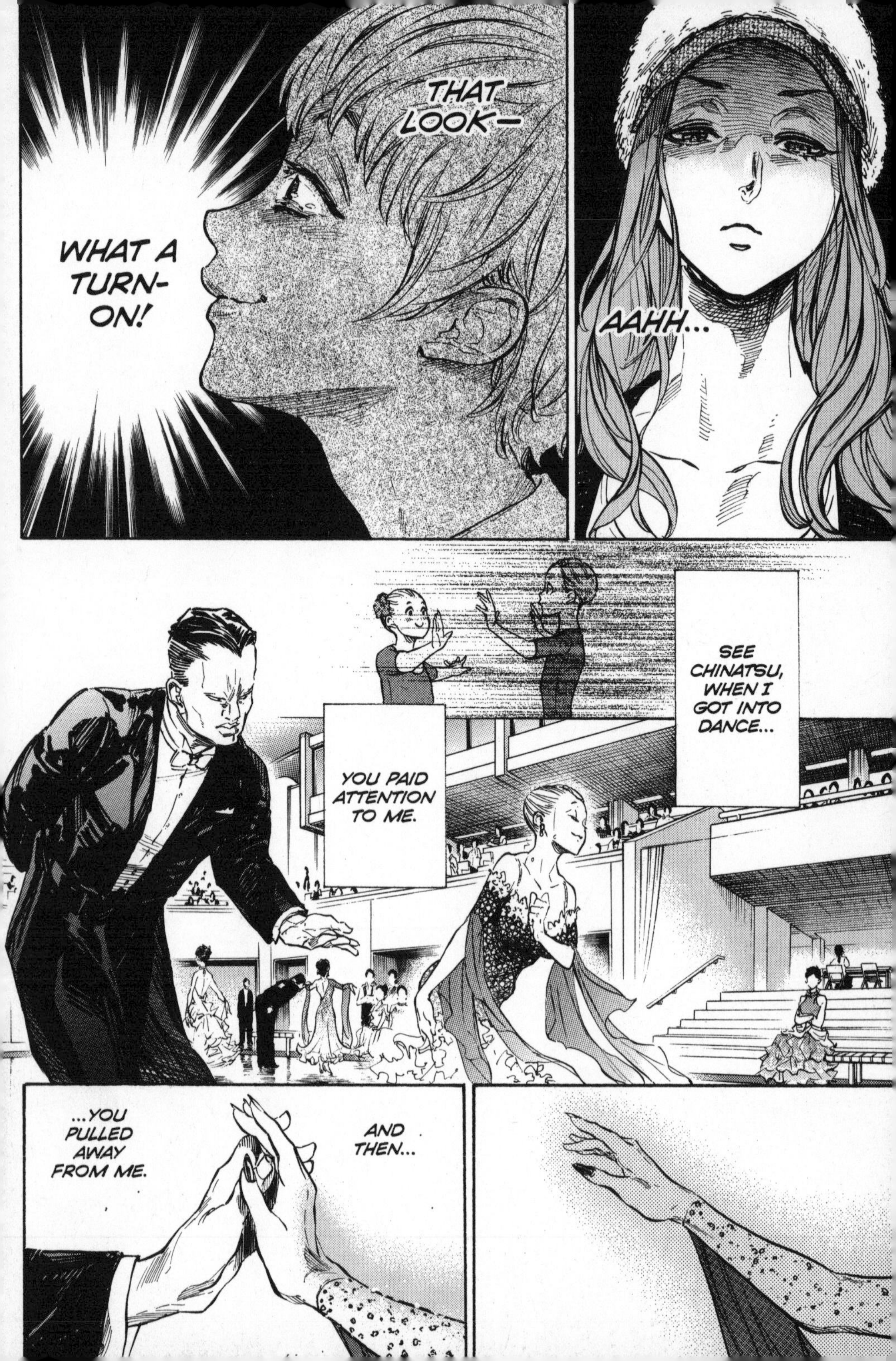
AAHH...
THAT LOOK—
WHAT A TURN-ON!
SEE CHINATSU, WHEN I GOT INTO DANCE...
YOU PAID ATTENTION TO ME.
AND THEN...
...YOU PULLED AWAY FROM ME.

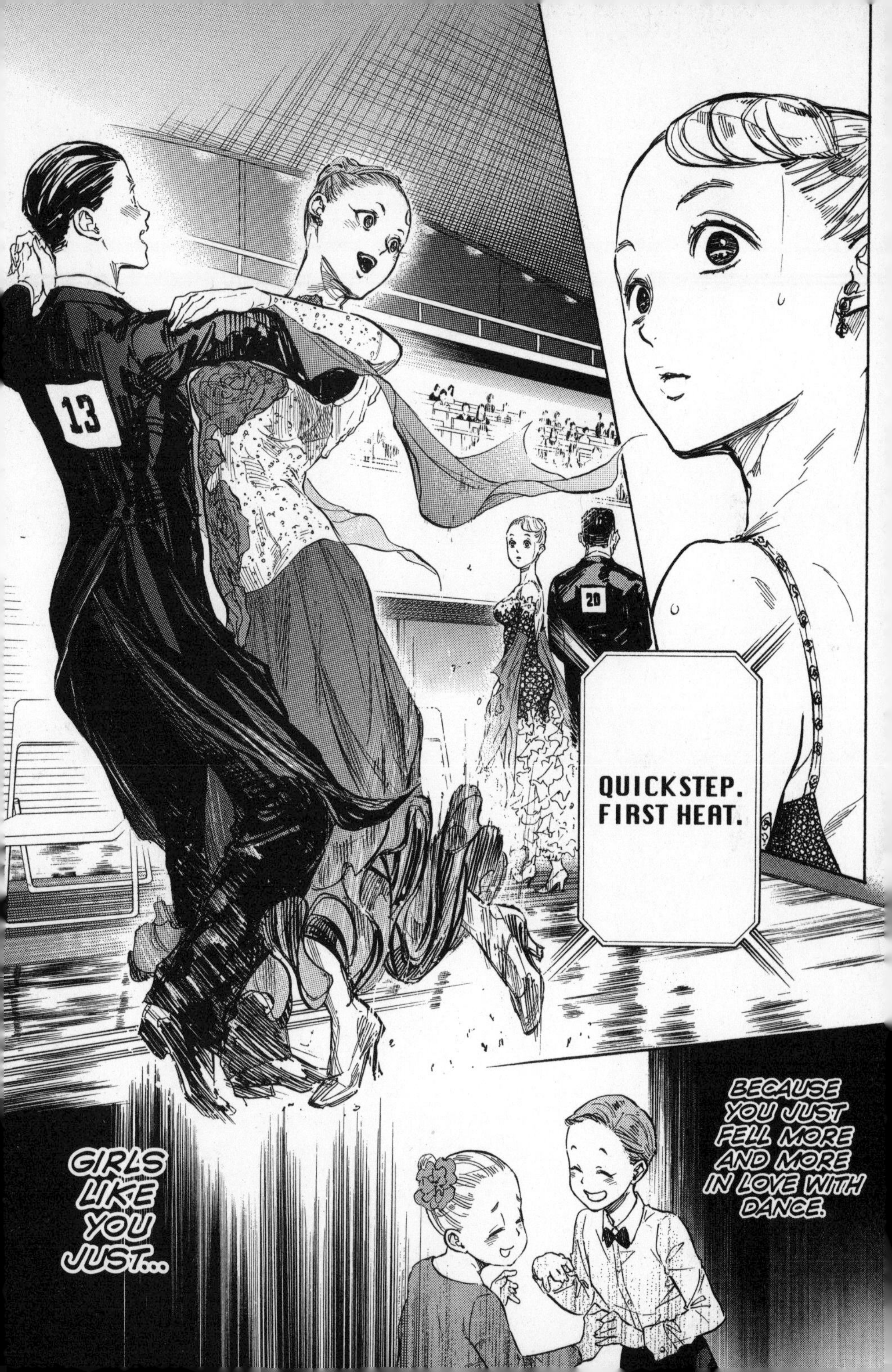

QUICKSTEP. FIRST HEAT.
20
13
BECAUSE YOU JUST FELL MORE AND MORE IN LOVE WITH DANCE.
GIRLS LIKE YOU JUST...

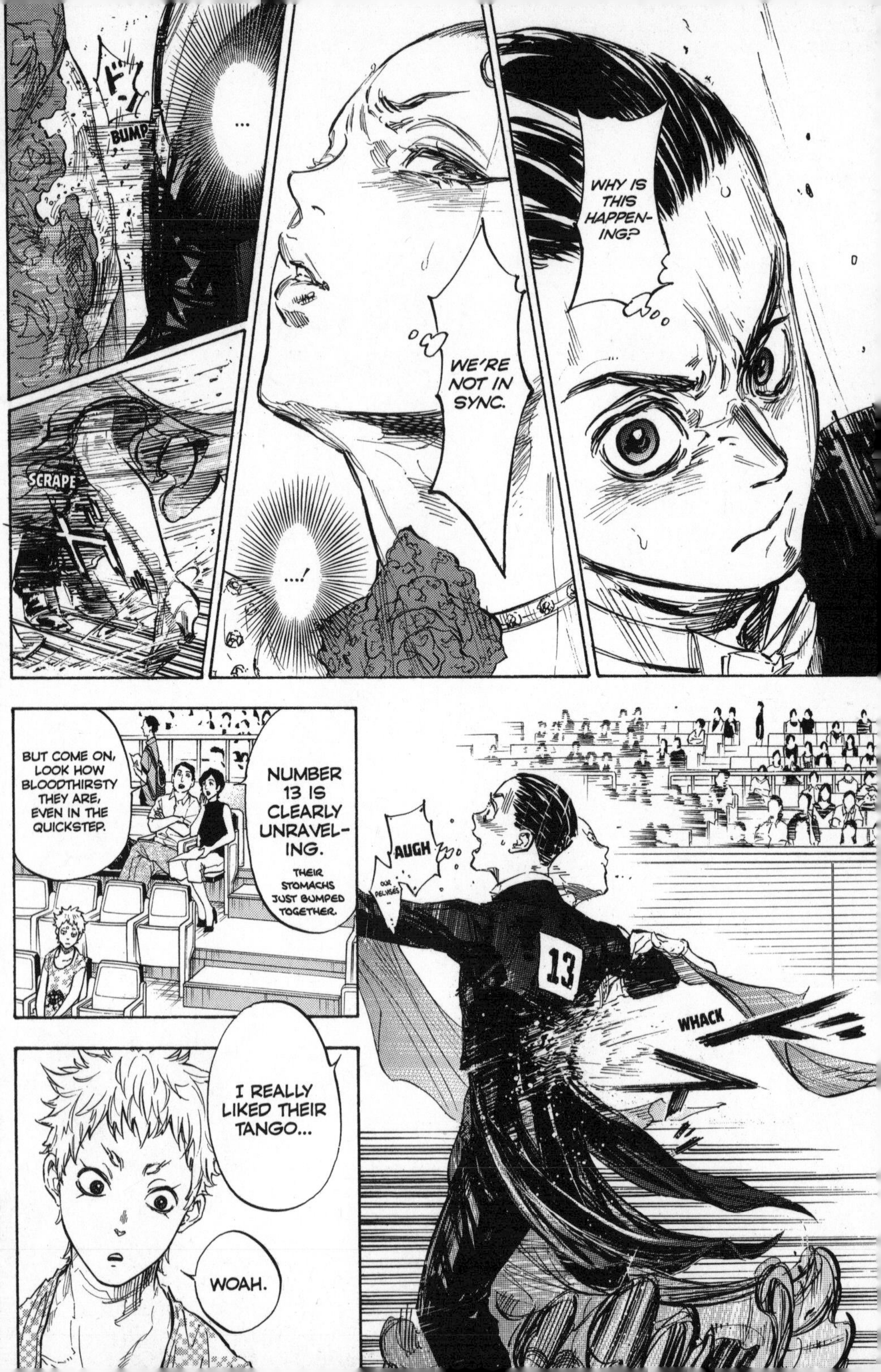
WHY IS THIS HAPPENING?
WE'RE NOT IN SYNC.
....!
...
BUMP
SCRAPE
AUGH
OUR PELVISES ...
...
WHACK
NUMBER 13 IS CLEARLY UNRAVELING.
THEIR STOMACHS JUST BUMPED TOGETHER.
BUT COME ON, LOOK HOW BLOODTHIRSTY THEY ARE, EVEN IN THE QUICKSTEP.
I REALLY LIKED THEIR TANGO...
WOAH.

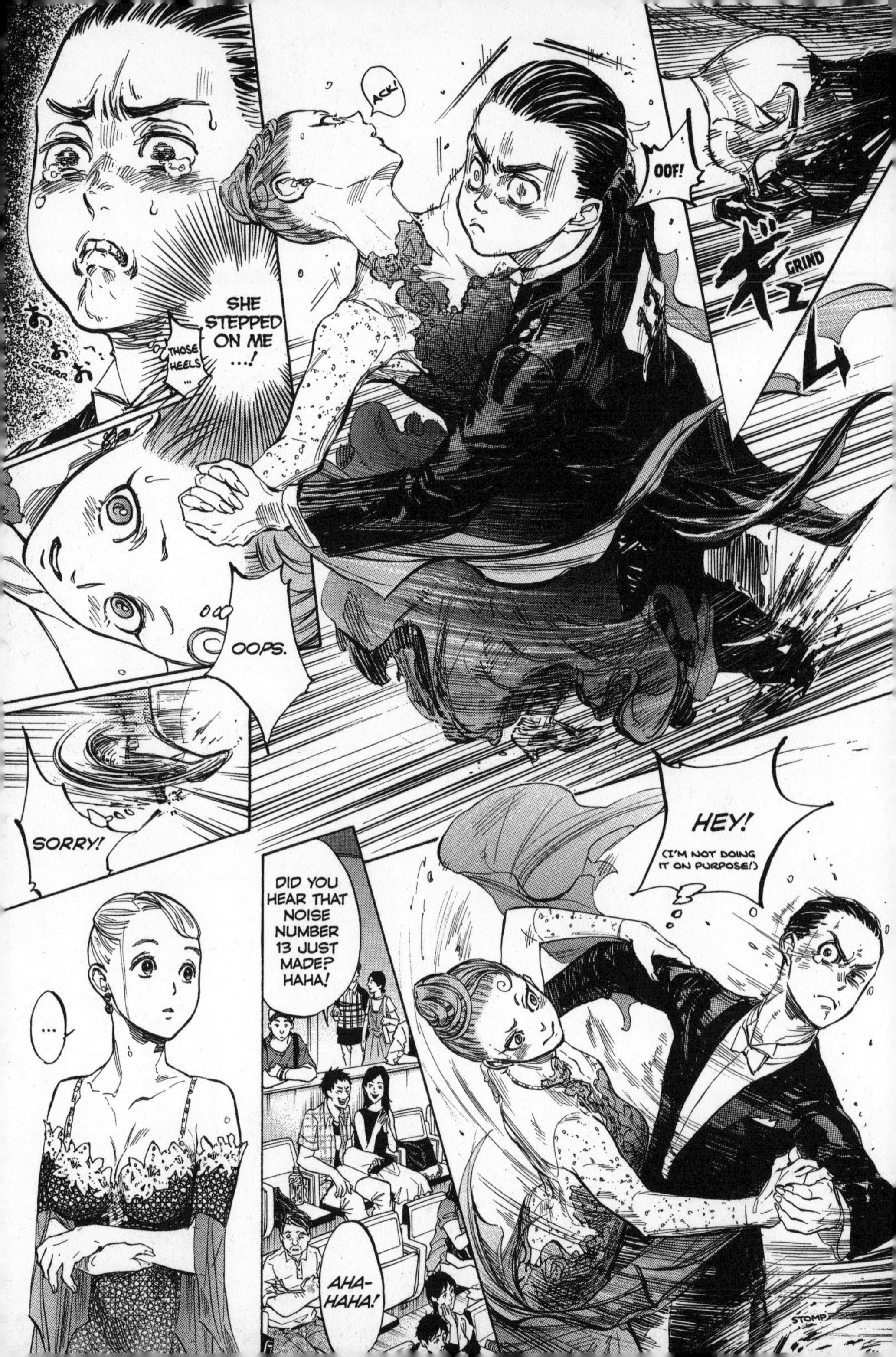
OOF!
GRIND
ACK!
SHE STEPPED ON ME ...!
THOSE HEELS ...
GRRRR
OOPS.
SORRY!
HEY!
(I'M NOT DOING IT ON PURPOSE!)
STOMP
DID YOU HEAR THAT NOISE NUMBER 13 JUST MADE? HAHA!
AHA-HAHA!
...

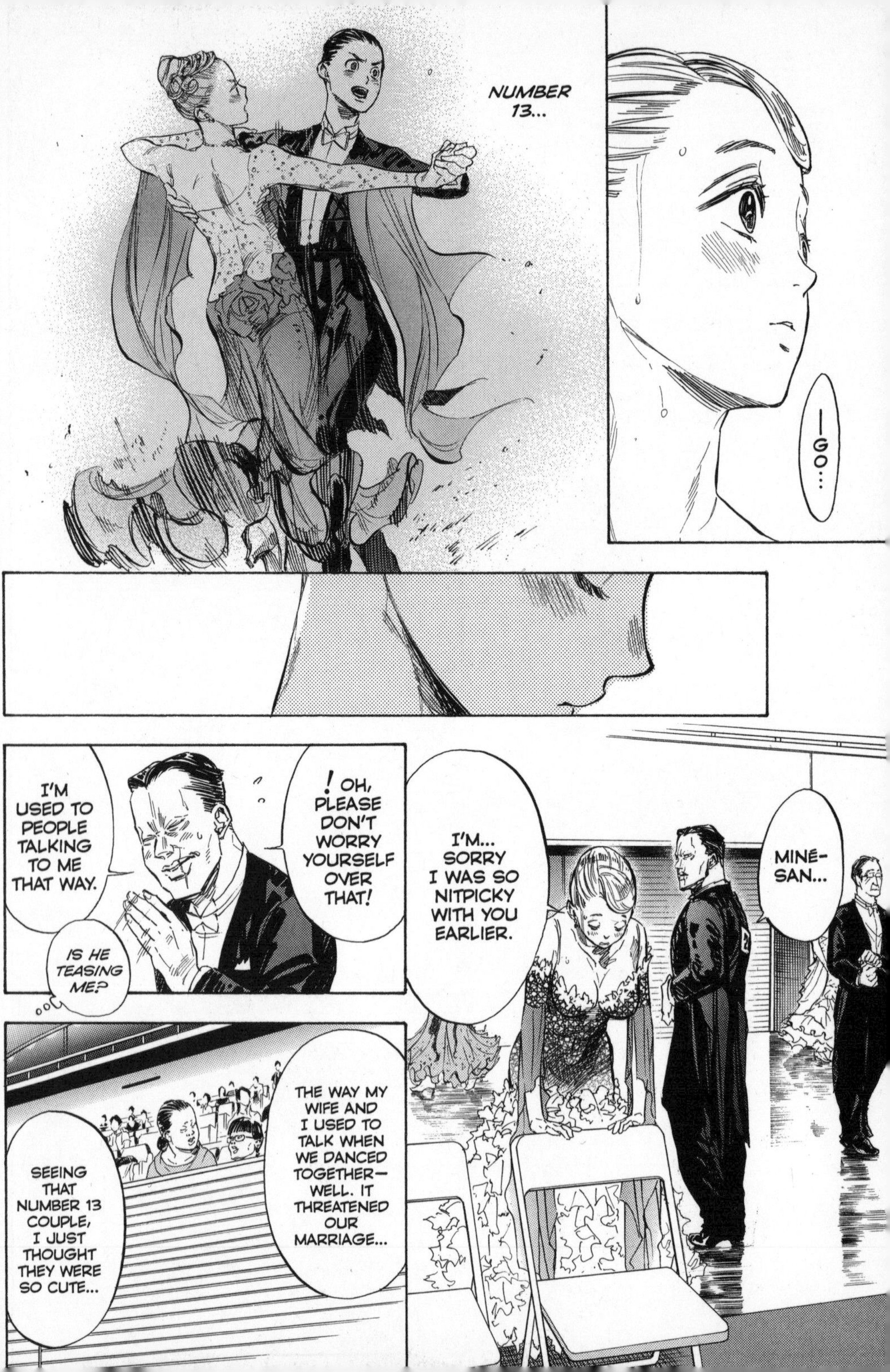
I GO...
NUMBER 13...
MINÉ-SAN...
I'M... SORRY I WAS SO NITPICKY WITH YOU EARLIER.
! OH, PLEASE DON'T WORRY YOURSELF OVER THAT!
I'M USED TO PEOPLE TALKING TO ME THAT WAY.
IS HE TEASING ME?
THE WAY MY WIFE AND I USED TO TALK WHEN WE DANCED TOGETHER—WELL. IT THREATENED OUR MARRIAGE...
SEEING THAT NUMBER 13 COUPLE, I JUST THOUGHT THEY WERE SO CUTE...

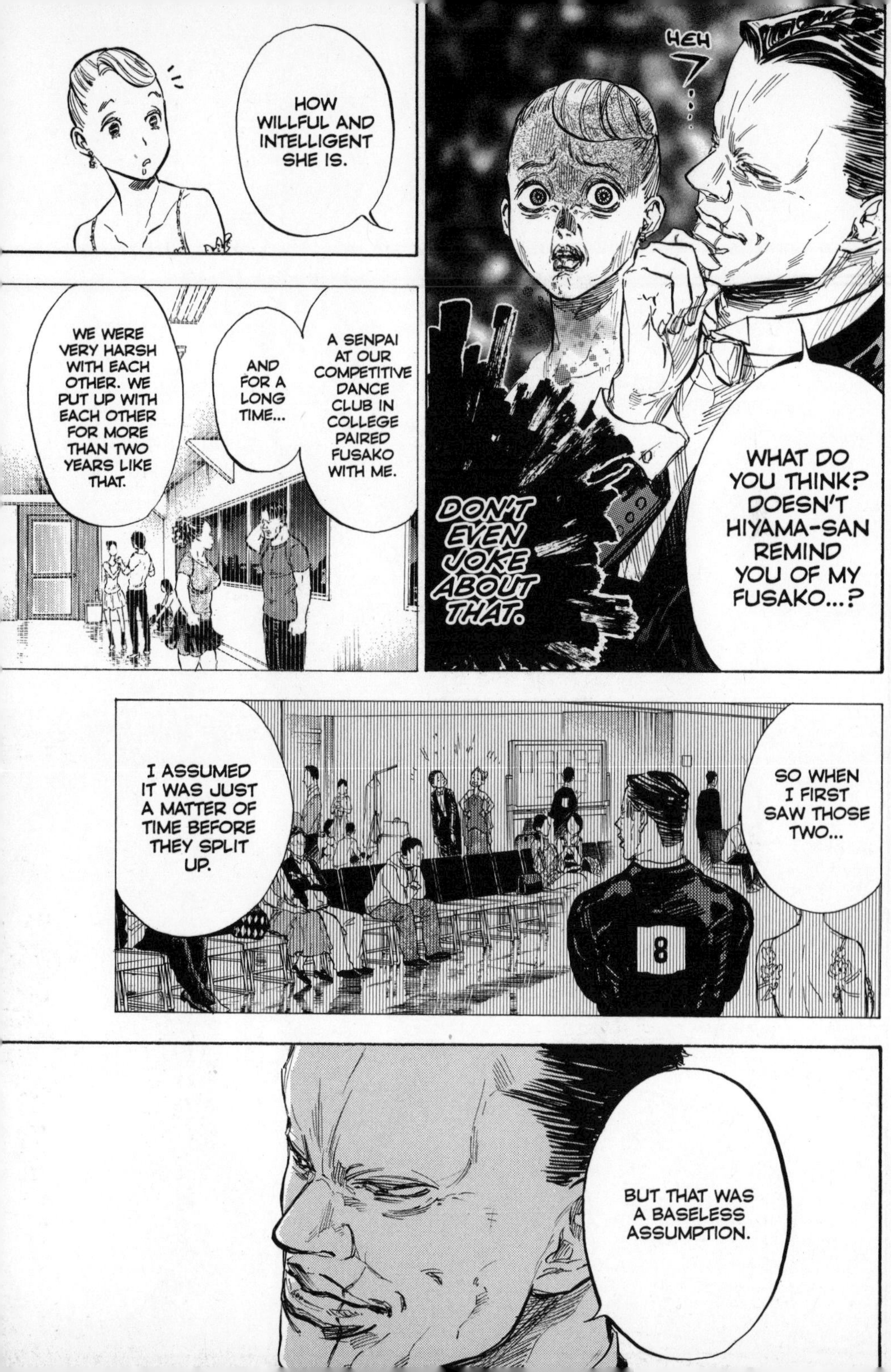
HEH
WHAT DO YOU THINK? DOESN'T HIYAMA-SAN REMIND YOU OF MY FUSAKO...?
DON'T EVEN JOKE ABOUT THAT.
HOW WILLFUL AND INTELLIGENT SHE IS.
A SENPAI AT OUR COMPETITIVE DANCE CLUB IN COLLEGE PAIRED FUSAKO WITH ME.
AND FOR A LONG TIME...
WE WERE VERY HARSH WITH EACH OTHER. WE PUT UP WITH EACH OTHER FOR MORE THAN TWO YEARS LIKE THAT.
SO WHEN I FIRST SAW THOSE TWO...
I ASSUMED IT WAS JUST A MATTER OF TIME BEFORE THEY SPLIT UP.
8
BUT THAT WAS A BASELESS ASSUMPTION.

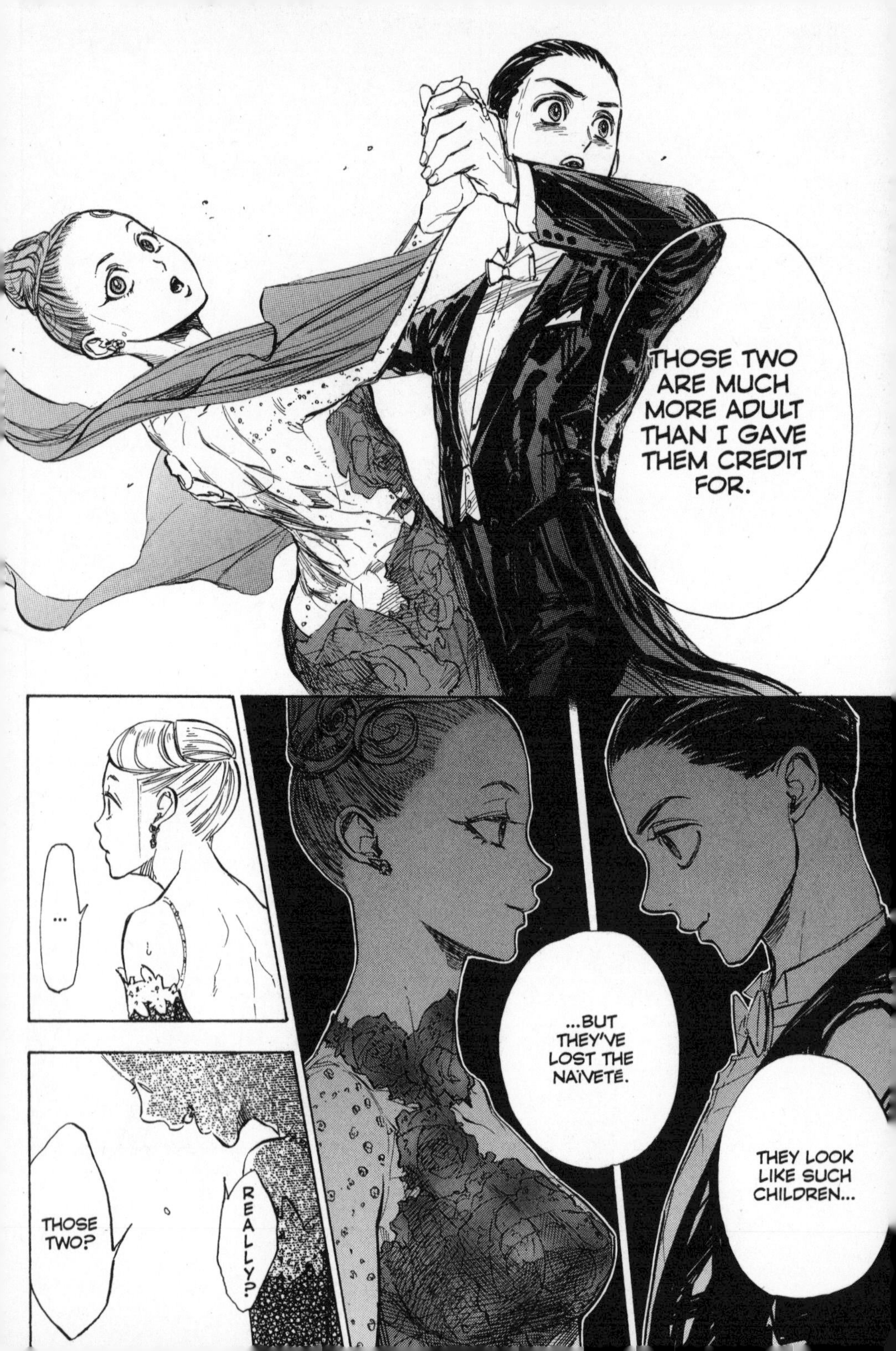
THOSE TWO ARE MUCH MORE ADULT THAN I GAVE THEM CREDIT FOR.
THEY LOOK LIKE SUCH CHILDREN...
...BUT THEY'VE LOST THE NAÏVETÉ.
...
REALLY?
THOSE TWO?

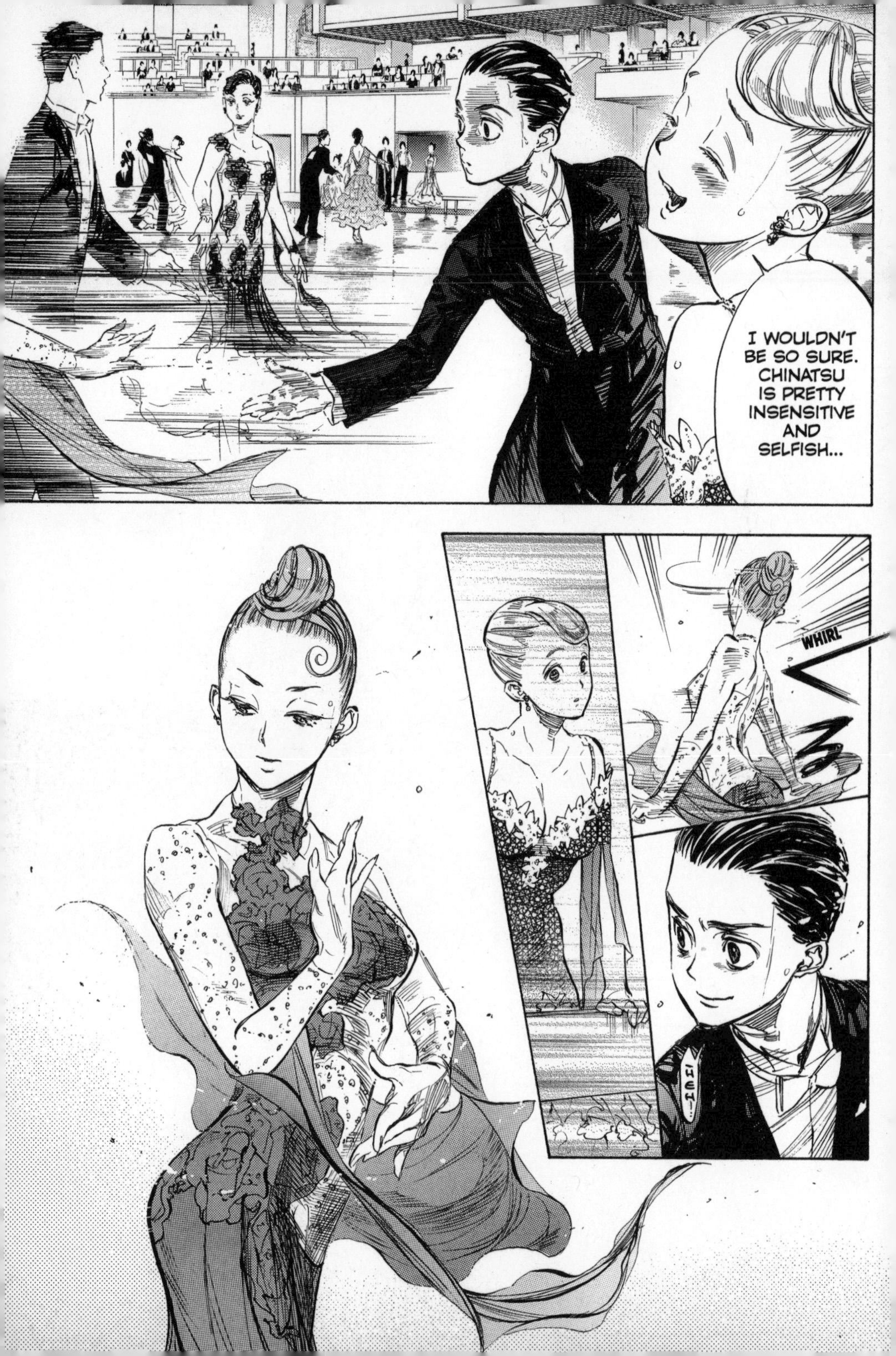
I WOULDN'T BE SO SURE. CHINATSU IS PRETTY INSENSITIVE AND SELFISH...
WHIRL
HEH!

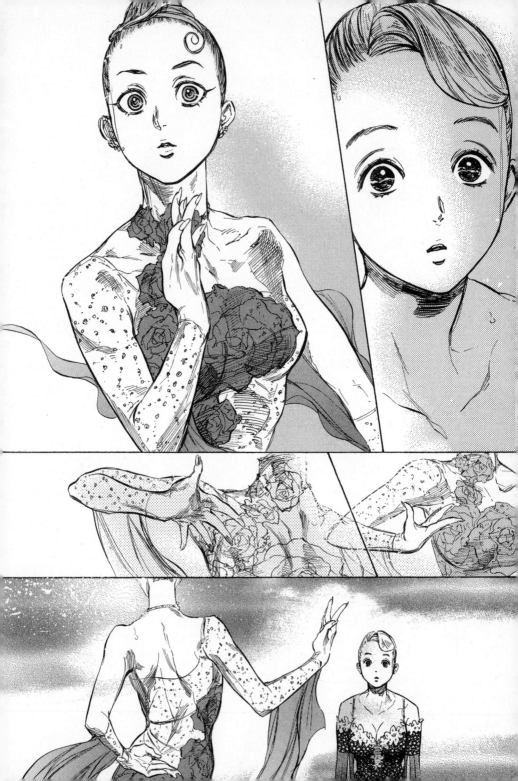

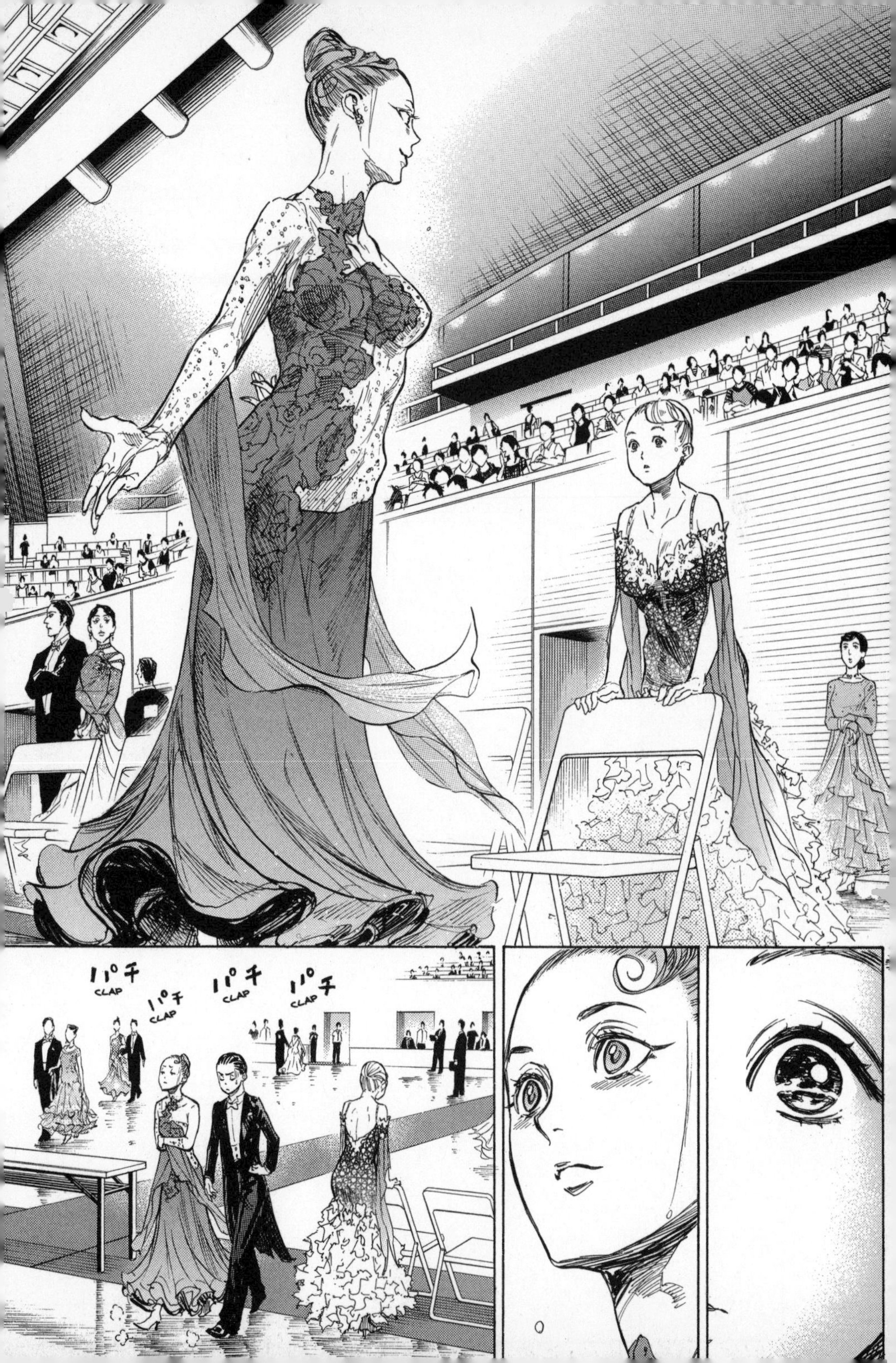
パチ CLAP
パチ CLAP
パチ CLAP
パチ CLAP

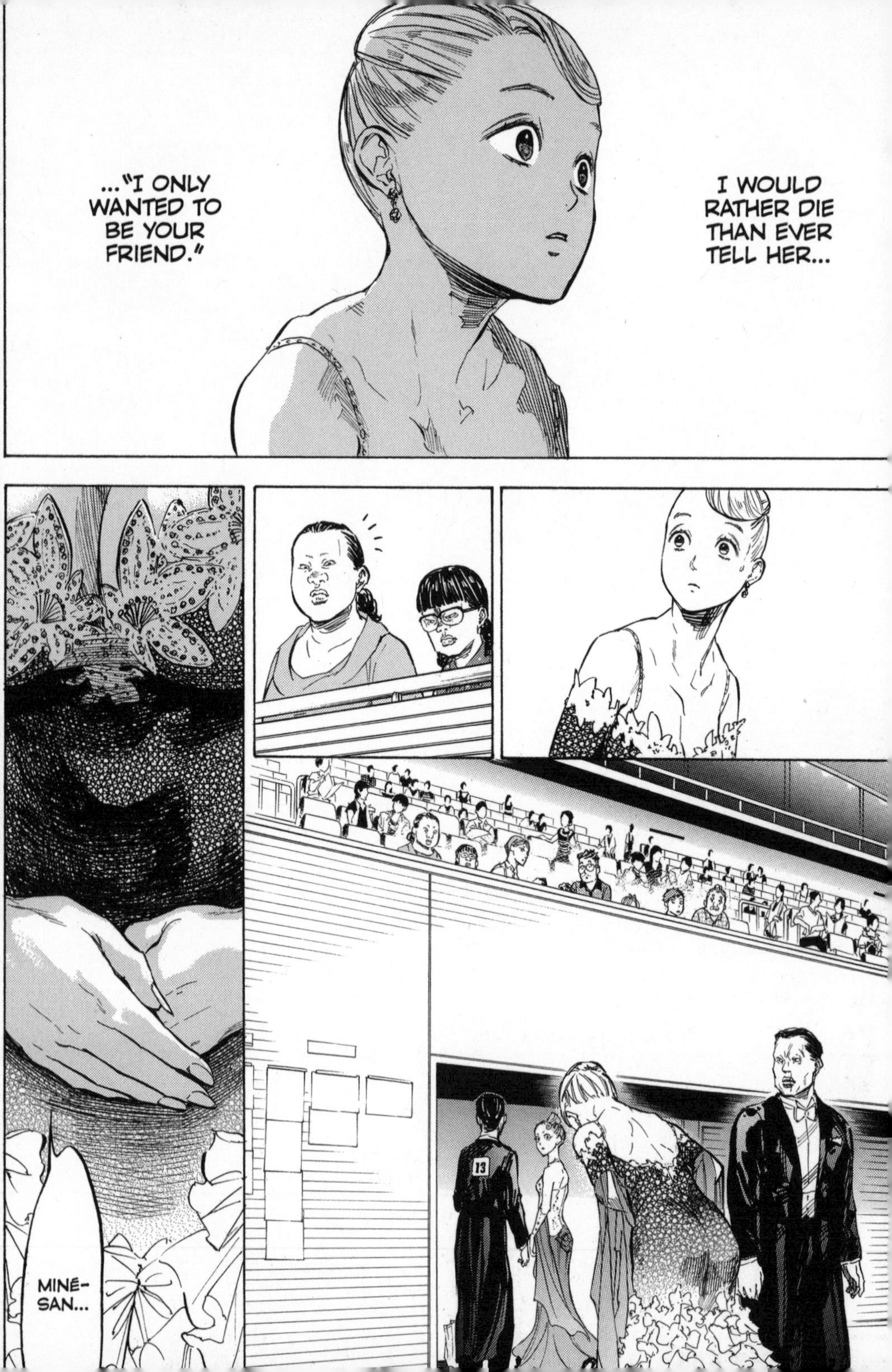
I WOULD RATHER DIE THAN EVER TELL HER...
..."I ONLY WANTED TO BE YOUR FRIEND."
MINÉ-SAN...

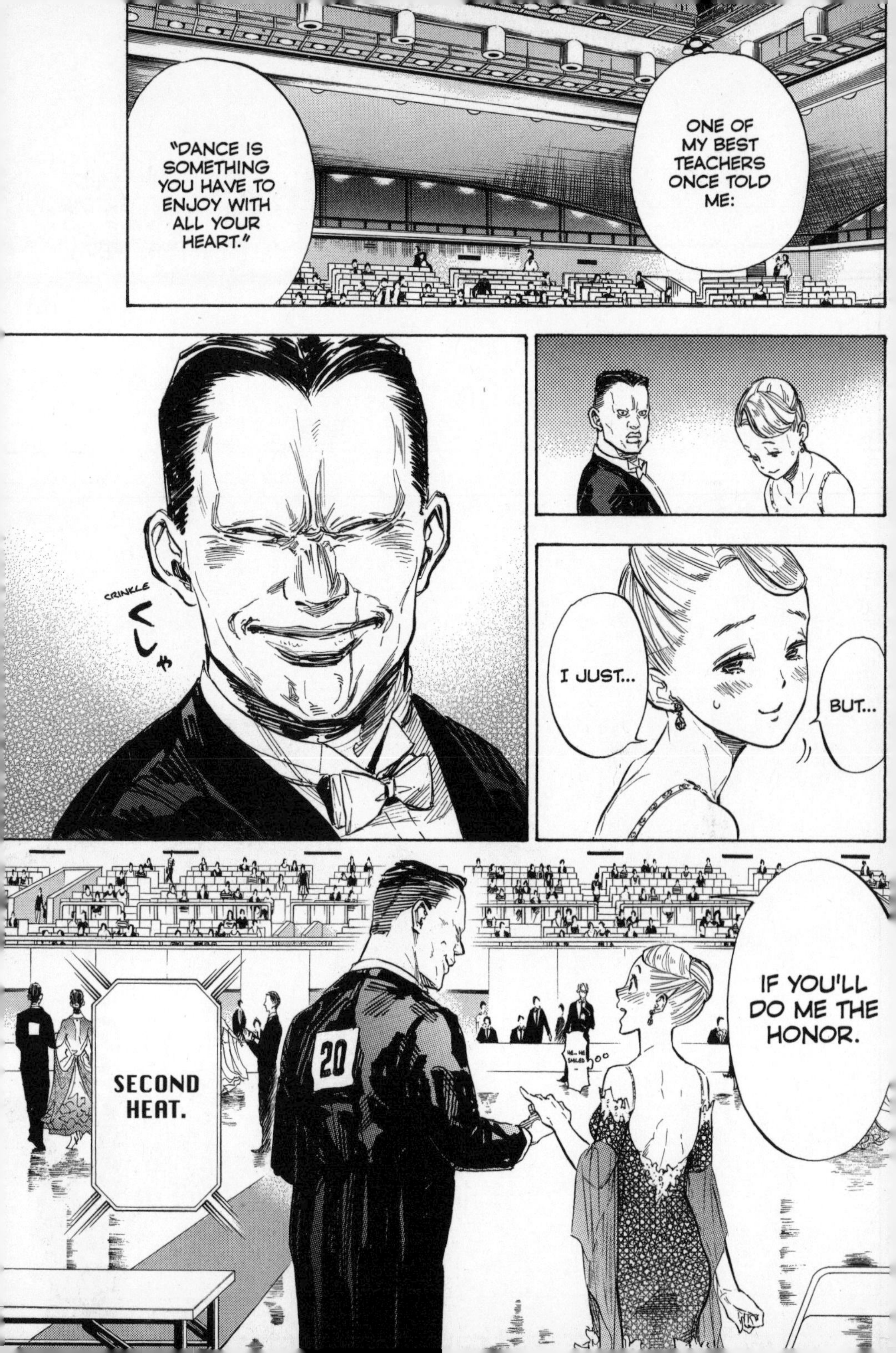
ONE OF MY BEST TEACHERS ONCE TOLD ME:
"DANCE IS SOMETHING YOU HAVE TO ENJOY WITH ALL YOUR HEART."
BUT...
I JUST...
CRINKLE
くしゃ
IF YOU'LL DO ME THE HONOR.
HE... HE SMILED
20
SECOND HEAT.

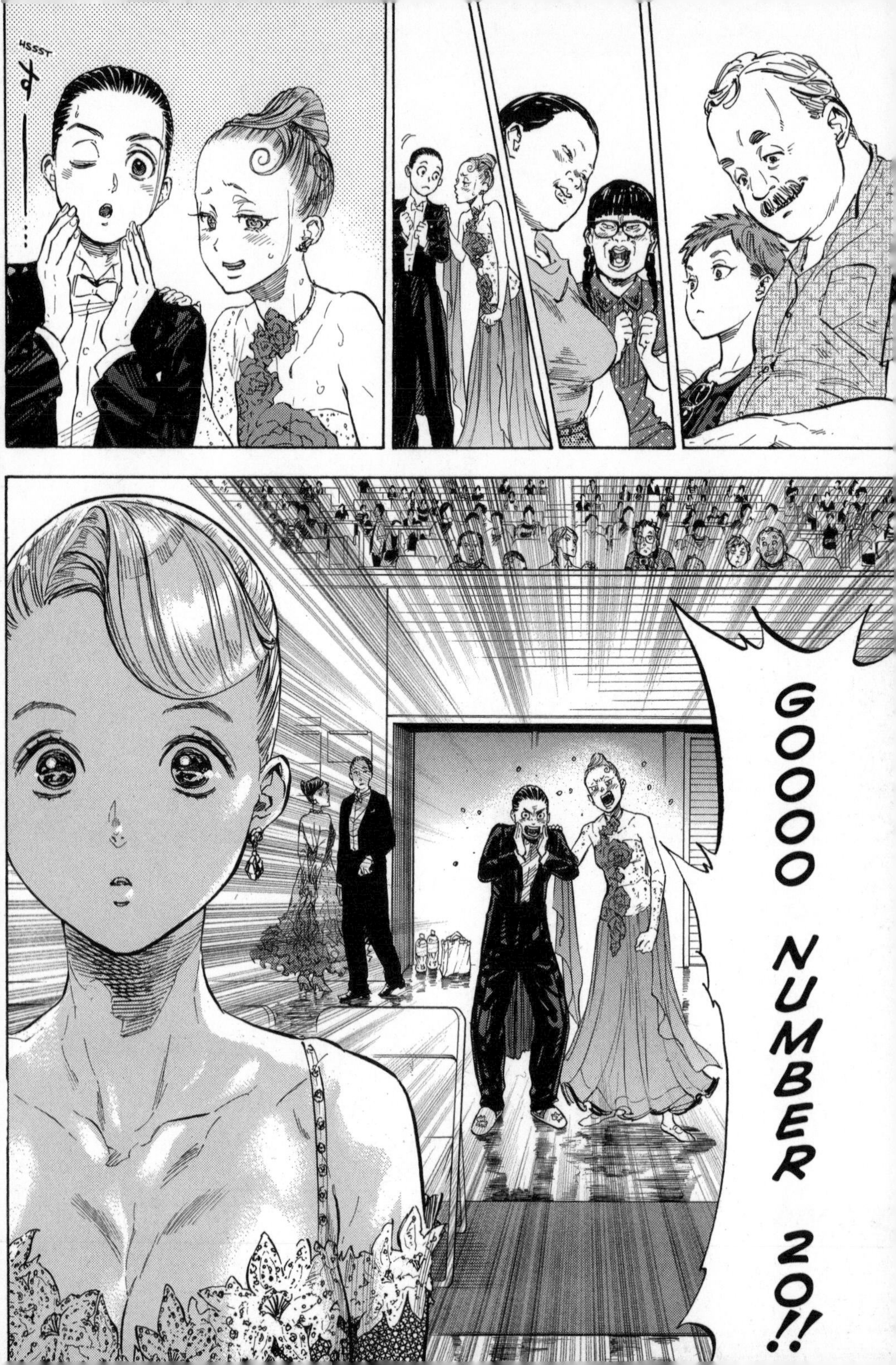
HSSST
すー…
GOOOOO NUMBER 20!!

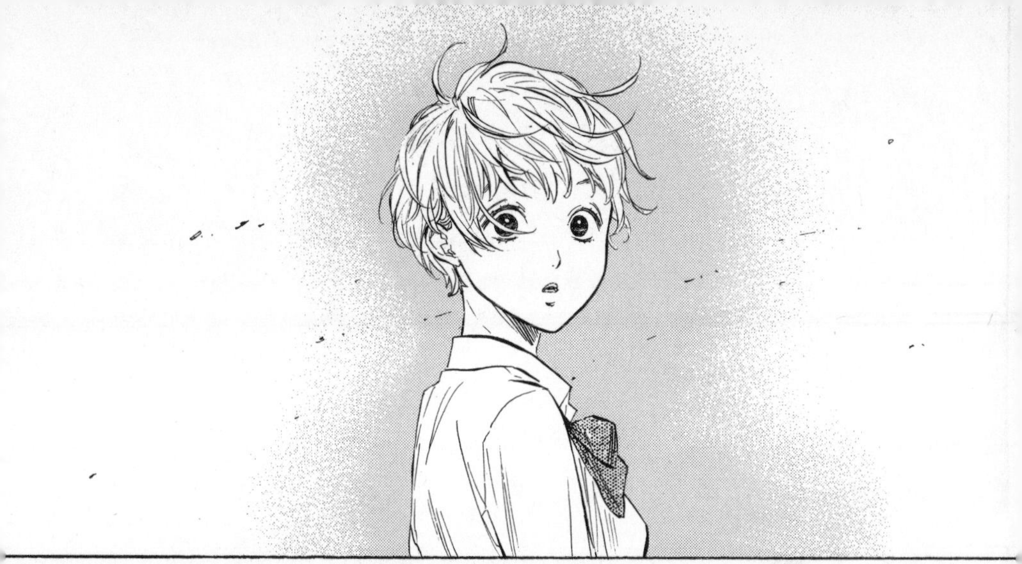
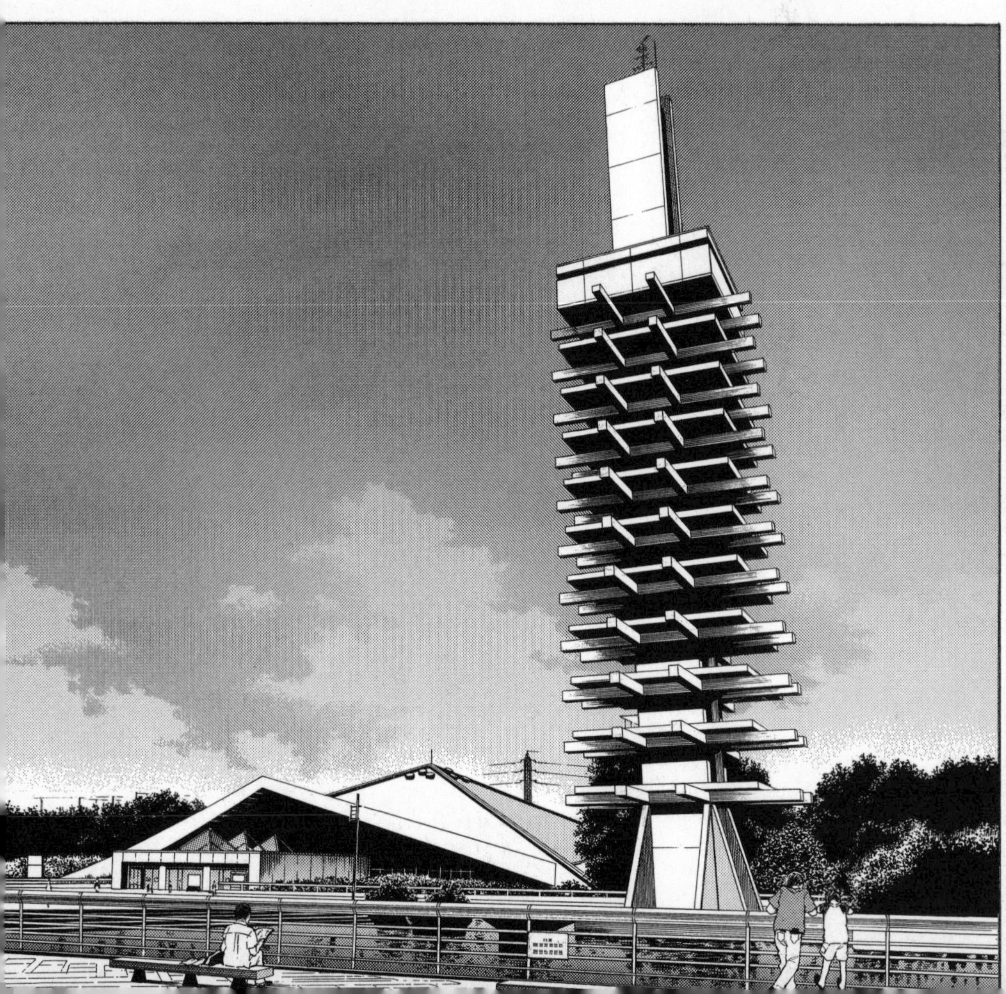

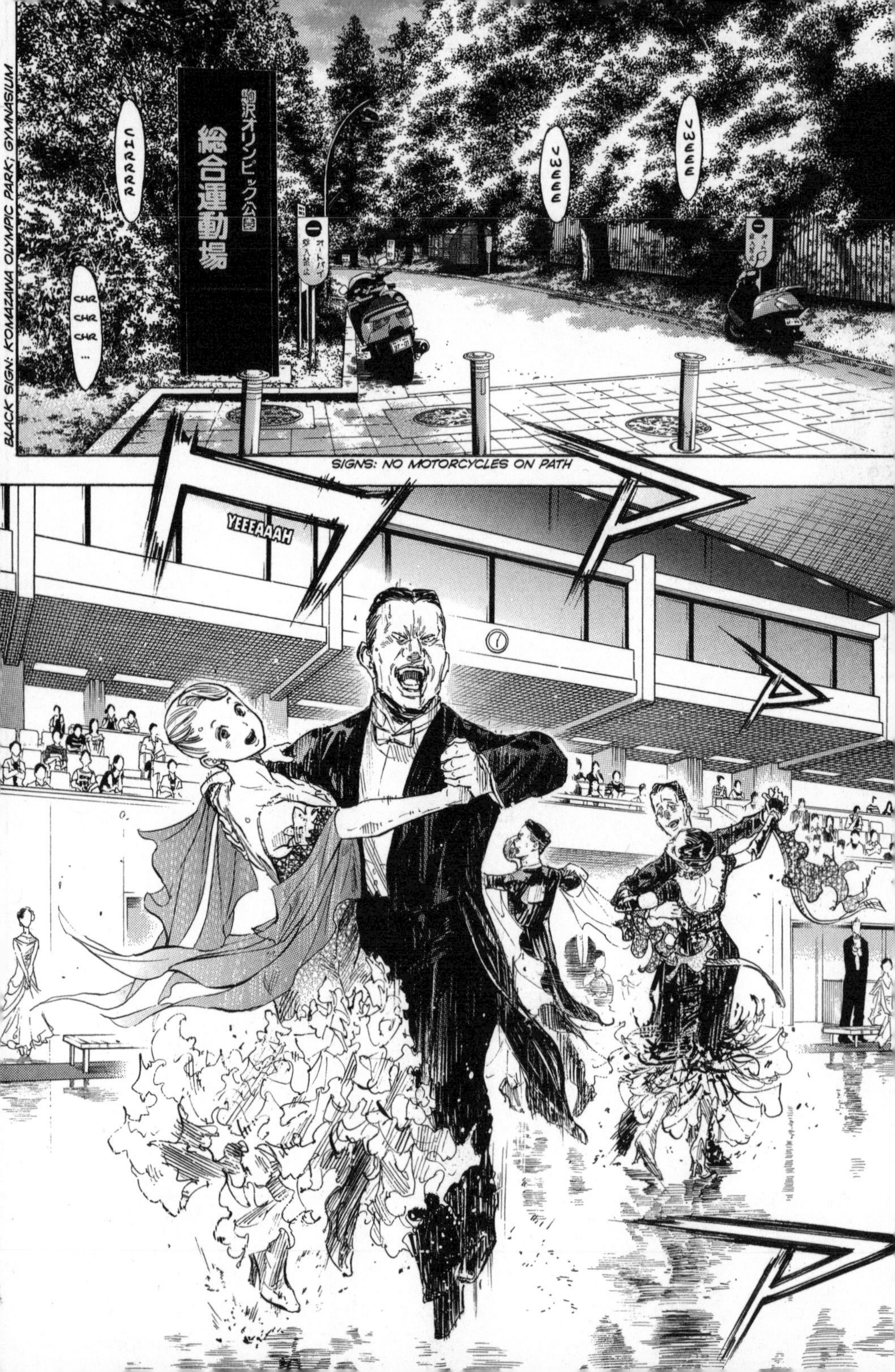

VWEEE
VWEEE
駒沢オリンピック公園
総合運動場
CHRRRR
CHR CHR CHR ...
BLACK SIGN: KOMAZAWA OLYMPIC PARK; GYMNASIUM
SIGNS: NO MOTORCYCLES ON PATH
YEEEAAAH

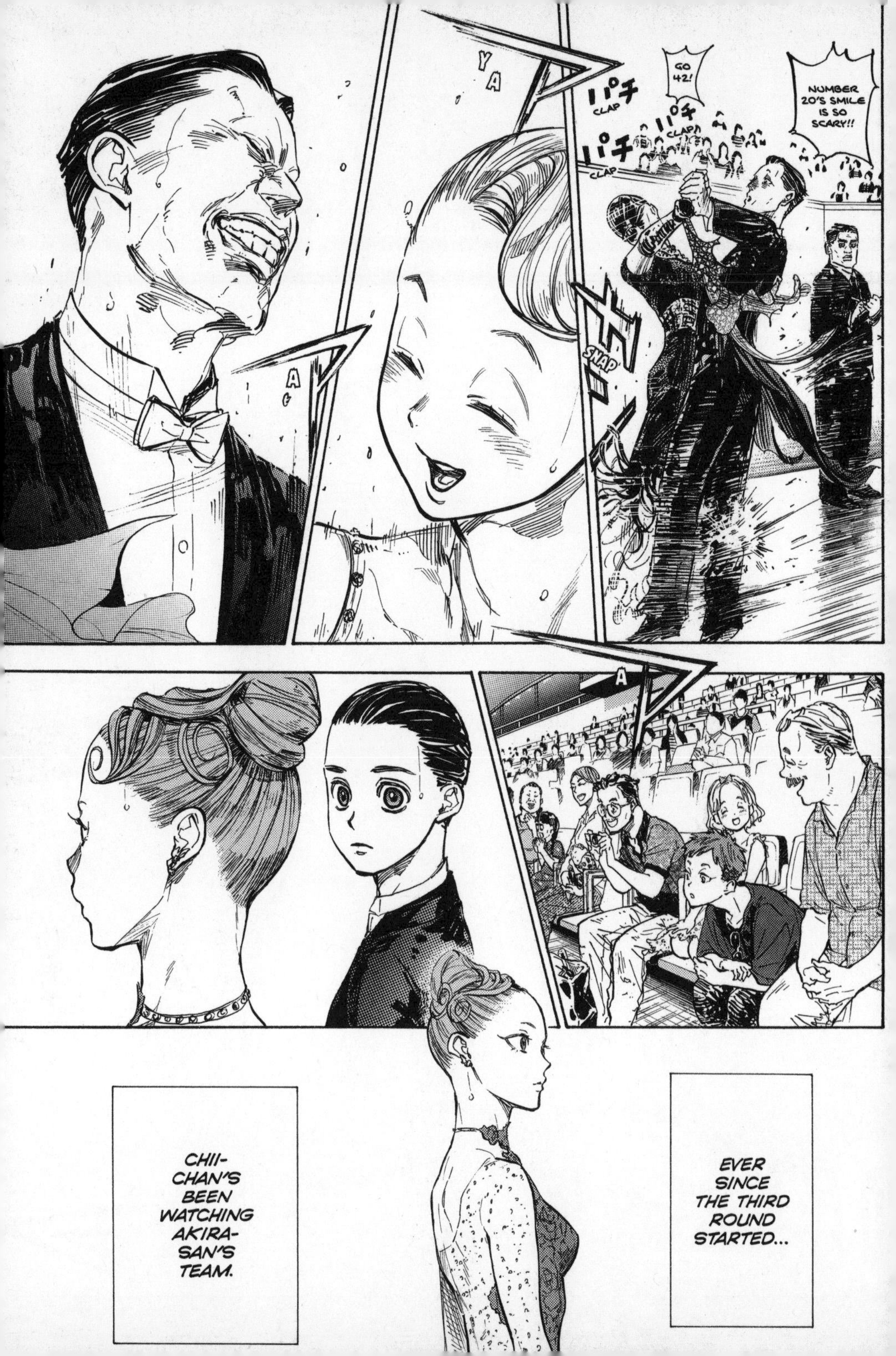
NUMBER 20'S SMILE IS SO SCARY!!
GO 42!
パチ CLAP
パチ CLAP
パチ CLAP
SNAP
YA
A
A
EVER SINCE THE THIRD ROUND STARTED...
CHII-CHAN'S BEEN WATCHING AKIRA-SAN'S TEAM.

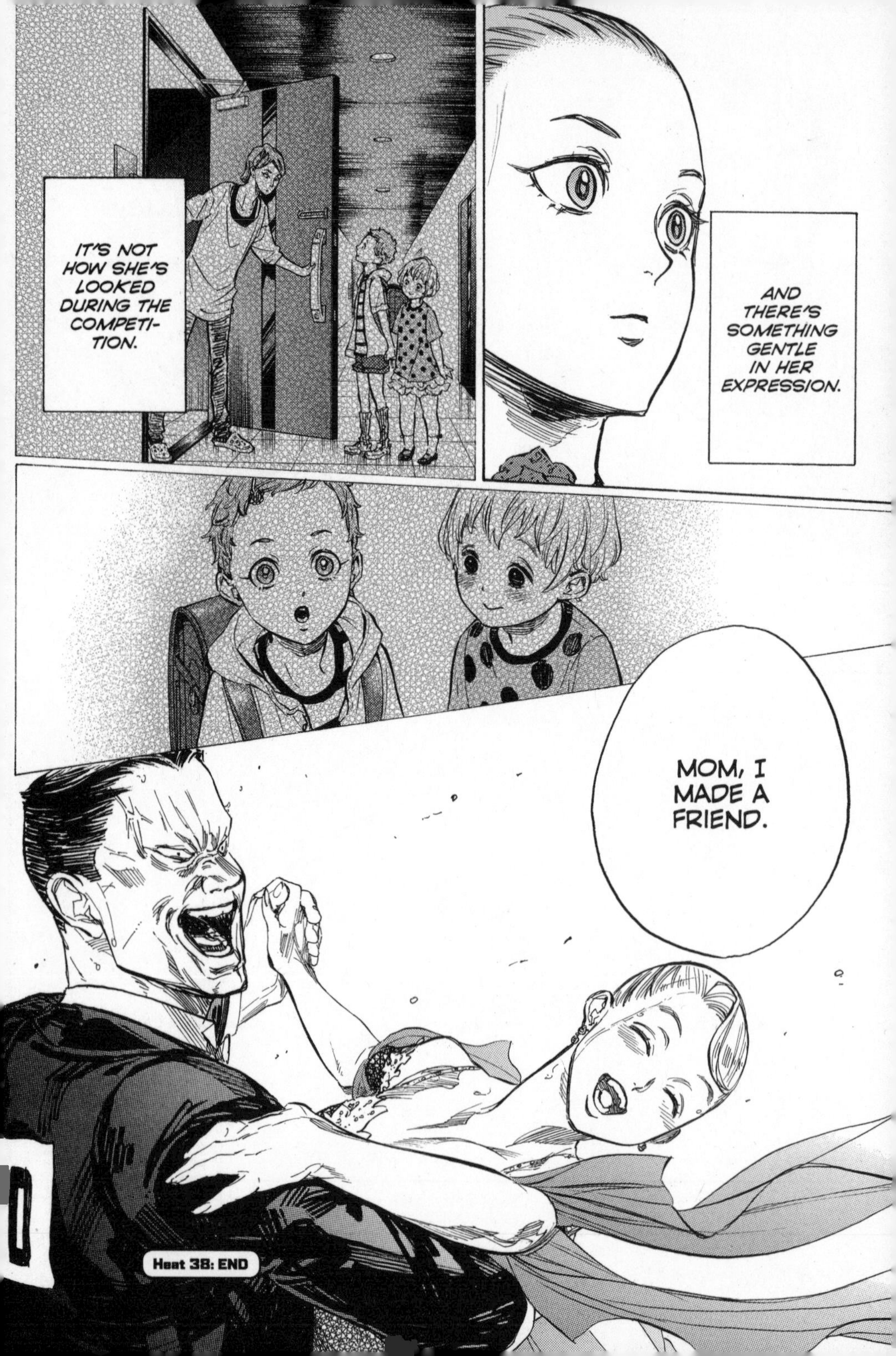
AND THERE'S SOMETHING GENTLE IN HER EXPRESSION.
IT'S NOT HOW SHE'S LOOKED DURING THE COMPETITION.
MOM, I MADE A FRIEND.
Heat 38: END

WELCOME TO THE BALLROOM

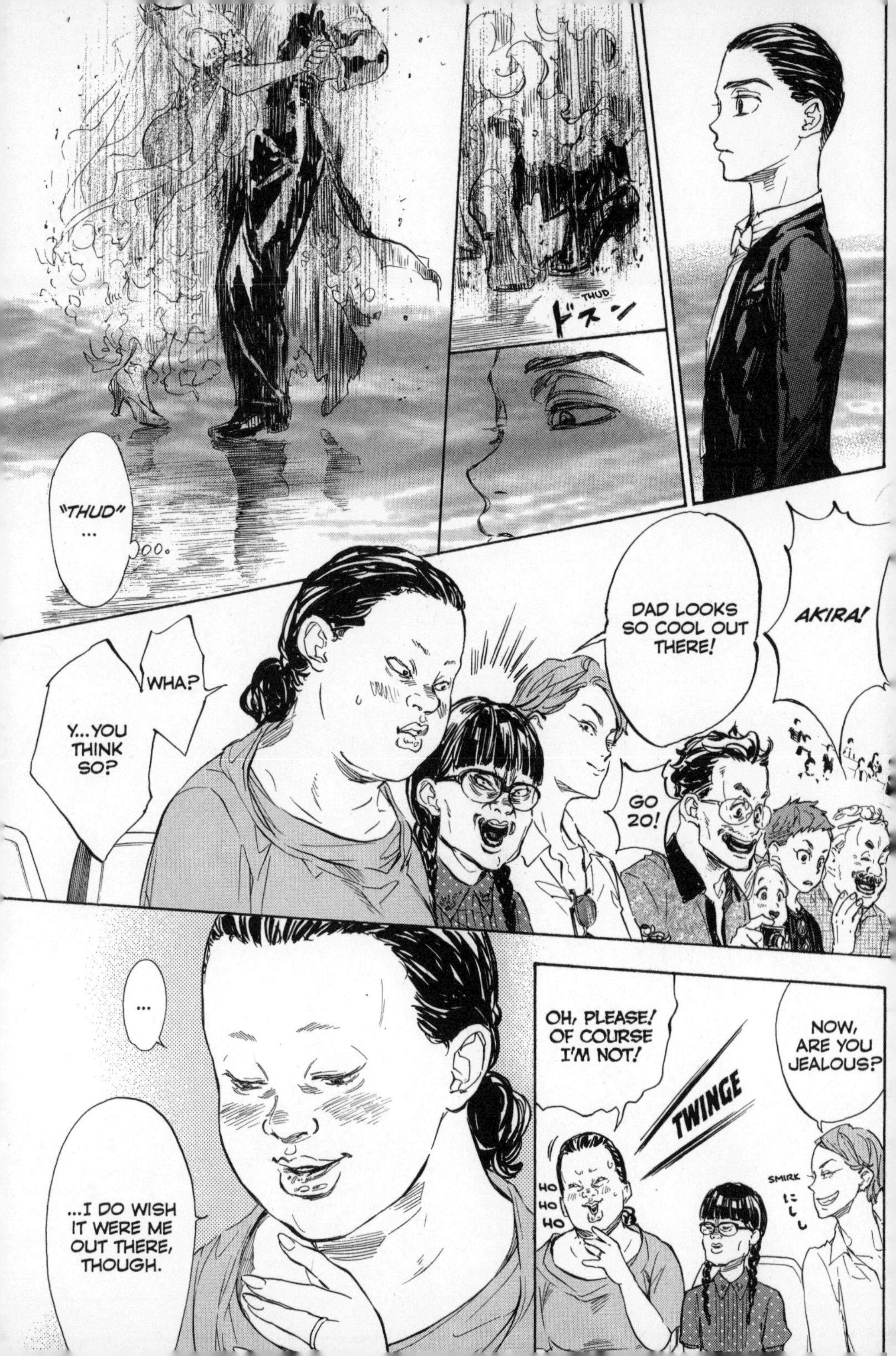
THUD
ドスン
"THUD"...
AKIRA!
DAD LOOKS SO COOL OUT THERE!
GO ZO!
WHA?
Y...YOU THINK SO?
NOW, ARE YOU JEALOUS?
SMIRK
にしし
TWINGE
OH, PLEASE! OF COURSE I'M NOT!
HO HO HO
...
...I DO WISH IT WERE ME OUT THERE, THOUGH.

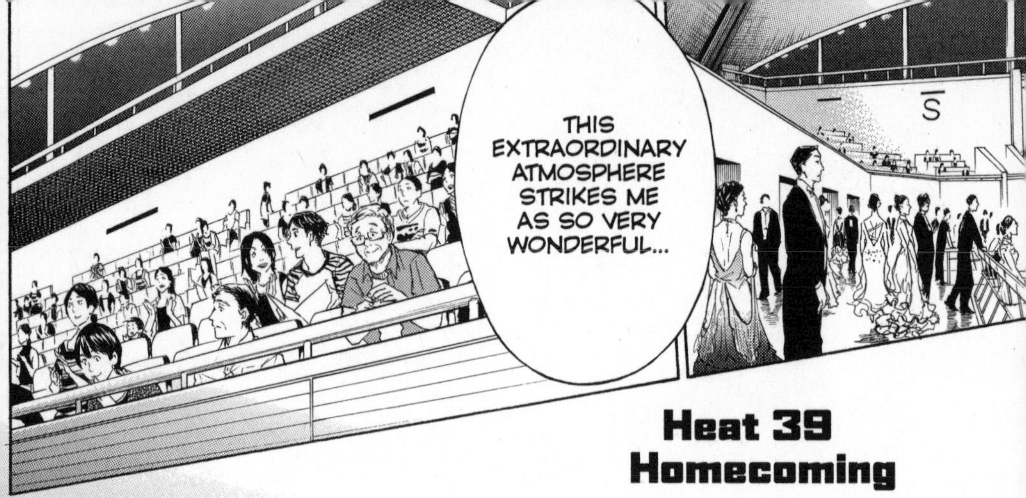
THIS EXTRAORDINARY ATMOSPHERE STRIKES ME AS SO VERY WONDERFUL...

Heat 39
Homecoming

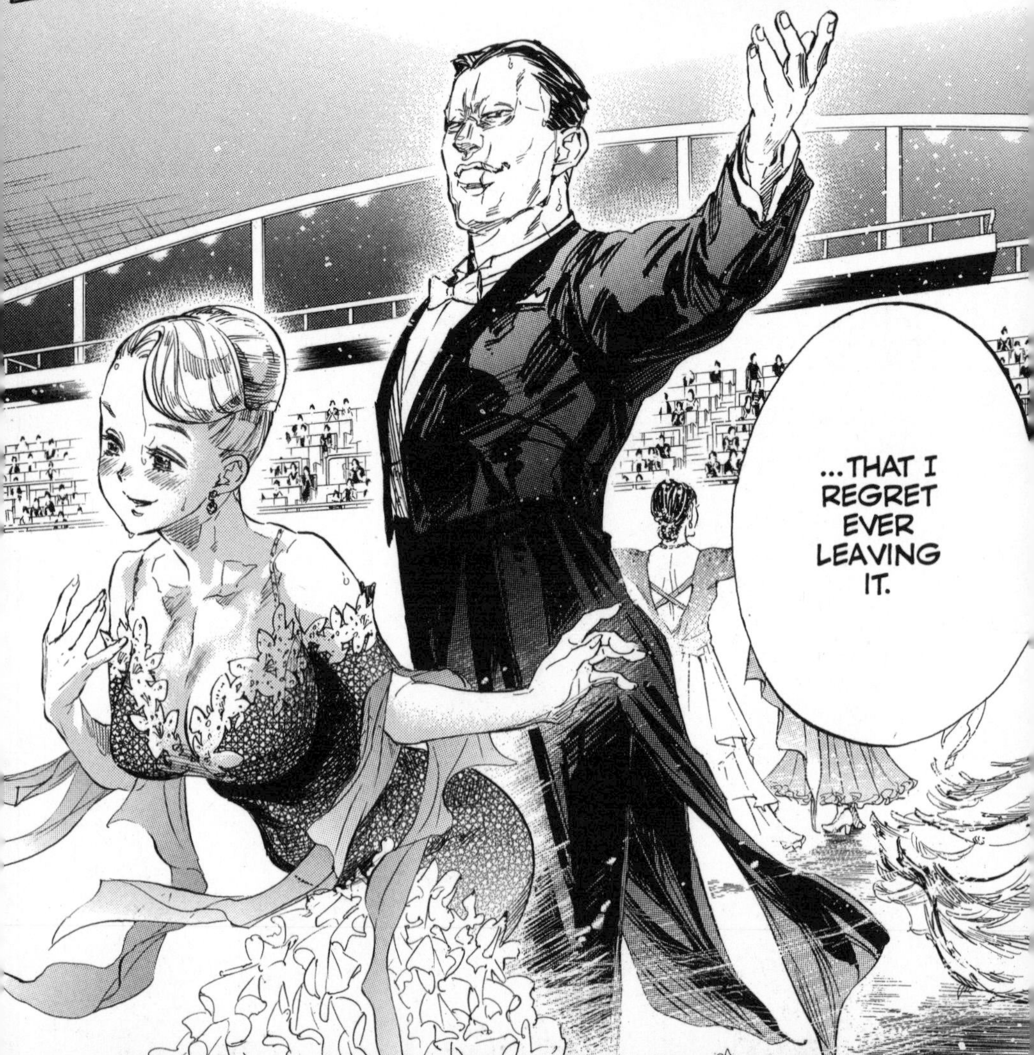
...THAT I REGRET EVER LEAVING IT.

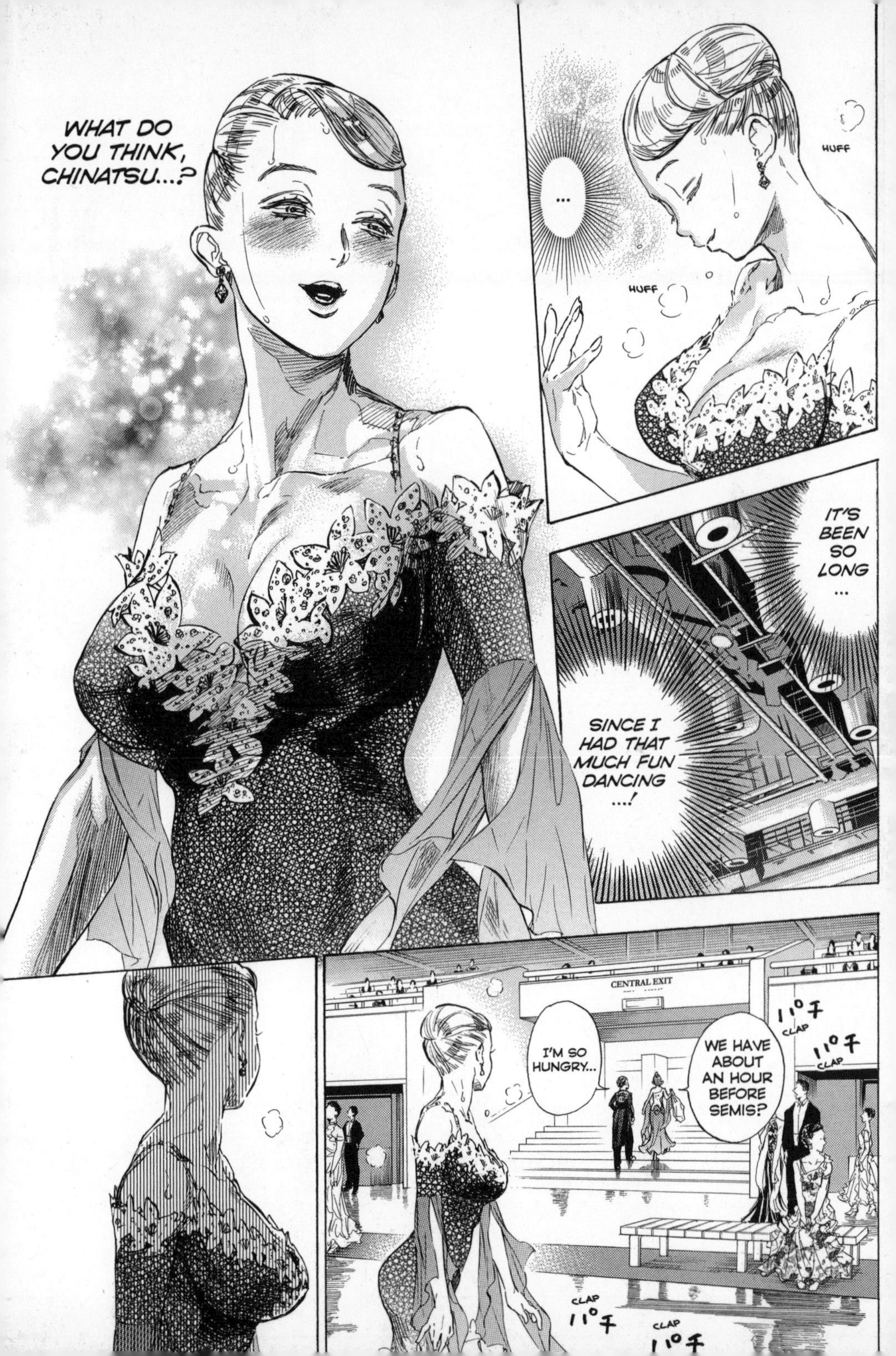
...
HUFF
HUFF
IT'S BEEN SO LONG ...
SINCE I HAD THAT MUCH FUN DANCING ...!
WHAT DO YOU THINK, CHINATSU...?
CENTRAL EXIT
パチ CLAP
パチ CLAP
WE HAVE ABOUT AN HOUR BEFORE SEMIS?
I'M SO HUNGRY...
CLAP パチ
CLAP パチ

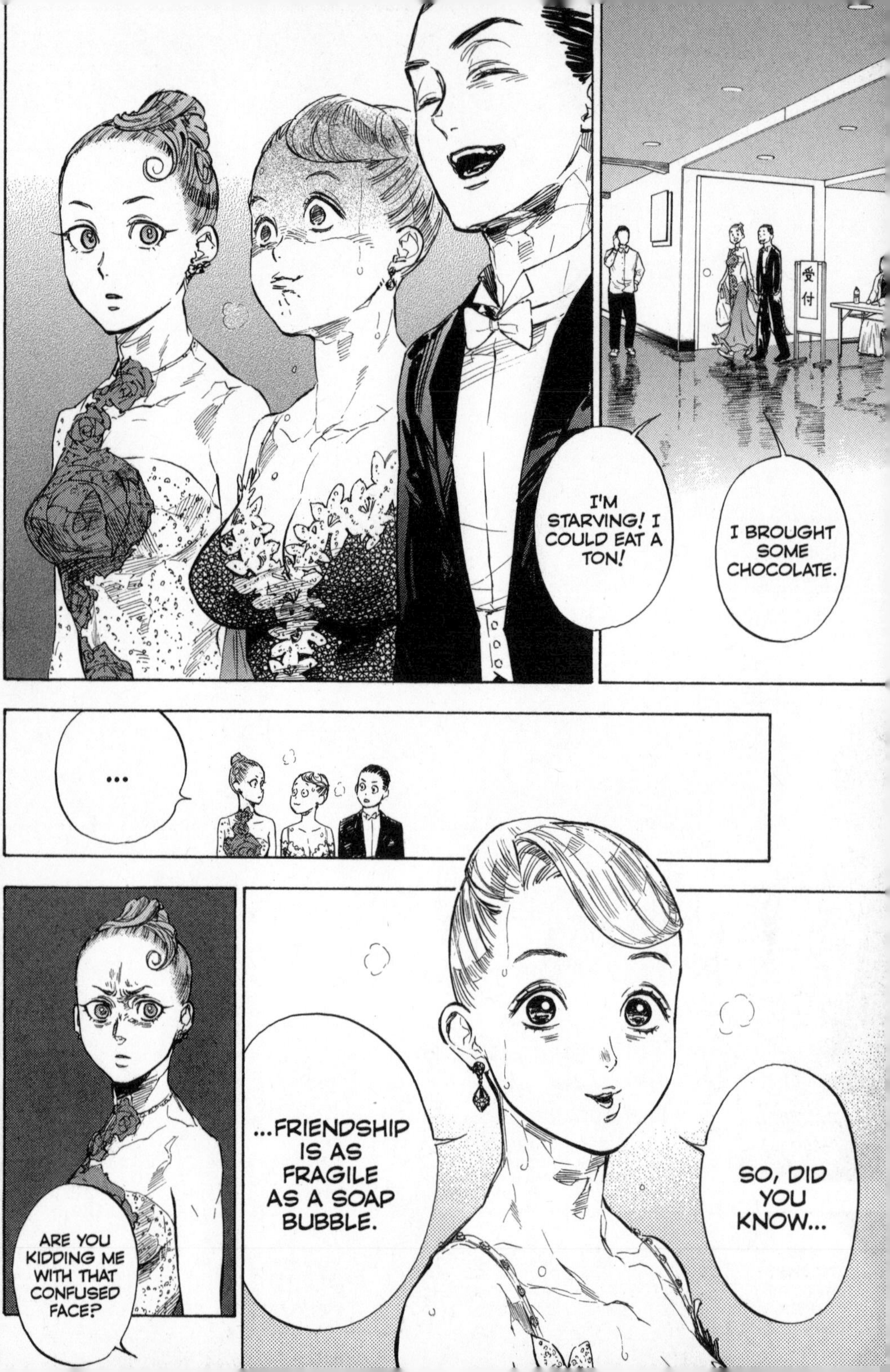
受付
I BROUGHT SOME CHOCOLATE.
I'M STARVING! I COULD EAT A TON!
...
SO, DID YOU KNOW...
...FRIENDSHIP IS AS FRAGILE AS A SOAP BUBBLE.
ARE YOU KIDDING ME WITH THAT CONFUSED FACE?

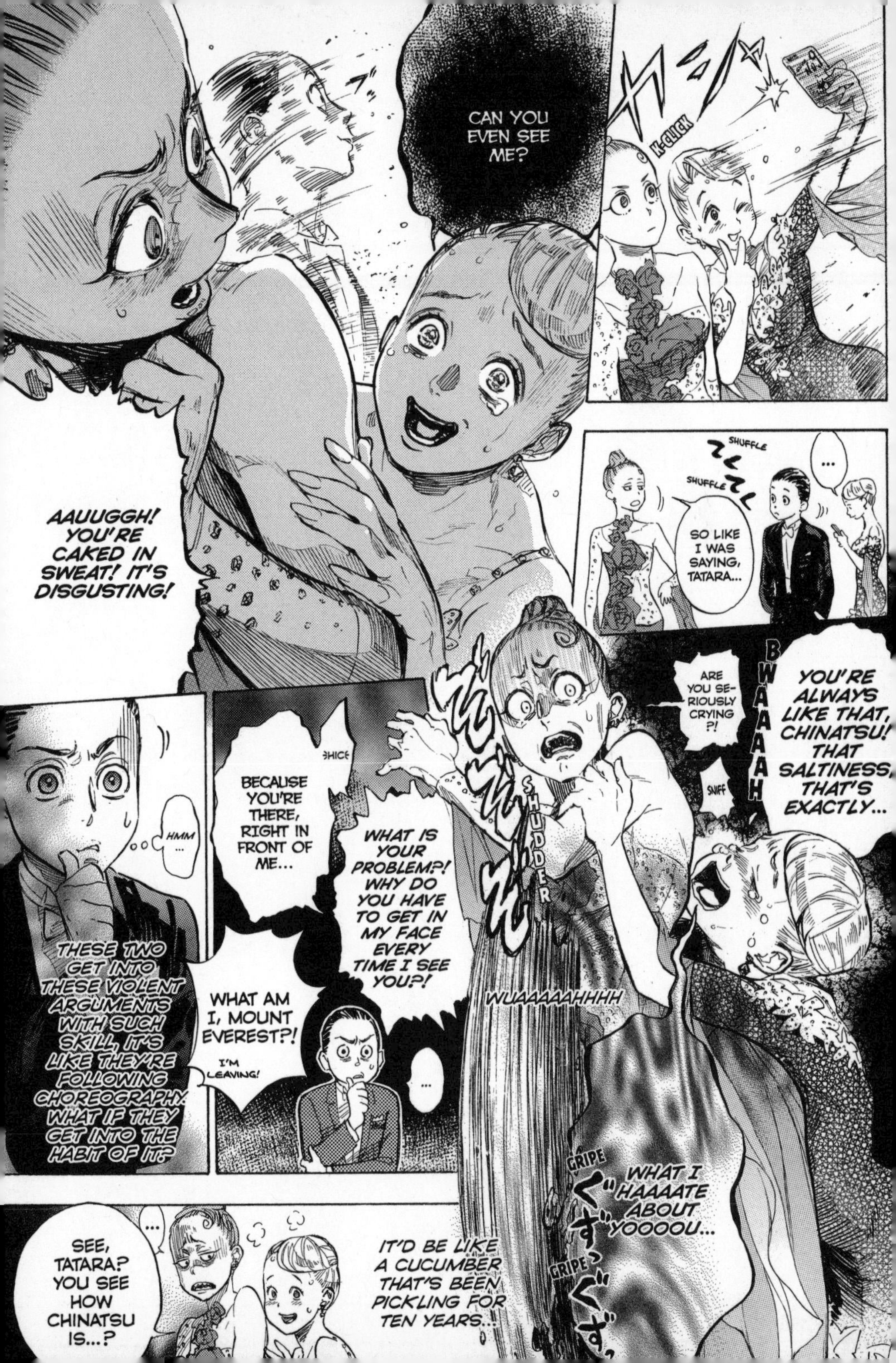

K-CLICK
SHUFFLE
SHUFFLE
...
SO LIKE I WAS SAYING, TATARA...
CAN YOU EVEN SEE ME?
AAUUGGH! YOU'RE CAKED IN SWEAT! IT'S DISGUSTING!
ARE YOU SE-RIOUSLY CRYING ?!
SNIFF
BWAAAAAH
YOU'RE ALWAYS LIKE THAT, CHINATSU! THAT SALTINESS, THAT'S EXACTLY...
SHUDDER
WHAT IS YOUR PROBLEM?! WHY DO YOU HAVE TO GET IN MY FACE EVERY TIME I SEE YOU?!
WUAAAAAHHHH
GRIPE
GRIPE
WHAT I HAAAATE ABOUT YOOOOU...
BECAUSE YOU'RE THERE, RIGHT IN FRONT OF ME...
WHAT AM I, MOUNT EVEREST?!
I'M LEAVING!
...
HMM...
THESE TWO GET INTO THESE VIOLENT ARGUMENTS WITH SUCH SKILL, IT'S LIKE THEY'RE FOLLOWING CHOREOGRAPHY. WHAT IF THEY GET INTO THE HABIT OF IT?
IT'D BE LIKE A CUCUMBER THAT'S BEEN PICKLING FOR TEN YEARS...
...
SEE, TATARA? YOU SEE HOW CHINATSU IS...?

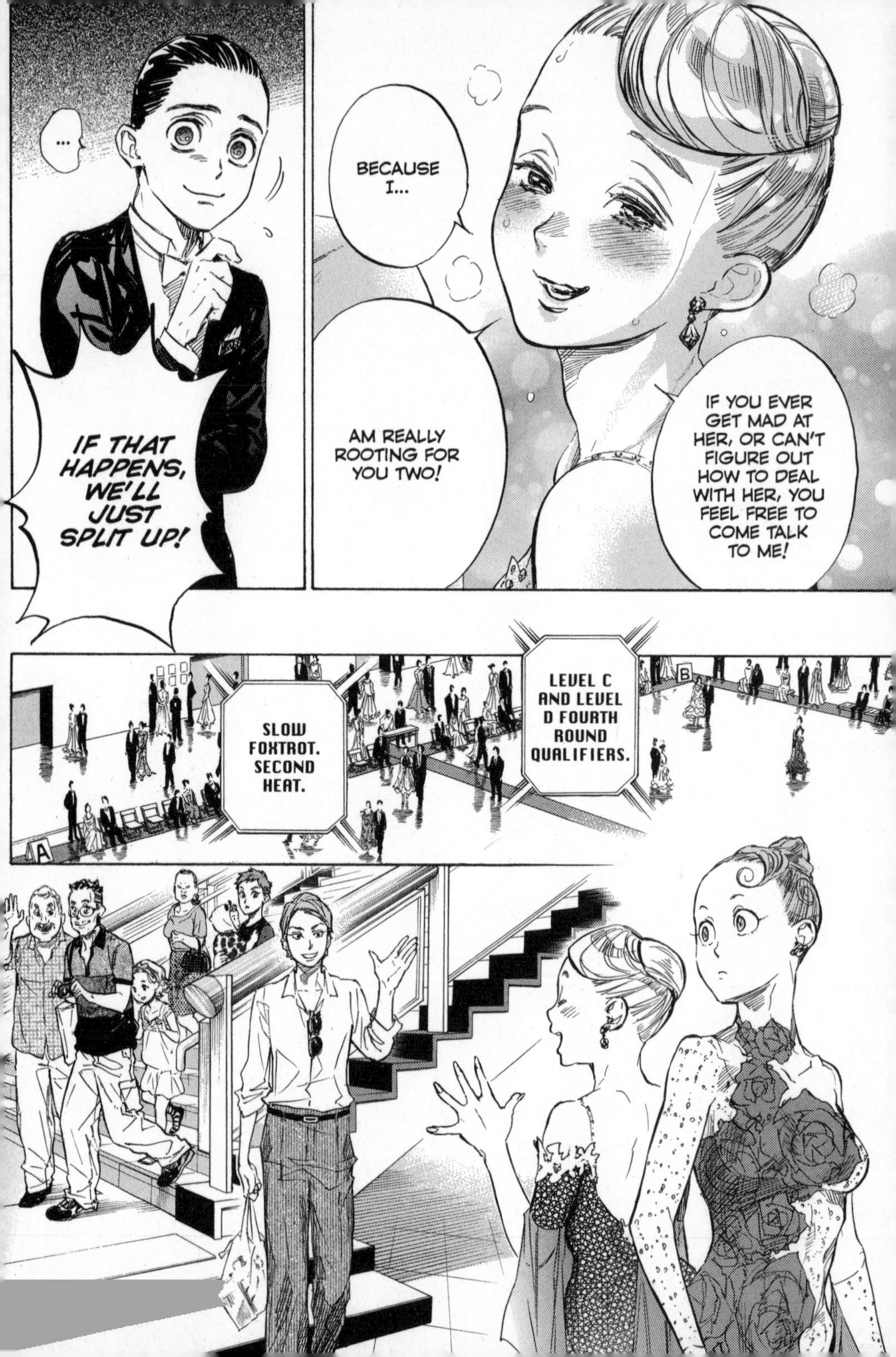
IF YOU EVER GET MAD AT HER, OR CAN'T FIGURE OUT HOW TO DEAL WITH HER, YOU FEEL FREE TO COME TALK TO ME!
BECAUSE I...
AM REALLY ROOTING FOR YOU TWO!
...
IF THAT HAPPENS, WE'LL JUST SPLIT UP!
LEVEL C AND LEVEL D FOURTH ROUND QUALIFIERS.
SLOW FOXTROT. SECOND HEAT.

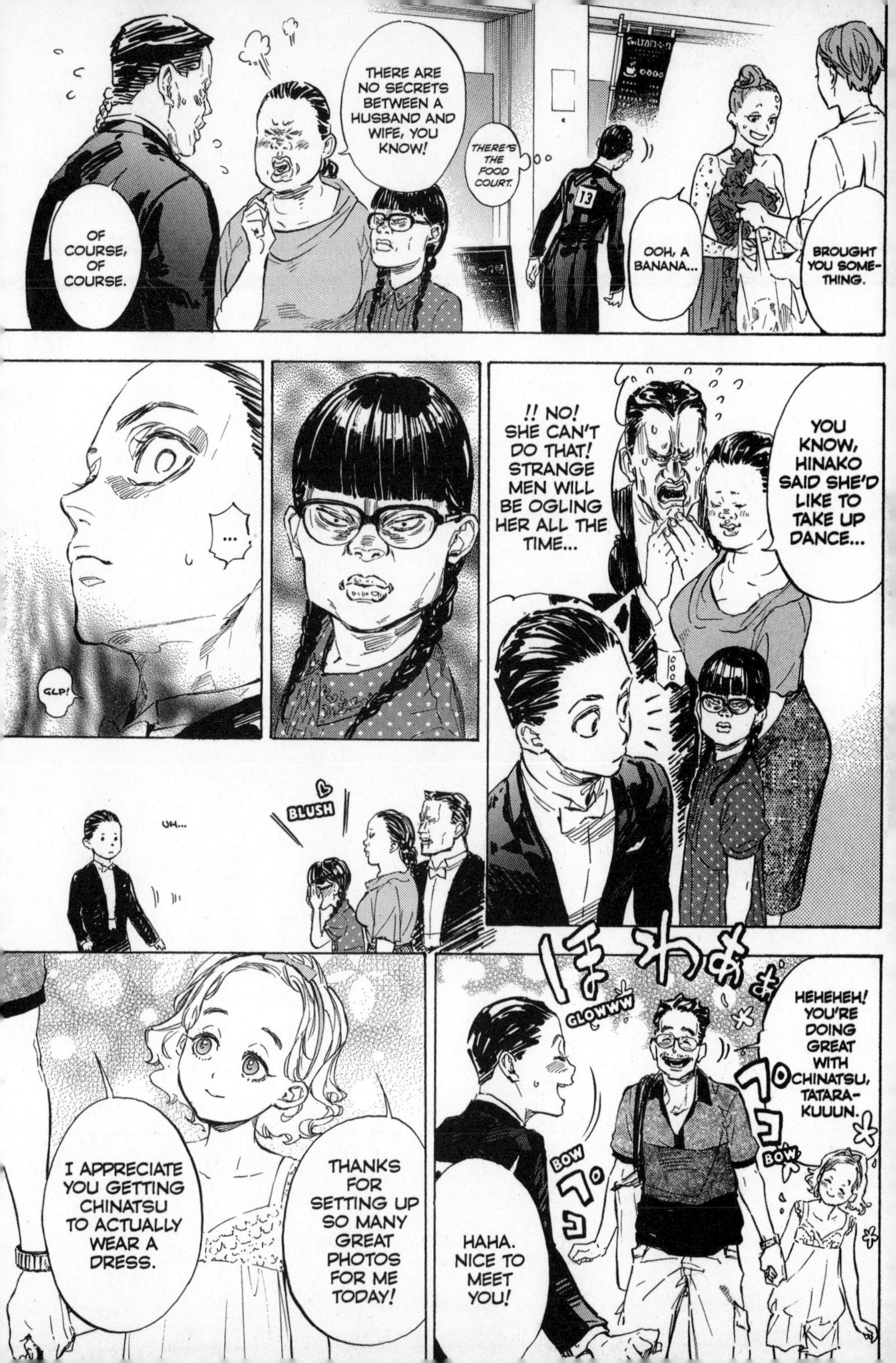
BROUGHT YOU SOMETHING.
OOH, A BANANA...
THERE ARE NO SECRETS BETWEEN A HUSBAND AND WIFE, YOU KNOW!
THERE'S THE FOOD COURT.
OF COURSE, OF COURSE.
YOU KNOW, HINAKO SAID SHE'D LIKE TO TAKE UP DANCE...
!! NO! SHE CAN'T DO THAT! STRANGE MEN WILL BE OGLING HER ALL THE TIME...
...
GLP!
BLUSH
UH...
GLOWWW
HEHEHEH! YOU'RE DOING GREAT WITH CHINATSU, TATARA-KUUUN.
BOW
BOW
HAHA. NICE TO MEET YOU!
THANKS FOR SETTING UP SO MANY GREAT PHOTOS FOR ME TODAY!
I APPRECIATE YOU GETTING CHINATSU TO ACTUALLY WEAR A DRESS.

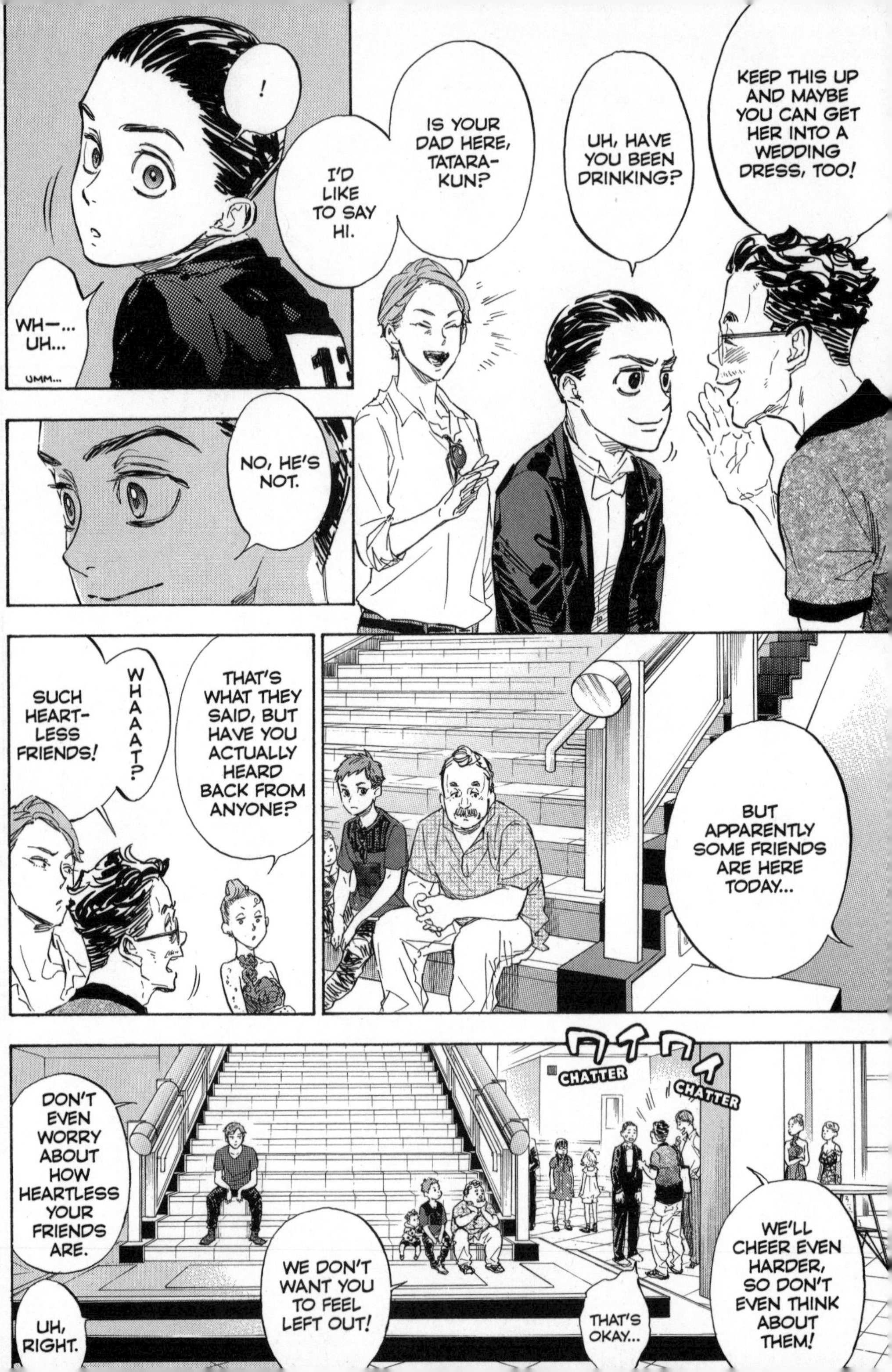
KEEP THIS UP AND MAYBE YOU CAN GET HER INTO A WEDDING DRESS, TOO!
UH, HAVE YOU BEEN DRINKING?
IS YOUR DAD HERE, TATARA-KUN?
I'D LIKE TO SAY HI.
!
WH—... UH...
UMM...
NO, HE'S NOT.
BUT APPARENTLY SOME FRIENDS ARE HERE TODAY...
THAT'S WHAT THEY SAID, BUT HAVE YOU ACTUALLY HEARD BACK FROM ANYONE?
WHAAAAT?
SUCH HEARTLESS FRIENDS!
ワイワイ
CHATTER
CHATTER
WE'LL CHEER EVEN HARDER, SO DON'T EVEN THINK ABOUT THEM!
THAT'S OKAY...
WE DON'T WANT YOU TO FEEL LEFT OUT!
DON'T EVEN WORRY ABOUT HOW HEARTLESS YOUR FRIENDS ARE.
UH, RIGHT.

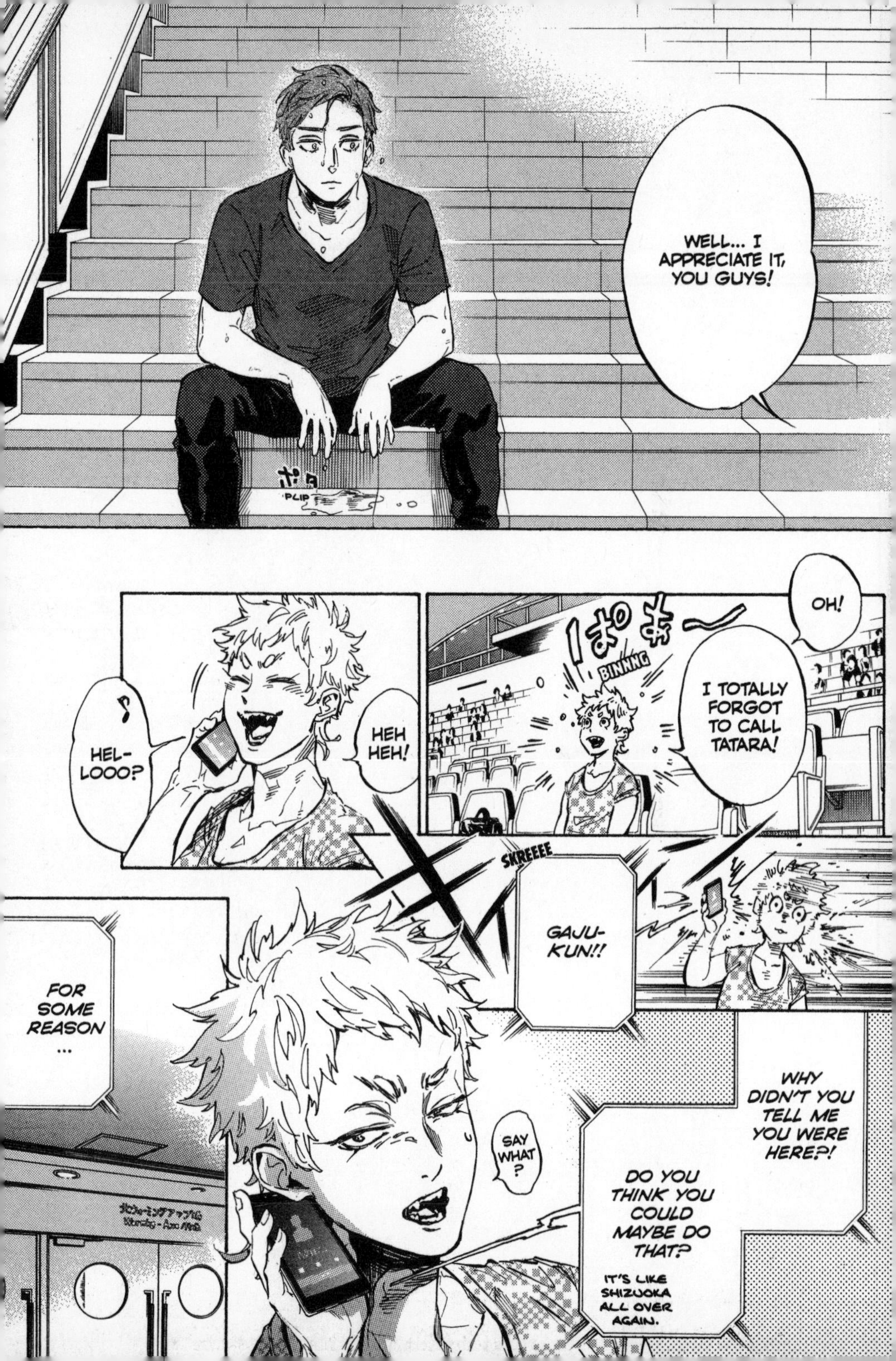
WELL... I APPRECIATE IT, YOU GUYS!
PLIP
OH!
BINNNG
I TOTALLY FORGOT TO CALL TATARA!
HEH HEH!
♪ HEL-LOOO?
SKREEEE
GAJU-KUN!!
WHY DIDN'T YOU TELL ME YOU WERE HERE?!
DO YOU THINK YOU COULD MAYBE DO THAT?
IT'S LIKE SHIZUOKA ALL OVER AGAIN.
SAY WHAT?
FOR SOME REASON...

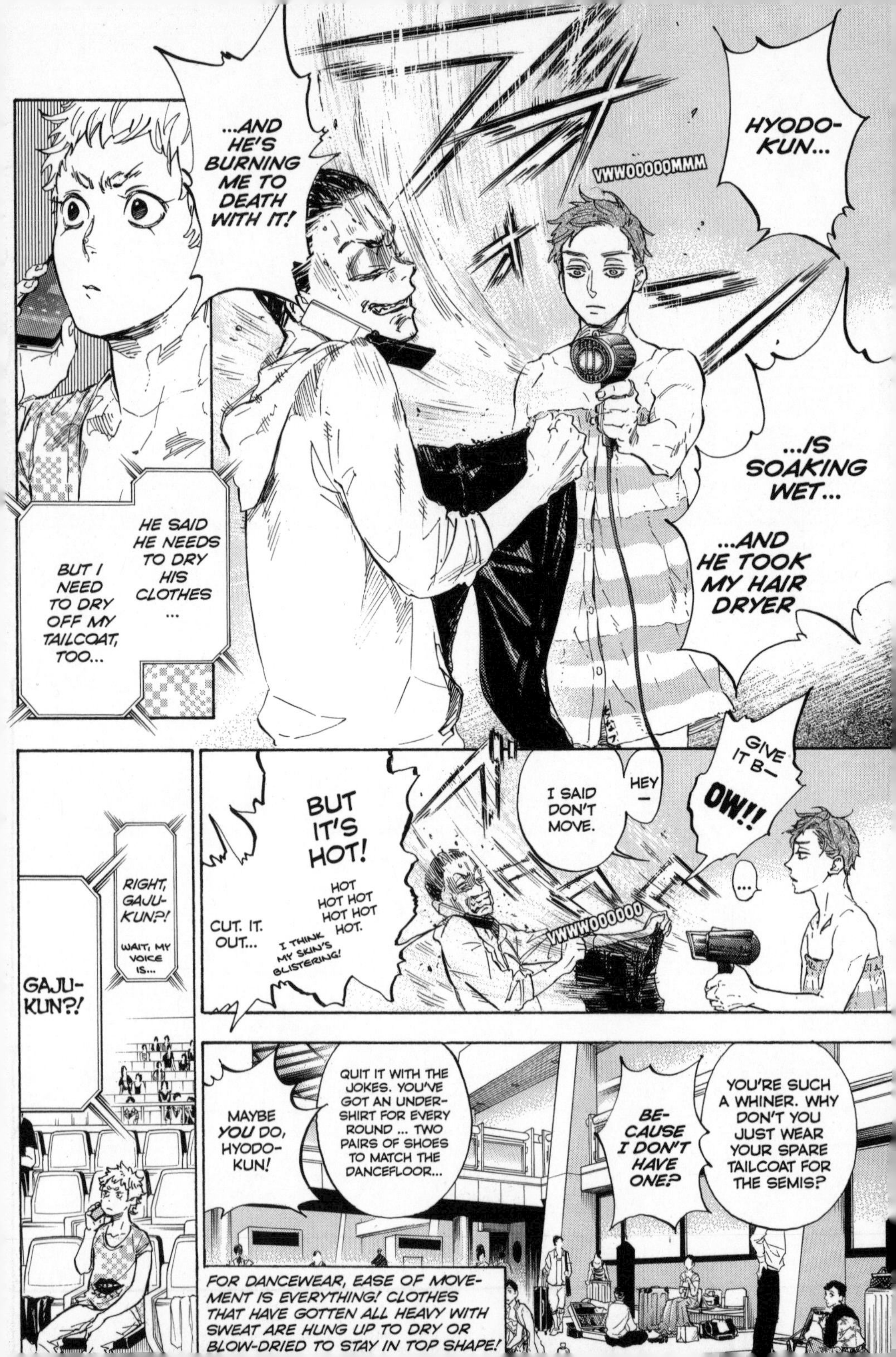
HYODO-KUN...
VWWOOOOOMMM
...IS SOAKING WET...
...AND HE TOOK MY HAIR DRYER
...AND HE'S BURNING ME TO DEATH WITH IT!
HE SAID HE NEEDS TO DRY HIS CLOTHES ...
BUT I NEED TO DRY OFF MY TAILCOAT, TOO...
GIVE IT B—
OW!!
HEY—
I SAID DON'T MOVE.
...
BUT IT'S HOT!
HOT HOT HOT HOT HOT HOT.
I THINK MY SKIN'S BLISTERING!
VWWWOOOOOO
CUT. IT. OUT...
RIGHT, GAJU-KUN?!
WAIT, MY VOICE IS...
GAJU-KUN?!
YOU'RE SUCH A WHINER. WHY DON'T YOU JUST WEAR YOUR SPARE TAILCOAT FOR THE SEMIS?
BE-CAUSE I DON'T HAVE ONE?
QUIT IT WITH THE JOKES. YOU'VE GOT AN UNDER-SHIRT FOR EVERY ROUND ... TWO PAIRS OF SHOES TO MATCH THE DANCEFLOOR...
MAYBE YOU DO, HYODO-KUN!
FOR DANCEWEAR, EASE OF MOVE-MENT IS EVERYTHING! CLOTHES THAT HAVE GOTTEN ALL HEAVY WITH SWEAT ARE HUNG UP TO DRY OR BLOW-DRIED TO STAY IN TOP SHAPE!

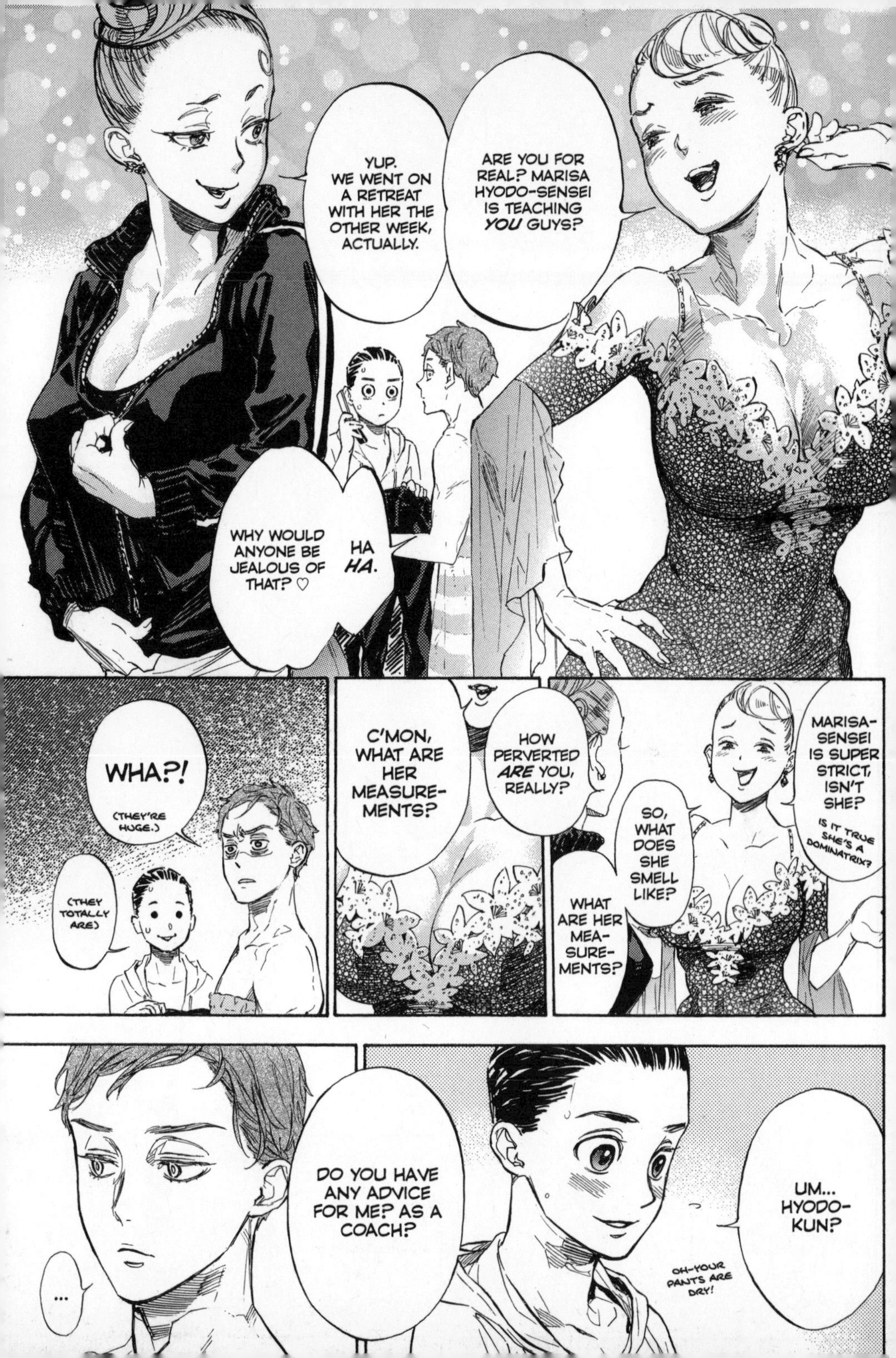
ARE YOU FOR REAL? MARISA HYODO-SENSEI IS TEACHING *YOU* GUYS?
YUP. WE WENT ON A RETREAT WITH HER THE OTHER WEEK, ACTUALLY.
HA *HA*.
WHY WOULD ANYONE BE JEALOUS OF THAT? ♡
MARISA-SENSEI IS SUPER STRICT, ISN'T SHE?
IS IT TRUE SHE'S A DOMINATRIX?
SO, WHAT DOES SHE SMELL LIKE?
WHAT ARE HER MEASUREMENTS?
HOW PERVERTED *ARE* YOU, REALLY?
C'MON, WHAT ARE HER MEASUREMENTS?
WHA?!
(THEY'RE HUGE.)
(THEY TOTALLY ARE)
UM... HYODO-KUN?
OH-YOUR PANTS ARE DRY!
DO YOU HAVE ANY ADVICE FOR ME? AS A COACH?
...

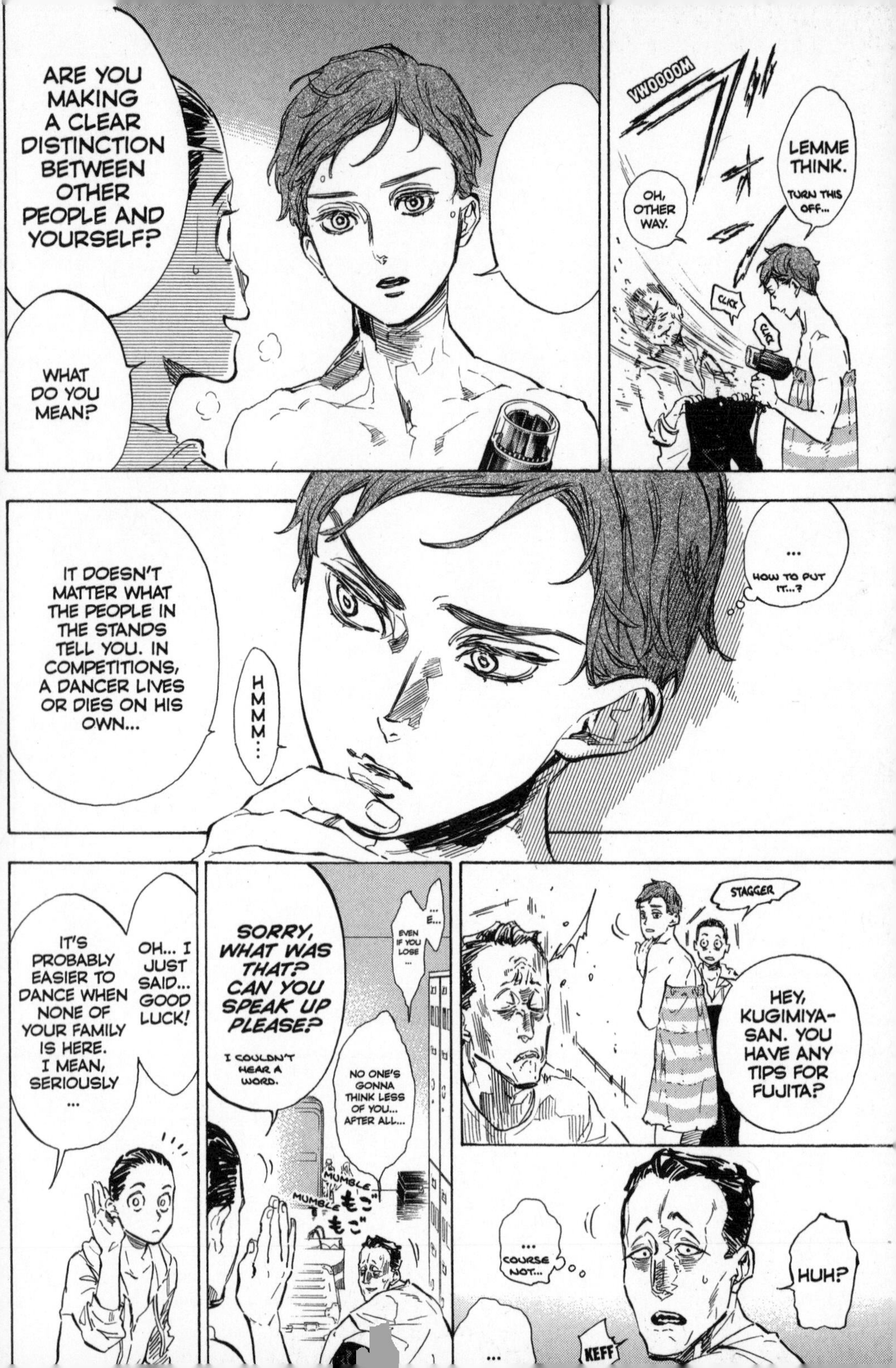
VWOOOOM
LEMME THINK.
TURN THIS OFF...
OH, OTHER WAY.
CLICK
CLICK
ARE YOU MAKING A CLEAR DISTINCTION BETWEEN OTHER PEOPLE AND YOURSELF?
WHAT DO YOU MEAN?
... HOW TO PUT IT...?
HMMM...
IT DOESN'T MATTER WHAT THE PEOPLE IN THE STANDS TELL YOU. IN COMPETITIONS, A DANCER LIVES OR DIES ON HIS OWN...
STAGGER
HEY, KUGIMIYA-SAN. YOU HAVE ANY TIPS FOR FUJITA?
HUH?
... COURSE NOT...
KEFF
...
... E... EVEN IF YOU LOSE ...
SORRY, WHAT WAS THAT? CAN YOU SPEAK UP PLEASE?
I COULDN'T HEAR A WORD.
NO ONE'S GONNA THINK LESS OF YOU... AFTER ALL...
MUMBLE もご
MUMBLE もご
OH... I JUST SAID... GOOD LUCK!
IT'S PROBABLY EASIER TO DANCE WHEN NONE OF YOUR FAMILY IS HERE. I MEAN, SERIOUSLY ...

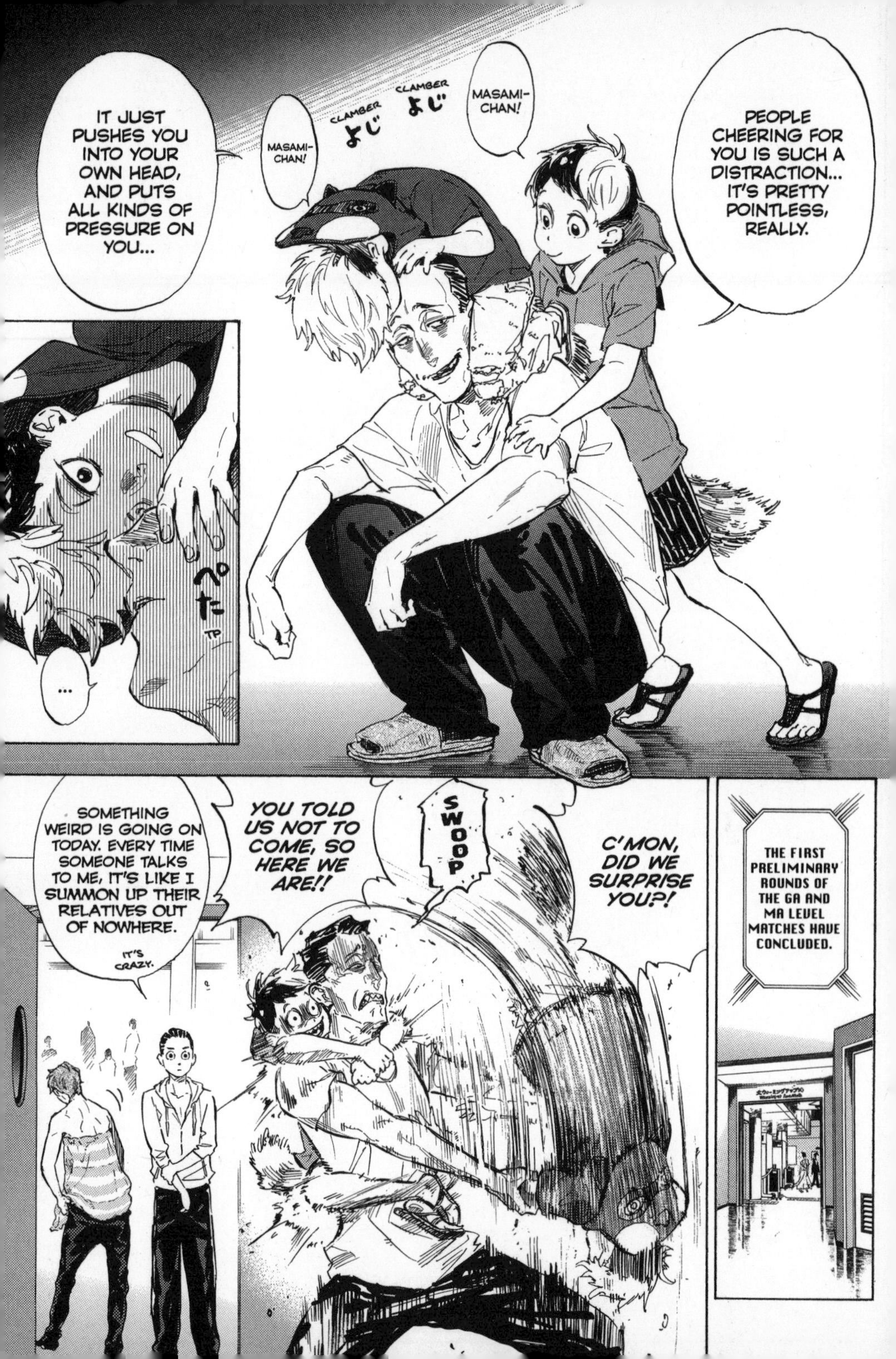
PEOPLE CHEERING FOR YOU IS SUCH A DISTRACTION... IT'S PRETTY POINTLESS, REALLY.
MASAMI-CHAN!
CLAMBER よじ
CLAMBER よじ
MASAMI-CHAN!
IT JUST PUSHES YOU INTO YOUR OWN HEAD, AND PUTS ALL KINDS OF PRESSURE ON YOU...
ぺた TP
...
THE FIRST PRELIMINARY ROUNDS OF THE GA AND MA LEVEL MATCHES HAVE CONCLUDED.
C'MON, DID WE SURPRISE YOU?!
SWOOP
YOU TOLD US NOT TO COME, SO HERE WE ARE!!
SOMETHING WEIRD IS GOING ON TODAY. EVERY TIME SOMEONE TALKS TO ME, IT'S LIKE I SUMMON UP THEIR RELATIVES OUT OF NOWHERE.
IT'S CRAZY.

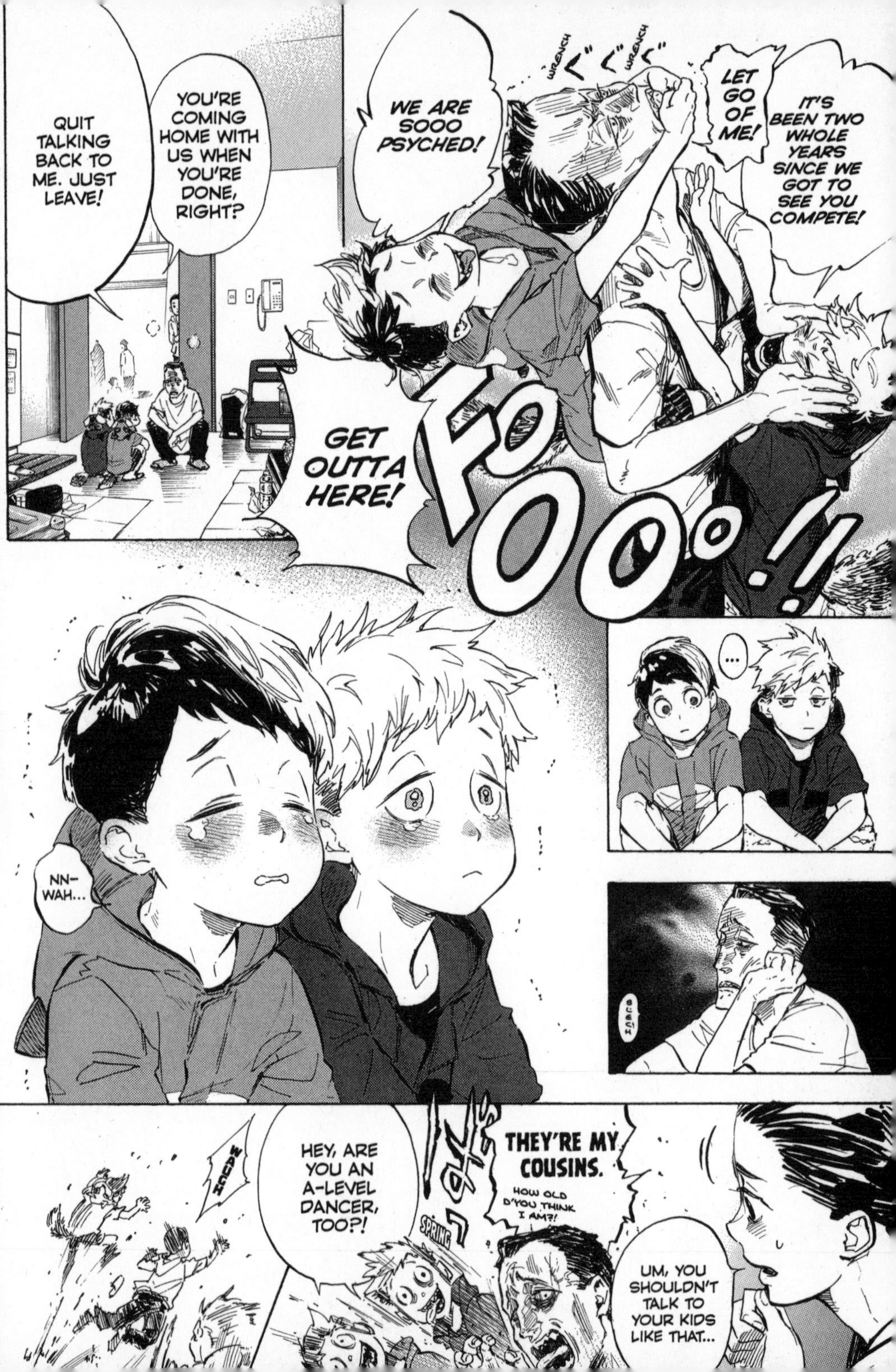
IT'S BEEN TWO WHOLE YEARS SINCE WE GOT TO SEE YOU COMPETE!
LET GO OF ME!
WRENCH
WRENCH
WE ARE SOOO PSYCHED!
FOOO!!
GET OUTTA HERE!
YOU'RE COMING HOME WITH US WHEN YOU'RE DONE, RIGHT?
QUIT TALKING BACK TO ME. JUST LEAVE!
...
NN-WAH...
UM, YOU SHOULDN'T TALK TO YOUR KIDS LIKE THAT...
THEY'RE MY COUSINS.
HOW OLD D'YOU THINK I AM?!
SPRING
HEY, ARE YOU AN A-LEVEL DANCER, TOO?!
WAUGH

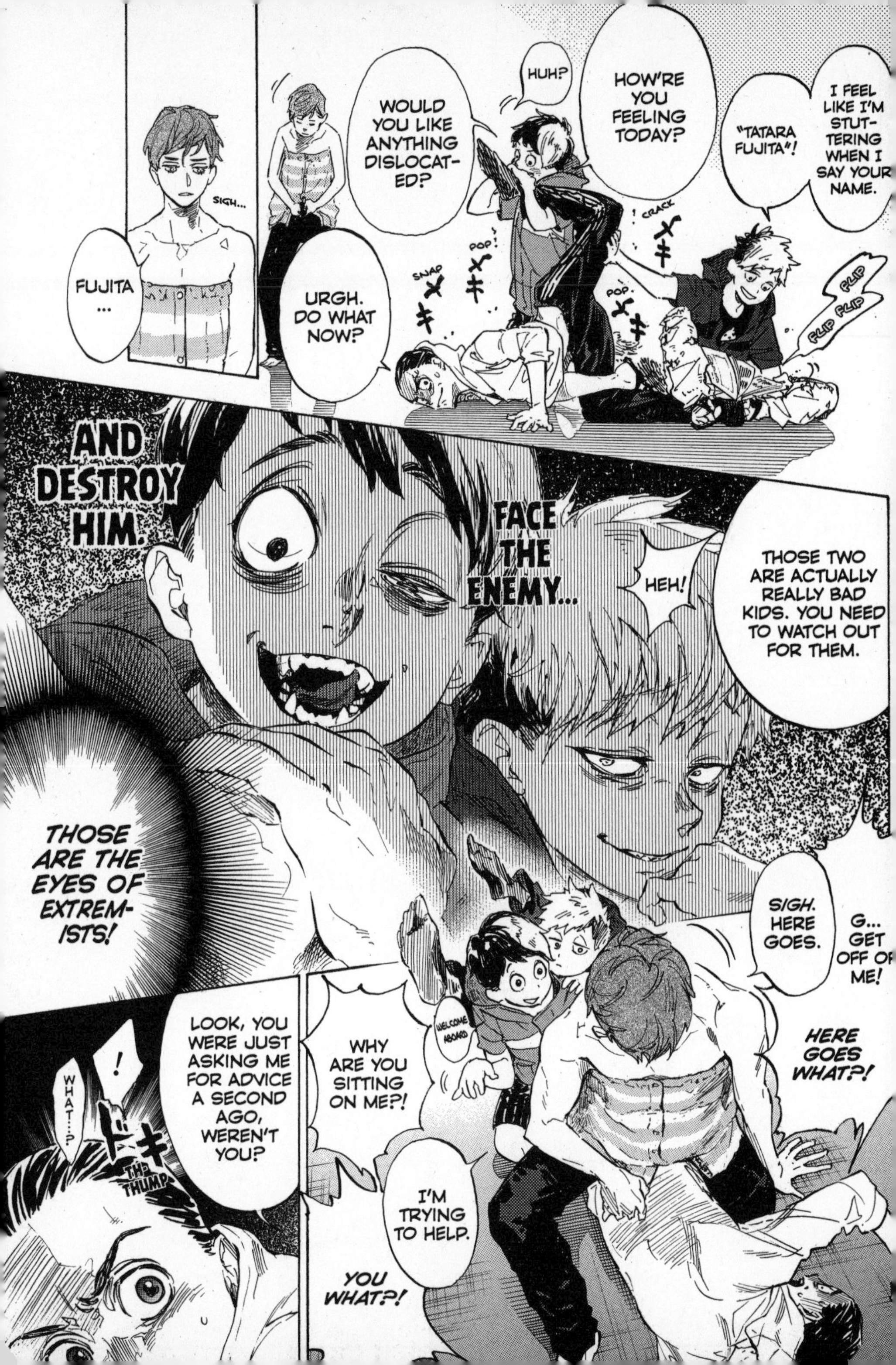
I FEEL LIKE I'M STUTTERING WHEN I SAY YOUR NAME.
"TATARA FUJITA"!
FLIP FLIP FLIP
HOW'RE YOU FEELING TODAY?
HUH?
CRACK
POP
POP
SNAP
WOULD YOU LIKE ANYTHING DISLOCATED?
URGH. DO WHAT NOW?
SIGH...
FUJITA...
THOSE TWO ARE ACTUALLY REALLY BAD KIDS. YOU NEED TO WATCH OUT FOR THEM.
HEH!
FACE THE ENEMY...
AND DESTROY HIM.
THOSE ARE THE EYES OF EXTREMISTS!
G... GET OFF OF ME!
SIGH. HERE GOES.
HERE GOES WHAT?!
WELCOME ABOARD
WHY ARE YOU SITTING ON ME?!
I'M TRYING TO HELP.
YOU WHAT?!
LOOK, YOU WERE JUST ASKING ME FOR ADVICE A SECOND AGO, WEREN'T YOU?
!
WHAT...?
THUMP
UM

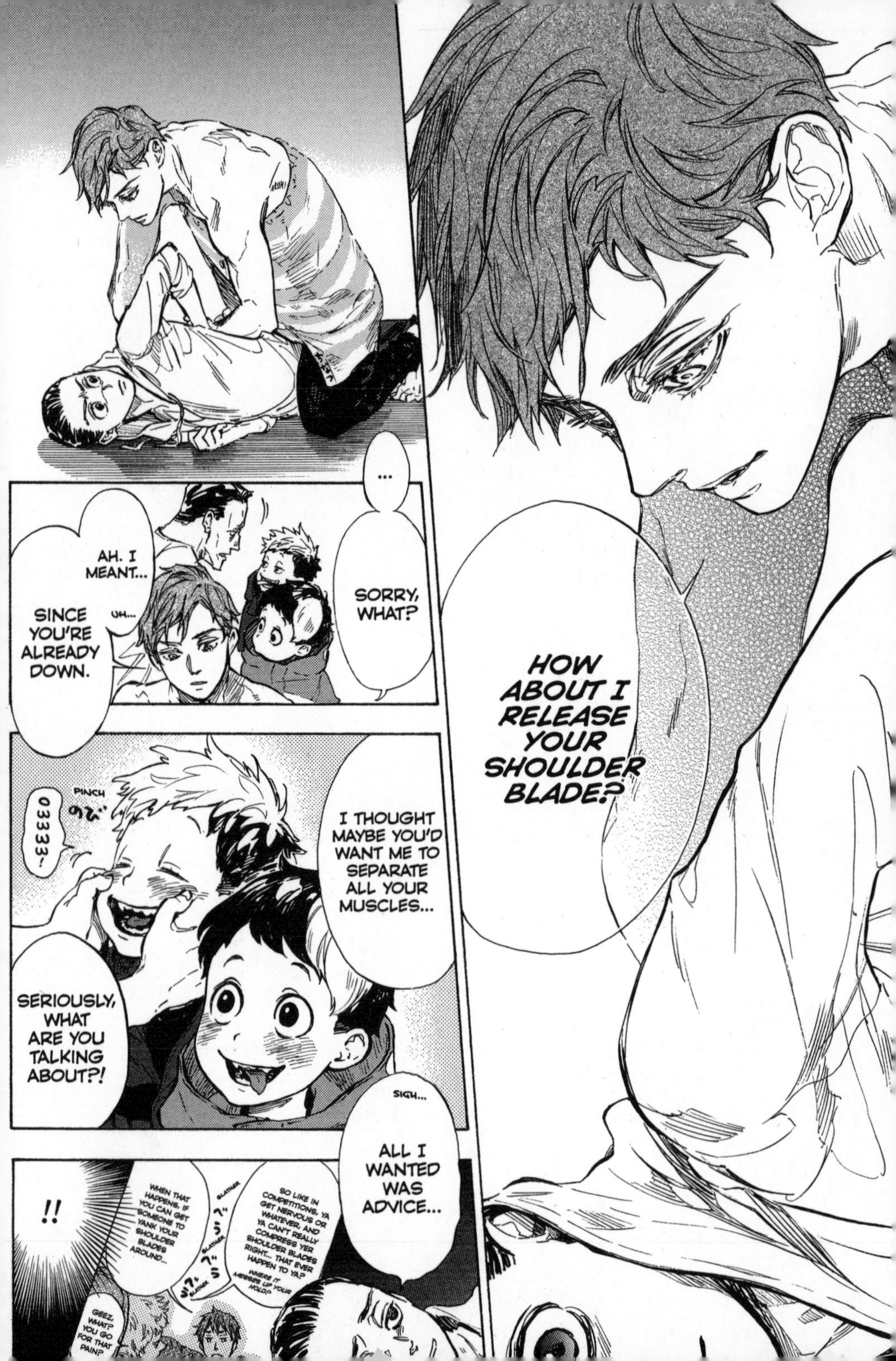
HOW ABOUT I RELEASE YOUR SHOULDER BLADE?
...
SORRY, WHAT?
AH. I MEANT...
UH...
SINCE YOU'RE ALREADY DOWN.
I THOUGHT MAYBE YOU'D WANT ME TO SEPARATE ALL YOUR MUSCLES...
PINCH
OWWWW-
SERIOUSLY, WHAT ARE YOU TALKING ABOUT?!
SIGH...
ALL I WANTED WAS ADVICE...
SO LIKE IN COMPETITIONS, YA GET NERVOUS OR WHATEVER, AND YA CAN'T REALLY COMPRESS YER SHOULDER BLADES RIGHT... THAT EVER HAPPEN TO YA?
WHERE IT MESSES UP YOUR HOLD?
SLATHER
SLATHER
SLATHER
WHEN THAT HAPPENS, IF YOU CAN GET SOMEONE TO YANK YOUR SHOULDER BLADES AROUND...
!!
GEEZ, WHAT? YOU GO FOR THAT PAIN?

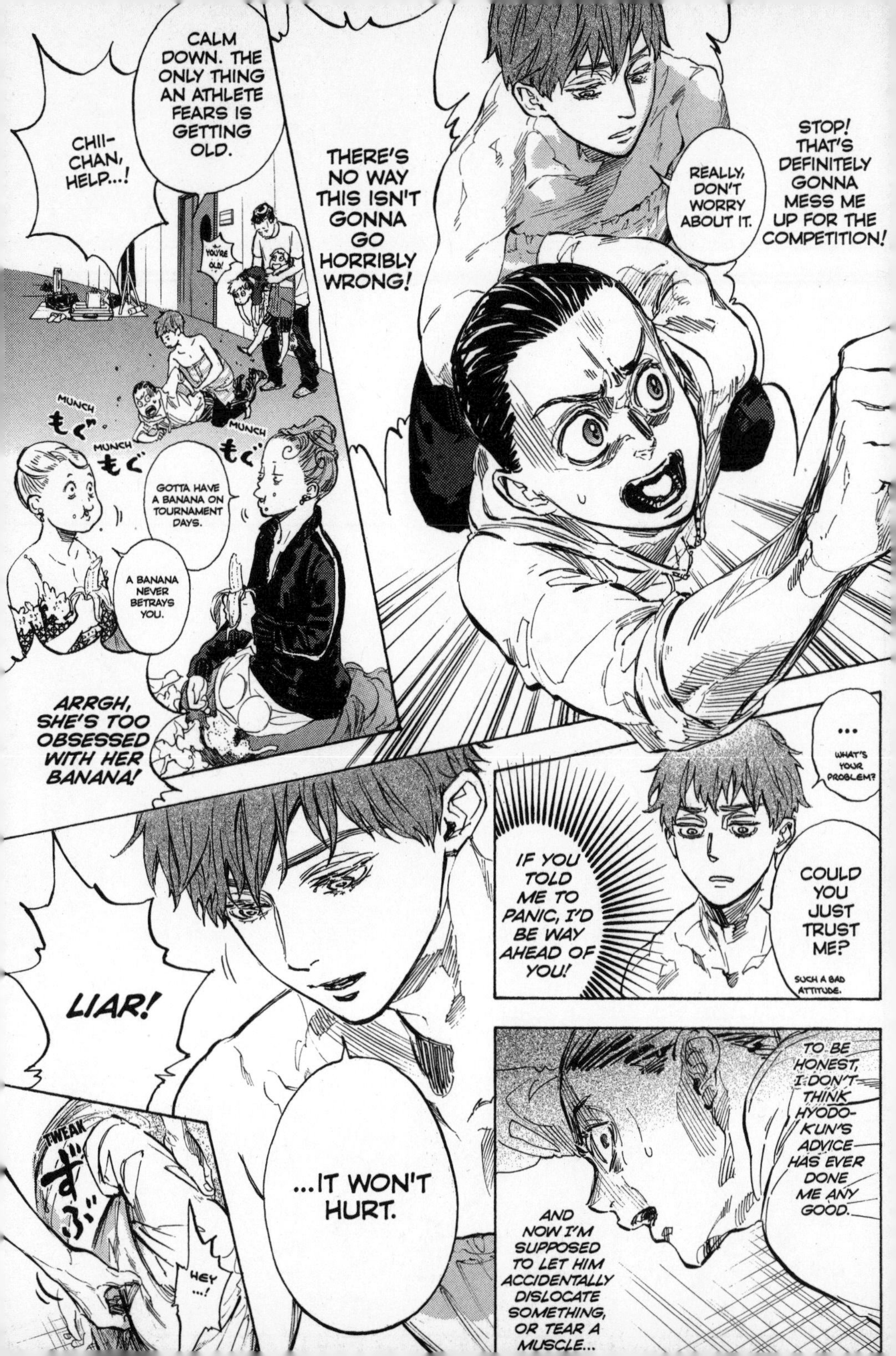

STOP! THAT'S DEFINITELY GONNA MESS ME UP FOR THE COMPETITION!
REALLY, DON'T WORRY ABOUT IT.
THERE'S NO WAY THIS ISN'T GONNA GO HORRIBLY WRONG!
CALM DOWN. THE ONLY THING AN ATHLETE FEARS IS GETTING OLD.
CHII-CHAN, HELP...!
YOU'RE OLD!
MUNCH もぐ
MUNCH もぐ
MUNCH もぐ
GOTTA HAVE A BANANA ON TOURNAMENT DAYS.
A BANANA NEVER BETRAYS YOU.
ARRGH, SHE'S TOO OBSESSED WITH HER BANANA!
...
WHAT'S YOUR PROBLEM?
COULD YOU JUST TRUST ME?
SUCH A BAD ATTITUDE.
IF YOU TOLD ME TO PANIC, I'D BE WAY AHEAD OF YOU!
TO BE HONEST, I DON'T THINK HYODO-KUN'S ADVICE HAS EVER DONE ME ANY GOOD.
AND NOW I'M SUPPOSED TO LET HIM ACCIDENTALLY DISLOCATE SOMETHING, OR TEAR A MUSCLE...
LIAR!
...IT WON'T HURT.
TWEAK ずぶ
HEY ...!

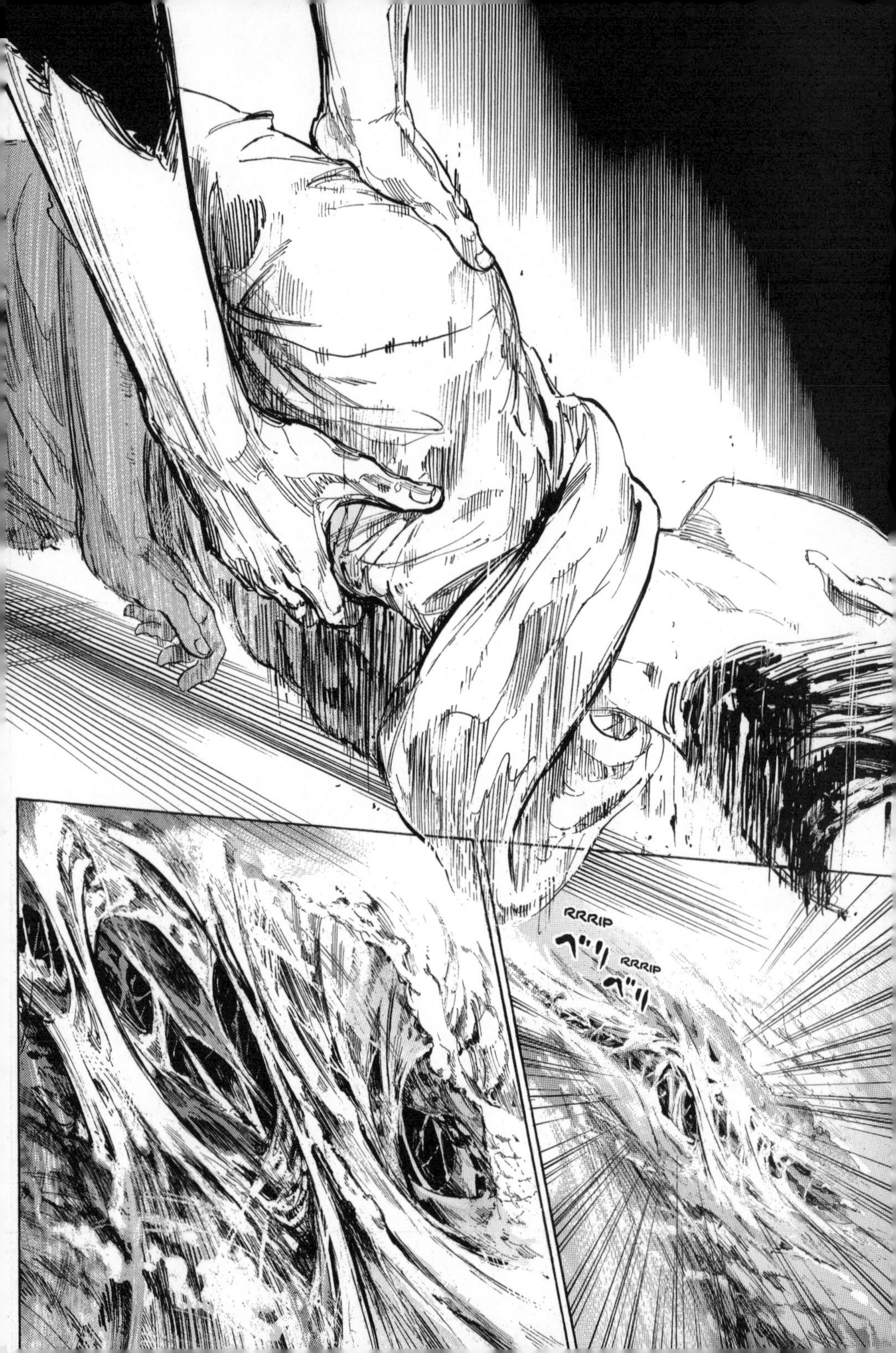
RRRIP
ベリ
RRRIP
ベリ

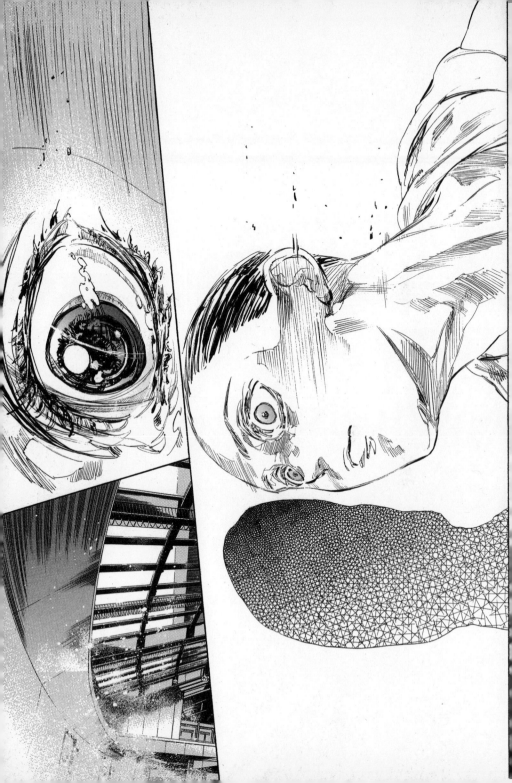

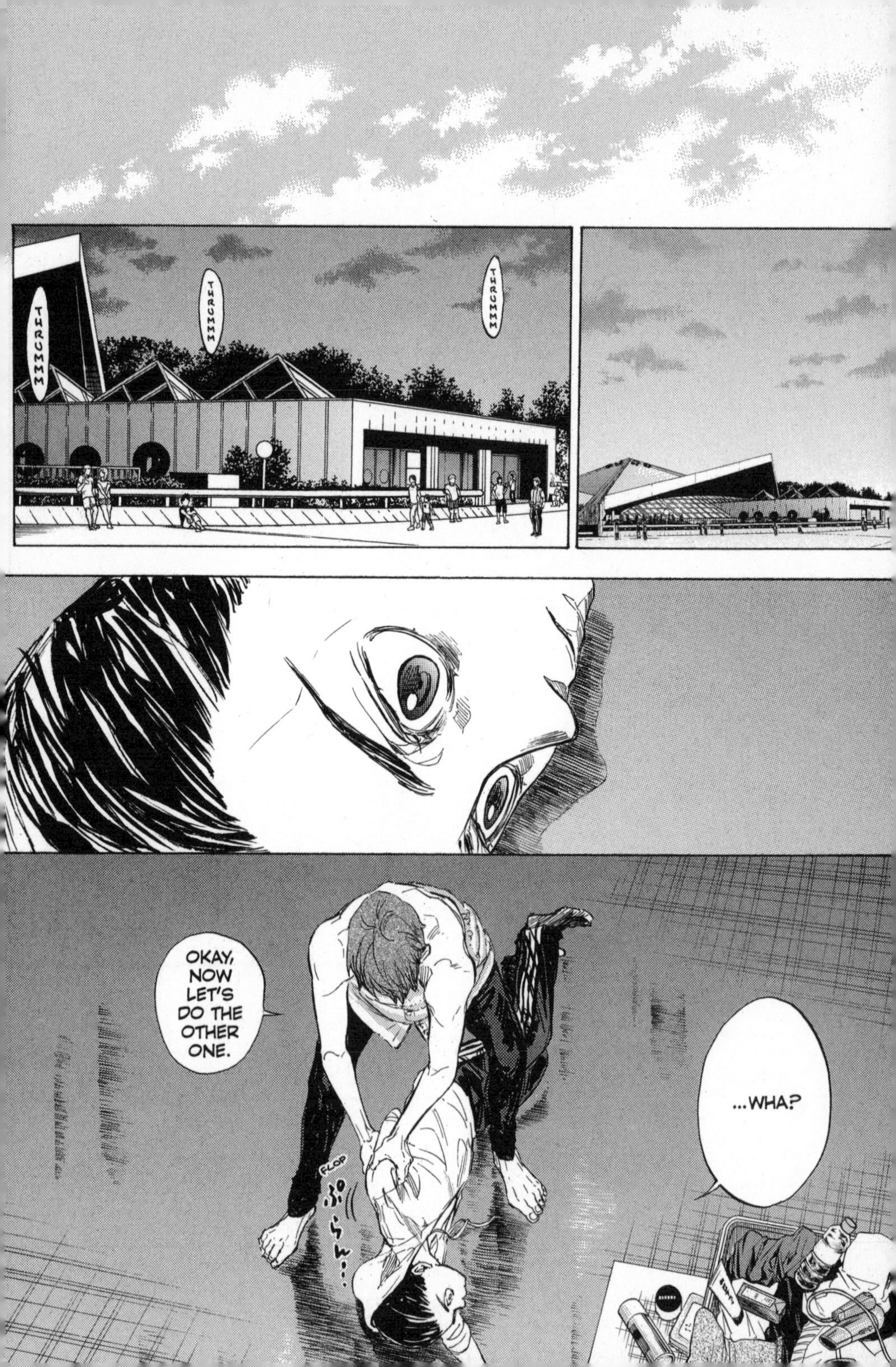
THRUMMM
THRUMMM
THRUMMM
OKAY, NOW LET'S DO THE OTHER ONE.
FLOP
ぷらん…
...WHA?

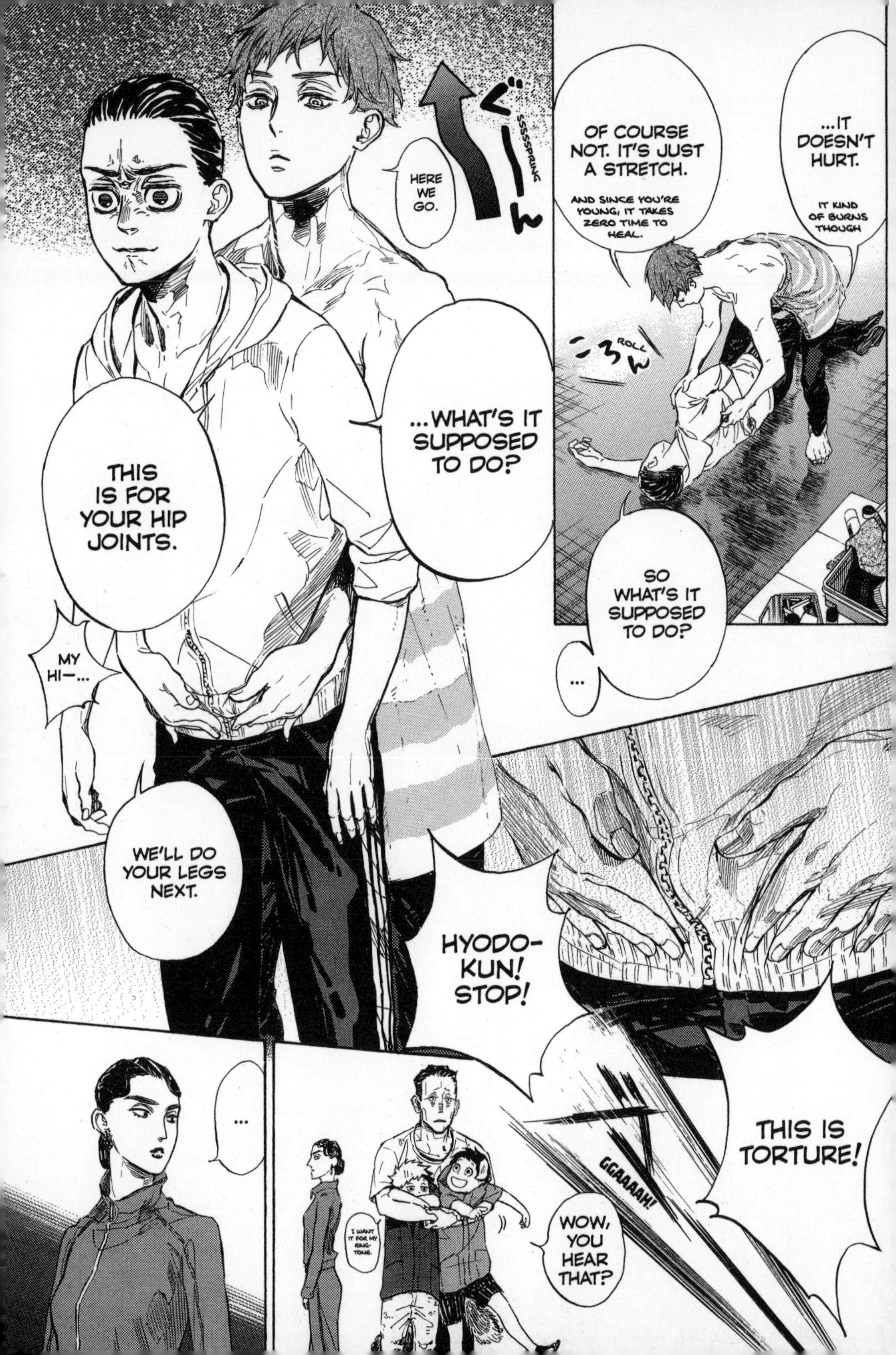
...IT DOESN'T HURT.
IT KIND OF BURNS THOUGH
OF COURSE NOT. IT'S JUST A STRETCH.
AND SINCE YOU'RE YOUNG, IT TAKES ZERO TIME TO HEAL.
ROLL
SO WHAT'S IT SUPPOSED TO DO?
...
SSSSPRING
HERE WE GO.
...WHAT'S IT SUPPOSED TO DO?
THIS IS FOR YOUR HIP JOINTS.
MY HI—...
WE'LL DO YOUR LEGS NEXT.
HYODO-KUN! STOP!
THIS IS TORTURE!
GGAAAAH!
WOW, YOU HEAR THAT?
I WANT IT FOR MY RING-TONE.
...

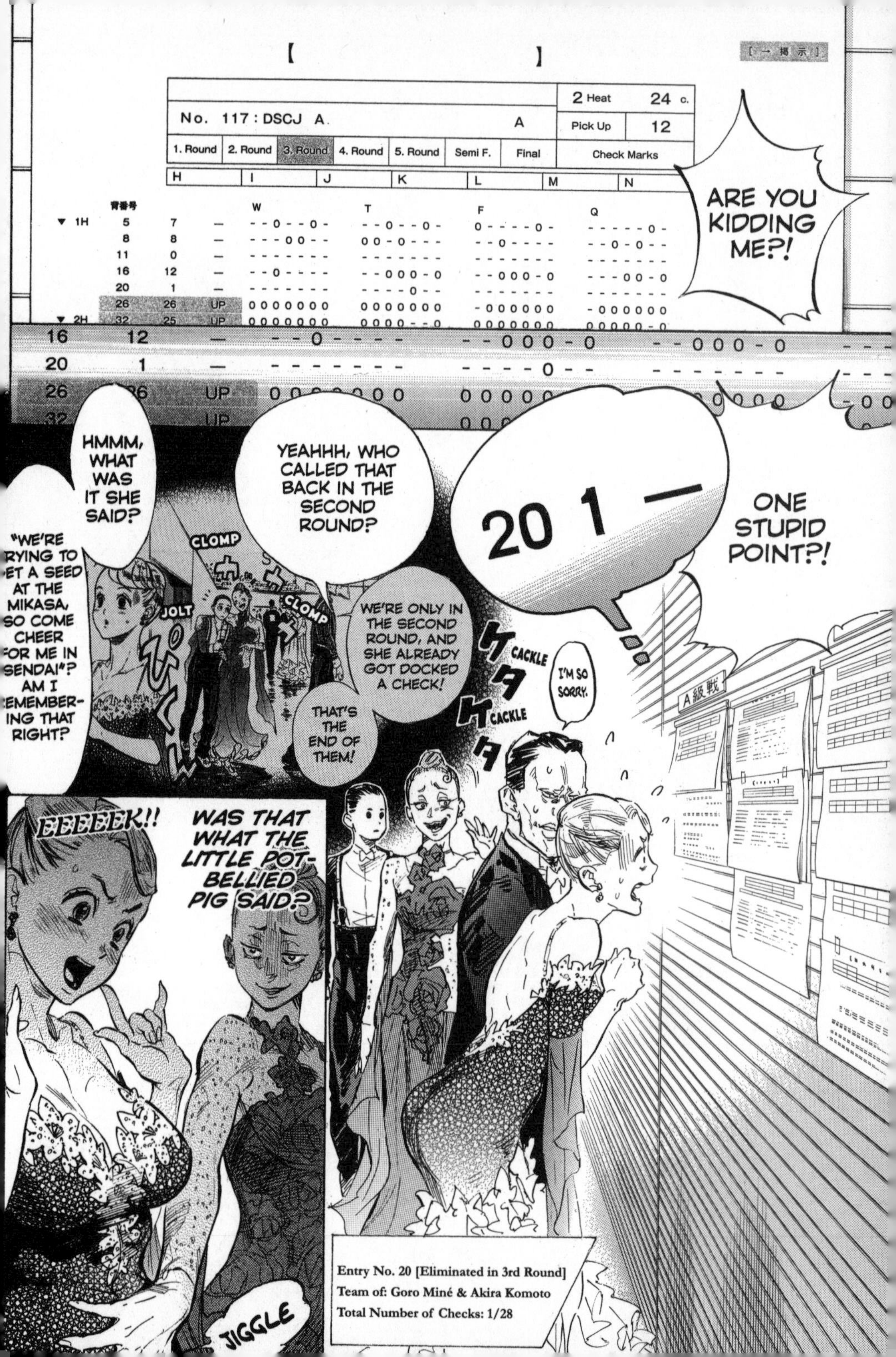

【 】
[一 掲 示]
No. 117 : DSCJ A. A
2 Heat 24 c.
Pick Up 12
1. Round
2. Round
3. Round
4. Round
5. Round
Semi F.
Final
Check Marks
H I J K L M N
背番号
W T F Q
▼ 1H 5 7 — - - 0 - - 0 - - - 0 - - 0 - 0 - - - - 0 - - - - - - 0 -
8 8 — - - - 0 0 - - 0 0 - 0 - - - - - 0 - - - - - - 0 - 0 - -
11 0 — -
16 12 — - - 0 - - - - - - 0 0 0 - 0 - - 0 0 0 - 0 - - - 0 0 - 0
20 1 — - - - - - - - - - - 0 - - - - - - - - - - - - - - - - - -
26 26 UP 0 0 0 0 0 0 0 0 0 0 0 0 0 0 - - - - - - - - - - - - - -
▼ 2H 32 25 UP 0 0 0 0 0 0 0
ARE YOU KIDDING ME?!
16 12 — - - 0 - - - - - - - 0 0 0 - 0 - - 0 0 0 - 0
20 1 — - - - - - - - - - - - - 0 - -
26 26 UP
20 1 —
ONE STUPID POINT?!
ケタケタ CACKLE CACKLE
I'M SO SORRY.
A級戦
WE'RE ONLY IN THE SECOND ROUND, AND SHE ALREADY GOT DOCKED A CHECK!
THAT'S THE END OF THEM!
Entry No. 20 [Eliminated in 3rd Round]
Team of: Goro Miné & Akira Komoto
Total Number of Checks: 1/28
YEAHHH, WHO CALLED THAT BACK IN THE SECOND ROUND?
CLOMP
CLOMP
JOLT
HMMM, WHAT WAS IT SHE SAID?
"WE'RE RYING TO ET A SEED AT THE MIKASA, SO COME CHEER FOR ME IN SENDAI"? AM I EMEMBERING THAT RIGHT?
WAS THAT WHAT THE LITTLE POT-BELLIED PIG SAID?
EEEEEK!!
JIGGLE

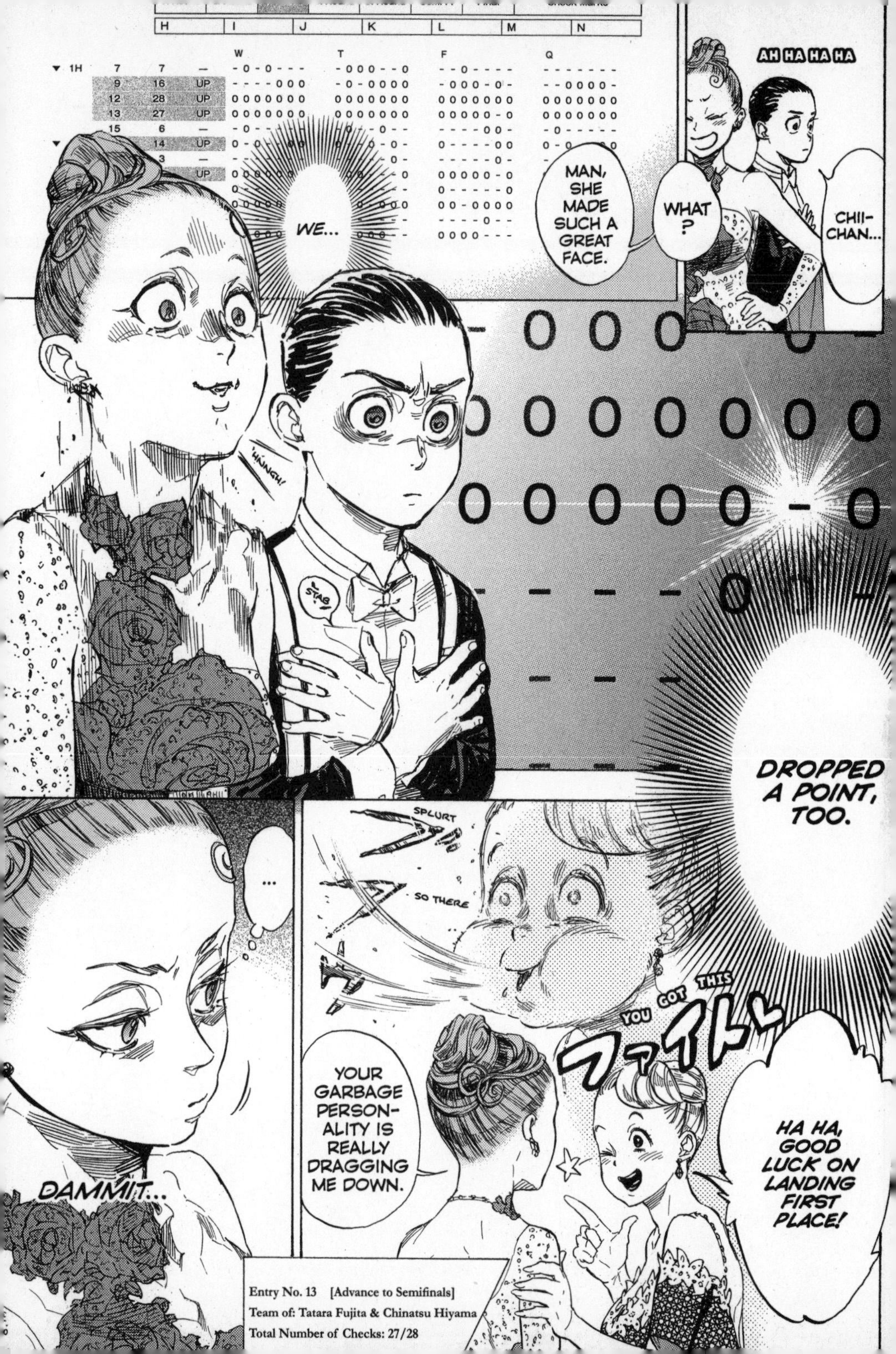
H I J K L M N
W T F Q
AH HA HA HA
CHII-CHAN...
WHAT?
MAN, SHE MADE SUCH A GREAT FACE.
WE...
HNNGH!
STAG
DROPPED A POINT, TOO.
SPLURT
SO THERE
YOU GOT THIS
ファイト♥
HA HA, GOOD LUCK ON LANDING FIRST PLACE!
YOUR GARBAGE PERSONALITY IS REALLY DRAGGING ME DOWN.
...
DAMMIT...
Entry No. 13 [Advance to Semifinals]
Team of: Tatara Fujita & Chinatsu Hiyama
Total Number of Checks: 27/28

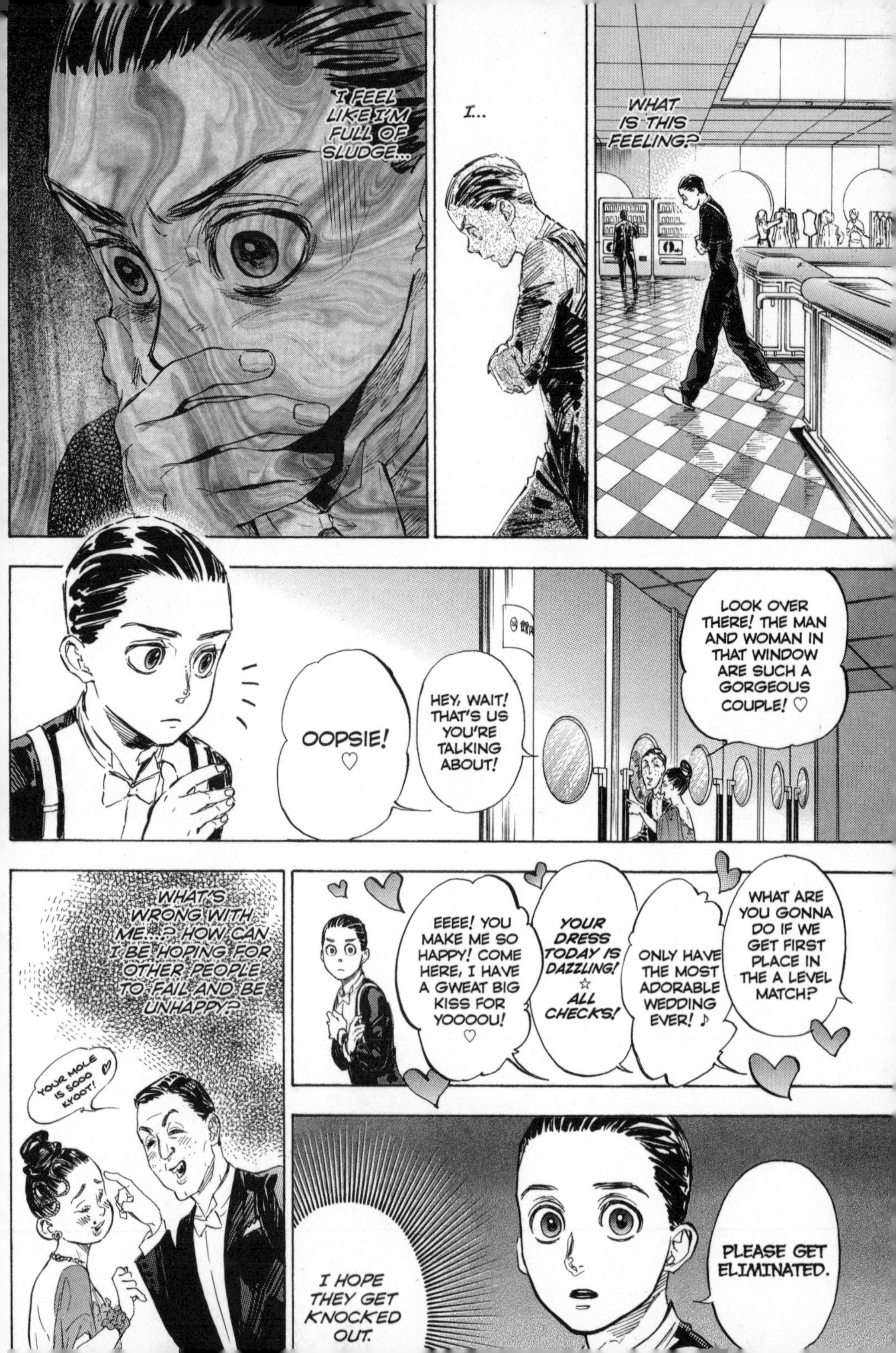
WHAT IS THIS FEELING?
I...
I FEEL LIKE I'M FULL OF SLUDGE...
LOOK OVER THERE! THE MAN AND WOMAN IN THAT WINDOW ARE SUCH A GORGEOUS COUPLE! ♡
HEY, WAIT! THAT'S US YOU'RE TALKING ABOUT!
OOPSIE! ♡
WHAT ARE YOU GONNA DO IF WE GET FIRST PLACE IN THE A LEVEL MATCH?
ONLY HAVE THE MOST ADORABLE WEDDING EVER! ♪
YOUR DRESS TODAY IS DAZZLING! ☆ ALL CHECKS!
EEEE! YOU MAKE ME SO HAPPY! COME HERE, I HAVE A GWEAT BIG KISS FOR YOOOOU! ♡
PLEASE GET ELIMINATED.
I HOPE THEY GET KNOCKED OUT.
WHAT'S WRONG WITH ME...? HOW CAN I BE HOPING FOR OTHER PEOPLE TO FAIL AND BE UNHAPPY?
YOUR MOLE IS SOOO KYOOT! ♡

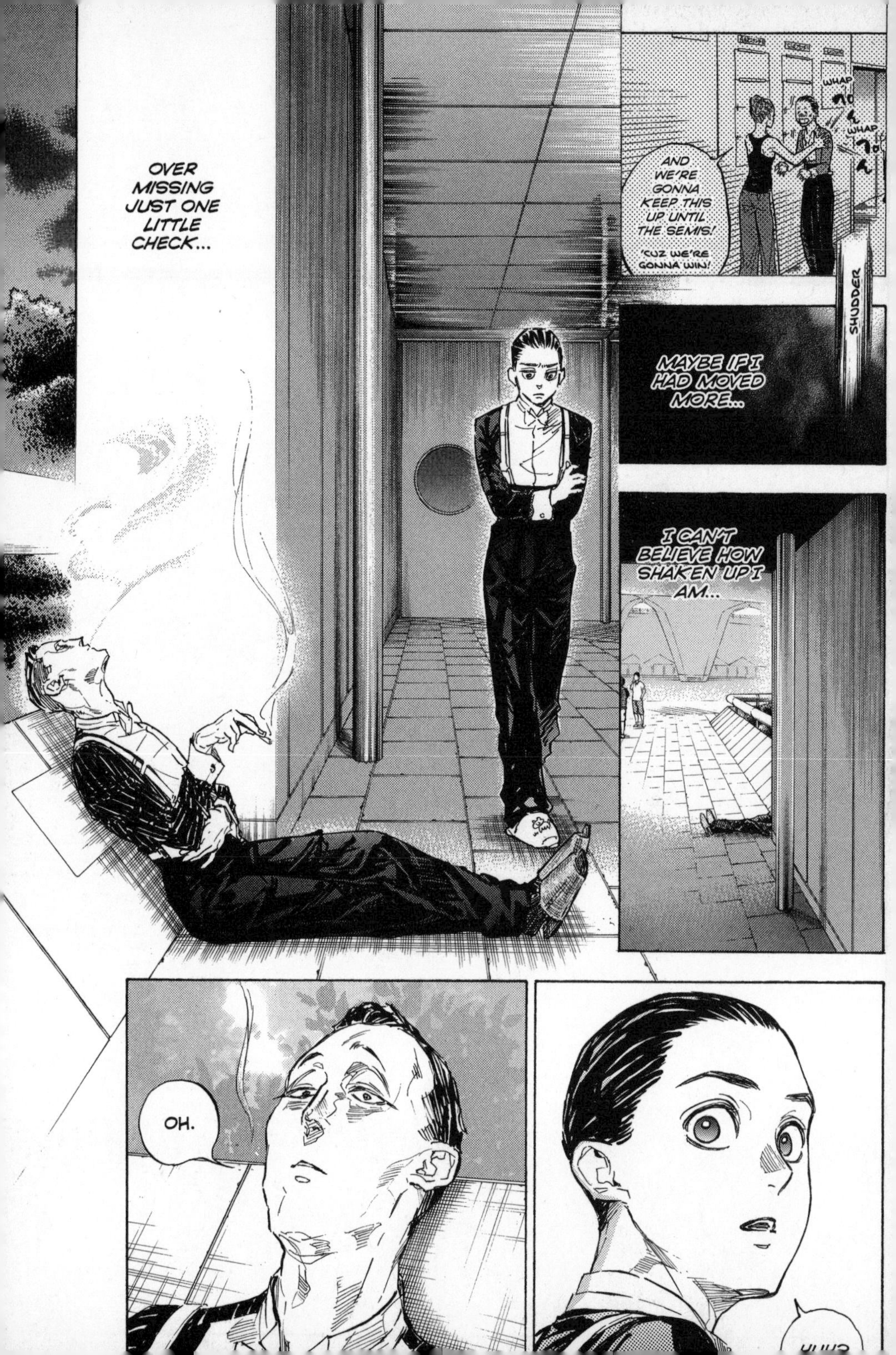
WHAP
WHAP
AND WE'RE GONNA KEEP THIS UP UNTIL THE SEMIS!
'CUZ WE'RE GONNA WIN!
SHUDDER
MAYBE IF I HAD MOVED MORE...
I CAN'T BELIEVE HOW SHAKEN UP I AM...
OVER MISSING JUST ONE LITTLE CHECK...
HUH?
OH.

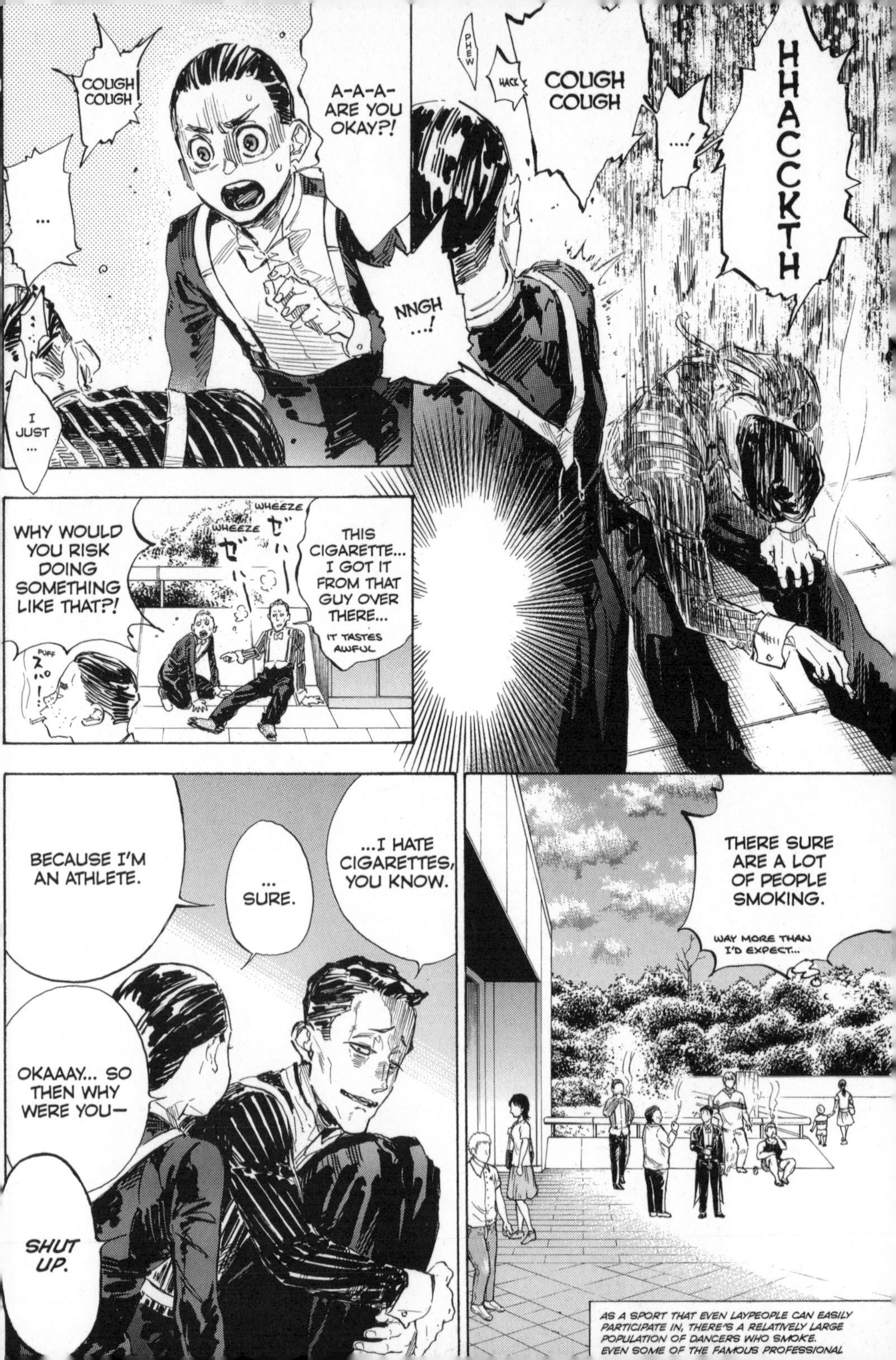
HHACCKTH
....!
COUGH COUGH
HACK
PHEW
NNGH ....!
A-A-A- ARE YOU OKAY?!
COUGH COUGH
...
I JUST ...
THIS CIGARETTE... I GOT IT FROM THAT GUY OVER THERE...
IT TASTES AWFUL
WHEEZE
WHEEZE
WHY WOULD YOU RISK DOING SOMETHING LIKE THAT?!
PUFF
THERE SURE ARE A LOT OF PEOPLE SMOKING.
WAY MORE THAN I'D EXPECT...
AS A SPORT THAT EVEN LAYPEOPLE CAN EASILY PARTICIPATE IN, THERE'S A RELATIVELY LARGE POPULATION OF DANCERS WHO SMOKE. EVEN SOME OF THE FAMOUS PROFESSIONAL
...I HATE CIGARETTES, YOU KNOW.
... SURE.
BECAUSE I'M AN ATHLETE.
OKAAAY... SO THEN WHY WERE YOU—
SHUT UP.

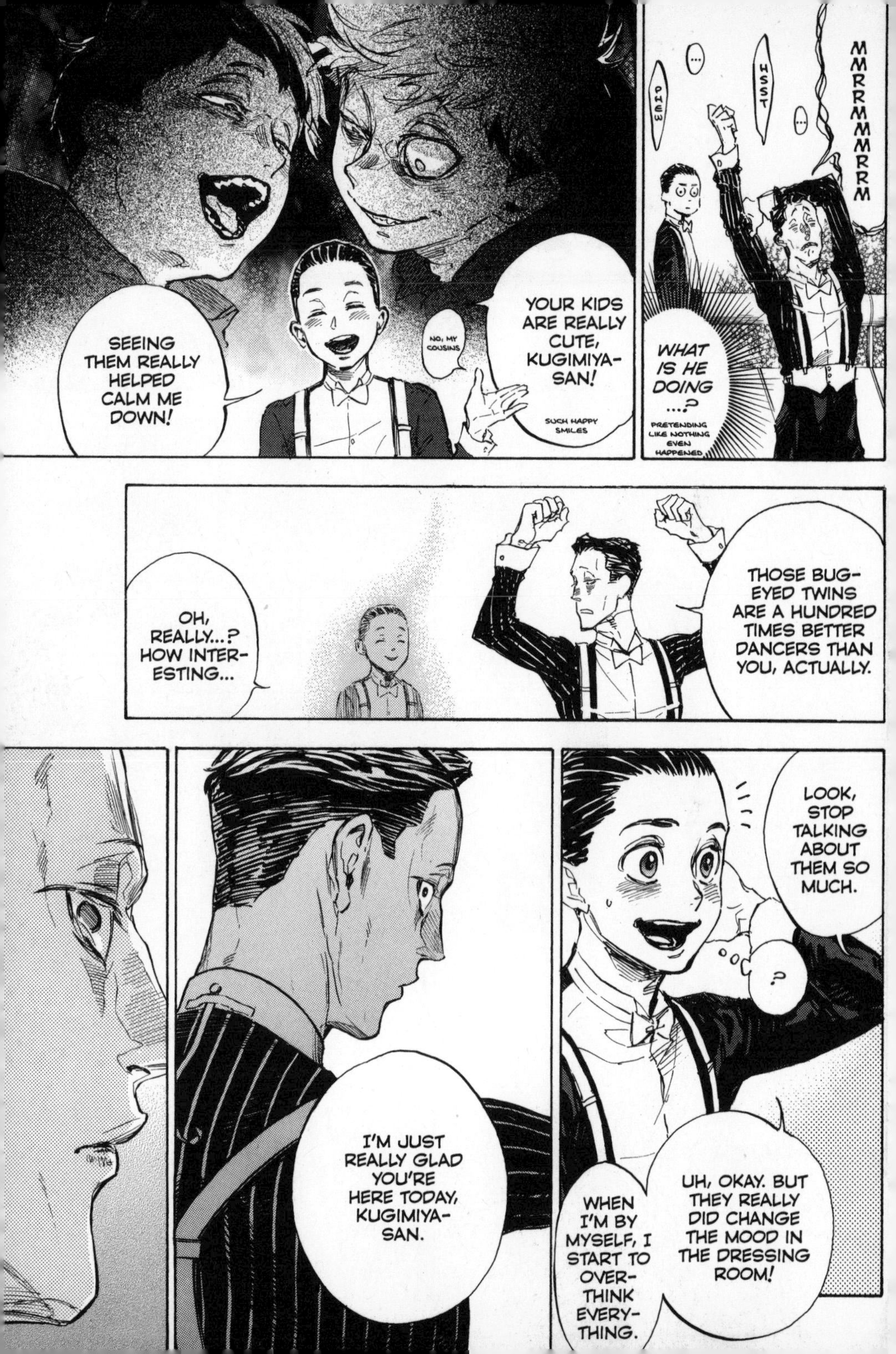
MMRRMMMRRM
...
HSST
...
PHEW
WHAT IS HE DOING ...?
PRETENDING LIKE NOTHING EVEN HAPPENED
YOUR KIDS ARE REALLY CUTE, KUGIMIYA-SAN!
SUCH HAPPY SMILES
NO, MY COUSINS
SEEING THEM REALLY HELPED CALM ME DOWN!
THOSE BUG-EYED TWINS ARE A HUNDRED TIMES BETTER DANCERS THAN YOU, ACTUALLY.
OH, REALLY...? HOW INTER-ESTING...
LOOK, STOP TALKING ABOUT THEM SO MUCH.
?
UH, OKAY. BUT THEY REALLY DID CHANGE THE MOOD IN THE DRESSING ROOM!
WHEN I'M BY MYSELF, I START TO OVER-THINK EVERY-THING.
I'M JUST REALLY GLAD YOU'RE HERE TODAY, KUGIMIYA-SAN.

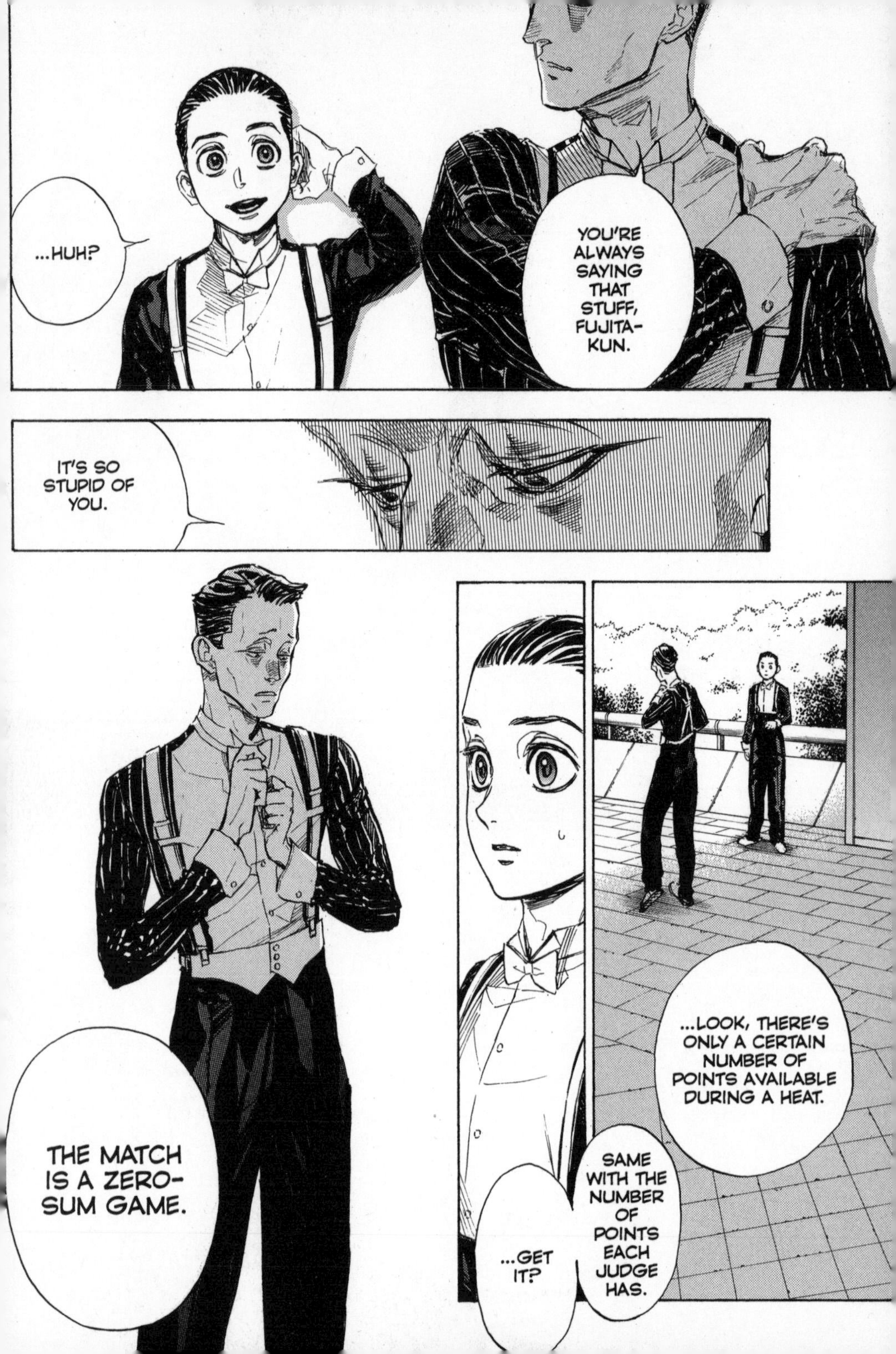
YOU'RE ALWAYS SAYING THAT STUFF, FUJITA-KUN.
...HUH?
IT'S SO STUPID OF YOU.
...LOOK, THERE'S ONLY A CERTAIN NUMBER OF POINTS AVAILABLE DURING A HEAT.
SAME WITH THE NUMBER OF POINTS EACH JUDGE HAS.
...GET IT?
THE MATCH IS A ZERO-SUM GAME.

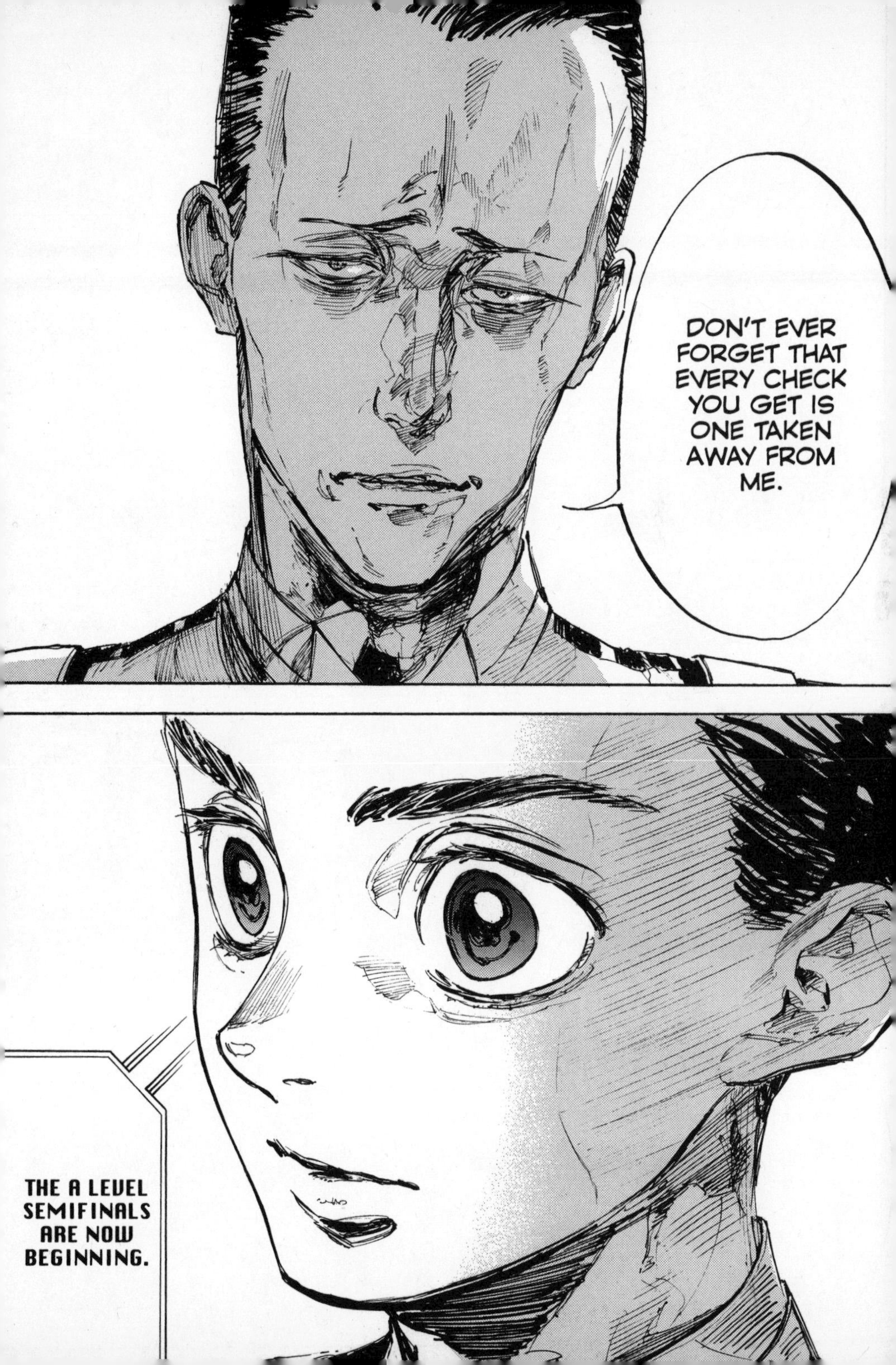
DON'T EVER FORGET THAT EVERY CHECK YOU GET IS ONE TAKEN AWAY FROM ME.
THE A LEVEL SEMIFINALS ARE NOW BEGINNING.

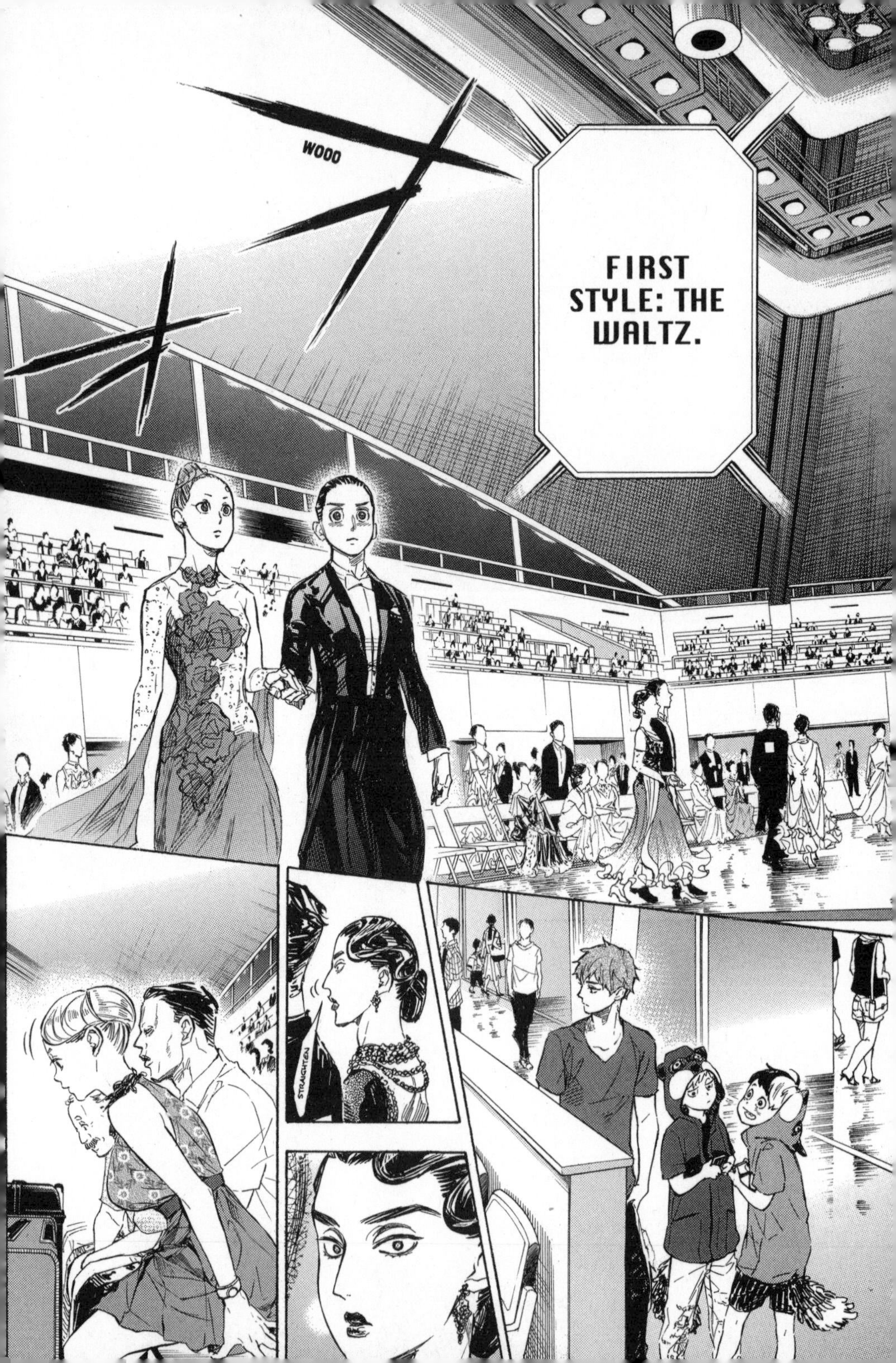
WOOO
FIRST STYLE: THE WALTZ.
STRAIGHTEN

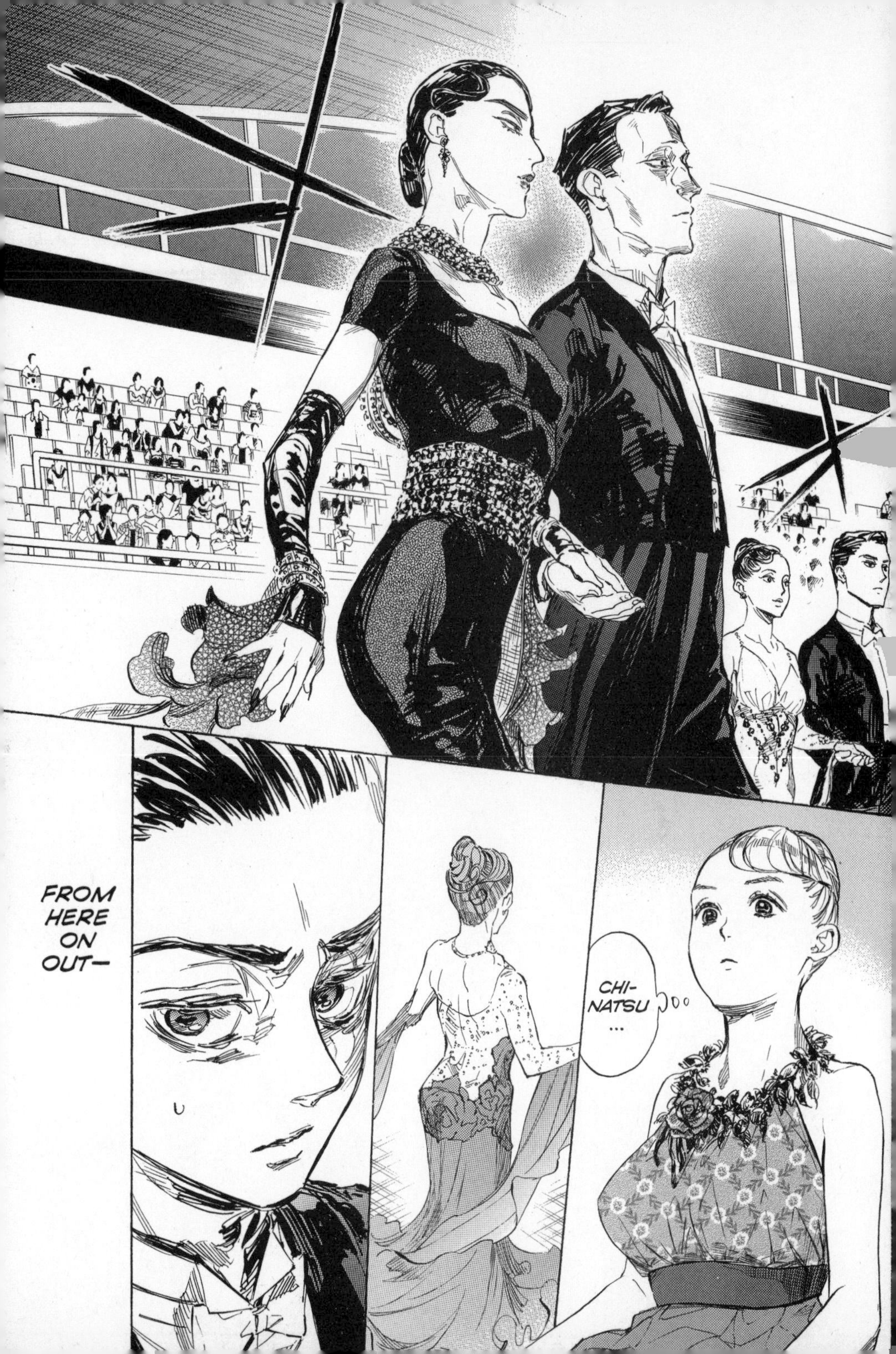
CHI-NATSU ...
FROM HERE ON OUT—

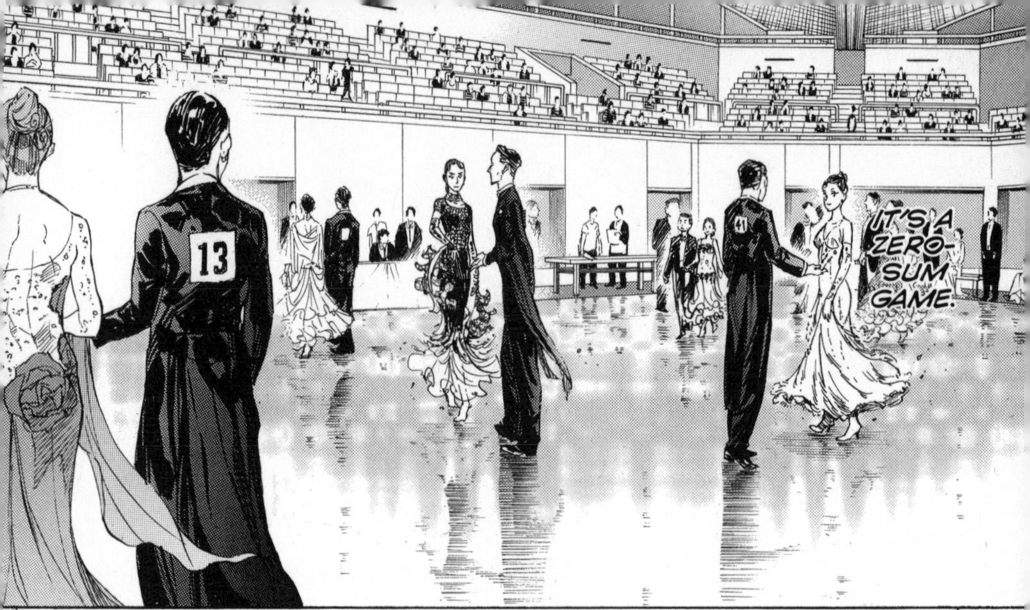
IT'S A ZERO-SUM GAME.
13
41

1-5	6-10	11-15	16-20

PARTICIPANT TRANSMITTAL

[PART. CONF. / COMP. / SAVE]
[ORG.]

No. 122 : DSCJ A-LEVEL STANDARD FLOOR A						
1. Round	2. Round	3. Round	4. Round	5. Round	Semi F.	Final

1 Heat	12 c.
Pick Up	6
Check Marks	

D a n c e				—
W	T	V	F	Q
S	C	R	P	J

Couple No	9	12	13	26	30	32	39	41	42	45	46	49								
1 Heat	YAZAWA	SAI	FUJITA	NAGATA	OTSUBO	MURAKAWA	SATO	NAKAMURA	KUGIMIYA	TAZAWA	HARAGUCHI	KINOSHITA								

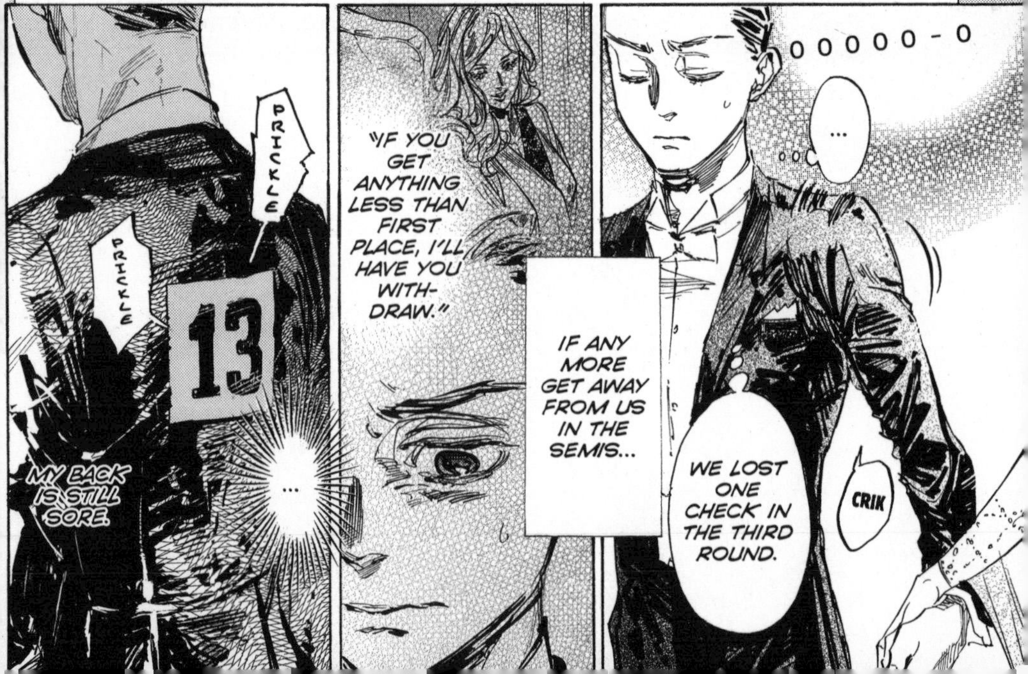
00000-0
...
WE LOST ONE CHECK IN THE THIRD ROUND.
CRIK
IF ANY MORE GET AWAY FROM US IN THE SEMIS...
"IF YOU GET ANYTHING LESS THAN FIRST PLACE, I'LL HAVE YOU WITHDRAW."
...
PRICKLE
PRICKLE
13
MY BACK IS STILL SORE.

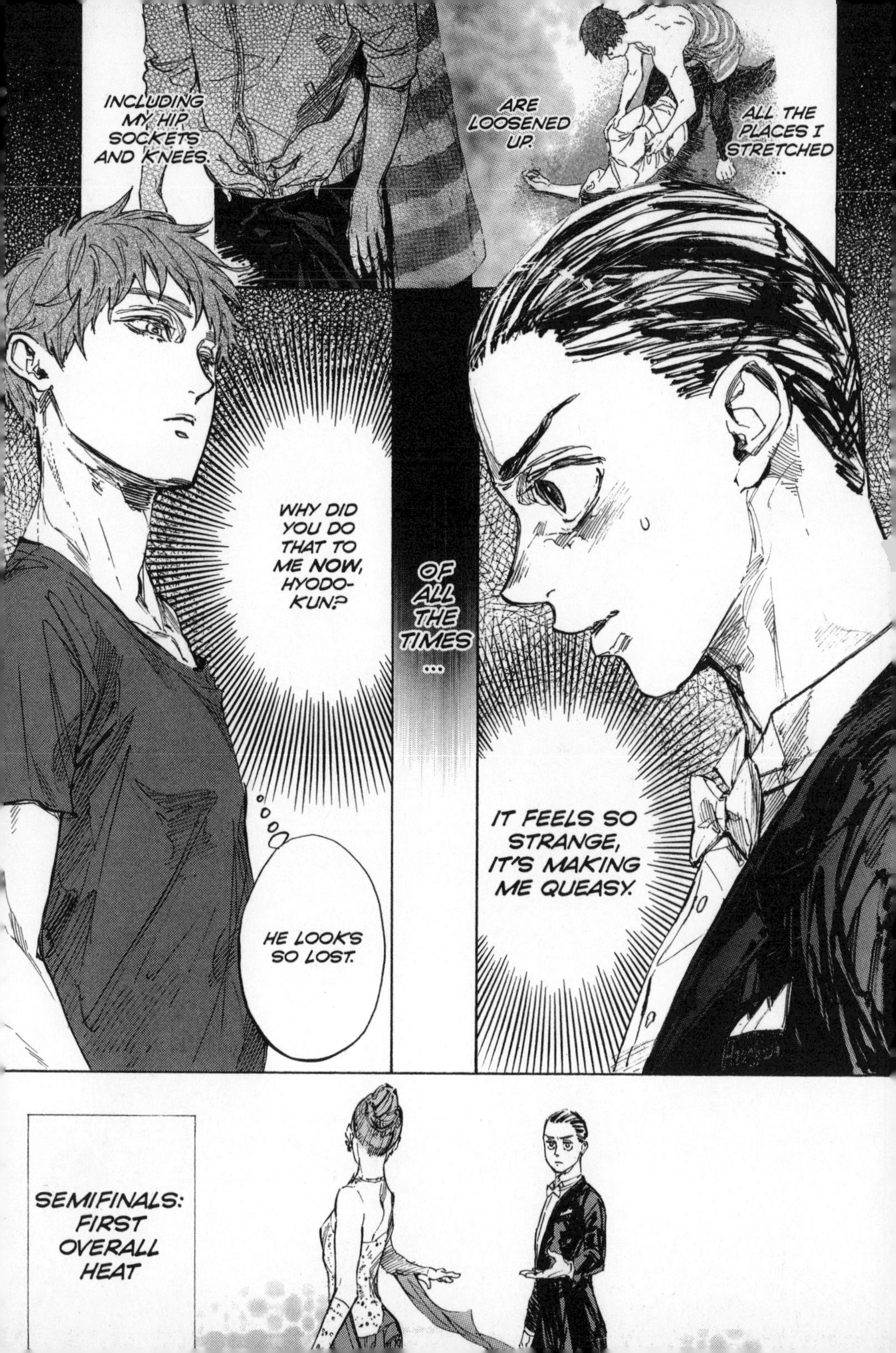
ALL THE PLACES I STRETCHED ...
ARE LOOSENED UP.
INCLUDING MY HIP SOCKETS AND KNEES.
OF ALL THE TIMES ...
WHY DID YOU DO THAT TO ME NOW, HYODO-KUN?
IT FEELS SO STRANGE, IT'S MAKING ME QUEASY.
HE LOOKS SO LOST.
SEMIFINALS: FIRST OVERALL HEAT

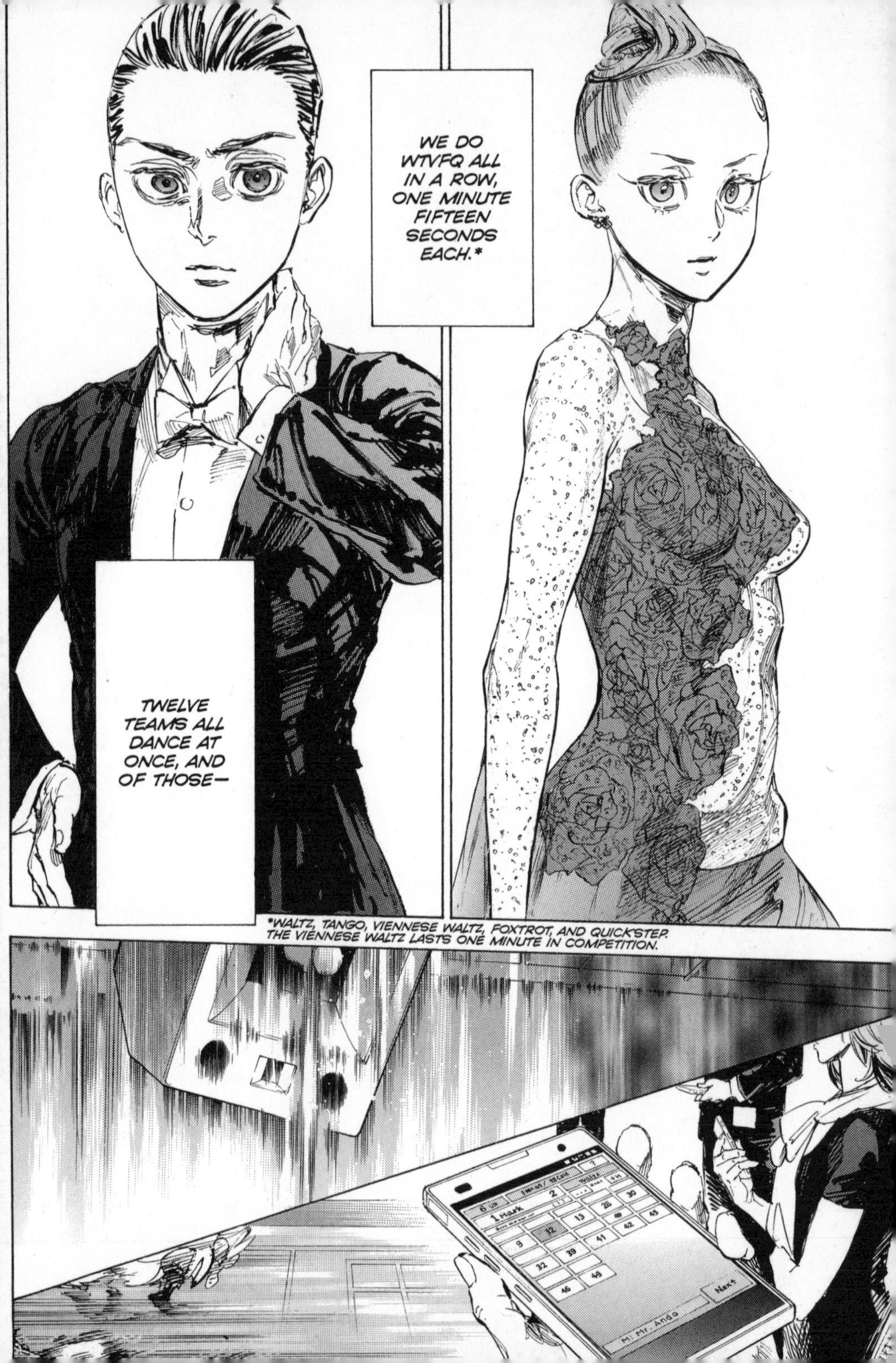

WE DO WTVFQ ALL IN A ROW, ONE MINUTE FIFTEEN SECONDS EACH.*
TWELVE TEAMS ALL DANCE AT ONCE, AND OF THOSE—
*WALTZ, TANGO, VIENNESE WALTZ, FOXTROT, AND QUICKSTEP. THE VIENNESE WALTZ LASTS ONE MINUTE IN COMPETITION.

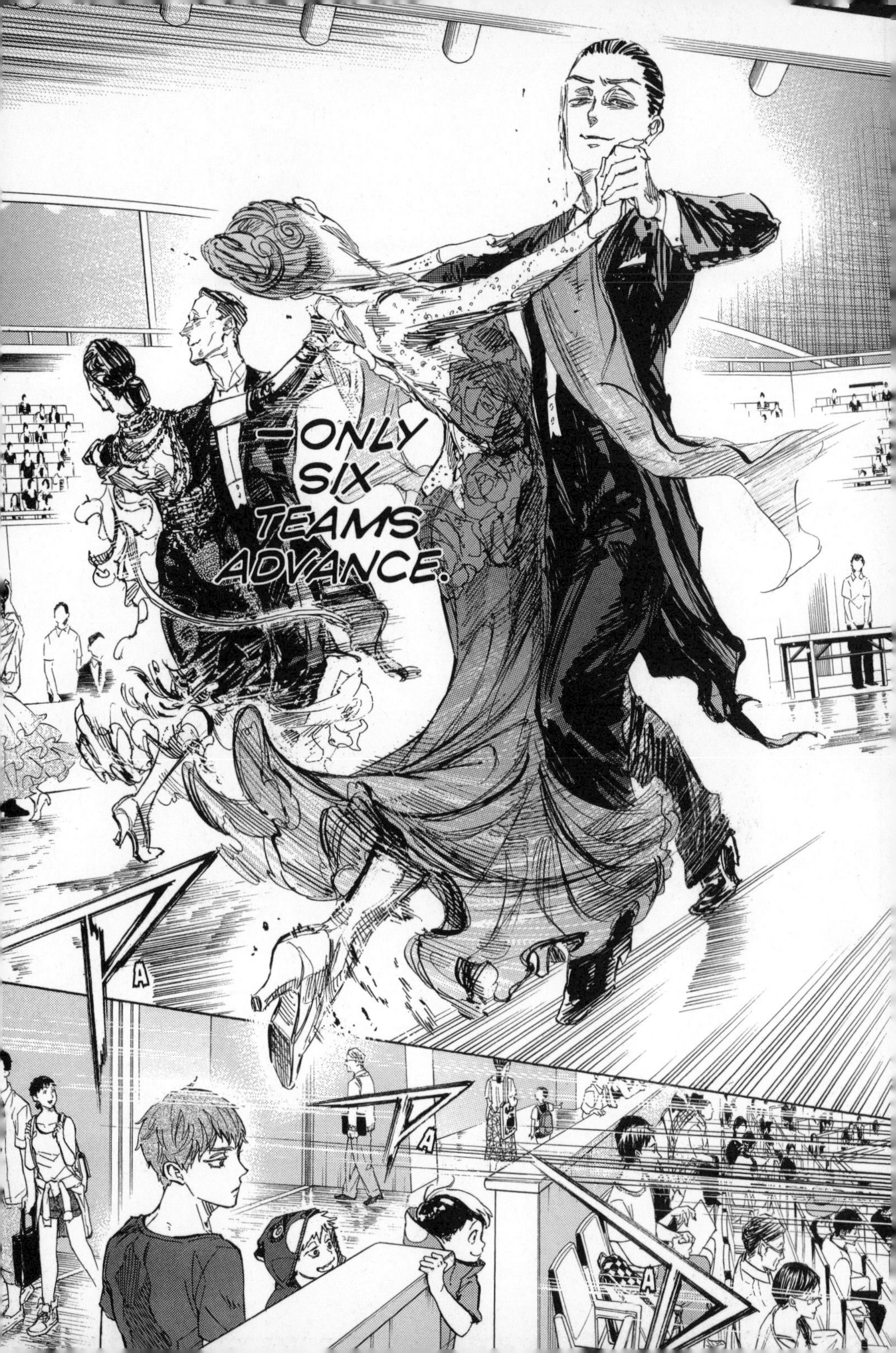
—ONLY SIX TEAMS ADVANCE.
PA
PA
PA

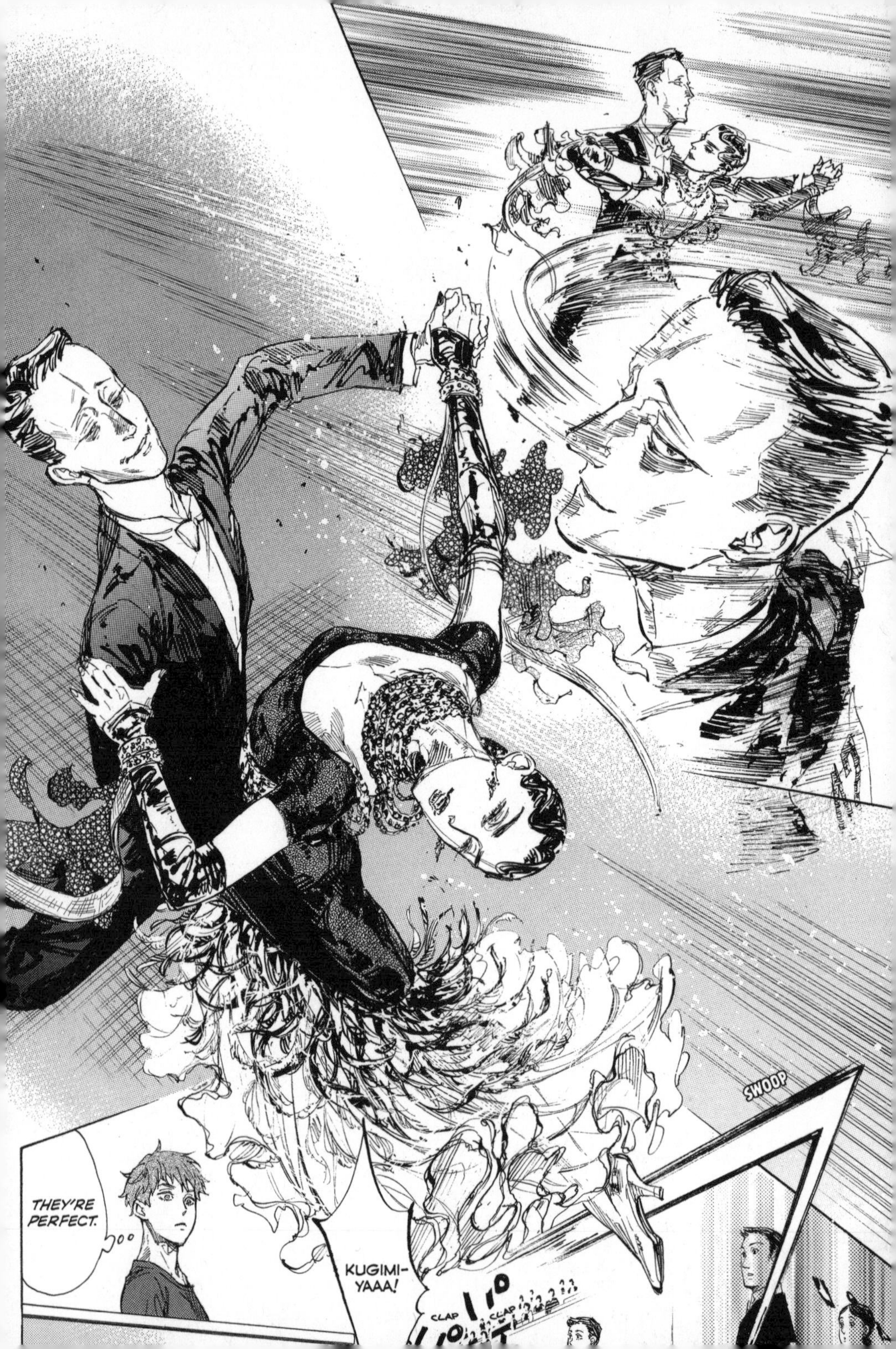
SWOOP
KUGIMI-YAAA!
CLAP CLAP
THEY'RE PERFECT.

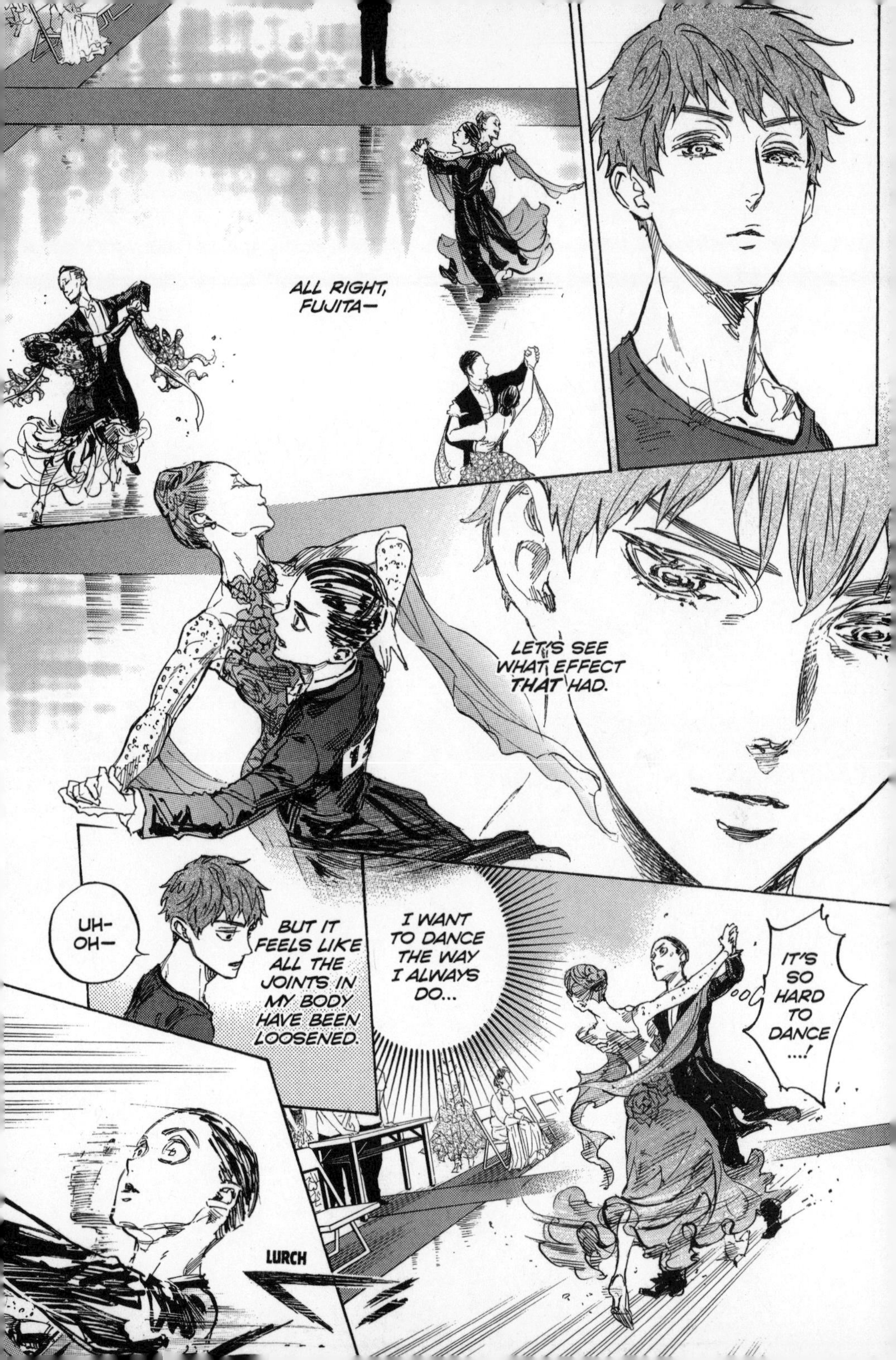
ALL RIGHT, FUJITA—
LET'S SEE WHAT EFFECT THAT HAD.
IT'S SO HARD TO DANCE...!
I WANT TO DANCE THE WAY I ALWAYS DO...
BUT IT FEELS LIKE ALL THE JOINTS IN MY BODY HAVE BEEN LOOSENED.
UH-OH—
LURCH

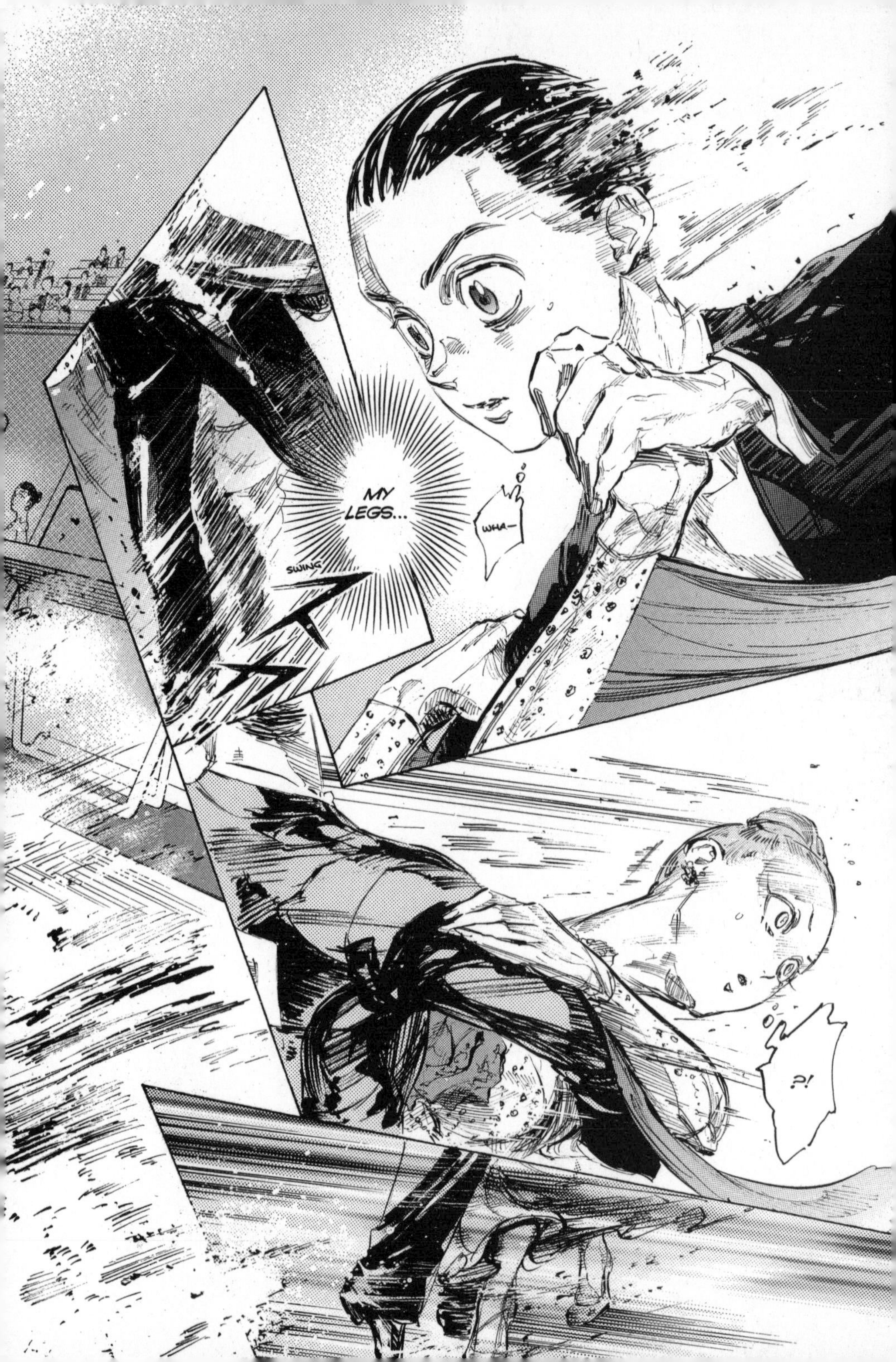
WHA-
MY LEGS...
SWING
?!

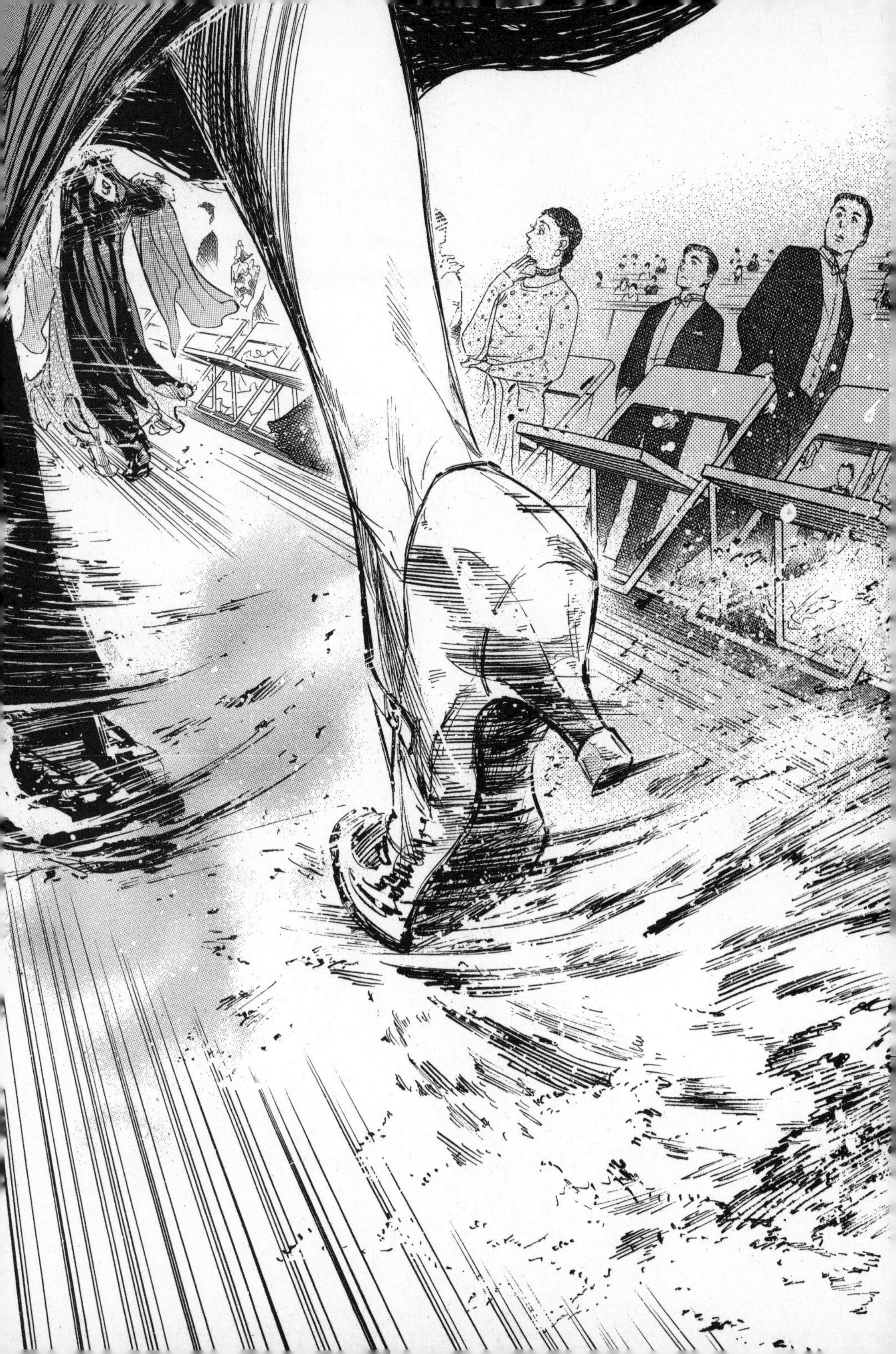

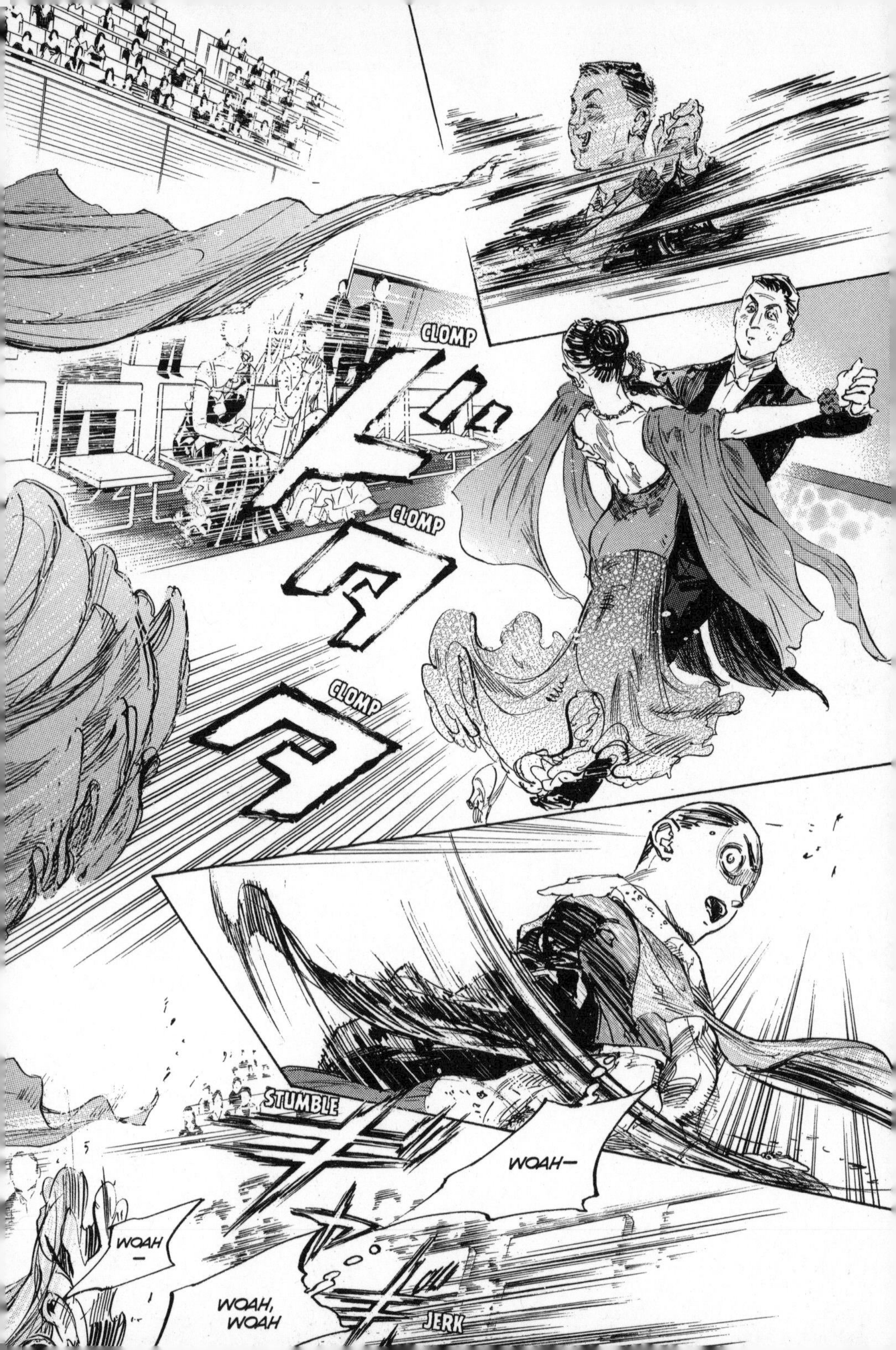

CLOMP
CLOMP
CLOMP
WOAH—
STUMBLE
JERK
WOAH —
WOAH, WOAH

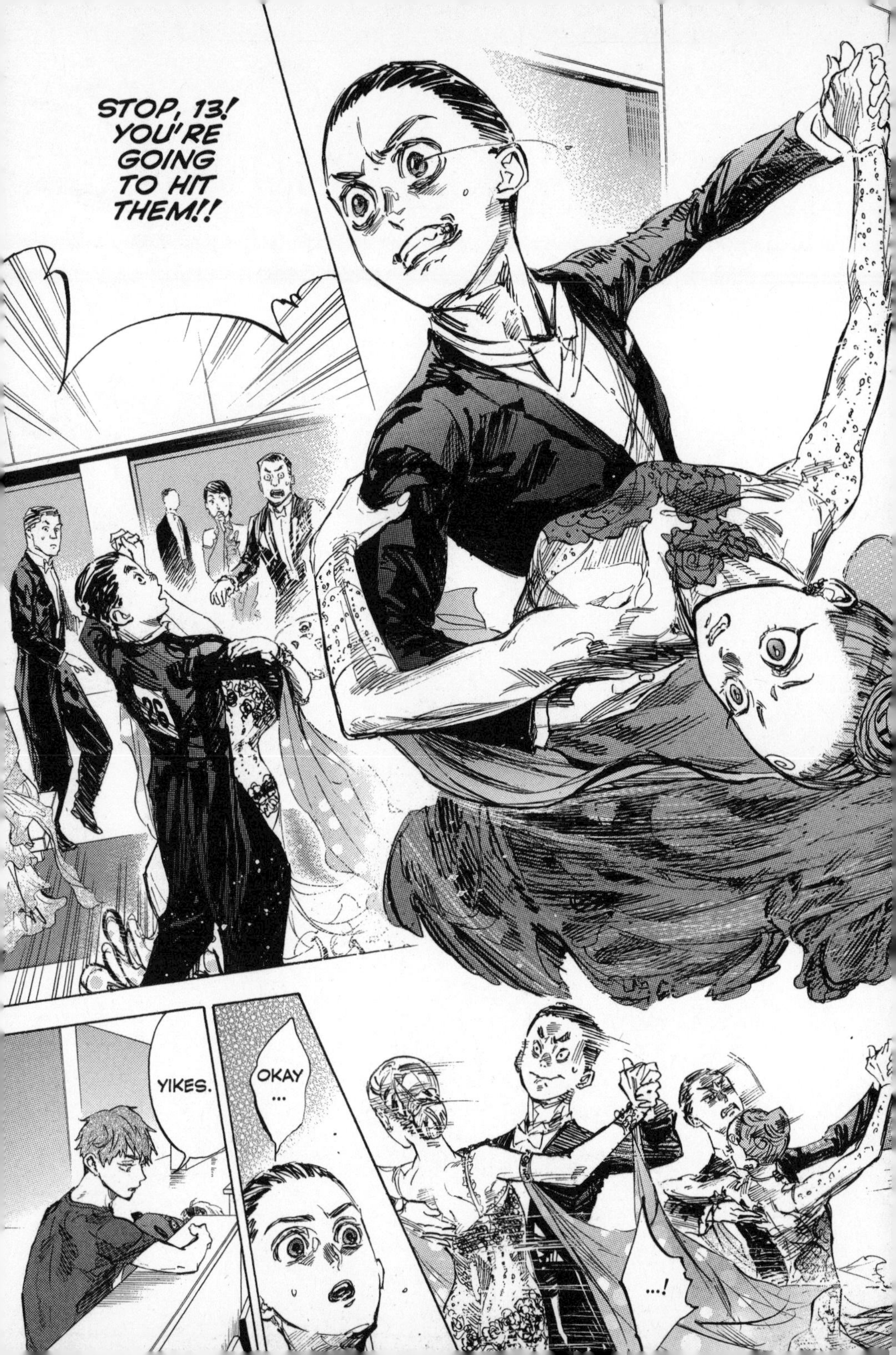
STOP, 13! YOU'RE GOING TO HIT THEM!!
...!
OKAY ...
YIKES.

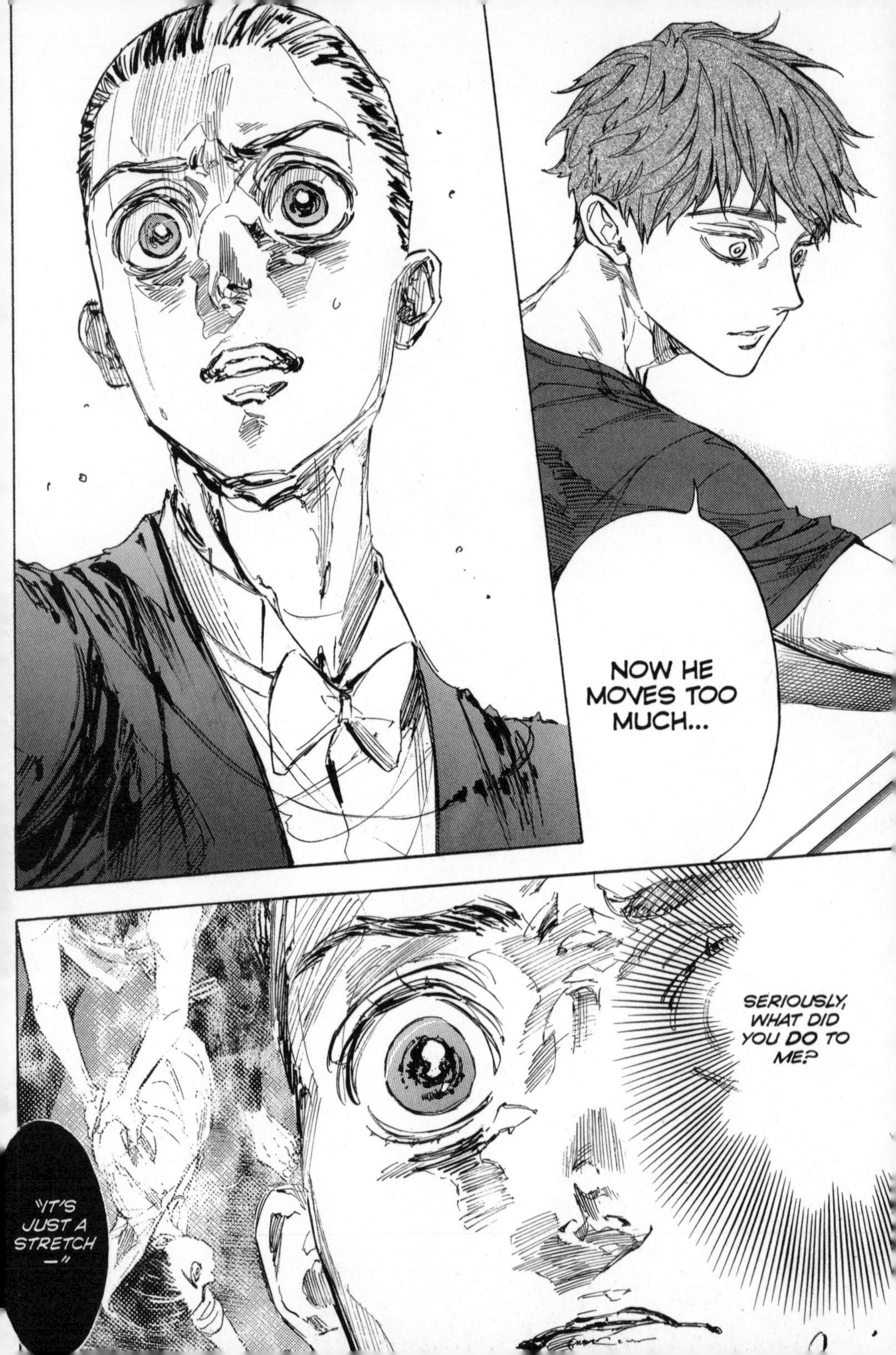
NOW HE MOVES TOO MUCH...
SERIOUSLY, WHAT DID YOU DO TO ME?
"IT'S JUST A STRETCH—"

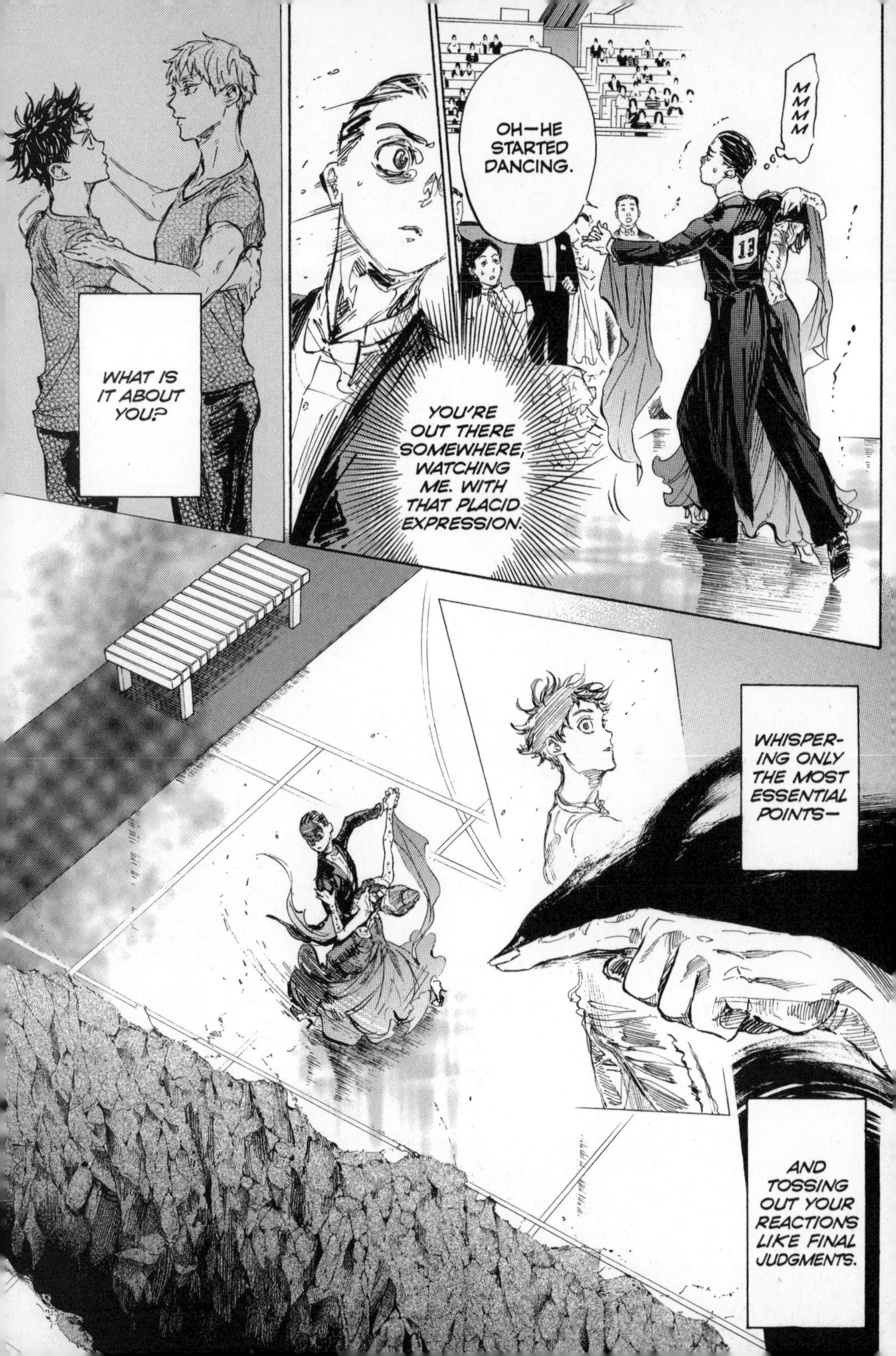
MMMM
OH—HE STARTED DANCING.
YOU'RE OUT THERE SOMEWHERE, WATCHING ME. WITH THAT PLACID EXPRESSION.
WHAT IS IT ABOUT YOU?
WHISPER-ING ONLY THE MOST ESSENTIAL POINTS—
AND TOSSING OUT YOUR REACTIONS LIKE FINAL JUDGMENTS.

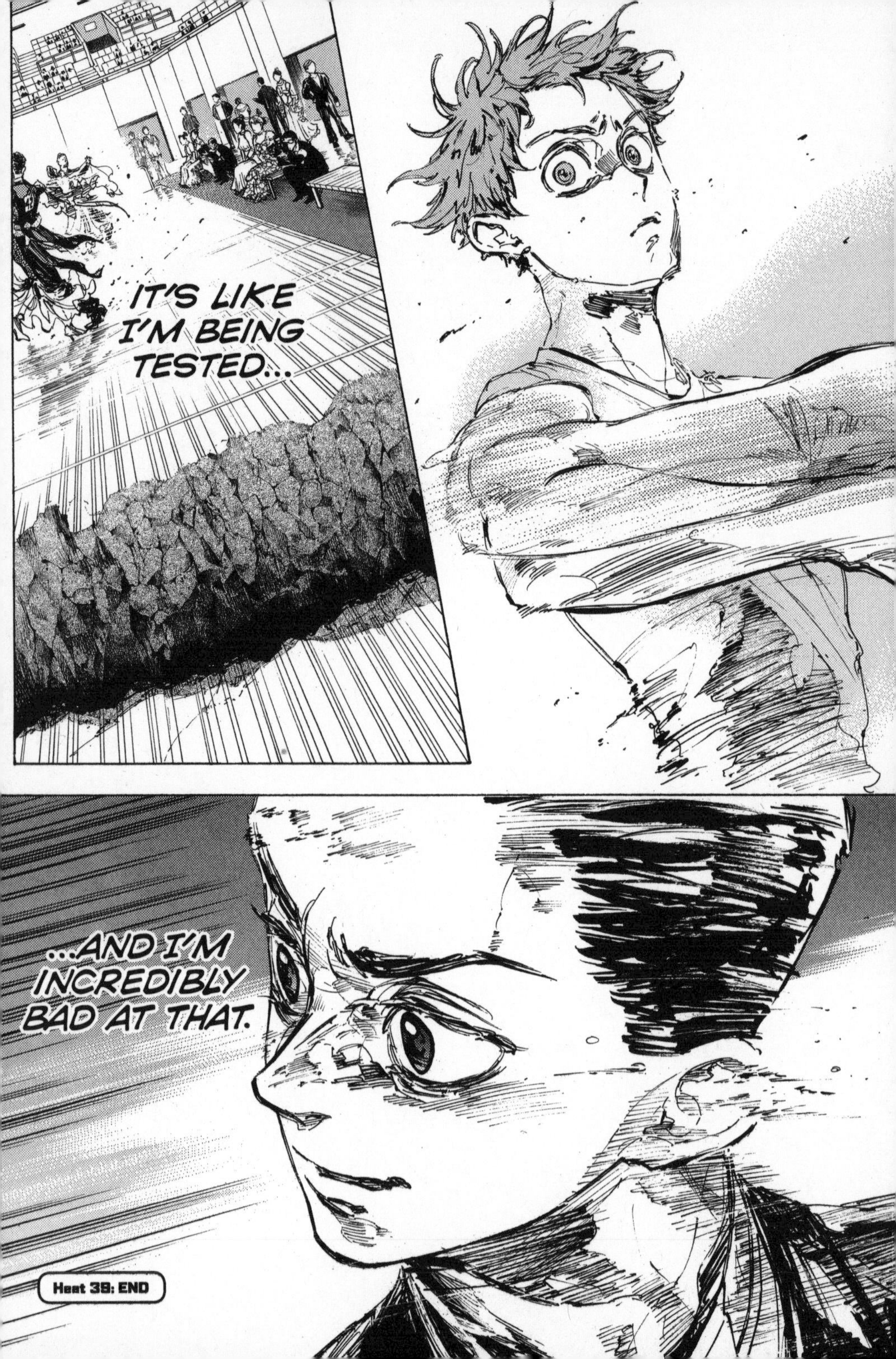
IT'S LIKE I'M BEING TESTED...
...AND I'M INCREDIBLY BAD AT THAT.
Heat 39: END

WELCOME TO THE BALLROOM

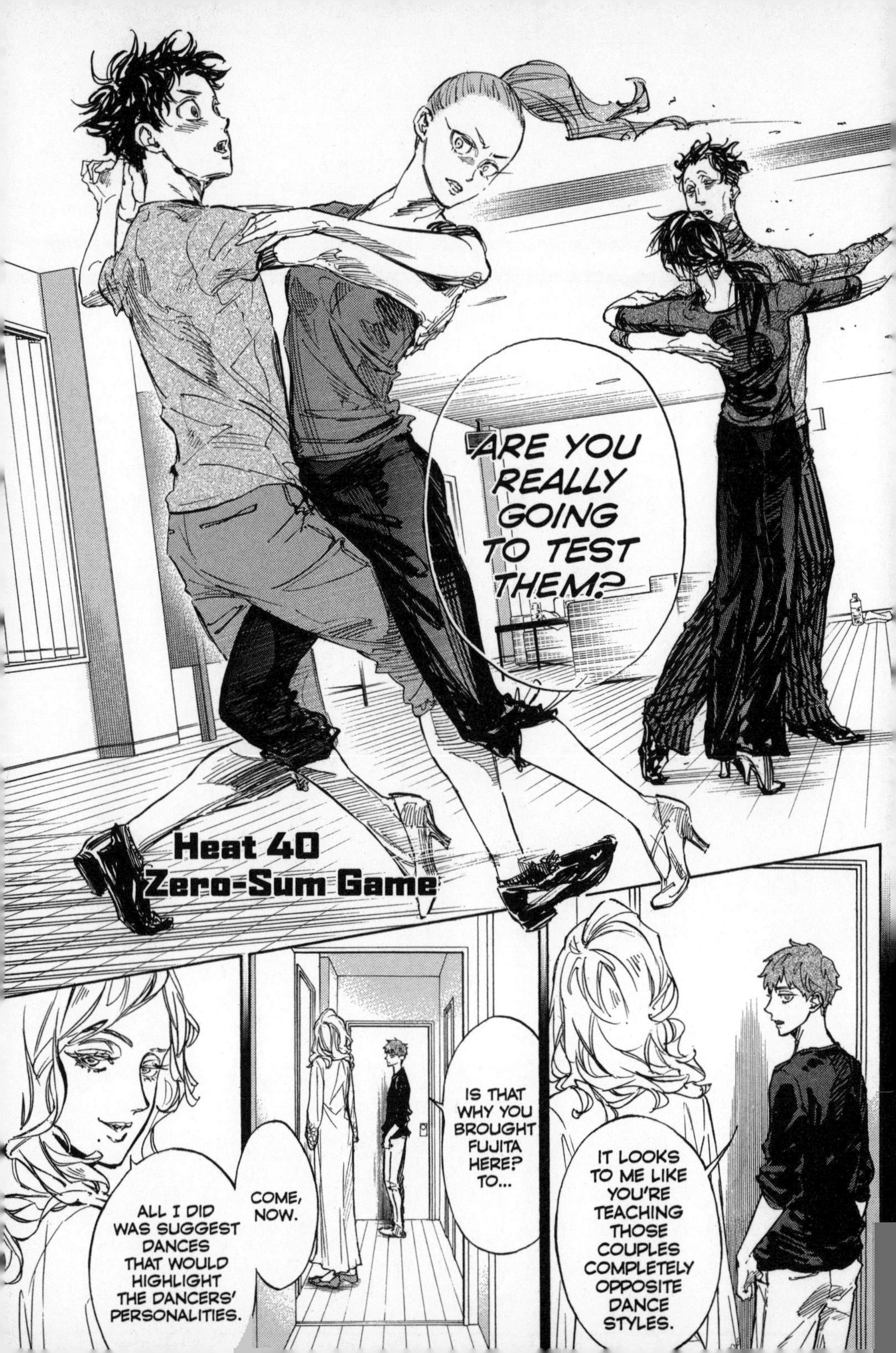
ARE YOU REALLY GOING TO TEST THEM?
Heat 40
Zero-Sum Game
IT LOOKS TO ME LIKE YOU'RE TEACHING THOSE COUPLES COMPLETELY OPPOSITE DANCE STYLES.
IS THAT WHY YOU BROUGHT FUJITA HERE? TO...
COME, NOW.
ALL I DID WAS SUGGEST DANCES THAT WOULD HIGHLIGHT THE DANCERS' PERSONALITIES.

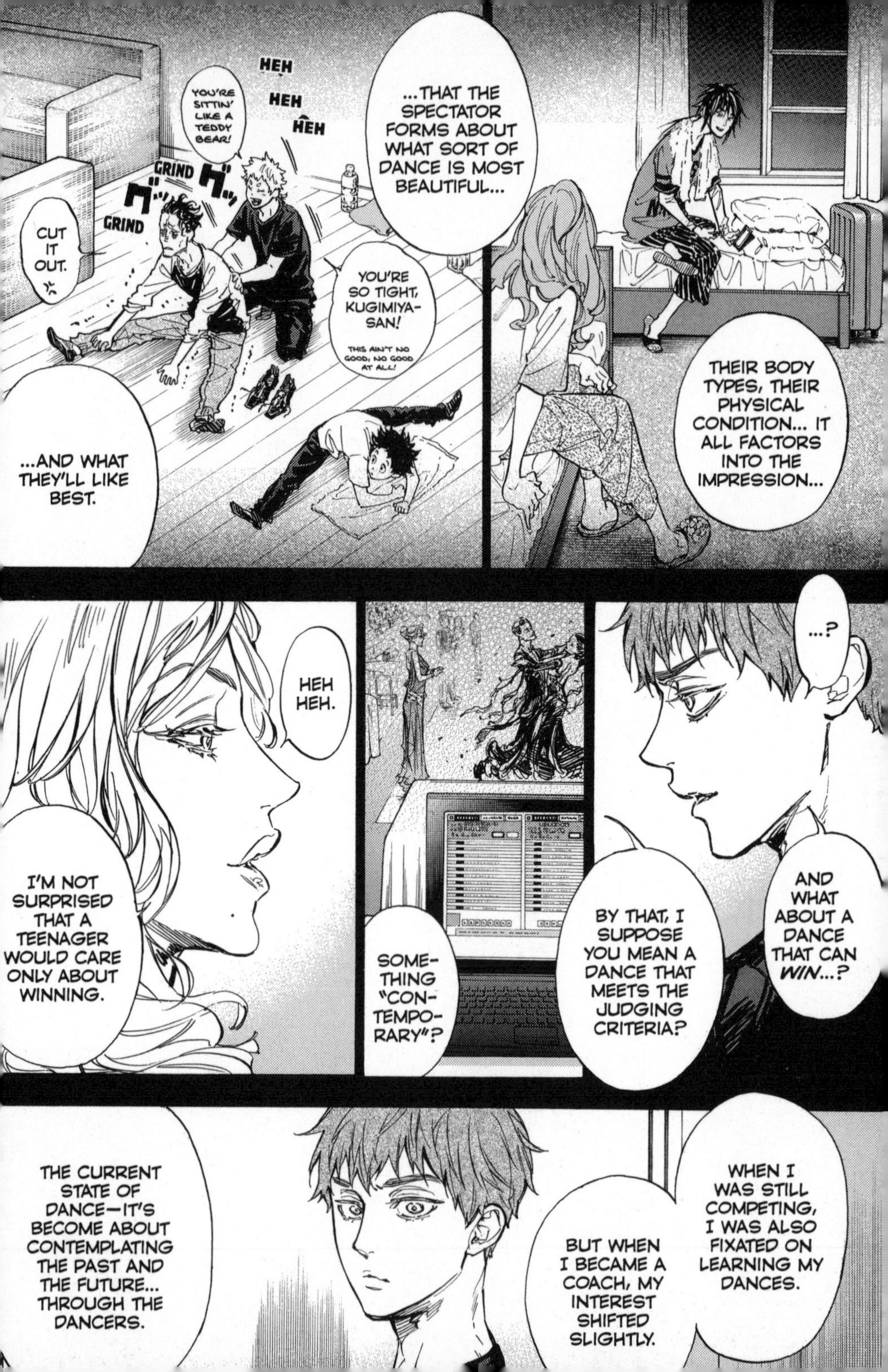
THEIR BODY TYPES, THEIR PHYSICAL CONDITION... IT ALL FACTORS INTO THE IMPRESSION...
...THAT THE SPECTATOR FORMS ABOUT WHAT SORT OF DANCE IS MOST BEAUTIFUL...
HEH HEH HEH
YOU'RE SITTIN' LIKE A TEDDY BEAR!
GRIND GRIND
CUT IT OUT.
YOU'RE SO TIGHT, KUGIMIYA-SAN!
THIS AIN'T NO GOOD, NO GOOD AT ALL!
...AND WHAT THEY'LL LIKE BEST.
...?
AND WHAT ABOUT A DANCE THAT CAN *WIN*...?
BY THAT, I SUPPOSE YOU MEAN A DANCE THAT MEETS THE JUDGING CRITERIA?
SOME-THING "CON-TEMPO-RARY"?
HEH HEH.
I'M NOT SURPRISED THAT A TEENAGER WOULD CARE ONLY ABOUT WINNING.
WHEN I WAS STILL COMPETING, I WAS ALSO FIXATED ON LEARNING MY DANCES.
BUT WHEN I BECAME A COACH, MY INTEREST SHIFTED SLIGHTLY.
THE CURRENT STATE OF DANCE—IT'S BECOME ABOUT CONTEMPLATING THE PAST AND THE FUTURE... THROUGH THE DANCERS.

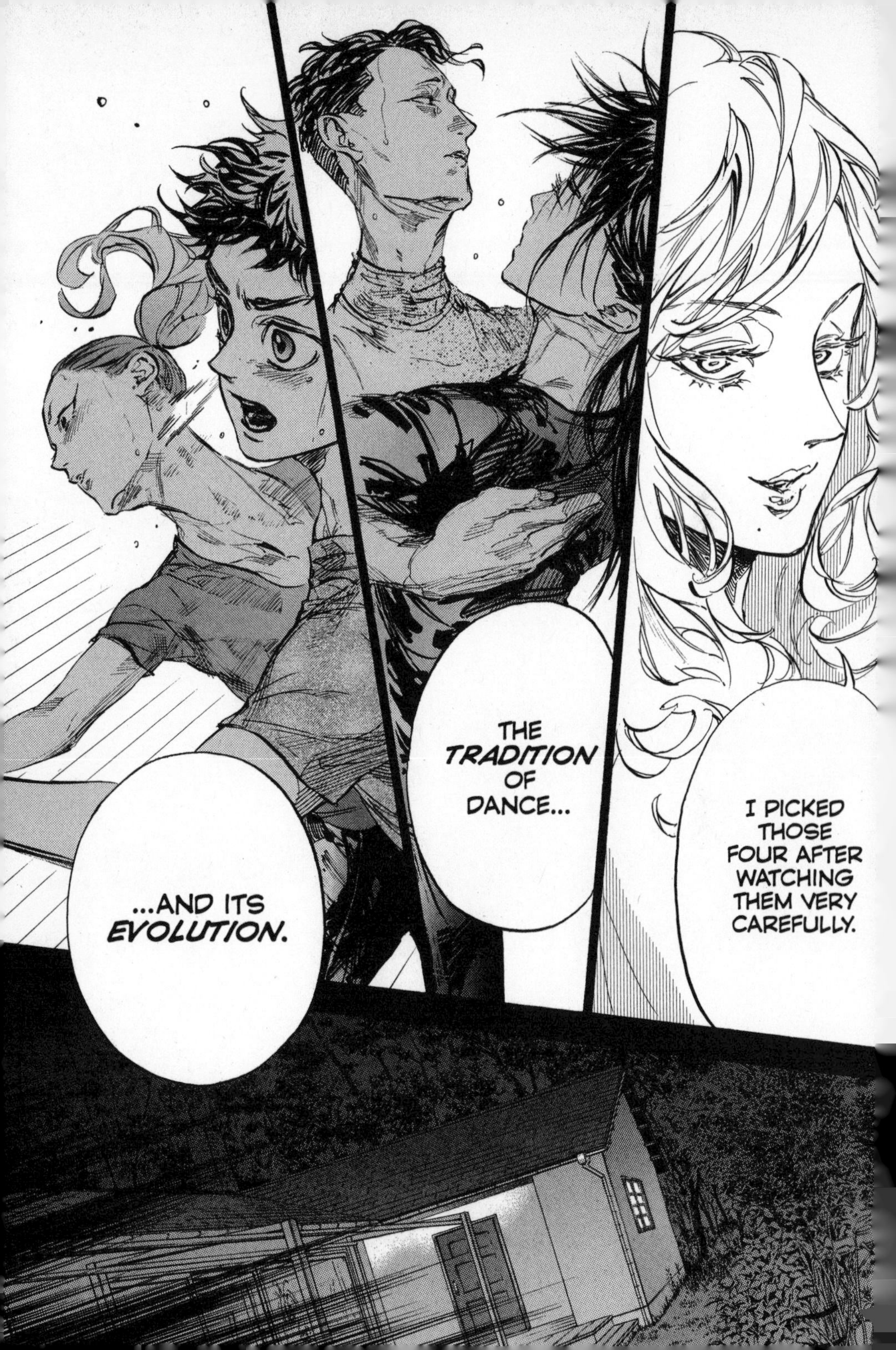
I PICKED THOSE FOUR AFTER WATCHING THEM VERY CAREFULLY.
THE *TRADITION* OF DANCE...
...AND ITS *EVOLUTION*.

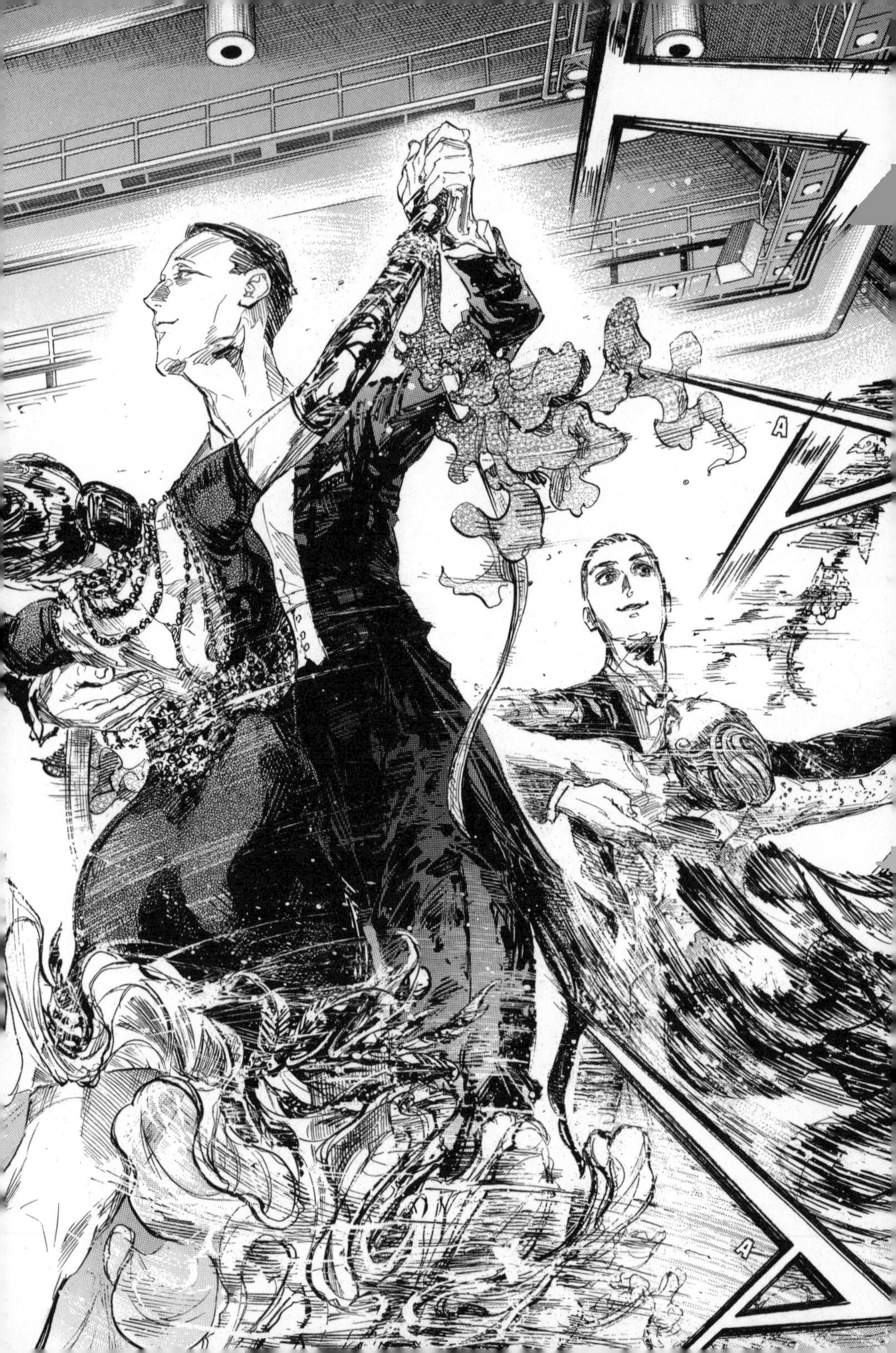

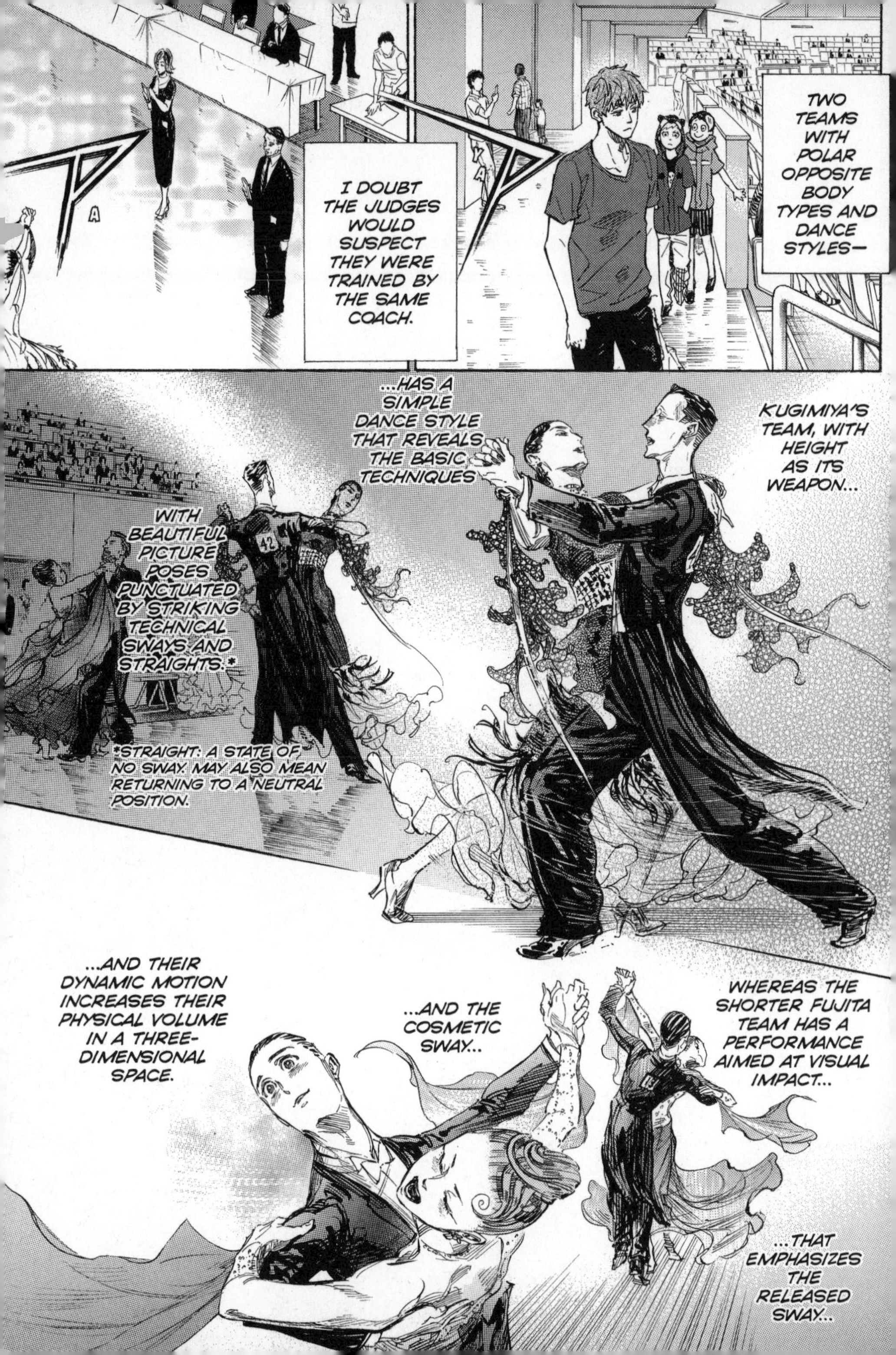
TWO TEAMS WITH POLAR OPPOSITE BODY TYPES AND DANCE STYLES—
I DOUBT THE JUDGES WOULD SUSPECT THEY WERE TRAINED BY THE SAME COACH.
KUGIMIYA'S TEAM, WITH HEIGHT AS ITS WEAPON...
...HAS A SIMPLE DANCE STYLE THAT REVEALS THE BASIC TECHNIQUES
WITH BEAUTIFUL PICTURE POSES PUNCTUATED BY STRIKING TECHNICAL SWAYS AND STRAIGHTS.*
*STRAIGHT: A STATE OF NO SWAY. MAY ALSO MEAN RETURNING TO A NEUTRAL POSITION.
WHEREAS THE SHORTER FUJITA TEAM HAS A PERFORMANCE AIMED AT VISUAL IMPACT...
...THAT EMPHASIZES THE RELEASED SWAY...
...AND THE COSMETIC SWAY...
...AND THEIR DYNAMIC MOTION INCREASES THEIR PHYSICAL VOLUME IN A THREE-DIMENSIONAL SPACE.

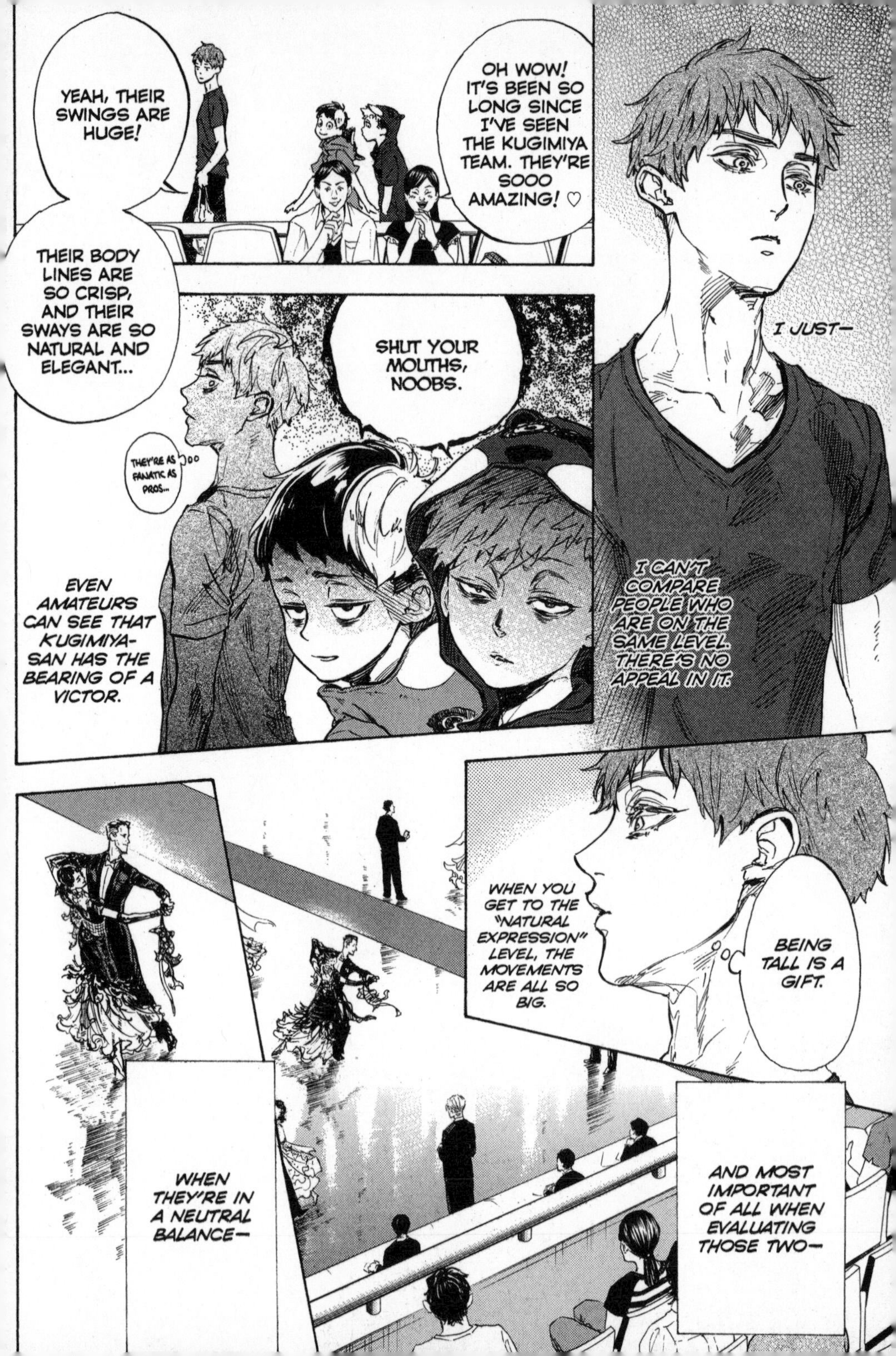

I JUST—
I CAN'T COMPARE PEOPLE WHO ARE ON THE SAME LEVEL. THERE'S NO APPEAL IN IT.
OH WOW! IT'S BEEN SO LONG SINCE I'VE SEEN THE KUGIMIYA TEAM. THEY'RE SOOO AMAZING! ♡
YEAH, THEIR SWINGS ARE HUGE!
THEIR BODY LINES ARE SO CRISP, AND THEIR SWAYS ARE SO NATURAL AND ELEGANT...
SHUT YOUR MOUTHS, NOOBS.
THEY'RE AS FANATIC AS PROS...
EVEN AMATEURS CAN SEE THAT KUGIMIYA-SAN HAS THE BEARING OF A VICTOR.
WHEN YOU GET TO THE "NATURAL EXPRESSION" LEVEL, THE MOVEMENTS ARE ALL SO BIG.
BEING TALL IS A GIFT.
AND MOST IMPORTANT OF ALL WHEN EVALUATING THOSE TWO—
WHEN THEY'RE IN A NEUTRAL BALANCE—

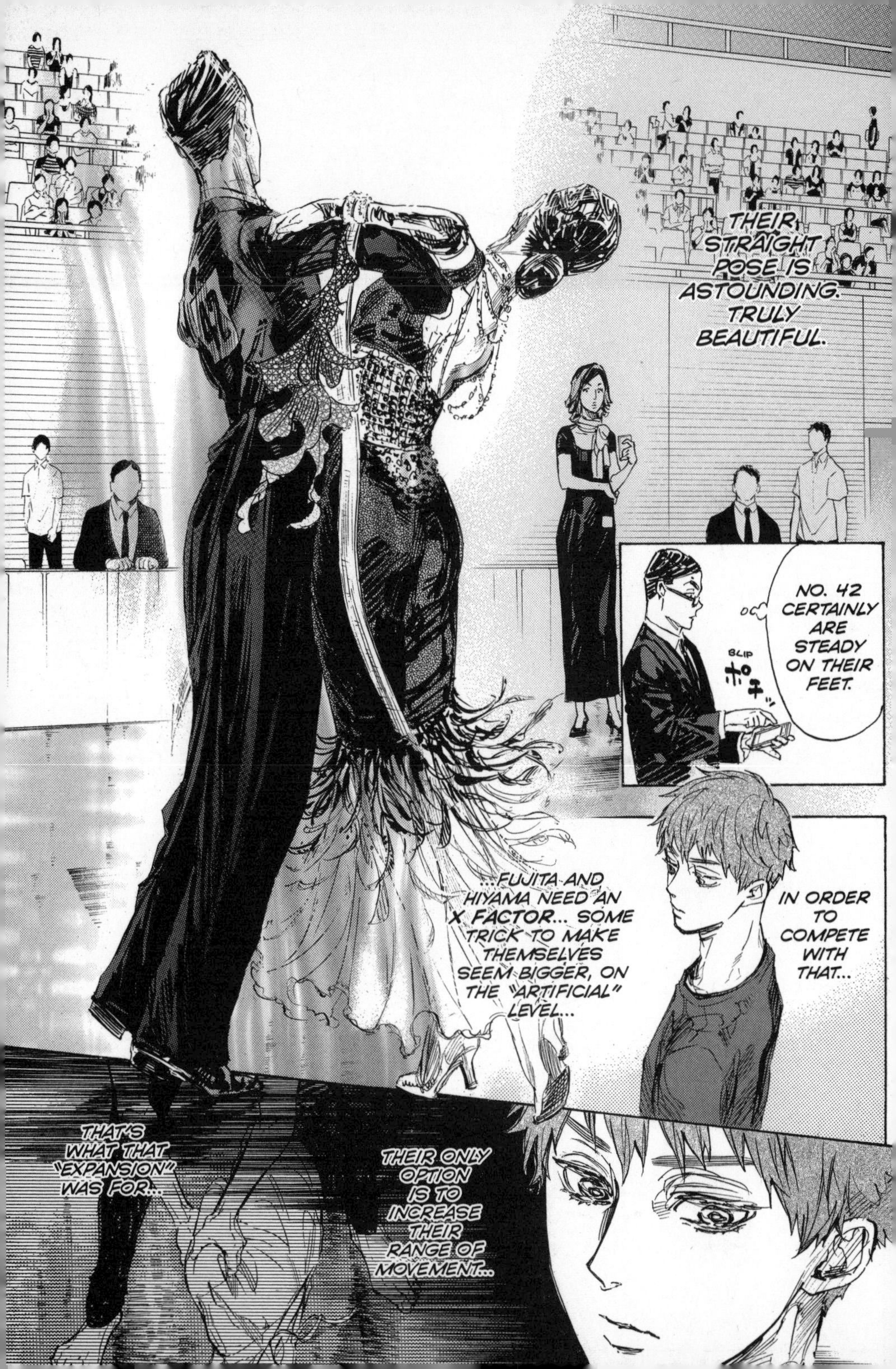
THEIR STRAIGHT POSE IS ASTOUNDING. TRULY BEAUTIFUL.
NO. 42 CERTAINLY ARE STEADY ON THEIR FEET.
SLIP
ポキッ
IN ORDER TO COMPETE WITH THAT...
...FUJITA AND HIYAMA NEED AN X FACTOR... SOME TRICK TO MAKE THEMSELVES SEEM BIGGER, ON THE "ARTIFICIAL" LEVEL...
THEIR ONLY OPTION IS TO INCREASE THEIR RANGE OF MOVEMENT...
THAT'S WHAT THAT "EXPANSION" WAS FOR...

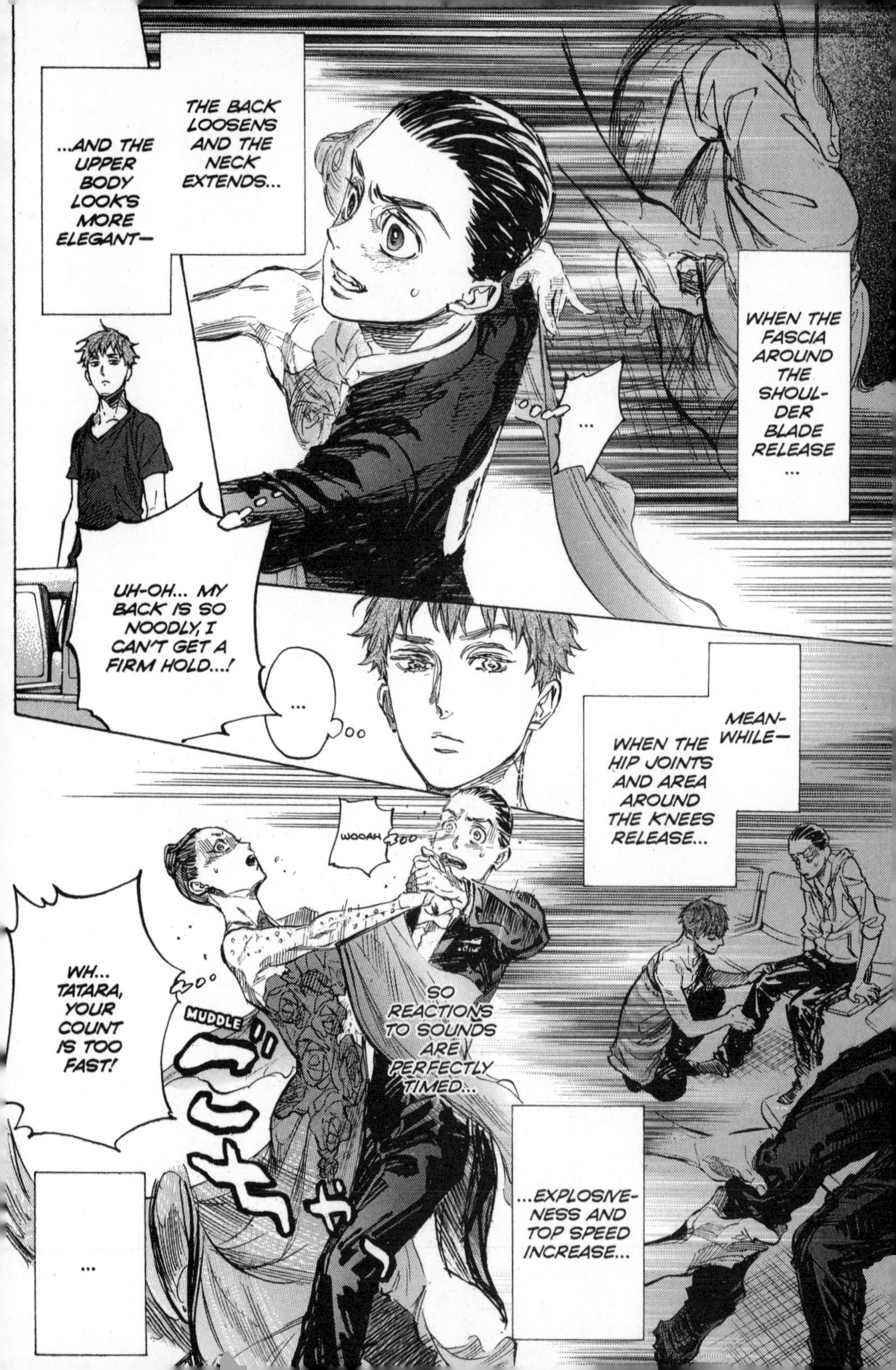
WHEN THE FASCIA AROUND THE SHOULDER BLADE RELEASE...
...
THE BACK LOOSENS AND THE NECK EXTENDS...
...AND THE UPPER BODY LOOKS MORE ELEGANT—
MEAN-WHILE—
...
UH-OH... MY BACK IS SO NOODLY, I CAN'T GET A FIRM HOLD...!
WHEN THE HIP JOINTS AND AREA AROUND THE KNEES RELEASE...
...EXPLOSIVE-NESS AND TOP SPEED INCREASE...
SO REACTIONS TO SOUNDS ARE PERFECTLY TIMED...
WOOAH
WH... TATARA, YOUR COUNT IS TOO FAST!
MUDDLE
...

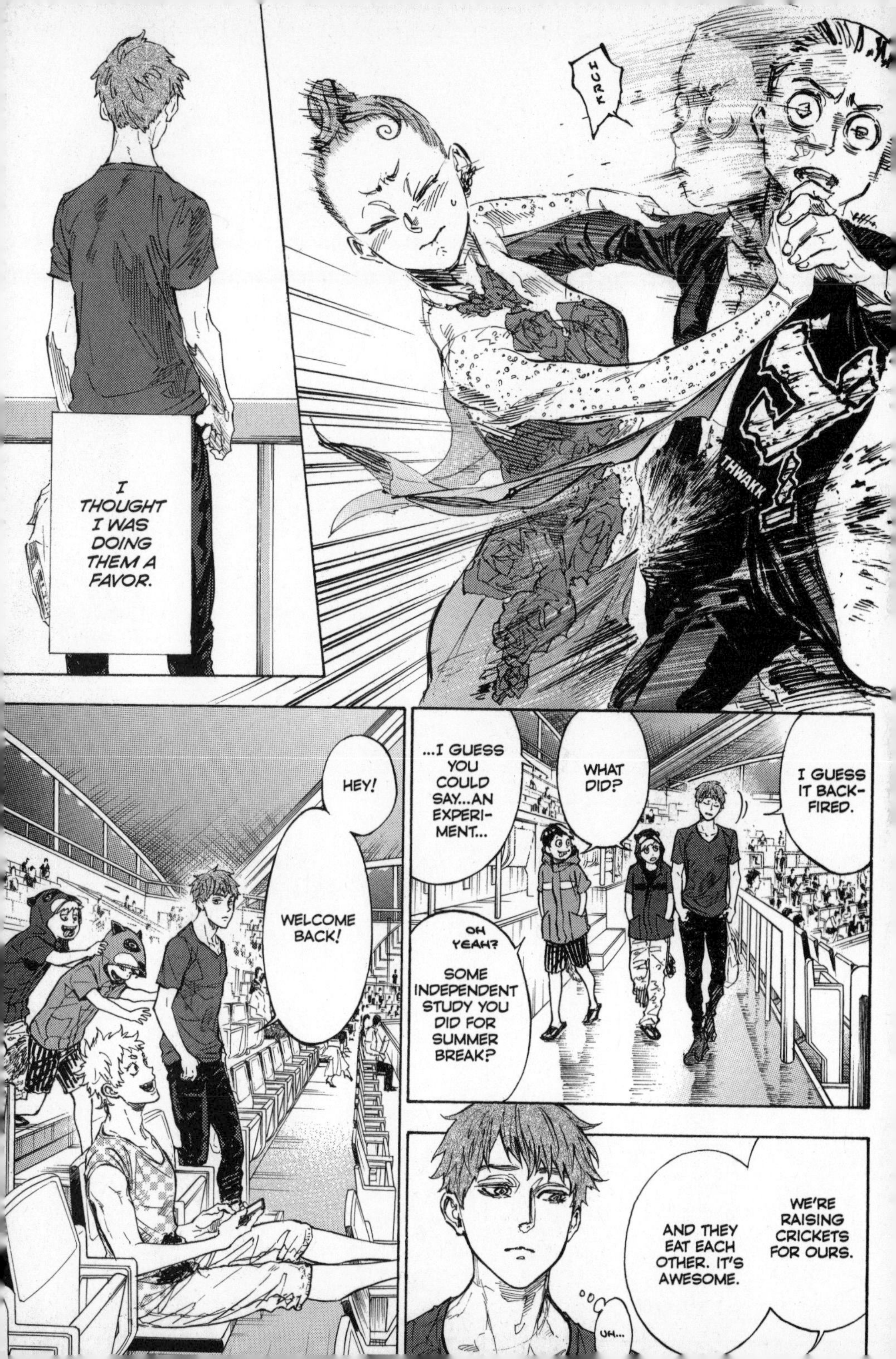
HURK
THWAKK
I THOUGHT I WAS DOING THEM A FAVOR.
I GUESS IT BACK-FIRED.
WHAT DID?
...I GUESS YOU COULD SAY...AN EXPERIMENT...
OH YEAH?
SOME INDEPENDENT STUDY YOU DID FOR SUMMER BREAK?
WE'RE RAISING CRICKETS FOR OURS.
AND THEY EAT EACH OTHER. IT'S AWESOME.
UH...
HEY!
WELCOME BACK!

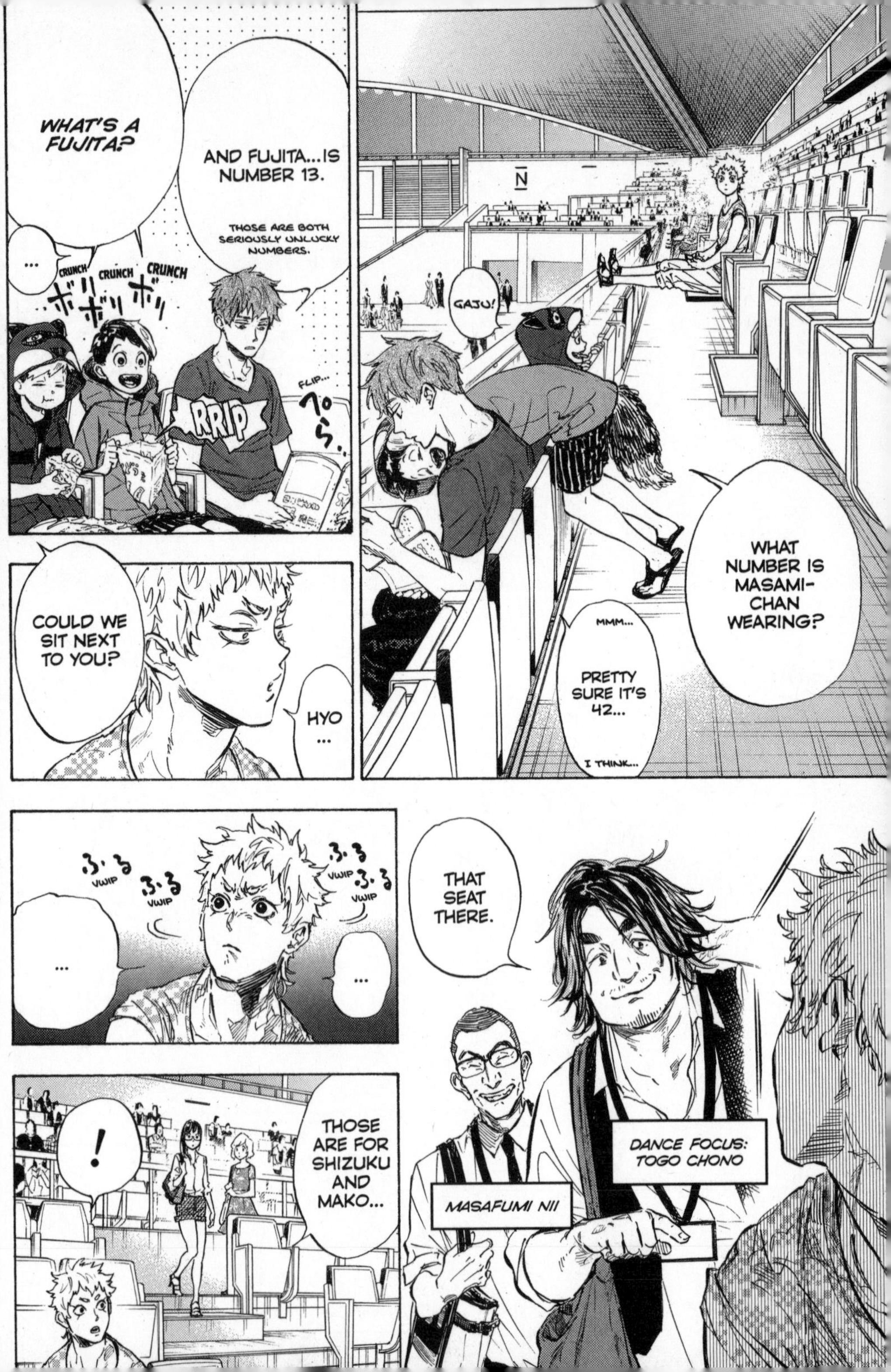
GAJU!
WHAT NUMBER IS MASAMI-CHAN WEARING?
MMM...
PRETTY SURE IT'S 42...
I THINK...
AND FUJITA...IS NUMBER 13.
THOSE ARE BOTH SERIOUSLY UNLUCKY NUMBERS.
WHAT'S A FUJITA?
...
CRUNCH ボリ
CRUNCH ボリ
CRUNCH ボリ
RRIP
FLIP... ぺら...
COULD WE SIT NEXT TO YOU?
HYO ...
THAT SEAT THERE.
DANCE FOCUS: TOGO CHONO
MASAFUMI NII
ふる VWIP
ふる VWIP
ふる VWIP
ふる VWIP
...
...
THOSE ARE FOR SHIZUKU AND MAKO...
!

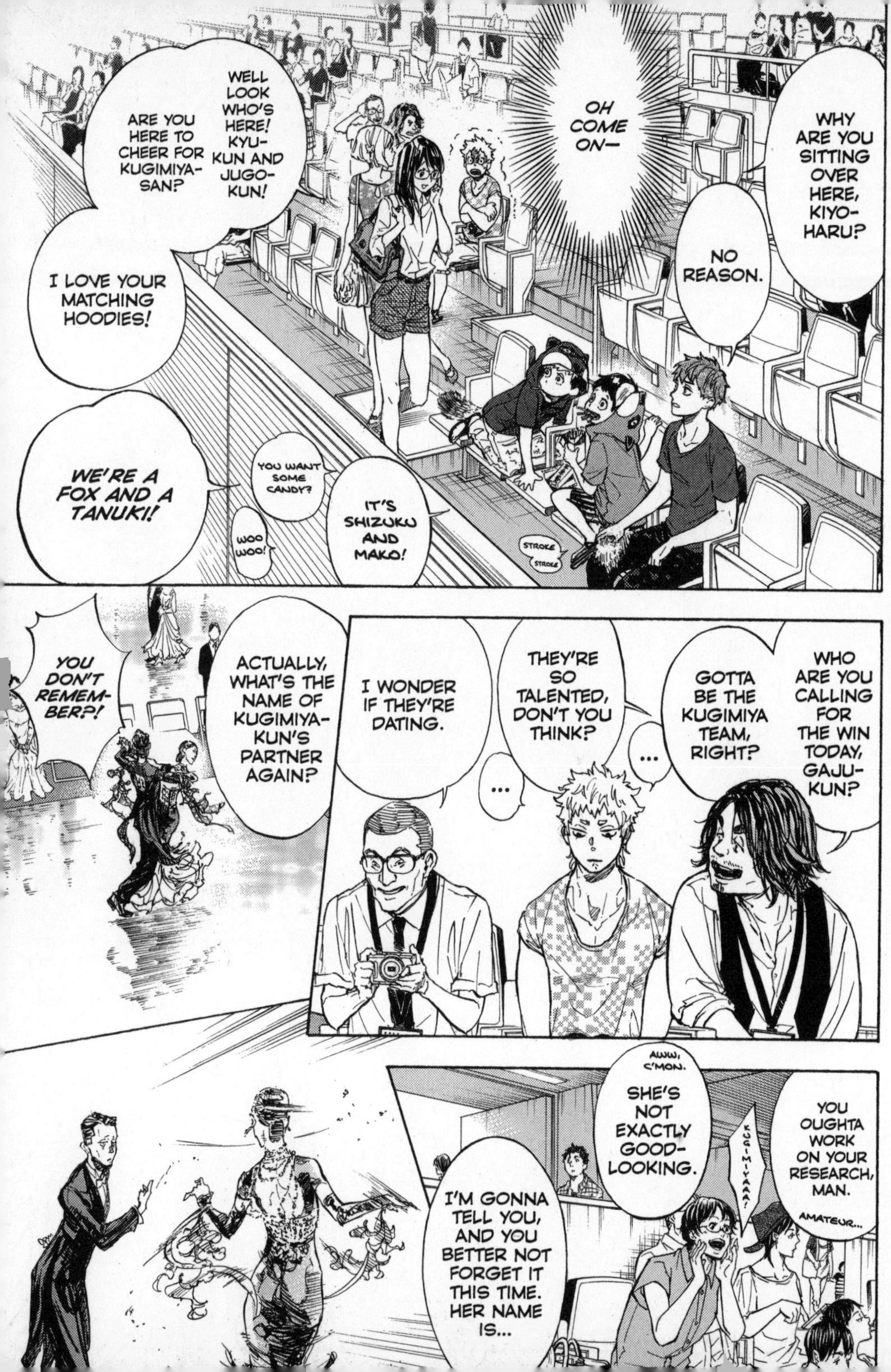
WHY ARE YOU SITTING OVER HERE, KIYO-HARU?
NO REASON.
OH COME ON—
WELL LOOK WHO'S HERE! KYU-KUN AND JUGO-KUN!
ARE YOU HERE TO CHEER FOR KUGIMIYA-SAN?
I LOVE YOUR MATCHING HOODIES!
WE'RE A FOX AND A TANUKI!
IT'S SHIZUKU AND MAKO!
YOU WANT SOME CANDY?
WOO WOO!
STROKE
STROKE
WHO ARE YOU CALLING FOR THE WIN TODAY, GAJU-KUN?
GOTTA BE THE KUGIMIYA TEAM, RIGHT?
...
THEY'RE SO TALENTED, DON'T YOU THINK?
...
I WONDER IF THEY'RE DATING.
ACTUALLY, WHAT'S THE NAME OF KUGIMIYA-KUN'S PARTNER AGAIN?
YOU DON'T REMEMBER?!
YOU OUGHTA WORK ON YOUR RESEARCH, MAN.
AMATEUR...
AWW, C'MON.
SHE'S NOT EXACTLY GOOD-LOOKING.
KUGIMIYAA!
I'M GONNA TELL YOU, AND YOU BETTER NOT FORGET IT THIS TIME. HER NAME IS...

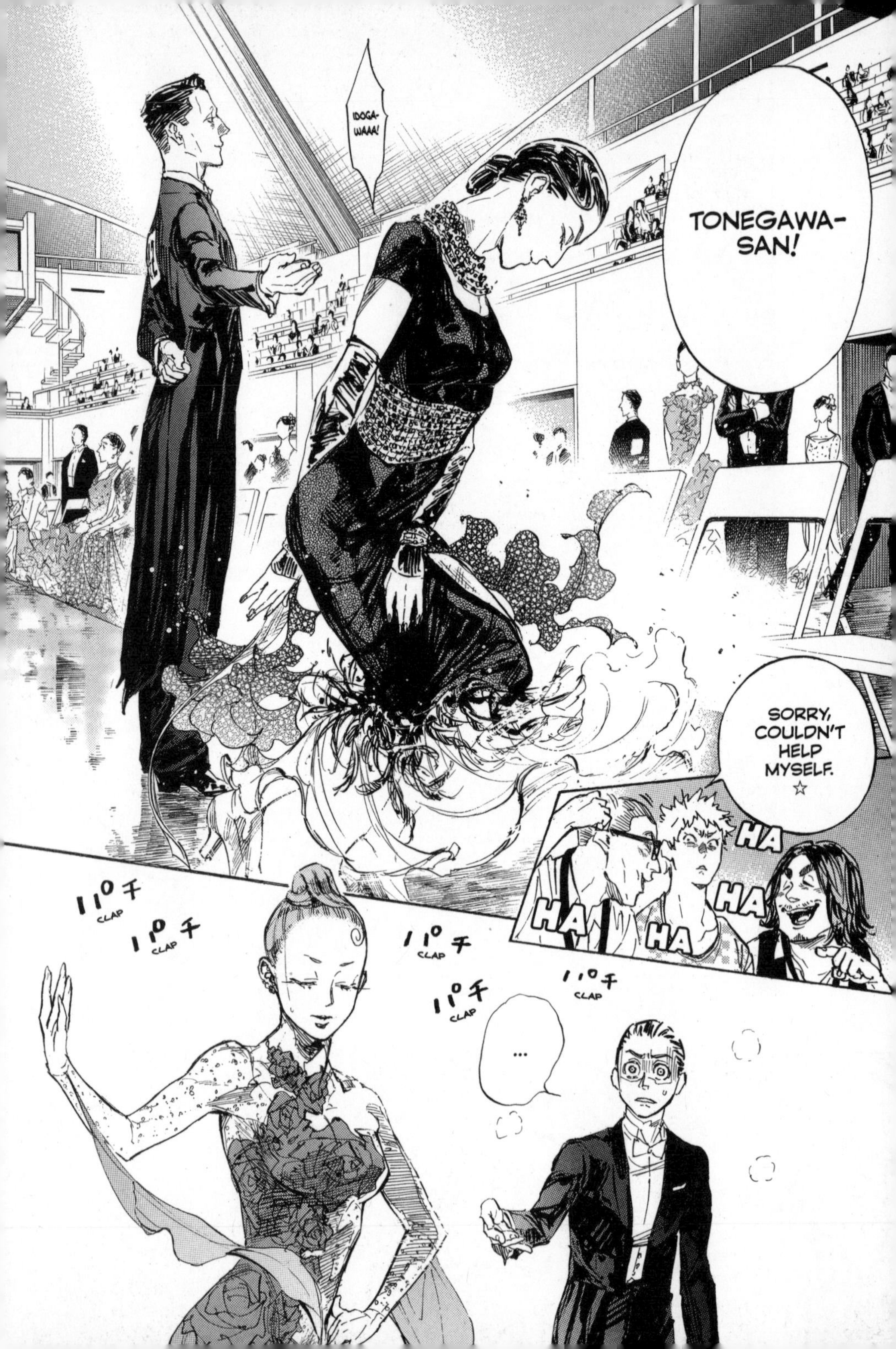
TONEGAWA-SAN!
IDOGA-WAAA!
SORRY, COULDN'T HELP MYSELF. ☆
HA
HA
HA
HA
パチ CLAP
パチ CLAP
パチ CLAP
パチ CLAP
パチ CLAP
...

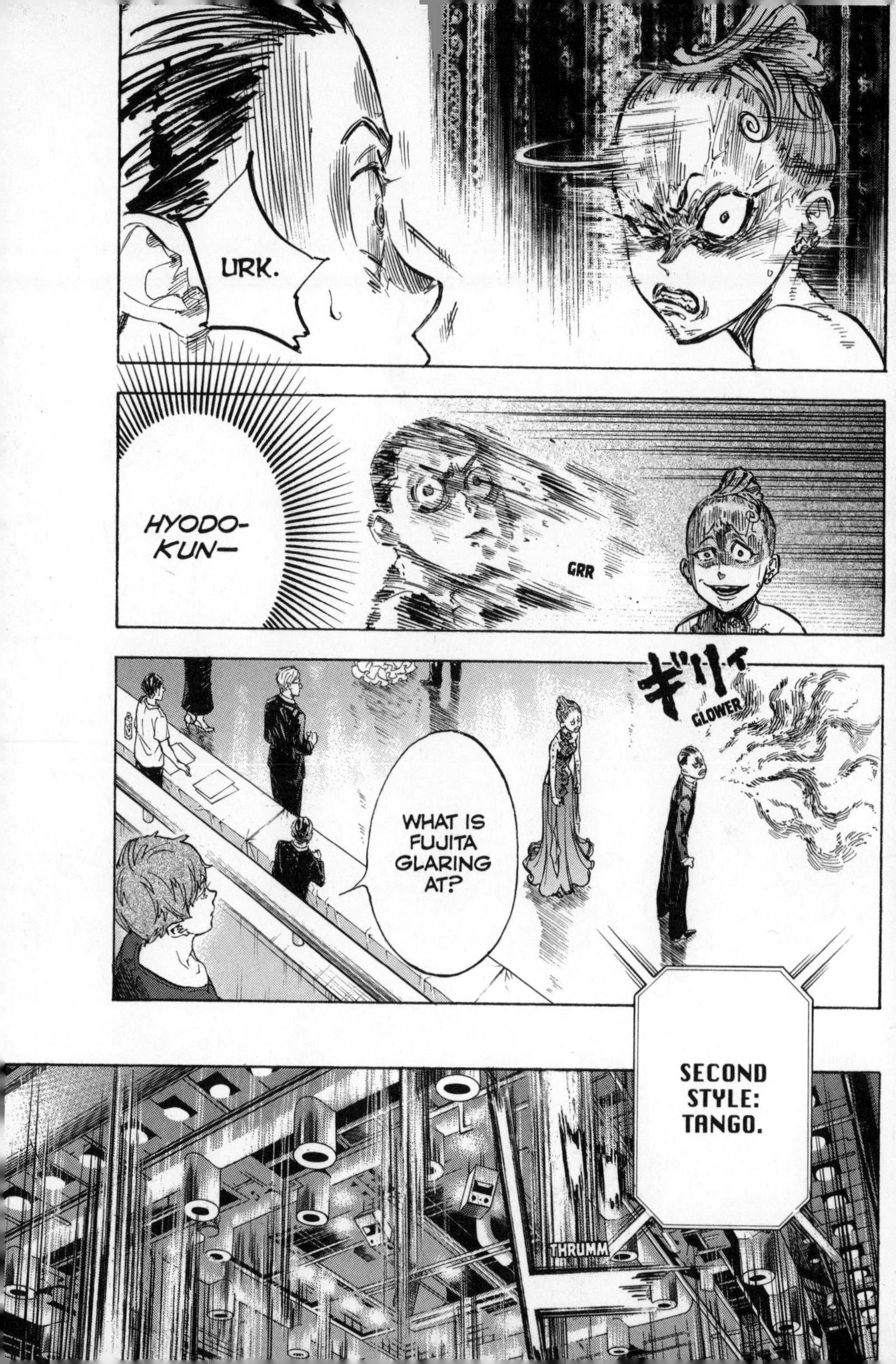
URK.
HYODO-KUN—
GRR
ギリィ
GLOWER
WHAT IS FUJITA GLARING AT?
SECOND STYLE: TANGO.
THRUMM

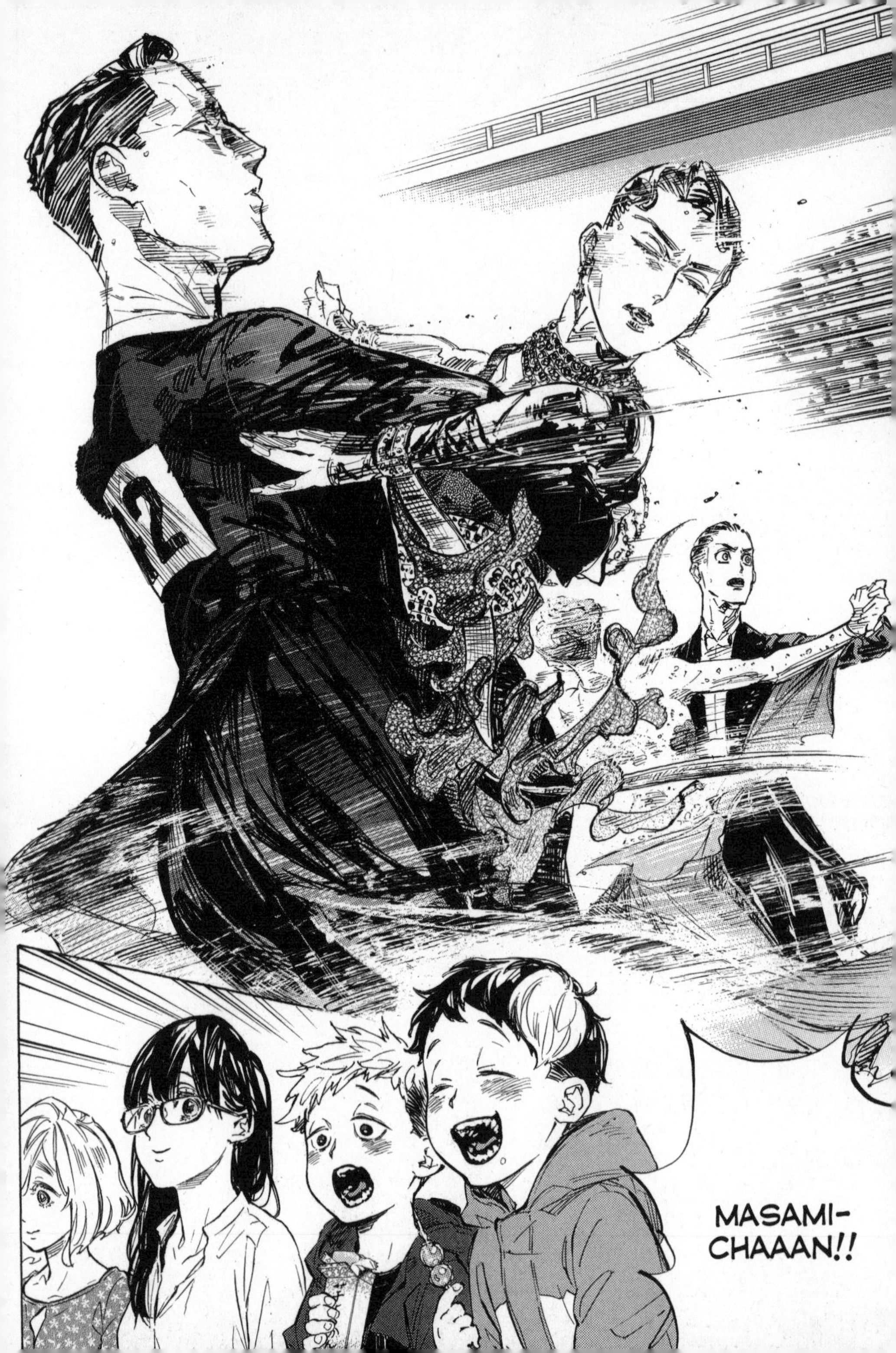
12
MASAMI-
CHAAAN!!

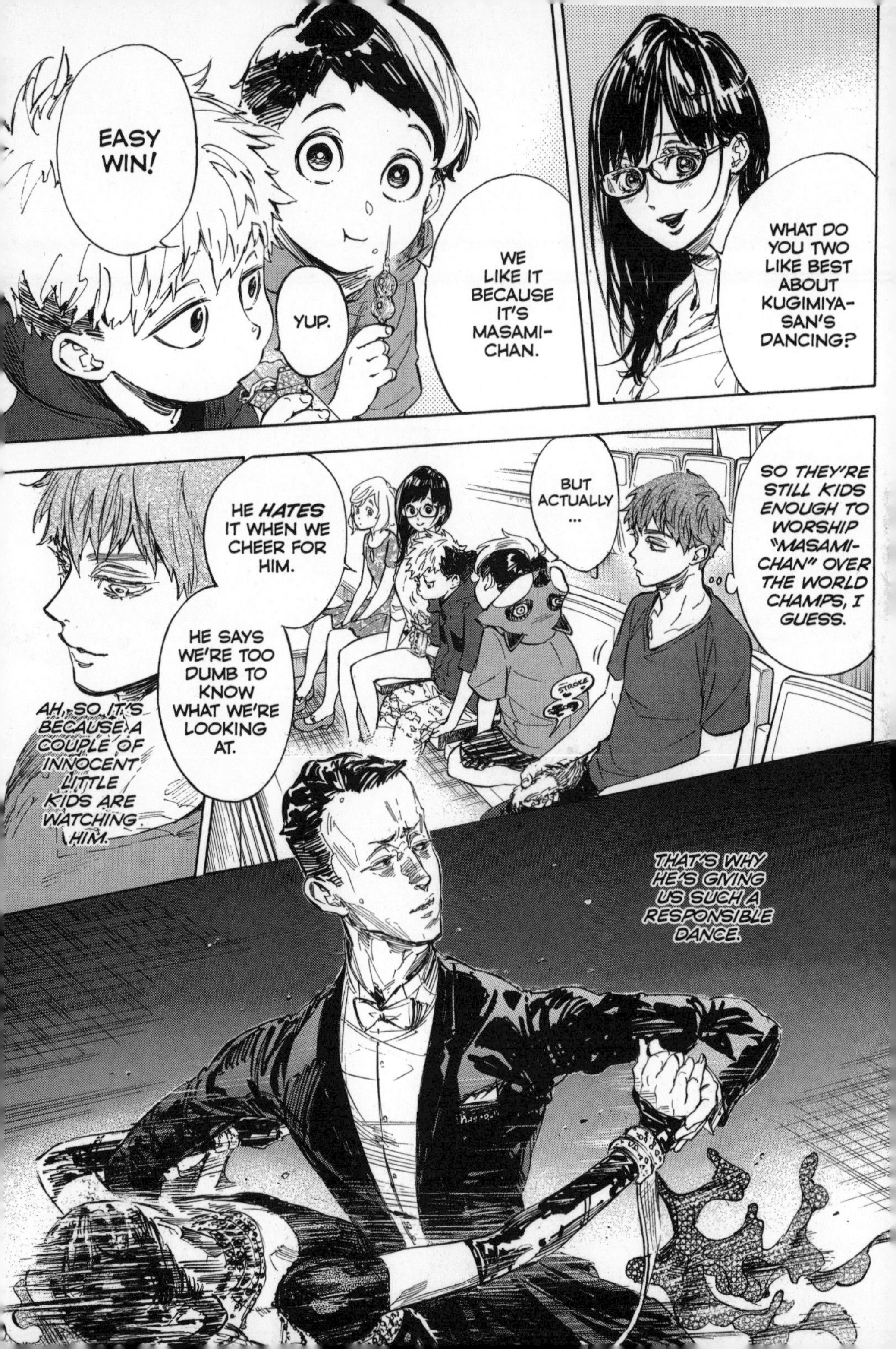
WHAT DO YOU TWO LIKE BEST ABOUT KUGIMIYA-SAN'S DANCING?
WE LIKE IT BECAUSE IT'S MASAMI-CHAN.
YUP.
EASY WIN!
SO THEY'RE STILL KIDS ENOUGH TO WORSHIP "MASAMI-CHAN" OVER THE WORLD CHAMPS, I GUESS.
BUT ACTUALLY ...
HE *HATES* IT WHEN WE CHEER FOR HIM.
HE SAYS WE'RE TOO DUMB TO KNOW WHAT WE'RE LOOKING AT.
AH, SO IT'S BECAUSE A COUPLE OF INNOCENT LITTLE KIDS ARE WATCHING HIM.
THAT'S WHY HE'S GIVING US SUCH A RESPONSIBLE DANCE.

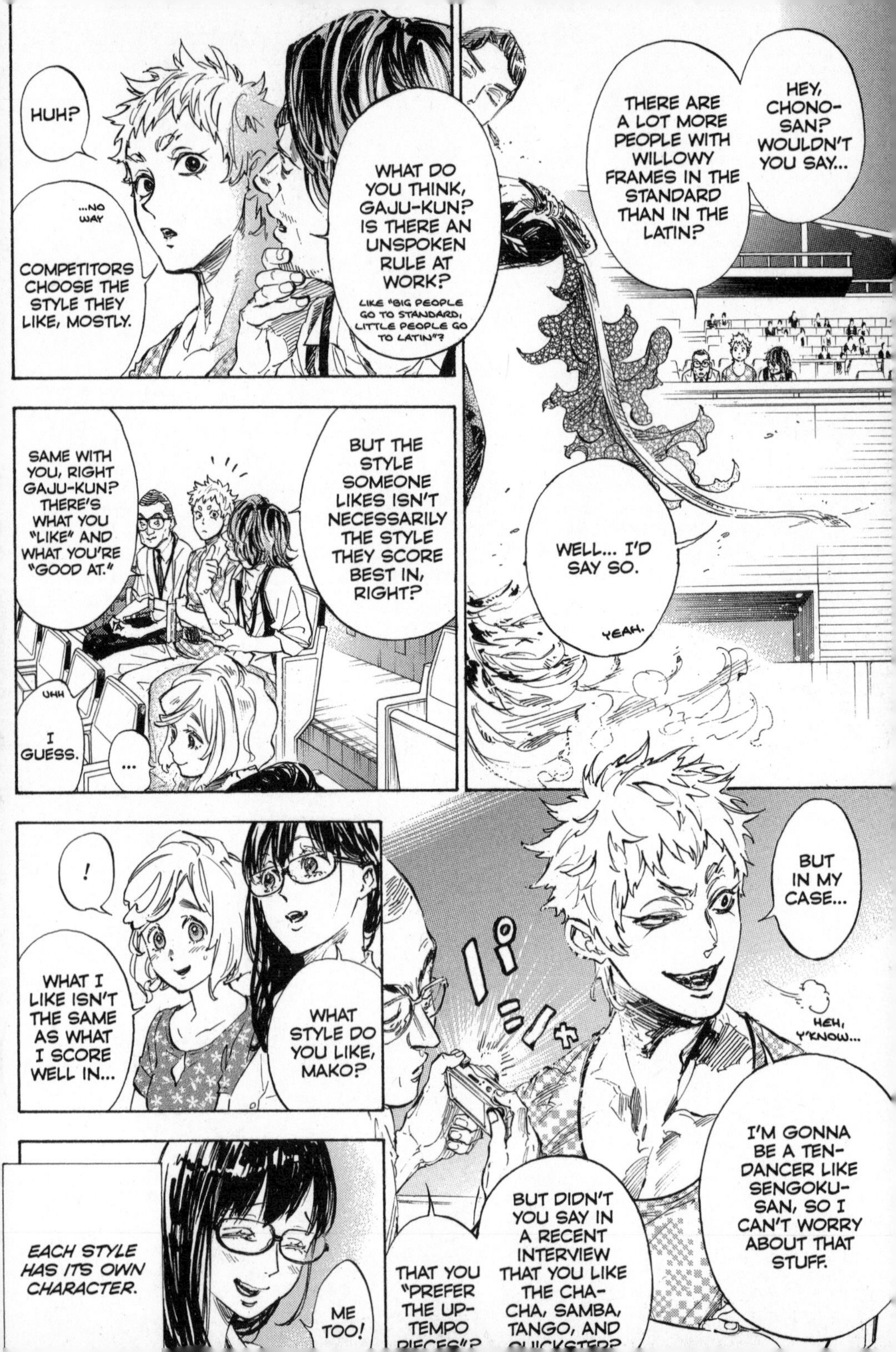
HEY, CHONO-SAN? WOULDN'T YOU SAY...
THERE ARE A LOT MORE PEOPLE WITH WILLOWY FRAMES IN THE STANDARD THAN IN THE LATIN?
WELL... I'D SAY SO.
YEAH.
WHAT DO YOU THINK, GAJU-KUN? IS THERE AN UNSPOKEN RULE AT WORK?
LIKE "BIG PEOPLE GO TO STANDARD; LITTLE PEOPLE GO TO LATIN"?
HUH?
...NO WAY
COMPETITORS CHOOSE THE STYLE THEY LIKE, MOSTLY.
BUT THE STYLE SOMEONE LIKES ISN'T NECESSARILY THE STYLE THEY SCORE BEST IN, RIGHT?
SAME WITH YOU, RIGHT GAJU-KUN? THERE'S WHAT YOU "LIKE" AND WHAT YOU'RE "GOOD AT."
...
UHH
I GUESS.
BUT IN MY CASE...
HEH, Y'KNOW...
I'M GONNA BE A TEN-DANCER LIKE SENGOKU-SAN, SO I CAN'T WORRY ABOUT THAT STUFF.
パシャ
BUT DIDN'T YOU SAY IN A RECENT INTERVIEW THAT YOU LIKE THE CHA-CHA, SAMBA, TANGO, AND
THAT YOU "PREFER THE UP-TEMPO
!
WHAT STYLE DO YOU LIKE, MAKO?
WHAT I LIKE ISN'T THE SAME AS WHAT I SCORE WELL IN...
ME TOO!
EACH STYLE HAS ITS OWN CHARACTER.

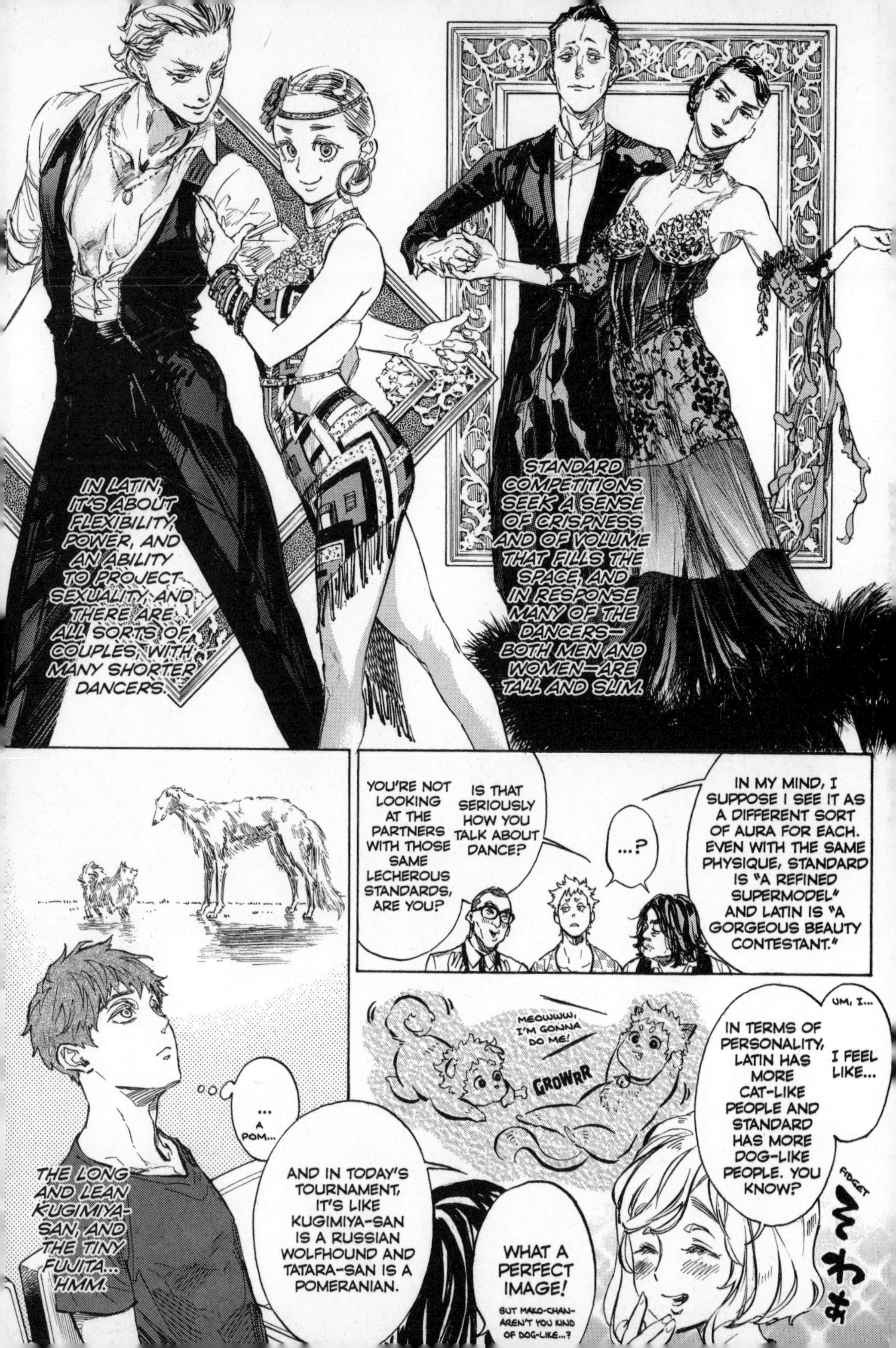
STANDARD COMPETITIONS SEEK A SENSE OF CRISPNESS AND OF VOLUME THAT FILLS THE SPACE, AND IN RESPONSE MANY OF THE DANCERS—BOTH MEN AND WOMEN—ARE TALL AND SLIM.
IN LATIN, IT'S ABOUT FLEXIBILITY, POWER, AND AN ABILITY TO PROJECT SEXUALITY, AND THERE ARE ALL SORTS OF COUPLES, WITH MANY SHORTER DANCERS.
IN MY MIND, I SUPPOSE I SEE IT AS A DIFFERENT SORT OF AURA FOR EACH. EVEN WITH THE SAME PHYSIQUE, STANDARD IS "A REFINED SUPERMODEL" AND LATIN IS "A GORGEOUS BEAUTY CONTESTANT."
...?
IS THAT SERIOUSLY HOW YOU TALK ABOUT DANCE?
YOU'RE NOT LOOKING AT THE PARTNERS WITH THOSE SAME LECHEROUS STANDARDS, ARE YOU?
UM, I...
I FEEL LIKE...
IN TERMS OF PERSONALITY, LATIN HAS MORE CAT-LIKE PEOPLE AND STANDARD HAS MORE DOG-LIKE PEOPLE. YOU KNOW?
FIDGET
MEOWWW, I'M GONNA DO ME!
GROWRR
WHAT A PERFECT IMAGE!
BUT MAKO-CHAN- AREN'T YOU KIND OF DOG-LIKE...?
AND IN TODAY'S TOURNAMENT, IT'S LIKE KUGIMIYA-SAN IS A RUSSIAN WOLFHOUND AND TATARA-SAN IS A POMERANIAN.
... A POM...
THE LONG AND LEAN KUGIMIYA-SAN, AND THE TINY FUJITA... HMM.

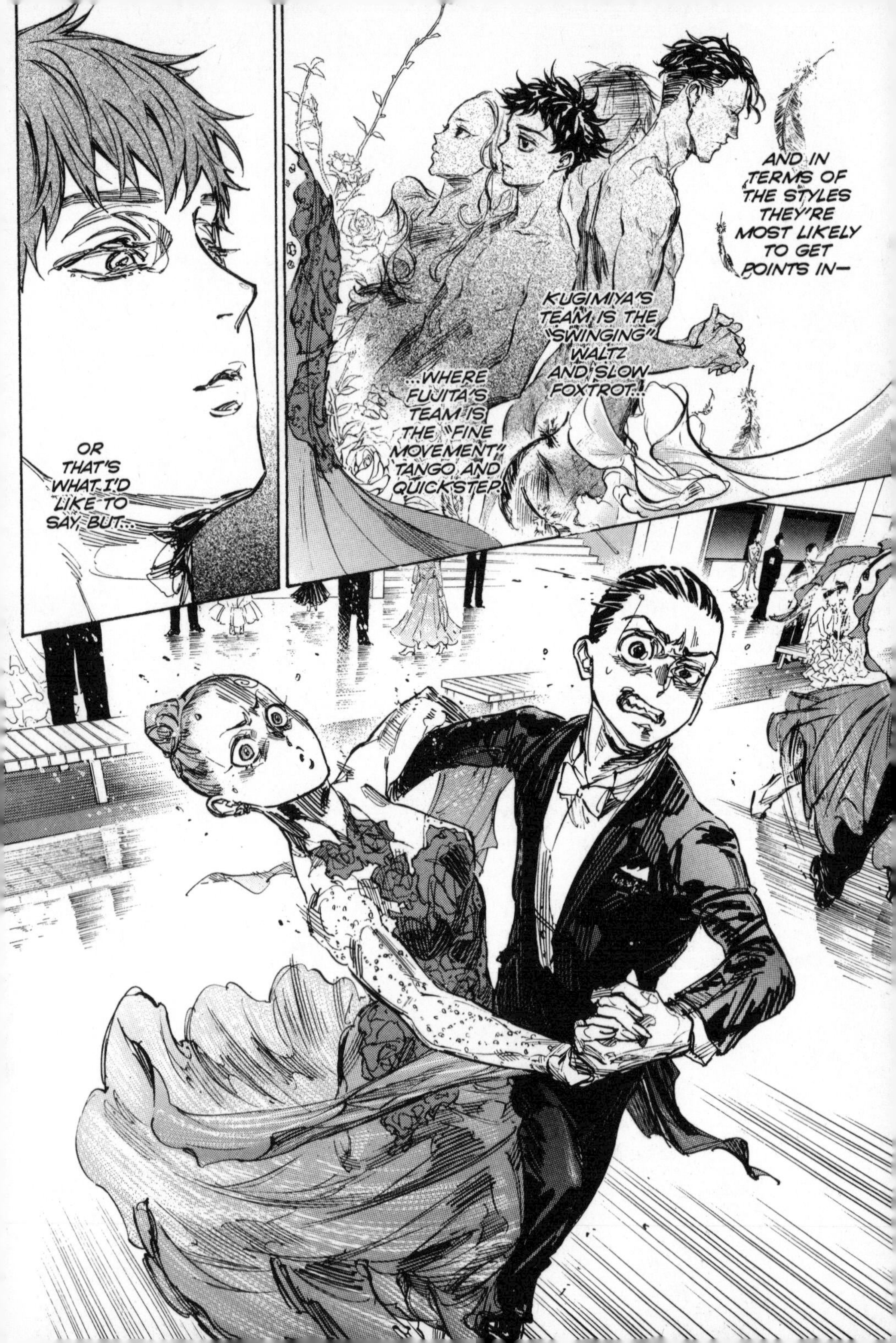
AND IN TERMS OF THE STYLES THEY'RE MOST LIKELY TO GET POINTS IN—
KUGIMIYA'S TEAM IS THE "SWINGING" WALTZ AND SLOW FOXTROT...
...WHERE FUJITA'S TEAM IS THE "FINE MOVEMENT" TANGO AND QUICKSTEP.
OR THAT'S WHAT I'D LIKE TO SAY, BUT...

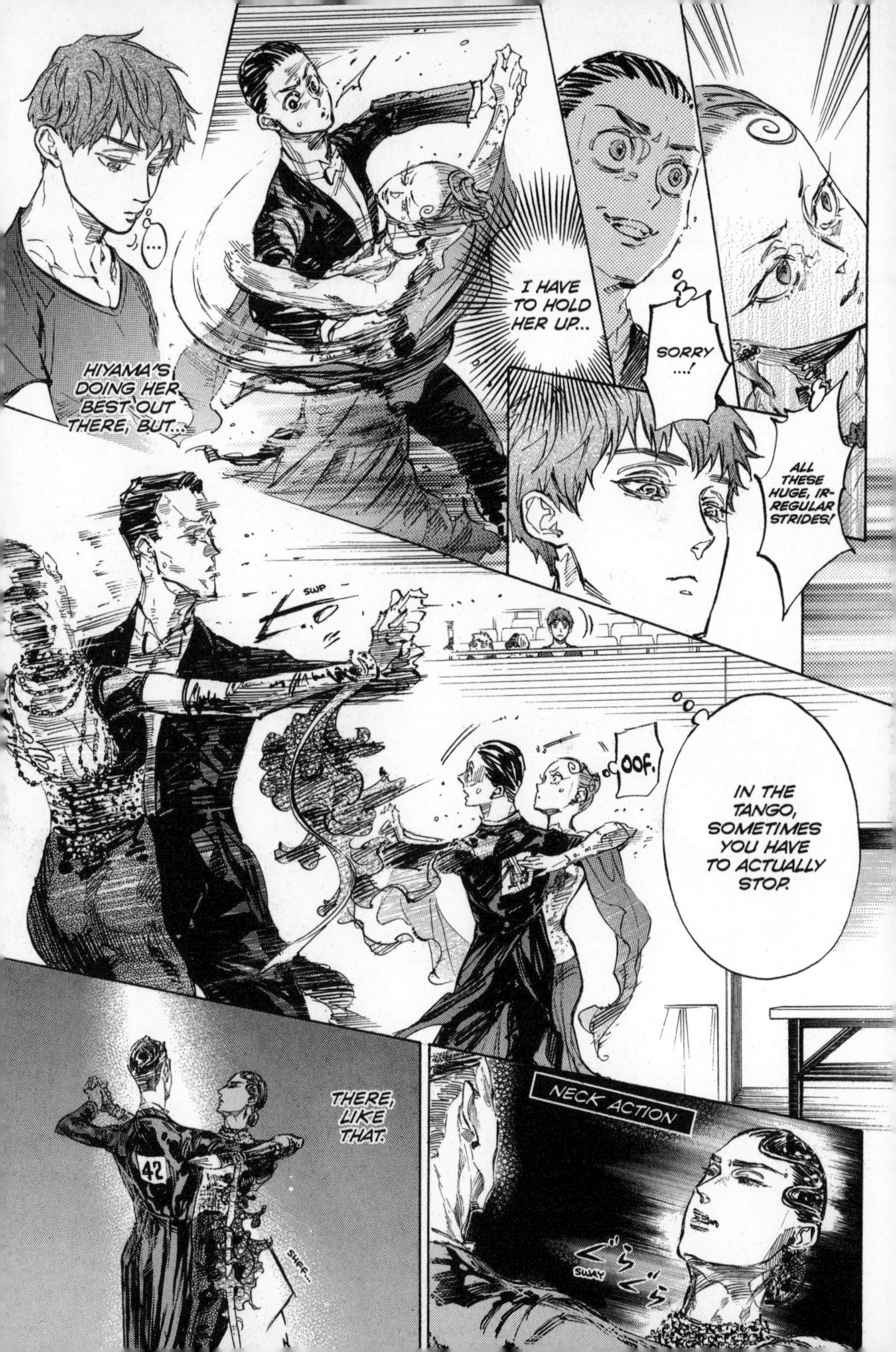

SORRY ...!
I HAVE TO HOLD HER UP...
...
HIYAMA'S DOING HER BEST OUT THERE, BUT...
ALL THESE HUGE, IR-REGULAR STRIDES!
IN THE TANGO, SOMETIMES YOU HAVE TO ACTUALLY STOP.
OOF.
SWP
NECK ACTION
SWAY
THERE, LIKE THAT.
SHFF...

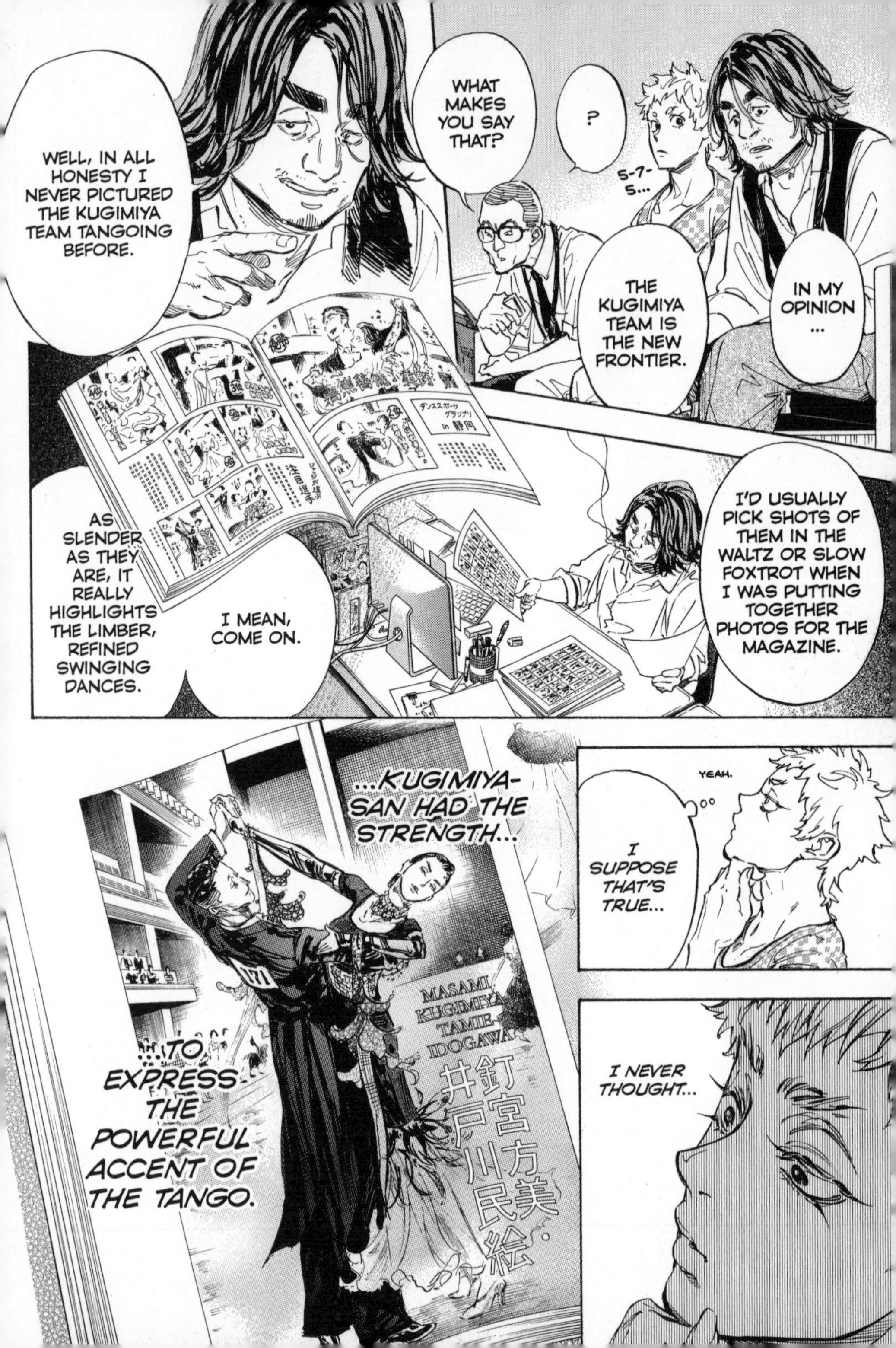
IN MY OPINION ...
THE KUGIMIYA TEAM IS THE NEW FRONTIER.
?
5-7-5...
WHAT MAKES YOU SAY THAT?
WELL, IN ALL HONESTY I NEVER PICTURED THE KUGIMIYA TEAM TANGOING BEFORE.
ダンススポーツグランプリ in 静岡
I'D USUALLY PICK SHOTS OF THEM IN THE WALTZ OR SLOW FOXTROT WHEN I WAS PUTTING TOGETHER PHOTOS FOR THE MAGAZINE.
I MEAN, COME ON.
AS SLENDER AS THEY ARE, IT REALLY HIGHLIGHTS THE LIMBER, REFINED SWINGING DANCES.
YEAH.
I SUPPOSE THAT'S TRUE...
I NEVER THOUGHT...
...KUGIMIYA-SAN HAD THE STRENGTH...
...TO EXPRESS THE POWERFUL ACCENT OF THE TANGO.
MASAMI KUGIMIYA TAMIE IDOGAWA
釘宮方美・井戸川民絵

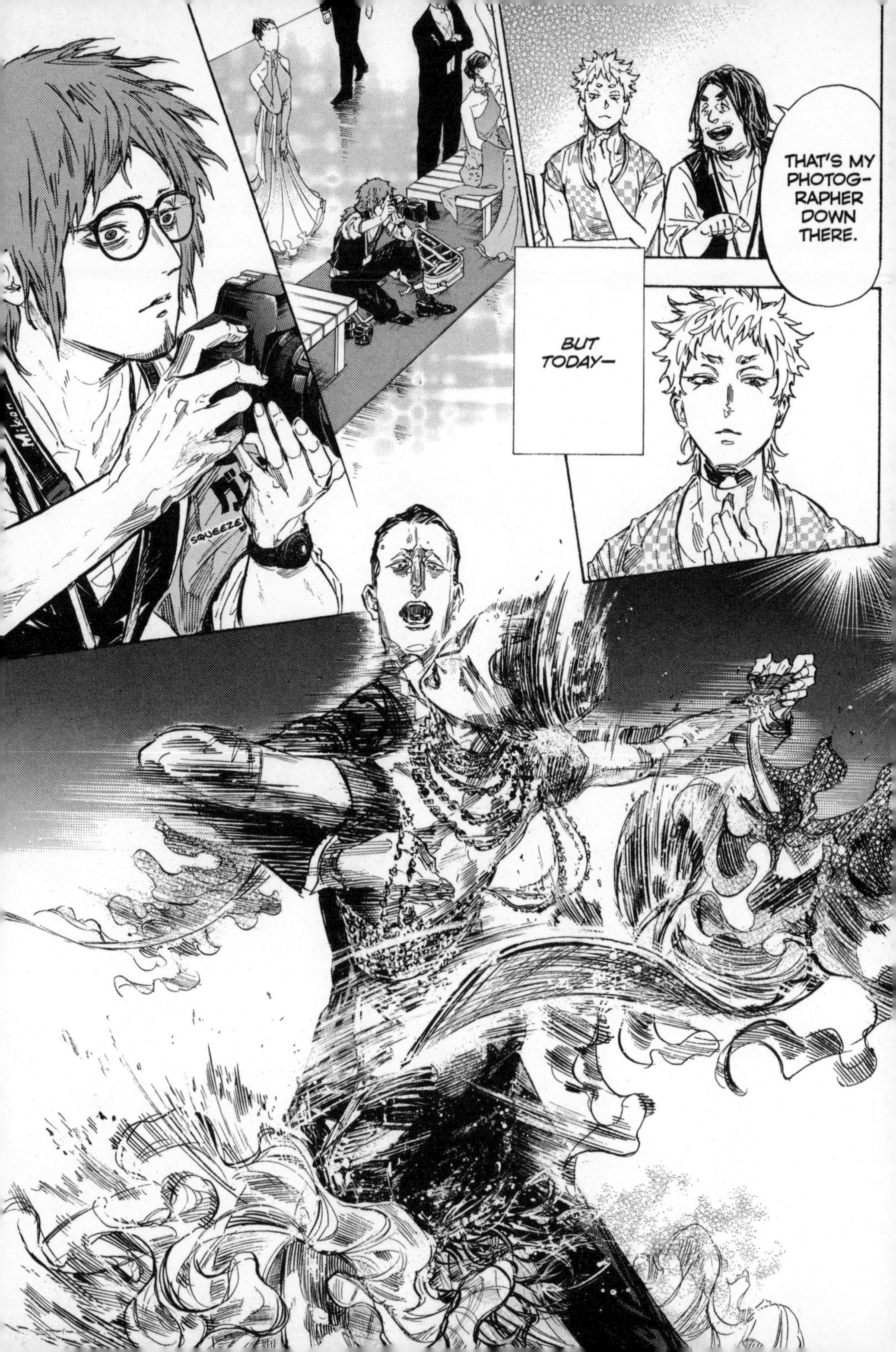
THAT'S MY PHOTOG-RAPHER DOWN THERE.
BUT TODAY—
Mikon
SQUEEZE

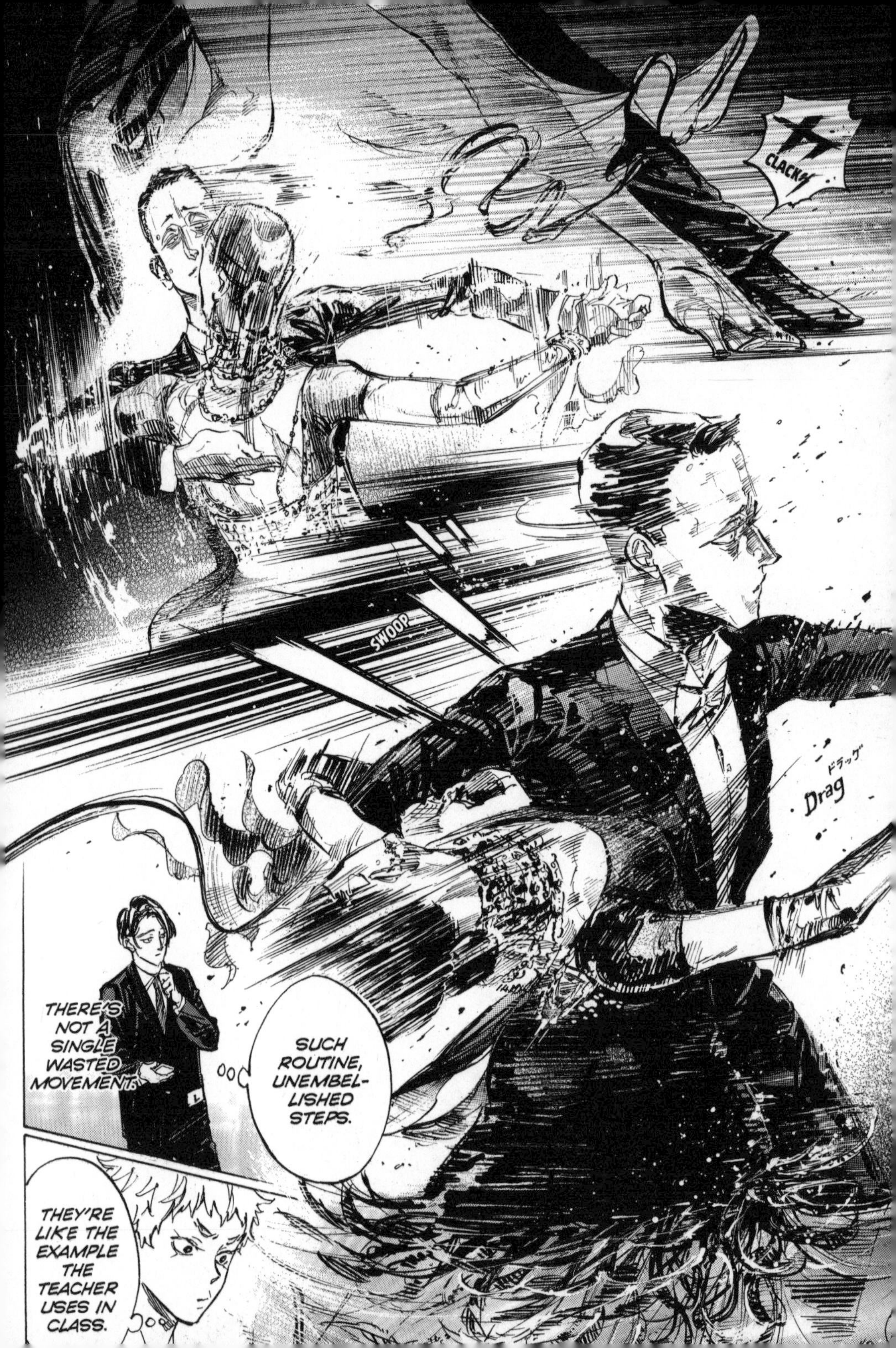
CLACK
SWOOP
ドラッグ
Drag
SUCH ROUTINE, UNEMBELLISHED STEPS.
THERE'S NOT A SINGLE WASTED MOVEMENT.
THEY'RE LIKE THE EXAMPLE THE TEACHER USES IN CLASS.

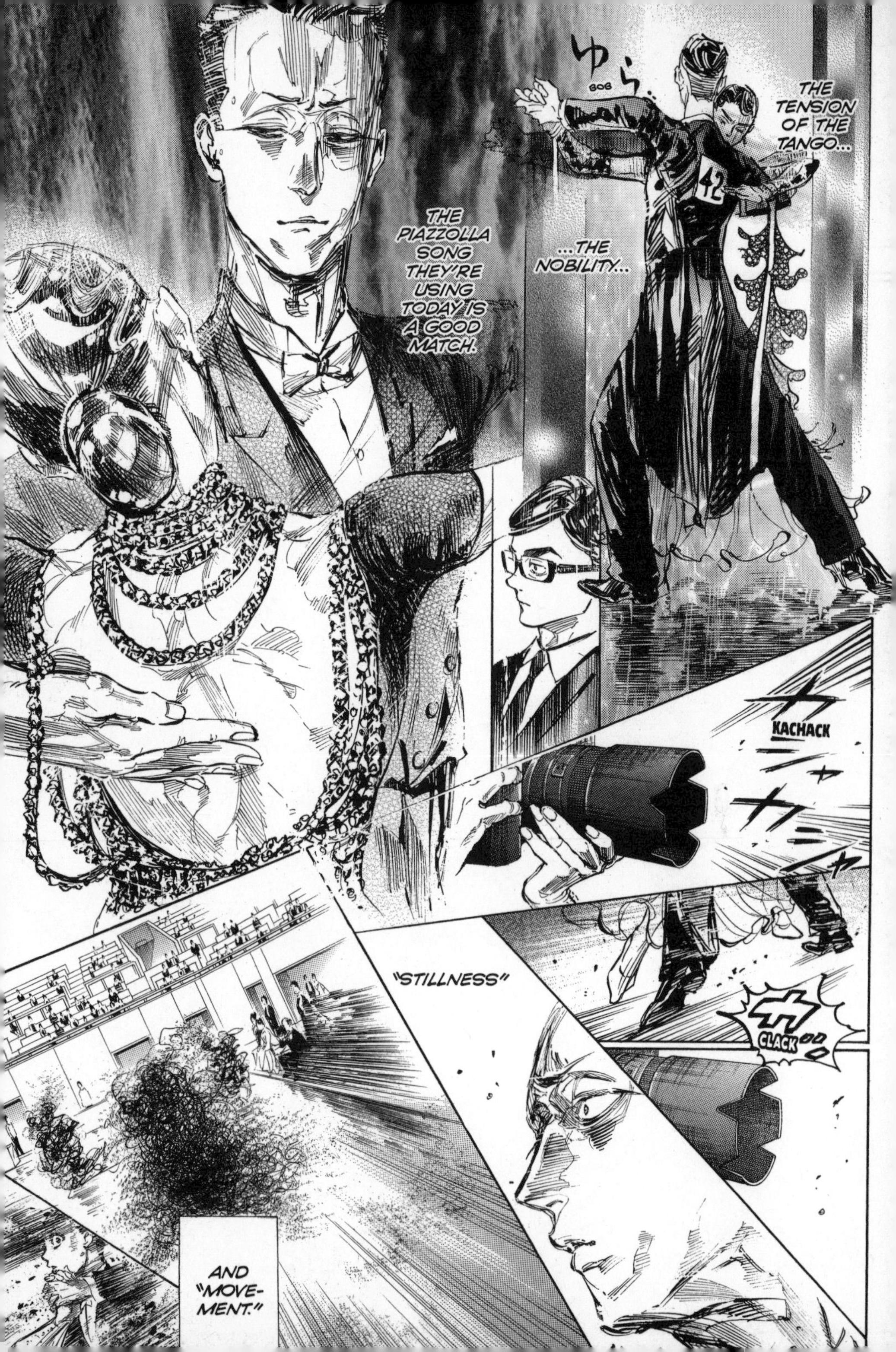

ゆら
BOB
THE TENSION OF THE TANGO...
...THE NOBILITY...
THE PIAZZOLLA SONG THEY'RE USING TODAY IS A GOOD MATCH.
KACHACK
CLACK
"STILLNESS"
AND "MOVEMENT."

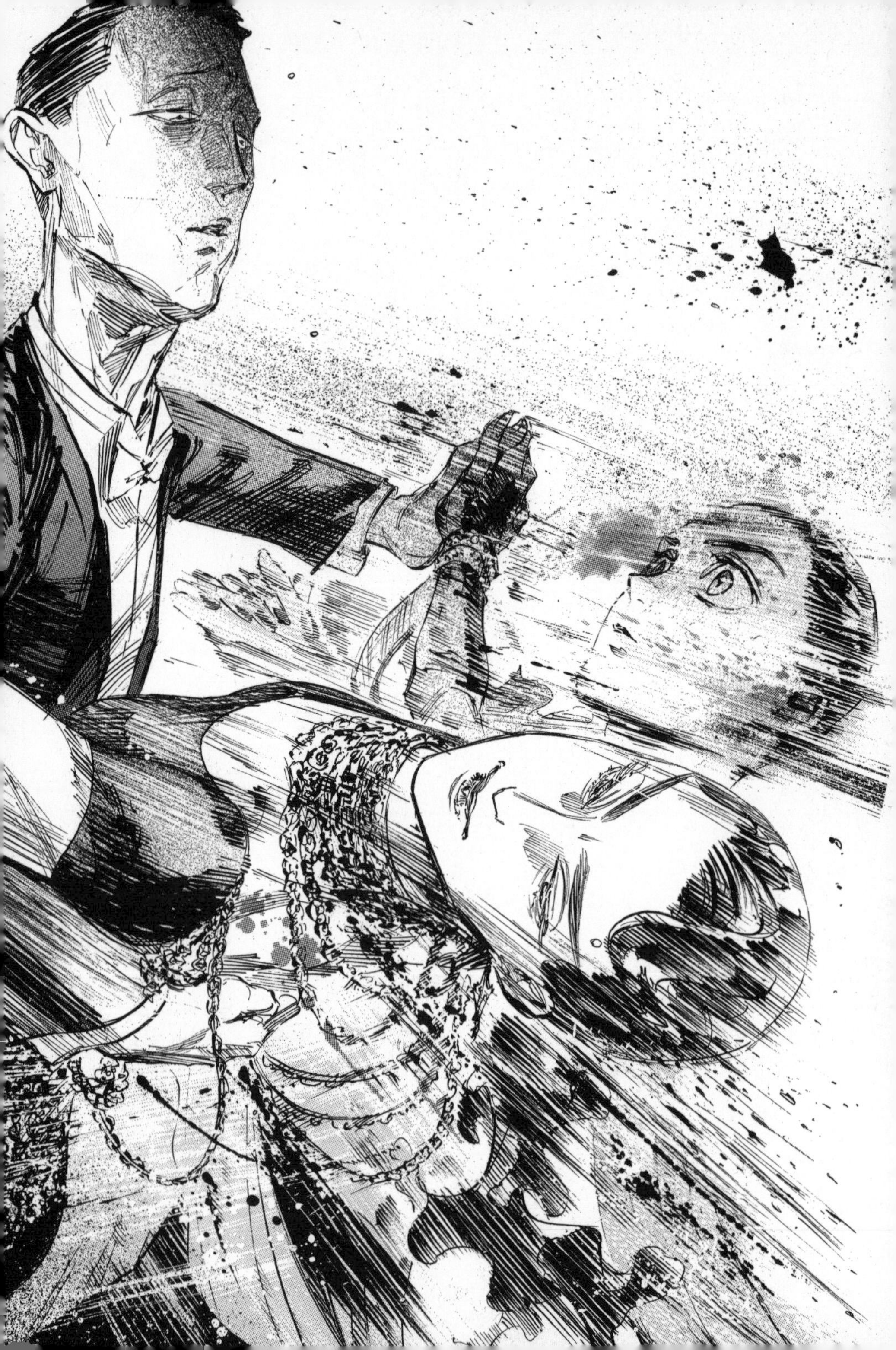

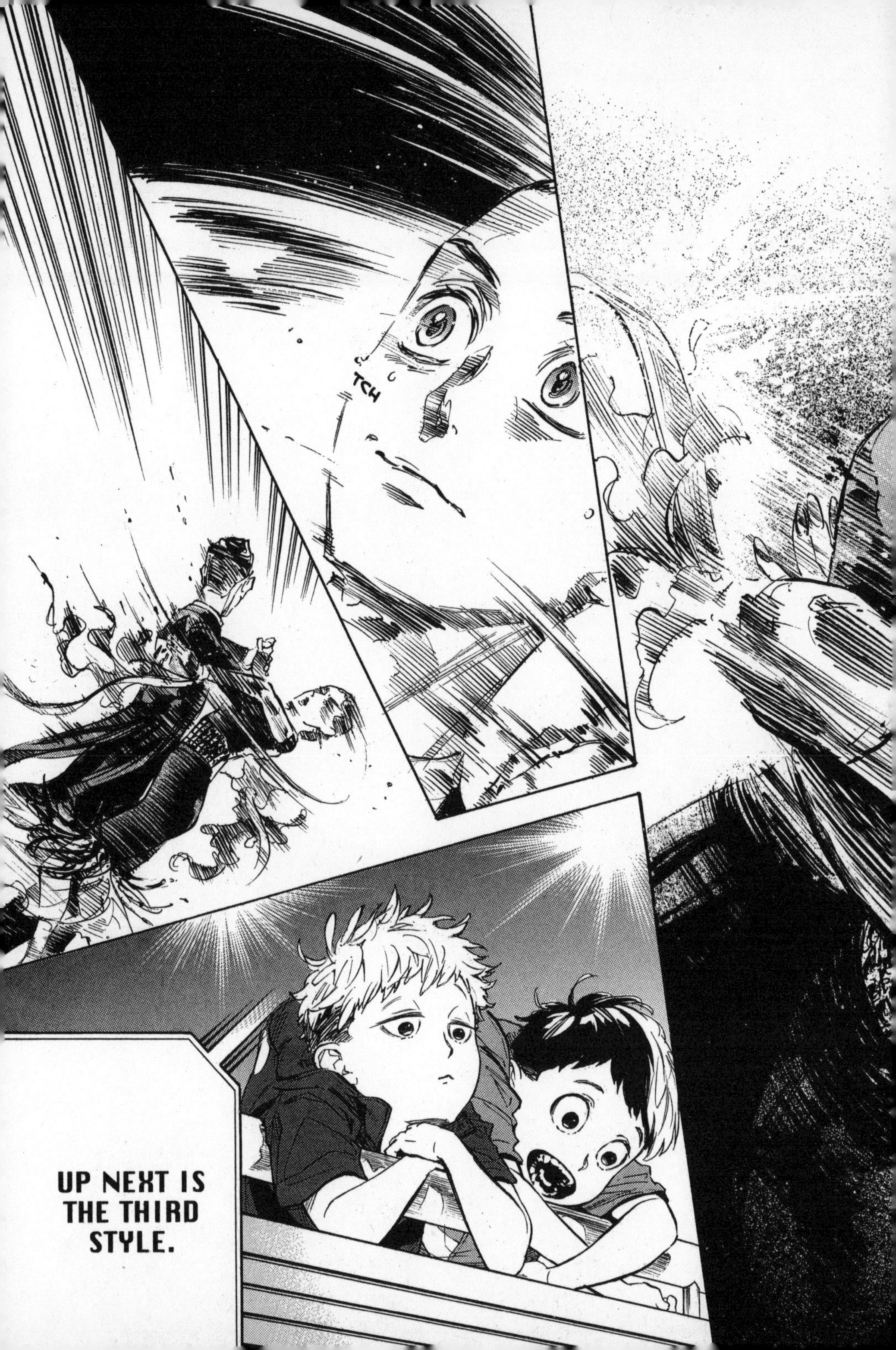
TCH
UP NEXT IS THE THIRD STYLE.

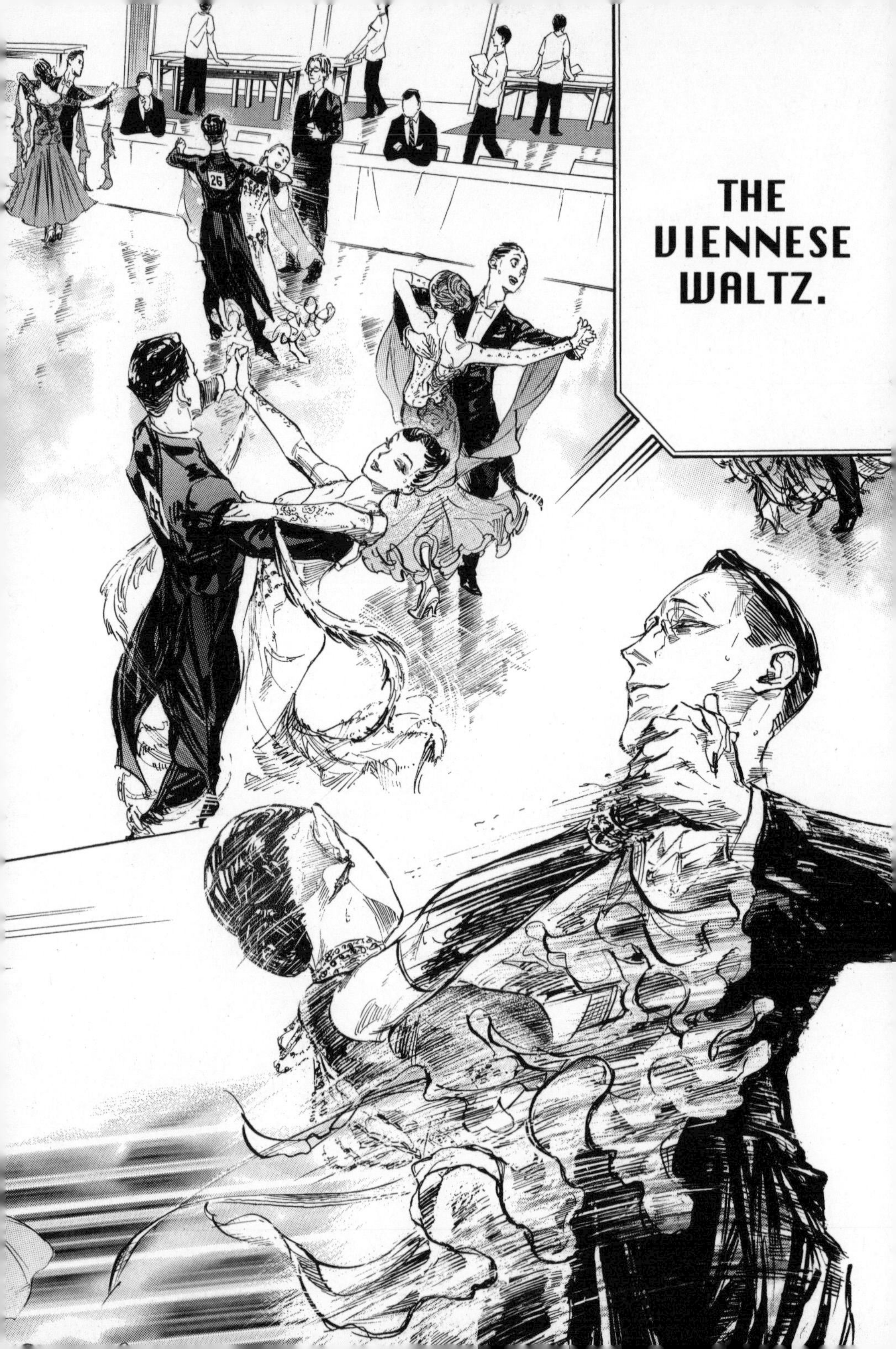
THE VIENNESE WALTZ.

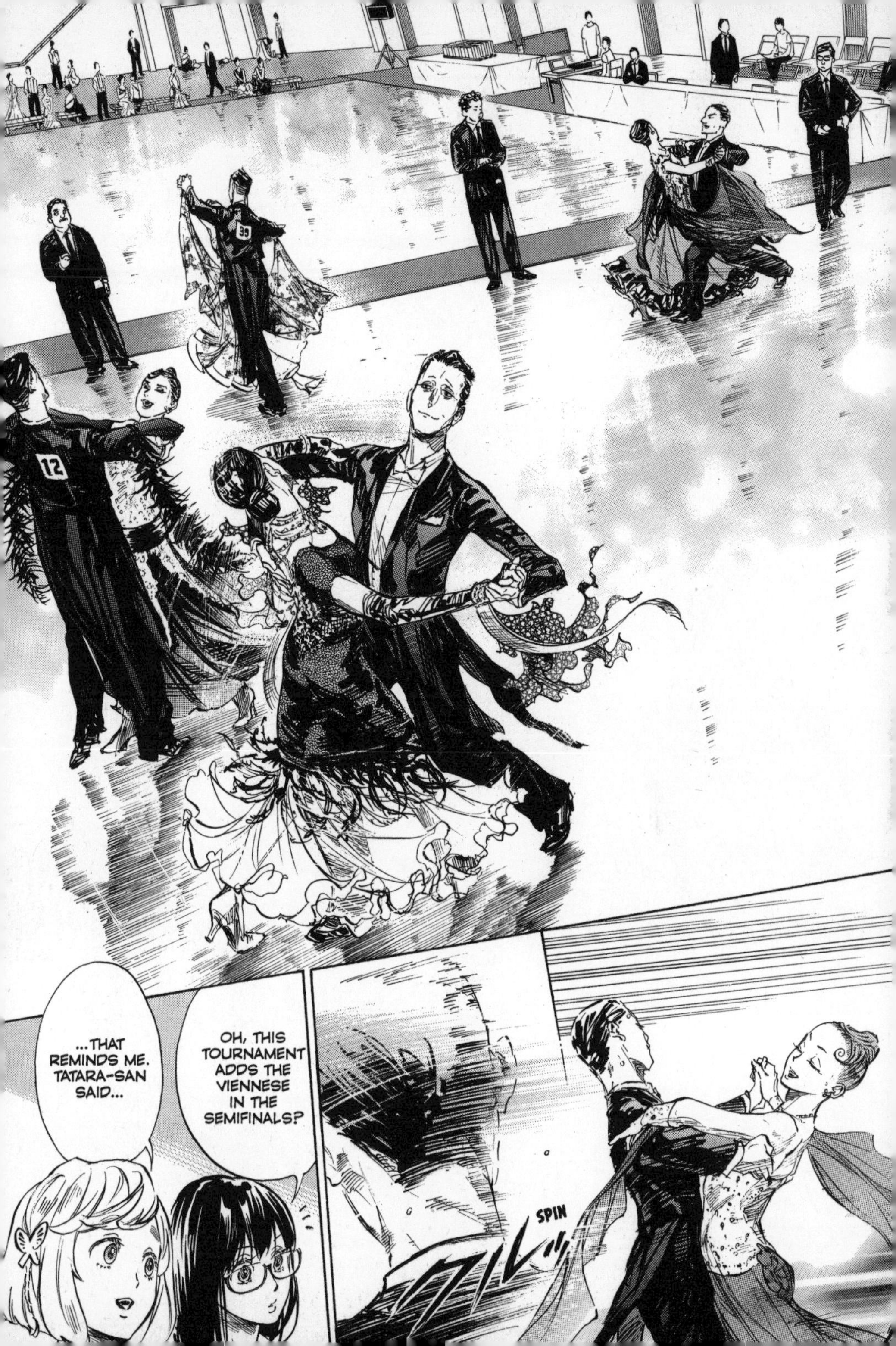
SPIN
OH, THIS TOURNAMENT ADDS THE VIENNESE IN THE SEMIFINALS?
...THAT REMINDS ME. TATARA-SAN SAID...

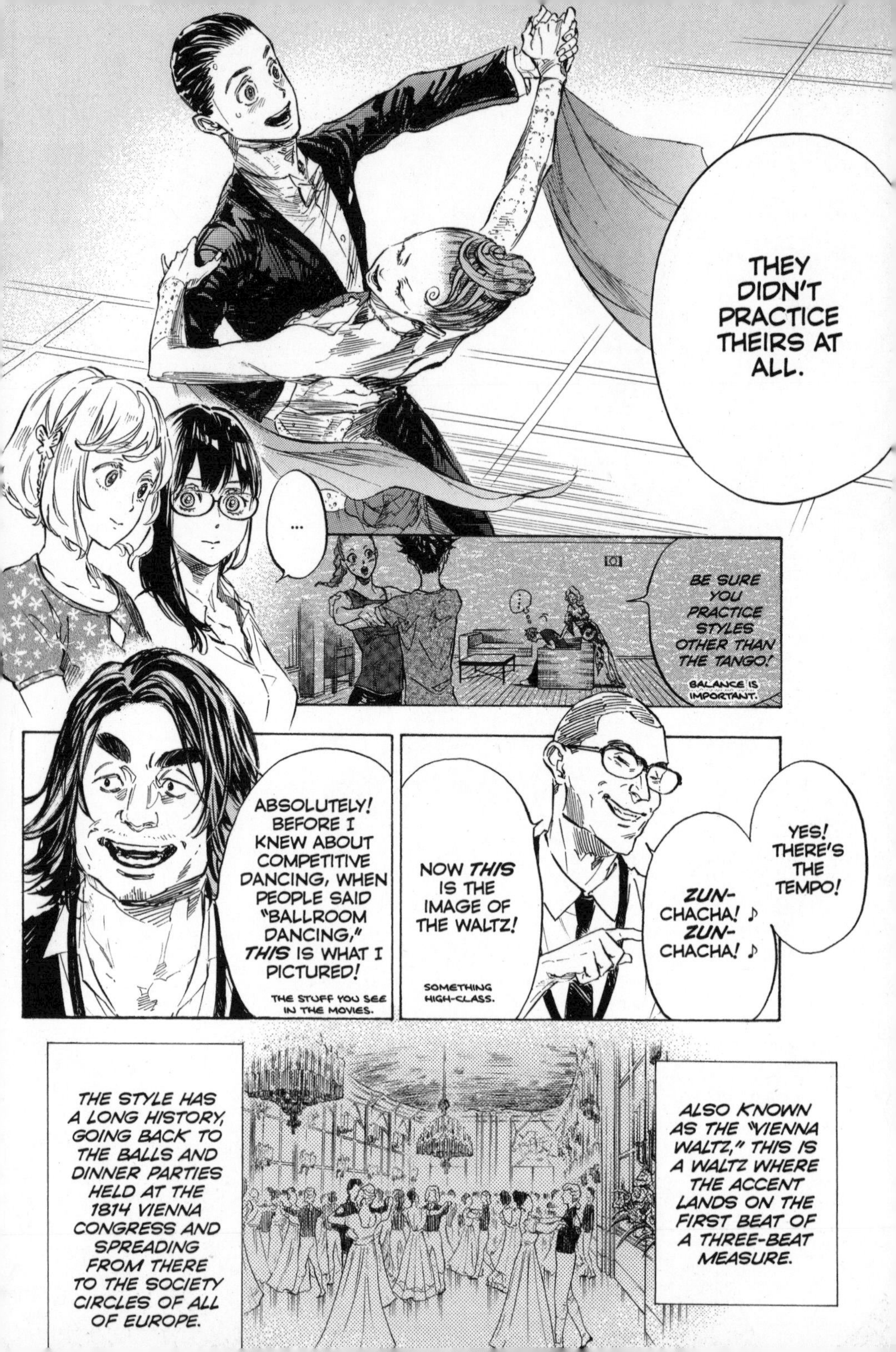
THEY DIDN'T PRACTICE THEIRS AT ALL.
...
BE SURE YOU PRACTICE STYLES OTHER THAN THE TANGO!
BALANCE IS IMPORTANT.
YES! THERE'S THE TEMPO!
ZUN-CHACHA! ♪ ZUN-CHACHA! ♪
NOW THIS IS THE IMAGE OF THE WALTZ!
SOMETHING HIGH-CLASS.
ABSOLUTELY! BEFORE I KNEW ABOUT COMPETITIVE DANCING, WHEN PEOPLE SAID "BALLROOM DANCING," THIS IS WHAT I PICTURED!
THE STUFF YOU SEE IN THE MOVIES.
ALSO KNOWN AS THE "VIENNA WALTZ," THIS IS A WALTZ WHERE THE ACCENT LANDS ON THE FIRST BEAT OF A THREE-BEAT MEASURE.
THE STYLE HAS A LONG HISTORY, GOING BACK TO THE BALLS AND DINNER PARTIES HELD AT THE 1814 VIENNA CONGRESS AND SPREADING FROM THERE TO THE SOCIETY CIRCLES OF ALL OF EUROPE.

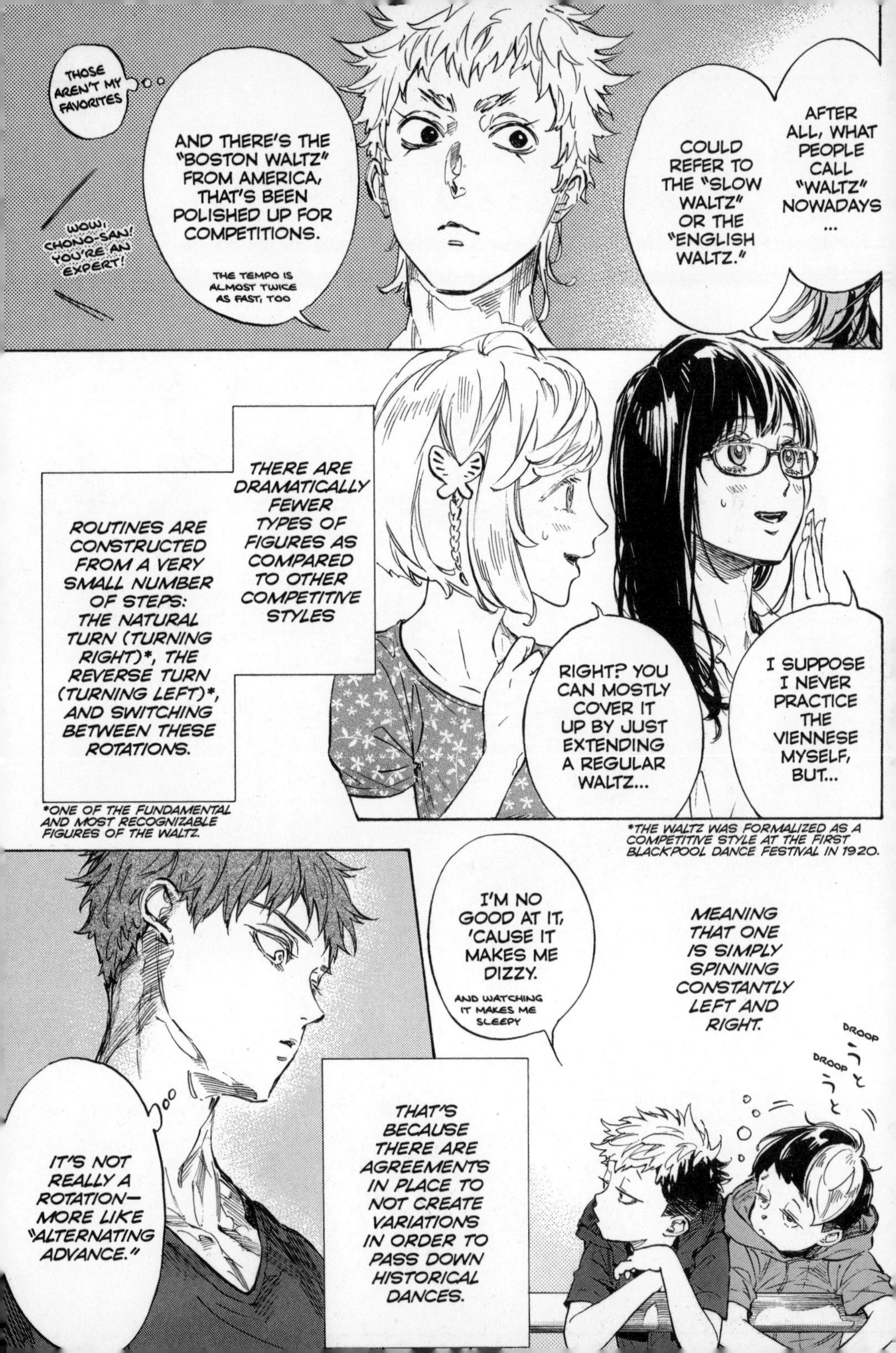
AFTER ALL, WHAT PEOPLE CALL "WALTZ" NOWADAYS ...
COULD REFER TO THE "SLOW WALTZ" OR THE "ENGLISH WALTZ."
AND THERE'S THE "BOSTON WALTZ" FROM AMERICA, THAT'S BEEN POLISHED UP FOR COMPETITIONS.
THE TEMPO IS ALMOST TWICE AS FAST, TOO
THOSE AREN'T MY FAVORITES
WOW, CHONO-SAN! YOU'RE AN EXPERT!
I SUPPOSE I NEVER PRACTICE THE VIENNESE MYSELF, BUT...
RIGHT? YOU CAN MOSTLY COVER IT UP BY JUST EXTENDING A REGULAR WALTZ...
*THE WALTZ WAS FORMALIZED AS A COMPETITIVE STYLE AT THE FIRST BLACKPOOL DANCE FESTIVAL IN 1920.
THERE ARE DRAMATICALLY FEWER TYPES OF FIGURES AS COMPARED TO OTHER COMPETITIVE STYLES
ROUTINES ARE CONSTRUCTED FROM A VERY SMALL NUMBER OF STEPS: THE NATURAL TURN (TURNING RIGHT)*, THE REVERSE TURN (TURNING LEFT)*, AND SWITCHING BETWEEN THESE ROTATIONS.
*ONE OF THE FUNDAMENTAL AND MOST RECOGNIZABLE FIGURES OF THE WALTZ.
MEANING THAT ONE IS SIMPLY SPINNING CONSTANTLY LEFT AND RIGHT.
DROOP
DROOP
I'M NO GOOD AT IT, 'CAUSE IT MAKES ME DIZZY.
AND WATCHING IT MAKES ME SLEEPY
THAT'S BECAUSE THERE ARE AGREEMENTS IN PLACE TO NOT CREATE VARIATIONS IN ORDER TO PASS DOWN HISTORICAL DANCES.
IT'S NOT REALLY A ROTATION— MORE LIKE "ALTERNATING ADVANCE."

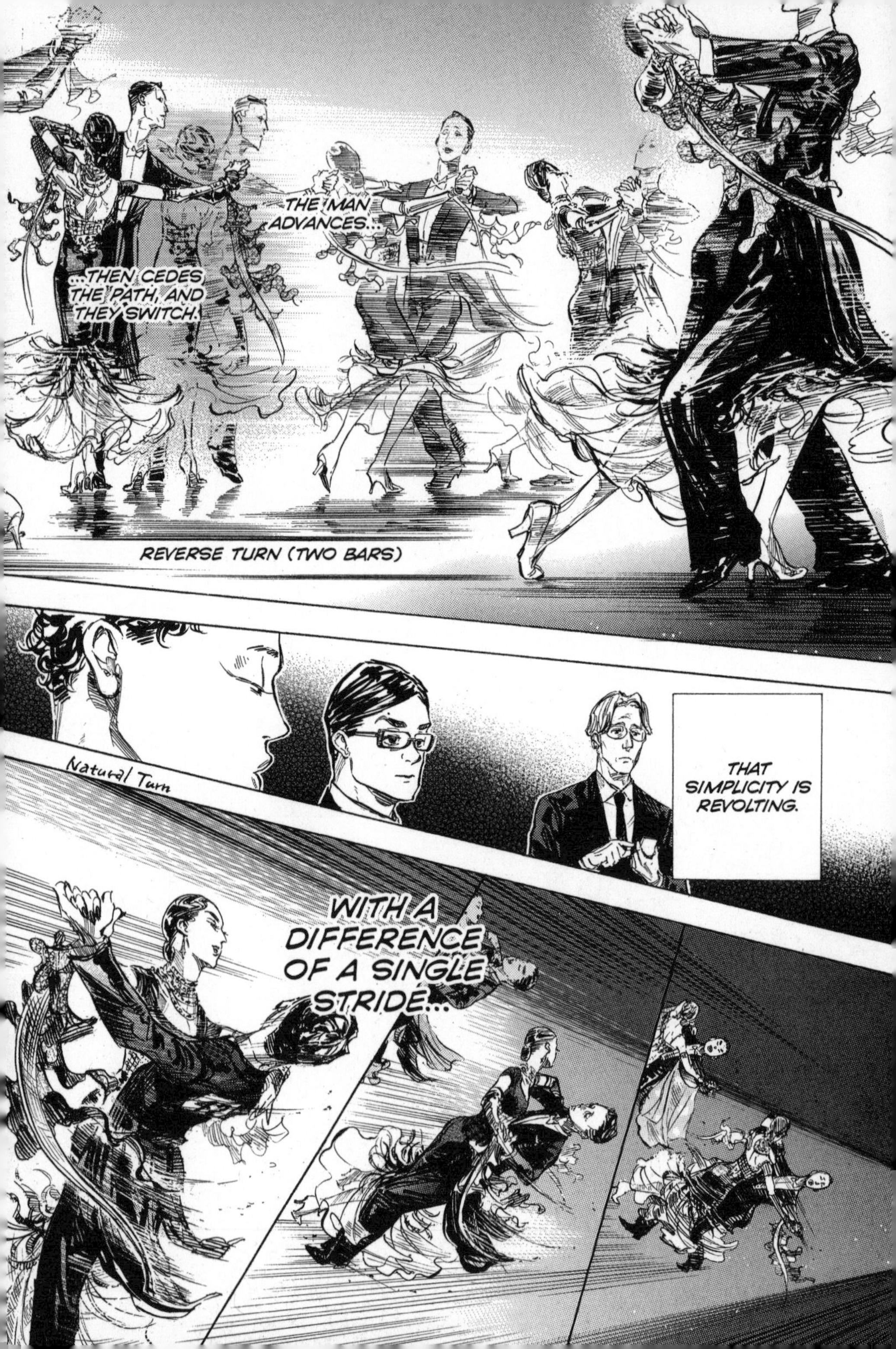
THE MAN ADVANCES...
...THEN CEDES THE PATH, AND THEY SWITCH.
REVERSE TURN (TWO BARS)
THAT SIMPLICITY IS REVOLTING.
Natural Turn
WITH A DIFFERENCE OF A SINGLE STRIDE...

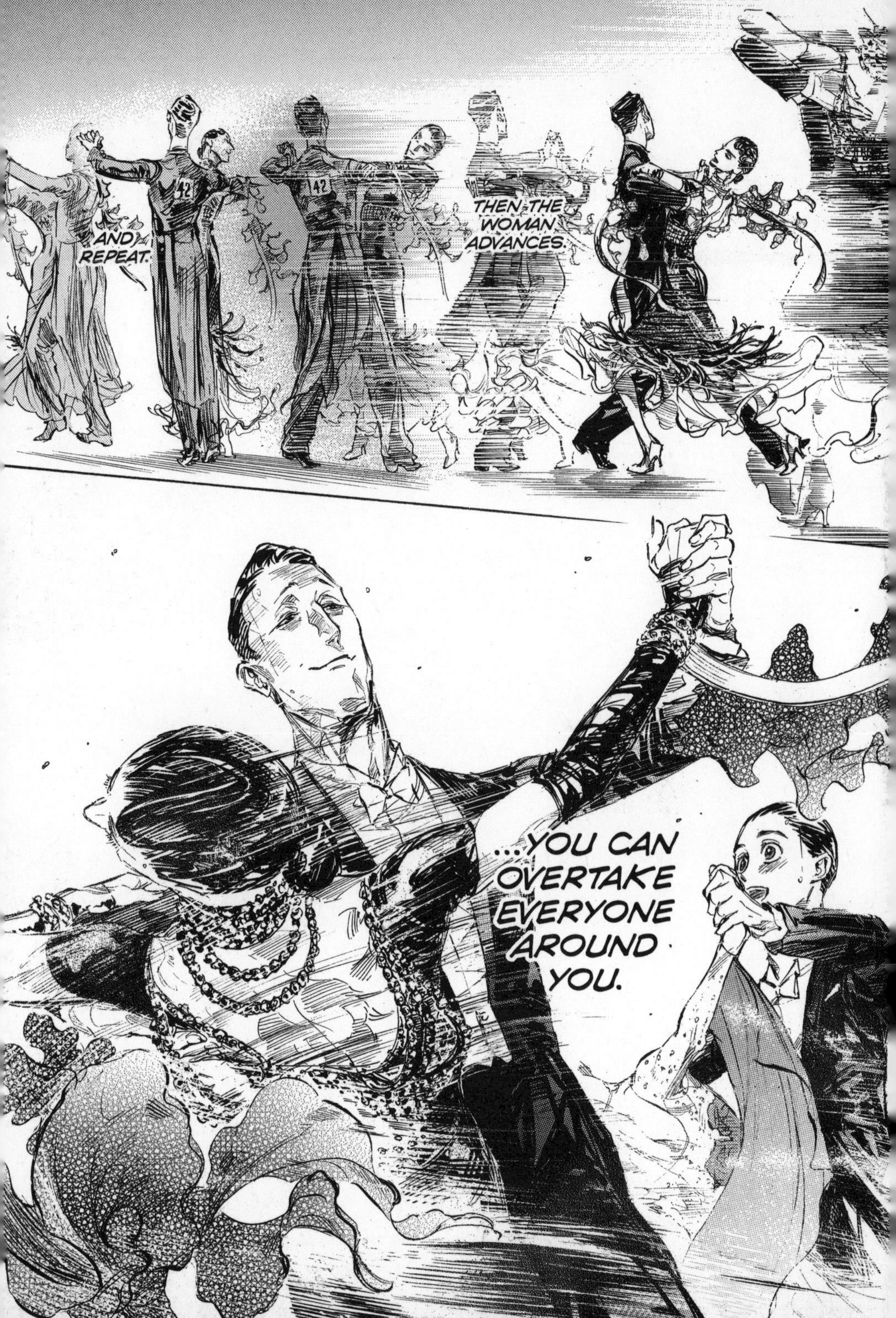
THEN THE WOMAN ADVANCES.
AND REPEAT.
...YOU CAN OVERTAKE EVERYONE AROUND YOU.

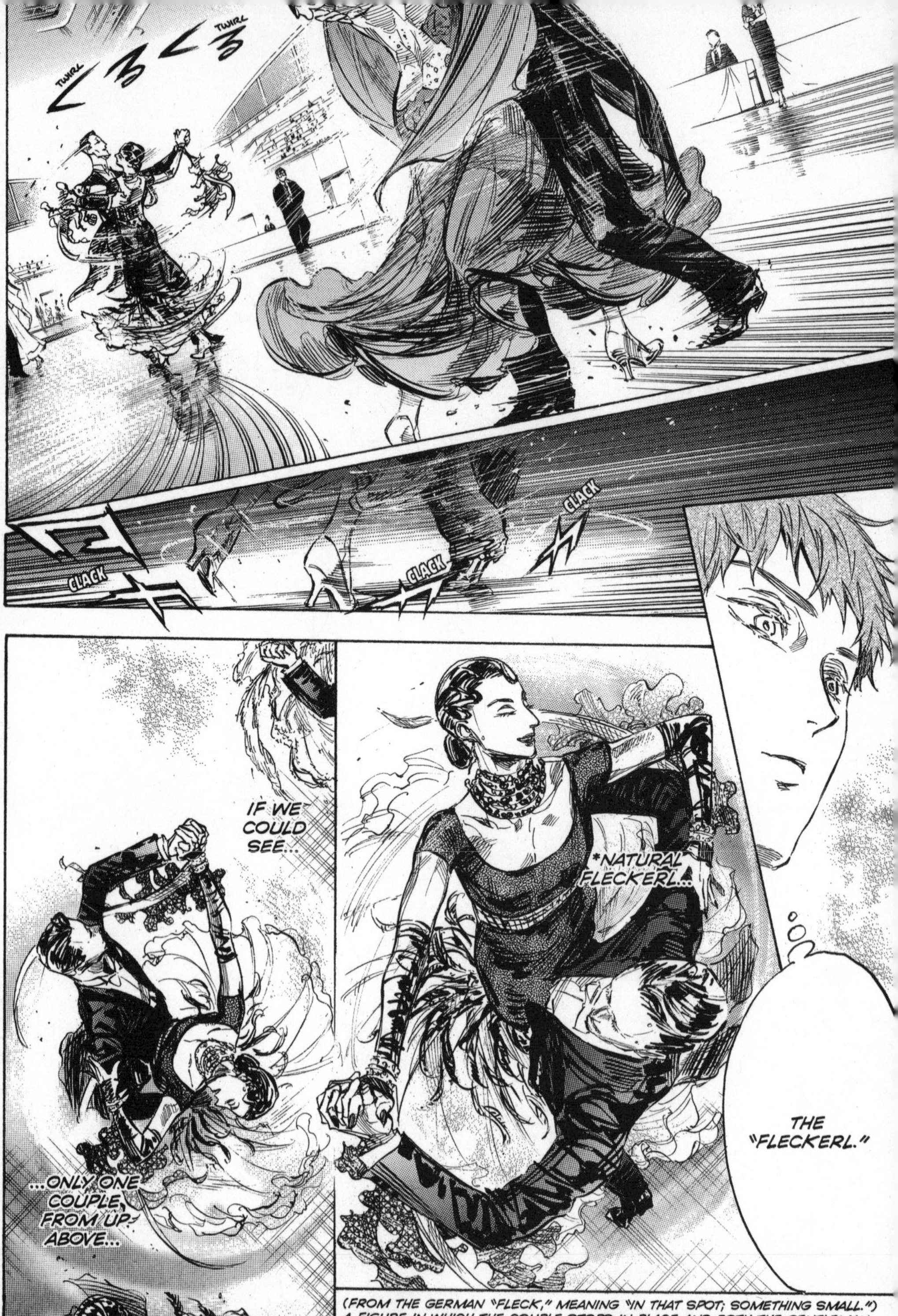

TWIRL
くるくる
TWIRL
CLACK
CLACK
CLACK
THE "FLECKERL."
*NATURAL FLECKERL...
IF WE COULD SEE...
...ONLY ONE COUPLE, FROM UP ABOVE...

(FROM THE GERMAN "FLECK," MEANING "IN THAT SPOT; SOMETHING SMALL.") A FIGURE IN WHICH THE COUPLE STOPS IN PLACE AND BOTH THE GENTLEMAN AND LADY TAKE ONE STEP AT A TIME ACROSS THE BODY WHILE TURNING IN PLACE. OFTEN DANCED AT THE CENTER OF THE DANCE FLOOR.

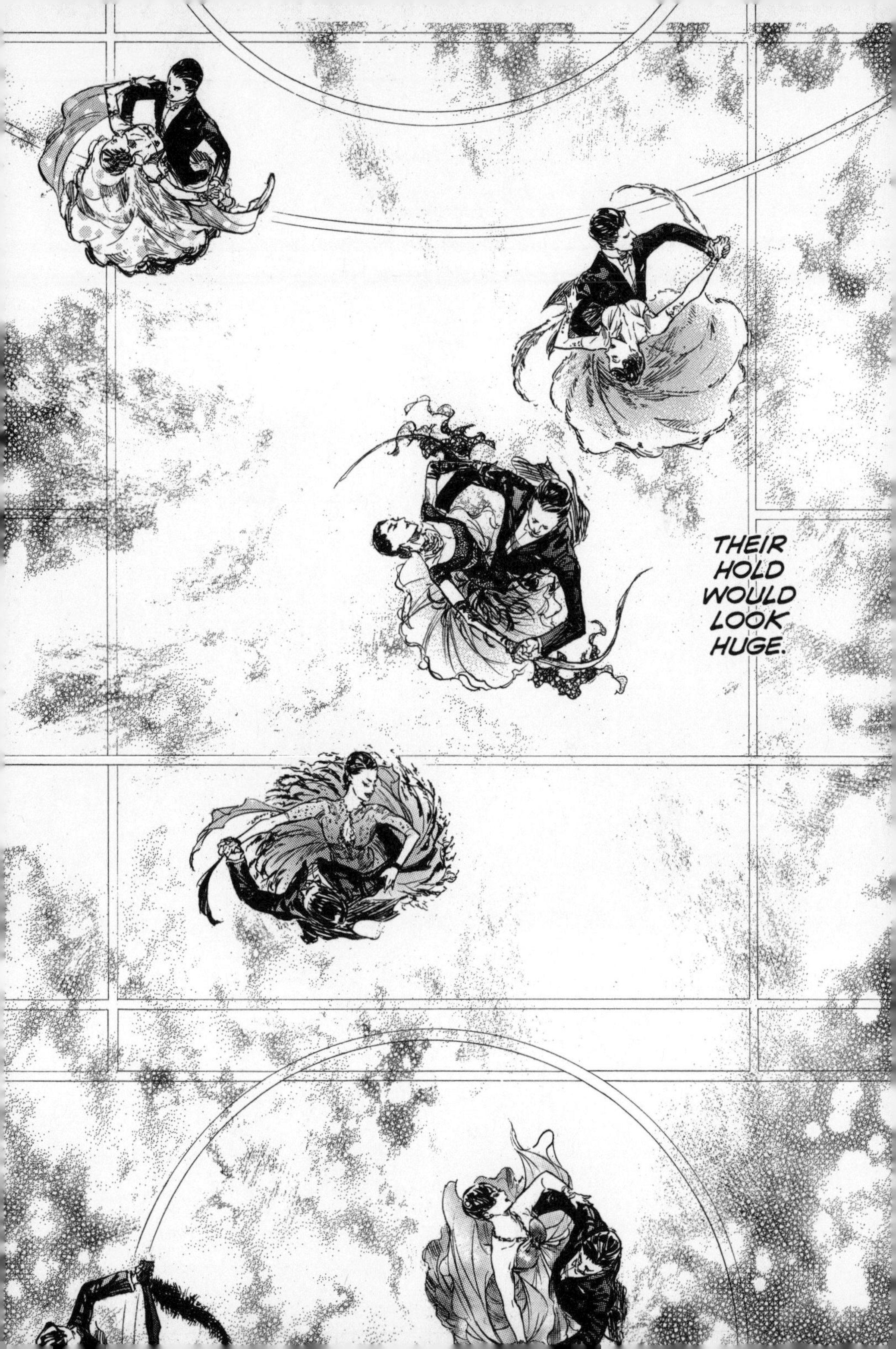
THEIR HOLD WOULD LOOK HUGE.

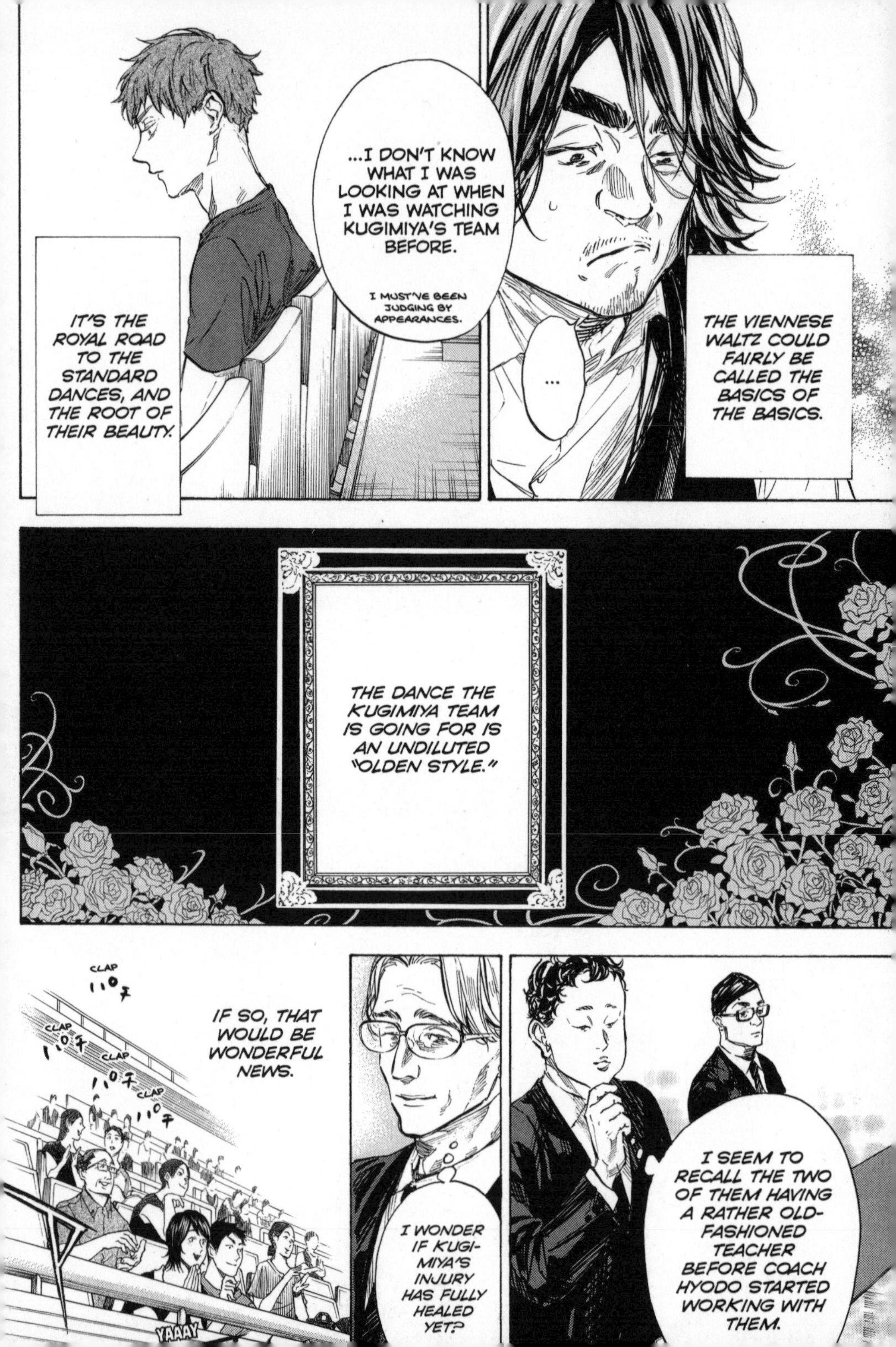
...I DON'T KNOW WHAT I WAS LOOKING AT WHEN I WAS WATCHING KUGIMIYA'S TEAM BEFORE.
I MUST'VE BEEN JUDGING BY APPEARANCES.
...
THE VIENNESE WALTZ COULD FAIRLY BE CALLED THE BASICS OF THE BASICS.
IT'S THE ROYAL ROAD TO THE STANDARD DANCES, AND THE ROOT OF THEIR BEAUTY.
THE DANCE THE KUGIMIYA TEAM IS GOING FOR IS AN UNDILUTED "OLDEN STYLE."
I SEEM TO RECALL THE TWO OF THEM HAVING A RATHER OLD-FASHIONED TEACHER BEFORE COACH HYODO STARTED WORKING WITH THEM.
I WONDER IF KUGIMIYA'S INJURY HAS FULLY HEALED YET?
IF SO, THAT WOULD BE WONDERFUL NEWS.
CLAP
CLAP
CLAP
CLAP
YAAAY

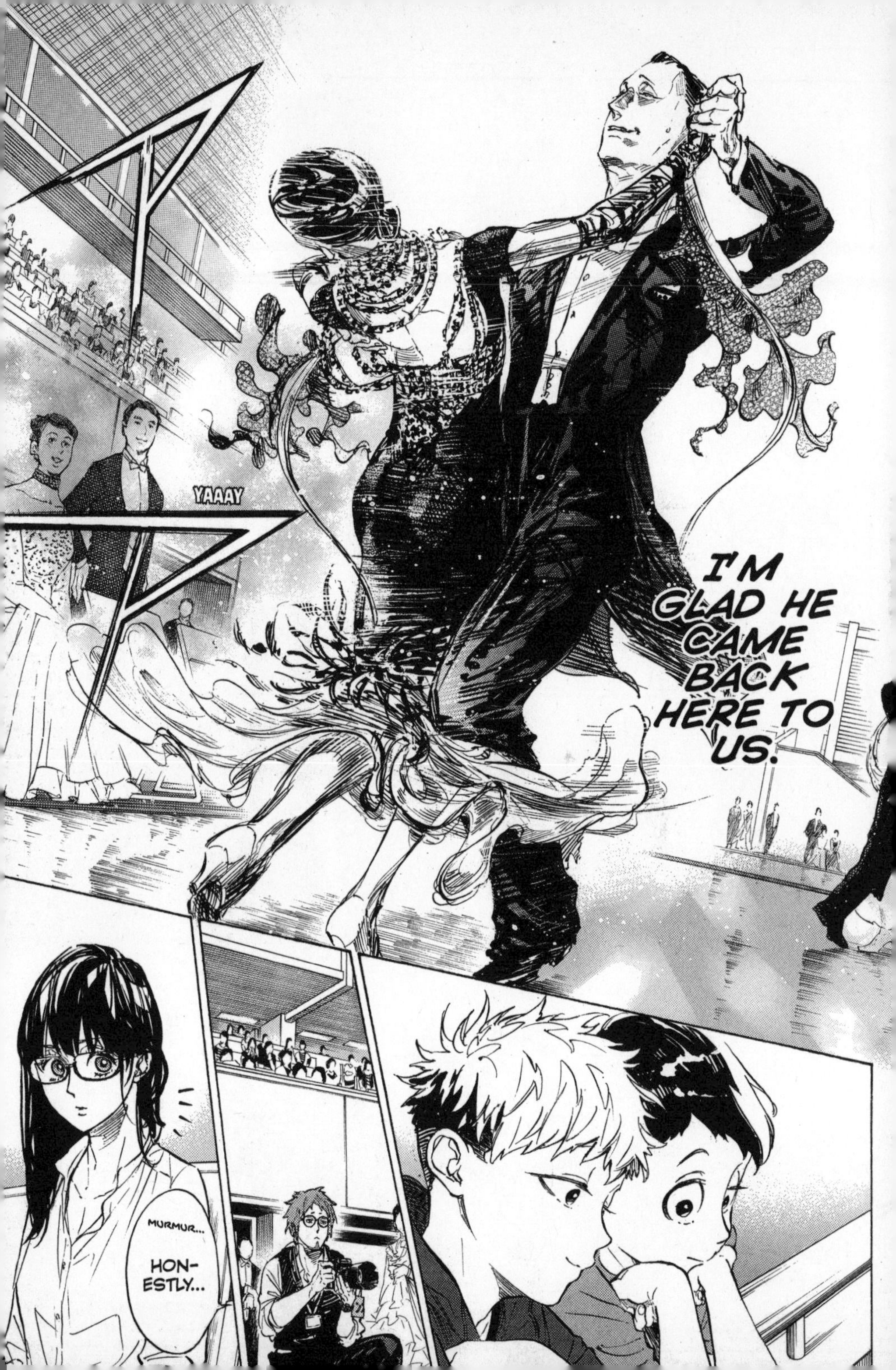
YAAAY
I'M GLAD HE CAME BACK HERE TO US.
MURMUR...
HON-ESTLY...

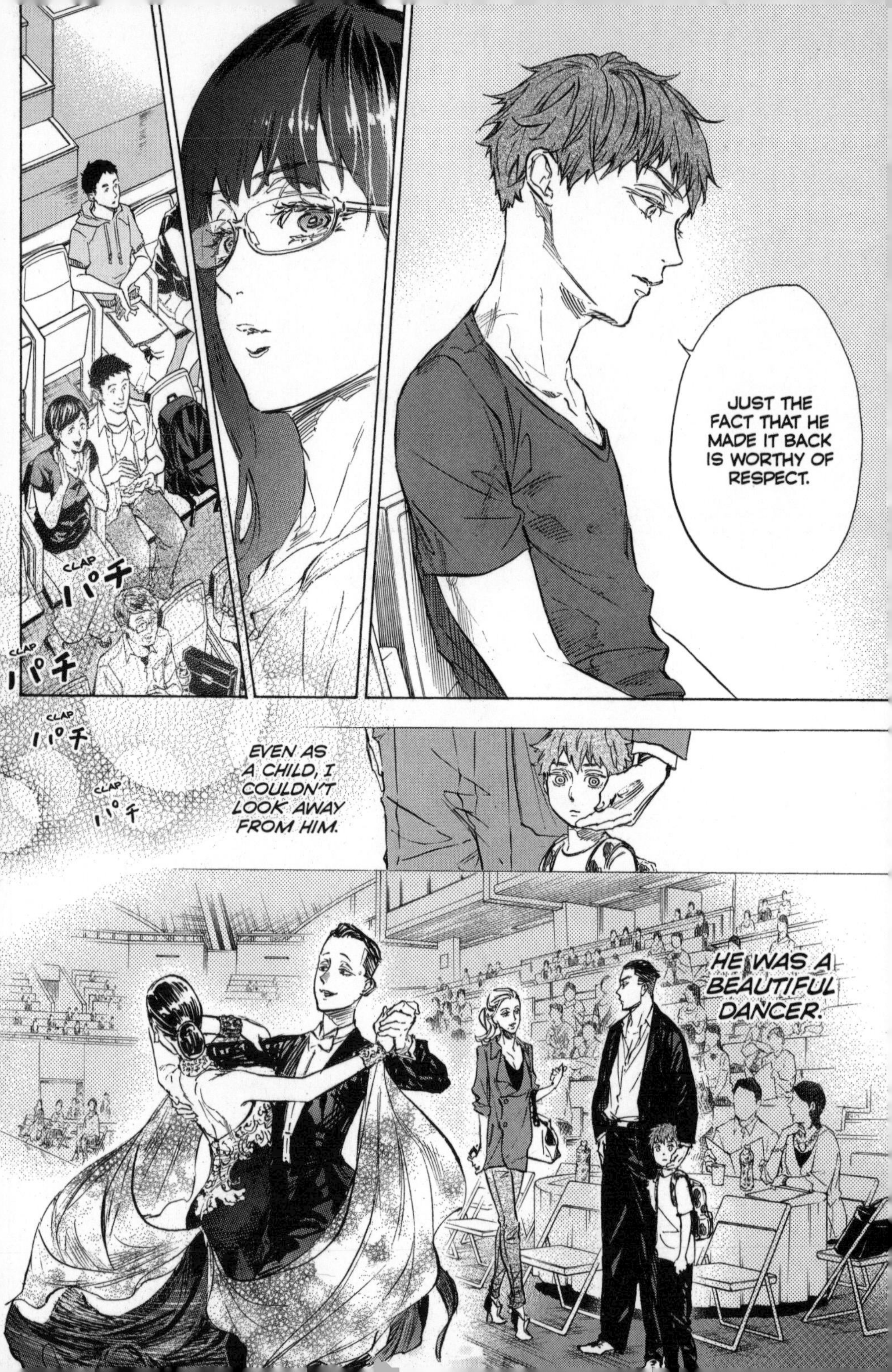
JUST THE FACT THAT HE MADE IT BACK IS WORTHY OF RESPECT.
CLAP
パチ
CLAP
パチ
CLAP
パチ
CLAP
パチ
EVEN AS A CHILD, I COULDN'T LOOK AWAY FROM HIM.
HE WAS A BEAUTIFUL DANCER.

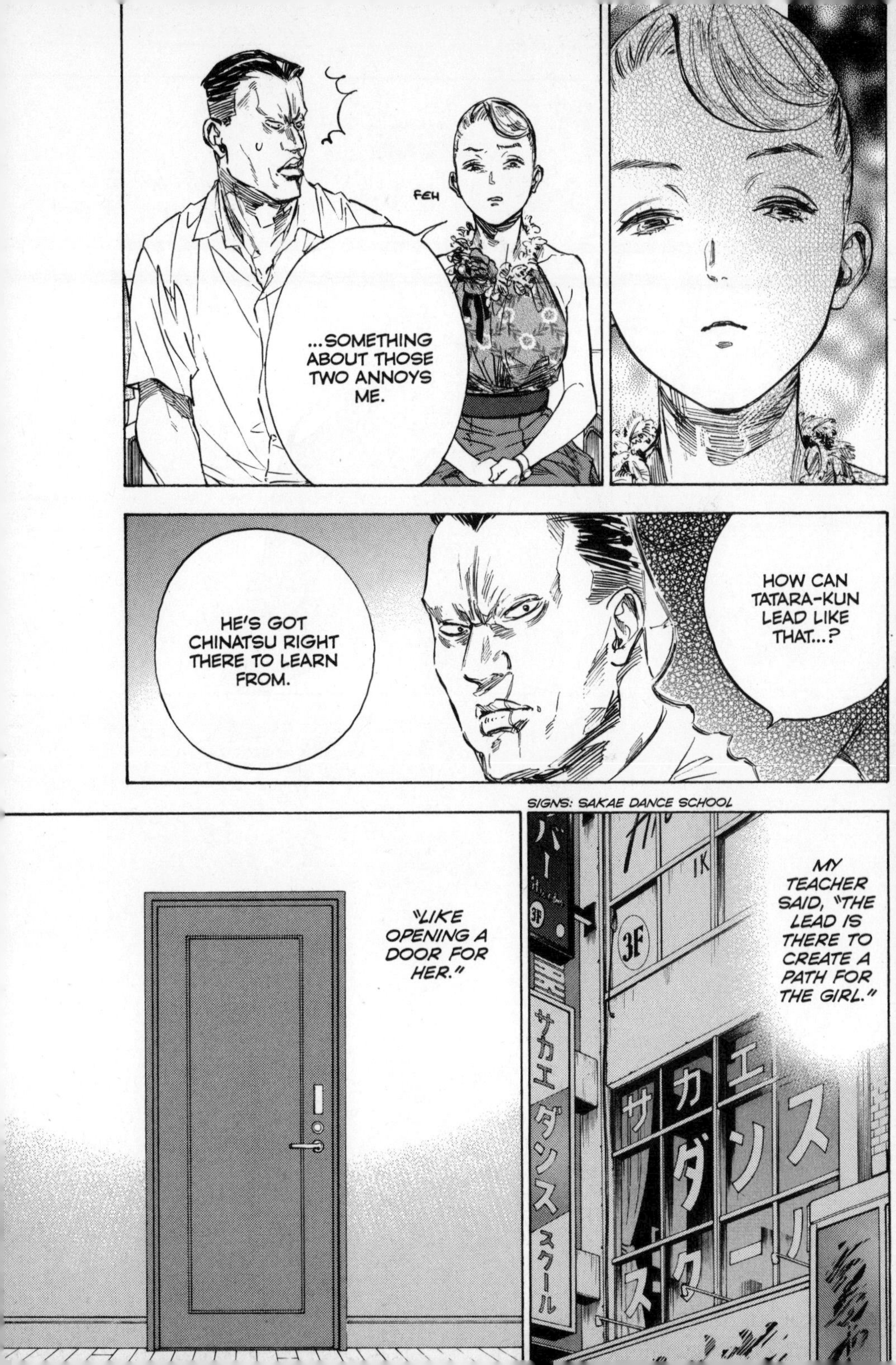
FEH
...SOMETHING ABOUT THOSE TWO ANNOYS ME.
HOW CAN TATARA-KUN LEAD LIKE THAT...?
HE'S GOT CHINATSU RIGHT THERE TO LEARN FROM.
SIGNS: SAKAE DANCE SCHOOL
MY TEACHER SAID, "THE LEAD IS THERE TO CREATE A PATH FOR THE GIRL."
3F
サカエダンススクール
サカエ ダンス スクール
"LIKE OPENING A DOOR FOR HER."

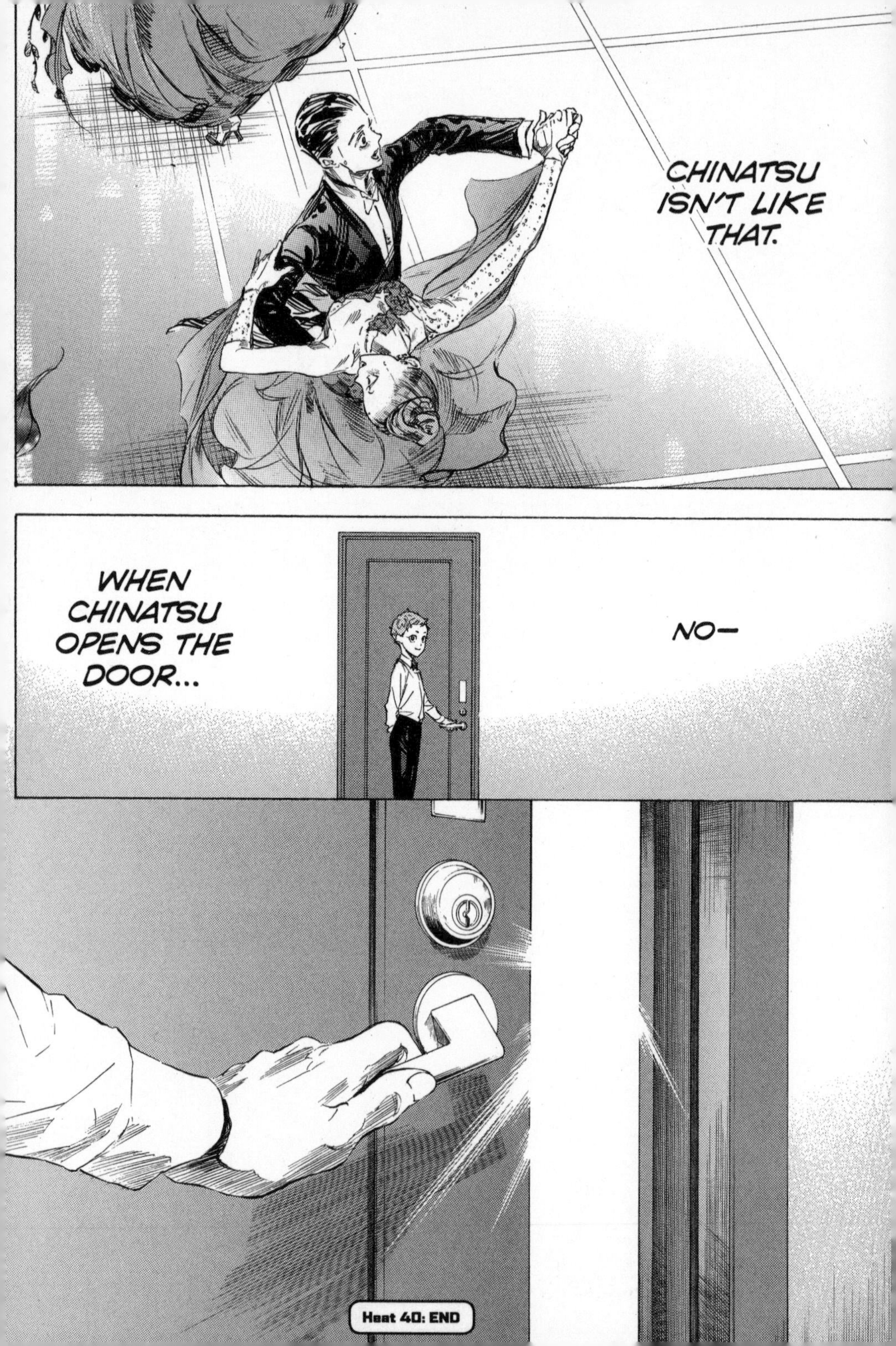
CHINATSU ISN'T LIKE THAT.
NO—
WHEN CHINATSU OPENS THE DOOR...
Heat 40: END

WELCOME TO THE BALLROOM

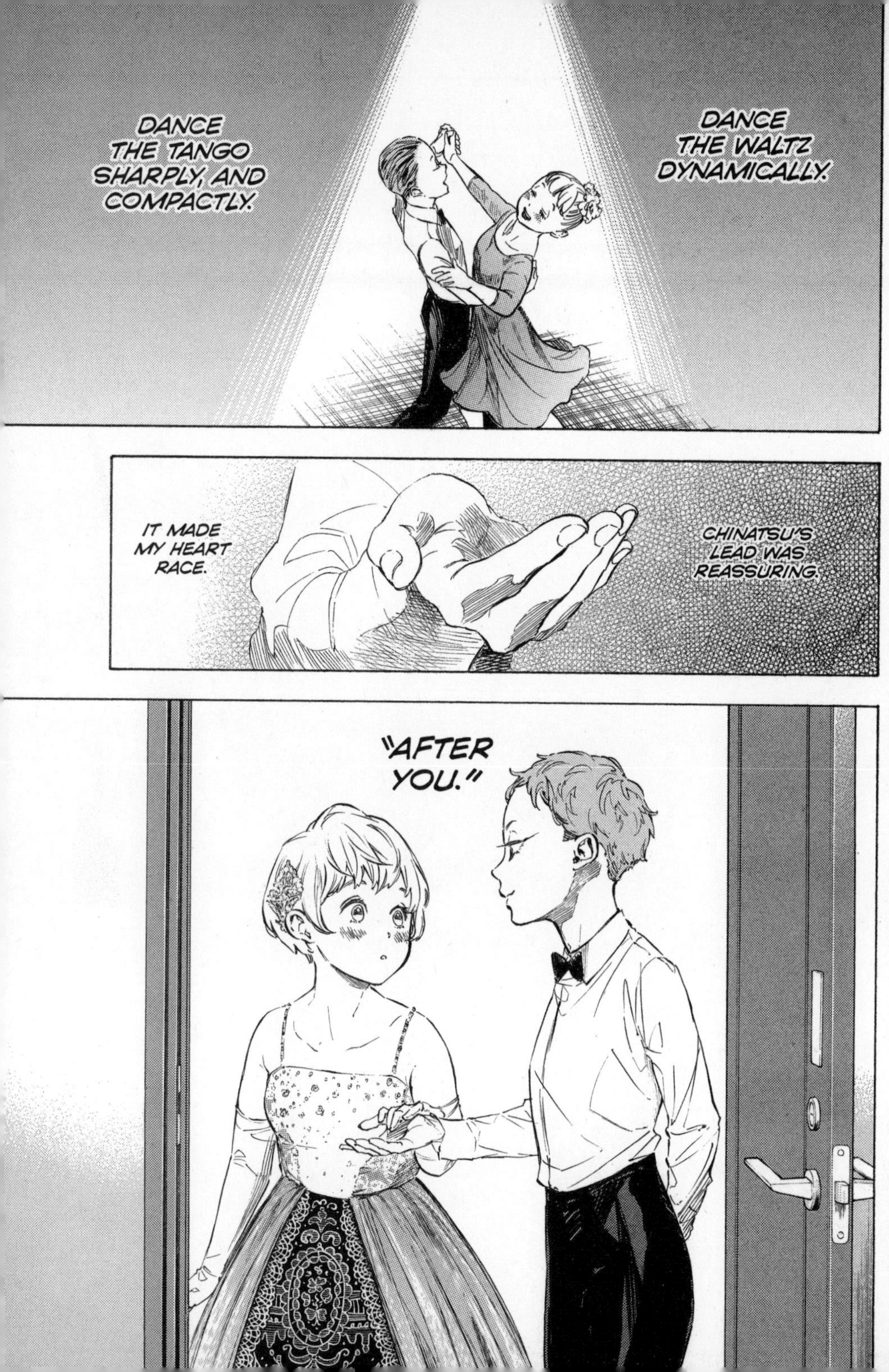
DANCE THE WALTZ DYNAMICALLY.
DANCE THE TANGO SHARPLY, AND COMPACTLY.
CHINATSU'S LEAD WAS REASSURING.
IT MADE MY HEART RACE.
"AFTER YOU."

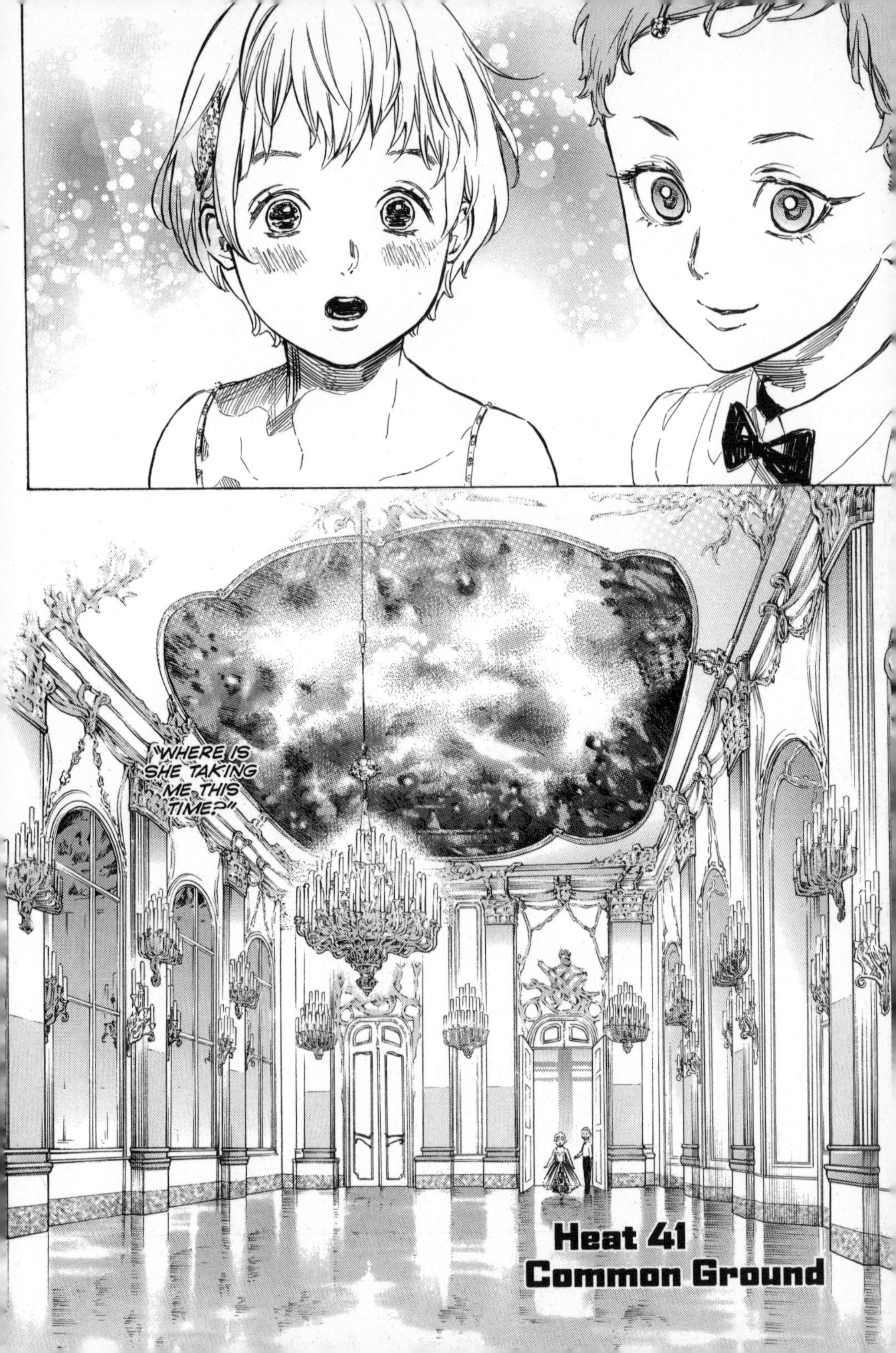
"WHERE IS SHE TAKING ME THIS TIME?"
Heat 41
Common Ground

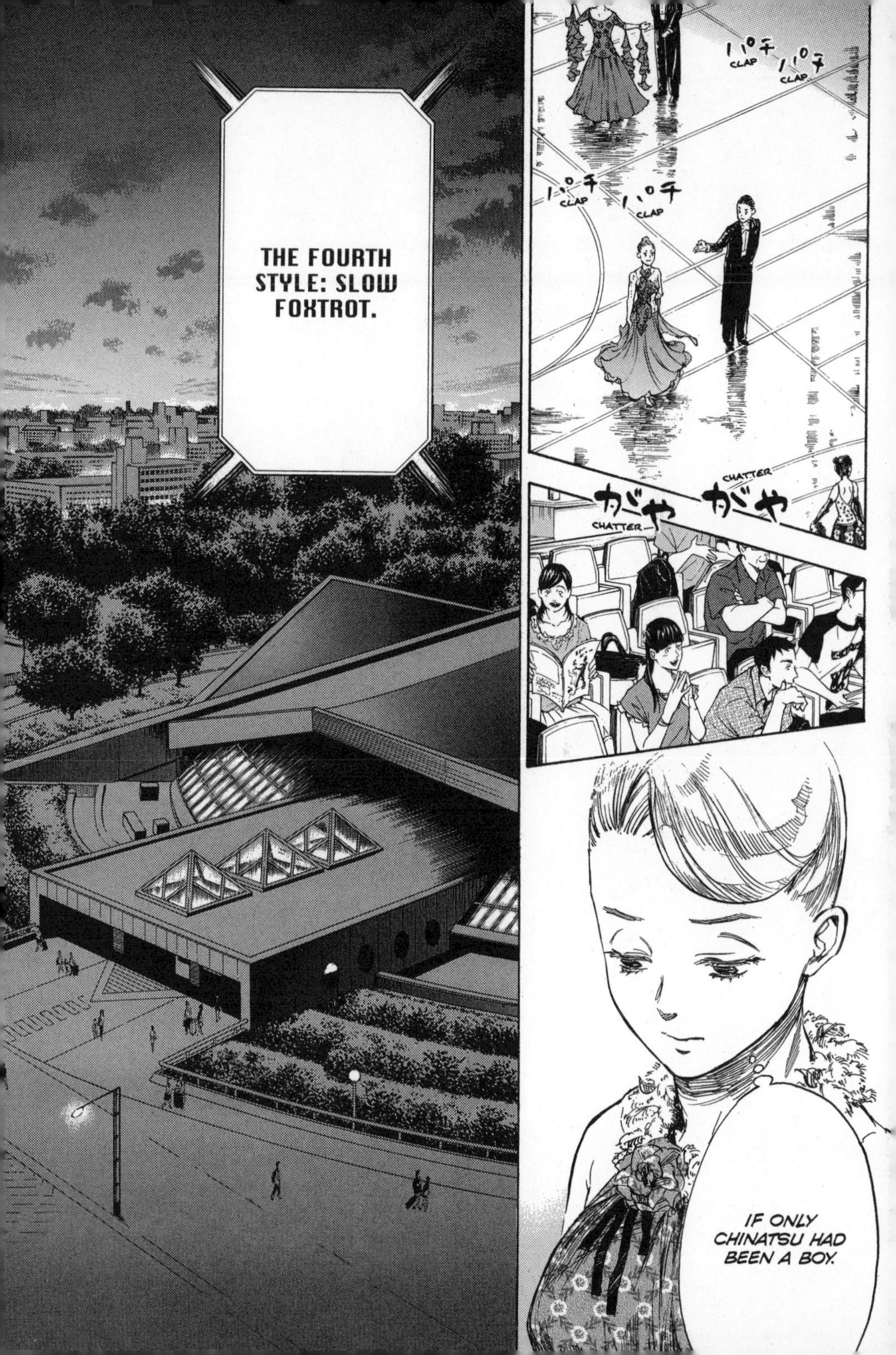
パチ
CLAP
パチ
CLAP
パチ
CLAP
パチ
CLAP
ガヤ
CHATTER
ガヤ
CHATTER
IF ONLY CHINATSU HAD BEEN A BOY.
THE FOURTH STYLE: SLOW FOXTROT.

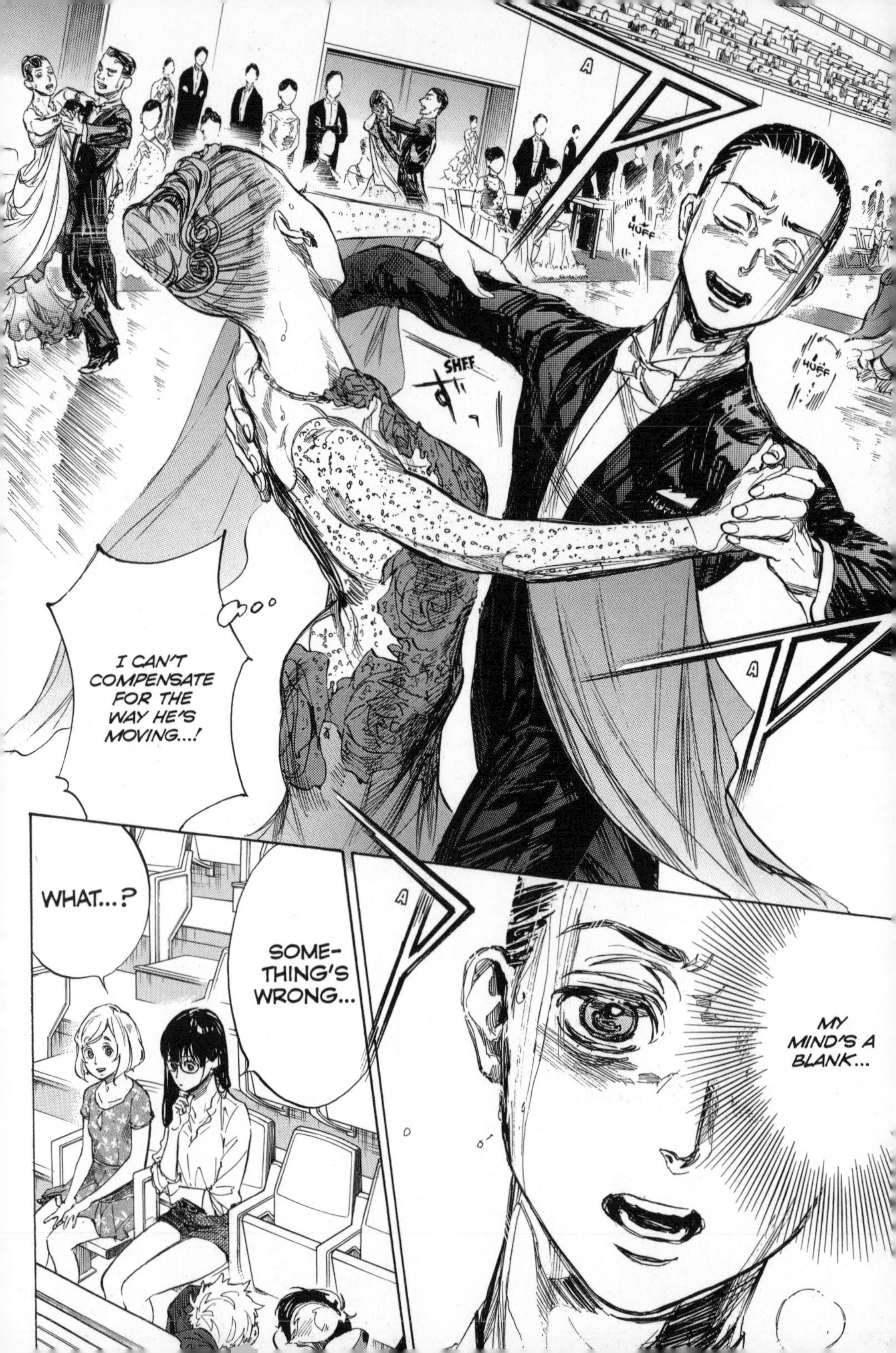
A
HUFF
HUFF
SHFF
A
I CAN'T COMPENSATE FOR THE WAY HE'S MOVING...!
MY MIND'S A BLANK...
A
SOME-THING'S WRONG...
WHAT...?

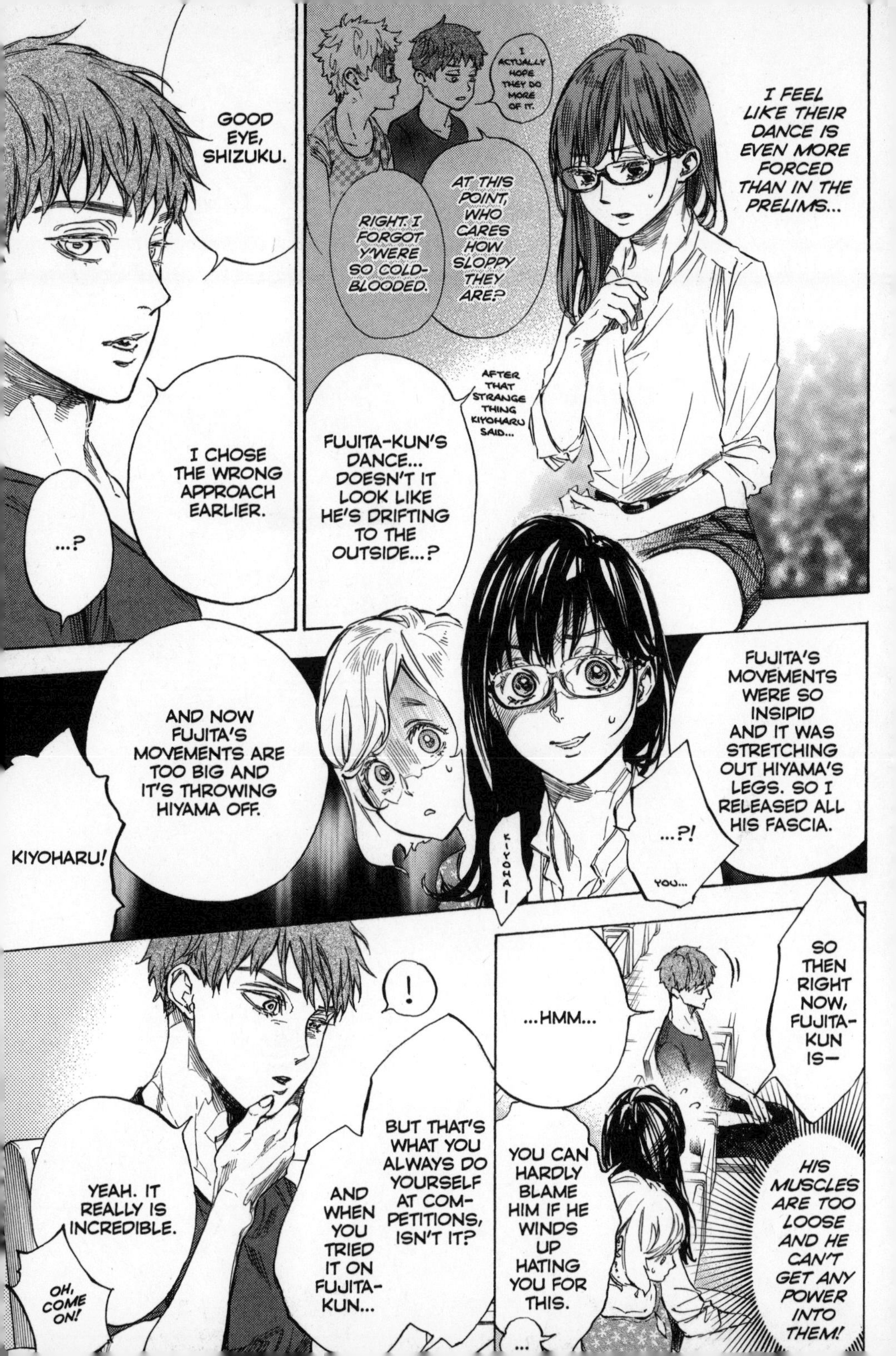
I FEEL LIKE THEIR DANCE IS EVEN MORE FORCED THAN IN THE PRELIMS...
I ACTUALLY HOPE THEY DO MORE OF IT.
AT THIS POINT, WHO CARES HOW SLOPPY THEY ARE?
RIGHT. I FORGOT Y'WERE SO COLD-BLOODED.
AFTER THAT STRANGE THING KIYOHARU SAID...
FUJITA-KUN'S DANCE... DOESN'T IT LOOK LIKE HE'S DRIFTING TO THE OUTSIDE...?
GOOD EYE, SHIZUKU.
I CHOSE THE WRONG APPROACH EARLIER.
...?
FUJITA'S MOVEMENTS WERE SO INSIPID AND IT WAS STRETCHING OUT HIYAMA'S LEGS. SO I RELEASED ALL HIS FASCIA.
...?!
YOU...
KIYOHA—
AND NOW FUJITA'S MOVEMENTS ARE TOO BIG AND IT'S THROWING HIYAMA OFF.
KIYOHARU!
SO THEN RIGHT NOW, FUJITA-KUN IS—
HIS MUSCLES ARE TOO LOOSE AND HE CAN'T GET ANY POWER INTO THEM!
...HMM...
YOU CAN HARDLY BLAME HIM IF HE WINDS UP HATING YOU FOR THIS.
...
!
BUT THAT'S WHAT YOU ALWAYS DO YOURSELF AT COMPETITIONS, ISN'T IT?
AND WHEN YOU TRIED IT ON FUJITA-KUN...
YEAH. IT REALLY IS INCREDIBLE.
OH, COME ON!

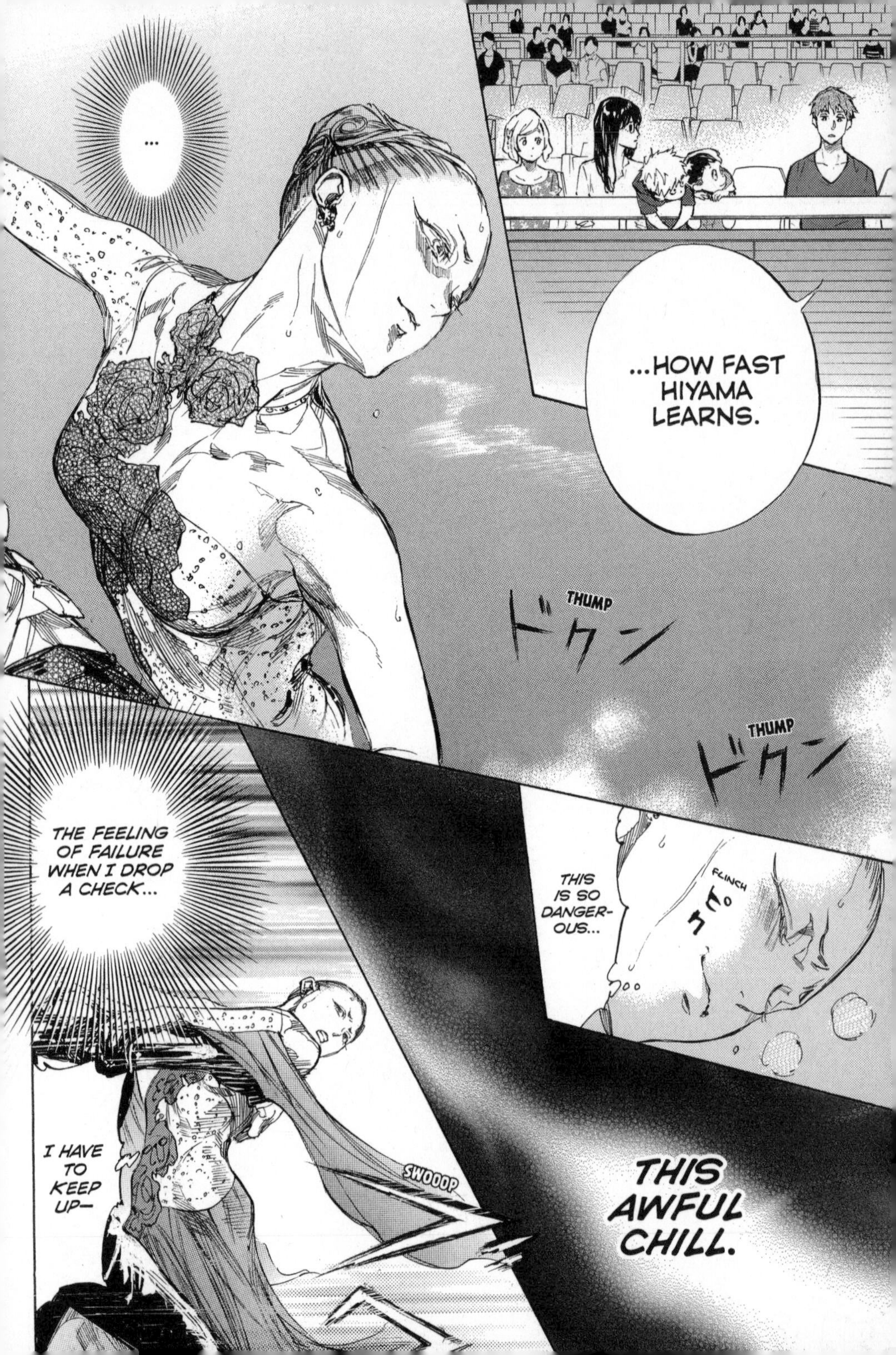

...HOW FAST HIYAMA LEARNS.
...
THUMP
ドクン
THUMP
ドクン
THIS IS SO DANGEROUS...
FLINCH
THE FEELING OF FAILURE WHEN I DROP A CHECK...
I HAVE TO KEEP UP—
SWOOOP
THIS AWFUL CHILL.

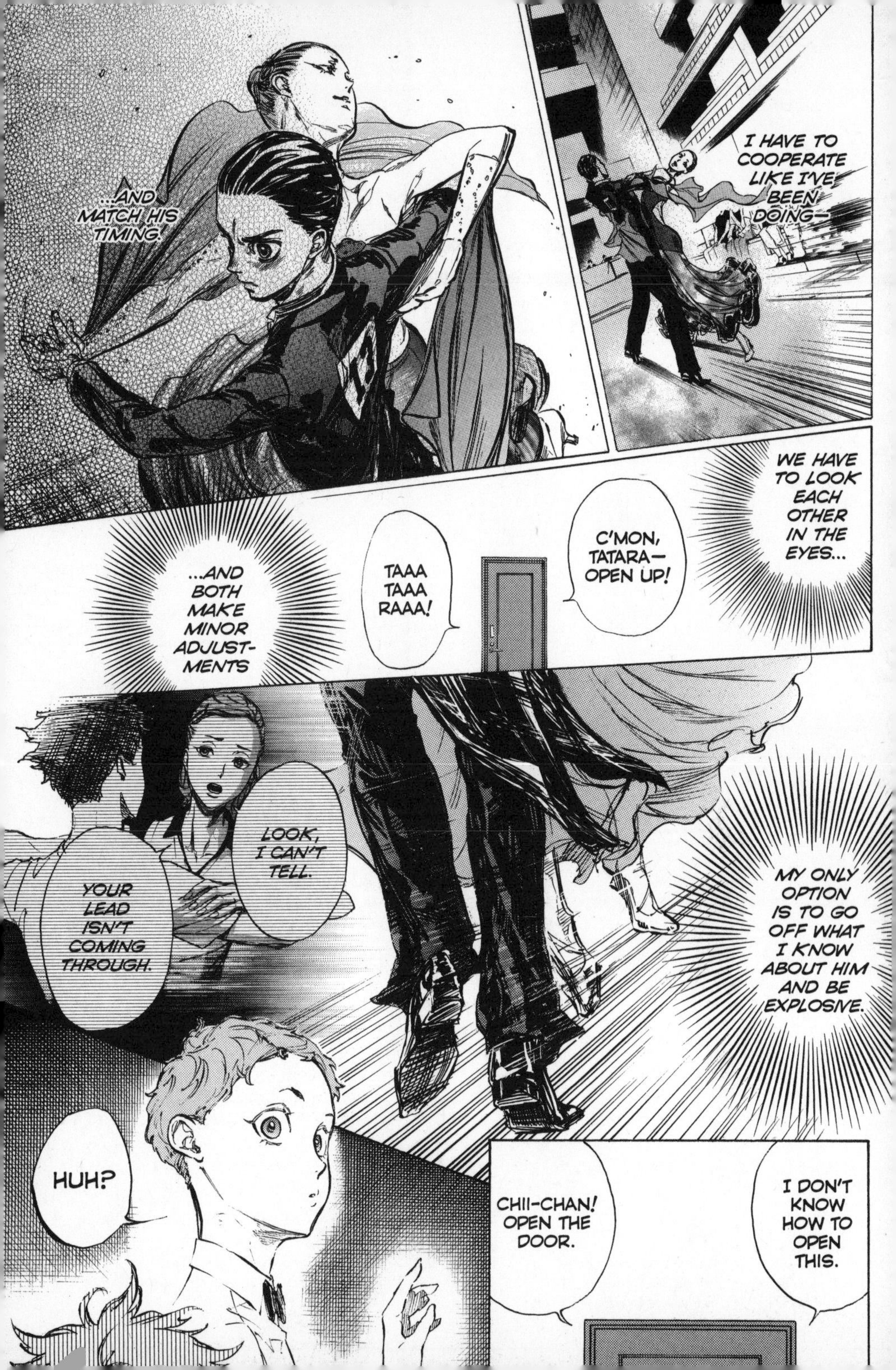
I HAVE TO COOPERATE LIKE I'VE BEEN DOING—
...AND MATCH HIS TIMING.
WE HAVE TO LOOK EACH OTHER IN THE EYES...
C'MON, TATARA—OPEN UP!
TAAA TAAA RAAA!
...AND BOTH MAKE MINOR ADJUST-MENTS
MY ONLY OPTION IS TO GO OFF WHAT I KNOW ABOUT HIM AND BE EXPLOSIVE.
LOOK, I CAN'T TELL.
YOUR LEAD ISN'T COMING THROUGH.
I DON'T KNOW HOW TO OPEN THIS.
CHII-CHAN! OPEN THE DOOR.
HUH?

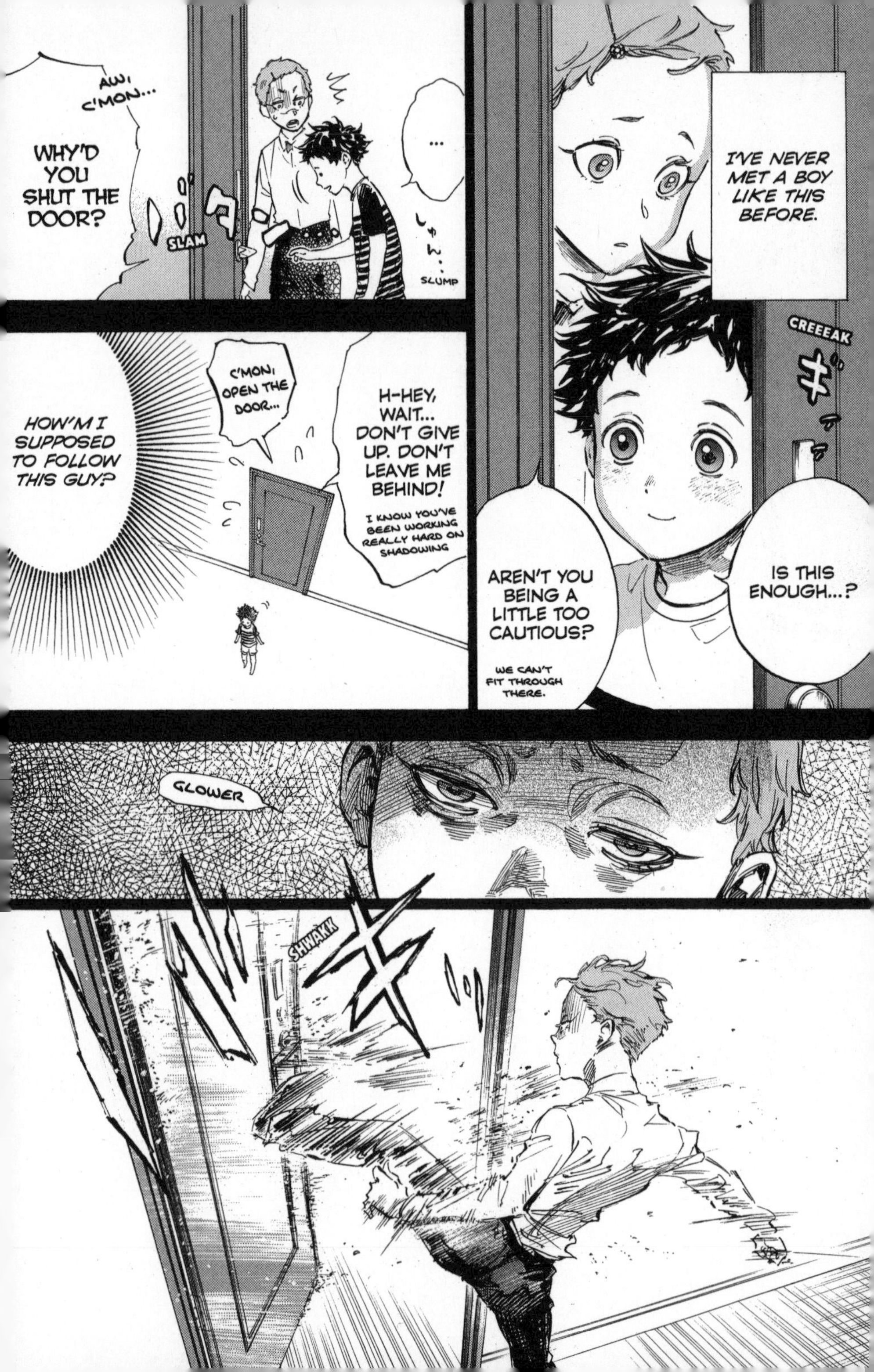
I'VE NEVER MET A BOY LIKE THIS BEFORE.
CREEEAK
IS THIS ENOUGH...?
AREN'T YOU BEING A LITTLE TOO CAUTIOUS?
WE CAN'T FIT THROUGH THERE.
...
しゅん‥
SLUMP
SLAM
AW, C'MON...
WHY'D YOU SHUT THE DOOR?
H-HEY, WAIT... DON'T GIVE UP. DON'T LEAVE ME BEHIND!
I KNOW YOU'VE BEEN WORKING REALLY HARD ON SHADOWING
C'MON, OPEN THE DOOR...
HOW'M I SUPPOSED TO FOLLOW THIS GUY?
GLOWER
SHWAKK

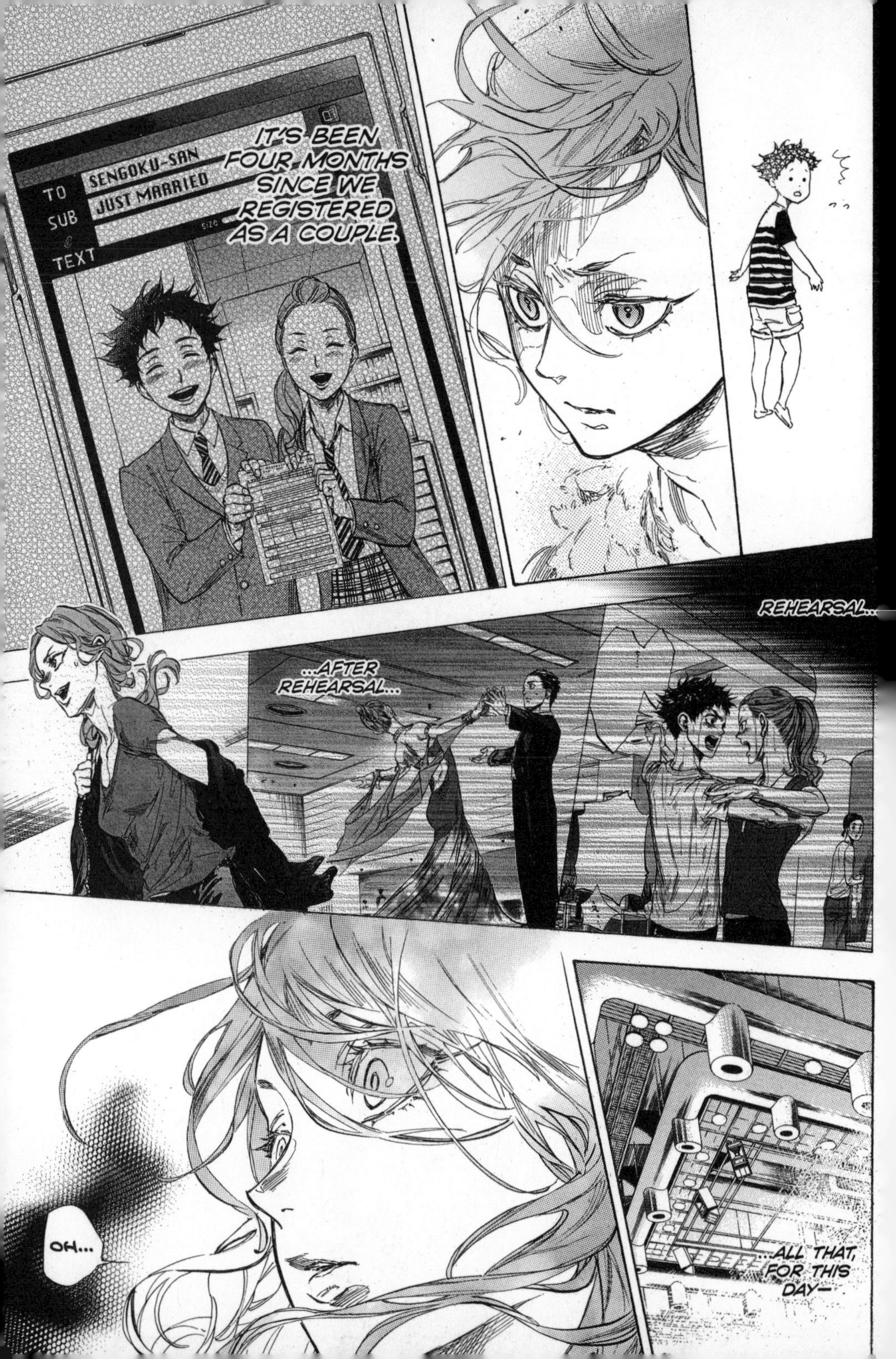
TO SENGOKU-SAN
SUB JUST MARRIED
TEXT
IT'S BEEN FOUR MONTHS SINCE WE REGISTERED AS A COUPLE.
REHEARSAL...
...AFTER REHEARSAL...
...ALL THAT, FOR THIS DAY—
OH...

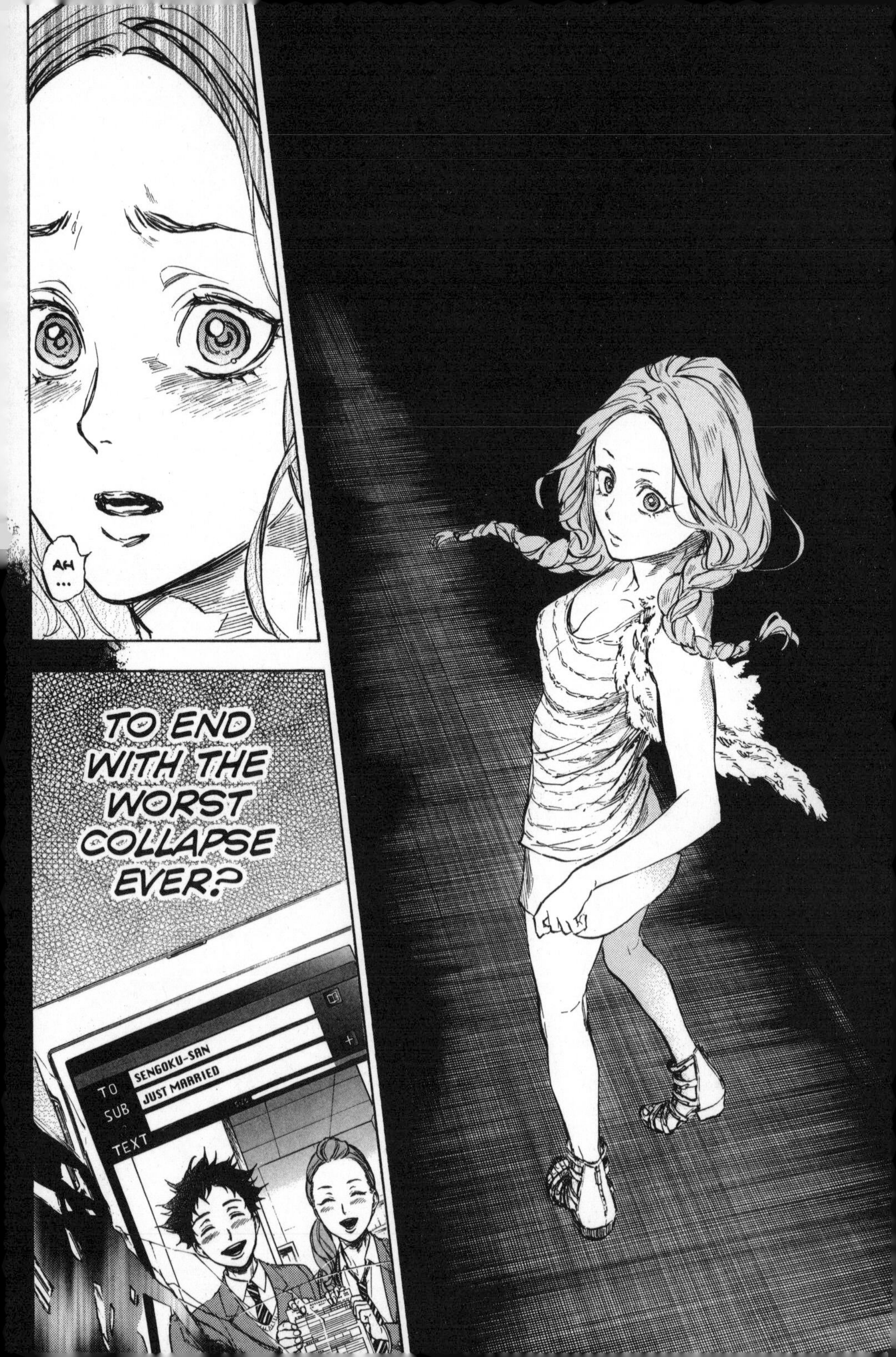
AH ...
TO END WITH THE WORST COLLAPSE EVER?
TO SENGOKU-SAN
SUB JUST MARRIED
TEXT

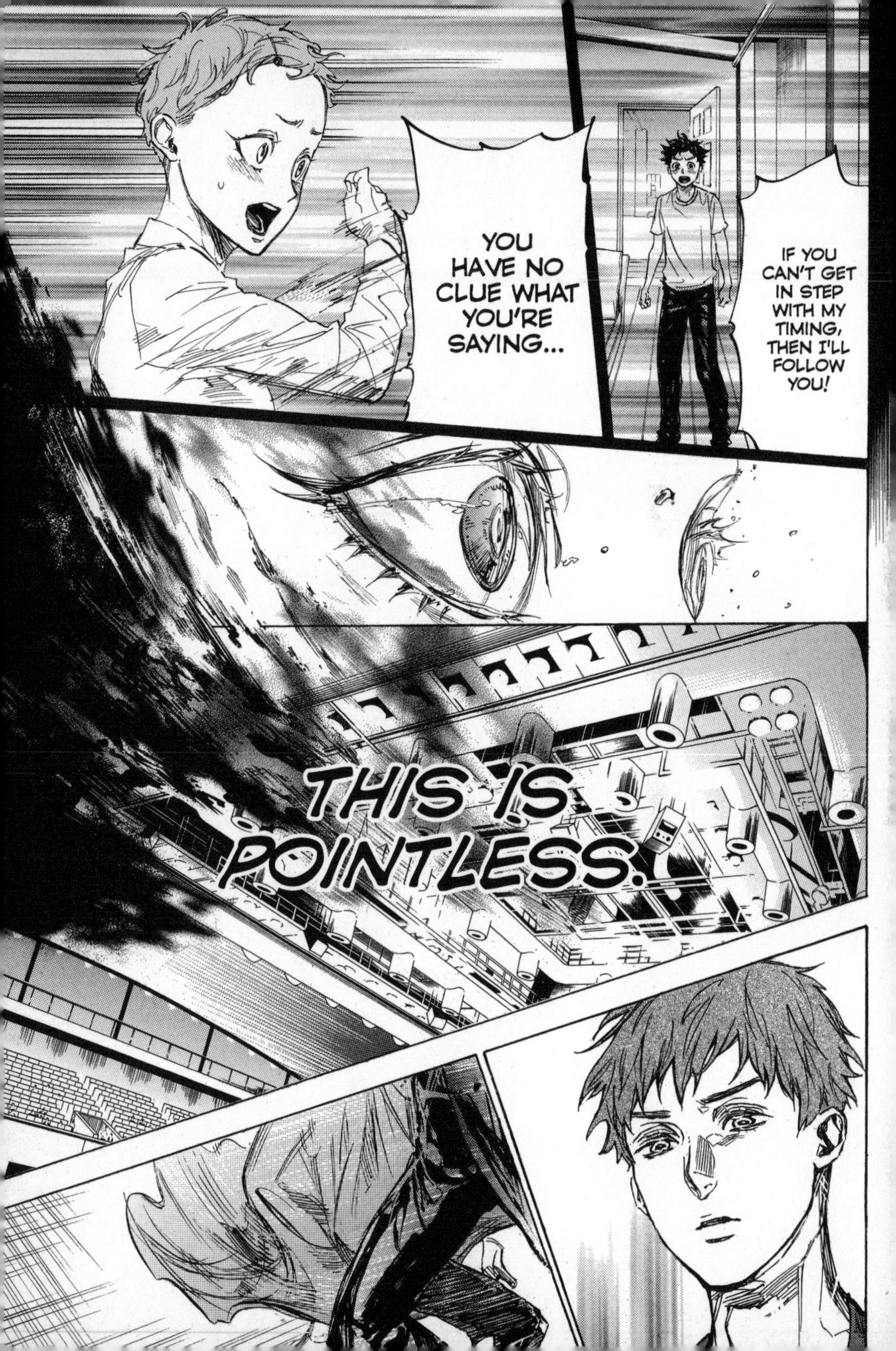
IF YOU CAN'T GET IN STEP WITH MY TIMING, THEN I'LL FOLLOW YOU!
YOU HAVE NO CLUE WHAT YOU'RE SAYING...
THIS IS POINTLESS.

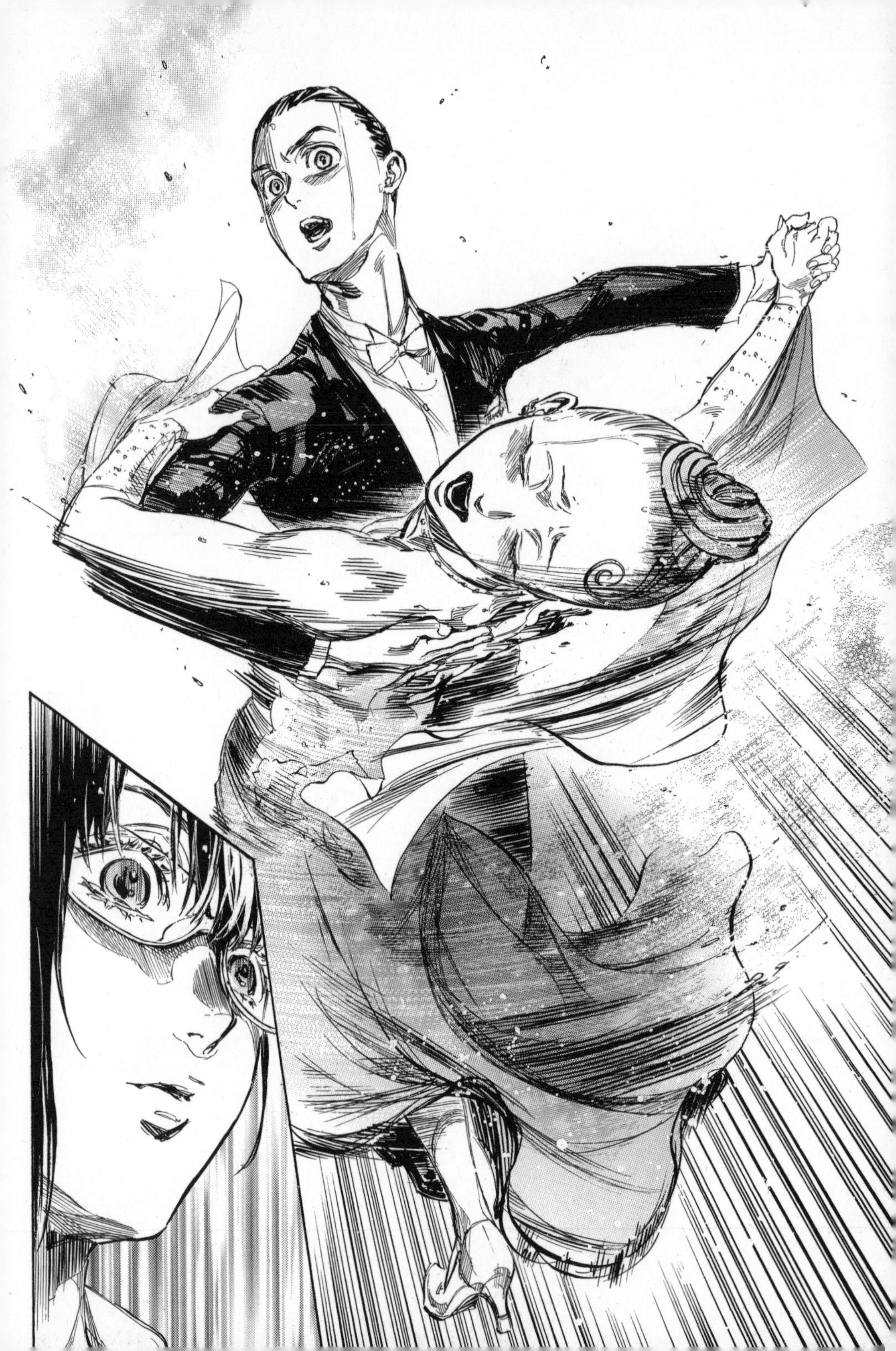

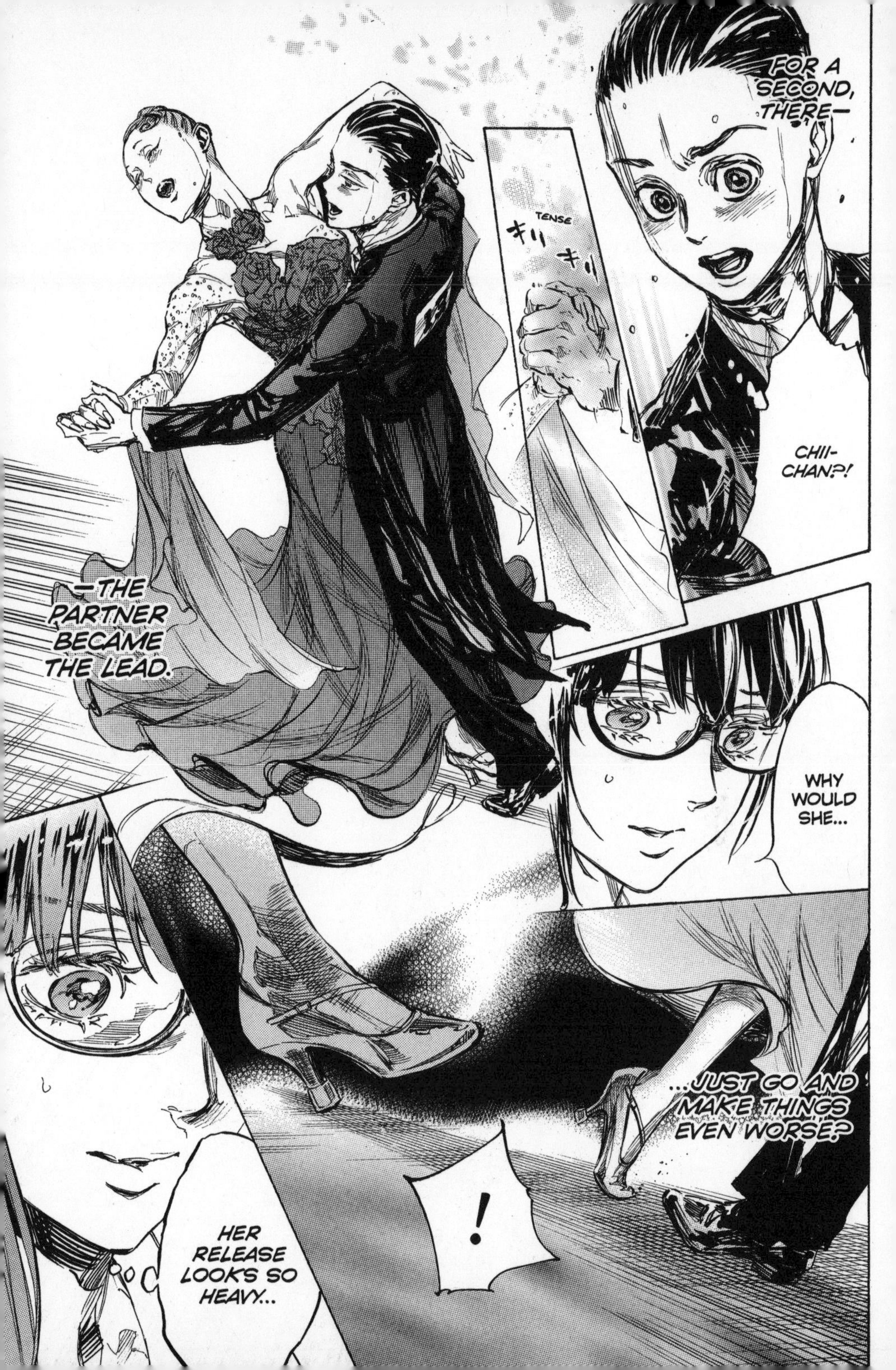

FOR A SECOND, THERE—
CHII-CHAN?!
TENSE
キリ キリ
—THE PARTNER BECAME THE LEAD.
WHY WOULD SHE...
...JUST GO AND MAKE THINGS EVEN WORSE?
!
HER RELEASE LOOKS SO HEAVY...

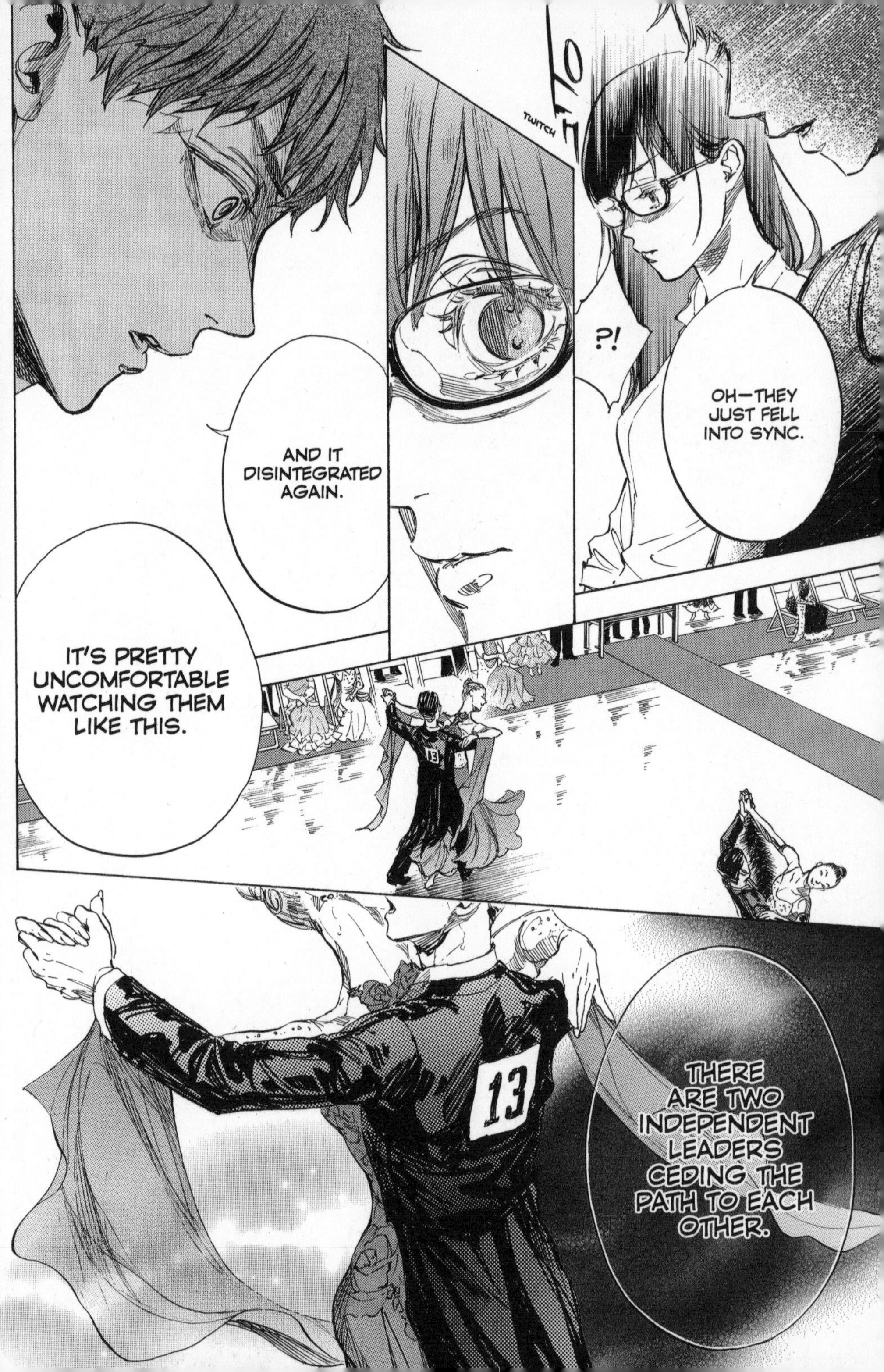
TWITCH
?!
OH—THEY JUST FELL INTO SYNC.
AND IT DISINTEGRATED AGAIN.
IT'S PRETTY UNCOMFORTABLE WATCHING THEM LIKE THIS.
13
13
THERE ARE TWO INDEPENDENT LEADERS CEDING THE PATH TO EACH OTHER.

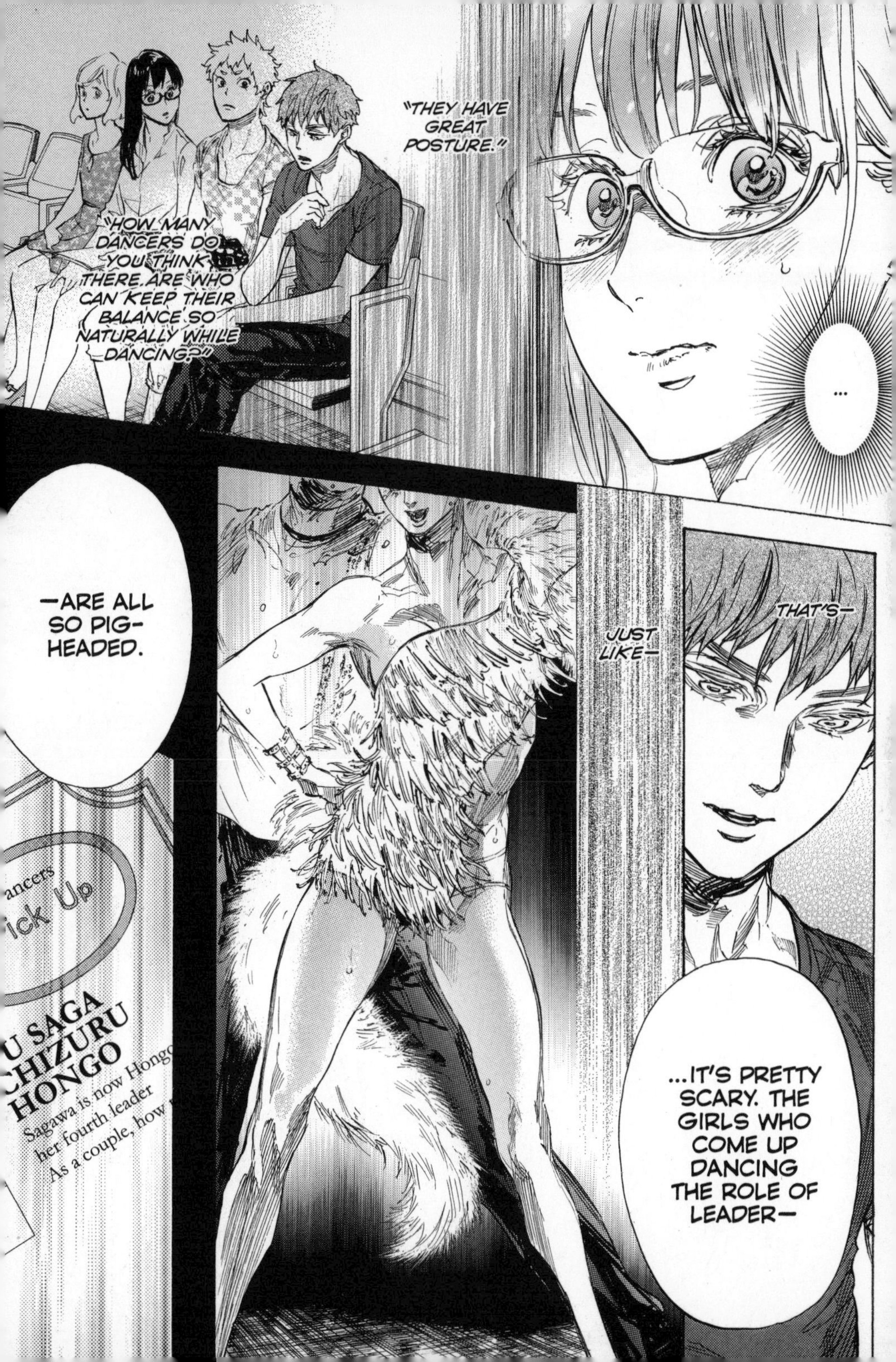
...
"THEY HAVE GREAT POSTURE."
"HOW MANY DANCERS DO YOU THINK THERE ARE WHO CAN KEEP THEIR BALANCE SO NATURALLY WHILE DANCING?"
THAT'S—
JUST LIKE—
...IT'S PRETTY SCARY. THE GIRLS WHO COME UP DANCING THE ROLE OF LEADER—
—ARE ALL SO PIG-HEADED.
ancers
ick Up
U SAGA
CHIZURU
HONGO
Sagawa is now Hongo
her fourth leader
As a couple, how

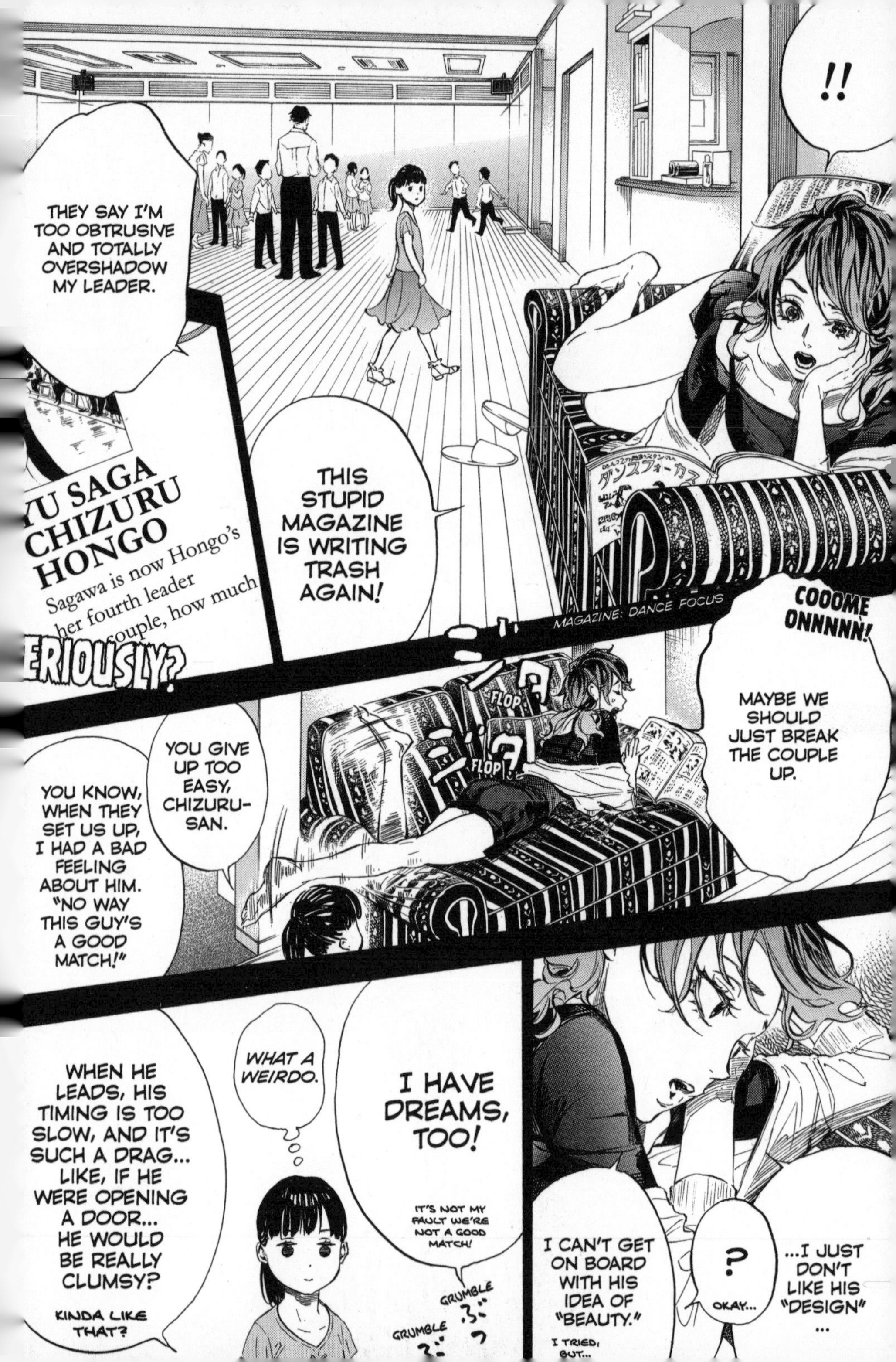

!!
THIS STUPID MAGAZINE IS WRITING TRASH AGAIN!
ダンスフォーカス
MAGAZINE: DANCE FOCUS
THEY SAY I'M TOO OBTRUSIVE AND TOTALLY OVERSHADOW MY LEADER.
YU SAGA
CHIZURU HONGO
Sagawa is now Hongo's
her fourth leader
couple, how much
ERIOUSLY?
COOOME ONNNNN!
MAYBE WE SHOULD JUST BREAK THE COUPLE UP.
FLOP
FLOP
YOU GIVE UP TOO EASY, CHIZURU-SAN.
YOU KNOW, WHEN THEY SET US UP, I HAD A BAD FEELING ABOUT HIM. "NO WAY THIS GUY'S A GOOD MATCH!"
...I JUST DON'T LIKE HIS "DESIGN"...
?
OKAY...
I CAN'T GET ON BOARD WITH HIS IDEA OF "BEAUTY."
I TRIED, BUT...
I HAVE DREAMS, TOO!
IT'S NOT MY FAULT WE'RE NOT A GOOD MATCH!
GRUMBLE
GRUMBLE
WHAT A WEIRDO.
WHEN HE LEADS, HIS TIMING IS TOO SLOW, AND IT'S SUCH A DRAG... LIKE, IF HE WERE OPENING A DOOR... HE WOULD BE REALLY CLUMSY?
KINDA LIKE THAT?

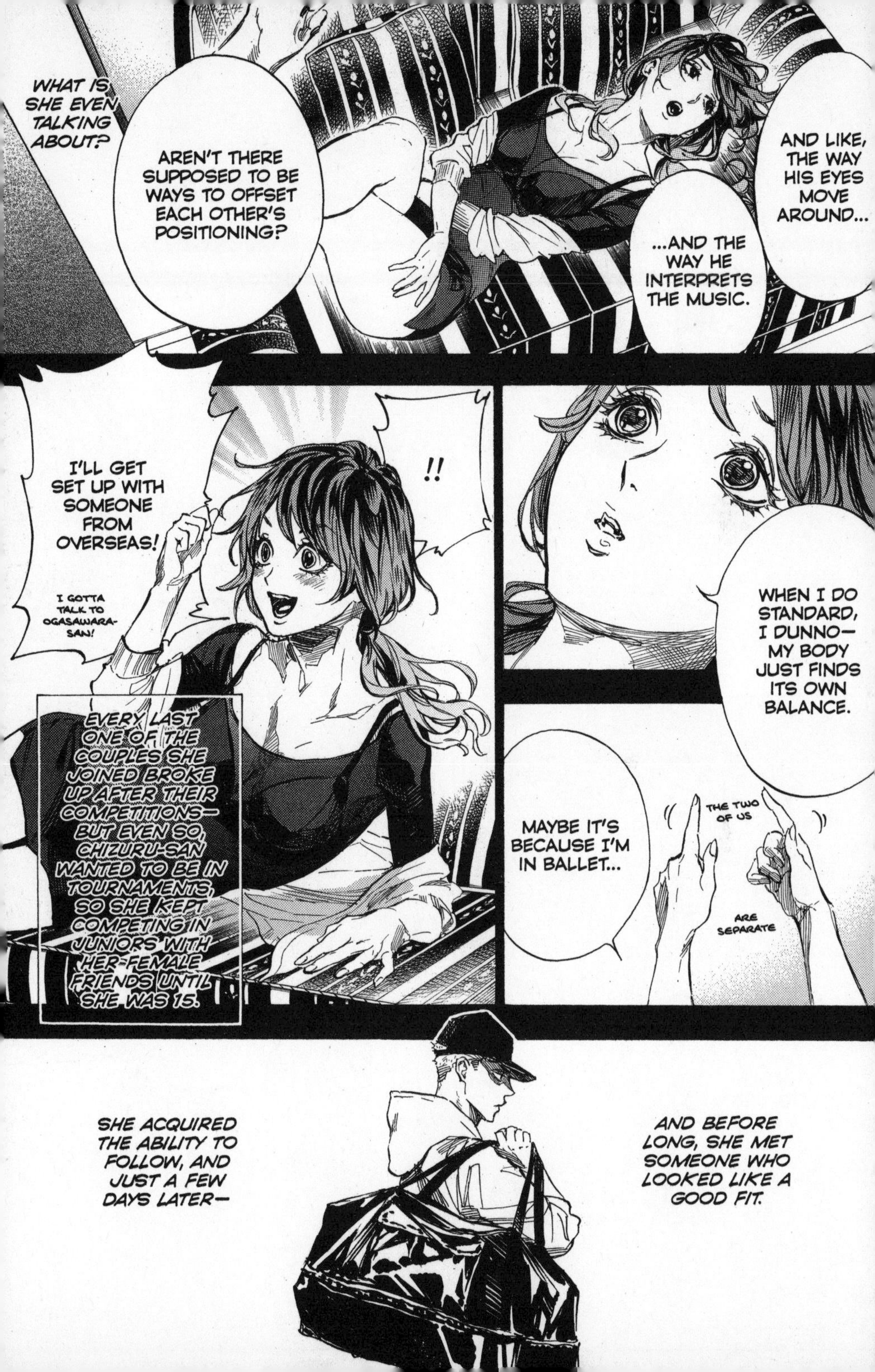
AND LIKE, THE WAY HIS EYES MOVE AROUND...
...AND THE WAY HE INTERPRETS THE MUSIC.
AREN'T THERE SUPPOSED TO BE WAYS TO OFFSET EACH OTHER'S POSITIONING?
WHAT IS SHE EVEN TALKING ABOUT?
WHEN I DO STANDARD, I DUNNO— MY BODY JUST FINDS ITS OWN BALANCE.
THE TWO OF US
ARE SEPARATE
MAYBE IT'S BECAUSE I'M IN BALLET...
!!
I'LL GET SET UP WITH SOMEONE FROM OVERSEAS!
I GOTTA TALK TO OGASAWARA-SAN!
EVERY LAST ONE OF THE COUPLES SHE JOINED BROKE UP AFTER THEIR COMPETITIONS— BUT EVEN SO, CHIZURU-SAN WANTED TO BE IN TOURNAMENTS, SO SHE KEPT COMPETING IN JUNIORS WITH HER FEMALE FRIENDS UNTIL SHE WAS 15.
SHE ACQUIRED THE ABILITY TO FOLLOW, AND JUST A FEW DAYS LATER—
AND BEFORE LONG, SHE MET SOMEONE WHO LOOKED LIKE A GOOD FIT.

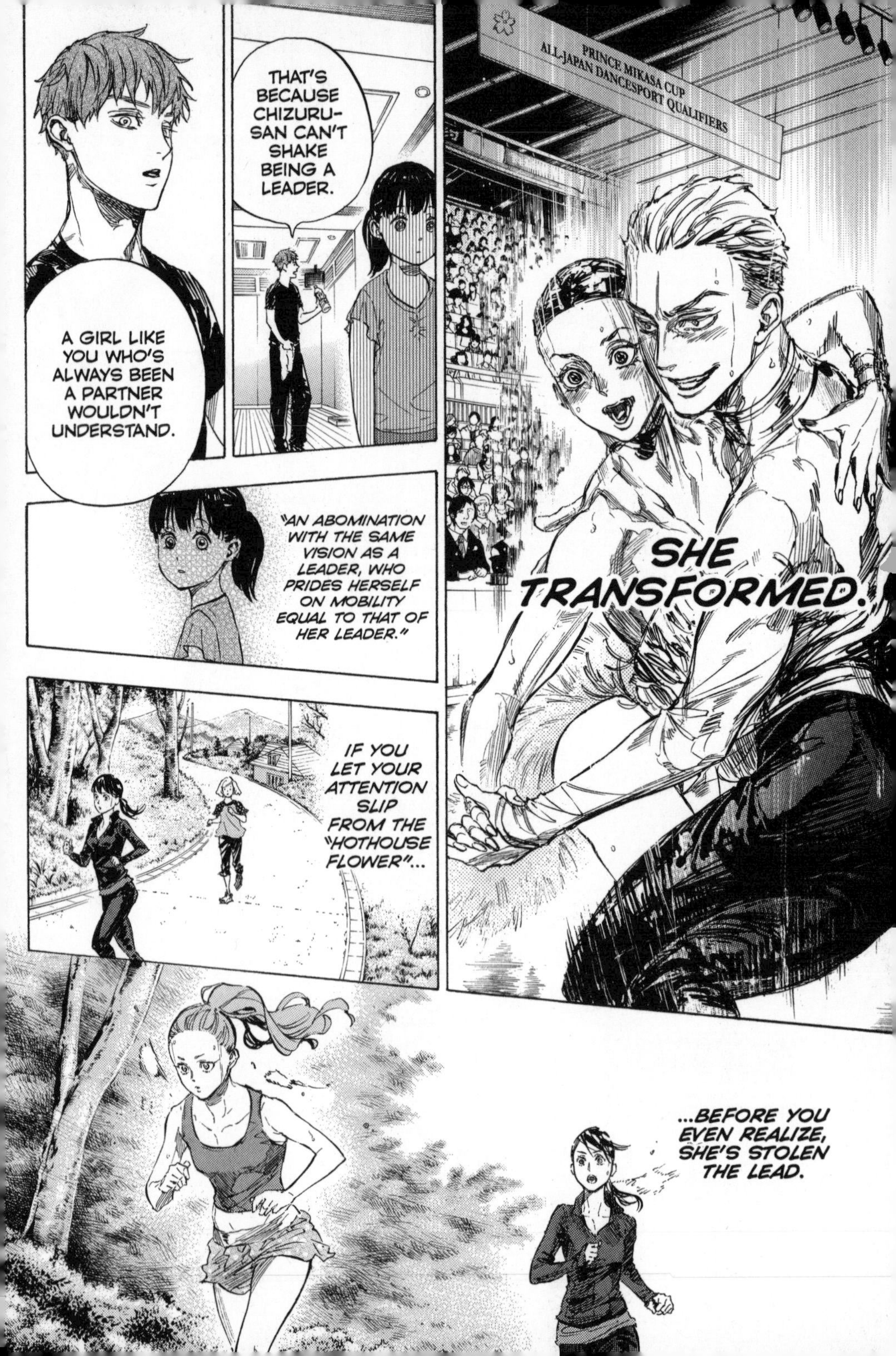
PRINCE MIKASA CUP
ALL-JAPAN DANCESPORT QUALIFIERS
SHE TRANSFORMED.
THAT'S BECAUSE CHIZURU-SAN CAN'T SHAKE BEING A LEADER.
A GIRL LIKE YOU WHO'S ALWAYS BEEN A PARTNER WOULDN'T UNDERSTAND.
"AN ABOMINATION WITH THE SAME VISION AS A LEADER, WHO PRIDES HERSELF ON MOBILITY EQUAL TO THAT OF HER LEADER."
IF YOU LET YOUR ATTENTION SLIP FROM THE "HOTHOUSE FLOWER"...
...BEFORE YOU EVEN REALIZE, SHE'S STOLEN THE LEAD.

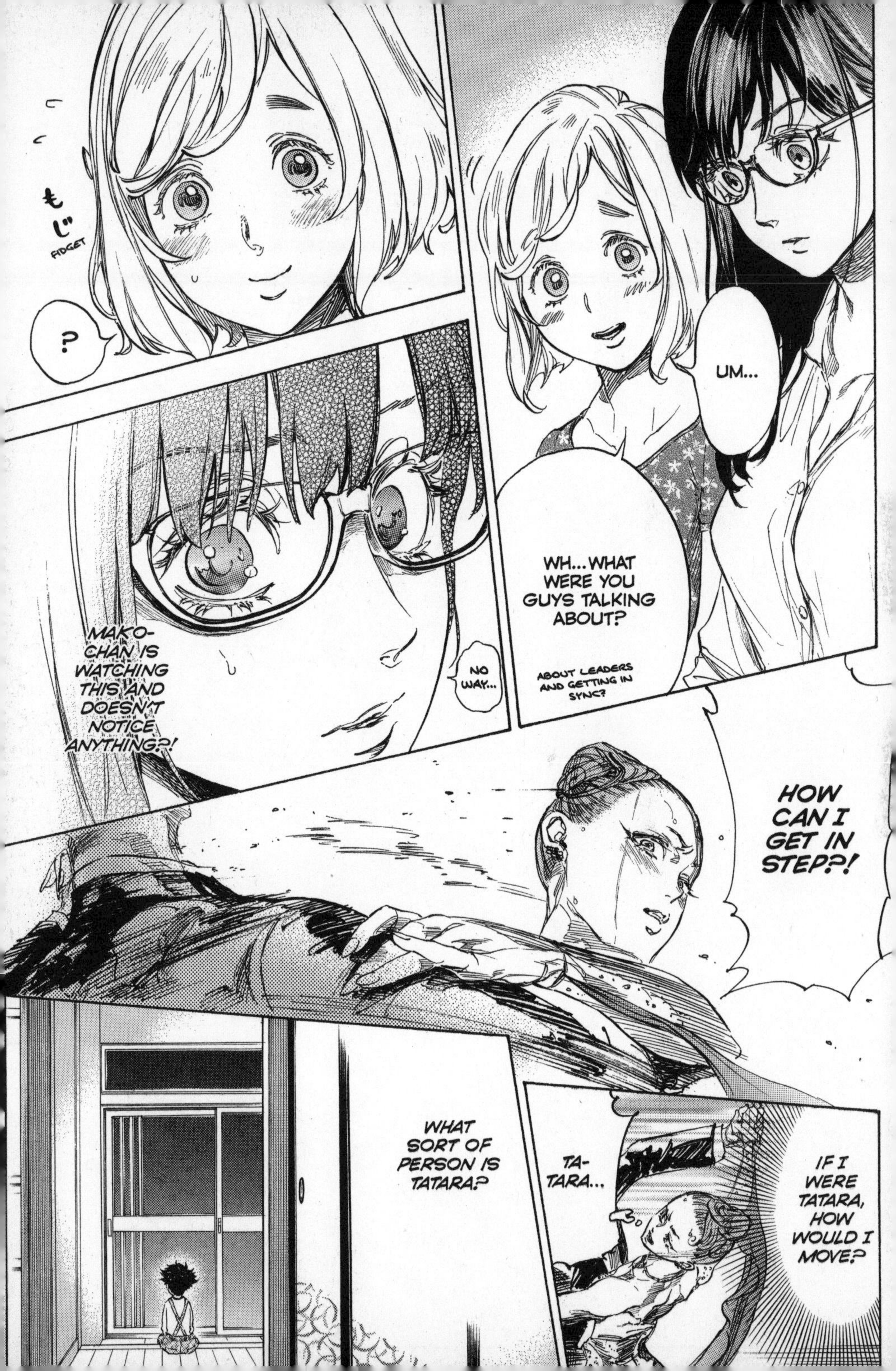
UM...
WH... WHAT WERE YOU GUYS TALKING ABOUT?
ABOUT LEADERS AND GETTING IN SYNC?
もじ
FIDGET
?
NO WAY...
MAKO-CHAN IS WATCHING THIS AND DOESN'T NOTICE ANYTHING?!
HOW CAN I GET IN STEP?!
IF I WERE TATARA, HOW WOULD I MOVE?
TA-TARA...
WHAT SORT OF PERSON IS TATARA?

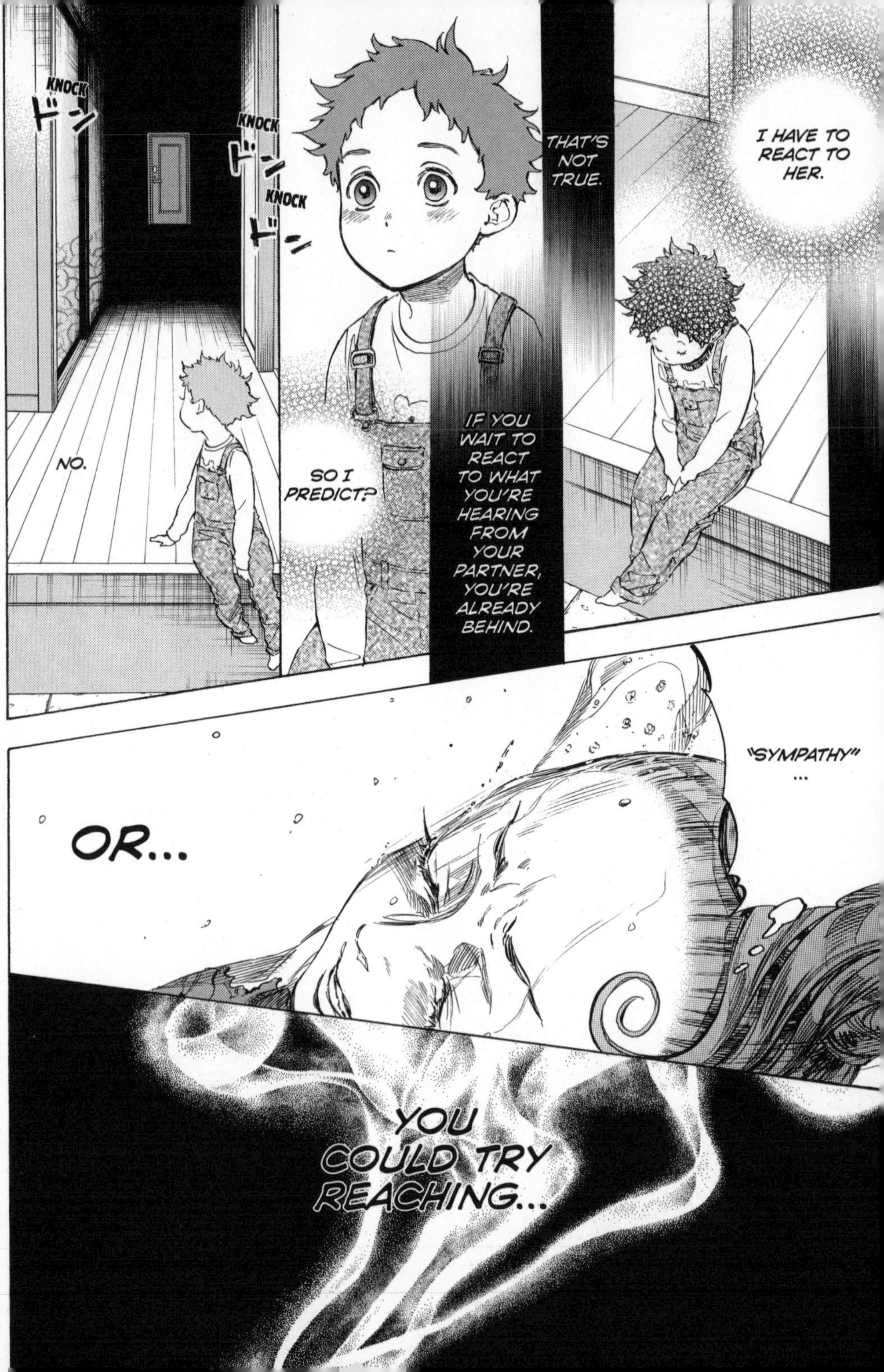
I HAVE TO REACT TO HER.
THAT'S NOT TRUE.
IF YOU WAIT TO REACT TO WHAT YOU'RE HEARING FROM YOUR PARTNER, YOU'RE ALREADY BEHIND.
SO I PREDICT?
KNOCK
ドン
KNOCK
ドン
KNOCK
ドン
NO.
"SYMPATHY" ...
OR...
YOU COULD TRY REACHING...

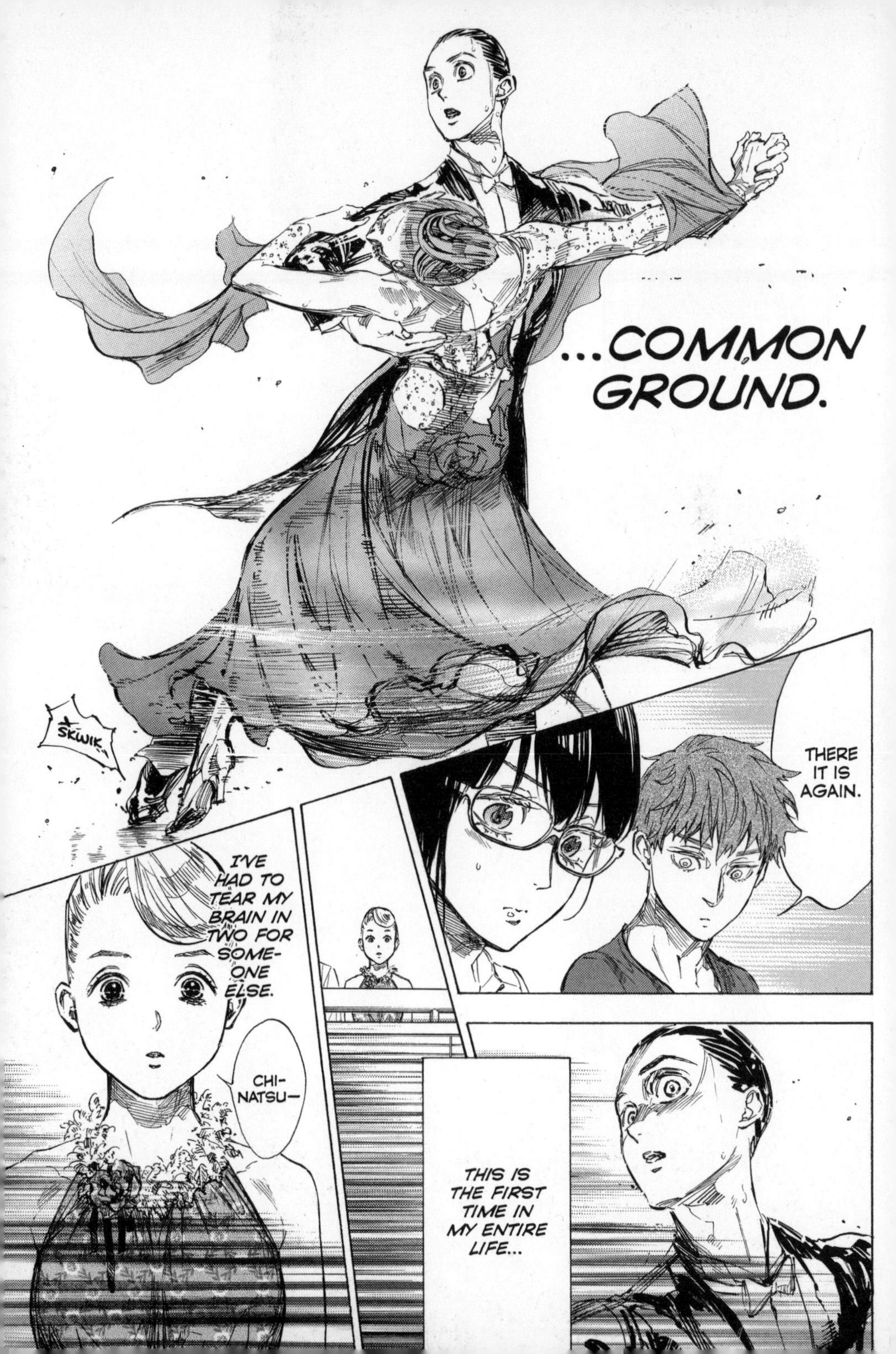
...COMMON GROUND.
SKWIK
THERE IT IS AGAIN.
THIS IS THE FIRST TIME IN MY ENTIRE LIFE...
I'VE HAD TO TEAR MY BRAIN IN TWO FOR SOMEONE ELSE.
CHI-NATSU—

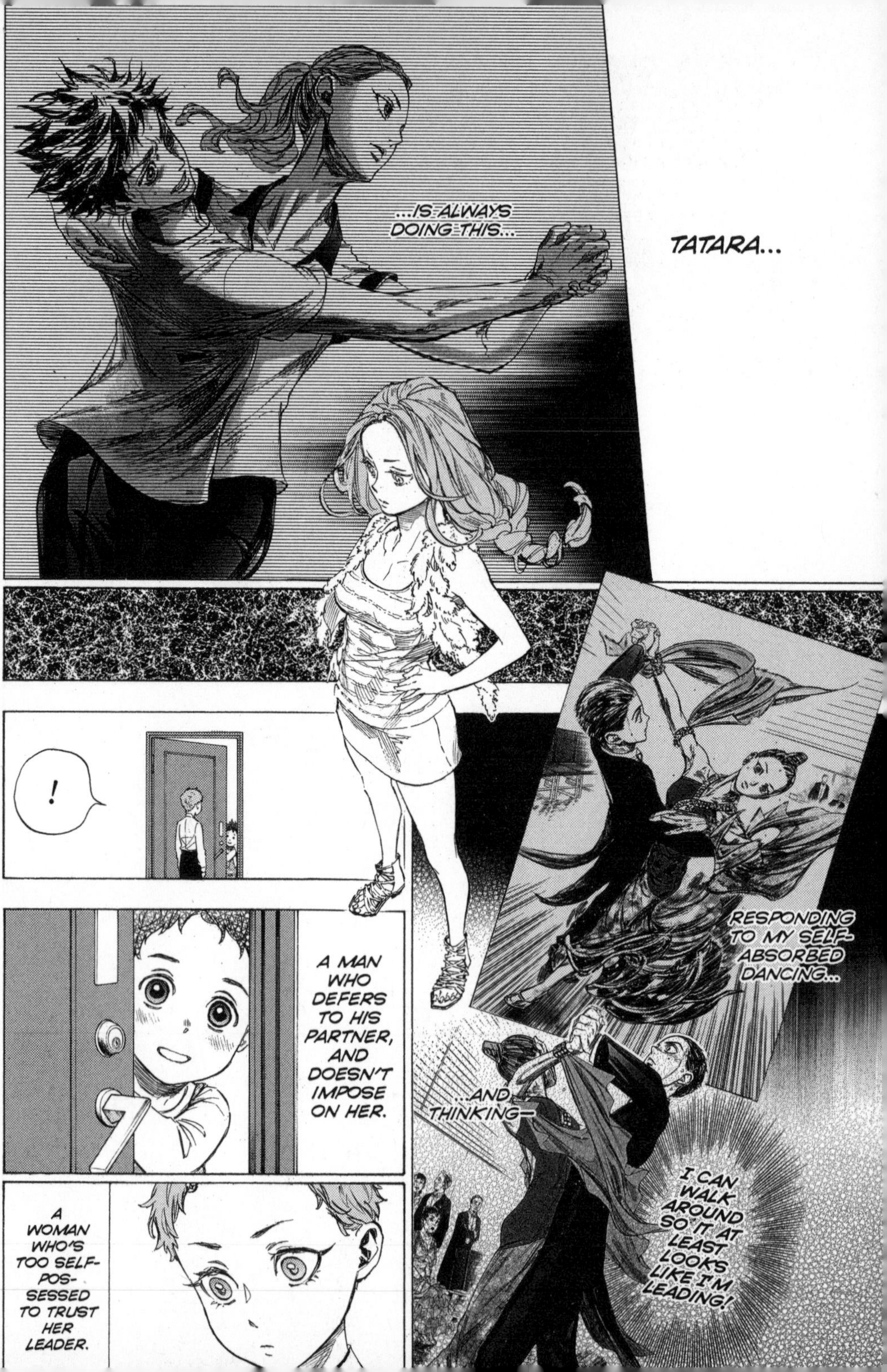
TATARA...
...IS ALWAYS DOING THIS...
RESPONDING TO MY SELF-ABSORBED DANCING...
...AND THINKING—
I CAN WALK AROUND SO IT AT LEAST LOOKS LIKE I'M LEADING!
!
A MAN WHO DEFERS TO HIS PARTNER, AND DOESN'T IMPOSE ON HER.
A WOMAN WHO'S TOO SELF-POSSESSED TO TRUST HER LEADER.

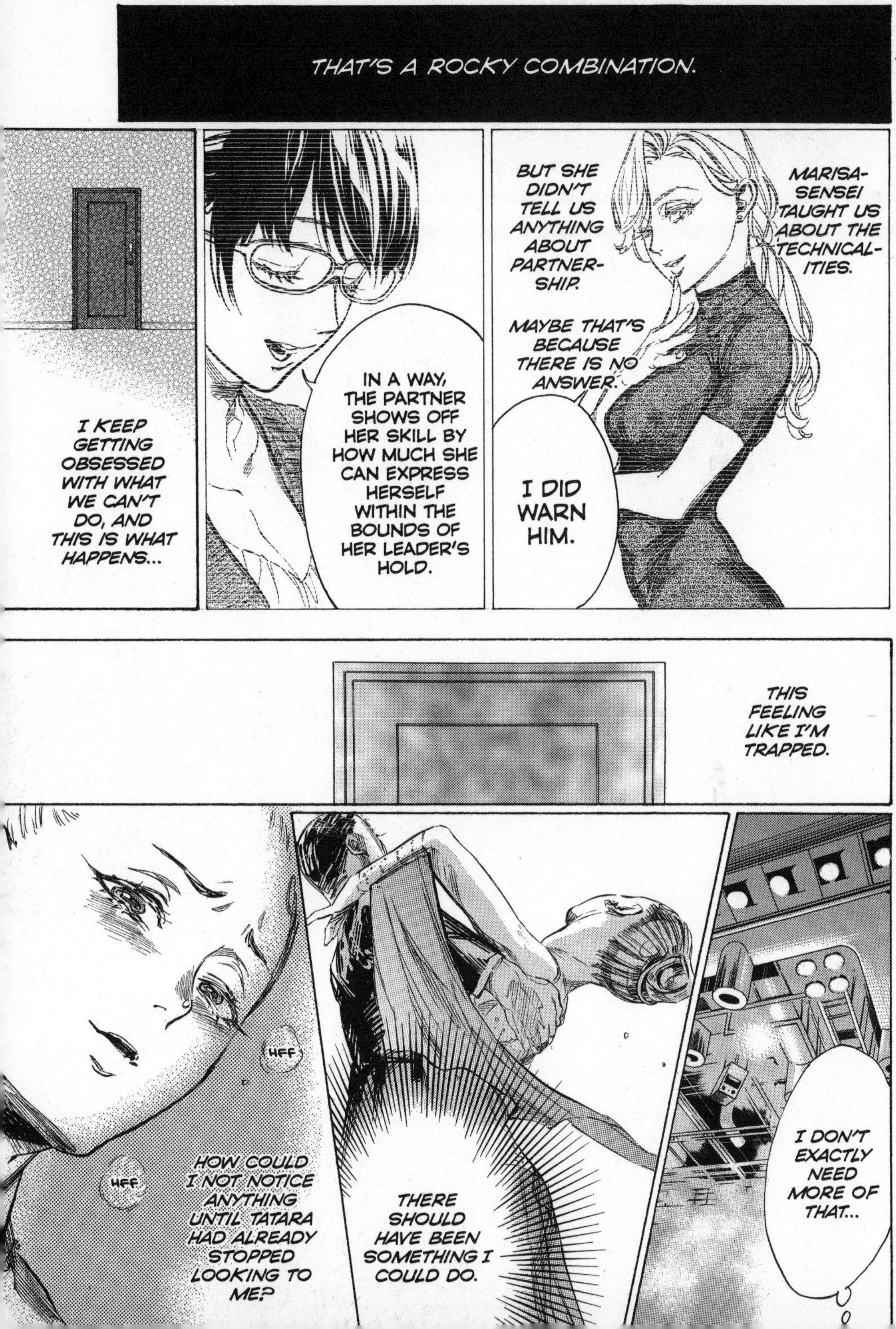
THAT'S A ROCKY COMBINATION.
MARISA-SENSEI TAUGHT US ABOUT THE TECHNICAL-ITIES.
BUT SHE DIDN'T TELL US ANYTHING ABOUT PARTNER-SHIP.
MAYBE THAT'S BECAUSE THERE IS NO ANSWER.
I DID WARN HIM.
IN A WAY, THE PARTNER SHOWS OFF HER SKILL BY HOW MUCH SHE CAN EXPRESS HERSELF WITHIN THE BOUNDS OF HER LEADER'S HOLD.
I KEEP GETTING OBSESSED WITH WHAT WE CAN'T DO, AND THIS IS WHAT HAPPENS...
THIS FEELING LIKE I'M TRAPPED.
I DON'T EXACTLY NEED MORE OF THAT...
THERE SHOULD HAVE BEEN SOMETHING I COULD DO.
HFF
HFF
HOW COULD I NOT NOTICE ANYTHING UNTIL TATARA HAD ALREADY STOPPED LOOKING TO ME?

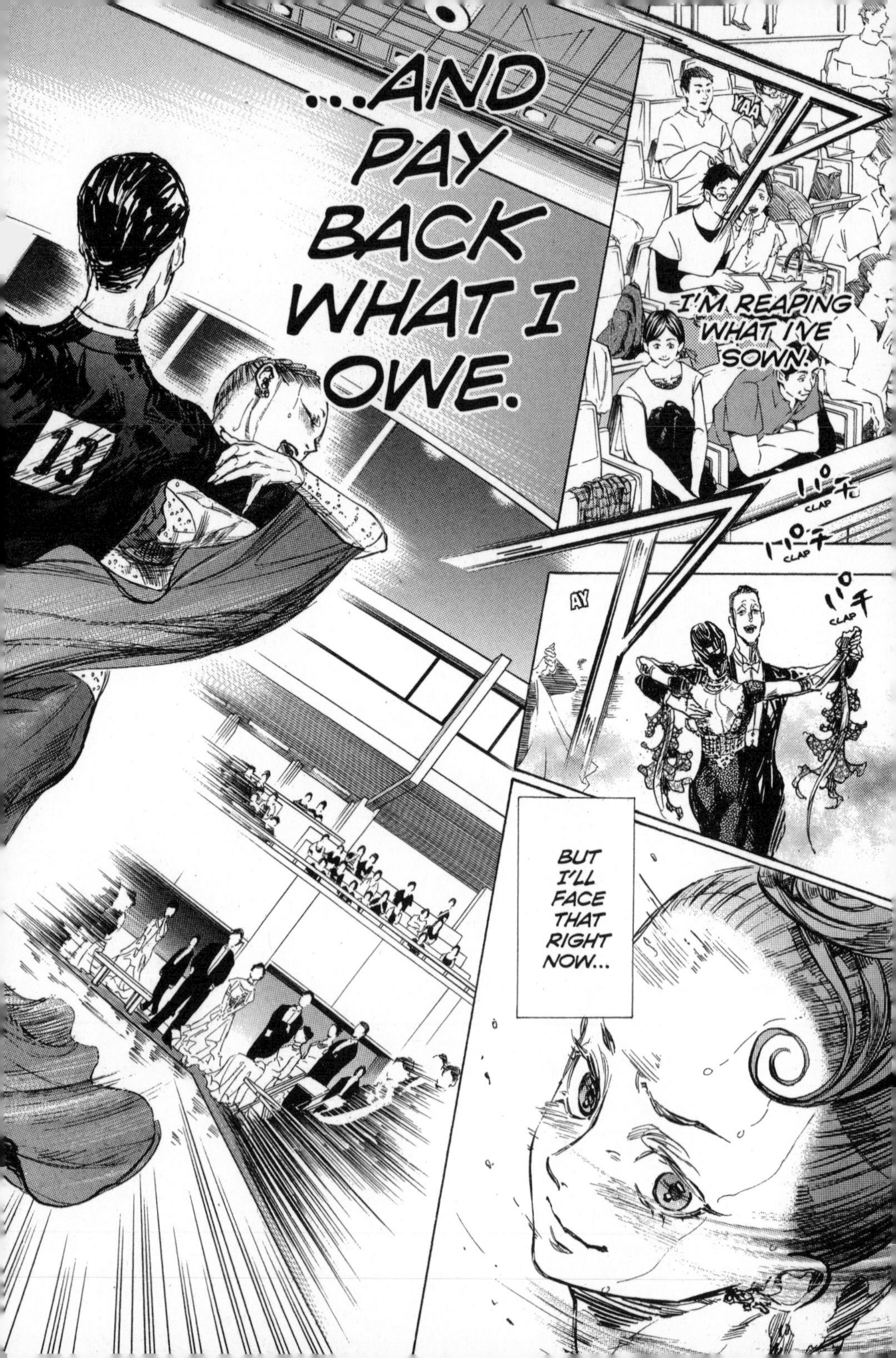

YAA
I'M REAPING WHAT I'VE SOWN.
パチ CLAP
パチ CLAP
AY
パチ CLAP
BUT I'LL FACE THAT RIGHT NOW...
...AND PAY BACK WHAT I OWE.

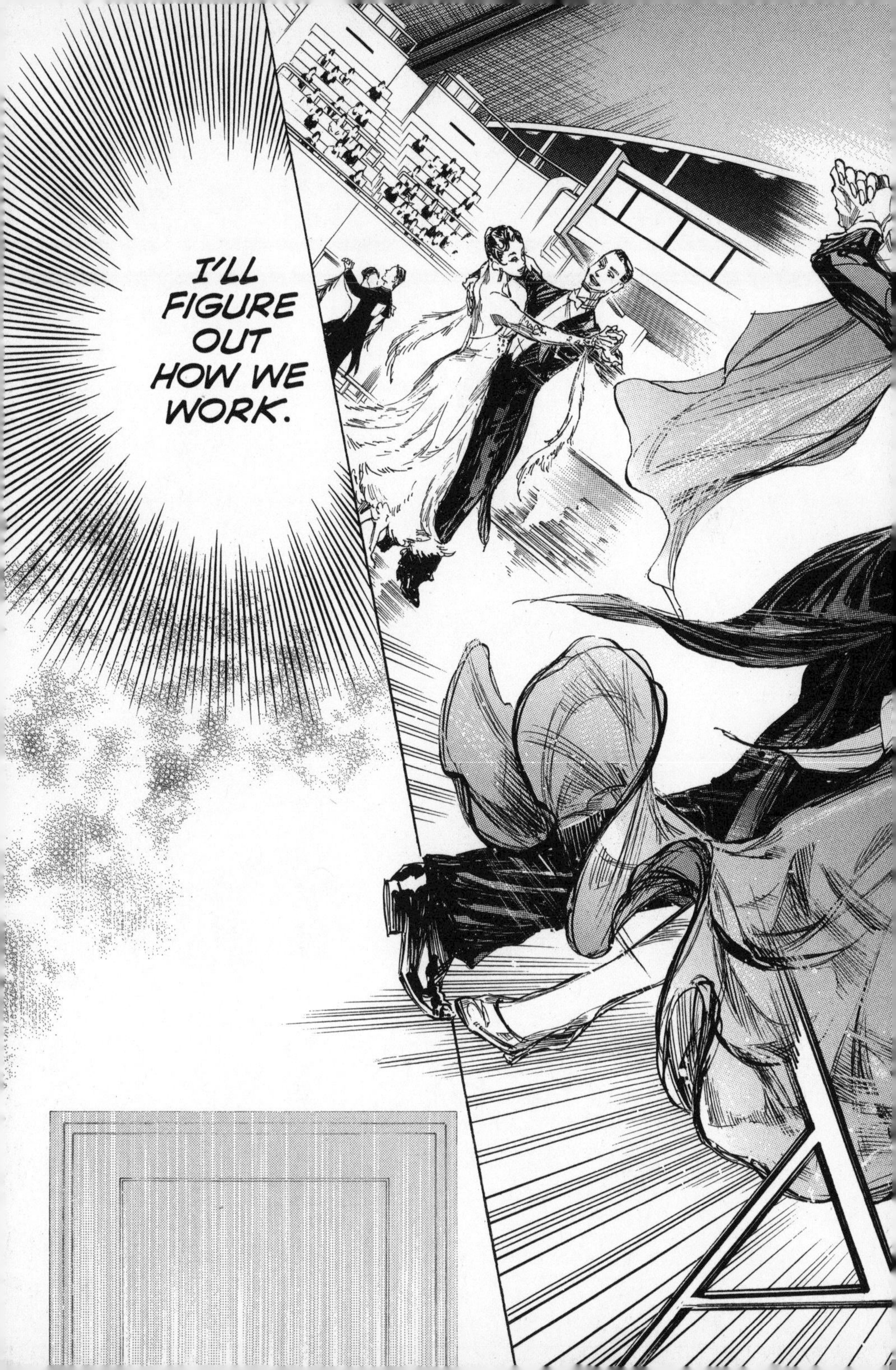
I'LL FIGURE OUT HOW WE WORK.

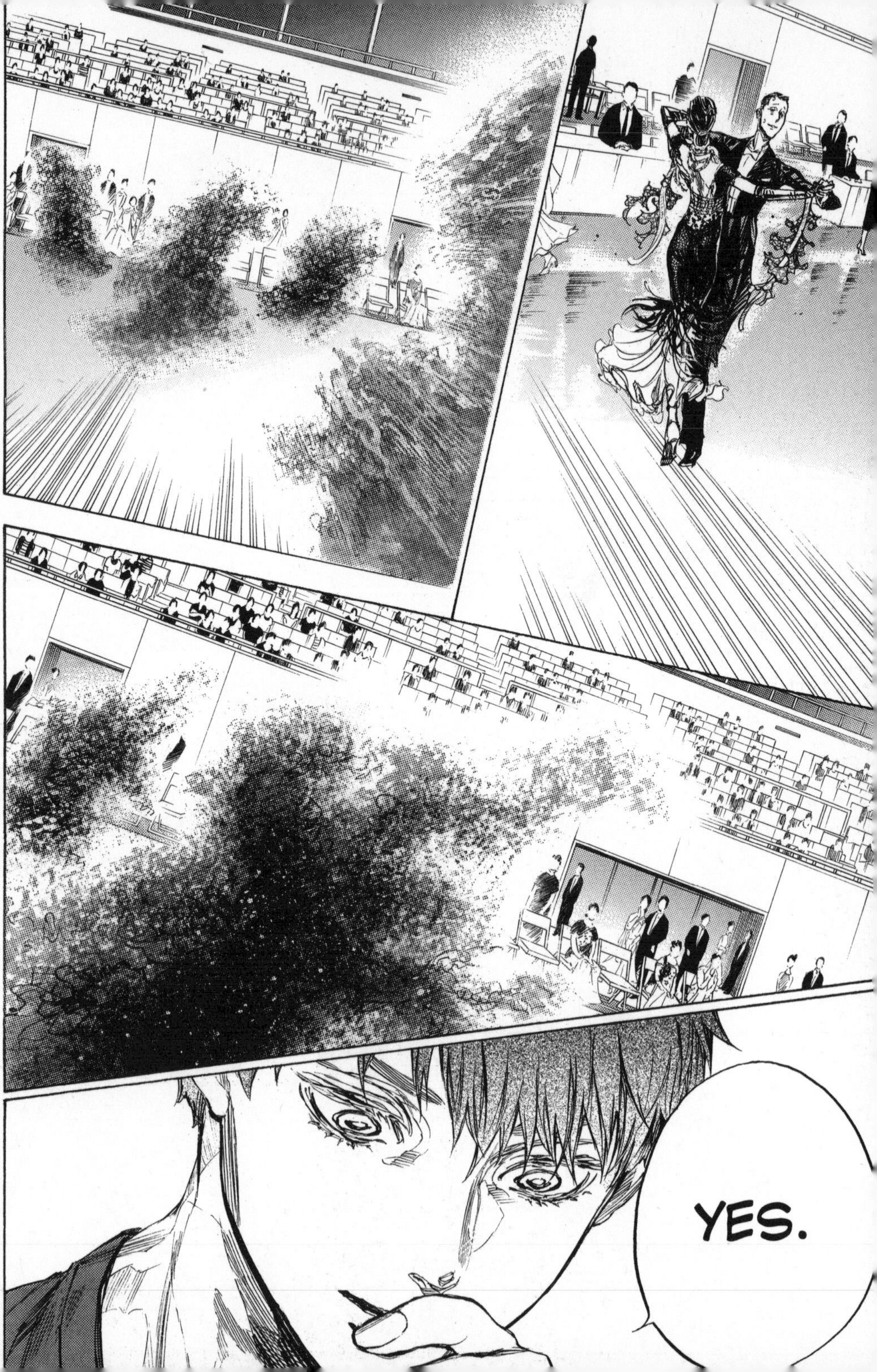
YES.

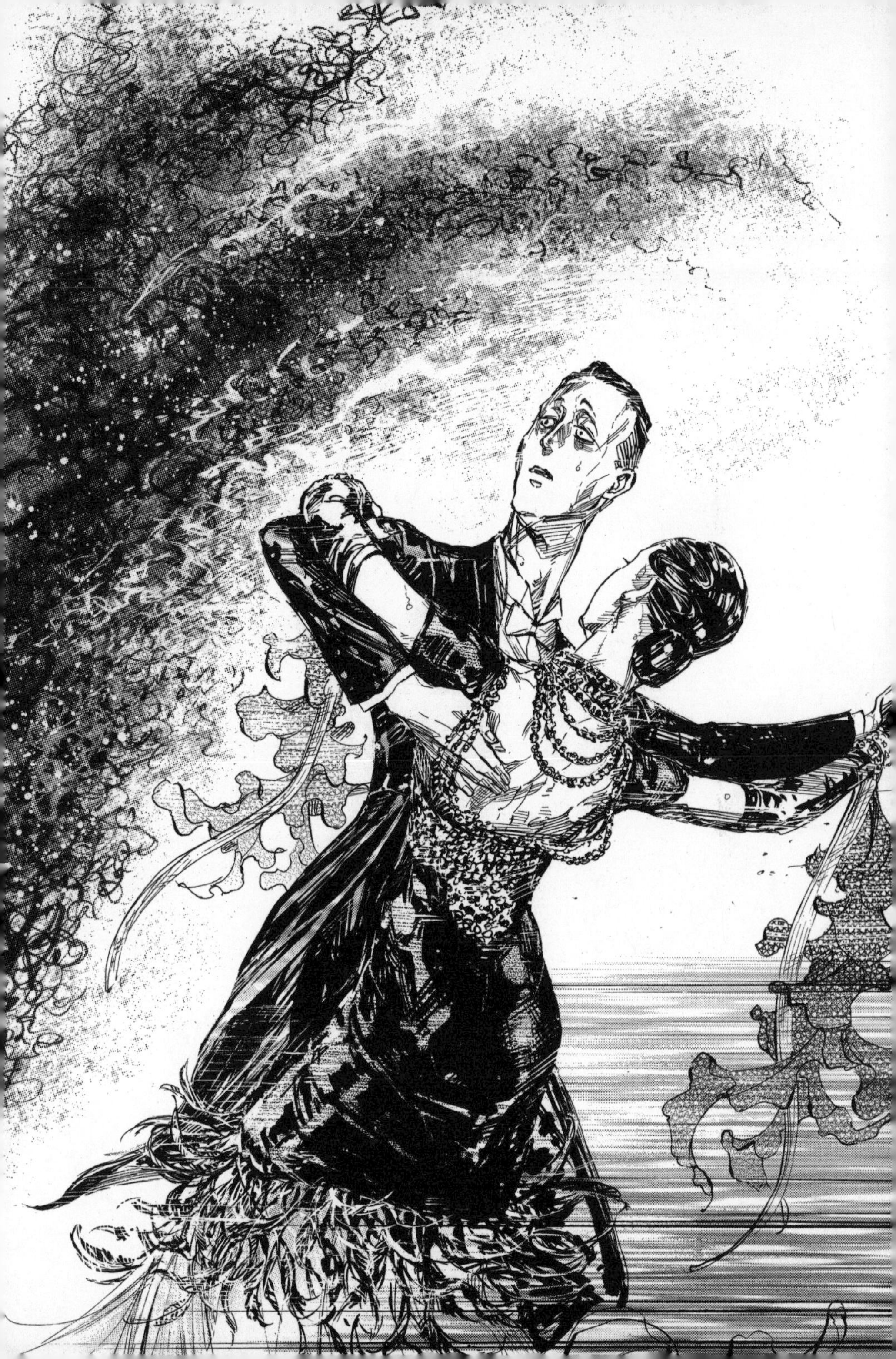

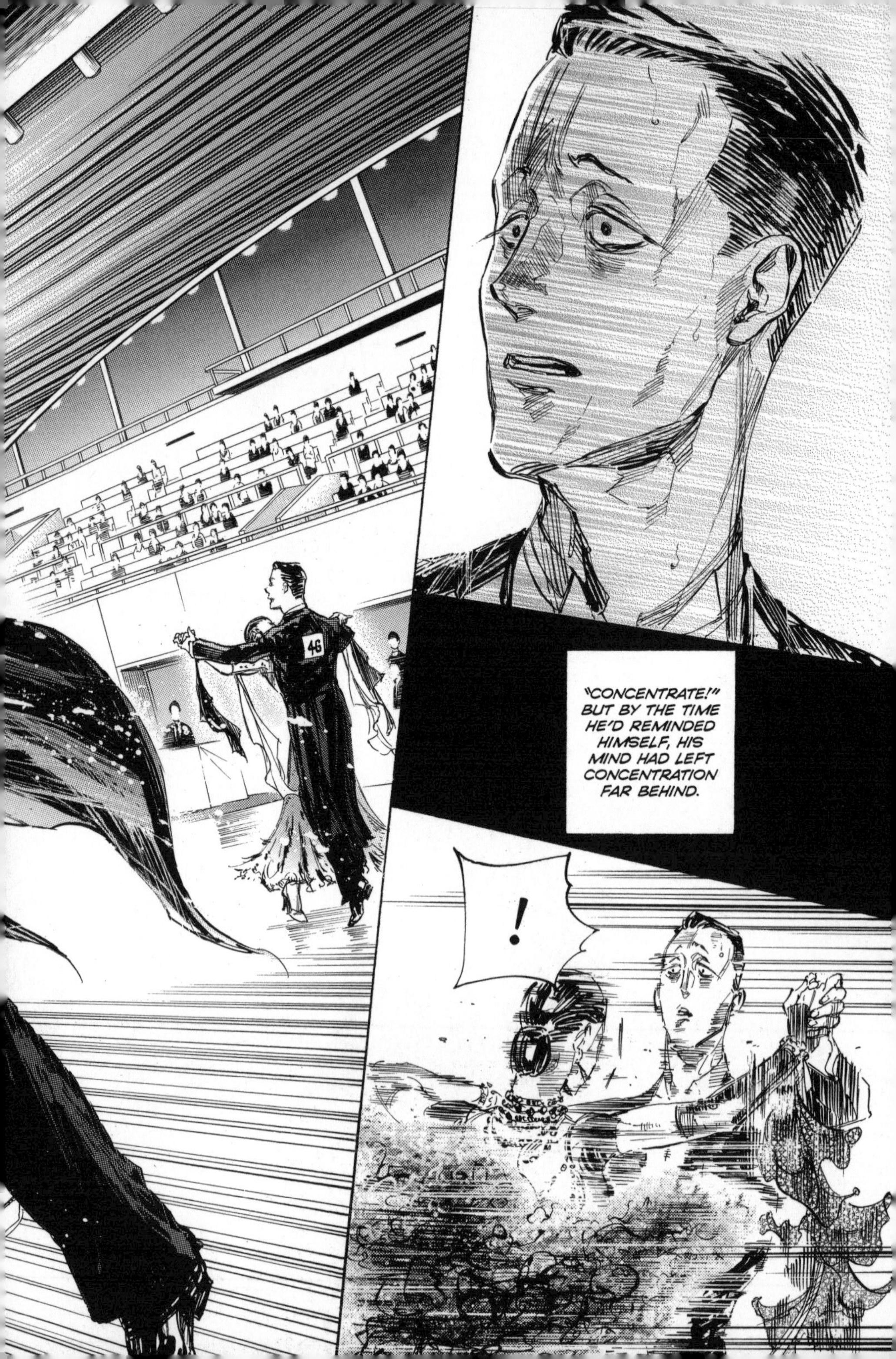
"CONCENTRATE!" BUT BY THE TIME HE'D REMINDED HIMSELF, HIS MIND HAD LEFT CONCENTRATION FAR BEHIND.
!
4G

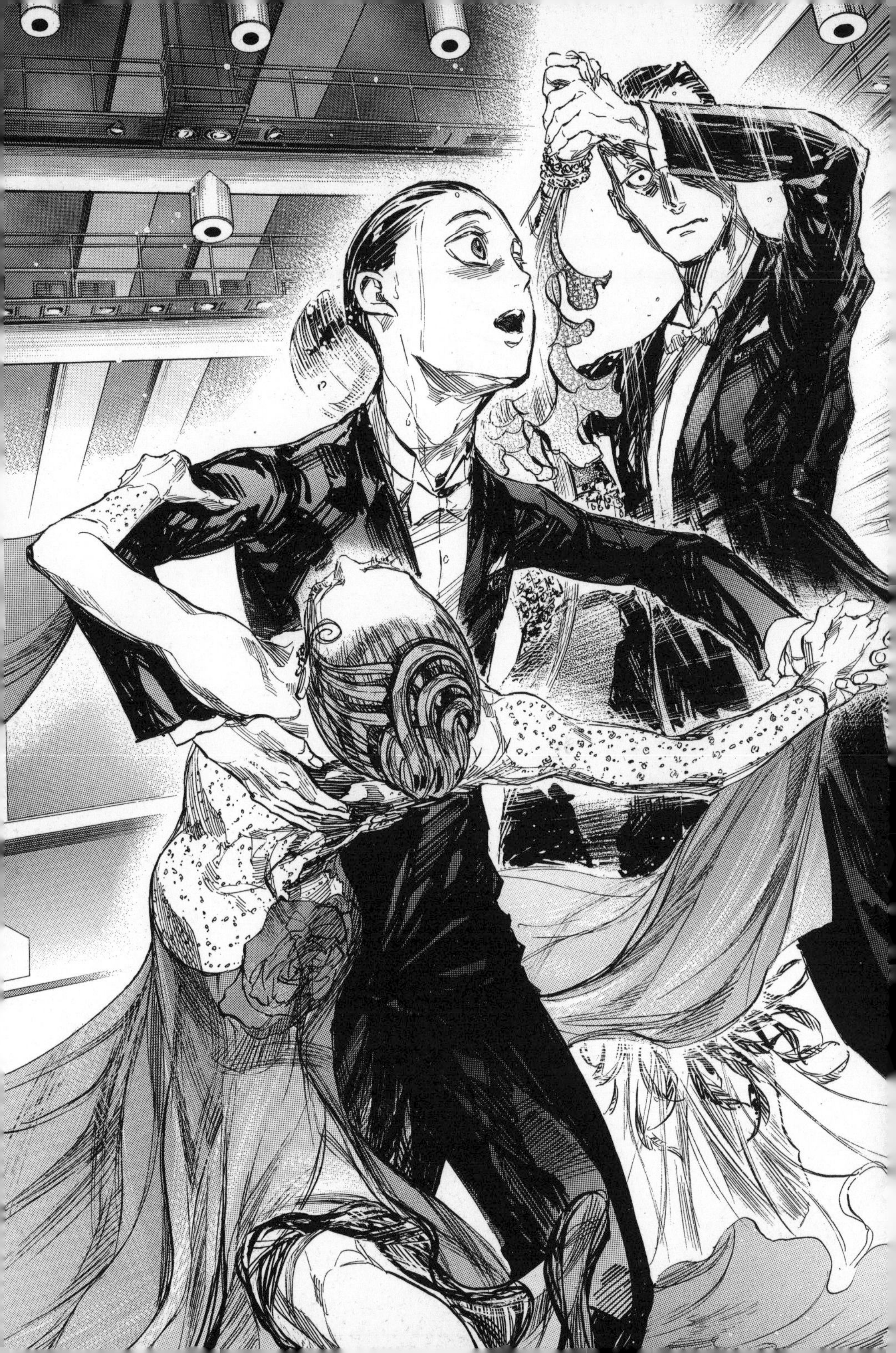

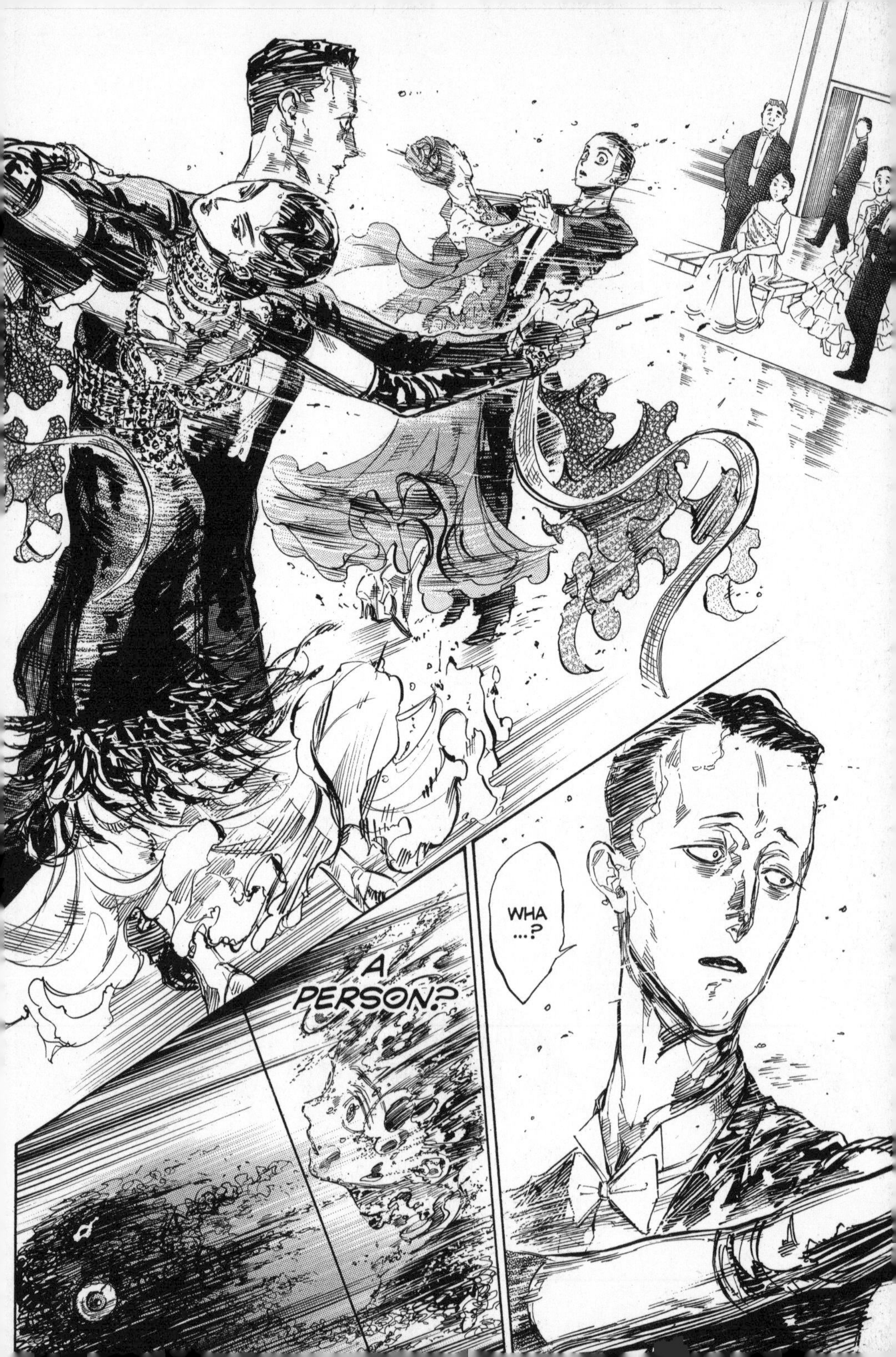
WHA ...?
A PERSON?

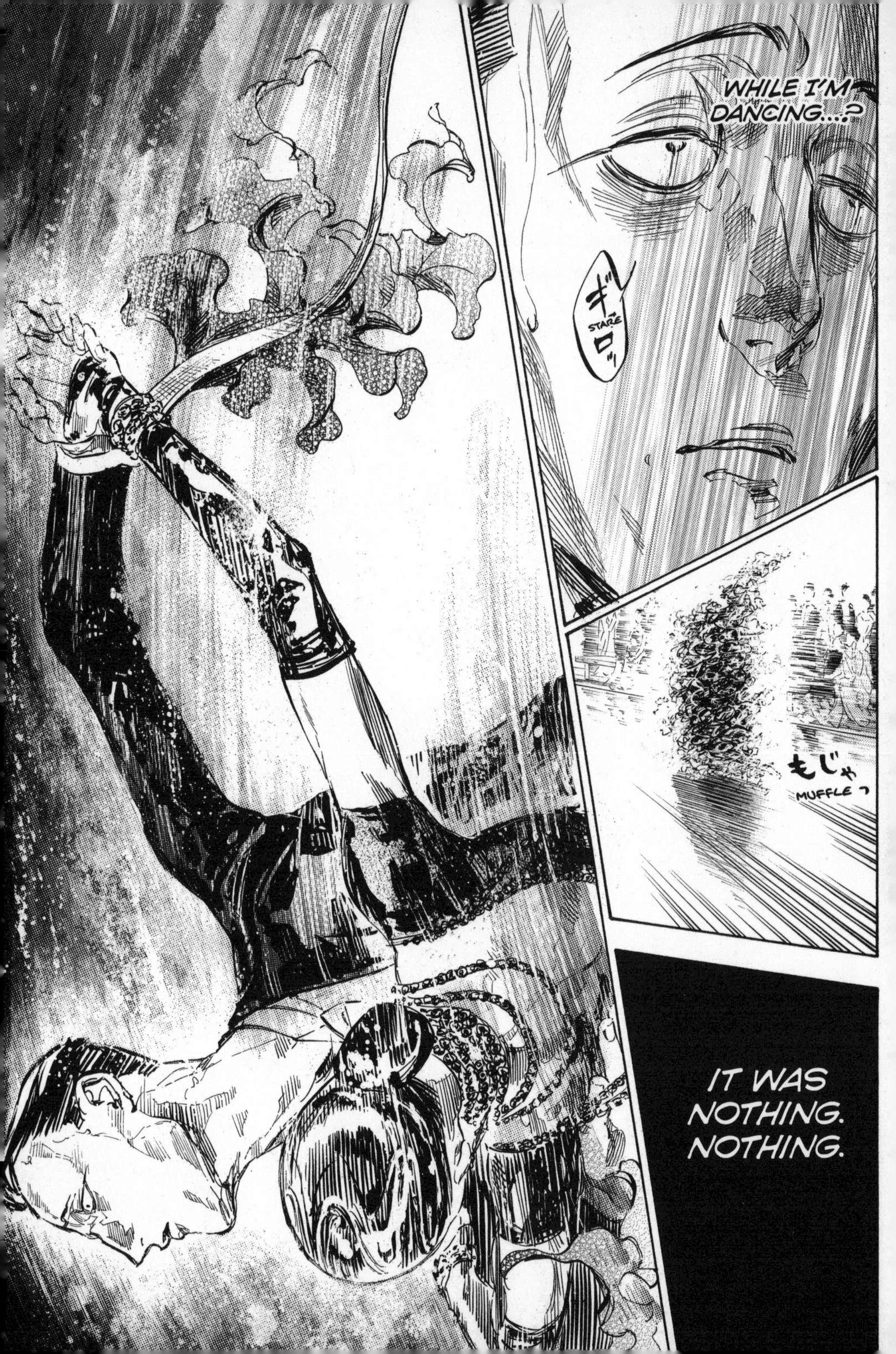
WHILE I'M DANCING...?
ギロッ
STARE
もじゃ
MUFFLE
IT WAS NOTHING. NOTHING.

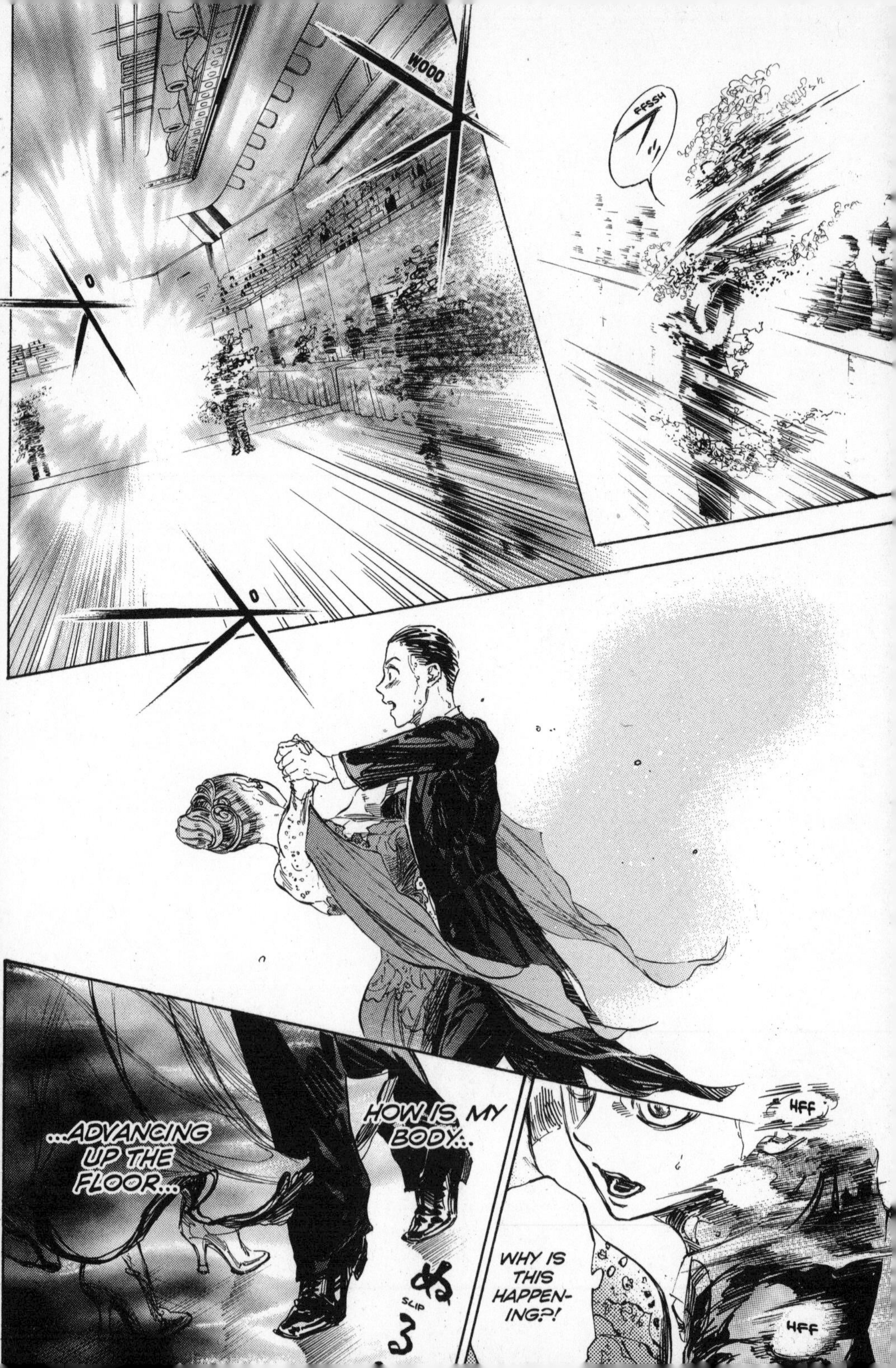
FFSSH
WOOO
O
O
HFF
WHY IS THIS HAPPENING?!
HFF
HOW IS MY BODY...
...ADVANCING UP THE FLOOR...
SLIP

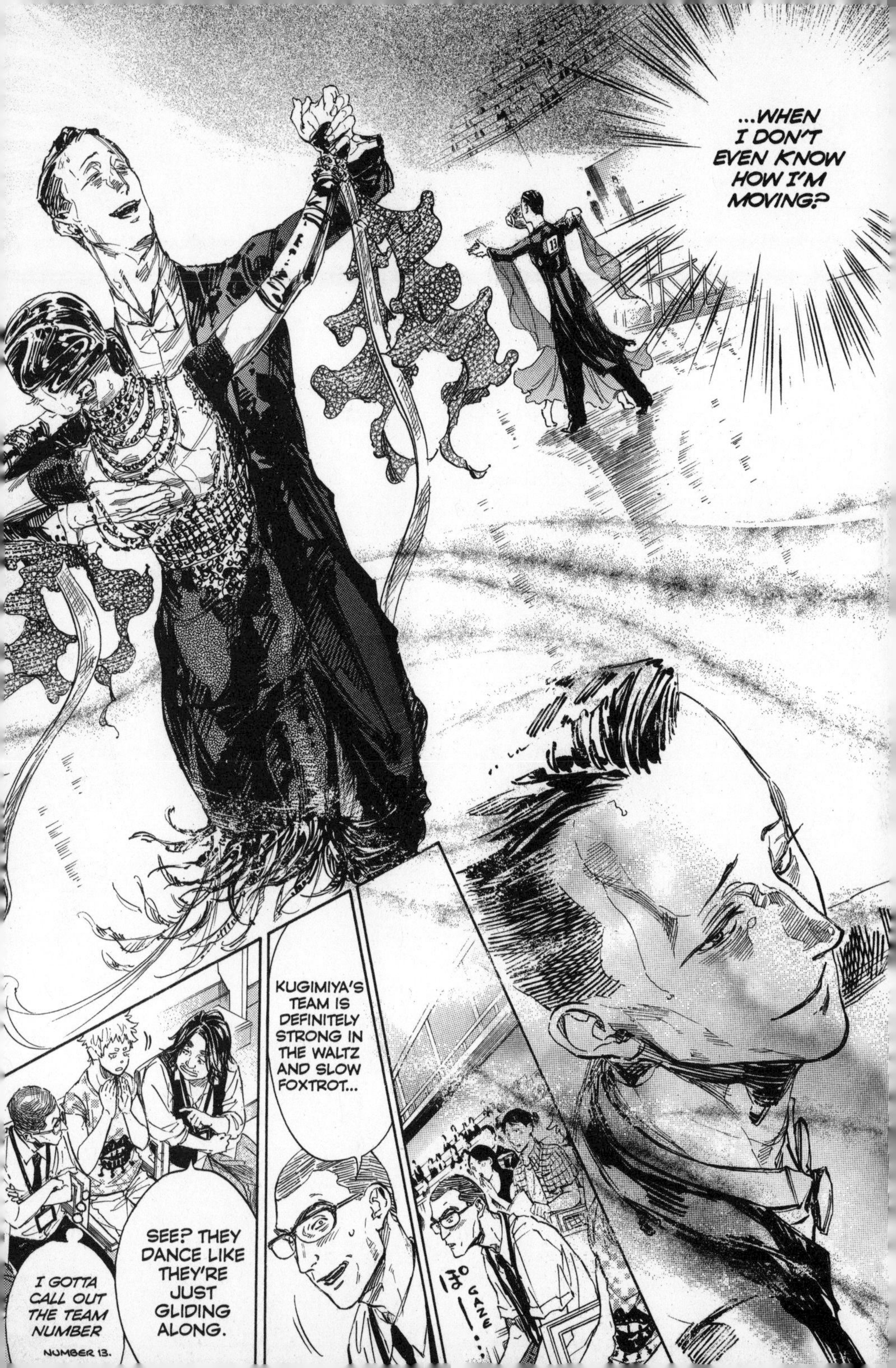
...WHEN I DON'T EVEN KNOW HOW I'M MOVING?
GAZE
KUGIMIYA'S TEAM IS DEFINITELY STRONG IN THE WALTZ AND SLOW FOXTROT...
SEE? THEY DANCE LIKE THEY'RE JUST GLIDING ALONG.
I GOTTA CALL OUT THE TEAM NUMBER
NUMBER 13.

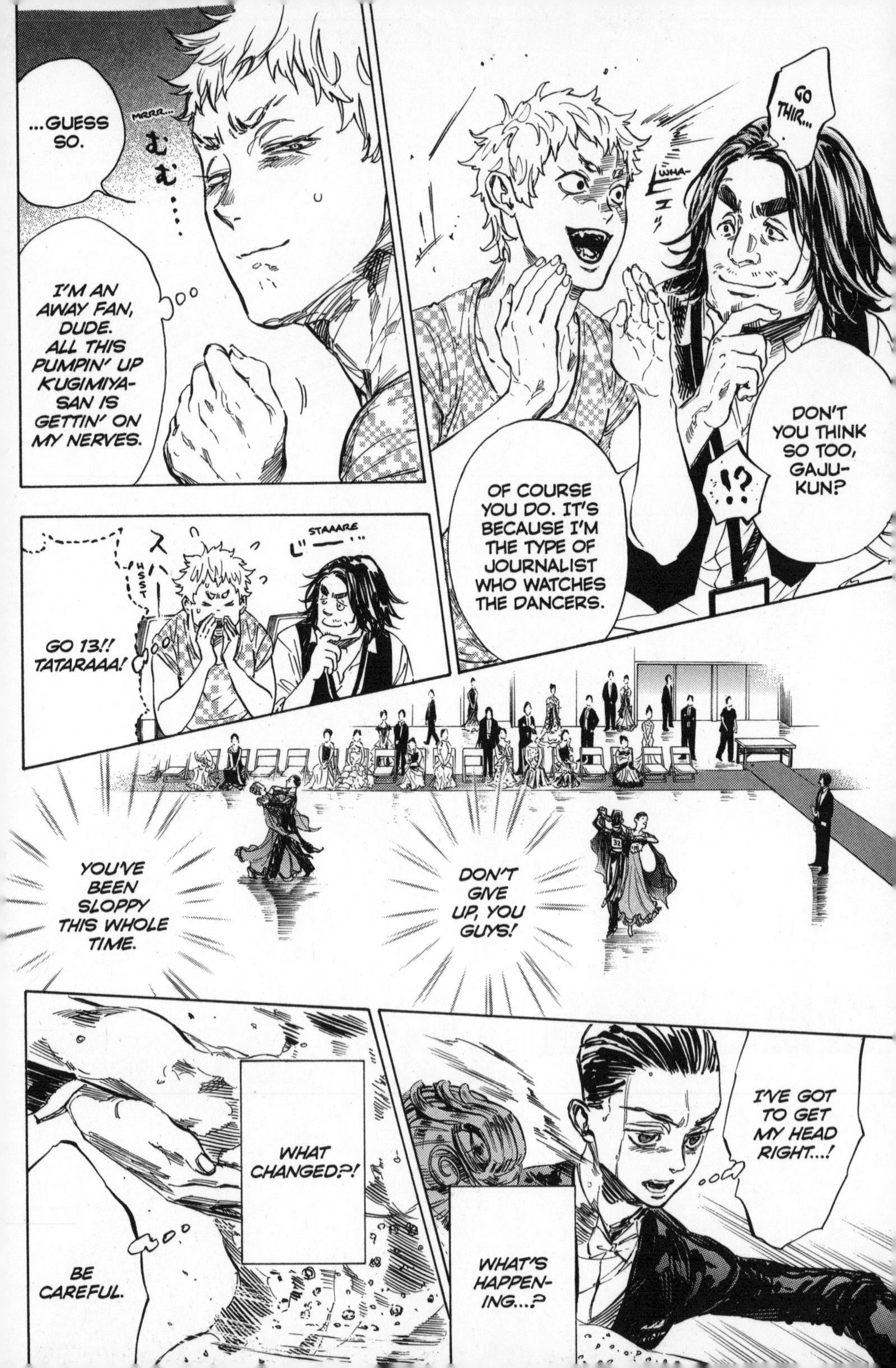

GO THIR...
WHA-
DON'T YOU THINK SO TOO, GAJU-KUN?
!?
OF COURSE YOU DO. IT'S BECAUSE I'M THE TYPE OF JOURNALIST WHO WATCHES THE DANCERS.
...GUESS SO.
MRRR...
I'M AN AWAY FAN, DUDE. ALL THIS PUMPIN' UP KUGIMIYA-SAN IS GETTIN' ON MY NERVES.
STAAARE
HSST
GO 13!! TATARAAA!
DON'T GIVE UP, YOU GUYS!
YOU'VE BEEN SLOPPY THIS WHOLE TIME.
I'VE GOT TO GET MY HEAD RIGHT...!
WHAT'S HAPPENING...?
WHAT CHANGED?!
BE CAREFUL.

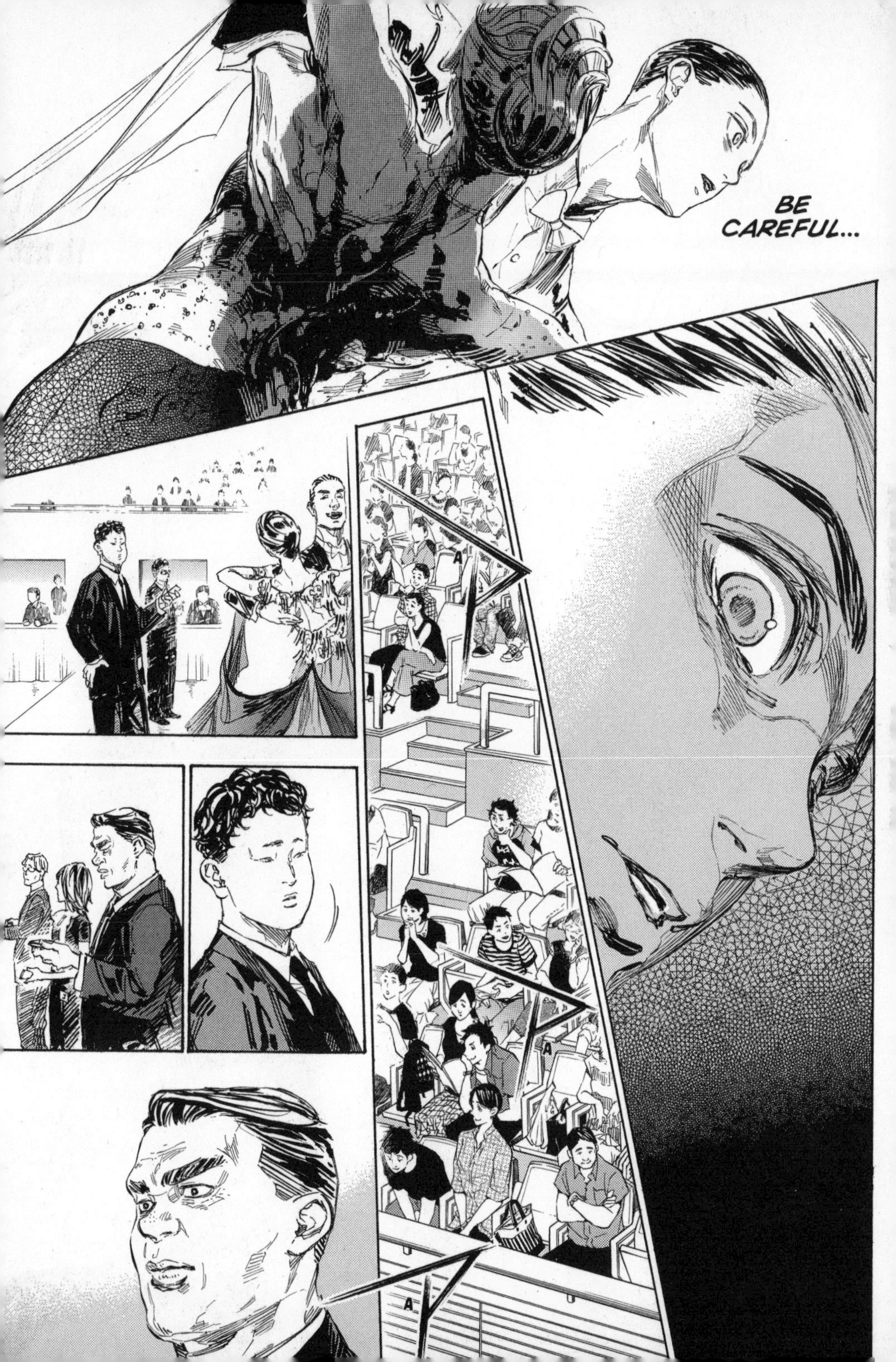
BE CAREFUL...

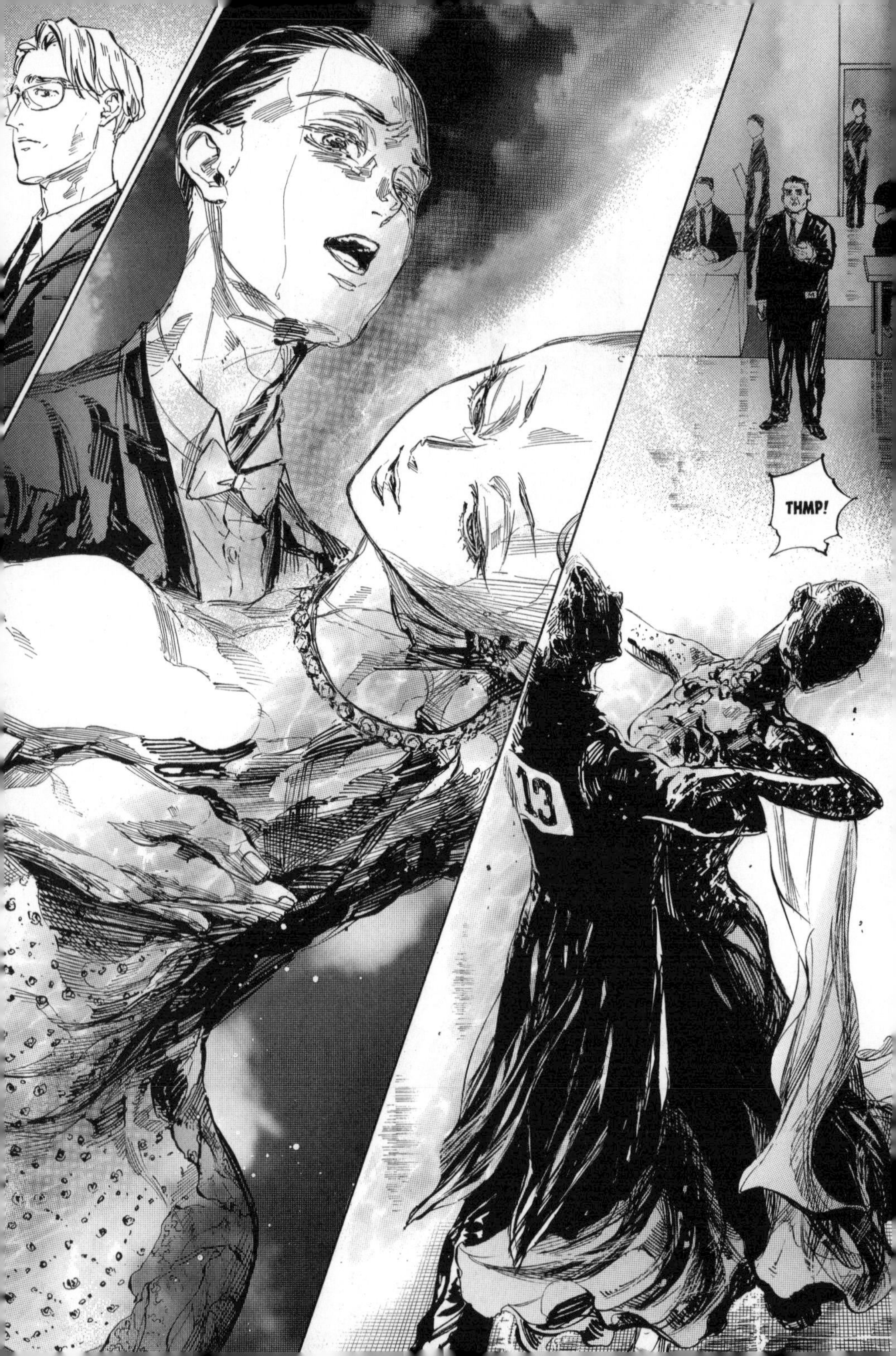
THMP!

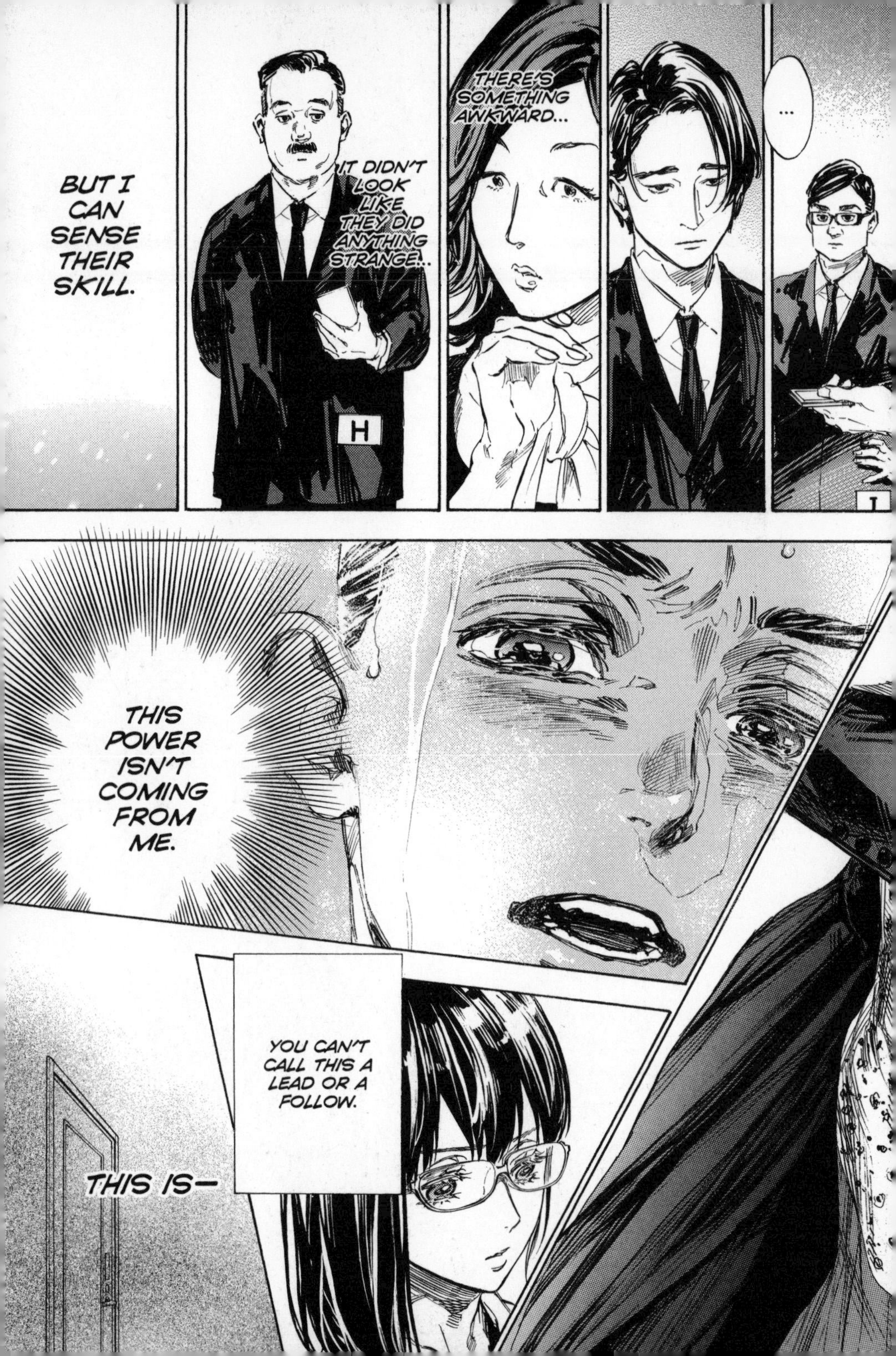
...
THERE'S SOMETHING AWKWARD...
IT DIDN'T LOOK LIKE THEY DID ANYTHING STRANGE...
BUT I CAN SENSE THEIR SKILL.
THIS POWER ISN'T COMING FROM ME.
YOU CAN'T CALL THIS A LEAD OR A FOLLOW.
THIS IS—

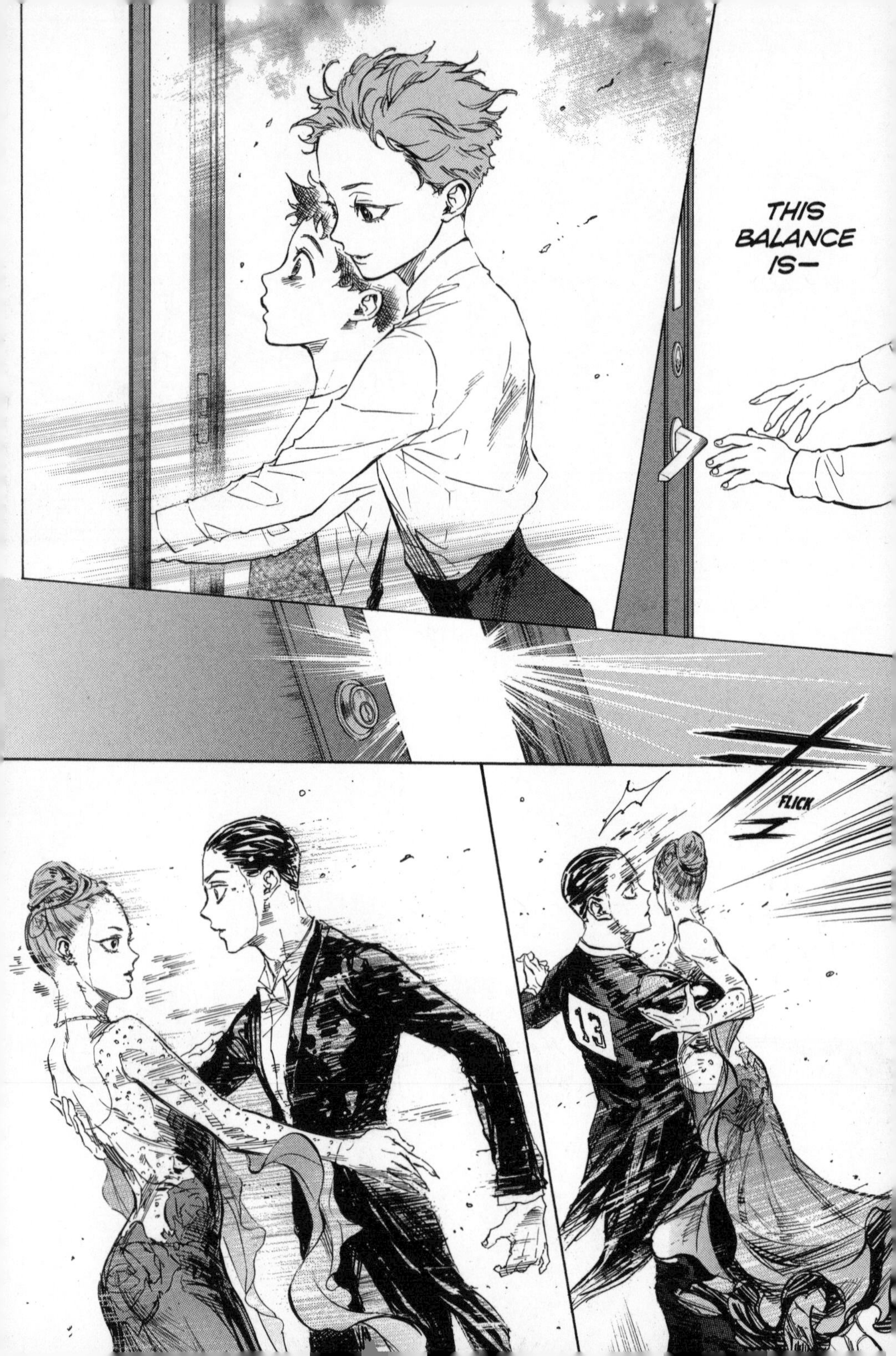
THIS BALANCE IS—
FLICK

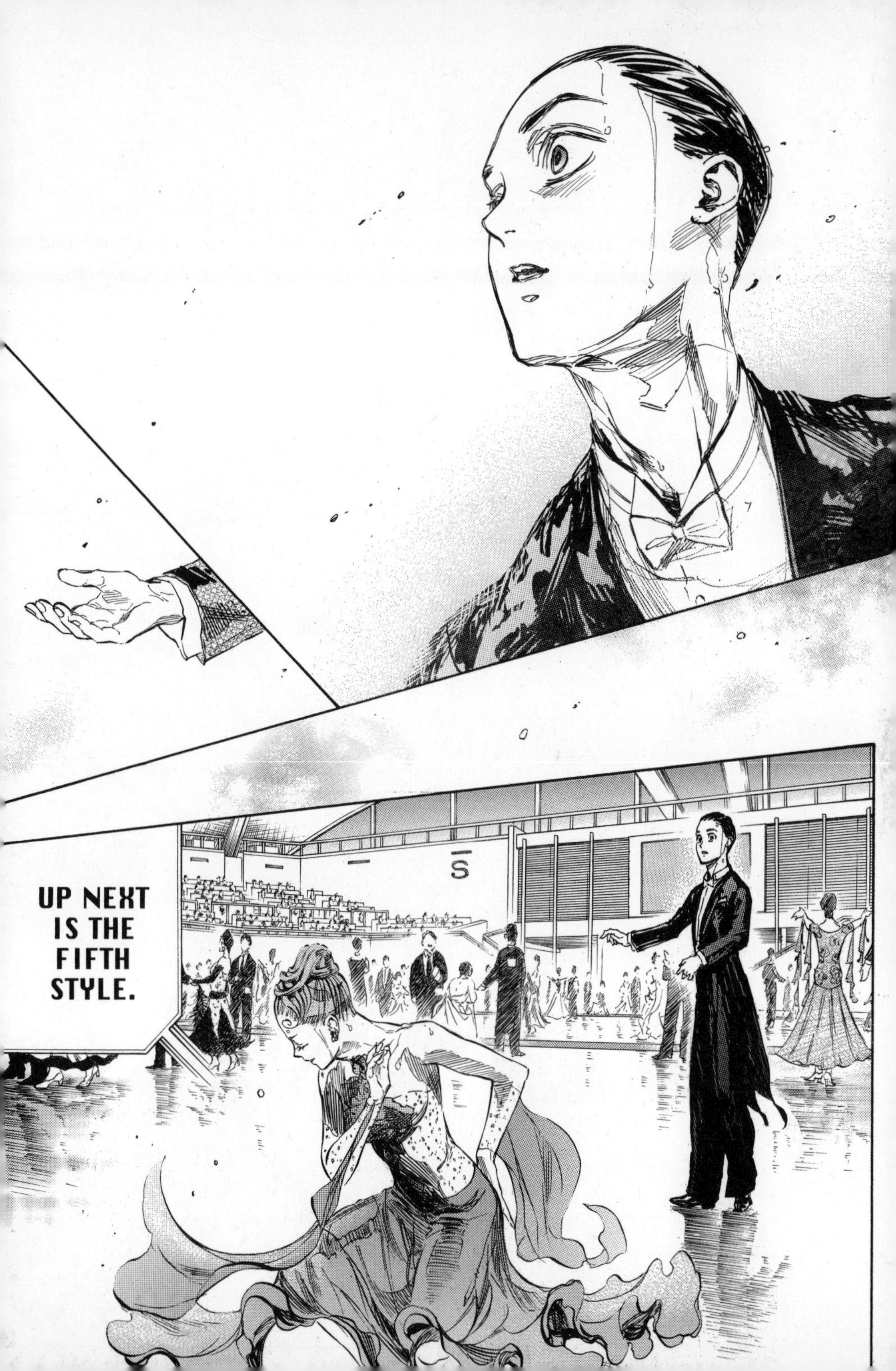
UP NEXT IS THE FIFTH STYLE.

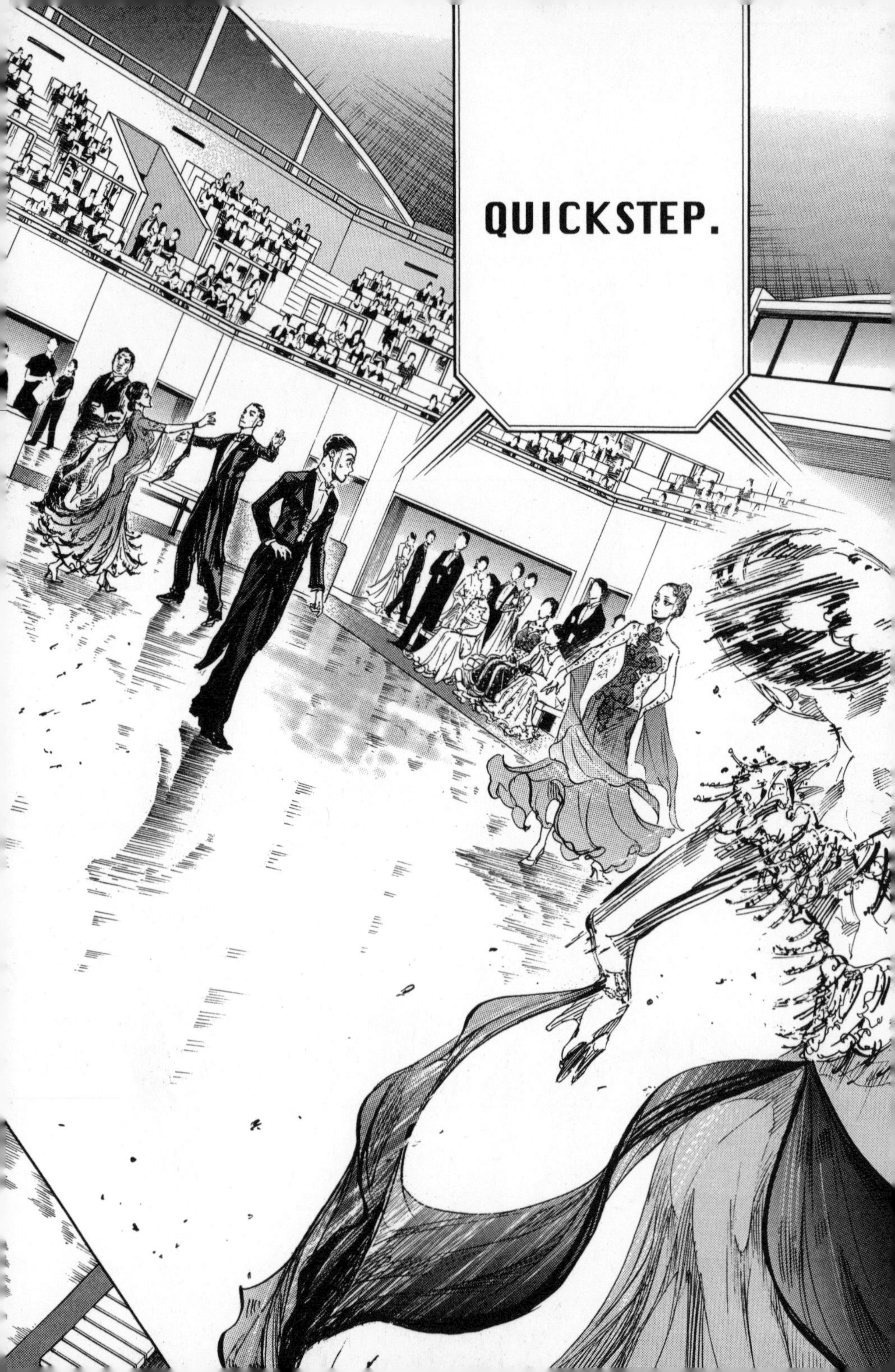
QUICKSTEP.

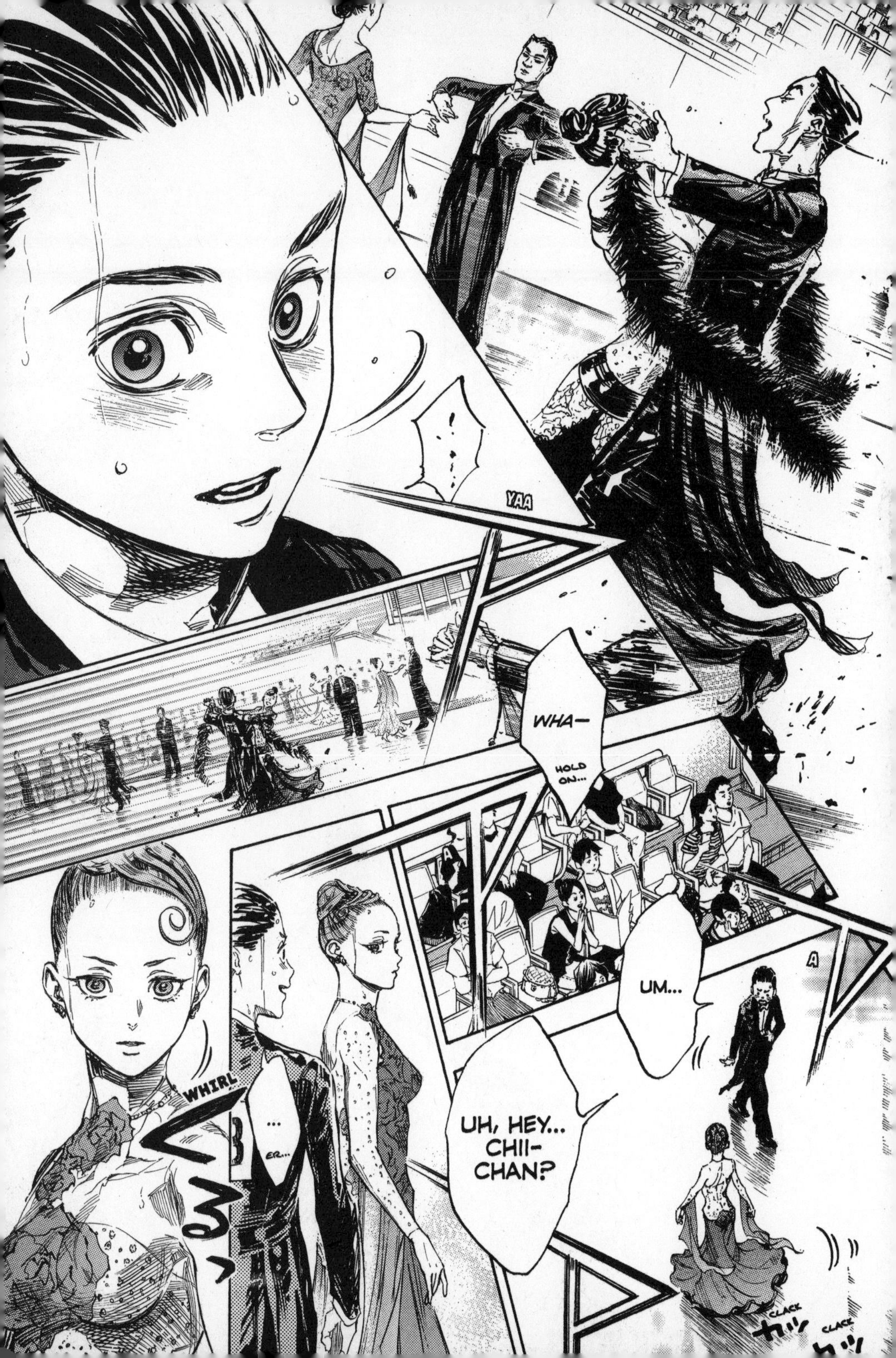
YAA
WHA—
HOLD ON...
UM...
UH, HEY... CHII-CHAN?
CLACK
CLACK
WHIRL
...
ER...

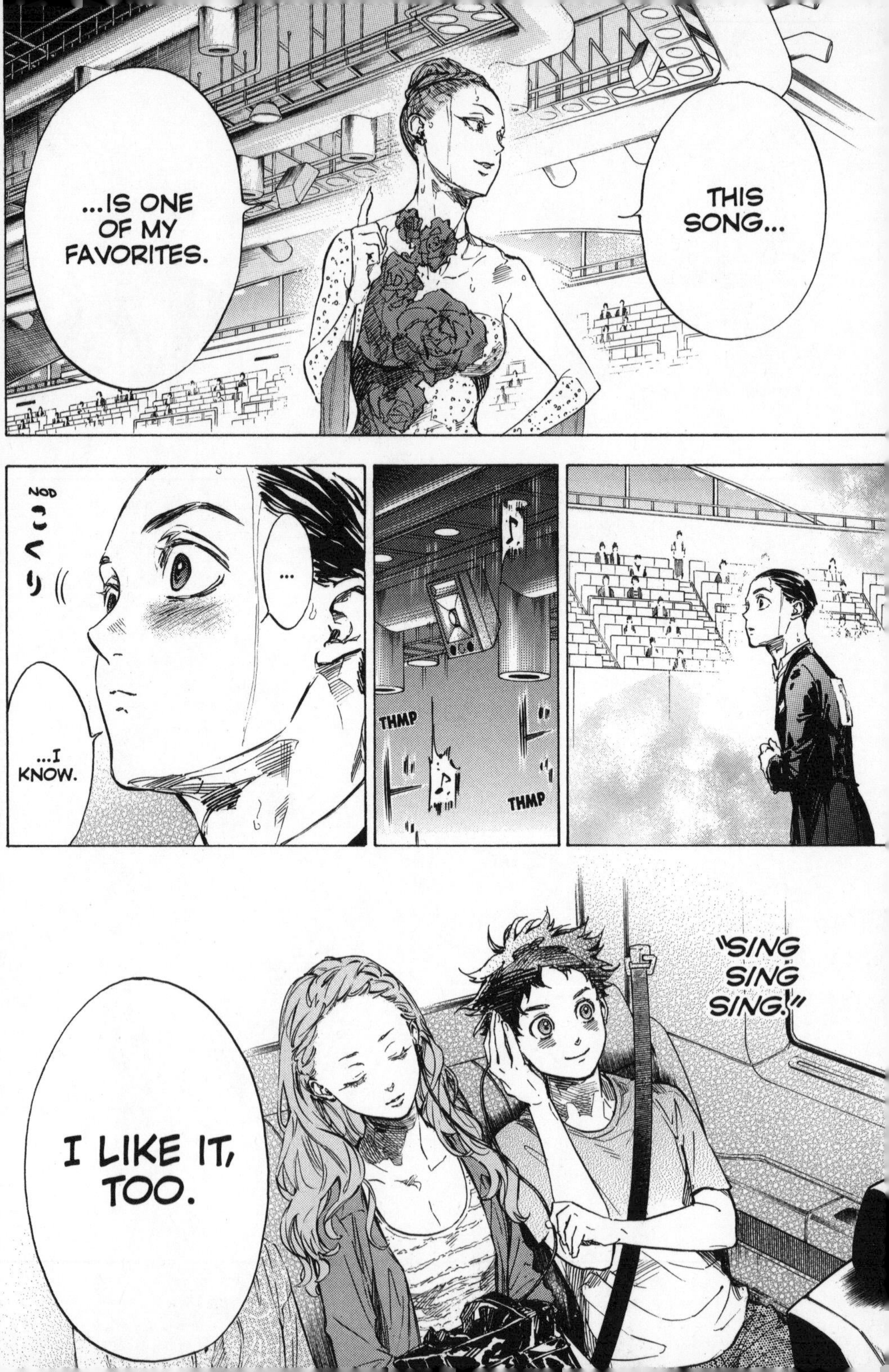
THIS SONG...
...IS ONE OF MY FAVORITES.
THMP
THMP
NOD
こくり
...
...I KNOW.
"SING SING SING."
I LIKE IT, TOO.

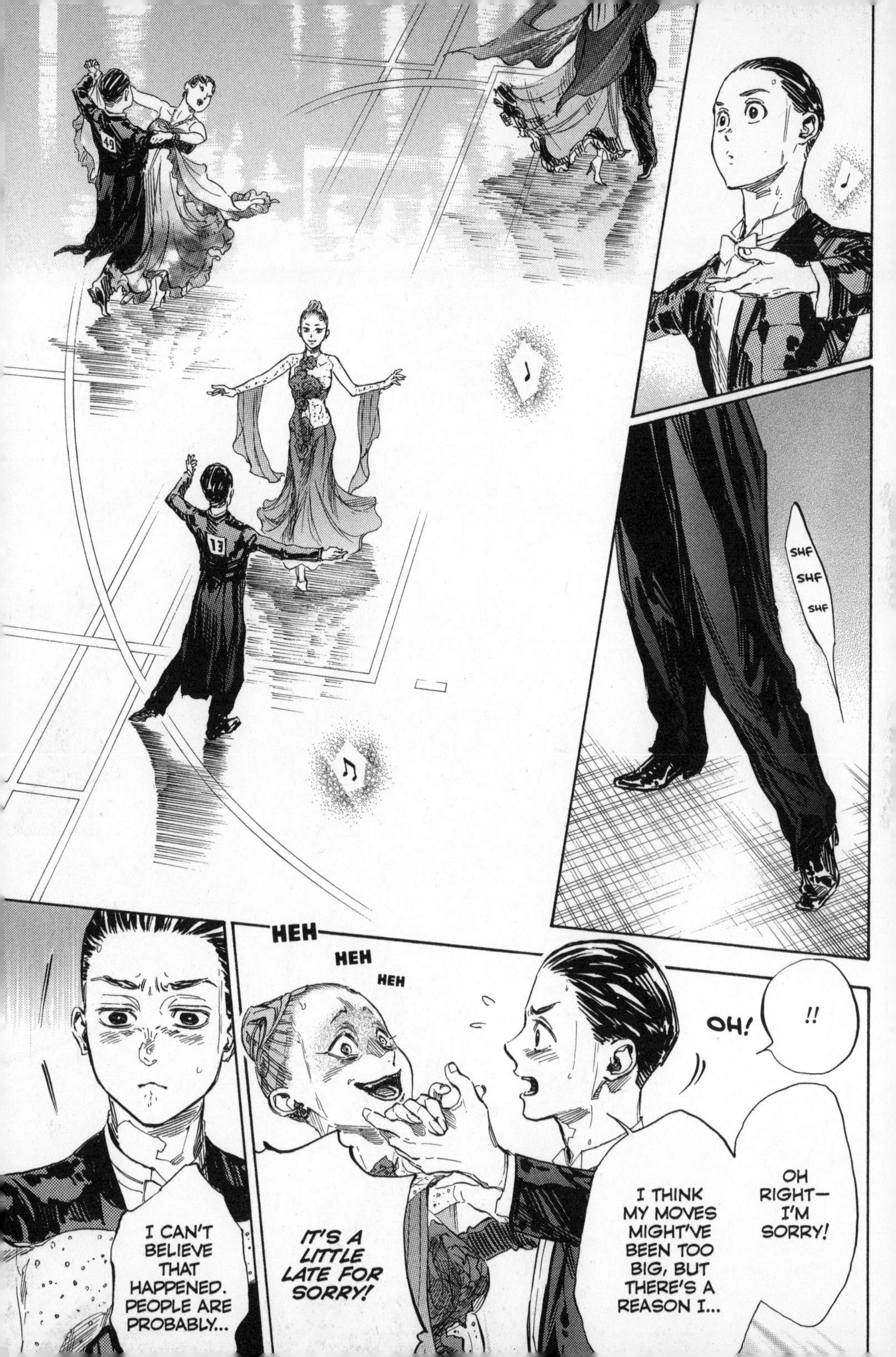
SHF
SHF
SHF
!!
OH!
HEH
HEH
HEH
OH RIGHT— I'M SORRY!
I THINK MY MOVES MIGHT'VE BEEN TOO BIG, BUT THERE'S A REASON I...
IT'S A LITTLE LATE FOR SORRY!
I CAN'T BELIEVE THAT HAPPENED. PEOPLE ARE PROBABLY...

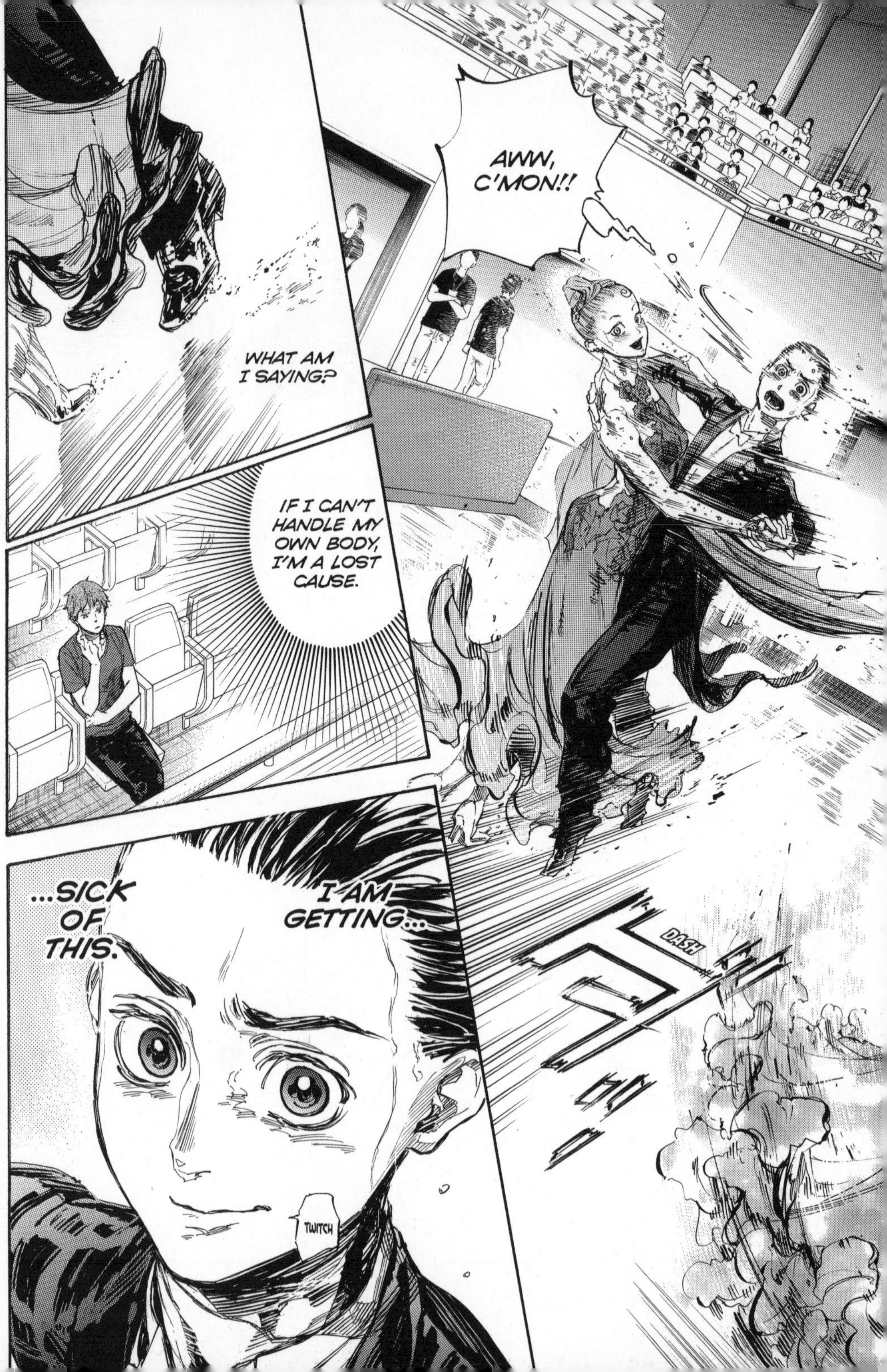
AWW, C'MON!!
DASH
WHAT AM I SAYING?
IF I CAN'T HANDLE MY OWN BODY, I'M A LOST CAUSE.
I AM GETTING...
...SICK OF THIS.
TWITCH

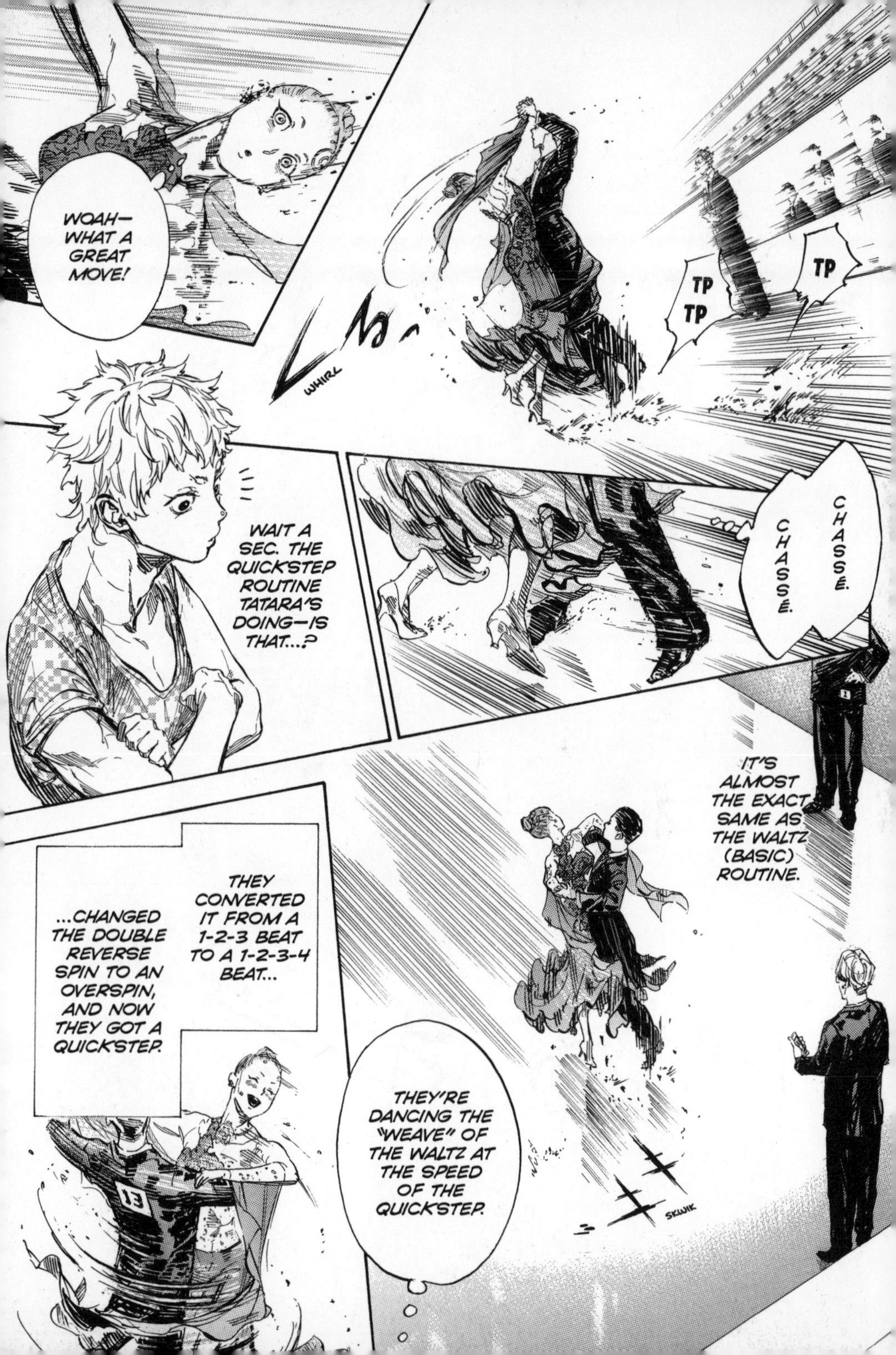
TP
TP TP
WHIRL
WOAH—WHAT A GREAT MOVE!
CHASSÉ.
CHASSÉ.
WAIT A SEC. THE QUICKSTEP ROUTINE TATARA'S DOING—IS THAT...?
IT'S ALMOST THE EXACT SAME AS THE WALTZ (BASIC) ROUTINE.
THEY'RE DANCING THE "WEAVE" OF THE WALTZ AT THE SPEED OF THE QUICKSTEP.
SKWIK
THEY CONVERTED IT FROM A 1-2-3 BEAT TO A 1-2-3-4 BEAT...
...CHANGED THE DOUBLE REVERSE SPIN TO AN OVERSPIN, AND NOW THEY GOT A QUICKSTEP.

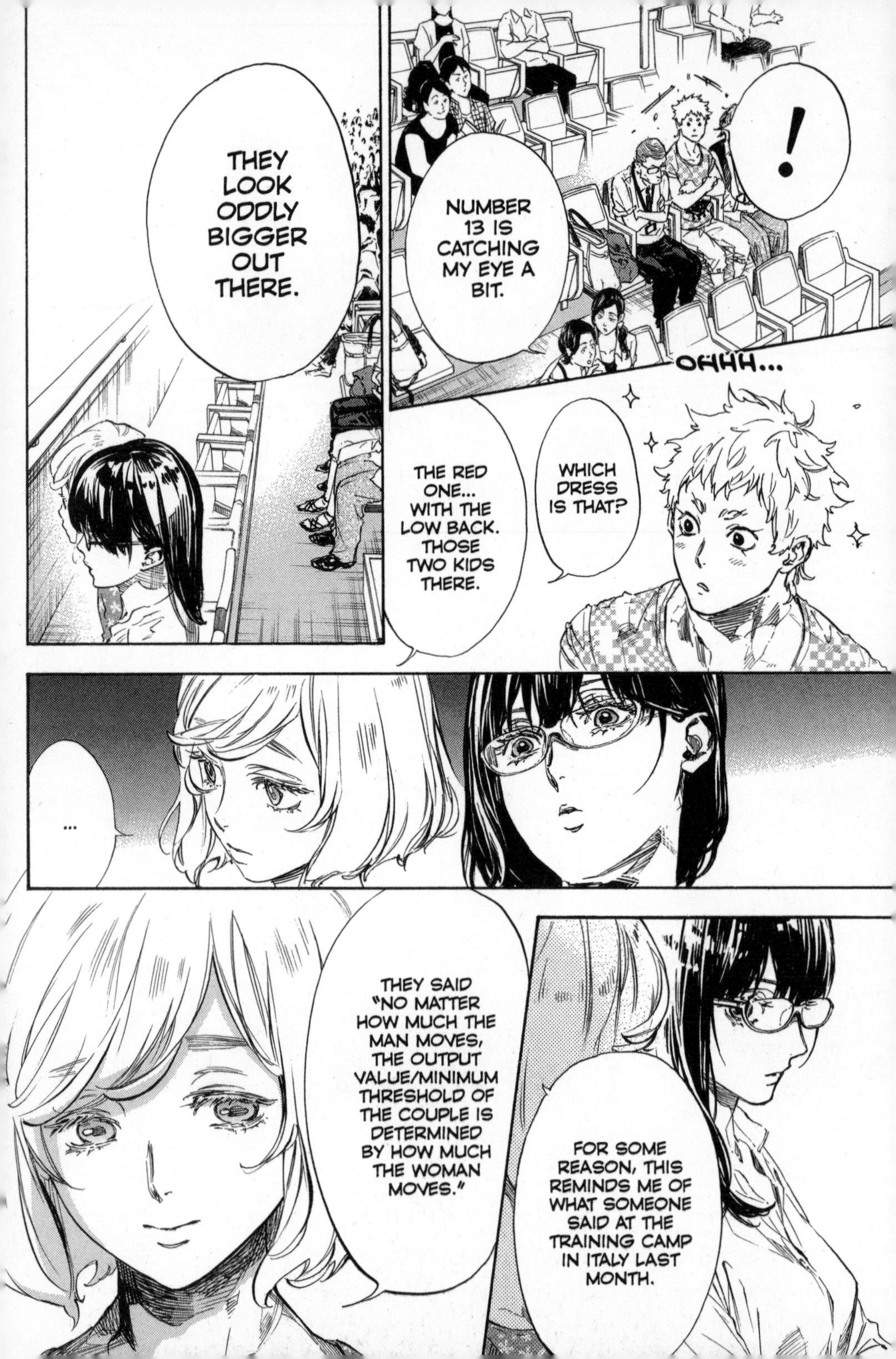
!
NUMBER 13 IS CATCHING MY EYE A BIT.
OHHH...
WHICH DRESS IS THAT?
THE RED ONE... WITH THE LOW BACK. THOSE TWO KIDS THERE.
THEY LOOK ODDLY BIGGER OUT THERE.
...
FOR SOME REASON, THIS REMINDS ME OF WHAT SOMEONE SAID AT THE TRAINING CAMP IN ITALY LAST MONTH.
THEY SAID "NO MATTER HOW MUCH THE MAN MOVES, THE OUTPUT VALUE/MINIMUM THRESHOLD OF THE COUPLE IS DETERMINED BY HOW MUCH THE WOMAN MOVES."

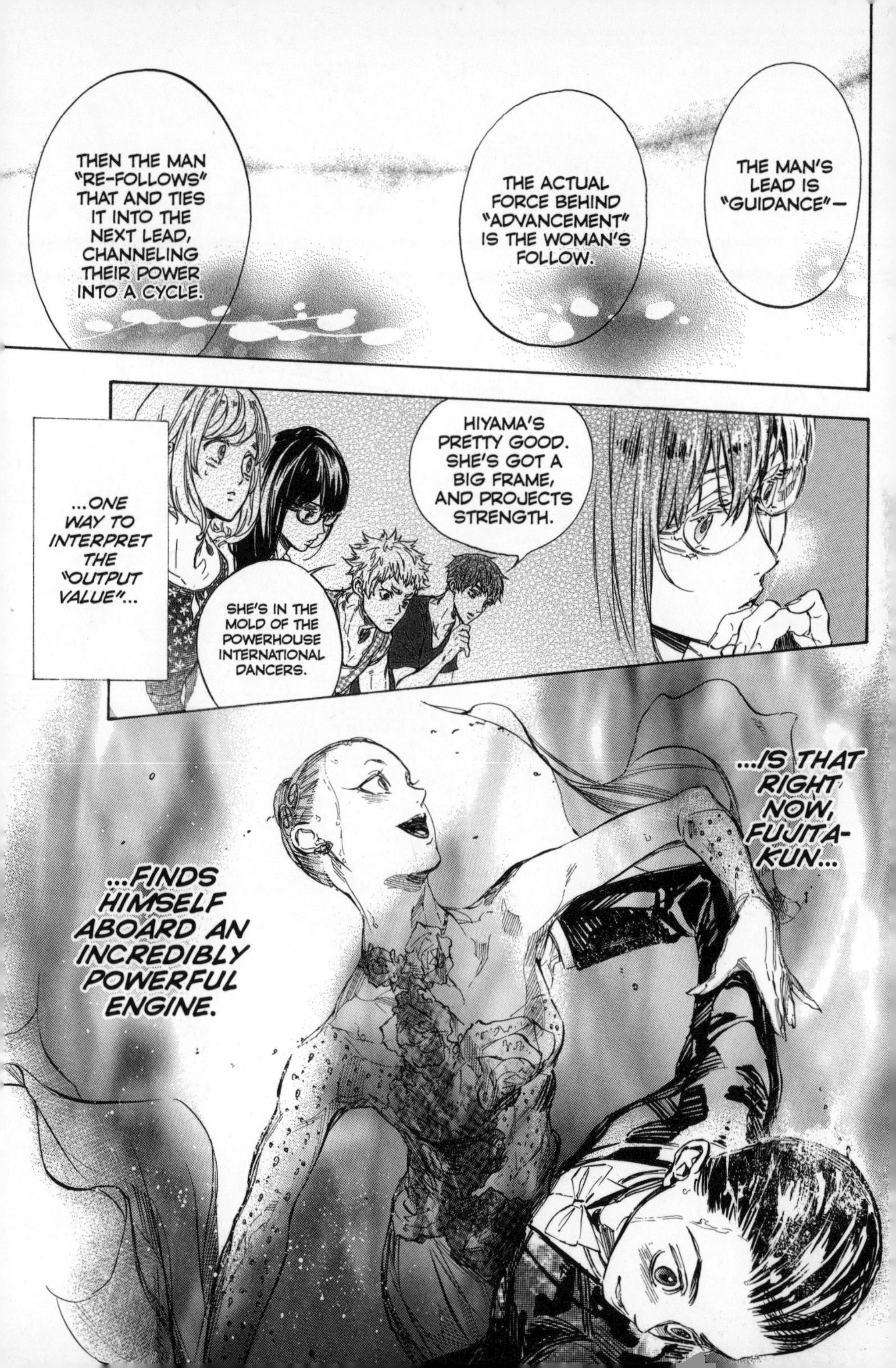
THE MAN'S LEAD IS "GUIDANCE"—
THE ACTUAL FORCE BEHIND "ADVANCEMENT" IS THE WOMAN'S FOLLOW.
THEN THE MAN "RE-FOLLOWS" THAT AND TIES IT INTO THE NEXT LEAD, CHANNELING THEIR POWER INTO A CYCLE.
HIYAMA'S PRETTY GOOD. SHE'S GOT A BIG FRAME, AND PROJECTS STRENGTH.
SHE'S IN THE MOLD OF THE POWERHOUSE INTERNATIONAL DANCERS.
...ONE WAY TO INTERPRET THE "OUTPUT VALUE"...
...IS THAT RIGHT NOW, FUJITA-KUN...
...FINDS HIMSELF ABOARD AN INCREDIBLY POWERFUL ENGINE.

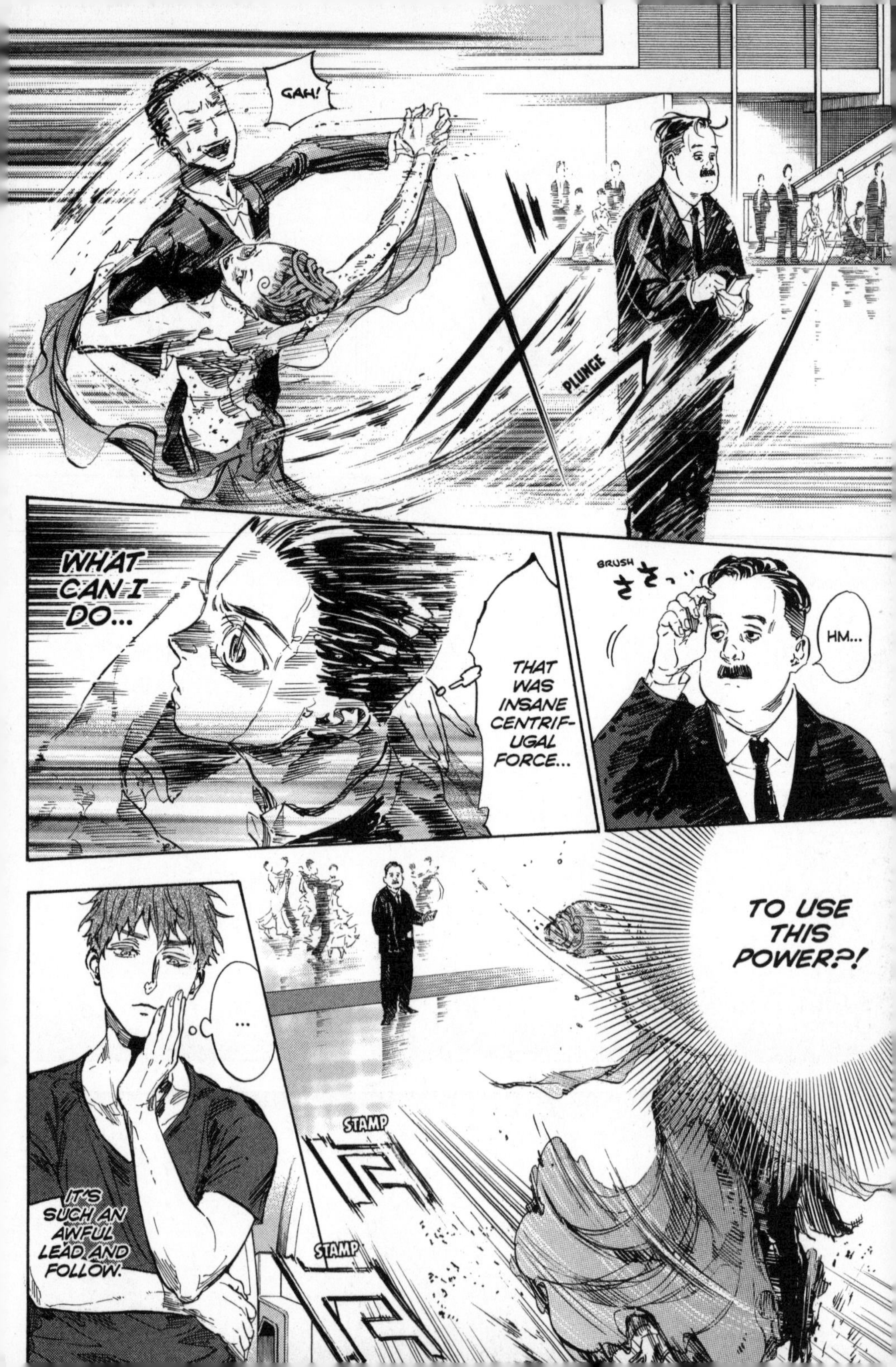
GAH!
PLUNGE
BRUSH
さささっ
HM...
WHAT CAN I DO...
THAT WAS INSANE CENTRIF-UGAL FORCE...
TO USE THIS POWER?!
STAMP
STAMP
...
IT'S SUCH AN AWFUL LEAD AND FOLLOW.

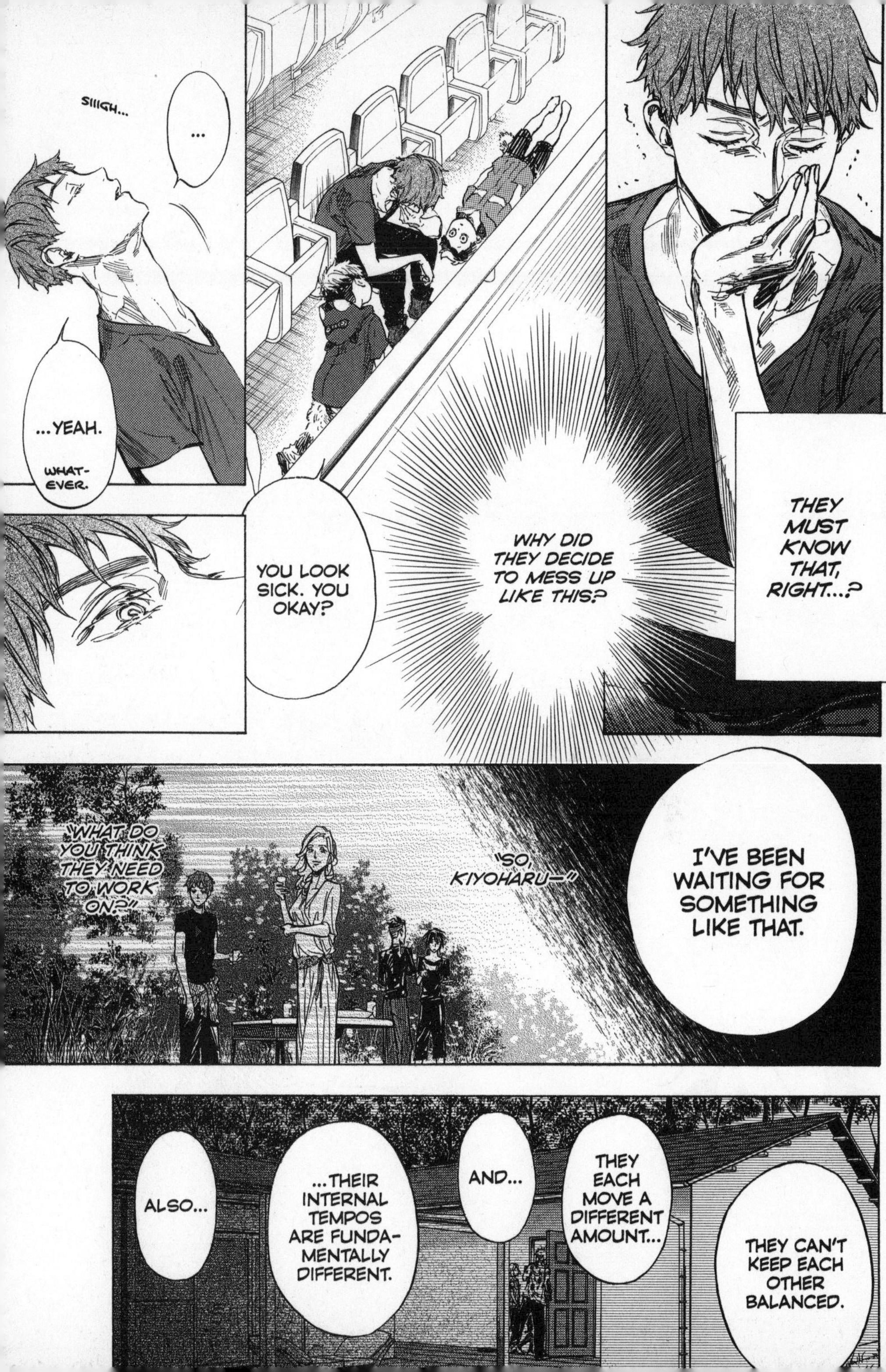

THEY MUST KNOW THAT, RIGHT...?
WHY DID THEY DECIDE TO MESS UP LIKE THIS?
...
SIIGH...
...YEAH.
WHAT-EVER.
YOU LOOK SICK. YOU OKAY?
I'VE BEEN WAITING FOR SOMETHING LIKE THAT.
"SO, KIYOHARU—"
"WHAT DO YOU THINK THEY NEED TO WORK ON?"
THEY CAN'T KEEP EACH OTHER BALANCED.
THEY EACH MOVE A DIFFERENT AMOUNT...
AND...
...THEIR INTERNAL TEMPOS ARE FUNDA-MENTALLY DIFFERENT.
ALSO...

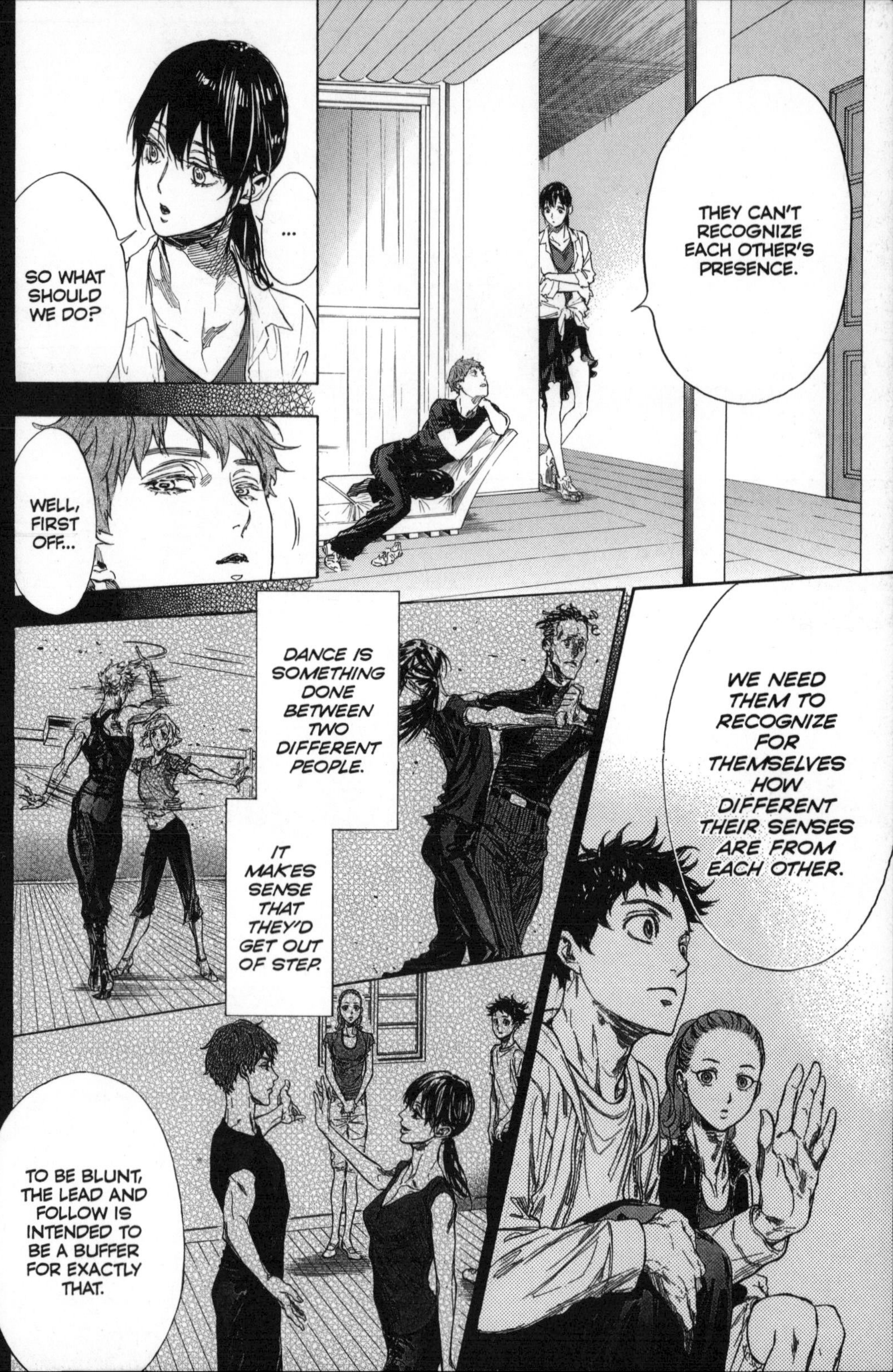
THEY CAN'T RECOGNIZE EACH OTHER'S PRESENCE.
...
SO WHAT SHOULD WE DO?
WELL, FIRST OFF...
WE NEED THEM TO RECOGNIZE FOR THEMSELVES HOW DIFFERENT THEIR SENSES ARE FROM EACH OTHER.
DANCE IS SOMETHING DONE BETWEEN TWO DIFFERENT PEOPLE.
IT MAKES SENSE THAT THEY'D GET OUT OF STEP.
TO BE BLUNT, THE LEAD AND FOLLOW IS INTENDED TO BE A BUFFER FOR EXACTLY THAT.

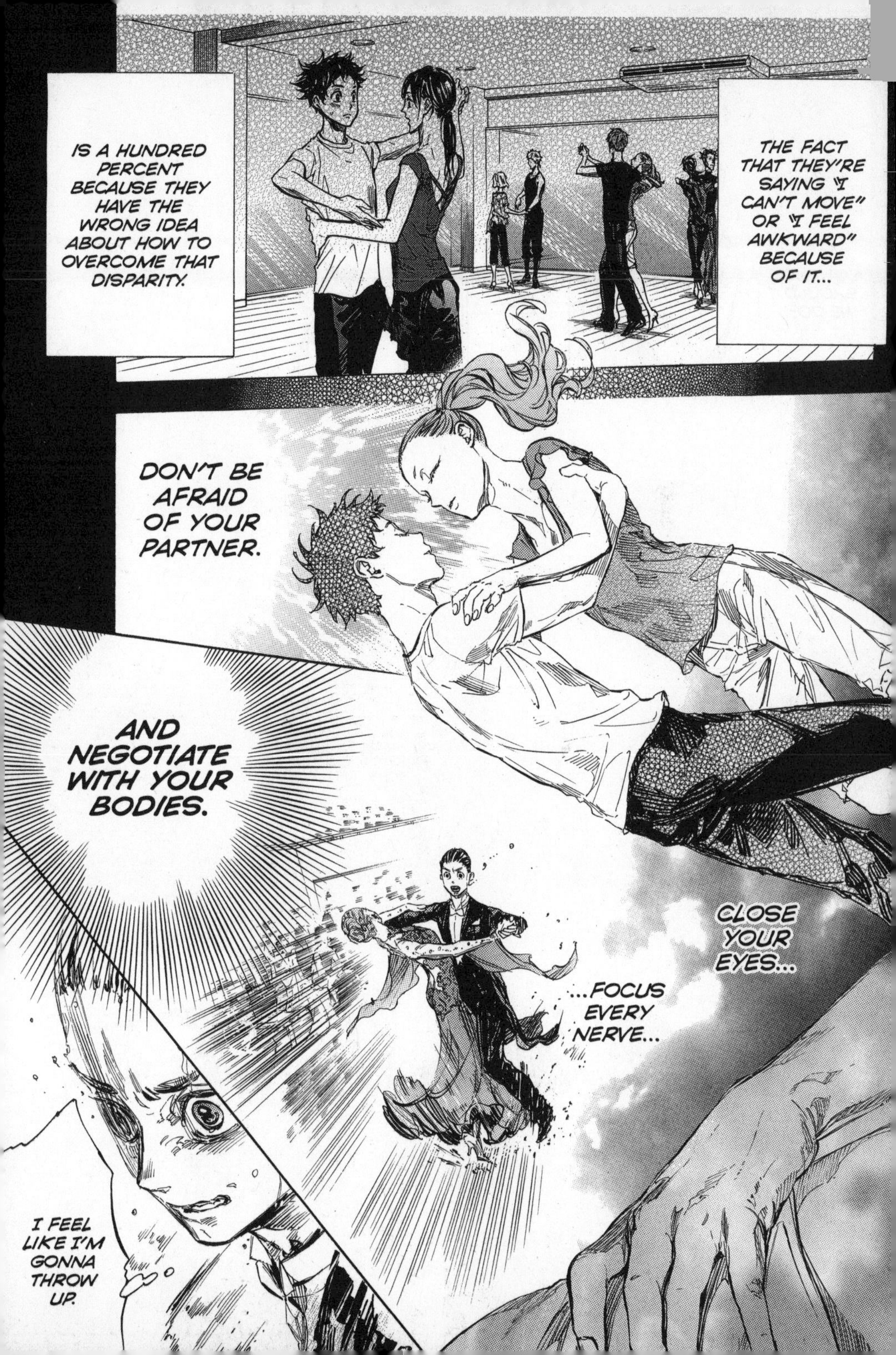
THE FACT THAT THEY'RE SAYING "I CAN'T MOVE" OR "I FEEL AWKWARD" BECAUSE OF IT...
IS A HUNDRED PERCENT BECAUSE THEY HAVE THE WRONG IDEA ABOUT HOW TO OVERCOME THAT DISPARITY.
DON'T BE AFRAID OF YOUR PARTNER.
AND NEGOTIATE WITH YOUR BODIES.
CLOSE YOUR EYES...
...FOCUS EVERY NERVE...
I FEEL LIKE I'M GONNA THROW UP.

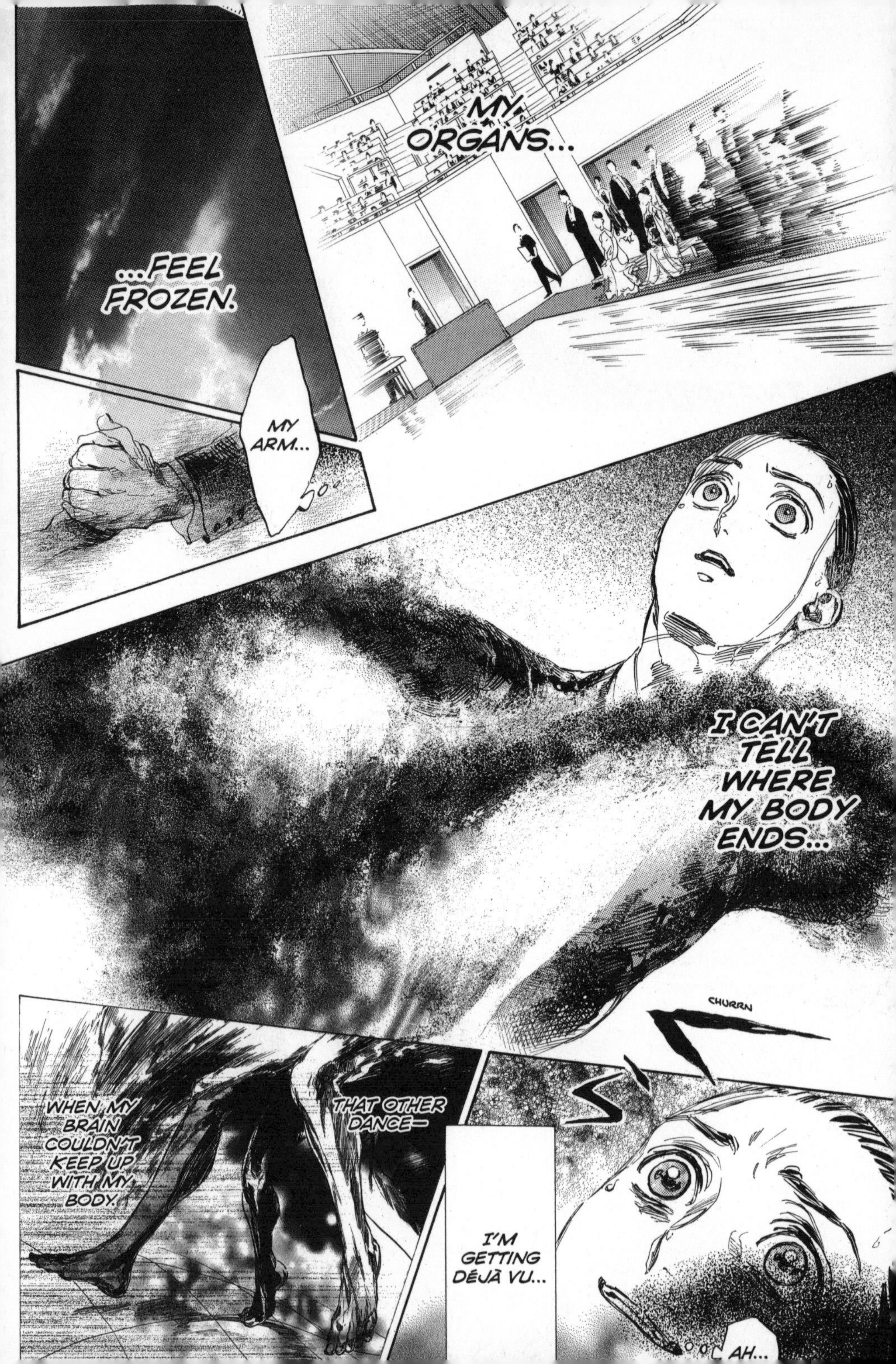
MY ORGANS...
...FEEL FROZEN.
MY ARM...
I CAN'T TELL WHERE MY BODY ENDS...
CHURRN
I'M GETTING DÉJÀ VU...
AH...
THAT OTHER DANCE—
WHEN MY BRAIN COULDN'T KEEP UP WITH MY BODY.

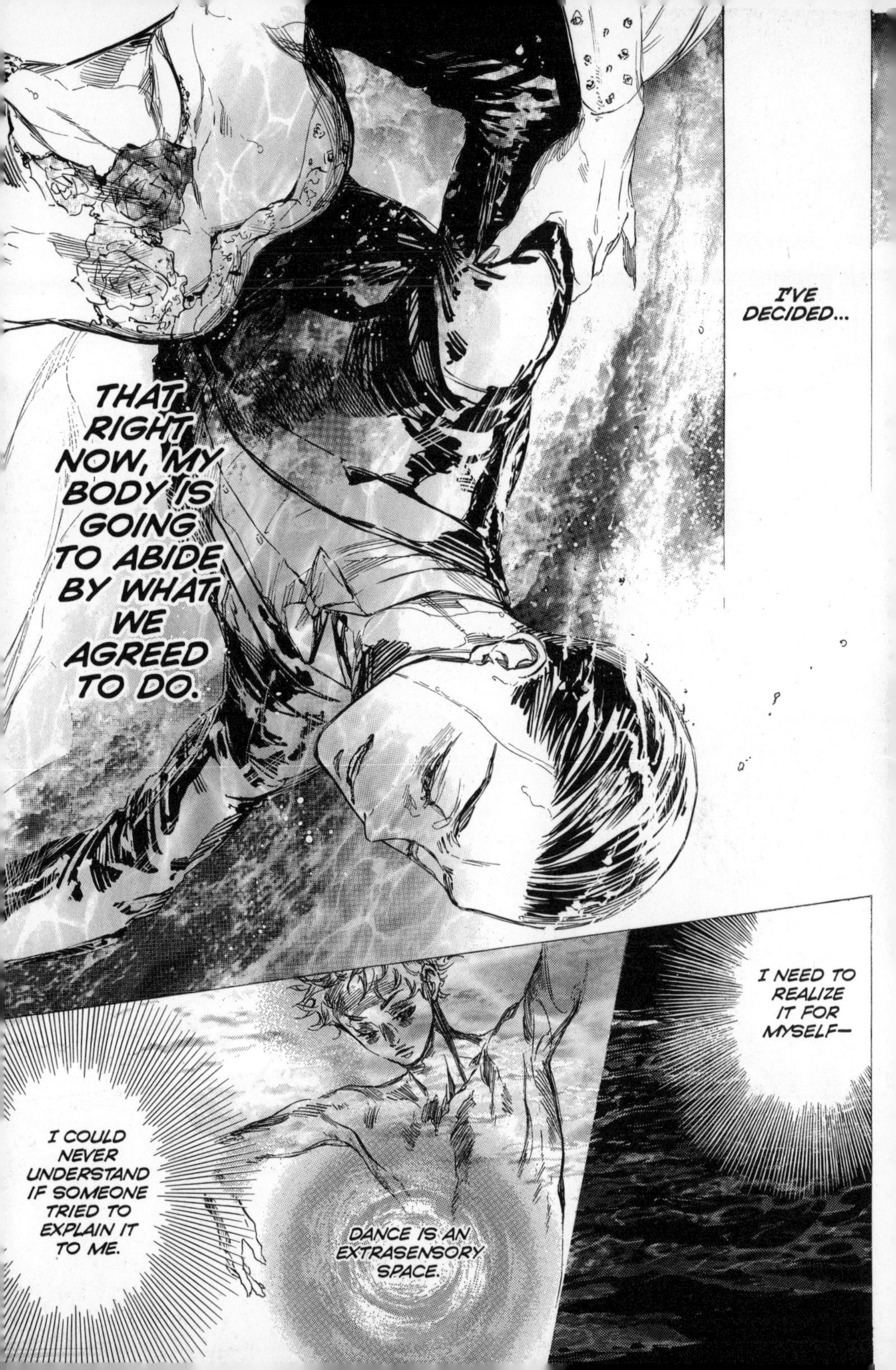
I'VE DECIDED...
THAT RIGHT NOW, MY BODY IS GOING TO ABIDE BY WHAT WE AGREED TO DO.
I NEED TO REALIZE IT FOR MYSELF—
I COULD NEVER UNDERSTAND IF SOMEONE TRIED TO EXPLAIN IT TO ME.
DANCE IS AN EXTRASENSORY SPACE.

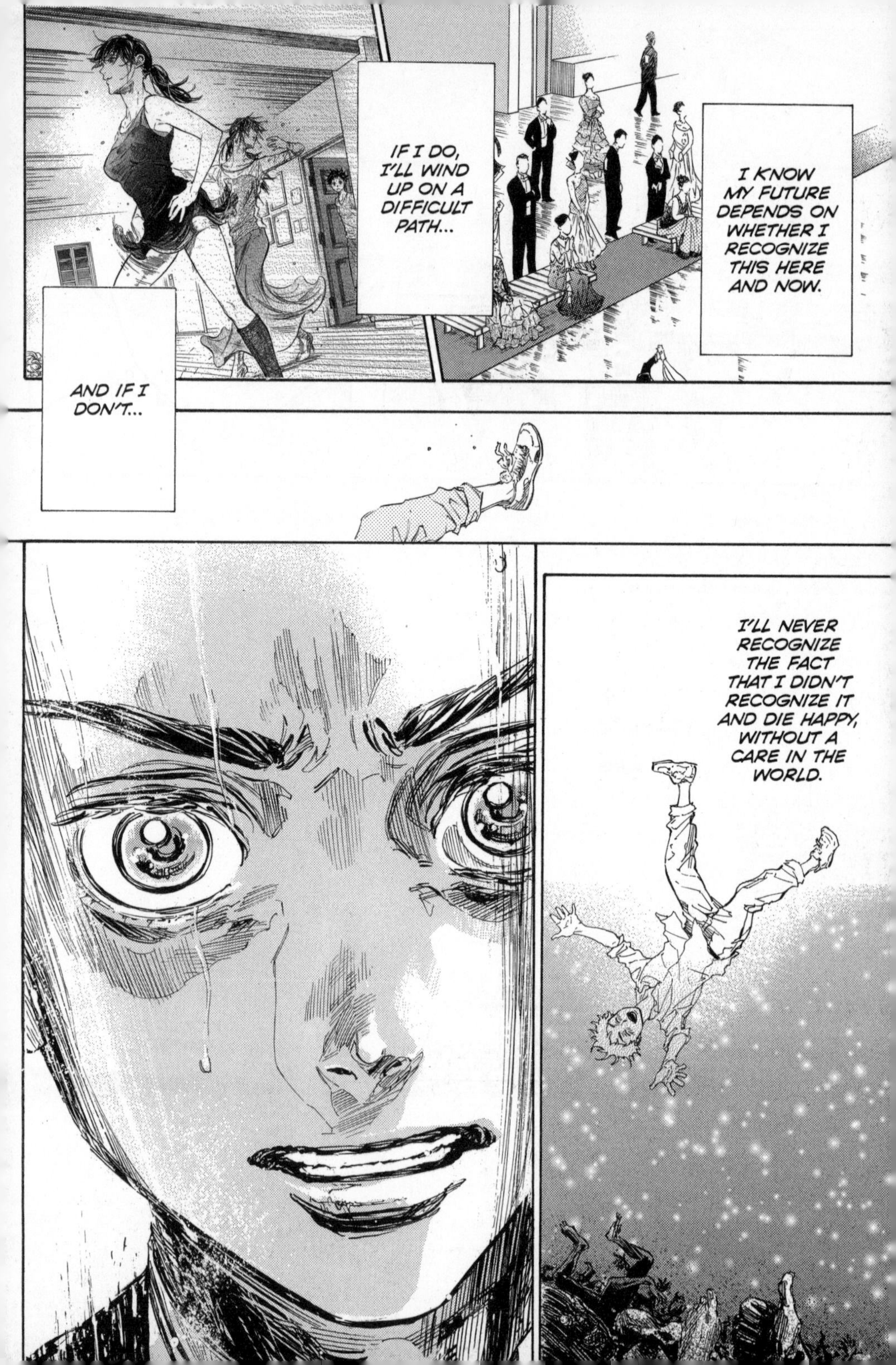
I KNOW MY FUTURE DEPENDS ON WHETHER I RECOGNIZE THIS HERE AND NOW.
IF I DO, I'LL WIND UP ON A DIFFICULT PATH...
AND IF I DON'T...
I'LL NEVER RECOGNIZE THE FACT THAT I DIDN'T RECOGNIZE IT AND DIE HAPPY, WITHOUT A CARE IN THE WORLD.

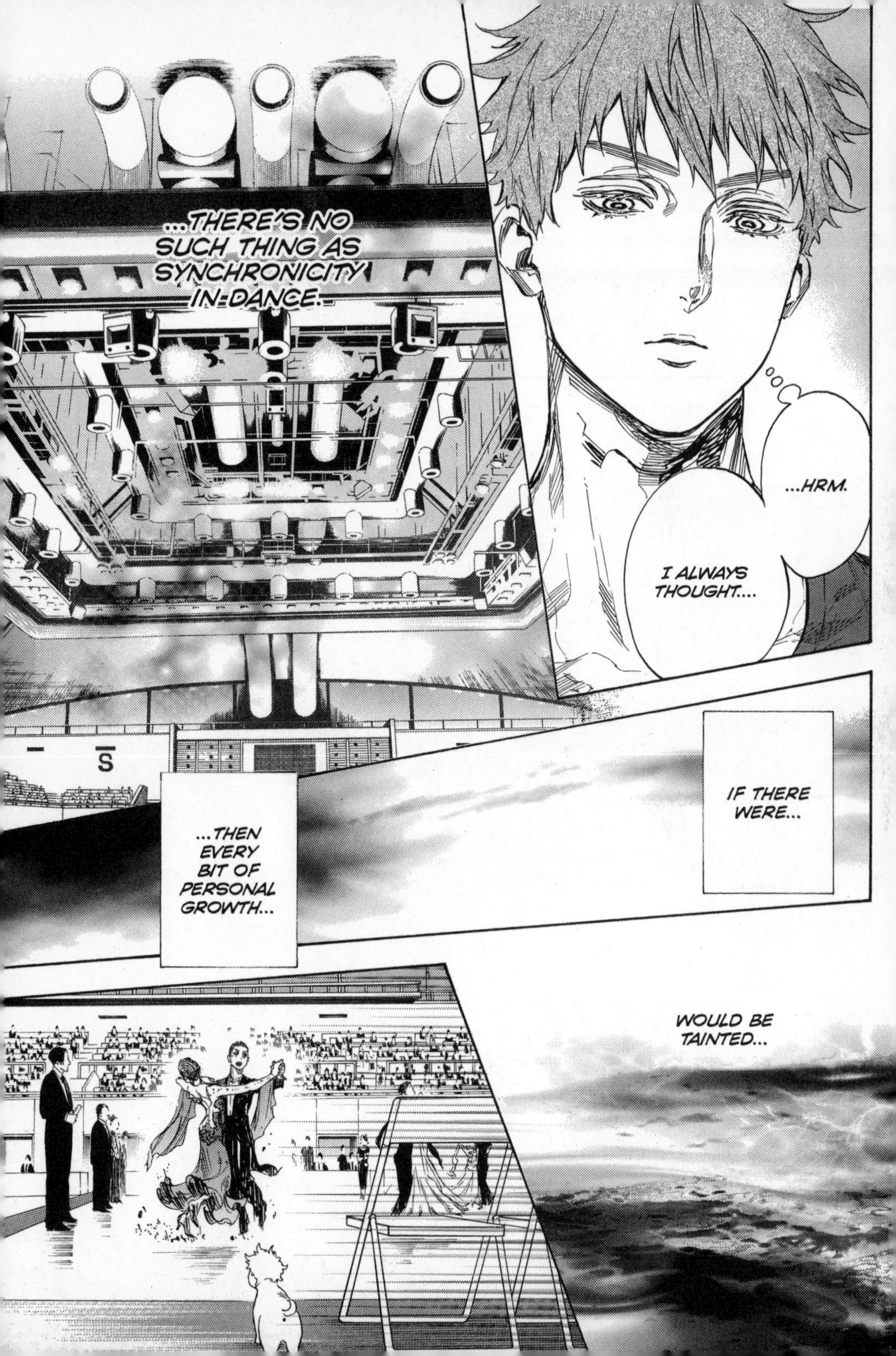
...HRM.
I ALWAYS THOUGHT....
...THERE'S NO SUCH THING AS SYNCHRONICITY IN DANCE.
IF THERE WERE...
...THEN EVERY BIT OF PERSONAL GROWTH...
WOULD BE TAINTED...

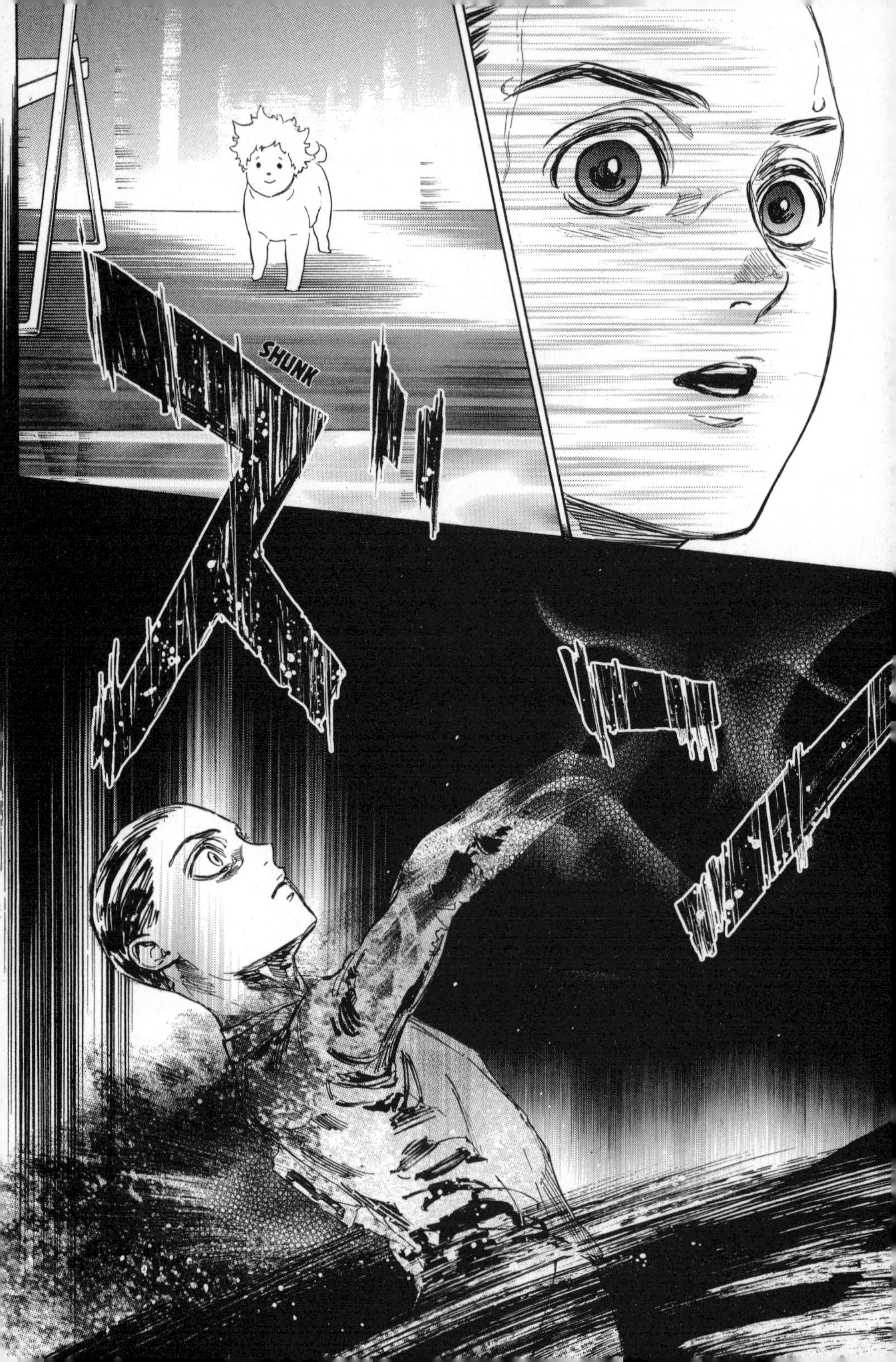
SHUNK

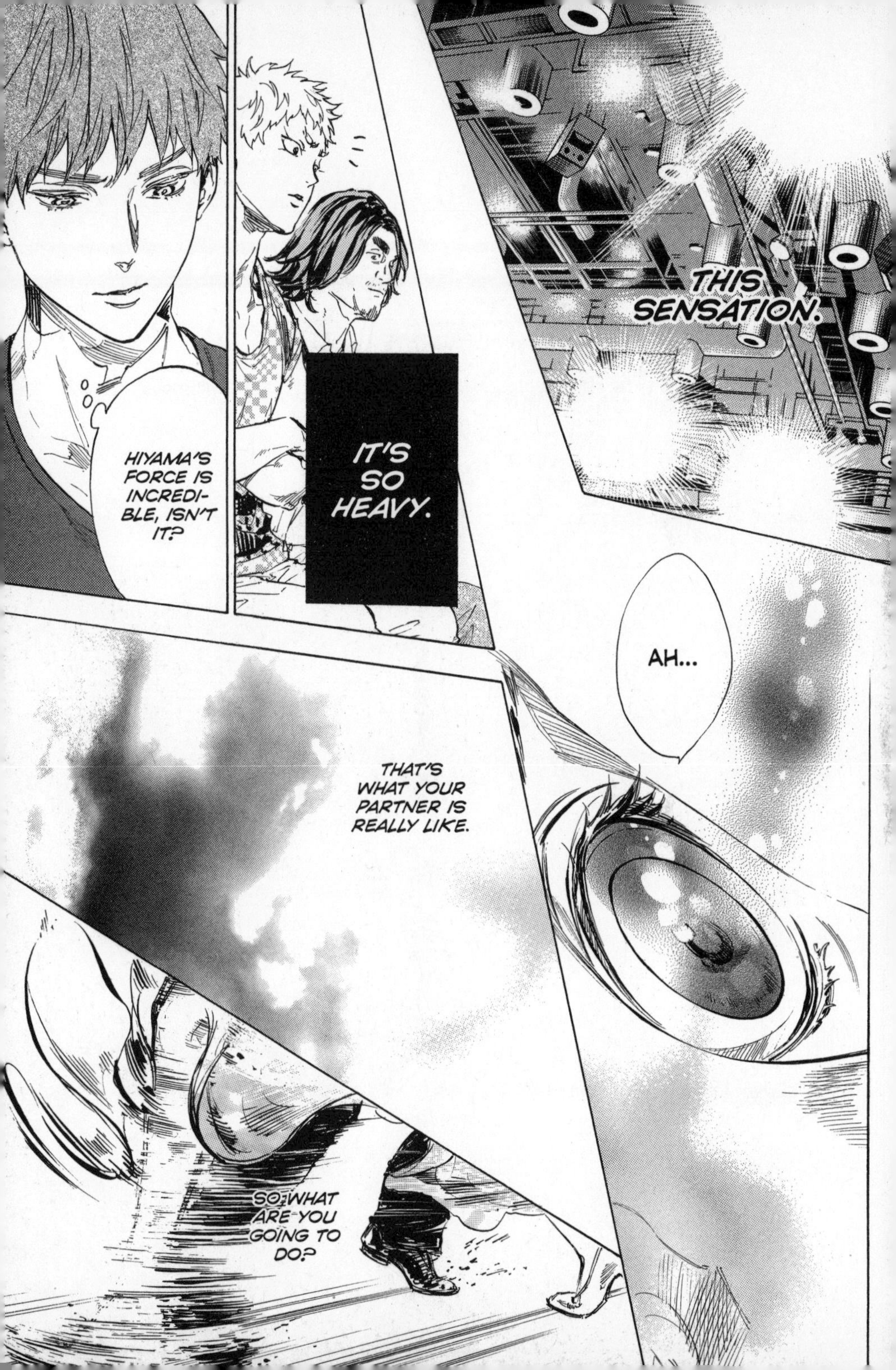
THIS SENSATION.
IT'S SO HEAVY.
HIYAMA'S FORCE IS INCREDIBLE, ISN'T IT?
AH...
THAT'S WHAT YOUR PARTNER IS REALLY LIKE.
SO WHAT ARE YOU GOING TO DO?

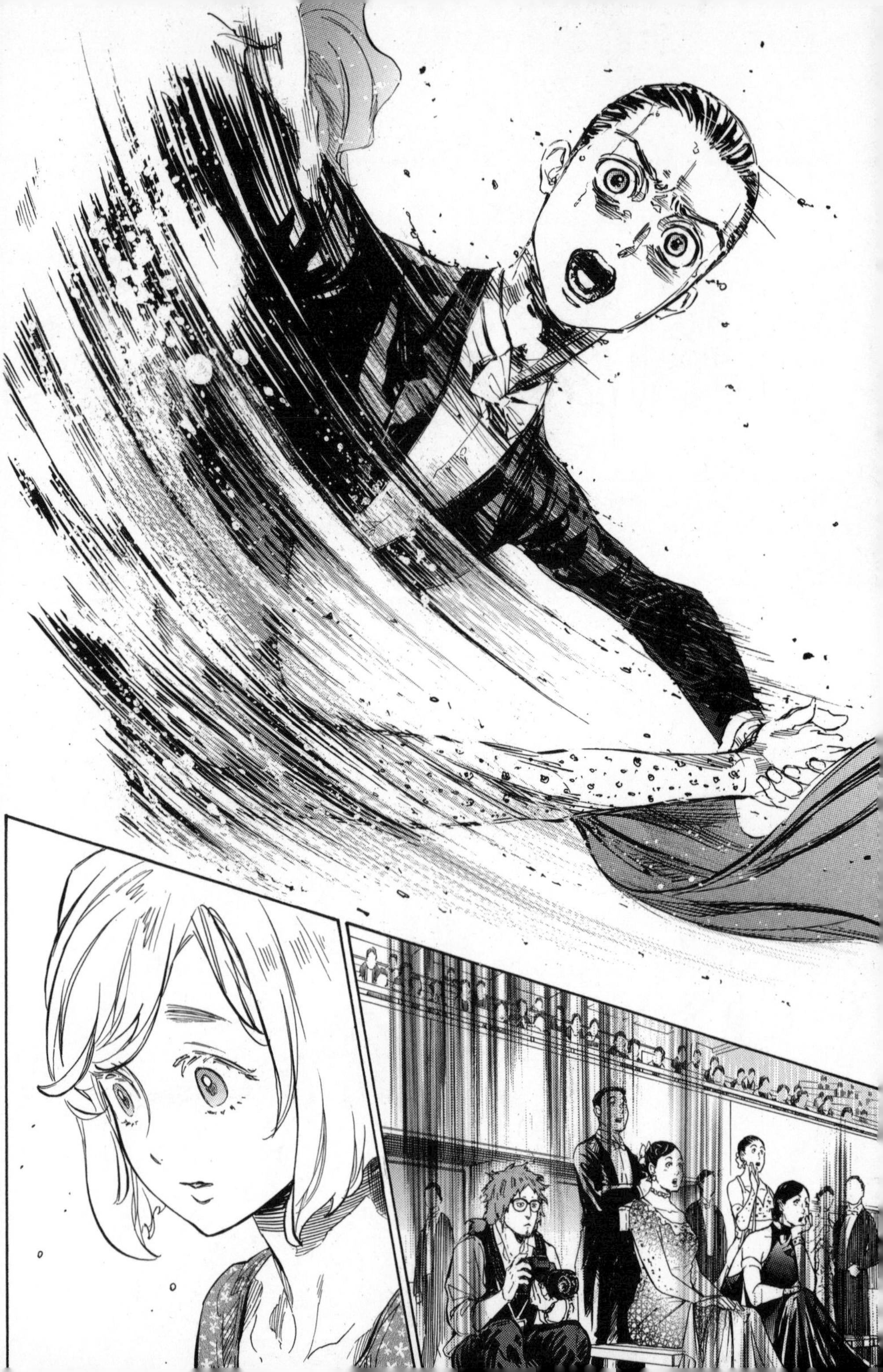

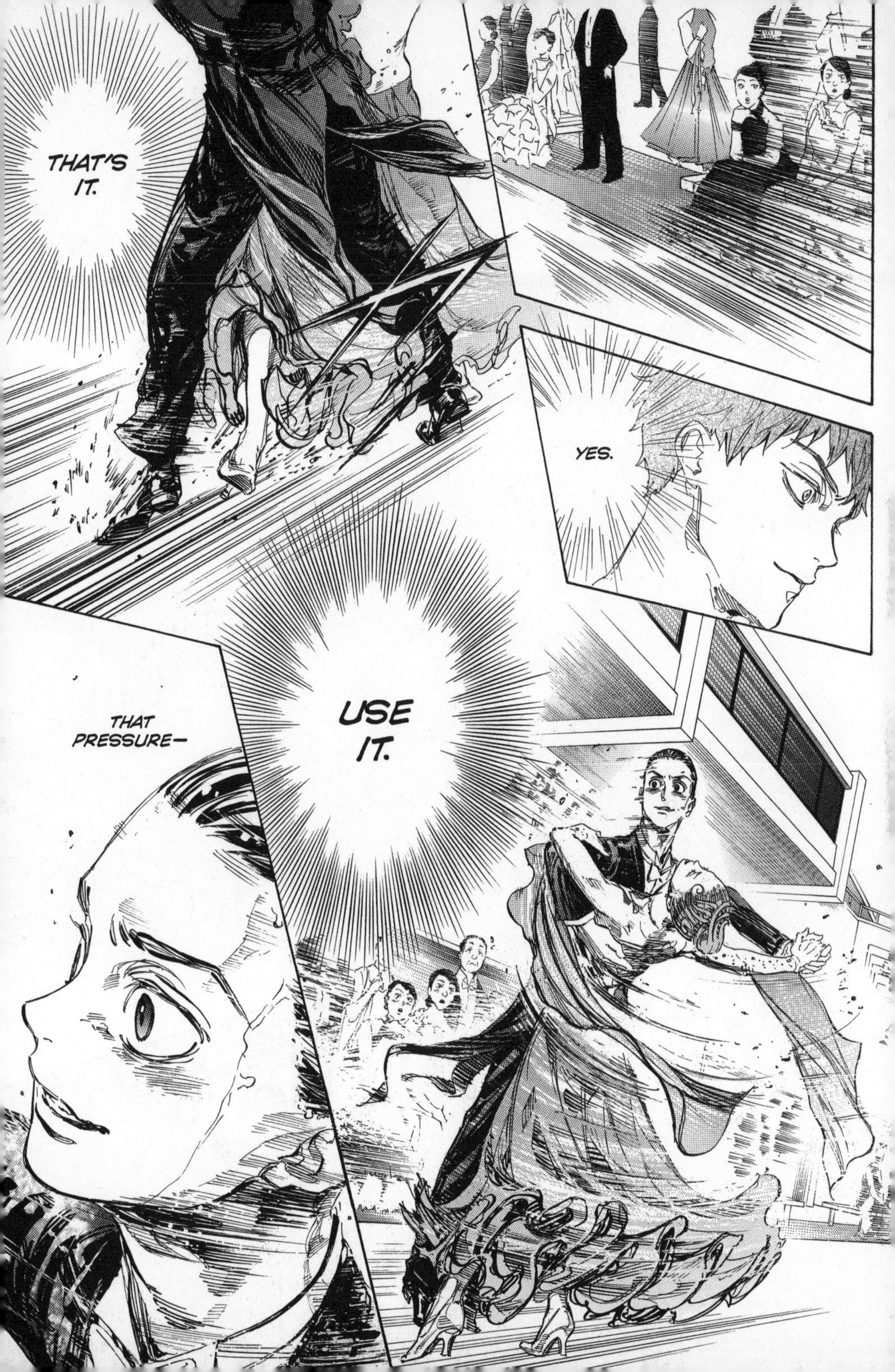
THAT'S IT.
YES.
THAT PRESSURE—
USE IT.

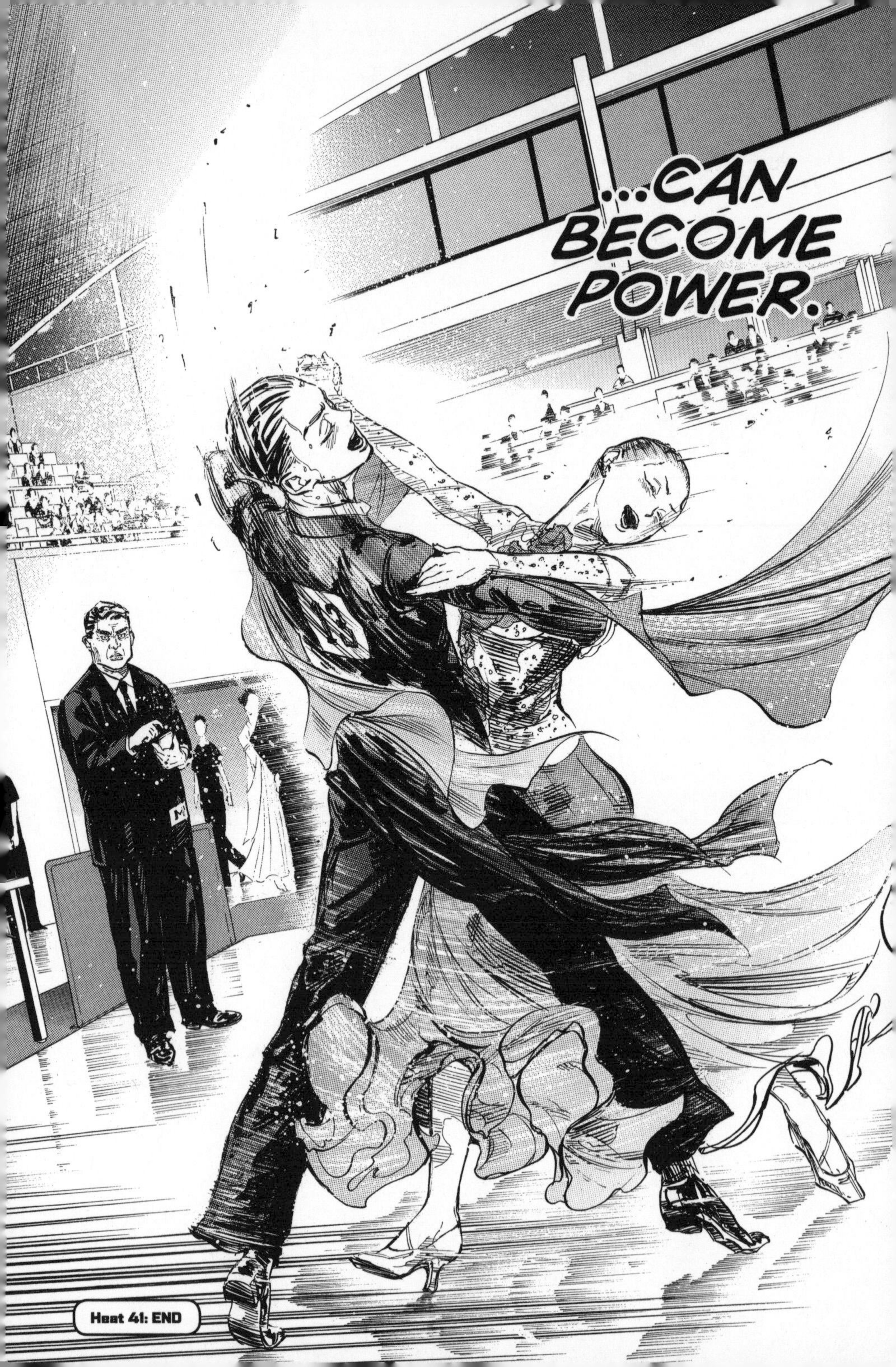
...CAN BECOME POWER.
Heat 41: END

Special Thanks!

For help with variations
Mr. Minato Kojima
Ms. Megumi Morita
Mr. Shin Wakashiro
Ms. Yuria Tatsumi

For help with background
Sakane Dance School

Translation Notes

Page 18
"Swallowtail"
Another name for the formal tailcoat.

Page 19
"good tailcoat can cost over ¥350,000 for the full set"
This corresponds to well over $3000 in U.S. dollars.

Page 23
"Cosmetic sway"
In the original Japanese, this term is further explained via superscript as a kind of sway from the collarbone up.

Page 32
"Did I just force an older man to apologize to me…?!"
Best-known to Westerners through the "sensei" and student relationship, and to fans of anime and manga through the senpai/kohai relationship, Japanese society still retains a strongly hierarchical infrastructure. In almost all cases, the young must defer to the old. In addition, though often glossed over in Western society, in Japan an apology is more explicitly understood to be humbling or "lowering" oneself relative to the person to whom one is apologizing. So despite Akira's brash personality, when a teenage girl scolds a man old enough to be her father, she would likely expect to be ignored or (at best) corrected. That the older man sees himself at a lower rank and apologizes to her is pretty surprising.

Page 41
"Spaghetti and meatball!!"
The boy actually uses a Japanese word (honetsuki-niku) that literally means "meat with bone," and refers to culinary presentations like "bone-in ribeye" or meat lollipops.

Page 57
"cram school"
In Japan, the school a person attends is often not determined by where they live. Middle schools and high schools require that prospective students achieve a certain score on an SAT-like exam—except that each school often has its own, individual exam. Therefore, students must devote a huge amount of time to studying a broad range of subjects in depth, and must take a large number of tests when transferring from elementary school to middle school, and again when moving from middle school to high school.

Page 95
"What am I, Mount Everest?!"
This is a reference to the famous quote by mountaineer George Mallory (1886-1924), one of the first Westerners to attempt to reach the summit of Mount Everest in the 1920s. When asked "Why do you want to climb Mount Everest?" Mallory replied, "Because it's there."

Page 146
"Those are both seriously unlucky numbers."
Though Tatara's number 13 is obviously unlucky to a Western reader, Kugimiya's number 42 is just as obviously unlucky to a Japanese reader. This is because the numbers 4 and 2 in Japanese are read shi and ni, which together are shini—a homonym for "death."

Page 147
"We're a fox and a tanuki!"
In English, a tanuki is properly called a "Japanese raccoon dog." They have a broad resemblance to raccoons, but are canines, rather than procyonidae. The tanuki of Japanese folklore is usually a trickster (though sometimes dull-witted) and a shapeshifter. Similarly, in Japanese legend, the fox can assume human form to infiltrate human society, sometimes for mischief and sometimes for romance.

Page 148
"Tonegawa-san!"
This is a reference to manga character named Yukio Tonegawa, who originally appeared as a boss in the gambling manga *Tobaku Mokushiroku Kaiji*, and now has his own ongoing gag manga titled *Chukan Kanriroku Tonegawa* about the trials and tribulations of middle management (his day job). The character has a very prominent, hooked nose.

Page 159
"Piazzolla"
Astor Piazzolla (1921-1992) was an Argentine composer ofwhose innovations helped to transform traditional tango music, incorporating inspirations from both jazz and classical music.

A Kodansha Comics Trade Paperback Original.

Welcome to the Ballroom volume 9 copyright © 2017 Tomo Takeuchi
English translation copyright © 2018 Tomo Takeuchi

Published in the United States by Kodansha Comics, an imprint of Kodansha USA Publishing, LLC, New York.

Publication rights for this English edition arranged through Kodansha Ltd., Tokyo.

First published in Japan in 2017 by Kodansha Ltd., Tokyo, as *Booruruumu e Youkoso* volume 9.

ISBN 978-1-63236-580-4

Printed in the United States of America.

www.kodanshacomics.com

9 8 7 6 5 4 3 2 1

Translator: Karen McGillicuddy
Lettering: Brndn Blakeslee
Editing: Paul Starr
Kodansha Comics edition cover design by Phil Balsman